# CONTENTS

**1  Family Law: An Introduction**                                      1
1.1 The changing state of family law and society — 1.2 The family —
1.2.1 What is 'the family'? — 1.2.2 Is the family under threat? — 1.3 The
scope and nature of family justice — 1.3.1 Rules and discretion in family law
— 1.3.2 The growth of mediation — 1.4 Policy issues in family law —
1.5 Approaches to family law — 1.5.1 A functionalist approach — 1.5.2 The
private and the public — 1.5.3 The social science perspective

**2  Marriage and Cohabitation**                                      29
2.1 Marriage: an introduction — 2.2 Who has a 'right' to marry? —
2.2.1 The grounds for void and voidable marriages — 2.2.2 Transsexuals and
marriage — 2.2.3 Same-sex marriages — 2.3 Separate but equal legal
personalities — 2.4 Should entry into marriage be controlled? — 2.5 The
future of marriage — 2.6 Cohabitation — 2.6.1 What is cohabitation? —
2.6.2 Why do people cohabit rather than marry? — 2.6.3 Should marriage-
type obligations be imposed on cohabitants?

**3  Family Property**                                                 55
3.1 Property rights of married couples — 3.1.1 Separation of property —
3.1.2 Matrimonial property statutes — 3.1.3 Ownership of personal property
during marriage — 3.1.4 Occupation of the matrimonial home —
3.2 Property rights of cohabitants — 3.2.1 Cohabitants in a disadvantageous

# PREFACE

While family law is a fascinating subject because it deals with life and the human condition, it can at the same time be frustrating to study because of its width and the vast range of different materials that must be absorbed. This book aims to remove that frustration by providing students and teachers with a 'portable library' of essential cases and materials. It is to be hoped that the extracts I have chosen will not only be stimulating to read but also that they will provide readers with a deeper understanding of family law and its policies and practices. Obviously it has not been possible in a book of this size to provide an exhaustive collection of materials, and it is inevitable that there will be some bias towards topics which I find particularly interesting.

Another aim has been to provide a book which can form the basis for a seminar-style of teaching. The questions throughout the book will provide some useful starting points for group discussion.

I would like to thank all those members of the 'family law community' who have allowed me to publish their work. Without their permission this book would not have been possible. I am particularly indebted to Richard Hudson of Jordans Ltd for giving me permission to use extracts not only from the *Family Law Reports*, but from the *Family Law* journal and the *Child and Family Law Quarterly*. My thanks also go to those at Blackstone Press who have assisted me in this enterprise.

Finally, I would like to thank my husband John for his assistance with this book, and for his patient and good-humoured support throughout. This book is dedicated to him and to our children, Tom and Lizzie.

*Kate Standley*
*28 February 1997*

# ACKNOWLEDGMENTS

The author and publishers would like to thank the following for permission to reproduce copyright material:

The Editor in Chief of the *All England Law Reports* for extracts from the *All England Law Reports*.

Andrew Bainham, 'Sexual Abuse in the Lords' (1996) CLJ 209.

J. S. Bell, Editor of *Legal Studies* for an extract from Brazier, Margaret and Bridge, Caroline, 'Coercion or Caring: Analysing Adolescent Autonomy' (1996) 16 *Legal Studies* 84.

Blackwell Publishers for the following extracts from *The Modern Law Review*: Bainham, Andrew, 'The Privatisation of the Public Interest in Children' (1990) 53 MLR 206; Gardner, Simon, 'A Woman's Work' (1991) 55 MLR 126; Hayes, Mary, 'The Law Commission and the Family Home' (1990) 53 MLR 222; Ingleby, Richard, 'Court Sponsored Mediation: The Case Against Mandatory Participation' (1993) 56 MLR 441; King, Michael, 'Children's Rights as Communication: Reflections on Autopoietic Theory and the United Nations Convention' (1994) 57 MLR 385; Lowe, Nigel and Juss, Harvinder, 'Medical Treatment — Pragmatism and the Search for Principle' (1993) 56 MLR 865.

Butterworths for an extract from Eekelaar, John, *Family Law and Social Policy*, 2nd edn, 1984.

Cavendish Publishing Ltd. for an extract from Dewar, John, 'Is Marriage Redundant?' (1992) *The Student Law Review* 46.

John Eekelaar for extracts from *Family Security and Family Breakdown*, London: Penguin Books, 1971.

Her Majesty's Stationery Office (HMSO) for extracts from the following publications, for which Crown copyright is reproduced with the permission of the Controller of Her Majesty's Stationery Office: Law Commission, *Facing the Future: A Discussion Paper on the Ground for Divorce*, Law Com No.

170, 1988; Law Commission, *Family Law: Matrimonial Property*, Law Com
No. 175, 1988; Law Commission, *Domestic Violence and Occupation of the
Family Home*, Law Com No. 207, 1992; Department of the Environment,
Department of Health, and Welsh Office, *Homelessness Code of Guidance for
Local Authorities*, 3rd edn (revised), 1994; Law Commission, *Report on
Guardianship and Custody*, Law Com No. 172, 1988; *Report of the Matrimonial
Causes Procedure* (Chairman: The Hon Mrs Justice Booth DBE); Department
of Health, *Introduction to the Children Act 1989*, 1991; Department of Health,
*The Children Act: Guidance and Regulations*, vol. 1 Court Orders, 1991, and
vol. 3 Family Placements, 1991; *Working Together under the Children Act 1989:
A Guide to Arrangements for Inter-Agency Cooperation for the Protection of
Children from Abuse*, 1991; *Report of the Inquiry into Child Abuse in Cleveland
1987*, Cm 412, 1987; DHSS, *Review of Child Care Law — Report to Ministers
of an Interdepartmental Working Party*, 1985; DHSS, *Report of the Committee of
Inquiry into the Care and Supervision Provided in Relation to Maria Colwell*
(Chairman: T. G. Field-Fisher QC), 1974; *Children Come First*, The Govern-
ment's Proposals on the Maintenance of Children, vol. 1, Cm 1264, 1990;
*Improving Child Support*, Cm 2745, 1995; Department of Health and Welsh
Office, *Review of Adoption Law*, Report to Ministers of an Interdepartmental
Working Group (A Consultation Paper), 1992; *Adoption — A Service for
Children* (Adoption Bill — Consultative Document), 1996; *Interdepartmental
Review of Adoption Law*, Discussion Paper No 4 on Intercountry Adoption.

The Incorporated Council of Law Reporting for England and Wales for
extracts from *The Law Reports* and the *Weekly Law Reports*.

The Institute of Economic Affairs, Health and Welfare Unit for an extract
from Morgan, Patricia, *Farewell to the Family — Public Policy and Family
Breakdown*, 1995.

Jordans Ltd (Family Law) for extracts from the *Family Law Reports* and for
the following extracts from *Family Law*: Ayton, Lyn, 'Preserving the Family
Home in the Face of Bankruptcy' [1993] Fam Law 180; Beevers, Kisch,
'Child Abduction — Welfare or Comity?' [1996] Fam Law 365; Bisphan,
Jennifer, and Greaney, Angeline, 'Child Support Act: Contra-indications for
Ancillary Relief and Contact' [1993] Fam Law 525; Bissett-Johnson,
Alastair and Barton, Chris, 'The Divorce White Paper' [1995] Fam Law 349;
Bradney, Anthony, 'Transsexuals and the Law' [1987] Fam Law 350;
Burrows, David, 'A Child's Understanding' [1974] Fam Law 579; Clarke,
Linda and Edmunds, Rod, '*H* v *M*: Equity and the Essex Cohabitant' [1992]
Fam Law 523; Clarke, Peter J., 'The Family Home: Intention and Agree-
ment' [1992] Fam Law 72; Cretney, Stephen, 'Divorce — A Smooth
Transition?' [1992] Fam Law 472; Cretney, Stephen, 'The Divorce White
Paper — Some Reflections' [1995] Fam Law 302; Deech, Ruth, 'Comment:
Not Just Marriage Breakdown' [1994] Fam Law 121; Edwards, S. and
Halpern A., 'Parental Responsibility — An Instrument of Social Policy'
[1992] Fam Law 113; His Honour Judge Nigel Fricker, 'Family Law is
Different' [1995] Fam Law 306; Halsey, A. H., 'Individualism and the
Decline of the Family' [1993] Fam Law 152; Hewitt, Patricia, 'Family

Values' [1994] Fam Law 160; Jolly, Simon and Sandland, R., 'Political Correctness and the Adoption White Paper' [1994] Fam Law 30; Lawson-Cruttenden, Tim and Odutola, Adetutu, 'Constructive Trusts — A Practical Guide' [1995] Fam Law 560; Lewis, Jane, 'Marriage Saving Revisited' [1996] Fam Law 423; Maclean, Mavis: 'Comment: Divorce and the Professionals' [1993] Fam Law 3; Maclean, M. and Johnston J., 'Alimony or Compensation' [1990] Fam Law 148; Singes, L., 'FDR and the Holy Grail' [1996] Fam Law 751; The Honourable Mr Justice Wall, 'The Status of the Family Division' [1995] Fam Law 374.

Jordans Ltd (Family Law) for the following extracts from the *Child and Family Law Quarterly*: Bailey-Harris, Rebecca, 'Law and the Unmarried Couple — Oppression or Liberation?' [1996] 8 CFLQ 137; Broberg, Morten P., 'The Registered Partnership for Same-Sex Couples in Denmark' [1996] 8 CFLQ 149; Keating, Heather, 'Shifting Standards in the House of Lords: *Re H and Others (Minors) (Sexual Abuse: Standard of Proof)*' [1996] 6 CFLQ 157; Richards, Margaret, "It Feels Like Someone Keeps Moving the Goalposts' — Regulating Post-Adoption Contact, *Re T (Adopted Children: Contact)*' [1996] 8 CFLQ 175; Richards, Martin, 'But What About the Children? Some Reflections on the Divorce White Paper' [1995] 7 CFLQ 223.

Jordans Ltd (Family Law) for extracts from Murch, Mervyn and Hooper, Douglas, *The Family Justice System*, 1994.

Kluwer International for extracts from: Asquith, Stewart and Hill, Malcolm (eds), *Justice for Children*, 1994, Martinus Nijhoff (all rights reserved © 1994 Kluwer Academic Publishers); and from Freeman, Michael D. A., 'The Limits of Children's Rights', in Freeman Michael D. A and Veerman P. (eds), *The Ideologies of Children's Rights*, Martinus Nijhoff (all rights reserved © 1992 Kluwer Academic Publishers).

The Law Society for extracts from *Memorandum: Maintenance and Capital Provision on Divorce*, 1991.

Oxford University Press for the following extracts from the *International Journal of Law and the Family*: Maclean, Mavis and Eekelaar, John 'Child Support: The British Solution' (1993) 7 IJL&F 205; Jackson, Emily and Wasoff, Fran with Maclean, Mavis and Emerson Dobash, Rebecca, ' Financial Support on Divorce: The Right Mixture of Rules and Discretion' (1993) 7 IJL&F 230; and Joshi, H. and Davies, H., 'Pensions, Divorce and Wives' Double Burden' (1992) 6 IJL & F 289.

Oxford University Press for extracts from: Davis, Gwynn, Cretney, Stephen and Collins, Jean, *Simple Quarrels*, 1994; Alston, P., Parker, S., and Seymour, J. (eds), *Children, Rights and the Law*, 1992; Martin Richards, 'Divorcing — Children: Roles for Parents and the State' in Maclean, Mavis and Kurczewski, Jacek (eds), *Families, Politics and the Law*, 1994, chap. 4.

Oxford University Press for the following extract from the *Oxford Journal of Legal Studies*: Eekelaar, John, 'The Emergence of Children's Rights' (1986) 6 Oxford Journal of Legal Studies 161.

Pluto Press for extracts from O'Donovan, Katherine, *Family Law Matters*, 1993.

M. J. Pritchard, Editor of *The Cambridge Law Journal*, and Andrew Bainham for an extract from Bainham, Andrew, 'Sexual Abuse in the Lords' (1996) CLJ 209.

F. M. B. Reynolds, Editor of *The Law Quarterly Review* and authors for the following extracts from *The Law Quarterly Review*: Bainham, 'The Judge and the Competent Minor' (1992) 108 LQR 194; Cane, Peter, 'Suing Public Authorities in Tort' (1996) 112 LQR 13; Deech, Ruth, 'Divorce Law and Empirical Studies' (1990) 106 LQR 229; Dickens, Bernard, 'The Modern Function and Limits of Parental Rights' (1981) 97 LQR 462; Eekelaar, John 'What is "Critical" Family Law?' (1989) 105 LQR 244; Eekelaar, John, 'The Eclipse of Parental Rights' (1986) 102 LQR 4; Eekelaar, John and Maclean, Mavis, 'Divorce Law and Empirical Studies — A Reply' (1990) 106 LQR 621; Eekelaar, John, 'Parental Responsibility — A New Legal Status?' (1996) 112 LQR 233; Gardner, Simon, 'Rethinking Family Property' (1993) 109 LQR 263; Hayes, Mary, 'Cohabitation Clauses in Financial Provision and Property Adjustment Orders — Law, Policy and Justice' (1994) 110 LQR 124; Thompson, J. M., 'A Right of Access?' (1989) 105 LQR 6.

Carl E. Schneider and the American Bar Association for an extract from 'The Tension Between Rules and Discretion in Family Law: A Report and a Reflection' (1993) vol. 27 no. 2 *Family Law Quarterly* p. 229, reprinted by permission of the American Bar Association, © 1993 American Bar Association.

The Solicitors' Family Law Association (SFLA) for permission to reproduce the Association's Code of Practice.

Stephen D. Sugarman and the American Bar Association for an extract from the 'Report of the American Bar Family Law Association, Family Law for the Next Century' (1993) vol. 27 no. 2 *Family Law Quarterly*, p. 175, © 1993 American Bar Association.

Sweet & Maxwell for an extract from Murch, Mervyn, *Justice and Welfare in Divorce*, 1980.

Times Newspapers Ltd for an editorial from *The Times*, 14 October 1991.

Geoffrey P. Wilson and John Dewar for an extract from Dewar, John, 'Policy Issues in Law and the Family', in Wilson, Geoffrey P. (ed), *Frontiers of Legal Scholarship*, John Wiley, 1995, chap. 5.

*The Yale Law Journal* for an extract from Mnookin, Robert H. and Kornhauser, Lewis, 'Bargaining in the Shadow of the Law' (1979) vol. 88 Yale LJ 950 reprinted by permission of *The Yale Law Journal Company* and Fred B. Rothman.

# ABBREVIATIONS OF STATUTES

| | | | |
|---|---|---|---|
| AA 1976 | Adoption Act 1976 | HFEA 1990 | Human Fertilisation and Embryology Act 1990 |
| CA 1989 | Children Act 1989 | | |
| CAA 1984 | Child Abduction Act 1984 | | |
| CACA 1985 | Child Abduction and Custody Act 1985 | I(PFD)A 1975 | Inheritance (Provision for Family and Dependants) Act 1975 |
| CSA 1991 | Child Support Act 1991 | | |
| CSA 1995 | Child Support Act 1995 | LPA 1925 | Law of Property Act 1925 |
| DPMCA 1978 | Domestic Proceedings and Magistrates' Courts Act 1978 | LP(MP)A 1989 | Law of Property (Miscellaneous Provisions) Act 1989 |
| DVMPA 1976 | Domestic Violence and Matrimonial Proceedings Act 1976 | MCA 1973 | Matrimonial Causes Act 1973 |
| | | MHA 1983 | Matrimonial Homes Act 1983 |
| FLA 1986 | Family Law Act 1986 | MFPA 1984 | Matrimonial and Family Proceedings Act 1984 |
| FLA 1996 | Family Law Act 1996 | | |
| FLRA 1969 | Family Law Reform Act 1969 | MWPA 1882 | Married Women's Property Act 1882 |
| FLRA 1987 | Family Law Reform Act 1987 | MWPA 1964 | Married Women's Property Act 1964 |
| HA 1985 | Housing Act 1985 | TLATA 1996 | Trusts of Land and Appointment of Trustees Act 1996 |
| HA 1996 | Housing Act 1996 | | |

# ABBREVIATIONS OF ARTICLES

| | | | |
|---|---|---|---|
| CFLQ | *Child and Family Law Quarterly* | JCL | *Journal of Child Law* |
| CLJ | *Cambridge Law Journal* | JSWL | *Journal of Social Welfare Law* |
| Conv | *Conveyancer* | JSWFL | *Journal of Social Welfare and Family Law* |
| Fam Law | *Family Law* | | |
| Fam LQ | *Family Law Quarterly* | LQR | *Law Quarterly Review* |
| ICLQ | *International and Comparative Law Quarterly* | MLR | *Modern Law Review* |
| IJL&F | *International Journal of Law and the Family* | NLJ | *New Law Journal* |
| | | Oxford J Legal Stud | *Oxford Journal of Legal Studies* |
| | | Yale LJ | *Yale Law Journal* |

# TABLE OF CASES

# TABLE OF STATUTES

# 1 FAMILY LAW: AN INTRODUCTION

## 1.1 THE CHANGING STATE OF FAMILY LAW AND SOCIETY

Family law has been and continues to be in a state of considerable flux. Not only have there been fundamental changes in the last ten years or so (e.g., the removal of discrimination against non-marital children by the Family Law Reform Act 1987, the introduction of a comprehensive civil code for children by the Children Act 1989, as well as changes to child maintenance under the Child Support Act 1991), but radical reforms are imminent. Fundamental reforms of divorce law are due to come into force in 1999 under Parts I and II, Family Law Act 1996, and fundamental changes to the law of domestic violence and occupation of the family home on 1 October 1997 under Part IV of the same Act. Major changes to adoption law are also proposed, and an area of law currently under discussion is that relating to the property rights of cohabitants. In addition to these reforms, changes in the way in which family disputes are managed continue to take place. Mediation, which provides an alternative to the court-based resolution of family disputes, has greatly increased, and is likely to increase further when the divorce reforms come into force.

As well as radical legal developments, there have been important demographic and social developments which have, and will continue to have, an impact on the development of family law and policy.

**Murch, Mervyn and Hooper, Douglas, *The Family Justice System***
Bristol: Jordans, 1994, pp. 9–15

Family life is undergoing dramatic demographic upheavals. Social values are altering and family structures are becoming more varied. The United Kingdom, like all

modern western industrial societies, is passing through a period in which traditional forms and images of family life based on Judeo/Christian marriage are giving way to more diverse and often less permanent family structures. The institutions of law, like those of health and welfare, are constantly having to adjust policies and practices to deal with complex issues of justice and family welfare thrown up by these changes. Moreover in a European context, with the arrival of the internal market in 1992 and its enhanced labour mobility, it will no longer be satisfactory to address family justice issues and related social policy questions simply from a national perspective. Increasingly we will be finding ourselves dealing with trans-national marriages, divorces, adoptions and other matters within a European and an even wider international framework.
. . .

## 1.  Divorce

In England and Wales the number of divorce petitioners increased sixfold between 1960 and 1980. By 1985 it had risen to about 160,000 but has since levelled to around 150,000. Divorce rates doubled during the 1960s from 6 per 1000 marriages to 12 per 1000 marriages but has remained roughly level throughout the 1980s. Even so Britain continues to have one of the highest divorce rates in Western Europe, a rate which has increased more rapidly than almost any other country although still remaining lower than in the USA.
. . .

## 2.  Children of Divorced and Separated Parents

Two thirds of divorcing couples have dependent children. Projections suggest that one in five of all children will have experienced a parental divorce by the time they are 16. By the turn of the century it has been estimated that 3.7 million children will have experienced at least one parental divorce. Most children who are not living with both parents now live with their birth mother and stepfather in a reconstituted family formed by cohabitation or remarriage (9% of all children under 16 in 1985) or with their mother in a lone parent family (10% of all children in 1985). We should also point out that 10% of all lone parent families comprise children being cared for by father. . . .

## 3.  Changing Patterns of Marriage and Cohabitation

### (i)  Marriage rates

The age of marriage has been clearly demonstrated to be associated with the incidence of later divorce. Since the early 1970s, in contrast to trends prevailing in the 1950s and 1960s, there has been a discernible trend towards older marriage with fewer teenage brides. Since 1971 the median age at first marriage of women increased from 21.4 years to 23.3 while that for men increased from 23.4 years to 25.3 years. There has also been a marked growth in the proportion of single women in the population. In 1970 only 13% of women in the 25–29 age bracket had never married. By 1987 this proportion had risen to 31% . . .

### (ii)  The rise of cohabitation

While marriage rates fell throughout the 1970s during the 1980s there has been a dramatic rise in the proportion of young people in cohabiting unions. Thus the proportion of single cohabiting women increased from 8% in 1981 to 17% in 1987. Estimates indicate a threefold increase in the number of single women cohabiting between 1979 and 1987 from a figure of 185,000 to 617,000. Even so the *duration* of cohabitation has remained fairly constant at about 18 months. Two major trends can be discerned from the available data about cohabitation rates.

First it has become increasingly common for single never previously married women to cohabit before marriage; a rise from 7% in the early 1970s to 48% in 1987. Second, cohabitation before second marriage of previously divorced women is now virtually the norm, applying to 70% of such marriages.

. . .

### (iii)   The increase in unmarried parenthood

One of the most remarkable demographic trends that emerged in the 1980s was the doubling of the numbers of children born outside marriage, from 77,000 in 1980 to 177,000 in 1988. These figures represent a rise in the proportion of extra-marital births to all births from 12% in 1980 to 25% in 1988, the majority born to women under the age of 25 years.

. . . Breakdowns in cohabitation bring their own particular set of legal and child-welfare problems — as yet less well studied and understood than the problems associated with marriage breakdown. Moreover it is generally recognised that in a number of respects, particularly in relation to taxation, social security and inheritance, the law tends to discriminate against cohabitation. Also the framework in which the law works when a cohabitation breaks up is different from that concerning marriage breakdown.

. . . It seems clear that in the coming decades increasing attention will have to be given to the implications of these trends both for social policy, and for the policies and practices of the family justice system.

### 4.   Remarriage and Reconstituted Families

The high incidence of remarriage after divorce, often now preceded by a period of cohabitation, indicates that the institution of marriage remains popular. Data from the 1986 General Household survey show that 39% of women and 53% of men divorced during 1979–1982 had remarried within two years and 57% of women and 72% of men divorcing during 1977–1980 had remarried within five years. We also know that despite the popularity of remarriage, remarriages are more likely than first marriages to break down. Those where both partners have children from previous marriages have the highest risk of doing so while couples where only one partner was previously married and where there are no resident step-children have the lowest risk.

### 5.   Child Abuse and Neglect: the problem of measuring trends

Compared with the numbers of children involved in divorce proceedings, those who become subject to care and protection proceedings are fortunately far fewer. Although child neglect and abuse arouse deep public concern, the subject suffers from remarkably poor basic information about its incidence, even in relation to the more obviously visible numbers of children who are subject to care and protection proceedings.

. . .

### 6.   Changing Patterns in Adoption

The number of children adopted in England and Wales declined by about two thirds between 1970 and 1986 from 22,373 to 7,892. Nearly twice as many babies were being adopted in 1970 as in 1986. On the other hand, the proportion of older children being adopted has increased. Thus the overall pattern of adoption proceedings has changed substantially since the Houghton Committee reported in 1972. . . .

. . .

### 7.   The Care Of The Elderly And The Family Justice System

Another major demographic feature of contemporary Britain is the increasing number of elderly people. Between 1901 and 1991 the proportion of people over 65 in the

population increased from 1.7 million (or 4.7% of the total) to 8.8 million (or 15.8% of the total). By the year 2027 it is expected to grow to 11 million or 19.2% of the population. Growth will be greater amongst the very elderly who, as the ministerial report 'Caring for People' pointed out, are most likely to be disabled and in need of community care. In 1988 there were 2.1 million people aged 80 or over, nearly 50% more than in 1961. Between 1981 and the year 2001 it is estimated that the number of people over 85 will double to over one million. . . .
. . .

The aging of the population is a major policy concern for our health, welfare and social security systems. It also has major implications for the development of family law. . . .

*Question*
Which developments in society in the last 40 or 50 years do you consider to have had the greatest impact on the family justice system, and which are likely to have the most significant impact in the next century?

## 1.2  THE FAMILY

### Preamble to the UN Convention on the Rights of the Child 1989

. . . *Convinced* that the family, as the fundamental group of society and the natural environment for the growth and well-being of all its members and particularly children, should be afforded the necessary protection and assistance so that it can fully assume its responsibilities within the community . . .

### European Convention for the Protection of Human Rights and Fundamental Freedoms 1950

**Article 8   Right to respect for family and private life**
1.   Everyone has the right to respect for his private and family life, his home and his correspondence.
2.   There shall be no interference by a public authority with the exercise of this right except such as is in accordance with the law and is necessary in a democratic society in the interests of national security, public safety or the economic well-being of the country, for the prevention of disorder or crime, for the protection of health or morals, or for the protection of the rights and freedoms of others.

**Article 12   Right to marry**
Men and women of marriageable age have the right to marry and to found a family, according to the national laws governing the exercise of this right.

*Note*
Articles 8 and 12 have been used by transsexuals to challenge English rules on the validity of marriages and UK rules on birth registration (see Chapter 2).

*Further reading*
Mr Justice Thorpe, 'The Influence of Strasbourg on Family Law' [1990] Fam Law 509.

## Eekelaar, John, *Family Security and Family Breakdown*
### London: Penguin, 1971, pp. 11, 12, 17–18, 25, and 44–47

**Definition and functions of the family**
The breakdown of a marriage involves more than the cessation of a relationship between two individuals, for it signifies the ultimate collapse of what is the most important social group in the community. This at once justifies the use by the community of social control through its laws over situations leading up to and resulting from that disturbance. But the law has not created the family. The family is a social organism which arises to fulfil certain needs of society and of individuals and which is subject to natural processes of decay and ultimate dissolution. Society cannot eradicate these processes, yet it can, by social pressure and by law, so channel them as to lessen the risk of family disruption. To this end it employs the purely legal concept of marriage to confer special recognition upon certain family groups in order to enable them better to perform some of the functions required of them in society.

Although these functions have varied from culture to culture and from age to age and many might, in theory, be fulfilled by agencies other than the family, no convincing alternative has yet been discovered. The universality of the family has often been remarked upon by sociologists and anthropologists. Differences have arisen over the correct classification of the types of family group evident in diverse societies. The group to which we are accustomed in the West is the so-called *nuclear* family which consists solely of a married man and woman and their offspring. But there is also to be found the *polygamous* family, where there will be a plural marriage by a spouse with two or more of the opposite sex and the *extended* family which includes, in addition to the married parents and the children, the spouses of those children. . . .

It is unnecessary to enter into controversies of definition. But it is important to notice from the evidence of anthropologists that some form of institutionalized cohabitation between individuals of opposite sexes on a more or less permanent basis and at least for the period necessary for the rearing of children is to be found practically everywhere. . . .

. . . The decline of the use of the family for alliance and descent and a supposed weakening of the influence of the extended family have led some to conclude that the twentieth century has seen the disintegration of marriage and the family system. That this is a gross exaggeration, indeed, distortion, has been demonstrated by McGregor (1957) and by Fletcher (1966). . . .

**Family disintegration**
A family has to be complete before it can properly be said to suffer a process of decline. But many families are incomplete. These are the families of unmarried mothers. Other families succeed in completing their formation, publicly attested by the marriage of the partners but fail in varying degrees to fulfil their social role. This may take place even though the partners are cohabiting and to a certain extent satisfying their own personal needs. The children may be so neglected that the family, far from acting as a unit catering for their physical and emotional needs, becomes a positive danger to them. In this category are to be found mainly that class of family described as the 'problem' family. A further step towards disintegration, though one not necessarily related to problem families, is that of separation between the spouses, which often, but not always, ends in the final dissolution by divorce. And finally there is by far the largest cause of dissolution, and that is the death of one or both of the partners to the marriage. . . .

**The role of the law**

... What is the role of the legal process in this interplay of forces? It is often alleged that the law has little influence on the social mores of a society; that 'true' law is to be found in the way people in fact behave and not in the examination of the written law. Indeed, it is said that, at best, the official law is simply a reflection of attitudes already adopted by society as a whole, and often a delayed one at that. For this view there is considerable evidence. Judges, after all, are drawn from their own contemporary society and will, by and large, express opinions consistent with those by which their society has moulded them during their formative years. ...

Yet such a pessimistic view of the utility of law as a means of social control is not justified. While it remains true that a law which deviates too drastically from communal opinion may fail (in the absence of a measure of coercion which would be considered unacceptable in a democratic society), toleration by the majority of reform coupled with its promotion by a few can have effective results. Thus the practice of 'baby-farming', by which strangers 'cared' for children for reward often in deplorable conditions, which was revealed on a scandalous scale at the end of the nineteenth century, has been largely eliminated by the enactment of child protection legislation. Legislation of this type requires a supervising agency to ensure its enforcement, but there are subtler ways by which legislation, or the absence of it, can affect population behaviour. ... Legal provisions may deter people from seeking advice or reconciliation, or they may encourage them to do so. Facultative provisions may be enacted to meet the problems of special groups of people as, for example, in the case of the adoption law. The economic security of wives and children can be regulated. Family allowances and taxation benefits can provide incentives or disincentives for or against certain activities. In a cohesive and comparatively closely regulated society, legal pressures of this kind might have a measurable effect. More difficult to calculate is whether statements of principle by the legislature can influence community attitudes. It is often claimed that, if the legislature was to proclaim the principle of divorce by consent obtained by simple registration, this would lessen the respect with which marriage is held in the eyes of the community as a whole. ...

... Although the family as an institution has its critics, ... the overwhelmingly dominant view is that social policy should support it, and when it functions inadequately, should devise measures to restore it rather than attempt to supplant it. Making this basic assumption, legal policy towards the family can simultaneously adopt two approaches. The first is to attempt to minimize the risk of family breakdown by seeking to prevent those situations arising where that risk is high and by promoting situations favourable to family cohesion. This 'preventive' role of the law therefore has both a negative and a positive side to it. The other approach is necessitated by recognition of the fact that the preventive function of the law in this area meets with limited success. Therefore it is necessary for legal provision to assume a remedial, therapeutic character. In all societies, no matter what the state of the law, there will always be children born outside marriage there will always be breakdown of marriages. It becomes necessary, therefore, to devise the most effective means of re-adjustment by which the law may mitigate the harmful consequences of illegitimacy and marital breakdown and to provide some measure of compensation for the frustration of the expectations entertained by the parties concerned. There will naturally be some overlap in the operation of these two functions as some legal provisions may serve both purposes simultaneously. Nevertheless, policy is conceptually divisible into this dual role. ...

*Note*

The references to McGregor and Fletcher in the above extract are:
McGregor, O.R., *Divorce in England*, London: Heinemann, 1957, and

Fletcher, R., *The Family and Marriage in Britain*, revised edn., London: Penguin, 1966.

*Questions*
1.  In the above extract the families of unmarried mothers are described as 'incomplete'. Is this true or have things changed since the extract was written?
2.  Should the European Convention for the Protection of Human Rights be incorporated into English law? Many countries (e.g. Italy and Ireland) have their own constitutional guarantees protecting and upholding the institution of the family and the primary importance of family life. What is the advantage of this, and should the UK do the same?

### 1.2.1   What is 'the family'?

### O'Donovan, Katherine, *Family Law Matters*
London: Pluto Press, 1993, p. 34

. . . The legal problem is that despite idealisation of the nuclear heterosexual family, there is no consistent model of what a family is. . . . Examination of varying judicial pronouncements on the definition of family reveals no continuous thread. No consistent philosophy is to be found, rather a case-by-case reaction to differing legislative provisions. . . .

### Boyd, Susan, 'What is a "Normal" Family?
*C v C (A Minor) (Custody: Appeal)*' (1992) 55 MLR 269

*C v C* [[1991] 1 FLR 223, a Court of Appeal decision on lesbian parenting] . . . demonstrates the power that the idea, if not the reality, of the heterosexual nuclear family continues to hold in English custody law. . . .
    Cases like *C v C* illustrate, however, the ways in which a dominant notion of the 'normal family' can marginalise other familial forms, such as black families and lesbian families. They raise the possibility that many white feminists and women of colour have been talking at cross purposes, at least to some extent. There has been a tendency to blur the important distinction between dominant ideological notions of 'family' and lived experience within families. For instance, white feminist critiques of the family have not so much been directed at diminishing the positive aspects that can be provided by familial life, particularly for individuals who experience racism or homophobia outside the familial realm. Rather, the point is to demonstrate how public policy has privileged one type of family which has predominated in modern western societies. Among other things, this family has been characterised by a rather strict division of labour between women and men, in the home and in the labour market, which often leaves women impoverished and lacking in self-esteem. This same public policy has had a way of diminishing the ability of alternative familial forms, such as same-sex families and black families, to flourish.
    This is not to say that many points raised by black feminists have not been valid. Most white feminist critics of 'the family' have *not* been careful to make it clear that they were addressing a particular·idealised family form probably more relevant to white women than black women in western societies. Many have not considered the relevance of race to the differential material and ideological circumstances of black and

white women's lives. Most white feminists writing on familial ideologies have not addressed the notion that ideologies of womanhood are race and class-specific. That white feminists have often been blind to issues of race does not necessarily mean, however, that *all* insights of their work are mistaken.

It is, then, crucial to continue to develop a critique of dominant ideas of 'family,' but a critique which is sensitive to the ways in which various ideologies or discourses on 'family' may differ according to race, class and sexual orientation. We must develop a critical stance on 'the family' which retains a sense of the different and often contradictory levels at which we think of family, for instance dominant and very powerful ideological notions of family as opposed to discourses of resistance developed through experience in alternative familial forms. A sense of the strengths one can derive from familial relationships which challenge traditional power configurations can be developed, while recognising that these strengths will often be diminished by the dominant ideologies on the family. Seeking to shift these dominant ideologies requires illumination of the differential experiences of real and diverse families in relation to them. Challenges must continue to be made to the way in which the legal system tends to reinforce an idea of the 'normal family' which inhibits healthy and open development of alternative familial forms.

*Note*
In *C* v *C (A Minor) (Custody: Appeal)* [1991] 1 FLR 223, the Court of Appeal overturned the decision of the county court judge and held that, while lesbianism *per se* would not deprive a mother of custody (now residence), lesbianism was an important consideration for the court, as the ideal environment in which to bring up a child was in the home of caring heterosexual parents.

### 1.2.2   Is the family under threat?

Some consider that the institution of the family is threatened because of the high incidence of family breakdown.

### Eekelaar, John, *Family Law and Social Policy*
2nd edn, London: Weidenfeld and Nicolson, 1984, p. 25

. . . The ideology western societies hold with respect to family living and their economic structure combine to perpetuate the family as the major institution within which children, especially very young children, are reared. But the perceived ideological and economic gains of delegating the task of nurturing the new generation to families must be offset against the inequalities and instability of the family system. Within some families children may be badly brought up. Other families will disintegrate. . . .

### Halsey, A. H., 'Individualism and the Decline of the Family'
[1993] Fam Law 152

. . . [I]ndividualistic policy, despite its many benefits to industry and commerce, . . . spreads by its own logic into the family. Marriage becomes not a sacred long-run compact but merely a contract, to be broken at the will of either party; and children become consumables, quality products, no doubt, but nevertheless objects like cars or washing machines If people choose to 'buy' them that is their right and their responsibility. Caveat emptor: if only one parent is left (usually the mother) it is largely up to her to look after the interest of the child. Some libertarians deem this a reasonable price for freedom. Many turn their faces away from the evidence that on average the children of broken or one-parent families have impoverished life chances — literally chances of survival, of health, of educational attainment, of conviviality, of jobs, of avoidance of marital breakdown in their own lives, and so on.

The point about Mrs Thatcher in this context is that she tacitly assumed that the individualistic ethic, untrammelled, could not enter the family; but in fact it did, and was vigorously encouraged by 'egotistic socialists' as well as libertarian individualists. Meanwhile, and pre-dating Thatcher, the State moved systematically to undermine support for the traditional family by eroding family allowances, promoting regressive national insurance contributions, individualising tax returns and, in short, shifting subsidy away from families, horizontally to individuals and vertically from the poor to the rich. Increasingly, we see a closer association of parenting with poverty and, most ominously, a new generation of males with little experience of, or interest in, responsible fatherhood.

It could all be turned around by determined action, but not by mindless reaction. The old respectable working-class family system worked, but at high cost (the double standard of morality, the harsh treatment of 'fallen women' and 'bastards', the kitchen containment of mothers, the taboo on male participation in 'women's work'). Clearly, those traditional conflicts and confinements are neither desirable nor any longer possible. Nevertheless, there are positive policy possibilities open to a richer country through serious reform of the schools, of working arrangements, through 'third-age' grandparents, properly provided family-friendly social services — a whole new programme of reform which dethrones the market mania of present government and turns instead to a wiser civilisation.

### Morgan, Patricia, *Farewell to the Family — Public Policy and Family Breakdown*
London: IEA Health and Welfare Unit, Choice in Welfare Series No. 21, Chapter 4, 'By Chance or Design?', 1995, pp. 83, 84 and 86

. . .

Suggestions that family trends owe a great deal to the actions of policymakers — whether or not the outcomes were intended — are contrary to the dogma that government is incapable of influencing developments in this field. It may seem particularly unusual to pay special attention to the economic basis of family life. Despite the way in which people are forever discussing what they can afford, even many of those who give pride of place to the role of economics in behaviour are among the first to deny that material considerations make any difference to family and marital decisions. The belief that family trends cannot be explained in economic terms shades into the belief that these are beyond understanding, yet there is no reason why they are any more unintelligible or beyond human influence than other social or physical phenomena.

To emphasise the extent to which economic factors influence people's decisions about marriage and childbearing is not to say that money is the only consideration, or the most important consideration. A host of factors are involved in the process of family formation and family stability and these affect each other. However, a pool of securely employed males is usually a necessary condition for a viable marriage market,

just as the capacity to run a household which does not absorb two wages facilitates
marital childbearing.

In spite of this we are repeatedly told that people just do what they want to do; that
'Today's plurality is the consequence of personal lifestyle decisions', or, according to
Malcolm Wicks, when he was director of the Family Policies Studies Centre, that:

> There are fewer marriages, more cohabitation, more children born out-of-wedlock,
> high divorce rates and more one-parent families. These are powerful forces and,
> faced with them, the governments are relatively powerless. The trends of the last 12
> years were not for turning.

At this point, an *is*, or a *will be*, tends to slip into an *ought*, and we often find standards
being read off from the direction of trends, which we are bidden to embrace and
accommodate just because they are happening. Extrapolations which have 50 per cent
of children being reared outside the conventional family after the turn of the century
are presented as if projections were prophecies, and these were already established
facts which, furthermore, possessed a kind of moral authority which we are obliged to
work towards. Hence, it is not just impossible to 'squeeze the toothpaste back into the
tube'; we are meant to help history squeeze it out.

. . . Nevertheless, whilst the nuclear family remains the statistical norm, it is also true
that the number of nuclear family households is decreasing, and that not all of this
decrease can be accounted for by the changing age structure of the population. So
what are the new, emerging family forms which we are hearing about? Malcolm Wicks
and Kathleen Kiernan describe these new families in terms of 'cohabitation, of having
children outside of marriage, of marital breakdown, and the rise in the number of lone
mothers'. However, there is nothing new about these groupings — they have always
existed. Whatever sort of family structure is regarded as the norm in a society, there
have always been irregular marriages, concubinage, adulteries and prohibited coup-
lings. The really original aspect of statistics showing changing household types in
recent years is the growth in *one-person* households from 14 per cent of all households
in 1961 to 27 per cent in 1992, with the biggest increase for men under pensionable
age. However, this is not a new family type, but *the absence of any family at all.*

The one-parent family is the result of the break-up of families, or procreation
outside of family structures, not a new family form. Despite attempts to find cultural
precedents for the institutionalisation of the lone mother as the norm, we have no
reason to revise Malinowski's view of the fatherless family as an aberration.
. . .

*Note*
The references in the above extract are as follows: 'Today's plurality is the
consequence of personal lifestyle decisions', Dormer, D., *The Relationship
Revolution*, London: One Plus One, 1982, p. 4; 'There are fewer marriages
. . .', Wicks, M., *Daily Telegraph*, 11 October 1991; Kiernan, K. and Wicks,
M., *Social Justice, Children and Families*, London: Institute for Public Policy
Research, 1993, p. 9.

*Questions*
What is 'the family'? What do politicians mean by 'traditional' family values?
What is the 'normal' family, or has this concept no meaning today? Is the
family under threat? If so, why and how? What functions does the family
perform? Could these be performed in other ways?

## 1.3    THE SCOPE AND NATURE OF FAMILY JUSTICE

### The Honourable Mr Justice Wall, 'The Status of the Family Division'
[1995] Fam Law 374

. . .

There is no doubt that the work we do is enormously diverse, and crosses all social and ethnic, as well as most professional and legal boundaries. In financial disputes at one extreme are complex family disputes of the degree of sophistication usually associated with tax avoidance or commercial fraud, and which involve consideration of offshore trusts and foreign Anstalts. Other cases throw up difficult points of trust, bankruptcy, company, and pension law (see, as a modest example of the latter, *Brooks v Brooks* [1994] 2 FLR 10). At the other end of the financial scale are the difficult problems which arise when financial provision has to be allocated among those whose income resources fall within or on the margins of the social security system.

In child law, we range in the private field from the implementation of the Hague and European Conventions on International Child Abduction (where the judges of the Division and the Court of Appeal are creating a growing jurisprudence) to an infinite variety of painful and often poignant family disputes over children. In the public law field we have to deal with the range of orders contained in Part IV of the Children Act 1989; with the fundamental questions of social policy which routinely arise and in which difficult social work, paediatric or psychiatric issues are common.

In addition, there are the numerous questions of statutory construction, both in its public and its private law sections which the Children Act 1989 has thrown up. . . .

### His Honour Judge Nigel Fricker, 'Family Law is Different'
[1995] Fam Law 306

**The Essential Conceptual Difference of Family Law**

The experience of lawyers and litigants varies considerably according to the area of law in which they are or become involved. Criminal law, the law of torts or civil wrongs, and the law of contract and commercial dealings each give rise to experience different from the others. The practice of family law involves particular sensitivity to the welfare needs of children, the trauma of separation and divorce and the consequent emotional and psychological changes, and the diverse cultural expectations and family structures of various ethnic groups. These and other practical circumstances arising in the practice of family law make experience of it different from other areas of legal practice, but do not distinguish family law as essentially different in any conceptual way. There is an additional and fundamental respect in which family law is distinct from most other areas of legal practice.

Most litigation and adjudication is concerned with the determination of, and giving effect to, vested legal rights arising from past events. In most adjudications the court has to determine the legal rights and obligations which have accrued to the litigants, and achieve a 'verdict' upon past events, before moving on to the grant of appropriate legal remedies to give effect to vested legal rights. In trial of crime, torts or contract, the process of reaching the verdict requires the court to decide, as objectively as humanly possible, what has happened in the past and what is the correct applicable law. There is no room for discretion in this requirement for objectivity, even though the jury or judge as human beings may find it difficult, when assessing the evidence, to exclude their subjective views and agendas. There may be room for discretion when the court moves on to decide what remedy to grant, for example the amount of damages for personal injury, or the severity of sentence for a crime or whether a remedial sentence is more appropriate. But deciding the remedy is secondary to, and consequential upon, reaching the verdict.

Most family litigation is concerned with the welfare and upbringing of children, the financial support of former spouses and of children, the occupation of the family home, and the protection from violence and molestation. A judge deciding a dispute about arrangements for a child, financial support or occupation of the family home, is making a choice which belongs to the parties. A judge deciding whether to grant a legal remedy for the protection of a child from a parent, or for protection of a person from a spouse or partner or relative, has to decide whether the court should intervene in issues of personal responsibility and behaviour which belong to the persons concerned. Judges have to make such decisions, determining choices about future behaviour and responsibilities, only because members of a family do not or cannot adequately fulfil, or reach agreement on, responsibilities which belong to them. Although in dealing with these issues the court may have to reach objective decisions about past facts and events, the critical function of the court is to evaluate the present and future needs and responsibilities of the several members of the family. The decision-making process involves making value assessments of future behaviour and ability to fulfil responsibilities, and the exercise of judicial discretion. This core function of family adjudication, while it requires objectivity on the part of the judge, is different from the objective process involved in reaching a verdict required in most other areas of law.

An adjudication which turns on the exercise of judicial discretion based on value judgments about present and future needs and responsibilities is inherently different from reaching a verdict on past events and discernment of consequent vested legal rights, which is the critical function of the adjudication in most areas of legal dispute resolution.

There are other significant areas of social tension, conflict and legal dispute resolution which seem similar to family proceedings, in being focused on present and future social needs and responsibilities. In respect of family issues, equality of opportunity, race relations and industrial relations, while substantive law may be appropriate for defining basic responsibilities, successful dispute resolution by negotiation controlled by the parties, within given legal boundaries, is likely to be more beneficial than conversion of the tensions into litigation and adjudication controlled by lawyers. However, protection by legal remedy for a vulnerable member of a family, or for someone vulnerable as a member of an ethnic group or as an employee, in some circumstances is a responsibility of the State.

. . .

### 1.3.1  Rules and discretion in family law

The following extract was written in the context of an United States Bar conference on 'Family Law for the Next Century'.

### Schneider, Carl E., 'The Tension Between Rules and Discretion in Family Law: A Report and Reflection'
#### (1993) 27 Fam LQ 229

The history of law is many things. But one of them is the story of an unremitting struggle between rules and discretion. The tension between these two approaches to legal problems continues to pervade and perplex the law today. Perhaps nowhere is that tension more pronounced and more troubling than in family law. It is probably

impossible to practice family law without wrestling with the imponderable choice between rules and discretion.
. . .

### Discretion

What, then, are the attractions of discretion? Perhaps its leading virtue is that it gives a judge authority to respond to the full range of circumstances a case presents and thus to do justice in each individual case. The conferees agreed without noticeable dissent that the need for individualized justice in family law is particularly pressing. People organize and conduct their family lives in a burgeoning and bewildering variety of ways. And a court's resolution of a family dispute will matter to the parties more deeply and durably than in perhaps any other kind of civil litigation.
. . .

A number of the conferees saw another substantial merit in discretion. They pointed out that we seem to be undergoing a period of rapid social change in those parts of life family law seeks to regulate. They observed that rules are intended to, and often do, change grudgingly and ponderously. Discretion, on the other hand, allows the judge to respond expeditiously to society's evolving preferences and practices.

Flexibility, then, is the leading positive argument for discretion. . . .

### Rules

. . . [T]he conferees felt that a primary attraction of rules is that they conduce to 'efficiency.' Rules reduce the possible range of decisions, thereby saving the time and tempers of courts, lawyers, and clients.

. . . 'Efficiency' is not a goal family law has historically valued. It is a cold virtue for so warm a subject. But several conferees proposed that efficiency is more desirable than we often think. They noted that most divorcing couples have little property to divide and no money to spare for legal fees. Even if they needed individualized justice (and some of the conferees believed that the problems of such couples were often not complex and regularly fell into identifiable patterns), they simply could not afford it.

Efficiency is not the only goal rules are usually thought to serve well. The planning function is another. People need to know what the law says so that they can organize their lives rationally. Rules seem likelier than discretion to inform people what the law is and what courts will do. Rules are, after all, publicly stated and thus are, relatively, accessible to prospective litigants. And rules are precisely an attempt to state in advance how cases should be decided.

In family law, the planning function may be relevant in two ways. First, people may want to know what the law is while they are married so that they can maximize their chances in any eventual divorce action. Second, people may want to understand the law when they are seeking a divorce so that they can 'bargain in the shadow of the law.'

. . . As I have been reporting, the conferees broadly agreed that rules generally serve law's efficiency and planning functions better than discretion. They were also alert to another way in which rules might be preferable to discretion in family law. They frequently remarked that rules often promote better than discretion law's 'expressive' function. The expressive function is mobilized when the law is used to make statements that have symbolic importance.

The law of child custody provides several illuminating examples of the use and usefulness of the law's expressive function. . . .

Finally some conferees saw a virtue in rules where other conferees had seen a virtue in discretion. These conferees argued that rules could enhance litigants' satisfaction (or, more accurately, reduce their dissatisfaction) better than discretion. Litigants may feel that a decision based observably on rules is at least not arbitrary and discriminatory. As one lawyer commented, 'Clients want to be treated the same way as everybody else.' Rules make even-handedness easier to demonstrate and to perceive.

Along these lines, several lawyers commented that rules helped them in their relations with their clients. As one lawyer observed, 'Sometimes clients have very unreasonable expectations, and clear rules help control them.' ('Control' here meant guiding the client toward claims that stood some chance of success and toward the hope of settling the dispute on reasonable terms.) . . .

These observations about how rules can promote the satisfaction of litigants could be expanded to make a more general point. Rules may serve better than discretion the goal of treating like cases alike. If each decision-maker has discretion to decide case by case what principles to apply and how to apply them, cases that are essentially similar are likely to be decided differently. Rules, on the other hand, work to suppress differences of opinion among decision-makers. Furthermore, rules serve as record-keeping devices, so that decision-makers can more easily cordinate their rulings over time and among themselves.

. . .

Many of the conferees were afraid that we today are witnessing the bureaucratization of family law. They saw the recent federal requirement that states adopt child-support guidelines as a telling step in that direction. They believed that that bureaucratization was being hastened along by another trend — the federalization of family law. Federal child-support legislation is one example of this trend; federal responses to the problem of child abuse are another. The conferees feared that, the more family law responds to central commands, the more bureaucratic it must become.

The bureaucratization of family law, of course, has deep and extensive consequences for the balance between rules and discretion. The essential question of bureaucratic organization is how to control and make consistent the similar decisions of legions of parallel decision-makers. The standard answer to that question is to impose rules of an effectively binding sort on those decision-makers — to deprive them of their discretion.

Some conferees certainly appreciated the advantages of the bureaucratization of family law. A number of people asked whether we can afford to offer individualized justice in an area where the demand for it is great, its cost is overwhelming, and its success is questionable. Nevertheless, the movement toward bureaucratization disturbed some of the conferees acutely.

The conferees who were concerned about the trend toward bureaucratization worried about what such a routinization of family law could mean for them professionally. They feared that judges deprived of discretion could hardly be distinguished from computers and that lawyers who argued to such judges could hardly be more than low-level data processors.

But these conferees also saw the trend as frustrating their clients in the way bureaucracies frustrate everyone — by being elaborately rule-bound and unable to respond to the individual circumstances of real people. 'But we're supposed to be lawyers looking for justice,' protested one conferee. And we all wondered how far this might be possible in the new world we face.

*Notes*
*1.* The discretionary nature of family justice is exemplified in the rule relating to appeals laid down in *G* v *G* *(Minors: Custody Appeal)* [1985] 1

WLR 647, [1985] 2 All ER 225, where the House of Lords held that the appellate courts should not interfere with the exercise of judicial discretion in the lower courts unless the judge had exceeded the generous ambit within which judicial disagreement was reasonably possible and the decision was plainly wrong. *G* v *G* concerned a custody dispute, but the same rule is applied to appeals in other family matters.

2.   One of the Government's justifications for introducing a mathematical formula for assessing child maintenance was because discretionary court decisions led to widely different results in similar cases (see Chapter 9).

*Questions*
What are the advantages and disadvantages of discretion? In which areas of family law is there wide discretion? Are the statutory guidelines in s. 25 of the Matrimonial Causes Act 1973 and in s. 1(3) of the Children Act 1989 intended to control discretion? Is there too much discretion in family law?

*Further reading*
Jackson, E. *et al,* 'Financial Support on Divorce: The Right Mixture of Rules and Discretion?' (1993) 7 IJL&F 230.
Hawkins, K., *The Uses of Discretion*, Oxford: Clarendon Press, 1992.

### 1.3.2   The growth of mediation

Mediation is a form of alternative dispute resolution (ADR) in which both parties to a dispute meet voluntarily with a neutral third person (a mediator) who helps them explore the possibility of reaching their own agreements about arrangements for the future. Mediation incorporates two main features. One is that family disputes should be resolved with the least possible bitterness and hostility, and the other is that important decisions following marriage breakdown should, where possible, be made by the couple themselves. There are other forms of ADR besides mediation. Negotiation between solicitors is another form, and so is the use of pre-trial hearings. Mediation is set to increase dramatically with the implementation of the divorce reforms under the Family Law Act 1996 (see Chapter 4).

Mediation techniques were initially developed in court and out of court to settle disputes between parents about arrangements for their children on divorce. This practice was known as conciliation (for an excellent survey of the development of conciliation, see the judgment of Sir Thomas Bingham MR in *Re D (Minors) (Conciliation: Privilege)* [1993] 1 FLR 932, CA, in Chapter 9). It was increasingly realised, however, that conciliation techniques were also suitable for solving disputes about property and finance on divorce. The term 'mediation' was originally used only in the context of property and financial disputes on divorce, but it is now used to cover the whole spectrum of disputes on family breakdown. Although mediation may be an ideal solution in some cases, it may not be a panacea for every dispute. In fact, mediation and negotiation may have their own sets of problems for those who are 'bargaining in the shadow of the law'.

**Eekelaar, John, and Maclean, Mavis, *Family Law and Social Policy*,
2nd edn**
London: Weidenfeld and Nicolson, 1984, p. 59

. . .

Objection to the promotion of conciliation over adjudication can take at least two forms. It can be argued that leaving the parties to come to their own arrangements, and giving these arrangements binding force, risks both the exploitation of one party by the other and the subordination of the children's (and possibly, the state's) interests to those of the two adults. Additionally, it may be said that the introduction of 'social work' oriented personnel to oversee the arrangements made by the parties promotes excessive regulatory intrusion into private affairs which are better protected by legal and procedural formality. . . .

**Ingleby, Richard, 'Court Sponsored Mediation: The Case Against
Mandatory Participation'**
(1993) 56 MLR 441

. . . The uncritical sponsorship of mediation is problematic from two angles. First, is 'settlement' always desirable? Should we necessarily assume that failure to settle or achieve settlement is a negative, dissonant feature in an otherwise well-ordered and satisfactorily functioning world? On the contrary, some conflict may be constructive and the submersion of at least some types of conflict harmful. Second, even if these goals are deemed desirable, is there any evidence that mediation, and in particular, mandated mediation, can meet them? . . .

One of the classic discussions of 'private ordering' on divorce is that of Mnookin and Kornhauser.

**Mnookin, Robert H., and Kornhauser, Lewis, 'Bargaining in
the Shadow of the Law'**
(1979) 88 *Yale Law Journal* 950

. . . We see the primary function of contemporary divorce law not as imposing order from above, but rather as providing a framework within which divorcing couples can themselves determine their postdissolution rights and responsibilities. This process by which parties to a marriage are empowered to create their own legally enforceable commitments is a form of 'private ordering'.
. . .

*The Advantages of Private Ordering*
. . . There are obvious and substantial savings when a couple can resolve distributional consequences of divorce without resort to courtroom adjudication. The financial cost of litigation, both private and public, is minimized. The pain of a formal adversary proceeding is avoided. Recent psychological studies indicate that children benefit when parents agree on custodial arrangements. Moreover, a negotiated agreement allows the parties to avoid the risks and uncertainties of litigation, which may involve

all-or-nothing consequences. Given the substantial delays that often characterize contested judicial proceedings, agreement can often save time and allow each spouse to proceed with his or her life. Finally, a consensual solution is by definition more likely to be consistent with the preferences of each spouse, and acceptable over time, than would a result imposed by a court.

In divorces that involve no minor children, divorcing couples should have very broad powers to make their own arrangements; significant limitations are inconsistent with the premises of no-fault divorce. After all, who can better evaluate the comparative advantages of alternative arrangements than the parties themselves? . . .

. . .

We believe divorcing parents should be given considerable freedom to decide custody matters — subject only to the same minimum standards for protecting the child from neglect and abuse that the state imposes on *all* families. A negotiated resolution is desirable from the child's perspective for several reasons. First, a child's social and psychological relationships with both parents ordinarily continue after the divorce. A process that leads to agreement between the parents is preferable to one that necessarily has a winner and a loser. A child's future relationship with each of his parents is better ensured and his existing relationship less damaged by a negotiated settlement than by one imposed by a court after an adversary proceeding. . . .

Second, the parents will know more about the child than will the judge.

. . .

*The Roles of Lawyers*

If one accepts the proposition that the primary function of the legal system should be to facilitate private ordering and dispute resolution, then several important questions come into sharp focus. To what extent does the participation of lawyers facilitate dispute resolution? Are there fairer and less costly procedures in which lawyers would play a lesser role?

Many observers are very critical of the way some lawyers behave in divorce negotiations. Lawyers may make negotiations more adversarial and painful, and thereby make it more difficult and costly for the spouses to reach agreement.

Indeed, lawyers may be more likely than lay people to adopt negotiating strategies involving threats and the strategic misrepresentation of their clients' true preferences in the hope of reaching a more favorable settlement. . . .

Yet, there are also arguments that lawyers facilitate dispute settlement. Lawyers may make negotiations more rational, minimize the number of disputes, discover outcomes preferable to both parties, increase the opportunities for resolution out of court, and ensure that the outcomes reflect the applicable legal norms.

. . .

Mnookin and Kornhauser conclude by drawing attention to the limits of private ordering:

          .

Viewing the process of divorce from the perspective of private ordering does not make previously intractable family law problems disappear. If anything, the world seems even more complex, since the analysis requires us to examine the effects of alternative rules and procedures on informal and formal bargaining about which we have little understanding.

*Note*
Despite Mnookin and Kornhauser's emphasis on the benefits of private ordering, under English law a couple may not by agreement oust the court's power to supervise their arrangements (*Hyman* v *Hyman* [1929] AC 601), and the court must scrutinise any agreement placed before it (see Lord Scarman in *Minton* v *Minton* [1979] AC 593 at p. 605).

Many lawyers adopt conciliatory approaches to family disputes by seeking to achieve and encourage agreement through negotiation rather than by litigation in the courts. Some family lawyers in fact work alongside the mediation services and some employ mediators on their staff. The Code of Practice of the Solicitors' Family Law Association (SFLA), to which members of that association subscribe, encourages conciliatory approaches to the resolution of family disputes. The Family Law Bar Association adopts a similar philosophy.

## Code of Practice of the Solicitors' Family Law Association

**General**
1.1 At an early stage the solicitor should inform the client of the approach he adopts in family law work.

1.2 The solicitor should advise, negotiate and conduct matters so as to encourage and assist the parties to achieve a constructive settlement of their differences as quickly as may be reasonable whilst recognising that the parties may need time to come to terms with their new situation.

1.3 The solicitor should ensure that the client appreciates that the interests of the children should be the first concern. The solicitor should encourage the client to see the advantages to the family of a constructive and non-adversarial approach as a way of resolving their differences. The solicitor should explain to the client that in cases where there are children the attitude of the client to the other family members in any negotiations will affect the family as a whole and may affect the relationship of the children with the parents.

1.4 The solicitor should encourage the attitude that a family dispute is not a contest in which there is one winner and one loser, but rather a search for fair solutions. He should avoid using words or phrases that imply a dispute when no serious dispute necessarily exists.

1.5 Because of the involvement of personal emotions in family disputes the solicitor should where possible avoid heightening such emotions in any way.

1.6 The solicitor should have regard to the impact of correspondence on the other party when writing a letter of which a copy may be sent to that party. He should also consider carefully the impact of correspondence on his own client before sending copies of letters to the client. The solicitor should avoid expressing personal opinions as to the conduct of the other party.

1.7 The solicitor should aim to avoid mistrust between parties by encouraging at an early stage full, frank and clear disclosure of information and openness in dealings.

**2. Relationship with Client**
2.1 The solicitor should ensure that his relationship with his client is such that his objectivity is preserved and his own personal emotions do not cloud his judgment.

2.2 Whilst recognising the need to advise firmly and guide the client, the solicitor should ensure that where the decision is properly that of the client, it is taken by the client and that its consequences are fully understood, both as to its effect on any children involved and financially.

2.3 The solicitor should always ensure that the client is fully aware of the impact of costs on any chosen course of action. The solicitor should throughout have regard to the cost of negotiations and proceedings.

2.4 The solicitor should ensure that the client is aware of the existence and range of all other services which may be of assistance in bringing about a resolution and helping members of the family through the process of family breakdown, such as mediation and counselling.

## 3. Dealings with other Solicitors
3.1 In all dealings with other solicitors, the solicitor should show courtesy and endeavour to create and maintain a good working relationship.

3.2 The solicitor should not denigrate the other solicitors involved in the case to the client.

## 4. Dealings with the other party in person
4.1 In dealings with another party who is not legally represented the solicitor should take particular care to be courteous and restrained. Special care should be taken to express letters and other communication clearly, avoiding technical language where it is not readily understandable to the layman or might be misunderstood.

4.2 Wherever any party is not legally represented, that party should, in the interests of both parties and the family, be advised to consult a solicitor.

## 5. Court Proceedings
5.1 The taking of any action or proceedings which is likely to cause or increase animosity between the parties must be balanced against the likely benefit to the client and the family.

5.2 Where the purpose of taking a particular step in proceedings may be misunderstood or appear hostile, the solicitor should consider explaining it, at the first practical opportunity, to the other party or his solicitors.

5.3 Before filing a petition, the solicitor should consider with the client whether the other party or his solicitor should be contacted in advance as to the intention to petition, the 'facts' on which the petition is to be based and/or the particulars to be alleged, with a view to proceeding by agreement. A client should be advised that filing a petition and/or Statement of Arrangements without first attempting to agree the contents is likely to increase feelings of contentiousness and hostility, making any settlement much more difficult to achieve. It may also earn the disapproval of the Court and may have a bearing on the issue of costs.

5.4 The solicitor should advise the client that on receipt for approval from the other spouse of a Petition or Statement of Arrangements, and other than in exceptional circumstances, a client should not first file their own petition without giving their spouse at least 5 working days' written notice of the intention to do so.

5.5 The solicitor should discourage a Petitioner client from naming a Co-Respondent unless there is a compelling reason to do so.

5.6   A solicitor should conduct family law proceedings, including the preparation, advocacy and implementation, in the most cost-effective manner and in such a way as not to increase hostility unnecessarily and as to allow reasonable opportunity for settlement.

## 6.  Children

6.1   The solicitor should, in advising, negotiating and conducting proceedings, encourage both his client and other family members to regard the welfare of the child as the first and paramount consideration.

6.2   The solicitor should aim to promote co-operation between parents in decisions concerning the child, and should consider encouraging arrangements to be reached direct or through mediation.

6.3   Issues of arrangements for the children on the one hand and finance on the other must be kept separate. They should be referred to in separate letters.

6.4   The solicitor must remember that the interests of the child may not coincide with those of either parent, and in exceptional cases it may be appropriate for the child to be separately represented; this may be by the Official Solicitor, a Panel Guardian (in specified proceedings) or in the case of a 'mature' child by a solicitor direct.

## 7.  The Child as client

7.1   A solicitor should only accept instructions from a child direct if the solicitor has the requisite training and expertise in this field. The solicitor should make a personal commitment to undertake all preparation and advocacy for the child and give the child the same respect afforded to an adult as client.

7.2   A difficult and continuing duty for the solicitor is to assess the child's capacity to give instructions.

7.3   The solicitor should ensure that the child has sufficient information throughout the proceedings to make informed decisions; advice and information should be presented in a clear and understandable form. The solicitor must be aware that certain information may be harmful to the child.

7.4   The child's solicitor should maintain a neutral approach as between each parent, the local authority and other parties.

7.5   Detailed guidelines have been drawn up by the SFLA for those members acting for children.

*Note*

The Solicitors' Family Law Association, responding to the Consultation Paper on Divorce (see Chapter 4), stated ([1994] Fam Law 179) that:

[Mediation] is not . . . suited by any means to all of the divorcing population. It is inappropriate to extrapolate the current success of mediation and build a whole new system upon it. . . . Lawyers are not the cause of cost in the divorce process; it is the complexity of present day life and the emotions which can be generated upon separation. Mediation will not automatically resolve these emotional difficulties. Cheap processes produce inferior results. . . .

*Questions*
What are the advantages and disadvantages of the trend towards a greater emphasis on mediation as opposed to legal advice and court adjudication? Is there a threat of 'lawyerless' justice and also a danger that many family issues which are best dealt with by the courts will not be? Is there a danger that women and children may suffer as a result of the increasing trend towards mediation?

*Further reading*
Davis, G., *Partisans and Mediators*, Oxford: Oxford University Press, 1988.
Eekelaar, J., 'A Jurisdiction in Search of a Mission: Family Proceedings in England and Wales' (1994) 57 MLR 839.
Fisher, T. (ed.), *Family Conciliation within the UK*, Bristol: Jordans, 1990.
McCarthy, P., and Walker, I., Involvement of Lawyers in the Mediation Process' [1996] Fam Law 154.
Roberts, S., 'Alternative Dispute Resolution and Civil Justice: An Unresolved Relationship' (1993) 56 MLR 452.

## 1.4   POLICY ISSUES IN FAMILY LAW

**Dewar, John, 'Policy Issues in Law and the Family',
in Wilson, Geoffrey P. (ed), *Frontiers of Legal Scholarship***
Chichester: John Wiley, 1995, Chapter 5, p. 62

Like social policy in the United Kingdom, legal policy with respect to the family over the last 25 years been characterised by a number of differing, and sometimes competing, objectives.

Three features characterised legal policy in the wake of the divorce reforms of 1969 and 1970. The first was that divorce should be more easily available than previously (both in terms of the substantive grounds and state funding of proceedings), and that the courts should have a wide ranging discretion to redistribute family assets and to make orders for income transfers on divorce. Second, marriage occupied an almost unquestioned centrality in lawyer's thinking about family matters: there was very limited provision for unmarried couples and the concept of illegitimacy was not to be removed from the law until 1987. Finally, the social security system, sometimes acknowledged as the 'third system' of Family Law, continued to be grounded on the post-war consensus that the role of the state was to guarantee the well being of family members to a basic level. The 1973 Finer Committee Report on One Parent Families, for example, did not regard it as politically unacceptable to propose new forms of state assistance for single parents, a group identified as facing particular economic hardship.

The shortcomings of this state of affairs became increasingly apparent during the 1980s. Divorce rates continued to rise with disastrous financial consequences for women and children, something which the divorce court, even when armed with its wide order-making powers, was powerless to prevent. Research showed that for many couples, the divorce court's jurisdiction to make financial provision was a luxury afforded by only a few; for increasing numbers of divorcing couples, the reality of divorce meant making the most of the state benefits available, particularly supplementary and related benefits (and especially the payment of mortgage interest). The courts colluded in this form of benefit planning, taking the view that men should support their new rather than former families. It became common practice for men to trade property for reduced child support; and although in theory such orders were not binding on the DHSS, there was a low level of recovery of support from 'liable relatives'. Further, it became apparent that never married mothers were an increasing and significant group of social security claimants, mirroring the rise in extra-marital cohabitation and non-marital births.

These developments had an impact on the public purse in two ways. The first was the growing cost of benefits paid to single mothers; the second was the rising cost to the Legal Aid budget of paying for a growing number of family disputes. The coming to power in 1979 of a Conservative government committed to reducing public expenditure meant that it was only a matter of time before this state of affairs came under official scrutiny. It duly did so, most obviously in the shape of the Government White Paper on Child Support (1990) and a later Green Paper on Divorce and Mediation (1993); less obviously in the shape of a steady erosion in legal aid eligibility and a restructuring of the state safety net by the Social Security Act 1988. These cost cutting measures were accompanied by an increasingly vehement rhetoric of parental (and individual) responsibility and a condemnation of 'abnormal' family lifestyles. Single mothers and feckless fathers were demonised.

Three trends in government and other official thinking appeared during the 1980s. The first was the growing recognition for legal purposes of family forms outside marriage. Growing diversity in patterns of family living forced a recognition that the creation and enforcement of effective support obligations would have to depend on something other than marriage. This, when coupled with other policy developments . . . led to the recognition of legal relationships (and especially obligations of support) that had nothing to do with marriage.

The second was that the traditional means of resolving family disputes were called into question: they were easily portrayed as expensive, unnecessarily elaborate for the majority of clients and likely to produce bad consequences for the welfare state. The third, linked to the second, was the disenchantment with the discretionary modes of decision-making that have come to characterise decision-making in family law in post-war years. This is seen to be productive of uncertainty and, thus, of inefficiency and injustice.

It could be argued that these trends were prompted exclusively by a desire on the part of the government to curb public spending; but there are two reasons why this argument should be treated with caution. The first is that public spending has exerted a grip over family law for some time. The introduction of the 'special procedure' in 1977, which arguably did more than the Divorce Reform Act 1969 to alter the nature of divorce, was prompted by a desire to remove legal aid from undefended divorces. Second, it is unlikely that these policy changes would have taken root if they did not reflect existing disenchantment with the system, or other policy shifts pointing in the same directions. The shift from marriage, for example, could be attributed as much to a policy of recentring legal concern on the child, rather than on the marital status of the parents, as to concern with the social security bill. The disenchantment with traditional methods of adjudication could be attributed as much to the conciliation/ mediation movement, and to research on the behaviour of judges and lawyers in the context of traditional litigation, as to concerns about the costs to the state of legal aid. The scepticism about discretion comes as much from a feminist perspective (especially discretionary decision-making in children and money cases) as from the perspective of justice and efficiency.

. . .

## 1.5   APPROACHES TO FAMILY LAW

### 1.5.1   A functionalist approach

**Kahn-Freund, O., and Wedderburn, K. W., editorial foreword
in Eekelaar, John, *Family Security and Family Breakdown***
London: Penguin, 1971

. . .

All legal principles affecting family life, marriage and divorce, family property, all legal principles governing the relation between parents and children, can be seen as directed to pathological situations, to 'family breakdown'. This function of the law is more prominent and more obvious in this context than anywhere else. The normal behaviour of directors of a company towards their shareholders, or of the officials of a local authority towards the councillors, is regulated by law, and must be. The normal behaviour of husband and wife or parents and children towards each other is beyond the law — as long as the family is 'healthy'. The law comes in when things go wrong. More than that, the mere hint by anyone concerned that the law may come in is the surest sign that things are or will soon be going wrong.

. . .

**Eekelaar, John, *Family Law and Social Policy*, 2nd edn**
London: Weidenfeld and Nicolson, 1984, p. 25

. . .

The first [function of family law] is to provide mechanisms and rules for *adjusting* the relationships between family members when family units break down. The second is to provide *protection* for individuals from possible harms suffered within the family. The third is to *support* the maintenance of family relationships. . . .
. . . The theory to be advanced . . . is that all children have an equal prima facie claim against the present adult world for optimal conditions of upbringing compatible with society's fundamental economic and ideological structure. It follows that the major (but not sole) criteria of evaluation of the three functions of family law delineated above will be child-centred. This is not to confine the evaluation to the concerns of the child itself, for a child-centred approach will also consider the interests of adults who have themselves contributed to the care of the child. . . .

*Questions*
1.   Is the statement by Kahn-Freund and Wedderburn, *supra*, true, or are there situations other than on family breakdown where family law is relevant?
2.   Which particular areas of family law perform the 'adjustment', 'protection' or 'support' functions? In which areas do these functions overlap?
3.   Should family law be more prescriptive, i.e. would it be a good idea, for instance, to define marital and parental obligations, or would this be too intrusive into family life?

### 1.5.2   The private and the public

Another way of looking at family law is in terms of the public/private dichotomy. Private family law may be regarded as the law governing the rights and relationships between family members, and public family law as the law which impacts on the family when the State becomes involved. Some commentators (e.g. Eekelaar, below) consider that the public/private dichotomy is a useless tool of legal analysis; but despite such comments, an approach to family law based on a consideration of the public/private dichotomy may provide us with a better understanding of the nature of family law and of the related but more philosophical question of to what extent the State should intervene in and govern private family life.

## Bainham, Andrew, 'The Privatisation of the Public Interest in Children'
### (1990) 53 MLR 206

The public–private dichotomy is a pervasive theme in legal writing and has been viewed by some as central to an understanding of the role of law in family life. Others have doubted the validity of a rigid demarcation between public and private spheres of activity and in particular the existence of a private, largely unregulated, area of family life. They point out that the so-called private realm is heavily influenced by structures external to it and that its boundaries are drawn up by the State. Thus, it is not naturally preconstituted or beyond legitimate State regulation. The far-ranging and radical reform of both the public and private law affecting children, which will be brought about by the Children Act 1989 (hereafter 'the 1989 Act'), provides a timely opportunity for considering the place of children in this public-private discourse.

Those who believe in a clear divide between the public and the private view the family as a largely unregulated area beyond the reach of law, 'the last outpost of *Gemeinschaft*'. There can be no doubt, at least in theory, that the nature of family privacy imposes significant legal and political constraints on state intervention. Mnookin has explained how, in the United States, there is broad agreement between Liberal Democrats and Conservative Republicans that there are limitations on the power of the Government to intrude into the family and that certain 'private' actions should be presumed to be beyond legitimate governmental control. The consensus there breaks down only when it comes to the definition of which activities should be considered to fall within this private sphere. Liberal Democrats would include within it a broad range of personal activities concerning, *inter alia*, sexuality, marriage and child-rearing. Conservative Republicans, in contrast, emphasise the importance of the family for the stability of society and therefore regard it as a primary social institution appropriate for legal regulation. Although there may be sharp political disagreement about where the boundaries of the public and private are to be drawn, the concept of family privacy is itself entrenched and legally protected under the constitution. Parents and children have constitutional rights not to be subjected to unwarranted state interference in their family life.

In Europe, similar interests are protected by the European Convention on Human Rights. Article 8(1), in particular, upholds the individual's right to 'respect for his private and family life, his home and his correspondence.' In the English domestic context, this meant that the child care legislation had to be reformed to ensure that parents and others were accorded procedural rights, particularly in relation to access, where local authorities attempted to take their children into compulsory care. A basic philosophy enshrined in the 1989 Act is that the state's role in the family is a primarily supportive one and that it should not intervene at all unless it is necessary to do so. There is nothing in the reformed legislation which contradicts (and a great deal which supports) the notion that the family, and specifically child care, is an area which ought to remain unregulated by law unless the need for regulation can be positively demonstrated.

Yet non-regulation or de-regulation is arguably as legally significant as regulation. O'Donovan has criticised lawyers for failing to appreciate the importance of the private sphere precisely because they have not grasped the essence of this. The short point is that the state has the necessary legal authority to regulate all aspects of family life. If it chooses not to do so, this amounts to an endorsement of the status quo. According to feminist theory, deliberate de-regulation of the family reinforces structural inequalities between the sexes.

The very susceptibility of the family to legal regulation may lead to a rejection of the public–private dichotomy as a tool of analysis. In a recent article John Eekelaar [see below] shows how, historically, the family was left substantially unregulated by law while it adequately performed functions which were thought to be in the public interest. Specifically, the legal protection of children came about initially because of the threat to the social order posed by large numbers of vagrant children in the early nineteenth century. This legal regulation was in effect a response to the failure of the family to operate as a 'sufficient mechanism of control.' He concludes that where the family is properly meeting the public interest the law plays only a small role in the definition or enforcement of societal values. But, since the family is in this sense performing a public service, it is inaccurate to view it as operating entirely outside the public sphere. Familial obligations, on the contrary, 'can be viewed as integral parts of the public law system as a whole'. It may thus be a mistake, according to this mode of analysis, to talk in terms of state intervention in the family as if this were an unproblematic concept. Child-rearing may be seen with equal justification as either a private matter, subject to state involvement only when public norms are transgressed, or as a public matter in the sense that the task of giving effect to the community's standards and expectations for child-rearing is delegated to parents. Each perspective according to Eekelaar, is equally valid and contradicts the existence of a well defined public–private dichotomy. In his view, the concept of 'the public interest' is a more valuable tool in understanding family law and 'the focus should be upon the nature of the conception of the *public interest* current at any given time within a community and not some presupposed classification which has small legal relevance'. His preferred approach entails examination of 'the process of transition from the perception that behaviour, whether within the private or public realm, adequately serves the public interest without the invocation of law to the conviction that the public interest demands a legal response.'

In this note I shall attempt to apply Eekelaar's analysis to certain aspects of the 1989 Act. It will be my contention that it is possible to observe the above process of transition in reverse. I shall argue . . . that the fundamental orientation of the legislation is away from the perception that the public interest in children demands a legal response and towards the position that it is best served by the private ordering of family relationships. In effect the Act does not deny the public interest in children but redefines it by identifying it more closely with support for parental discretion. In the more traditional language of the public–private division the latter sphere may be considered to have been enlarged at the expense of the former, since child rearing is likely to be viewed increasingly as a private matter unsuitable for legal regulation. . . .

*Note*

The references in the above extract are to: Mnookin, R., 'The Public/Private Dichotomy: Political Disagreement and Academic Repudiation' (1982) 130

*U Pa LR* 1429, at p. 1430; and O'Donovan, K., *Sexual Divisions in Law*, London: Weidenfeld and Nicolson, 1985, Chapter 1.

## Eekelaar, John, 'What is "Critical" Family Law?'
### (1989) 105 LQR 244

. . .

**(b)   The Public and Private: the Dichotomy Dissolved**
. . .
Instead of the language of 'public' and 'private,' I have preferred to employ the concept of public *interest*. The functioning of what is socially defined as private may often be a matter of public interest. It is always, therefore, susceptible to legal regulation, and has always been so. Marriage, the gateway to the 'private,' has long been under the control of public policy in most societies ('liberal' or otherwise). The law of nullity and divorce, which reached into the most intimate aspects of personal relationships, was no respecter of socially drawn categories. From the point of view of understanding family law, what requires analysis is the process of transition from the perception that behaviour, whether within the private or public realm, adequately serves the public interest without the invocation of law to the conviction that the public interest demands a legal response. This will involve consideration of the image a community holds of itself, and of what events constitute threats to that image. It will include examination of the historically-specific configuration of interest groups within a community and their control over or access to the process of lawmaking. In short, the focus should be upon the nature of the conception of the *public interest* current at any given time within a community and not some presupposed classification which has small legal relevance.
. . .

### 1.5.3   The social science perspective

Family law sometimes draws on social science to provide evidence of trends in family life and to establish whether the law should be reformed; and, if so, how (e.g. some of the Law Commission's arguments in favour of divorce reform (see Chapter 4) were based on statistical evidence gathered from market research, which was conducted to assess the public perception and experience of divorce). Ruth Deech has criticised the over-reliance on empirical social science research, particularly in the area of divorce reform.

## Deech, Ruth, 'Divorce Law and Empirical Studies'
### (1990) 106 LQR 229

. . . [T]he Law Commission reports [on divorce] illustrate the point that the use of statistics in family law today suffers from several hazards. They are gathered and presented by writers who hold preconceptions about the policy changes considered desirable; they are selective; they are used in international comparison while totally ignoring vital national differences; and their use and the different disciplines of the researchers have sapped the intellectual rigour and attractions of family law. Unquestioning reliance by family lawyers on what they perceive to be the conclusions to be drawn from works of social science threatens the rule of law in this field.

By selectivity in statistics is meant that contrasting conclusions may be drawn from the same sets of figures, and that some sets may be emphasised while others are not, or are not gathered when they might have been. Acting as devil's advocate, one could say that the two Law Commission reports on divorce have used only those materials that separate breakdown of marriage and the law, and have ignored those that relate the two and spell out that divorce is bad for the parties and the children.

. . .

One of the most statistically selective topics in family law is the Children Act 1989. Statistics were not used at all in the extensive debate surrounding its passage into law. . . . What would we have done with such figures? Probably we would, quite rightly, have ignored them in the interests of doing the right thing according to current notions of justice, European human rights and in deference to perceived public demand and politics. That is as it should be, and is an attitude which, it is suggested, ought to be substituted for the abject submission to figures, sometimes of the most sketchy and irrelevant variety, presently prevailing in most areas of family law.

. . .

Lawyers appear to have lost faith in their own role in family law and their ability to assess it and plan for the future. There has been an invasion of the divorce process by mediators, possibly at the expense of the parties' statutory rights. Social workers took over child care law and have had to be checked by statute; the statisticians and social scientists are taking over divorce law. It is significant that fewer young academic lawyers now seem to enter family law. This may be because the influence of the social scientists has led to an apparent reduction in the intellectual challenge and content of the law.

We should not in this field disregard the rules of law and the concept of justice in pursuit of aims defined by sociologists as welfare, and lawyers should not withdraw from the subject nor automatically defer to sets of figures. The civil liberties of spouses and children undergoing divorce may be under threat from the interlocking views of a group of social scientists who are not trained in law and lawyers who are not trained in social science. The lawyers appear to believe that their research is valid only when supported by statistics, and the social scientists are seeking a practical subject of study. But the aims of the two professions are, or should be, fundamentally different. Precedent and principle are valuable preservers of rights; the amateur and foreign social science permeating family law is not. Lawyers should be promoting judicial administration of family law, rather than disfranchisement in divorce by conciliation and untrammelled discretion. It is only by upholding legal standards, and by critique from a legal standpoint that academic family lawyers can command respect.

## Eekelaar, John, and Maclean, Mavis, 'Divorce Law and Empirical Studies — A Reply'
### (1990) 106 LQR 621

. . .

Although we have argued that most of Deech's strictures on empirical studies are misplaced, there is one possible effect of social science research on law reform which may explain her sense of anxiety. There may be a risk that absorption in social data becomes so complete that the normative role of the law is minimised or even forgotten. A classic example occurred when Goldstein, Freud and Solnit, impressed by their clinical findings of the disturbance caused to children by interaction with an absent parent, suggested that contact between child and such parent should be entirely within the control of the caregiving parent [*Beyond the Best Interests of the Child*, 1973]. A contrary mistake would be to conclude from the evidence of the weakness of the link between the absent parent and the child that it is not worth legal protection. There may be a similar danger that evidence on the sheer complexity of the social conditions which lead to marriage breakdown could lead policy makers to abandon belief in any normative role for the law in that area. But it is precisely because these fears have substance that we hope that the *combination* of legal and social science input will achieve a balanced response. Can we establish guidelines according to which socio-legal researchers can safely move from the descriptive to the normative?

First, socio-legal researchers should be clear-eyed about the social constructions of the world in which they move. Take the case of evidence of the adverse economic consequences suffered by women and children after divorce. A variety of explanations may be offered. One may be that absent parents are neglectful of their duties. Another that divorce is too easy. But explanation may equally be found in assertions about male dominance in the workplace, gender role divisions within marriage and child-rearing and the nuclear family system. Apart from making divorce more difficult, or tightening support obligations, remedies could range from abolishing the family and collectivising child care or the rigorous enforcement of child care responsibilities of fathers to providing employers with incentives to minimise contact between the sexes in the workplace or sponsoring a religious revival. Let us not allow our preconceptions to close any doors.

But socio-legal researchers are not, we think, in the business of making revolutions. Part of their purpose is to relate the aims of social policy as manifested in law or otherwise to social life. It is for this reason that their enterprise has been branded with the label of 'functionalism'. We encourage speculative thought which questions the premises of social organisation But socio-legal studies has its own intellectual challenge. It lies in searching for a reconciliation between the conflicting responses to the questions raised by considering social data (which Deech's article has revealed) and the normative function and juristic principles of a legal system. It can only complement, and never replace, traditional legal scholarship. . . .

*Note*

Other ways of considering the nature of family law might be from a social policy, an economic or a philosophical perspective. For an approach based on concepts taken from moral and political philosophy, see Park, Stephen, 'Rights and Utility in Anglo-Australian Family Law' (1992) 55 MLR 311.

# 2 MARRIAGE AND COHABITATION

The first part of this chapter deals with marriage. The second part deals with cohabitation, which perhaps poses a threat to the institution of marriage, for, while marriage is on the decrease, increasing numbers of couples are choosing to cohabit rather than to marry. In fact in 1993 there were just under 300,000 marriages, of which only 182,000 were first-time marriages — the lowest recorded figure ever. In 1979, by way of comparison, there were 426,000 marriages of which 340,000 were first-time marriages.

## 2.1 MARRIAGE: AN INTRODUCTION

### Hyde v Hyde and Woodmansee
(1866) LR 1 P & D 130, Court of Divorce and Matrimonial Causes

LORD PENZANCE: . . . Marriage has been well said to be something more than a contract, either religious or civil — to be an Institution. It creates mutual rights and obligations, as all contracts do, but beyond that it confers a status. The position or status of 'husband' and 'wife' is a recognised one throughout Christendom: the laws of all Christian nations throw about that status a variety of legal incidents during the lives of the parties, and induce definite rights upon their offspring. What, then, is the nature of this institution as understood in Christendom? Its incidents vary in different countries, but what are its essential elements and invariable features? If it be of common acceptance and existence, it must needs (however varied in different countries in its minor incidents) have some pervading identity and universal basis. I conceive that marriage, as understood in Christendom, may for this purpose be defined as the voluntary union for life of one man and one woman, to the exclusion of all others. . . .

### Eekelaar, John, *Family Law and Social Policy*, 2nd edn
London: Weidenfeld and Nicolson, 1984, p. 3

. . . The epicentre of family law has always evolved around the institution of marriage. Marriage is the basis of the legal family and has therefore provided the framework in which legal obligations of the adult parties towards each other and their children have been set. There are, however, many indications that marriage is losing this central position. Other forms of living arrangements which can broadly be considered 'familial' are becoming more common. Marriage is still the most significant of these, but it is becoming difficult to see with clarity what are the characteristics which distinguish it from other modes of family life and correspondingly harder to know what legal responses are appropriate to each of them. . . .

## O'Donovan, Katherine, *Family Law Matters*
London: Pluto Press, 1993, Chapter 4, at pp. 57–8

. . .

As befits an ancient institution, marriage has its iconography. Symbols are: engagement ring, church announcements, public notices, invitations, special clothes, wedding dress, veil, prescribed colours, flowers, bouquet, attendants, witnesses, wedding ring, ritualistic words, ceremony, music, signature and record. Marriage is a *rite de passage* to be celebrated with food, wine, speech; to be recorded on film. Consider how a few bars of Mendlessohn's Wedding March can invoke immediate images and the power of institution and ritual is evident. Later, photographs in silver frames, engagement and wedding rings serve as reminders of changed legal status, and as sign to others.

The legal and the social are mixed in wedding ritual, as is the political. For marriage provides 'the basic unit of our society. It is within the family that the next generation is nurtured' (Thatcher, *The Times*, 17 October 1981). There is a kind of uniform monotony in our fates. We are destined to marry or to enter similar relationships. . ..

It is not just the wedding which is ritual, but the lived experience of marriage. It is a material condition, a visible structure of everyday life. Experienced as a system of images, confirmed by wedding and family pictures, re-enacted through anniversary custom, its traces are visible everywhere. Despite deconstructionist critique, perhaps because of its all-embracing but unspecific nature, marriage endures as symbol. The marriage order, like the legal order, is a matter of what is lived, accepted and made familiar, or family. It may be presented as private but it is reinforced everywhere in public and in political discourse. Marriage has its own rituals, children, coupledom, Saturday nights out, reunions, a familiar tradition learned and transmitted at home. It does not have to be rational, its origins are sacred, it can call on mythology, an unconscious reservoir of memories, emblems, a fictive narrative. In a sense, the problem for those excluded from legal marriage is that, despite logic and rationality which may be marshalled to support change, there is no reason to listen, and their voices may not be heard. Children carry forward the tradition, unwritten, custom. Marriage hallucinates in a repetition of ritual. It matters not that obedience is dropped from the marriage vow or that the ceremony takes place without a church. It invokes and evokes timeless, unspoken memory. It can resist theorising and theory. To break free from marriage as a timeless, unwritten institution whose terms are unequal and unjust has been the ambition of feminist writers. Legal theorists have deconstructed marriage to point up the gendered nature of its terms. Yet others find a solution in a freely negotiated contract to be agreed by the partners. Contract as the model of political relations and the justification of the state is presented as a solution to marriage difficulties, as a principle of social association, and as a means of creating social relationship, such as couple agreements. This is reinforced by pointing to entry into marriage as free and voluntary. Recent work on family and social contract raises

doubts about this line of reasoning. In her powerful book *The Sexual Contract* Carole Pateman criticises the limitations of social contract theory in justifying current political arrangements. The sexual contract, which predated the social contract, gave men conjugal mastery over women, realised through marriage. Readings of major social contract theorists from Hobbes to Rousseau confirm that the family is taken as natural, as pre-given. Marriage, the foundation of family, ensures the subordination of women, which is presented as inevitable. The free individuals who contract in the social contract are male. The issue of whether or not women contract freely into the sexual contract is unresolved, and the way out for political theorists is to tell patriarchal stories in which marriage and family are 'natural'.
. . .

*Note*
The reference in the above extract is to Pateman, C., *The Sexual Contract*, Stanford University: Polity Press, 1988.

**Law Commission, *Facing the Future: A Discussion Paper on the Ground for Divorce*, Law Com. No. 170**
London: HMSO, 1988, pp. 9 and 10

. . .
2.19 Socio-economic developments seem to have led to a change in the nature of marriage in Western society. What has been called 'institutional' marriage, which largely entails economic functions and the provision of domestic services, has been replaced by what may be called 'companionate' marriage, which requires a continuing successful emotional relationship. The latter is obviously far more difficult to sustain than the former. A number of factors have been identified which may have contributed to this changed view of marriage. First, the values of society generally have changed, with greater emphasis on pursuit of individual success and happiness and less on religious and ethical doctrines. Secondly, income and wealth today depend upon trade and employment rather than inherited property. This has emancipated more young people from their parents' control. Combined with increased prosperity it has enabled couples to marry, or set up home together, as soon as they please, and even (it has been suggested) to apply consumer society's 'throwaway attitude' to marriage. Thirdly, the 'emancipation' of women has changed women's expectations of what marriage should provide for them. Interviews with divorcing couples reveal that often the spouses had widely differing conceptions both of what marriage meant and of what their own marriage had been like. . . .
2.20 The increased vulnerability of marriage would seem to be exacerbated by various other socio-economic causes, such as unemployment and greater social isolation caused by urban living, which create stresses in the marriage. Just as important as the factors which have increased the vulnerability of marriages are those developments which have provided increased opportunities for people, particularly women, who are disillusioned with their marriages to break away. Thus, greater educational and employment opportunities for women have meant that they are more likely to have or be able to achieve financial and social independence. Allied to this is the trend towards smaller, more consciously planned families. . . . The provision by the Welfare State of supplementary benefit, local authority housing (with priority given to child-carers) and legal aid and advice has given many women the means, previously only available to men, to end their marriages. The higher divorce rate itself may have

a catalyst effect by making divorce more familiar and removing the extra-legal deterrents. Thus, for example, divorce has carried less stigma and there are more social outlets for divorcees including an increased possibility of remarriage.

2.21   Lastly, although there has been a reduction in the rate of marriage over the past two decades and non-marital cohabitation and the rearing of children outside marriage have increased in incidence and social acceptability, there is no reason to suppose that marriage and the family are declining in popularity or significance. Indeed, it has been suggested that high divorce rates indicate that the institution of marriage is as healthy as ever, for two reasons. First, as discussed above, people tend to divorce '*not* because they are turned off marriage but, rather, because their expectations of marriage are so high that they will not settle for unsatisfactory approximations'. Thus, it has been suggested that divorce 'is mainly a backhanded compliment to the ideal of modern marriage, as well as a testimony to its difficulties'. Secondly, people often divorce in order to remarry. . . .

. . . [W]hat has changed is not the respect for marriage and the family, but people's expectations, attitudes and behaviour. These changes mean that ironically divorce often reflects the continued value attached by people to marriage.
. . .

*Questions*
1.   Do you agree with the Law Commission that marriage is as popular as it ever was?
2.   Has Lord Penzance's description of marriage, which is sometimes quoted in marriage ceremonies and sometimes appears on register office walls, any relevance today?
3.   Why do people marry? Why do same-sex partners want to marry?
4.   What is meant by the 'institution' of marriage? Is cohabitation an institution? What purpose does the institution of marriage serve?
5.   Should marriage as it is presently constituted be abolished and replaced by a contractual arrangement?

## 2.2   WHO HAS A 'RIGHT' TO MARRY?

## EUROPEAN CONVENTION FOR THE PROTECTION OF HUMAN RIGHTS AND FUNDAMENTAL FREEDOMS 1950

### Article 12   Right to marry
Men and women of marriageable age have the right to marry and to found a family, according to the national laws governing the exercise of this right.

### 2.2.1   The grounds for void and voidable marriages

### Matrimonial Causes Act 1973

**11.   Grounds on which a marriage is void**
A marriage . . . shall be void on the following grounds only, that is to say—
    (a)   that it is not a valid marriage under the provisions of the Marriage Acts 1949 to 1986 (that is to say where—
        (i)    the parties are within the prohibited degrees of relationship;
        (ii)   either party is under the age of sixteen; or
        (iii)  the parties have intermarried in disregard of certain requirements as to the formation of marriage);

(b)  that at the time of the marriage either party was already lawfully married;

(c)  that the parties are not respectively male and female;

(d)  in the case of a polygamous marriage entered into outside England and Wales, that either party was at the time of the marriage domiciled in England and Wales.

. . .

## 12.  Grounds on which a marriage is voidable

A marriage . . . shall be voidable on the following grounds only, that is to say—

(a)  that the marriage has not been consummated owing to the incapacity of either party to consummate it;

(b)  that the marriage has not been consummated owing to the wilful refusal of the respondent to consummate it;

(c)  that either party to the marriage did not validly consent to it, whether in consequence of duress, mistake, unsoundness of mind or otherwise;

(d)  that at the time of the marriage either party, though capable of giving a valid consent, was suffering (whether continuously or intermittently) from mental disorder within the meaning of the Mental Health Act 1983 of such a kind or to such an extent as to be unfitted for marriage;

(e)  that at the time of the marriage the respondent was suffering from venereal disease in a communicable form;

(f)  that at the time of the marriage the respondent was pregnant by some person other than the petitioner.

*Notes*

*1.*  A decree of annulment is not needed if a marriage is void, but the advantage of a decree is that it gives the court jurisdiction under Part II of the Matrimonial Causes Act (MCA) 1973 to make finance and property orders (see Chapter 5). Section 13 of the MCA 1973 lays down bars ('defences') to nullity petitions sought under s. 12. A void marriage is one that is void *ab initio* (i.e. there never was a valid marriage). A voidable marriage is a marriage which is valid and existing until the grant of a decree absolute of nullity (see MCA 1973, s. 16).

*2.*  Nullity petitions are rare (most people choose to divorce), but the law of nullity retains some residual significance where the parties have religious objections to divorce or where the parties have entered into an arranged marriage. Annulments in arranged marriage cases are usually sought on the grounds of non-consummation (MCA 1973, s. 12(a) or (b)) and/or lack of consent because of duress (s. 12(c)) (see, e.g., *Kaur* v *Singh* [1972] 1 WLR 105, [1972] 1 All ER 292, CA, and *Hirani* v *Hirani* (1983) 4 FLR 232, CA).

*3.*  The new divorce law (see Chapter 4) will leave the law on nullity intact, except for minor amendments to Part II of the MCA 1973 in respect of the court's powers to make orders for financial provision and property adjustment on a decree of nullity.

*Questions*

Have the following parties contracted valid marriages:

(a)  Just before the ceremony, John decided he did not wish to marry Mary, but after his best man had given him five double vodkas, he went ahead with the ceremony. He remembers nothing of the event. The marriage was consummated, but the next day he realised he had made a terrible mistake.

(b)    An Irishman and a Ghanaian woman living in England were married in Ghana according to customary law. The man, as instructed by a Ghanaian relative, provided £100 and a bottle of gin for the ceremony. During the ceremony, which the couple did not attend, the £100 was distributed to the family and some of the gin was drunk as a blessing? (For the answer, see *McCabe v McCabe* [1994] 1 FLR 410, CA, where these facts actually occurred.)

### 2.2.2    Transsexuals and marriage

## *Rees v United Kingdom*
### [1987] 2 FLR 111
### European Court of Human Rights

. . .

The term 'transsexual' is usually applied to those who while belonging physically to one sex, feel convinced that they belong to the other; they often seek to achieve a more integrated, unambiguous identity, by undergoing medical treatment and surgical operations to adapt their physical characteristics to their psychological nature.

Transsexuals who have been operated upon thus form a fairly well defined and identifiable group.

. . .

English law does not allow a transsexual to contract a valid marriage in the newly acquired sex, as the requirement that the parties to a marriage be respectively male and female (MCA 1973, s. 11(c), *supra*) has been narrowly interpreted. *Corbett v Corbett (Otherwise Ashley)* is the leading case.

## *Corbett v Corbett (Otherwise Ashley)*
### [1970] 2 WLR 1306
### Court of Appeal

*Facts*:  Corbett, the petitioner, married the respondent, April Ashley, knowing that she had been registered at birth as a boy but had later had a sex change operation (removal of the testicles and the construction of an artificial vagina). Corbett subsequently sought a declaration that the marriage was void under s. 11(c) of the MCA 1973, as the respondent was of the male sex. He alternatively petitioned for a decree of nullity on the ground that the marriage was voidable under s. 12(a) and (b) (incapacity or wilful refusal to consummate the marriage). The respondent in answer sought a decree of nullity on the ground of the petitioner's incapacity or wilful refusal to consummate the marriage.

*Held*: that whether the parties to a marriage were male or female was to be determined solely by biological criteria, so that, as the respondent at the date of the marriage ceremony was not a woman but a biological male, the marriage was void.

ORMROD J: . . . The fundamental purpose of law is the regulation of the relations between persons, and between persons and the state or community. For the limited purposes of this case, legal relations can be classified into those in which the sex of the individuals concerned is either irrelevant, relevant or an essential determinant of the nature of the relationship. Over a very large area the law is indifferent to sex. It is irrelevant to most of the relationships which give rise to contractual or tortious rights and obligations, and to the greater part of the criminal law. In some contractual relationships, e.g., life assurance and pensions schemes, sex is a relevant factor in determining the rate of premium or contributions. It is relevant also to some aspects of the law regulating conditions of employment and to various state-run schemes such as national insurance, or to such fiscal matters as selective employment tax. It is not an essential determinant of the relationship in these cases because there is nothing to prevent the parties to a contract of insurance or a pension scheme from agreeing that the person concerned should be treated as a man or as a woman, as the case may be. Similarly, the authorities, if they think fit, can agree with the individual that he shall be treated as a woman for national insurance purposes, as in this case. On the other hand sex is clearly an essential determinant of the relationship called marriage because it is and always has been recognised as the union of man and woman. It is the institution on which the family is built, and in which the capacity for natural hetero-sexual intercourse is an essential element. It has, of course, many other characteristics, of which companionship and mutual support is an important one, but the characteristics which distinguish it from all other relationships can only be met by two persons of opposite sex. . . .

Since marriage is essentially a relationship between man and woman, the validity of the marriage in this case depends, in my judgment, upon whether the respondent is or is not a woman. . . . The question then becomes, what is meant by the word 'woman' in the context of a marriage, for I am not concerned to determine the 'legal sex' of the respondent at large. Having regard to the essentially hetero-sexual character of the relationship which is called marriage, the criteria must, in my judgment, be biological, for even the most extreme degree of transsexualism in a male or the most severe hormonal imbalance which can exist in a person with male chromosomes, male gonads and male genitalia, cannot reproduce a person who is naturally capable of performing the essential role of a woman in marriage. In other words, the law should adopt in the first place, the first three of the doctors' criteria, i.e., the chromosomal, gonadal and genital tests, and if all three are congruent, determine the sex for the purpose of marriage accordingly, and ignore any operative intervention. The real difficulties, of course, will occur if these three criteria are not congruent. This question does not arise in the present case and I must not anticipate, but it would seem to me to follow from what I have said that the greater weight would probably be given to the genital criteria than to the other two. This problem and, in particular, the question of the effect of surgical operations in such cases of physical inter-sex, must be left until it comes for decision. My conclusion, therefore, is that the respondent is not a woman for the purposes of marriage but is a biological male and has been so since birth. It follows that the so-called marriage of September 10, 1963, is void.

## Armstrong, C. N., and Walton, T., 'Transsexuals and the Law'
[1990] 140 NLJ 1384

. . . *Corbett* . . . was responsible in this country for bringing all legal development on the law relating to transsexuals to a shuddering halt. Since then developments in scientific knowledge and understanding of the problem have rapidly and spectacularly outstripped the appreciation of the law, which is unable to keep pace.

Consider the case of a male to female transsexual who, armed with a passport in her 'new' role, complete with operation under the National Health Service and Employment Card, may still be made to use the gentlemen's bathroom, be thrown into a male part of hospital or prison and may not be the subject of rape.

... Many other countries have taken a different attitude: in South Australia, various states in the US, Provinces of Canada and some EEC countries and Scandinavia the transsexual enjoys full rights. In some this includes the right to marry. ...

*Note*

Armstrong and Walton go on to submit that 'psychological sex, psycho-sexuality and behaviour — is hormone determined and consequent upon the sex of the brain and is therefore biological'.

### The Cossey Case
### [1991] 2 FLR 492
### European Court of Human Rights

*Facts*: Miss Caroline Cossey, a male to female transsexual, alleged that the Registrar General's refusal to issue her with a birth certificate showing her sex as female and her inability to contract a valid marriage under English law, gave rise to a violation by the UK of arts 8 and 12 respectively of the European Convention of Human Rights. The UK Government contested her allegations.

*Held*: by 10 votes to 8 that there had been no violation of art. 8, and by 14 votes to 4 that there had been no violation of art. 12.

. . .

34. The Court thus concludes that the present case is not materially distinguishable on its facts from the *Rees* case.

II.  *Should the Court depart from its* Rees *judgment?*

. . .

A.  *Alleged violation of art. 8*

36. The applicant asserted that the refusal to issue her with a birth certificate showing her sex as female constituted an 'interference' with her right to respect for her private life, in that she was required to reveal intimate personal details whenever she had to produce a birth certificate. In her view, the Government had not established that this interference was justified under art. 8(2).

On this point, the Court remains of the opinion which it expressed in the *Rees* judgment . . . : refusal to alter the register of births, or to issue birth certificates whose contents and nature differ from those of the original entries, cannot be considered as an interference. What the applicant is arguing is not that the State should abstain from acting, but rather that it should take steps to modify its existing system. The question is, therefore, whether an effective respect for Miss Cossey's private life imposes a positive obligation on the UK in this regard.

37. As the Court has pointed out on several occasions, notably in the *Rees* judgment itself . . ., the notion of 'respect' is not clear-cut, especially as far as the positive obligations inherent in that concept are concerned: having regard to the

diversity of the practices followed and the situations obtaining in the Contracting States, the notion's requirements will vary considerably from case to case. In determining whether or not a positive obligation exists, regard must be had to the fair balance that has to be struck between the general interest of the community and the interests of the individual, the search for which balance is inherent in the whole of the Convention.

38.   In reaching its conclusion in the *Rees* judgment that no positive obligation of the kind now in issue was incumbent on the UK, the Court noted, inter alia, the following points . . . :

(a)   The requirement of striking a fair balance could not give rise to any direct obligation on the respondent State to alter the very basis of its system for the registration of births, which was designed as a record of historical facts, by substituting therefor a system of documentation, such as that used in some other Contracting States, for recording current civil status.

(b)   An annotation to the birth register, recording Mr Rees' change of sexual identity, would establish only that he belonged thenceforth — and not from the time of his birth — to the other sex. Furthermore, the change so recorded could not mean the acquisition of all the biological characteristics of the other sex. In any event, such an annotation could not, without more, constitute an effective safeguard for ensuring the integrity of his private life, as it would reveal the change in question.

(c)   That change, and the corresponding annotation, could not be kept secret from third parties without a fundamental modification of the existing system for maintaining the register of births, which was accessible to the public. Secrecy could have considerable unintended results and could prejudice the purpose and function of the register by, for instance, complicating factual issues arising in the fields of family and succession law. It would also take no account of the position of third parties, in that they would be deprived of information which they had a legitimate interest to receive.

39.   In the Court's view, these points are equally cogent in the present case, especially as regards Miss Cossey's submission that arrangements could be made to provide her either with a copy birth certificate stating her present sex, the official register continuing to record the sex at birth, or, alternatively, a short-form certificate, excluding any reference either to sex at all or to sex at the date of birth.

Her suggestions in this respect were not precisely formulated, but it appears to the Court that none of them would overcome the basic difficulties. Unless the public character of the register of births were altered, the very details which the applicant does not wish to have disclosed would still be revealed by the original entry therein or, if that entry were annotated, would merely be highlighted. Moreover, the register could not be corrected to record a complete change of sex since that is not medically possible.

40.   In the *Rees* judgment, the Court, having noted that the UK had endeavoured to meet Mr Rees' demands to the fullest extent that its system allowed — and this applies also in the case of Miss Cossey — pointed out that the need for appropriate legal measures concerning transsexuals should be kept under review, having regard particularly to scientific and societal developments. . . .

The Court has been informed of no significant scientific developments that have occurred in the meantime; in particular, it remains the case — as was not contested by the applicant — that gender reassignment surgery does not result in the acquisition of all the biological characteristics of the other sex.

. . .

42.   The Court accordingly concludes that there is no violation of art. 8. The Court would, however, reiterate the observations it made in the *Rees* judgment . . . .

It is conscious of the seriousness of the problems facing transsexuals and the distress they suffer. Since the Convention always has to be interpreted and applied in the light of current circumstances, it is important that the need for appropriate legal measures in this area should be kept under review.

B. *Alleged violation of art. 12*

43. In reaching its conclusion in the *Rees* judgment that there had been no violation of art. 12, the Court noted the following points . . .:

(a)  The right to marry, guaranteed by art. 12, referred to the traditional marriage between persons of opposite biological sex. This appeared also from the wording of the article, which made it clear that its main concern was to protect marriage as the basis of the family.

(b)  Article 12 laid down that the exercise of the right to marry shall be subject to the national laws of the Contracting States. The limitations thereby introduced must not restrict or reduce the right in such a way, or to such an extent, that the very essence of the right was impaired. However, the legal impediment in the UK on the marriage of persons who were not of the opposite biological sex could not be said to have an effect of this kind.

44. Miss Cossey placed considerable reliance, as did the Delegate of the Commission, on the fact that she could not marry at all: as a woman, she could not realistically marry another woman and English law prevented her from marrying a man.

In the latter connection, Miss Cossey accepted that art. 12 referred to marriage between a man and a woman, and she did not dispute that she had not acquired all the biological characteristics of a woman. She challenged, however, the adoption in English law of exclusively biological criteria for determining a person's sex for the purposes of marriage . . . and the Court's endorsement of that situation in the *Rees* judgment, despite the absence from art. 12 of any indication of the criteria to be applied for this purpose. In her submission, there was no good reason for not allowing her to marry a man.

45. As to the applicant's inability to marry a woman, this does not stem from any legal impediment and, in this respect, it cannot be said that the right to marry has been impaired as a consequence of the provisions of domestic law.

As to her inability to marry a man, the criteria adopted by English law are in this respect in conformity with the concept of marriage to which the right guaranteed by art. 12 refers. . . .

46. Although some Contracting States would now regard as valid a marriage between a person in Miss Cossey's situation and a man, the developments which have occurred to date . . . cannot be said to evidence any general abandonment of the traditional concept of marriage. In these circumstances, the Court does not consider that it is open to it to take a new approach to the interpretation of art. 12 on the point at issue. It finds, furthermore, that attachment to the traditional concept of marriage provides sufficient reason for the continued adoption of biological criteria for determining a person's sex for the purposes of marriage, this being a matter encompassed within the power of the Contracting States to regulate by national law the exercise of the right to marry.

. . .

48. The Court thus concludes that there is no violation of art. 12.

*Notes*

*1.* The European Court of Human Rights held that *Cossey* was indistinguishable on its facts from *The Rees Case* [1987] 2 FLR 111, ECHR, in which

the European Court, while recognising Mr Rees's anguish and suffering and the intensity of his desire to adopt a new sexual role, held by 12 votes to 3 that there had been no breach of art. 8, and held unanimously that there had been no breach of art. 12. See also *B* v *France* [1992] 2 FLR 249, where the European Court of Human Rights distinguished *Rees* and *Cossey* on their facts and held by 15 votes to 6 that France had violated art. 8 by refusing to allow Miss B (a male to female transsexual) to re-register as a female in the civil status register and on social security, employment and banking documents and to register new forenames. Despite developments in medical science, however, the Court refused to overrule *Rees* and *Cossey*, holding (in para. 48) that there still remained 'some uncertainty as to the essential nature of transsexualism' and there was 'no sufficiently broad consensus between the Member States of the Council of Europe to persuade the court to reach opposite conclusions to those in its *Rees* and *Cossey* judgments'.
2.    In *Re P and G (Transsexuals)* [1996] 2 FLR 90, QBD, two male to female transsexuals' applications for judicial review of the Registrar General's refusal to amend their birth certificates were dismissed, the court holding, *inter alia*, that the Registrar General was fully entitled to adhere to the tests for ascertaining the sex of the child approved in *Corbett, supra*.

Bradney has described *Corbett* as 'the linchpin of the law relating to trans-sexuality' and says that if the case were reversed 'the legal position of transsexuals would change dramatically'.

### Bradney, Anthony, 'Transsexuals and the Law'
### [1987] Fam Law 350

. . . The integrity of the judgment in *Corbett* is susceptible to challenge on a number of different grounds. One basis for the judgment in *Corbett* is the *Hyde* v *Hyde* dictum that marriage is the union of one man and one woman for life ((1866) LR 1 P & D 130 at p. 133). . . . If it is true that English marriage law specifies the union of man and woman then this is the only part of *Hyde* that is correct.

In fact, English law, interpreted literally, now specifies gender not sex; the contracting parties have to be male and female rather than man and woman (MCA 1973, s. 11(c)). It is possible to argue, on the basis of a rigorous application of doctrinal requirements, that, since marriage law is now couched in the language of gender not sex, *Corbett* is now merely persuasive authority. However, it seems unlikely that the appellate courts would permit such a summary dispatch of a decision which has found its way into the very interstices of the law relating to transsexuals. Nevertheless, one of the rocks on which *Corbett* is founded now seems curiously insubstantial.

The other basis for *Corbett* is the notion that marriage is a partnership with two different roles determined by a bifurcated biology. Ormrod J's references to the division of roles within marriage contain both positive and negative statements. Positively, Ormrod J asserted that the essential role of husband and wife is the capacity for heterosexual intercourse. . . . Negatively, he argued that a transsexual who is a post-operative woman is incapable in law of such intercourse (and, legally, would be incapable even if it was accepted that post-operative sex was determinant on legal sex). *Mutatis mutandis* this latter view would presumably also apply in the case of a transsexual who was a post-operative man.

Both the positive and the negative aspects of this part of *Corbett* give cause for concern. The rationale for the priority that Ormrod J gave to intercourse as the root of marriage is not immediately obvious. As he himself noted, there are several other contenders for this position of pre-eminence; companionship, for example, or mutual support. . . . The primacy given to intercourse cannot be due to its role in procreation. Childless marriages are neither void nor voidable. A marriage in which intercourse has not taken place may be voidable (MCA 1973, s. 12(a) and (b)) but will be fully valid until the moment of the decree of nullity (MCA 1973, s. 16). Socially, it is not clear that many, if any, marriages are contracted primarily with a view to intercourse.

The idea that a transsexual cannot consummate a marriage is based upon the proposition that an artificial vagina does not allow of that 'ordinary and complete intercourse' found necessary in *D-e* v *A-q* (1845) Rob Ecc 279 at p. 298. In his judgment, Ormrod J sought to distinguish the apparently contrary view found in the Court of Appeal decision in *SY* v *SY* [1963] P37. He argued first that this latter case concerned an artificially enlarged vagina and that those parts of the judgment which referred to wholly artificial vaginas were therefore *obiter*. Secondly, he argued that a distinction should be drawn beween an otherwise anatomically normal woman, as in *SY* v *SY*, who had had surgical treatment to her vagina and similar operations with respect to a transsexual. . . . This distinction would only be logical if those other features with which Ormrod J was concerned (possession of ovaries, for example) were of any legal significance in consummation. In fact, legally, consummation is concerned purely with the physical fact of intercourse and not with those potential consequences which usually flow from the act and for which features other than a vagina are necessary (*Baxter* v *Baxter* [1948] AC 274). A legal finding that consummation cannot take place if one party is transsexual is, in any event, at odds with the experience of satisfactory sexual relations in *Peterson* [noted in *The Times*, 12 July 1985] and *W* v *W* [(1976) (2) SA 308 (W)].

Even if the internal incoherence of the arguments in *Corbett* is ignored, the result of the judgment still seems anomalous. The sex which transsexuals must marry under becomes, by definition, the converse of the sex by which they live. This is to disregard the social nature of marriage in favour of a spurious pursuit of scientific niceties. Yet, as Professor Dewhurst observed in *Corbett*, 'we [doctors] do not determine sex — in medicine we determine the sex in which it is best for the individual to live'. . . . In *Corbett*, science is pursued beyond the point where scientists will go. 'Marriage,' held Ormrod J in *Corbett*, 'is a relationship which depends on sex and not on gender'. . . . Others have taken the contrary view. . . .

Marriage is a social institution which allows society to propagate itself in a particular way. It reinforces social patterns, educating individuals into the mores of their community. Whilst sex is a biological matter, gender is a question of social status. Marriage thus seems a creature of gender rather than sex. . . .

### Dr Russell Reid, 'Transsexualism: the Current Medical Viewpoint', 1995, produced as part of the work of the UK Parliamentary Forum on Transsexualism, para. 7.2 (cited in *Re P and G (Transsexuals)* (see note 2, *supra*), at p. 96)

Current medical knowledge recognises that an absolute etiology for transsexualism is not available although the present weight of evidence is in favour of a biologically based, multifactorial causality. It is considered, therefore, that scientific knowledge of transsexualism has progressed considerably since *Corbett* v *Corbett* and that the evidence presented there is no longer reliable.

*Notes and questions*

1.   A research report of Dr Russell Reid in January 1996 (cited in *Re P and G*) stated: 'This research indicates that, medically, the sex of an individual must be regarded as being decided by the construction of the brain; it is not an issue of 'psychological sex' but of 'physiological differentiation'. Other research, however, has shown Dr Russell Reid's research to be inconclusive.

2.   What objections are there to allowing a transsexual to marry a person of the same biological sex? Is the English court ever likely to accept that there is adequate medical evidence to justify overruling *Corbett*, or is the issue more than merely a question of medical science?

3.   In *P v S and Another (Sex Discrimination)* (Case C–13/94) [1996] 2 FLR 347 (referred to by counsel in *Re P and G, supra*), the European Court of Justice held that the dismissal of a transsexual for a reason related to a sex change was precluded by the Community Directive on Equal Treatment in Employment (Directive 76/207). Does this provide further fuel to the claims of transsexuals?

4.   Should transsexual couples be allowed to have families (i.e. by means of artificial reproduction, surrogacy or adoption), or is this contrary to the best interests of children?

### 2.2.3   Same-sex marriages

Homosexual partners are also putting pressure on governments to allow them to marry. In some countries (e.g., Denmark, Norway and Sweden) same-sex couples may register their partnership with the registration authorities whereupon their relationship is given limited legal recognition.

### Broberg, Morten, P., 'The Registered Partnership for Same-sex Couples in Denmark'
### [1996] 8 CFLQ 149

. . .

Until now the registered partnership has received the greatest attention in those countries which are normally considered to be the most liberal, that is the Scandinavian countries and the Netherlands. Nevertheless, it seems that the idea is gaining ground and it may be foreseen that the new 'concept' will be implemented in still more countries of the Western world in the years to come. The Danish model has shown that — technically speaking — introducing a registered partnership scheme is a legally surmountable task. As has been shown in this article, the problems encountered by the Danish model have been *vis-à-vis* the Church, the legality under EC law of the requirement that at least one of the partners must have a strong relationship with Denmark, the possibility of adopting children and the question of pensions — in particular widows' pensions. Solutions to the lack of a Church blessing and the problem concerning the adoption of stepchildren are presently being considered. The conflict with EC law will probably have to wait until a case is brought to the Court of Justice of the European Communities; while rights to adoption and joint custody which fully mirror those of married couples at present do not seem likely to be granted to registered partners. The problem with regard to pensions is likely to solve itself since, as it is illegal to discriminate between married couples and registered partners will acquire the same rights as married couples when entering into a new pension agreement. One further difficulty which is bound to be encountered in the future concerns the recognition of the registered partnership by foreign jurisdictions.

In modern society following one's sexual orientation is persuasively claimed to be a human right and, consequently, discriminating between homosexuals and heterosexuals is a breach of this right. The introduction of a registered partnership minimises such discrimination, but it does not mean that the discrimination has been brought to an end. The above examination has shown that the registered partnership differs from a marriage on a number of points. Thus registered partners are not 'married', they have only 'registered' their relationship; registered partners may not register in a church in the same way as heterosexuals may; registered partners may not adopt children; and under international private law registered partners cannot normally expect to be treated in the same way as married couples.

Regardless of the shortcomings which the Act may have and whether or not we as individuals like or dislike the idea of a registered partnership, the fact that it diminishes a rather obvious discrimination between heterosexuals and homosexuals, and recognises that following one's sexual orientation must be considered a human right, means that putting the idea into practice through legislation has much to commend it.

*Questions*
Will legislation in other member States of the European Union permitting same-sex couples to register their partnerships put pressure on the UK to do the same? Are the English courts likely to recognise the validity of a registered partnership entered into (e.g. in Holland) by two homosexual British citizens? Should family law adapt to the evolution of a society where partnerships other than marriage have evolved?

*Further reading*
Barton, C., 'The Homosexual in the Family' [1996] Fam Law 626.
Heinze, E., *Sexual Orientation: A Human Right — An Essay on International Human Rights Law*, Dordrecht: Martinus Nijhoff, 1995.
Norrie K., 'Reproductive Technology, Transsexualism and Homosexuality: New Problems for International Private Law' (1994) 43 ICLQ 757.
Wintemute, R., *Sexual Orientation and Human Rights — the United States Constitution, the European Convention and the Canadian Charter*, Oxford: Clarendon Press, 1995.
Zirin, J., 'Vows that Could Alter Marriage' [1996] *The Times*, 3 September, p. 37.

## 2.3  SEPARATE BUT EQUAL LEGAL PERSONALITIES

### *R v R*
[1991] 3 WLR 767
House of Lords

LORD KEITH: . . . [M]arriage is in modern times regarded as a partnership of equals, and no longer one in which the wife must be the subservient chattel of the husband. . . .

### *Midland Bank Trust Co. Ltd* v *Green (No. 3)*
[1982] Ch 529
Court of Appeal

LORD DENNING MR: . . . Nowadays, both in law and in fact, husband and wife are two persons, not one. They are partners — equal partners — in a joint enterprise, the enterprise of maintaining a home and bringing up children. Outside that joint enterprise they live their own lives and go their own ways — always, we hope, in consultation one with the other, in complete loyalty one with the other, each maintaining and deserving the trust and confidence of the other. They can and do own property jointly or severally or jointly and severally, with all the consequences that ownership entails. They can and do enter into contracts with others jointly or severally or jointly and severally, and can be made liable for breaches just as any other contractors can be. They can and do commit crimes jointly or severally and can be punished severally for them. They can and do commit wrongs jointly or severally and can be made liable jointly or severally just as any other wrong-doers. The severance in all respects is so complete that I would say that the doctrine of unity and its ramifications should be discarded altogether, except in so far as it is retained by judicial decision or by Act of Parliament.

Husbands and wives have a right to make independent and separate decisions about their own medical treatment. This right also extends to giving the wife the capacity to make a unilateral decision to abort the child conceived of the relationship.

### *Paton* v *British Pregnancy Advisory Service Trustees*
[1979] QB 276
Queen's Bench Division

*Facts*: Mr Paton applied for an injunction against the trustees of the British Pregnancy Advisory Service and his wife, the second defendant, to prevent her from having a legal abortion. On the same day his wife applied for a divorce.
*Held*: refusing the injunction, that the husband had no right to prevent his wife from having an abortion.

SIR GEORGE BAKER P: By a specially endorsed writ the plaintiff, who is the husband of the second defendant, seeks an injunction in effect to restrain the first defendants, a charitable organisation, and particularly his wife, the second defendant, from causing or permitting an abortion to be carried out upon his wife without his consent.

Such action, of course, arouses great emotions, and vigorous opposing views as was recently pointed out in 1972 in the Supreme Court of the United States by Blackmun J in *Roe* v *Wade* (1973) 93 S Ct 705, 708–709. In the discussion of human affairs and especially of abortion, controversy can rage over the moral rights, duties, interests, standards and religious views of the parties. Moral values are in issue. I am, in fact, concerned with none of these matters. I am concerned, and concerned only, with the law of England as it applies to this claim. My task is to apply the law free of emotion or predilection.

Nobody suggests that there has ever been such a claim litigated before the courts in this country. Indeed, the only case of which I have ever heard was in Ontario. It was unreported because the husband's claim for an injunction was never tried.

In considering the law the first and basic principle is that there must be a legal right enforceable in law or in equity before the applicant can obtain an injunction from the court to restrain an infringement of that right. That has long been the law.
. . .

The first question is whether this plaintiff has a right at all. The foetus cannot, in English law, in my view, have a right of its own at least until it is born and has a separate existence from its mother. That permeates the whole of the civil law of this country (I except the criminal law, which is now irrelevant), and is, indeed, the basis of the decisions in those countries where law is founded on the common law, that is to say, in America, Canada, Australia and, I have no doubt, in others.

For a long time there was great controversy whether after birth a child could have a right of action in respect of pre-natal injury. The Law Commission considered that and produced a Working Paper No. 47 in 1973, followed by a Final Report (Law Commission Report, No. 60 (Cmnd. 5709)), but it was universally accepted, and has since been accepted, that in order to have a right the foetus must be born and be a child. . . .

The father's case must therefore depend upon a right which he has himself. I would say a word about the illegitimate, usually called the putative, but I prefer myself to refer to the illegitimate father. Although American decisions to which I have been referred concern illegitimate fathers, and statutory provisions about them, it seems to me that in this country the illegitimate father can have no rights whatsoever except those given to him by statute. . . .

So this plaintiff must, in my opinion, bring his case, if he can, squarely within the framework of the fact that he is a husband. It is, of course, very common for spouses to seek injunctions for personal protection in the matrimonial courts during the pendency of or, indeed, after divorce actions, but the basic reason for the non-molestation injunction often granted in the family courts is to protect the other spouse or the living children, and to ensure that no undue pressure is put upon one or other of the spouses during the pendency of the case and during the breaking-up of the marriage.

There was, of course, the action for restitution of conjugal rights, a proceeding which always belied its name and was abolished in 1970. It arose because in ecclesiastical law the parties could not end the consortium by agreement. In a sense the action for restitution was something of a fiction. The court ordered the spouse to return to cohabitation. If the spouse did not return then that spouse was held to be in desertion. No more could happen. The court could not compel matrimonial intercourse: see *Forster* v *Forster* (1790) 1 Hag Con 144. So matrimonial courts have never attempted the enforcement of matrimonial obligations by injunction.

The law is that the court cannot and would not seek to enforce or restrain by injunction matrimonial obligations, if they be obligations, such as sexual intercourse or contraception (a non-molestation injunction given during the pendency of divorce proceedings could, of course, cover attempted intercourse). No court would ever grant an injunction to stop sterilisation or vasectomy. Personal family relationships in marriage cannot be enforced by the order of a court. An injunction in such circumstances was described by Judge Mager in *Jones* v *Smith* (1973) 278 So Rep 339 in the District Court of Appeal of Florida as 'ludicrous'.

I ask the question, 'If an injunction were ordered, what could be the remedy?' and I do not think I need say any more than that no judge could even consider sending a husband or wife to prison for breaking such an order. That, of itself, seems to me to cover the application here; this husband cannot by law stop his wife by injunction from having what is now accepted to be a lawful abortion within the terms of the Abortion Act 1967.

. . .

The husband, therefore, in my view, has no legal right enforceable in law or in equity to stop his wife having this abortion or to stop the doctors from carrying out the abortion.

*Note*

For a failed attempt by an unmarried father to prevent his ex-girlfriend aborting his child, see *C v S* [1988] QB 135, [1987] 1 All ER 1230 (but rumour has it that she went ahead and had the child and handed it over to the father) (see Deech, R., 'The Rights of Fathers: Sociological and Biological Concepts of Parenthood', in Eekelaar, J., and Šarčević, P. (eds), *Parenthood in Modern Society*, Dordrecht: Martinus Nijhoff, 1993, at p. 25).

*Questions*
1.  Do you agree with the decision in *Paton*?
2.  Is it illogical that had Mr Paton's baby been born, both he and his wife would have had parental responsibility for the child (see Chapter 8), and that he would have had a right to consent to the child's adoption (see Chapter 9)?

(For marital property rights, see Chapter 3; for parental responsibility, see Chapter 8; for a discussion of marital contracts, see Chapter 5.)

## 2.4   SHOULD ENTRY INTO MARRIAGE BE CONTROLLED?

Marriage breakdown is a traumatic experience for the parties and for their children and often has dramatic consequences, e.g. in terms of family poverty, housing and the emotional development of children. The question therefore arises as to whether there should be any controls on the parties at the point of entry into marriage.

### Sugarman, Stephen D., 'Report of the American Bar Family Law Association, Family Law for the Next Century'
(1993) 27 Fam LQ 175

. . .

Many observers of the family have been raising loud alarms about the harmful consequences of divorce on minor children. I do not resist these findings. For my purposes here I am quite prepared to assume that, on average, children of divorced parents seriously suffer psychologically, educationally, and socially as compared with those who spend their childhood living with their married parents. What can we expect the law to do to turn around that result? Probably not much.

. . .

One sweeping strategy would be to control entry into matrimony, discouraging or preventing marriage by those who are likely later to divorce with minor children in their care. In furtherance of this goal we might, for example, raise sharply the minimum age of marriage. Or we might require successful completion of a parenting training course as a condition of marriage. Or we might require premarital counselling and screening, after which those who appeared destined to divorce with minor children were then barred from (or at least strongly dissuaded from) marrying.

It is by no means clear, however, that this approach would have any significant positive effect. . . .

*Questions*
1.   Should there be some sort of marriage screening? Would it be a good idea to make marriage and parenthood skills a compulsory part of the National Curriculum? What about a mandatory waiting period for consideration and reflection before marriage just as there is under the new divorce law (see Chapter 4)? What about medical screening before marriage, e.g., for AIDs and genetically transmitted diseases?
2.   Should a legal definition of a valid marriage be enacted which would also include some of the minimum obligations of marriage and parenthood? As the law stands, the validity of a marriage is determined by looking at the grounds for proving its non-existence, and it is quite likely that until marriage breakdown many spouses will have no knowledge of spousal and parental obligations. Should family law be more prescriptive, or would this be a threat to family autonomy?

## 2.5   THE FUTURE OF MARRIAGE

### Dewar, John, 'Is Marriage Redundant?'
[1992] *Student Law Review* 46

. . . Legal marriage and its effects are concerned with the two powerful themes of sex and money. Eligibility for marriage rests on a privileged model of human sexual relations (derived either from religious conceptions of marriage or secular eugenic concerns). Its legal consequences hinge very largely around money and property either with reference to the state (as with tax law) or with reference to the parties themselves (as with claims for maintenance). The unmarried are excluded from this special treatment, thus creating a supposed legal disincentive to unmarried cohabitation but also incidentally creating an unregulated space for alternative models of family living.

An important issue that will dominate Family Law over the coming years is how far marriage can retain this privileged position in law, or indeed any legal significance at all. It may be that in reality marriage is already in retreat as the primary determinant of the legal rights and remedies of family members. The growth in unmarried cohabitation and more especially in births outside marriage has already shifted the focus of legal regulation towards parenthood as the state has sought to define and enforce financial obligations between family members irrespective of marriage in an attempt to reduce calls on the public purse. There is also an increasingly strong case for extending some elements of Family Law to those who are unmarried whether they have children or not. The power to allocate property at the end of a relationship, and perhaps to order some limited form of income support, would be strong candidates for this.

. . .

For present purposes, we may assume that marriage is legally significant in three respects. First, it marks out those who may be entitled to special treatment by the state, for example through tax law. Second, it specifies those who are to be obliged to provide, and those entitled to receive private inter-spousal financial support or share in family property. Third, it enables those who are married to make use of the specialist jurisdiction of the divorce court to sort out the financial and other consequences of the end of a relationship. By definition the powers of the divorce court are not available to those who are not married. If we take each of these in turn, we can see that marriage is not logically necessary for any of these purposes.

As far as the state is concerned, there is no obvious reason to promote marriage through favourable tax (or any other form of) treatment. A legitimate concern may be to assist parents to bear the costs of child rearing, but parenthood no longer has any necessary connection with marriage. To adopt a policy of discouraging parenting outside marriage would now seem odd. It is difficult to see what other reasons there might be for encouraging marriage as a matter of official policy. Sexual behaviour is now more effectively regulated either through the criminal law or by means that are not remotely concerned with law.

As far as the enforcement of money and property claims are concerned we may in any case doubt the significance of this supposed privileged status of married couples. Many couples will either be on income support (so that the divorce court's jurisdiction will be almost completely irrelevant) or will have at most an owner-occupied home mortgaged to a building society with one or two incomes. In the latter category the primary concern of the courts will be to meet the reasonable needs of the parties. It is difficult to understand why the courts should not be able to perform this limited adjustive funcion for unmarried couples as well instead of leaving them to the mercies of the law of property and implied trusts. There are also those wealthier spouses to whom the status rights conferred by marriage are undoubtedly significant, but should the spouse of a wealthy man or woman be able to claim a substantial share of their spouse's assets on divorce? Why not leave them to negotiate an enforceable premarriage contract (as the Law Society has recently suggested)?

. . . There are thus strong arguments for the view that marriage is legally unnecessary; indeed not only unnecessary but harmful in that it distorts our perceptions of what families need from Family Law. What, if anything, could take its place?

. . . One possibility would be to extend certain features of marriage to those who cohabit. A number of jurisdictions, such as Australia and Sweden, have done just this. In England the legal treatment of cohabitation is extremely *ad hoc*: people who live together 'as husband and wife' are accorded similar treatment to married couples for certain very limited purposes, but there is no generalised obligation of support. There would be no difficulty in defining cohabitation for legal purposes (just as there has been no perceived obstacle to defining 'separation' for the law of divorce. The problem would be to decide what consequences to attach to it.

. . . Marriage may be losing its appeal but parenthood is still something that (we may hope) people will continue to engage in. For a government concerned about the financial consequences of relationship breakdown and, in particular, the cost to the state of supporting one parent families there are obvious attractions in bypassing marriage altogether and attaching financial obligations to the fact of parenthood (but are the facts of parenthood always obvious?). The improvement in the law concerning private support of children (in Schedule 1 of the Children Act 1989), which empowers a court to make the full range of financial and property orders against a 'parent' (with or without 'parental responsibility'), together with the Child Support Act 1991 (which nowhere mentions 'marriage'), represent a significant move towards bringing parenthood to centre stage; and the powers under the Children Act 1989 to make orders in relation to children are available irrespective of the marital status of the parents. In future, for most families, the financial consequences of breakdown will be determined by the needs of children. . . .

*Questions*
1.  Should parenthood be the primary status, not that of being a married or cohabiting person?
2.  Will the divorce reforms in the Family Law Act 1996 (see Chapter 4) have any effect on marriage? If so, how?
3.  Is marriage really losing its central significance in today's society? Is increasing cohabitation likely to undermine the institution of marriage?

*Further reading*
Clive, E., 'Marriage: an Unnecessary Legal Concept?' in Eekelaar, J., and Katz, J. (eds), *Marriage and Cohabitation in Contemporary Societies*, London: Butterworths, 1980.
Freeman, M., 'Marriage and Divorce in England' (1995) 29 Fam LQ 549.

## 2.6  COHABITATION

### 2.6.1  What is 'cohabitation'?

**Hayes, Mary, "Cohabitation Clauses' in Financial Provision and Property Adjustment Orders — Law, Policy and Justice'**
**(1994) 110 LQR 124**

. . .

*The meaning of cohabitation*
The verb to cohabit has no clearly recognised meaning and is not normally used in common parlance. It is certainly not a mode of speech which would readily spring to the lips of the man or woman on the Clapham omnibus or, more pertinently, embroiled in divorce proceedings. Cohabitation is not even a concept of which it can be said 'there is no definition but everyone knows what it means.' 'To cohabit with another man' is a short-hand phrase used by lawyers, including judges, to describe a manner in which people live. This is somewhat surprising since it is nowhere statutorily defined. 'Living together as husband and wife' might make a little more sense to lay persons, though there is a certain irony in that phrase being proffered in a positive sense to those who will normally have experienced this relationship for some considerable time in the context of marriage breakdown. The phrase which lawyers and judges appear to avoid using, probably because they instinctively recognise that there is no such concept known to modern English domestic law, is 'common law husband or wife.' Paradoxically, it is suggested that not only do the general public have a common mental image of what 'common law husband' and 'common law wife' means, but also, most probably, many of them realise that it is a concept not really understood by English domestic law. Indeed, if they appreciate that the law is a bit

hazy about how and when the legal provisions which apply to spouses extend to those who are unmarried, this appreciation will correctly reflect the reality.

How then are courts going to be in a position to decide whether or not an unmarried couple are cohabiting, or living together as husband and wife, when the assertion that they are doing so is strenuously denied? It seems inevitable that they are going to be forced into developing a new common law concept, with little to guide them on what the concept should mean. However, because it has become increasingly commonplace for men and women to live together outside marriage, Parliament has enacted various statutes which give varying degrees of recognition to this fact of human behaviour. This legislation and its attendant case law is therefore an obvious source of guidance. A common feature of the legislation is that a cohabitant is included within its ambit in order that the protective arm of the law can be extended to him or her. It is only in the case of social security law that the fact of cohabitation may operate to the cohabitant's disadvantage. . . .

### 2.6.2   Why do people cohabit rather than marry?

**Scottish Law Commission, *The Effects of Cohabitation in Private Law*, 1990, Discussion Paper 86, pp. 2 and 3**

1.4   We have very little information in this country about the reasons or motivations which lead people to prefer cohabitation to marriage. Inability to marry because of a subsisting prior marriage is a reason in some cases . . . . However, . . . this is not a major reason nowadays. The high rates of cohabitation among divorced people may suggest a certain disillusionment with legal marriage or at least a view that it is not so necessary, or so expected by others, in their circumstances. It seems clear, from comments made by participants in current affairs programmes and others, that some couples are opposed to legal marriage on principle. They regard their relationship as based on an emotional bond or voluntary mutual commitment and regard the addition of any legal or religious bond as in some way diminishing this personal bond. They may also feel that a legal marriage implies the adoption of certain traditional assumptions about the roles of husbands and wives and restricts their freedom to form a type of relationship of their own choosing. These remarks apply to cohabitation as an alternative to legal marriage. In the case of pre-marital cohabitation the reasons for not marrying earlier are likely to be of a more practical nature. In such cases there is clearly no lasting objection to marriage as an institution.

### 2.6.3   Should marriage-type obligations be imposed on cohabitants?

**Scottish Law Commission, *The Effects of Cohabitation in Private Law*, 1990, Discussion Paper 86**

5.1   . . . We are aware of the danger of imposing marriage-related obligations on people who may have deliberately opted out of marriage in order to avoid such obligations. However, some of the rules on financial provision on divorce are related, not to the nature of marriage or of the commitments publicly undertaken on marriage, but to the simple redress of economic inequities arising out of the factual situation of cohabitation and child-bearing. It may be that the balance between liberty and protection would not be tipped too far in favour of protection if rules of this nature were applied to certain cohabitants. This, at least, seems to us to be an issue worth addressing. . . .

**Freeman, Michael D. A., 'Legal Ideologies, Patriarchal Precedents and Domestic Violence' in Freeman, Michael D. A., (ed.), *The State, the Law and the Family: Critical Perspectives***
London: Tavistock Publications, Sweet & Maxwell, 1984

. . . I view with some alarm the increasing tendency to treat cohabitation as if it were marriage. It seems that many who avoid marriage because of its ideological notions of subordination and dependence find the consequences attaching to marriage thrust on them whether they like it or not. It is almost as if women were being told they were not allowed to escape by cohabiting. . . .

**Bailey-Harris, Rebecca, 'Law and the Unmarried Couple —
Oppression or Liberation?'**
[1996] 8 CFLQ 137

. . . Is increased legal regulation oppressive of those who choose an alternative family form? Or, on the contrary, does the law not yet go far enough in offering the unmarried couple recognition, so that those who do not marry remain unjustifiably disadvantaged? At the outset one must bear in mind the range of relationships which must be considered — in contrast to the married, the unmarried couple may be either heterosexual or homosexual.

Policy dilemmas immediately emerge when one considers the law's role in relation to the unmarried couple. On the one hand, strong arguments can be mounted for an increased recognition by law of relationships outside marriage — in other words, that increased recognition means liberation for those concerned. The statistics speak for themselves — the incidence of cohabitation outside marriage has risen dramatically in recent years. Conversely, marriage rates are at their lowest since 1889, and the divorce rate is at its highest ever. The law cannot simply turn its back on social facts — the statistics demand a response. Legal paternalism — properly to be renamed legal maternalism — sees the proper role of the law (society's agent) as ensuring fairness and justice between family members, particularly when their relationship breaks down. It is proper for the law to redress any power imbalance or inequality between partners, whether the inequality be physical, emotional or financial. The nature of contemporary society also supports greater recognition by the law of family forms alternative to marriage. As society becomes increasingly diverse, socially, religiously and in its personal morality and value-systems, the law is obliged to recognise diversity by giving legal status to a range of different family relationships which individuals choose for themselves. Legal recognition is the authentication by society of alternative family structures. This argument finds some support from the Church of England in a report released in 1995. Anti-discrimination arguments are also persuasive — the law should not offer lesser protection by reason of the unmarried status of a relationship, nor on the basis of the sexuality of the partners. An anti-discrimination analysis encompasses not only the comparison of the married with the unmarried, but also of heterosexual and homosexual relationships. Finally, one can argue that society's evidently changing attitude to marriage — in particular, the transformation of marriage in less than 150 years from an institution predominantly characterised by its indissolubility to what is likely to become one readily terminable on the demand of either party — necessarily opens the door to a broader recognition of other relationships, since marriage has long since lost its unique character.

Yet arguments which at first sight may appear equally persuasive can be put for the other side — that legal regulation is oppressive. Why should the law impose regulation of those couples who have deliberately chosen not to marry? The respect accorded to individual self-determination in contemporary society requires that the choice to be different be given meaning. Moreover, the current political climate encourages a policy of general retreat from legal interference with the individual and with family life; greater regulation of unmarried relationships would be inconsistent with this trend. Finally, one frequently hears the argument that to give greater legal protection to unmarried couples weakens the institution of marriage. These points, whilst on their face attractive, may on closer examination reveal flaws. Party autonomy arguments assume freedom of choice and informed choice, an assumption which is by no means universally justified in the formation of family relationships. People drift into cohabitation, often with misconceptions about its legal consequences. There are dangers in society's retreat from legal regulation, which will be examined later. Moreover, it does not follow logically that the support of one institution necessarily undermines another — support of a variety of institutions may simply be a manifestation of the pluralism characterising contemporary society. . . .

[Bailey-Harris then considers the functions of family law and applies these to a discussion of cohabitation.]

. . . I identify first (perhaps seemingly paradoxically) the remedial role of the law — to regulate the consequences of family breakdown in a way that achieves a fair result between the parties. This role is of particular importance in respect of the financial consequences of relationship breakdown. The aim of the law on financial provision should be to achieve a fair distribution of assets between the former couple, giving proper recognition and value to the various different contributions (both financially and domestic) which they have made to the relationship, and making allowance for the way in which the relationship has affected their respective financial positions, for better or for worse. . . .

Once this function of the law is identified, it can be argued that there is no justification for distinguishing between different categories of domestic relationship according to their legal status or even the sexual orientation of the parties. If the remedial purpose of rules on financial provision is 'to respond to what actually happened in a relationship', why should the classification of the relationship have any significance? What is significant is how the role-division assumed within a relationship has determined the different contributions which each party has made and has affected their respective financial futures. Hence the law of financial provision should treat married and unmarried relationships alike. I argue that the same principles of maintenance and property distribution should apply to unmarried couples — both heterosexual and same-sex — as apply to married couples on divorce. Those principles should of course be sufficiently flexible to permit the outcome to be tailored to meet the justice of the particular case and to take account of the myriad ways in which couples arrange their lives. A broad statutory scheme which permits consideration of a wide range of factors — including contributions to the relationship both financial and non-financial, and future expectations from pension funds — should in substance be extended from its current operation on divorce to encompass the breakdown of any cohabitation relationship. . . . The proper purpose of the law here is to adjust assets in the light of role-division assumed during the relationship. It is the role-division adopted in a particular relationship which is important, not the sexual orientation of the parties. . . .

Another role and function of family law is protective — to protect family members from abuse and exploitation by others, in the situation where the family is dysfunctional. This role is particularly crucial where there is power-imbalance within a relationship. Violence within the family is the hallmark of inequality; a violent relationship is by nature unequal. We are now witnessing a welcome and growing recognition of the long-term disempowering effects of violence on the women and children who are its most usual victims. No one should dispute the proposition that the law's protection from violence within the family should be offered quite irrespective of the legal status of the relationship; a marriage certificate should be wholly irrelevant to the protection of the vulnerable adult or child. . . .

. . . Violence is the most serious form of exploitation within a family, but there are others, such as the economic exploitation of one adult by another, both during a relationship and on its breakdown. The law must protect one party from financial exploitation by the other, for example, where one unfairly refuses to give proper recognition to the other's contributions to the relationship. This role may be invoked in support of the reforms to the law of financial provision on the breakdown of unmarried relationships advocated above. Such reforms should be designed to ensure that the parties' different contributions to their relationship are properly reflected in a fair division of their assets on separation.

A third role of family law is the promotion of the welfare of children. This is not limited to their protection from physical and emotional abuse, but extends more widely to the promotion of their welfare in all aspects. That the law should aim to promote the welfare of children is wholly non-controversial as a general proposition, but the implementation of that principle in particular situations gives rise to more debate, raising, as it inevitably does, questions of competing values. The details of family law reflect underlying assumptions about family forms which are most likely to promote a child's welfare. To take two examples — under the Children Act 1989 an unmarried father — even one living in a long-term de facto relationship with the child's mother — is not by virtue of his paternity alone entitled to parental responsibility, but is required to take positive steps to acquire it either by formal agreement with the mother or by court order. His married counterpart, by contrast, is given parental responsibility automatically. The assumption underpinning this law must be that the unmarried father, even one living in a stable de facto relationship with the mother, is not presumed without more to be as capable of promoting his child's welfare as is his married counterpart. In contemporary society this assumption should be strongly questioned as outmoded and discriminatory. It fails to take proper account of the realities of the current rates of marriage breakdown — the married father cannot safely be regarded as a permanent feature in a child's household or even in his or her upbringing. The current law may be inconsistent with the UN Declaration on the Rights of the Child. The Scottish Law Commission in 1992 favoured the automatic conferral of parental rights on unmarried fathers, drawing *inter alia* on non-discrimination arguments, but the recent Children (Scotland) Act 1995 has declined to reform the law in this respect. . . . If automatic conferral of parental responsibility on *all* unmarried fathers is felt to be too drastic a reform in the English political climate, at least responsibilities could be conferred more conservatively in the context of heterosexual de facto relationships, i.e. on fathers living in a household with the mother at the time of the child's birth. The automatic conferral of joint responsibility on unmarried parents by the Children Act 1989 would convey a powerful message to all parents about the shared nature of parental obligation, both during a relationship and after its breakdown which is at the heart of the Act's policy.

As another example, consider the law of adoption. The governing principle in adoption law is that the welfare of the child is the first consideration. The objective of the adoption process is to create a new family with the optimum chance of success. In England the Adoption Act 1976 permits a couple to adopt a child jointly only if they are married. The White Paper *Adoption: The Future* released in November 1993 proposed no changes to the law in England determining the family structures which are deemed best suited to promote successful adoptions. . . . There can be no better illustration of stereotyping and the failure to respond to the realities of a diverse society. The White Paper unequivocally assumes that adopted children are best off being placed with married parents. This assumption should not go unchallenged. The fact that one is married today does not mean that one will remain married next year. Since the welfare of the individual child is the primary focus in social conditions which have severely reduced the numbers of children 'available' for adoption, the law's emphasis should shift to the assessment of the particular couple's capacity to provide a child's welfare, free from stereotyped assumptions based merely on the status of the applicant's relationship.

. . . I have already said that equality and non-discrimination arguments can be used to support an increased regulation of unmarried relationships. Yet it is important to understand that equal treatment does not necessarily mean identical treatment. Recent discussion of the concept of equality rejects formal equality (gender- and sexuality-neutral/identical treatment) in favour of a 'difference' approach. In the context of my current argument this means that the holistic question — to what extent should unmarried cohabitation be equated with marriage? — must be rejected as over-simplistic in that it fails to distinguish between various legal consequences in various areas of law. The extent to which married and unmarried cohabitation should be equated will, as argued earlier, depend on the examination of the purpose of legal regulation in a particular field.

The third and final key to law reform is to ask whether in a diverse society any limitations should be placed on the freedom of the individual to choose the form of family which best suits his or her personal aspirations. The Australian Law Reform Commission in its work on *Multiculturalism and the Law* [Australian Law Reform Commission Paper No. 47, 1991, para. 24] articulated a valuable approach to this issue, and one which is equally applicable in the United Kingdom.

> . . . generally speaking, the law should not inhibit the formation of family relationships and should recognise as valid the relationships people choose for themselves. Further, the law should support and protect those relationships. However, the law should restrict a person's choice to the extent that it is necessary to protect the fundamental rights and freedoms of others and should not support relationships in which the fundamental rights and freedoms of individuals are violated. Instead, it should intervene to protect them.

This approach is consistent with the arguments based on the law's remedial and protective roles, and on equality, which I have advocated earlier. A crucial role of the law is the protection of children's rights. The question of what placement best promotes the welfare of an individual child should be addressed without *a priori* assumptions about family structures.

Does the definition of relationships outside marriage pose insuperable problems for either the policy-maker or the draftsperson? I argue that, once a policy decision is taken, experiences both overseas and in English legislation to date prove that the translation of that policy into statutory formulation presents no great difficulties.

Three main issues must be addressed. Should the definition be gender/sexuality neutral, so as to encompass same-sex relationships? Is cohabitation (in the sense of sharing a home and an intimate life) to be a requirement? Is there to be a minimum qualifying period as an indicator of the stability of a relationship — if so, how long, and should the same period apply to all areas of law?

. . .

*Questions*

1.   Should cohabitants (heterosexual and homosexual) be given greater legal recognition? If so, how? Would this threaten the institution of marriage?

2.   Why do people cohabit rather than marry? Why has marriage decreased and cohabitation increased? Twenty years ago cohabiting before marriage or instead of marriage was considered to be 'living in sin'. Cohabitation is now an acceptable way of life. Why has there been this fundamental change of attitude to cohabitation, and why has it happened so quickly?

3.   Are cohabitation contracts the answer for cohabitants? Should the State control these contracts?

4.   To what extent are the protective, adjustive and support functions of the law applied to cohabiting families? Should these be extended?

5.   Is the different treatment for cohabitants and married couples and their families logical if the family may be considered to be a social, rather than a legal, unit?

*Further reading*

Kingdom, E., 'Cohabitation Contracts and Equality' (1990) 18 *International Journal of the Sociology of Law* 287.

Parry, M., *The Law Relating to Cohabitation*, 2nd edn, London: Sweet & Maxwell, 1993.

Priest, J., *Families Outside Marriage*, 2nd edn, Bristol: Jordans, 1993.

# 3  FAMILY PROPERTY

Although this chapter is concerned with the property rights of married and unmarried couples, virtually the same principles apply to any family member — hence the title of the chapter. Property orders for children are considered in Chapter 9.

Property disputes between married or cohabiting partners are rare during the relationship. It is on relationship breakdown that such disputes tend to arise. On marriage breakdown a property dispute may be dealt with under Part II of the MCA 1973 (see Chapter 5), which gives the divorce court jurisdiction to redistribute and reallocate matrimonial property according to the needs and resources of the parties, largely irrespective of their respective rights of ownership. Cohabiting couples, on the other hand, are not in such a fortunate position on relationship breakdown, as their entitlement to property is determined by the general rules of property and contract law. There is as yet no special statutory regime for adjusting their rights.

If there is a property dispute, it is likely to be about the family home because of its value both financially and as a provider of accommodation. In some cases the family home may have been used as security for a loan, and the dispute may not be between the parties themselves but between the parties and a third party (e.g., a mortgagee bank or building society, or trustee in bankruptcy).

## 3.1  PROPERTY RIGHTS OF MARRIED COUPLES

### 3.1.1  Separation of property

England and Wales has a system of separation of property, whereby each spouse may own property separately during marriage (although in practice many couples own property jointly). There is no special regime of shared property ownership for married couples, as there is in many European countries and some US states. Ownership of property depends on the principles of contract and trusts, although there are some statutory provisions which apply only to spouses (see below).

## Law Reform (Married Women and Tortfeasors) Act 1935

### 1. Capacity of married women
. . . a married woman shall—
    (a)   be capable of acquiring, holding and disposing of, any property; and
    (b)   be capable of rendering herself, and being rendered, liable in respect of any tort, contract, debt, or obligation; and
    (c)   be capable of suing and being sued, either in tort or in contract or otherwise; and
    (d)   be subject to the law relating to bankruptcy and to the enforcement of judgments and orders,
in all respects as if she were a feme sole.

### 2. Property of married women
    (1)  . . . all property which—
        (a)  . . .
        (b)   belongs at the time of her marriage to a woman married after the passing of this Act; or
        (c)   after the passing of this Act is acquired by or devolves upon a married woman,
shall belong to her in all respects as if she were a feme sole and may be disposed of accordingly.

### 3.1.2   Matrimonial property statutes

The following statutes make provision in respect of matrimonial property, but as married couples may claim interests under the general law of property, these provisions are rarely used in practice.

## Married Women's Property Act 1964

### 1. Money and property derived from housekeeping allowance
If any question arises as to the right of a husband or wife to money derived from any allowance made by the husband for the expenses of the matrimonial home or for similar purposes, or to any property acquired out of such money, the money or property shall, in the absence of any agreement between them to the contrary, be treated as belonging to the husband and the wife in equal shares.

## Matrimonial Proceedings and Property Act 1970

### 37. Contributions by spouse in money or money's worth to the improvement of property
. . . where a husband or wife contributes in money or money's worth to the improvement of real or personal property in which or in the proceeds of sale of which either or both of them has or have a beneficial interest, the husband or wife so

contributing shall, if the contribution is of a substantial nature and subject to any agreement between them to the contrary express or implied, be treated as having then acquired by virtue of his or her contribution a share or an enlarged share, as the case may be, in that beneficial interest of such an extent as may have been then agreed or, in default of such agreement, as may seem in all the circumstances just to any court before which the question of the existence or extent of the beneficial interest of the husband or wife arises (whether in proceedings between them or in any other proceedings).

## Married Women's Property Act 1882

### 17. Questions between husband and wife as to property to be decided in a summary way

In any question between husband and wife as to the title to or possession of property, either party may apply by summons or otherwise in a summary way to the High Court or such county court as may be prescribed and the court may, on such an application (which may be heard in private), make such order with respect to the property as it thinks fit. . . .

*Notes*
1.   Section 1 of the Married Women's Property Act 1964 is archaic and discriminatory. The Law Commission (*Family Law: Matrimonial Property*, Law Com No. 175, 1988) recommended its repeal, but nothing was done.
2.   Section 37 of the Matrimonial Proceedings and Property Act 1970 is hardly used in practice. Most claims are based on trust principles or those of proprietary estoppel.
3.   Proceedings under s. 17 of the Married Women's Property Act 1882 may also be brought by spouses within three years of divorce or nullity (Matrimonial Proceedings and Property Act 1970, s. 39) and by engaged couples within three years of the termination of the engagement (Law Reform (Miscellaneous Provisions) Act 1970, s. 2). Orders under s. 17 may be made in respect of property which is no longer in the other party's possession and can extend to the proceeds of sale and to other property representing the original (Matrimonial Causes (Property and Maintenance) Act 1958, s. 7). Once the court has declared the respective interests of the partners, it may make such order as it thinks fit, including an order for sale (s. 7(7) of the 1958 Act). Lord Diplock in *Pettitt* v *Pettitt* [1970] AC 777, at pp. 820 and 821, stated that s. 17 only gives the court jurisdiction to declare existing property rights, not to create or vary them.

### 3.1.3   Ownership of personal property during marriage

In its Report *Family Law: Matrimonial Property* (Law Com No. 175, 1988) the Law Commission criticised the law governing the ownership of matrimonial personal property (i.e. property other than land) and made proposals for reform. However, the proposals were not implemented, so that the way in which household goods and other personal property is owned during marriage still remains arbitrary.

Law Commission, *Family Law: Matrimonial Property*,
Law Com 175,
London: HMSO, 1988

. . .

## Co-ownership within marriage

2.1   In deciding who owns property acquired by the spouses during the marriage
the law at present places great weight on who paid for the property. Superficially this
may seem reasonable but two examples may serve to show how the results may not
reflect the spouses' wishes.

(i)   Husband and wife decide to buy a washing machine; one Saturday they
look together at various makes and decide to discuss it over the weekend. They decide
upon the make they want and on Monday, the husband, who happens to pass on his
way to work a shop which has the particular machine in stock, goes and buys the
machine. On sale, ownership of the machine passes to the husband.

(ii)   A husband is paid in cash, and his wife receives a monthly salary cheque.
Because of this, they use his money for rent, food and other day to day necessities,
and her money for bills and larger purchases. Consequently all the furniture in the
house belongs to her.

Further, the emphasis on who pays creates great disadvantages for a non-earning
spouse who, whatever other contributions he or she may be making to the couple's
life together, is likely to end up owning very little of the property which both of them
may well regard as 'joint'.

2.2   It might be thought that the couple could avoid these results by choosing
co-ownership. However, co-ownership cannot arise simply because the parties intend
to own property in this way. Intention alone is insufficient; there must be some act
which is effective to create the co-ownership. There are five ways in which co-
ownership might arise:

(i)   Purchase out of joint funds. If the couple have pooled their money, either
physically, or in a joint bank account, and they intend the account to be joint in equity
as well as in law, then property bought with that money will be co-owned.

(ii)   Transfer of legal title into joint names. This is quite difficult to do, and we
suspect that in practice it virtually never happens. Once property has been acquired
by one spouse, it can only be transferred into joint names by using the appropriate
formalities for that type of property. So far as chattels are concerned, there must either
be a deed, or the intention to transfer plus delivery. However, delivery between
spouses can be difficult to prove, and delivery where one wishes to create co-
ownership would be even more difficult to establish.

(iii)   Contribution to purchase. If one spouse contributes financially, either
directly or indirectly, to the purchase of property by the other, the property will
become co-owned if the contributing spouse is the wife (subject to evidence of an
intention on her part to make a gift to her husband, in which case the property will
be solely his). If the husband contributes towards a purchase by his wife, the
presumption of advancement will operate so that the property is solely his wife's,
subject to evidence of an intention that he should not make a gift to her.

(iv)   Proprietary estoppel. Similar to, and in some cases indistinguishable from
co-ownership arising from a contribution is co-ownership arising from proprietary
estoppel. Where one spouse leads the other to believe that property is to be co-owned,

co-ownership may arise if the other spouse takes some action which would otherwise be to his disadvantage in reliance on that belief.

(v)   Declaration of trust. It is possible for one spouse to declare that he, or she, is holding property on trust for both spouses. However the courts have long been reluctant to hold that someone has declared himself to be a trustee, because of the burden this imposes. Unless he makes it explicit that that is what he intends to be, a mere expression of a wish that someone else should have an interest is not usually enough.

(vi)   Married Women's Property Act 1964. The Act . . . does give rise to co-ownership, but only where an allowance is made by a husband to his wife.

2.3   It might also be suggested that the law of agency would produce co-ownership in cases where one spouse was in effect buying goods for them both. However, for this to happen, the husband would have to make a contract of sale with the shop on behalf of himself and his wife, thus rendering them both liable upon it, which is not what any of the parties intend. Alternatively, if he contracts personally with the shop, the property vests in him and does not pass to the wife until she pays him for the goods, which again is not what they intend.

2.4   The very brief account set out above demonstrates, we think that even when a married couple have thought about it and wish their property to be co-owned, creating co-ownership may present difficulties. In what we suspect is the more usual case, where the couple have not thought about it at all, but if asked would say that they *assumed* much of their property was co-owned, they would be wrong.

. . .

2.8   The present law is unsatisfactory because its application may not result in co-ownership of property even when a married couple desire this. Actual ownership may be held to depend on factors which neither party considered significant at the time of acquisition. In its treatment of money allowances and gifts of property the law discriminates between husband and wife.

. . .

5.1   We *recommend* that in future the purchase of property (with some exclusions) by one or both spouses for their joint use or benefit should give rise to joint ownership of that property subject to a contrary intention on the part of the purchasing spouse, known to the other spouse.

5.2   We further *recommend* that transfer of property by one spouse to the other for their joint use or benefit should give rise to joint ownership of that property subject to a contrary intention on the part of the transferring spouse, known to the other spouse. If the transferred property is not for joint use or benefit it should become the sole beneficial property of the spouse to whom it is transferred, subject to a contrary intention on the part of the transferring spouse, known to the other spouse.

5.3   These recommendations do *not* extend to property purchased or transferred for business purposes.

. . .

## Note

The Law Commission (at paras 3.3 ff) rejected, largely for pragmatic reasons, the introduction of a system of community of property. It also mooted the possibility of extending its recommendations to cohabitants (para. 4.21). In Scotland there is a presumption of joint ownership of household goods, except for gifts or inheritances acquired from third parties (Family Law

(Scotland) Act 1985, s. 25). 'Household goods' does not include money or securities, cars, caravans or other road vehicles or any domestic animal (s. 25(3)).

*Question*
Should legislation similar to the Scottish legislation be introduced in England, or does it really not matter much if personal property disputes rarely occur during marriage?

### 3.1.4 Occupation of the matrimonial home

(For occupation orders, etc. where there is violence in the home, see Chapter 6.)

A right of occupation may arise by virtue of ownership, or a right under a lease or a right arising under a licence to occupy property. Married persons also have statutory rights of occupation of the matrimonial home under the Matrimonial Homes Act (MHA) 1983.

## Matrimonial Homes Act 1983

**1.  Rights concerning matrimonial home where one spouse has no estate, etc**

(1)  Where one spouse is entitled to occupy a dwelling house by virtue of a beneficial estate or interest or contract or by virtue of any enactment giving him or her the right to remain in occupation, and the other spouse is not so entitled, then, subject to the provisions of this Act, the spouse not so entitled shall have the following rights (in this Act referred to as 'rights of occupation')—

(a)  if in occupation, a right not to be evicted or excluded from the dwelling house or any part thereof by the other spouse except with the leave of the court given by an order under this section;

(b)  if not in occupation, a right with the leave of the court so given to enter into and occupy the dwelling house.

(2)  So long as one spouse has rights of occupation, either of the spouses may apply to the court for an order—

(a)  declaring, enforcing, restricting or terminating those rights, or

(b)  prohibiting, suspending or restricting the exercise by either spouse of the right to occupy the dwelling house, or

(c)  requiring either spouse to permit the exercise by the other of that right.

(3)  On an application for an order under this section, the court may make such order as it thinks just and reasonable having regard to the conduct of the spouses in relation to each other and otherwise, to their respective needs and financial resources, to the needs of any children and to all the circumstances of the case. . . .

*Note*
Rights of occupation are binding on third parties only if they have been registered as a charge on the matrimonial home (MHA 1983, s. 2).

The MHA 1983 will be repealed when Part IV of the Family Law Act (FLA) 1996 comes into force (expected date 1 October 1997). Sections 30 and 31 and sch. 4 of the FLA 1996 make provision for 'matrimonial home rights'. Occupation orders for married couples, cohabitants and other persons will be available under ss. 33–41 (see Chapter 6).

## Family Law Act 1996

**30.  Rights concerning matrimonial home where one spouse has no estate, etc.**

(1)  This section applies if—
    (a)  one spouse is entitled to occupy a dwelling-house by virtue of—
        (i)  a beneficial estate or interest or contract; or
        (ii)  any enactment giving that spouse the right to remain in occupation; and
    (b)  the other spouse is not so entitled.

(2)  Subject to the provisions of [Part IV of this Act], the spouse not so entitled has the following rights ('matrimonial home rights')—
    (a)  if in occupation, a right not to be evicted or excluded from the dwelling-house or any part of it by the other spouse except with the leave of the court given by an order under section 33;
    (b)  if not in occupation, a right with the leave of the court so given to enter into and occupy the dwelling-house.
  . . .

*Note*
Section 31 makes provision in respect of the effect of matrimonial home rights as a charge on the dwelling-house. Section 32 and sch. 4 re-enact with consequential amendments and minor modifications the provisions of the MHA 1983.

(For the law on acquiring rights in the family home, see 3.3 below.)

## 3.2  PROPERTY RIGHTS OF COHABITANTS

### 3.2.1  Cohabitants in a disadvantageous position compared with divorcing spouses

Any property dispute between cohabitants on relationship breakdown is determined by the general principles of property law; the court has no statutory jurisdiction equivalent to that of the divorce court to adjust their property rights. As this lack of adjustive jurisdiction may cause injustice, the Law Commission is currently considering reforms in order to give the courts jurisdiction to adjust the property rights of cohabitants and other partnerships. The following case provides a good example of the disadvantage of being a cohabitant on relationship breakdown rather than a divorcing spouse.

*Burns* v *Burns*
[1984] Ch 317
Court of Appeal

*Facts*: The parties had cohabited for about 19 years and had two children. The home in which they had lived for 17 years had been purchased by Mr Burns in his sole name. Mrs Burns (she had changed her name) had made no direct contribution to the purchase price or to the mortgage. She was unable to earn money while she was bringing up their children, but later found employment and contributed towards housekeeping expenses, and bought fixtures and fittings and consumer durables for the house. She also decorated the interior. When their relationship broke down, she sought a declaration claiming she was entitled to a beneficial interest in the house by reason of her contributions to the household during the 17 years that they had lived there. At first instance her claim failed. She appealed to the Court of Appeal.

*Held*: dismissing the appeal, and applying *Pettitt* v *Pettitt* and *Gissing* v *Gissing*, that the court was unable to impute from the parties' conduct a common intention that Mrs Burns was to have a beneficial interest merely from the fact that she had lived with the defendant for 19 years, had looked after their children, performed domestic duties, bought chattels and re-decorated the house.

FOX LJ: The house with which we are concerned in this case was purchased in the name of the defendant and the freehold was conveyed to him absolutely. That was in 1963. If, therefore, the plaintiff is to establish that she has a beneficial interest in the property she must establish that the defendant holds the legal estate upon trust to give effect to that interest. That follows from *Gissing* v *Gissing* [1971] AC 886. For present purposes I think that such a trust could only arise (a) by express declaration or agreement *or* (b) by way of a resulting trust where the claimant has directly provided part of the purchase price *or* (c) from the common intention of the parties.

In the present case (a) and (b) can be ruled out. There was no express trust of an interest in the property for the benefit of the plaintiff; and there was no express agreement to create such an interest. And the plaintiff made no direct contribution to the purchase price. Her case, therefore, must depend upon showing a common intention that she should have a beneficial interest in the property. Whether the trust which would arise in such circumstances is described as implied, constructive or resulting does not greatly matter. If the intention is inferred from the fact that some indirect contribution is made to the purchase price, the term 'resulting trust' is probably not inappropriate. Be that as it may, the basis of such a claim, in any case, is that it would be inequitable for the holder of the legal estate to deny the claimant's right to a beneficial interest.

In determining whether such common intention exists it is, normally, the intention of the parties when the property was purchased that is important. As to that I agree with the observations of Griffiths LJ in *Bernard* v *Josephs* [1982] Ch 391, 404. As I understand it, that does not mean that for the purpose of determining the ultimate shares in the property one looks simply at the factual position as it was at the date of acquisition. It is necessary for the court to consider all the evidence, including the contributions of the parties, down to the date of separation (which in the case of man and mistress will generally, though not always, be the relevant date). Thus the law proceeds on the basis that there is nothing inherently improbable in the parties acting on the understanding that the woman

should be entitled to a share which was not to be quantified immediately upon the acquisition of the home but should be left to be determined when the mortgage was repaid or the property disposed of, on the basis of what would be fair having regard to the total contributions, direct or indirect, which each spouse had made by that date: (see *Gissing* v *Gissing* [1971] AC 886, 909, *per* Lord Diplock.)

That approach does not, however, in my view preclude the possibility that while, initially, there was no intention that the claimant should have any interest in the property, circumstances may subsequently arise from which the intention to confer an equitable interest upon the claimant may arise (e.g., the discharge of a mortgage or the effecting of capital improvements to the house at his or her expense). Further, subsequent events may throw light on the initial intention.

Looking at the position at the time of the acquisition of the house in 1963, I see nothing at all to indicate any intention by the parties that the plaintiff should have an interest in it. . . .

I come then to the position in the year after the house was purchased. I will deal with them under three heads, namely financial contributions, work on the house and finally housekeeping. There is some overlapping in these categories.

. . .

None of this expenditure, in my opinion, indicates the existence of the common intention which the plaintiff has to prove. What is needed, I think, is evidence of a payment or payments by the plaintiff which it can be inferred was referable to the acquisition of the house. . . .

. . . I think that the decoration undertaken by the plaintiff gives no indication of any such common intention as she must assert.

There remains the question of housekeeping and domestic duties. So far as housekeeping expenses are concerned, I do not doubt that (the house being bought in the man's name) if the woman goes out to work in order to provide money for the family expenses, as a result of which she spends her earnings on the housekeeping and the man is thus able to pay the mortgage instalments and other expenses out of his earnings, it can be inferred that there was a common intention that the woman should have an interest in the house — since she will have made an indirect financial contribution to the mortgage instalments. But that is not this case.

. . .

I think it would be quite unreal to say that, overall, she made a substantial financial contribution towards the family expenses. That is not in any way a criticism of her; it is simply the factual position.

But, one asks, can the fact that the plaintiff performed domestic duties in the house and looked after the children be taken into account? I think it is necessary to keep in mind the nature of the right which is being asserted. The court has no jurisdiction to make such order as it might think fair; the powers conferred by the Matrimonial Causes Act 1973 in relation to the property of married persons do not apply to unmarried couples. The house was bought by the defendant in his own name and, prima facie, he is the absolute beneficial owner. If the plaintiff, or anybody else, claims to take it from him, it must be proved the claimant has, by some process of law, acquired an interest in the house. What is asserted here is the creation of a trust arising by common intention of the parties. That common intention may be inferred where there has been a financial contribution, direct or indirect, to the acquisition of the house. But the mere fact that parties live together and do the ordinary domestic tasks is, in my view, no indication at all that they thereby intended to alter the existing property rights of either of them. As to that I refer to the passage from the speech of Lord Diplock in *Pettitt* v *Pettitt* [1970] AC 777, 826 which I have already mentioned; and also to the observations of Lord Hodson in *Pettitt* v *Pettitt* at p. 811 and of Lord Reid at p. 796. The undertaking of such work is, I think, what Lord Denning MR in *Button* v *Button* [1968] 1 WLR 457, 462 called the sort of things which are done for the benefit of the family without altering the title to property. The assertion that they do alter property rights seems to me to be, in substance, reverting to the idea of the 'family asset' which was rejected by the House of Lords in *Pettitt* v *Pettitt* [1970] AC 777. . . .

The result, in my opinion, is that the plaintiff fails to demonstrate the existence of any trust in her favour. . . .

For the reasons which I have given I think that the appeal must be dismissed. I only add this. The plaintiff entered upon her relationship with the defendant knowing that there was no prospect of him marrying her. And it is evident that in a number of respects he treated her very well. He was generous to her, in terms of money, while the relationship continued. And, what in the long term is probably more important he encouraged her to develop her abilities in a number of ways, with the result that she built up the successful driving instruction business. Nevertheless, she lived with him for 18 years as man and wife, and, at the end of it, has no rights against him. But the unfairness of that is not a matter which the courts can control. It is a matter for Parliament.

MAY LJ: This appeal raises a question which arises nowadays with increasing frequency. If a man and a woman marry, acquire a home, live in it together, bring up children, but sadly sooner or later separate and divorce, the courts have a wide discretion to adjust their subsequent respective financial situations under the provisions of the Matrimonial Causes Act 1973. In particular the court has power to determine the spouses' respective rights to the matrimonial home, which is usually the family's main asset, and by virtue of section 25(1) of the Act of 1973 is given a wide discretion to exercise its powers to place the parties, so far as it is practicable and just to do so, in the financial position in which they would have been if the marriage had not broken down and each had properly discharged his or her financial obligations and responsibilities towards the other.

However, it is becoming increasingly frequent that couples live together without being married, but just as if they were so. They acquire a home for themselves and their children whom they bring up in the same way as the family next door. Nevertheless it also happens, just like their married friends, that differences do arise between the couple and they separate. In some cases the man and the woman can agree what is to happen in those circumstances, for instance, to their erstwhile joint home. But if they do not agree, they come to the courts for the resolution of their dispute. In the case of an unmarried couple in these circumstances there is no statute which gives a court similar powers to those which it has as between husband and wife. In these cases the question therefore arises what principles is the court to apply?

For my part, I agree that the principles which the courts must apply are those laid down in *Pettitt* v *Pettitt* [1970] AC 777 and *Gissing* v *Gissing* [1971] AC 886. . . .

Further, in this particular field different people have very different views about the problems and relationships involved. In my view, as Parliament has not legislated for the unmarried couple as it has for those who have been married, the courts should be slow to attempt in effect to legislate themselves. . . .

[After reviewing all the authorities, his Lordship concluded:]

In the light of all these cases, I think that the approach which the courts should follow, be the couples married or unmarried, is now clear. . . .

. . . [W]hen the house is taken in the man's name alone, if the woman makes no 'real' or 'substantial' financial contribution towards either the purchase price, deposit or mortgage instalments by the means of which the family home was acquired, then she is not entitled to any share in the beneficial interest in that home even though over a very substantial number of years she may have worked just as hard as the man in maintaining the family in the sense of keeping the house, giving birth to and looking after and helping to bring up the children of the union.

On the facts of the instant case, which Waller LJ has outlined, I think that it is clear that the plaintiff falls into the last of the categories to which I have just referred and accordingly I too would dismiss this appeal. When one compares this ultimate result with what it would have been had she been married to the defendant, and taken appropriate steps under the Matrimonial Causes Act 1973, I think that she can justifiably say that fate has not been kind to her. In my opinion, however, the remedy for any inequity she may have sustained is a matter for Parliament and not for this court.

*Questions*
1. What might have been the outcome of the case if Mrs Burns had been married and divorcing (see Chapter 5)?
2. Why did Mrs Burns receive nothing, whereas Miss Mitchell (see *Hammond v Mitchell* at 3.3.2.2 below) received a half share of the home? Is this satisfactory? Was Mrs Burns unjustly treated?

### 3.2.2   Occupation rights

Cohabitants, unlike spouses, have no statutory rights of occupation. Cohabitants acquire rights of occupation only by being an owner or tenant of property, or by having a licence to remain in occupation of the property.

(For occupation orders where there is violence in the home, see Chapter 6, and for the law on acquiring rights in the home and reform of the law for cohabitants, see 3.3 and 3.4 below.)

## 3.3   THE FAMILY HOME: OWNERSHIP

(For the family home on divorce, see Chapter 5.)

### Lawson-Cruttenden, Tim, and Odutola, Adetutu, 'Constructive Trusts — A Practical Guide'
[1995] Fam Law 560

The real difficulty faced by the court is that most couples who set up home together, whether married or unmarried, do not normally discuss in a formal manner their respective proprietary interests in the property which is or is to be their home. These difficulties are compounded by the common misunderstanding that the cohabitation relationship is a 'legal shadow' of the marriage relationship. Many cohabitees labour under the misapprehension, at least, in relation to property, that they have rights not dissimilar to those under the Matrimonial Causes Act 1973, and that those rights are acquired by virtue of 'common law'. Hence the apparent and erroneous doctrine of 'common law wife'.

### Clarke, Peter J., 'The Family Home: Intention and Agreement'
[1992] Fam Law 72

In an ideal world, those who intend to own property or a share in it would do three things: they would agree what they intended to do; they would then record their intentions; and they would take legal advice to ensure that what they wanted had been achieved in a manner which the law recognises. However, as any practitioner or student of the law reports is well aware, life is not like that. At one stage the battleground was between spouses but, since the Matrimonial Proceedings and Property Act 1970 and the Matrimonial Causes Act 1973, that is now very seldom the case. However, tensions emerged in those days between two groups of judges: those who wished to do justice at the expense of certainty, Lord Denning being the obvious and most vociferous example, and those others — often in the House of Lords, or who had a Chancery background, or both — who believed that property rights, like the status of matrimony itself, should not be lightly acquired. Cases from that era include those *loci classici*, *Pettitt* v *Pettitt* [1970] AC 777 and *Gissing* v *Gissing* [1971] AC 886, which are still part of the law. The background of those cases may be important: judges who are happy with a result in a matrimonial situation may be less happy where heterosexual cohabitation — or another relationship — is involved.

The area of dispute has now shifted. There are, of course, still disputes over matrimonial property, but often not between the parties (at least, ostensibly); instead, a party to the marriage — whether or not acting as a 'front' for them both — is seeking to assert a right against a lender or a purchaser. Lenders have commonly had a bad press: many will remember the time when lenders — and even banks — were commonly solvent, and when banks were seeking business and attempting to be part of the caring society. The other fruitful source of litigation has been cohabiting couples; because there is no Matrimonial Causes Act, the judge-made law which was relevant to married couples is still relevant to the unmarried. . . .

### 3.3.1  Written formalities for land

Written formalities are needed for a transfer of the home, a declaration of a trust in respect of the home and a contract for its sale.

## Law of Property Act 1925

**53.  Instruments required to be in writing**
(1)  . . .
    (a)  no interest in land can be created or disposed of except by writing signed by the person creating or conveying the same, or by his agent thereunto lawfully authorised in writing, or by will, or by operation of law;
    (b)  a declaration of trust respecting any land or any interest therein must be manifested and proved by some writing signed by some person who is able to declare such trust or by his will;
. . .
    (2)  This section does not affect the creation or operation of resulting, implied or constructive trusts.

## Law of Property (Miscellaneous Provisions) Act 1989

**2.  Contracts for sale etc. of land to be made by signed writing**
(1)  A contract for the sale or other disposition of an interest in land can only be made in writing and only by incorporating all the terms which the parties have expressly agreed in one document or, where contracts are exchanged, in each.
(2)  The terms may be incorporated in a document either by being set out in it or by reference to some other document.

(3)   The document incorporating the terms or, where contracts are exchanged, one of the documents incorporating them (but not necessarily the same one) must be signed by or on behalf of each party to the contract.

(4)   . . .

(5) . . . nothing in this section affects the creation or operation of resulting, implied or constructive trusts.

### 3.3.2   Acquiring ownership under a trust

*Midland Bank plc* v *Cooke*
[1995] 2 FLR 915
Court of Appeal

WAITE LJ: . . . Equity has traditionally been a system which matches established principle to the demands of social change. The mass diffusion of home ownership has been one of the most striking social changes of our own time. The present case is typical of hundreds, perhaps even thousands, of others. When people, especially young people, agree to share their lives in joint homes they do so on a basis of mutual trust and in the expectation that their relationship will endure. Despite the efforts that have been made by many responsible bodies to counsel prospective cohabitants as to the risks of taking shared interests in property without legal advice, it is unrealistic to expect that advice to be followed on a universal scale. For a couple embarking on a serious relationship, discussion of the terms to apply at parting is almost a contradiction of the shared hopes that have brought them together. There will inevitably be numerous couples, married or unmarried, who have no discussion about ownership and who, perhaps advisedly, make no agreement about it. It would be anomalous, against that background, to create a range of home-buyers who were beyond the pale of equity's assistance in formulating a fair presumed basis for the sharing of beneficial title, simply because they had been honest enough to admit that they never gave ownership a thought or reached any agreement about it. . . .

*Note*

The non-owner (spouse or cohabitant, or any other person) may claim a right to a beneficial ownership in the family home under a trust, as interests under a trust can be acquired without the requirement of writing (see s. 53(2) of the Law of Property Act 1925 and s. 2(5) of the Law of Property (Miscellaneous Provisions) Act 1989 *supra*). Two types of trust can be used as a means of acquiring an interest: the purchase price resulting trust; and the common intention constructive trust. Different principles apply to each.

### 3.3.2.1   The purchase price resulting trust

*Dyer* v *Dyer*
(1788) 2 Cox, Eq Cas 92
Court of Exchequer

EYRE CB: . . . The clear result of all the cases, without a single exception, is that the trust of a legal estate . . . whether taken in the names of the purchasers and others jointly, or in the names of others without that of the purchaser; whether in one name or several; whether jointly or successive — results to the man who advances the purchase-money. . . .

*Note*

The successful claimant will be granted a share of the beneficial interest proportionate his or her financial contribution to the purchase price. It must be noted, however, that the payment of money raises a *presumption* of a resulting trust, i.e. a trust is presumed unless there is a contrary intention (e.g. that the money was an outright gift or a loan). The presumption of resulting trust was not rebutted in the following case.

### *Springette* v *Defoe*
### [1992] 2 FLR 388
### Court of Appeal

*Facts*: The parties, who were elderly cohabitants, bought their council house jointly under the 'right to buy' scheme, but there was nothing in the registered transfer quantifying their beneficial interests in the property. Each party contributed half of the mortgage instalments, but the plaintiff paid the balance of the purchase price, except for £180 paid by the defendant. When the relationship broke down the plaintiff Springette issued an originating summons claiming she was entitled to 75 per cent of the share of the proceeds of sale, representing her contribution to the purchase. The trial judge granted them an equal share of the beneficial interest, on the basis that it was their uncommunicated belief or intention that they were to share the property equally. The plaintiff appealed.

*Held*: allowing the appeal, that as there was no discussion between the parties as to their respective beneficial interests, there was nothing to rebut the presumption of resulting trust that the plaintiff was entitled to 75 per cent of the beneficial interest, representing her contribution to the purchase price.

DILLON LJ: This is yet another case in which it falls to the court to decide the proportions of the beneficial interests of a man and a woman, who are not married to each other, in the proceeds of sale of a house which they have acquired in their joint names for the purpose of living together in it.
. . .

The recorder directed himself by reference to a somewhat lengthy passage in my judgment in *Walker* v *Hall* [1984] FLR 126 at pp. 133D–135A, and also by reference to the decision to the same effect of Bush J in *Marsh* v *Von Sternberg* [1986] 1 FLR 526.

In *Walker* v *Hall*, I expressed the view at p. 134C that it was not open to this court, in the absence of specific evidence of the parties' intentions, to hold that the property there in question belonged beneficially to the two parties in equal shares, notwithstanding their unequal contributions to the purchase price, simply because it was bought to be their family home and they intended — or possibly one should say 'hoped' — that their relationship should last for life. The effect is that, in the absence of an express declaration of the beneficial interests, the court will hold that the joint purchasers hold the property on a resulting trust for themselves in the proportions in which they contributed directly or indirectly to the purchase price, unless there is sufficient specific evidence of their common intention that they should be entitled in other proportions — e.g. in equal shares notwithstanding unequal contributions — to rebut the presumption of a resulting trust.

There are many references to the intention of the parties in cases before and after *Walker* v *Hall.* For instance in *Gissing* v *Gissing* [1971] AC 886 at p. 909E, Lord Diplock, referring in particular to the date as at which the common intention should be ascertained, said:

> Where this was the most likely inference from their conduct it would be for the court to give effect to that common intention of the parties by determining what in all the circumstances was a fair share.

. . .

There are statements in some more recent authorities which appear at first glance to be expressed more widely.

Thus in *Stokes* v *Anderson* [1991] 1 FLR 391, Nourse LJ, in giving the leading judgment with which Lloyd and Ralph Gibson LJJ agreed, said at p. 16B of the transcript that 'the court must supply the common intention by reference to that which all the material circumstances have shown to be fair'. Nicholls LJ used a similar expression in *Passee* v *Passee* [1988] 1 FLR 263 at p. 271A, where he said:

> They intended, or are to be taken to have intended, that each would be entitled to a share to be determined . . . on the basis of what would be fair, having regard to the contributions which in total each had . . . made.

The common intention must be founded on evidence such as would support a finding that there is an implied or constructive trust for the parties in proportions to the purchase price. The court does not as yet sit, as under a palm tree, to exercise a general discretion to do what the man in the street, on a general overview of the case, might regard as fair.

But the common intention of the parties must, in my judgment, mean a shared intention communicated between them. It cannot mean an intention which each happened to have in his or her own mind but had never communicated to the other. I find some assistance in this respect in the observation of Lord Bridge of Harwich in *Lloyds Bank plc* v *Rosset* [1991] 1 AC 107, [1990] 2 FLR 155, where he said at pp. 135F and 163G respectively in relation to the question whether there had been any agreement, arrangement or understanding reached between the parties to the effect that a property was to be shared beneficially:

> The finding of an agreement or arrangement to share in this sense can only, I think, be based on evidence of express discussions between the partners, however imperfectly remembered and however imprecise their terms may have been.

It is not enough to establish a common intention which is sufficient to found an implied or constructive trust of land that each of them happened at the same time to have been thinking on the same lines in his or her uncommunicated thoughts, while neither had any knowledge of the thinking of the other.

Since, therefore, it is clear in the present case that there never was any discussion between the parties about what their respective beneficial interests were to be, they cannot, in my judgment, have had in any relevant sense any common intention as to the beneficial ownership of the property. I cannot therefore support the conclusion of the recorder that the beneficial interest was held by Miss Springette and Mr Defoe in equal shares. The presumption of a resulting trust is not displaced. Accordingly, I would allow this appeal and would declare instead that they are beneficially entitled in the proportions of 75 per cent to Miss Springette and 25 per cent to Mr Defoe. . . .

STEYN LJ: On the appeal the question is whether the assistant recorder was right in concluding on the evidence that an actual common intention at the time of the purchase to acquire the property in equal beneficial shares had been established.

When they gave evidence the parties were agreed on one point. There had been no discussion or communication between them as to the beneficial shares which they would have in the property. And the judge accepted that evidence, subject to minor and immaterial qualifications. On behalf of the respondent it was suggested that the parties must have communicated an intention that they should have equal shares at a subconscious level. I fear that will not do. Our trust law does not allow property rights to be affected by telepathy. Prima facie, therefore, the alleged actual common intention was not established. . . .

*Note*
See also *Sekhon* v *Alissa* [1989] 2 FLR 94, ChD, where a mother who had contributed to the purchase of a house owned by her daughter succeeded in a claim against her daughter, despite the daughter's defence that her mother's contribution was intended as a gift or alternatively as an unsecured loan and that she had only a moral, not a legal, obligation to repay it to her mother.

### 3.3.2.2 The common intention constructive trust
The existence of this sort of trust depends on the intentions of the parties. It is therefore referred to as the 'common intention' constructive trust, in order to distinguish it from constructive trusts which arise in other contexts (e.g. in cases of commercial fraud).

The principles applicable to a claim by way of constructive trust are laid down in a trilogy of House of Lords' decisions: *Pettitt* v *Pettitt*; *Gissing* v *Gissing* and *Lloyds Bank plc* v *Rosset*. *Pettitt* and *Gissing* involved claims by spouses to obtain a share of the matrimonial home in equity under a trust at a time when the divorce court had no jurisdiction to adjust property rights. Today each spouse would have applied for a property adjustment order under s. 24 of the MCA 1973 (see Chapter 5). *Rosset* involved a dispute between the spouses and a mortgagee bank. Although all three cases involved spouses, the same principles apply to disputes between cohabitants.

**Pettitt v Pettitt**
[1970] AC 777
House of Lords

*Facts*: On marriage breakdown the husband applied under s. 17 of the Married Women's Property Act 1882 (see 3.1.2 *supra*), claiming that he was entitled to a share in the proceeds of sale of the former matrimonial home owned by his wife on the basis that he had improved and redecorated it. He had done internal decorative work, built a wardrobe, and had laid a lawn and built an ornamental well and a side wall in the garden. The Court of Appeal granted him a share. The wife appealed.
*Held*: allowing the appeal, that the husband was not entitled to a share in the proceeds of sale, as his improvements to the property were nearly all of an ephemeral nature. He had done 'DIY' jobs which husbands normally do.

LORD REID: . . . [I]t is, I think, proper to consider whether, without departing from the principles of the common law, we can give effect to the view that, even where there was in fact no agreement, we can ask what the spouses, or reasonable people in their shoes, would have agreed if they had directed their minds to the question of what rights should accrue to the spouse who has contributed to the acquisition or improvement of property owned by the other spouse. There is already a presumption which operates in the absence of evidence as regards money contributed by one spouse towards the acquisition of property by the other spouse. So why should there not be a similar presumption where one spouse has contributed to the improvement of the property of the other? I do not think that it is a very convincing argument to say that, if a stranger makes improvements on the property of another without any agreement or any request by that other that he should do so, he acquires no right. The improvement is made for the common enjoyment of both spouses during the marriage. It would no doubt be different if the one spouse makes the improvement while the other spouse who owns the property is absent and without his or her knowledge or consent. But if the spouse who owns the property acquiesces in the other making the improvement in circumstances where it is reasonable to suppose that they would have agreed to some right being acquired if they had thought about the legal position, I can see nothing contrary to ordinary legal principles in holding that the spouse who makes the improvement has acquired such a right.

Some reference was made to the doctrine of unjust enrichment. I do not think that that helps. The term has been applied to cases where a person who has paid money sues for its return. But there does not appear to be any English case of the doctrine being applied where one person has improved the property of another. And in any case it would only result in a money claim whereas what a spouse who makes an improvement is seeking is generally a beneficial interest in the property which has been improved.

No doubt there would be practical difficulties in determining what the parties, or reasonable people in their shoes, would have agreed. But then there is almost equal difficulty in determining whether the spouses did in fact make an agreement, and, if they did, what are its terms. . . .

In whatever way the general question as to improvements is decided I think that the claim in the present case must fail for two reasons. These improvements are nearly all of an ephemeral character. Redecoration will only last for a few years and it would be unreasonable that a spouse should obtain a permanent interest in the house in return for making improvements of this character. And secondly I agree with the view of Lord Denning MR expressed in *Button* v *Button* [1968] 1 WLR 457, 461. He said with regard to the husband 'he should not be entitled to a share in the house simply by doing the "do-it-yourself" jobs which husbands often do': and with regard to the wife (at p. 462):

> The wife does not get a share in the house simply because she cleans the walls or works in the garden or helps her husband with the painting and decorating. Those are the sort of things which a wife does for the benefit of the family without altering the title to, or interests in, the property.

. . .

LORD UPJOHN: . . . My Lords, the facts of this case depend not upon the acquisition of property but upon the expenditure of money and labour by the husband in the way of improvement upon the property of the wife which admittedly is her own beneficial property. Upon this it is quite clearly established that by the law of England the expenditure of money by A upon the property of B stands in quite a different category from the acquisition of property by A and B.

It has been well settled in your Lordships' House (*Ramsden v Dyson* (1865) LR 1 HL 129) that if A expends money on the property of B, prima facie he has no claim on such property. And this, as Sir William Grant MR, held as long ago as 1810 in *Campion v Cotton* (1810) 17 Ves 263, is equally applicable as between husband and wife. If by reason of estoppel or because the expenditure was incurred by the encouragement of the owner that such expenditure would be rewarded, the person expending the money may have some claim for monetary reimbursement in a purely monetary sense from the owner or even, if explicitly promised to him by the owner, an interest in the land (see *Plimmer v Wellington Corpn.* (1884) 9 App Cas 699). But the respondent's claim here is to a share of the property and his money claim in his plaint is only a qualification of that. Plainly, in the absence of agreement with his wife (and none is suggested) he could have no monetary claim against her and no estoppel or mistake is suggested so, in my opinion, he can have no charge upon or interest in the wife's property. . . .

LORD DIPLOCK: . . . How, then, does the court ascertain the 'common intention' of spouses as to their respective proprietary interests in a family asset when at the time that it was acquired or improved as a result of contributions in money or money's worth by each of them they failed to formulate it themselves? It may be possible to infer from their conduct that they did in fact form an actual common intention as to their respective proprietary interests and where this is possible the courts should give effect to it. But in the case of transactions between husband and wife relating to family assets their actual common contemplation at the time of its acquisition or improvement probably goes no further than its common use and enjoyment by themselves and their children, and while that use continues their respective proprietary interests in it are of no practical importance to them. They only become of importance if the asset ceases to be used and enjoyed by them in common and they do not think of the possibility of this happening. In many cases, and most of those which come before the courts, the true inference from the evidence is that at the time of its acquisition or improvement the spouses formed no common intention as to their proprietary rights in the family asset. They gave no thought to the subject of proprietary rights at all.

But this does not raise a problem which is peculiar to transactions between husband and wife. It is one with which the courts are familiar in connection with ordinary contracts and to its solution they apply a familiar legal technique. The common situation in which a court has to decide whether or not a term is to be implied in a contract is when some event has happened for which the parties have made no provision in the contract because at the time it was made neither party foresaw the possibility of that event happening and so never in fact agreed as to what its legal consequences would be upon their respective contractual rights and obligations. Nevertheless the court imputes to the parties a common intention which in fact they never formed and it does so by forming its own opinion as to what would have been the common intention of reasonable men as to the effect of that event upon their contractual rights and obligations if the possibility of the event happening had been present to their minds at the time of entering into the contract. . . .

It is common enough nowadays for husbands and wives to decorate and to make improvements in the family home themselves, with no other intention than to indulge in what is now a popular hobby, and to make the home pleasanter for their common use and enjoyment. If the husband likes to occupy his leisure by laying a new lawn in the garden or building a fitted wardrobe in the bedroom while the wife does the shopping, cooks the family dinner or bathes the children, I, for my part, find it quite impossible to impute to them as reasonable husband and wife any common intention that these domestic activities or any of them are to have any effect upon the existing proprietary rights in the family home on which they are undertaken. It is only in the bitterness engendered by the break-up of the marriage that so bizarre a notion would enter their heads. . . .

The present case . . . in my view, clearly falls in the same category as *Button* v *Button* and *Appleton* v *Appleton* [[1965] 1 WLR 25]. I would allow this appeal.

### *Gissing* v *Gissing*
### [1971] AC 886
### House of Lords

*Facts*: The matrimonial home was purchased in the husband's name. There was no express agreement as to how the beneficial interest should be held and the wife had made no direct contribution to the purchase price, although she had paid for household goods and for clothes for herself and her son and for improving the lawn. The husband paid for outgoings on the house and for holidays and paid his wife a housekeeping allowance. When their relationship broke down the wife claimed a share of the beneficial interest in the home. The trial judge held that she had no beneficial interest. The Court of Appeal (Edmund Davies LJ dissenting) held that she was entitled to a half share. The husband appealed.

*Held*: allowing the appeal and unanimously restoring the trial judge's decision, that it was impossible to draw an inference on the facts that there was any intention that the wife should have a beneficial interest in the home.

LORD REID: My Lords, I agree with your Lordships that this appeal must be allowed. But, as in *Pettitt's case* [1970] AC 777, much wider questions have been raised than are necessary for the decision of the case. I adhere to the views which I expressed in *Pettitt's* case and I do not think that I am precluded from maintaining them by the decision in that case. But if I am, then in my view the law is left in a very unsatisfactory position.
. . .

If there has been no discussion and no agreement or understanding as to sharing in the ownership of the house and the husband has never evinced an intention that his wife should have a share, then the crucial question is whether the law will give a share to the wife who has made those contributions without which the house would not have been bought.

I agree that this depends on the law of trust rather than on the law of contract, so the question is under what circumstances does the husband become a trustee for his wife in the absence of any declaration of trust or agreement on his part. It is not disputed that a man can become a trustee without making a declaration of trust or evincing any intention to become a trustee. The facts may impose on him an implied, constructive or resulting trust. Why does the fact that he has agreed to accept these contributions from his wife not impose such a trust on him?

As I understand it, the competing view is that, when the wife makes direct contributions to the purchase by paying something either to the vendor or to the building society which is financing the purchase, she gets a beneficial interest in the house although nothing was ever said or agreed about this at the time: but that, when her contributions are only indirect by way of paying sums which the husband would otherwise have had to pay, she gets nothing unless at the time of the acquisition there was some agreement that she should get a share. I can see no good reason for this distinction and I think that in many cases it would be unworkable. Suppose the spouses have a joint bank account. In accordance with their arrangement she pays in enough money to meet the household bills and so there is enough to pay the purchase price instalments and their bills as well as their personal expenses. They never discuss whose money is to go to pay for the house and whose is to go to pay for other things. How can anyone tell whether she has made a direct or only an indirect contribution to paying for the house? It cannot surely depend on who signs which cheques. Is she to be deprived of a share if she says 'I can pay in enough to pay for the household bills,' but given a share if she says 'I can pay in £10 per week regularly.'

It is perfectly true that where she does not make direct payments towards the purchase it is less easy to evaluate her share. If her payments are direct she gets a share proportionate to what she has paid. Otherwise there must be a more rough and ready evaluation. I agree that this does not mean that she would as a rule get a half-share. I think that the high-sounding brocard 'equality is equity' has been misused. There will of course be cases where a half-share is a reasonable estimation, but there will be many others where a fair estimate might be a tenth or a quarter or sometimes even more than a half.

But then it is said that there will be few deserving cases where the court cannot find enough in the evidence to justify a finding that there was at the time of acquisition some kind of agreement or understanding or intention that the wife should have a share. I do not agree. In evidence the husband will say truthfully that the matter was never discussed and that he never considered the question of her having a share. Even if in cross-examination he were to say that if he had been asked he might have been willing to make some arrangement, that would be quite irrelevant if the law requires a contemporary agreement. And a candid and honest wife would agree that the matter was never discussed, that her husband never indicated any intention to give her a share, and that she never thought about it. On such evidence no judge could possibly infer that on a balance of probability there was an agreement. On the other hand a more sophisticated wife who had been told what the law was would probably be able to produce some vague evidence which would enable a sympathetic judge to do justice by finding in her favour. That would not be a very creditable state in which to leave the law.

Returning to the crucial question there is a wide gulf between inferring from the whole conduct of the parties that there probably was an agreement, and imputing to the parties an intention to agree to share even where the evidence gives no ground for such an inference. If the evidence shows that there was no agreement in fact then that excludes any inference that there was an agreement. But it does not exclude an imputation of a deemed intention if the law permits such an imputation. If the law is to be that the court has power to impute such an intention in proper cases then I am content, although I would prefer to reach the same result in a rather different way. But if it were to be held to be the law that it must at least be possible to infer a contemporary agreement in the sense of holding that it is more probable than not there was in fact some such agreement then I could not contemplate the future results of such a decision with equanimity.

LORD DIPLOCK: . . . Any claim to a beneficial interest in land by a person, whether spouse or stranger, in whom the legal estate in the land is not vested must be based upon the proposition that the person in whom the legal estate is vested holds it as trustee upon trust to give effect to the beneficial interest of the claimant as cestui que trust. The legal principles applicable to the claim are those of the English law of trusts and in particular, in the kind of dispute between spouses that comes before the courts, the law relating to the creation and operation of 'resulting, implied or constructive trusts.' Where the trust is expressly declared in the instrument by which the legal estate is transferred to the trustee or by a written declaration of trust by the trustee, the court must give effect to it. But to constitute a valid declaration of trust by way of gift of a beneficial interest in land to a cestui que trust the declaration is required by section 53(1) of the Law of Property Act, 1925, to be in writing. If it is not in writing it can only take effect as a resulting, implied or constructive trust to which that section has no application.

A resulting, implied or constructive trust — and it is unnecessary for present purposes to distinguish between these three classes of trust — is created by a transaction between the trustee and the cestui que trust in connection with the acquisition by the trustee of a legal estate in land, whenever the trustee has so conducted himself that it would be inequitable to allow him to deny to the cestui que trust a beneficial interest in the land acquired And he will be held so to have conducted himself if by his words or conduct he has induced the cestui que trust to act to his own detriment in the reasonable belief that by so acting he was acquiring a beneficial interest in the land.

. . . An express agreement between spouses as to their respective beneficial interests in land conveyed into the name of one of them obviates the need for showing that the conduct of the spouse into whose name the land was conveyed was intended to induce the other spouse to act to his or her detriment upon the faith of the promise of a specified beneficial interest in the land and that the other spouse so acted with the intention of acquiring that beneficial interest. The agreement itself discloses the common intention required to create a resulting, implied or constructive trust.

But parties to a transaction in connection with the acquisition of land may well have formed a common intention that the beneficial interest in the land shall be vested in them jointly without having used express words to communicate this intention to one another; or their recollections of the words used may be imperfect or conflicting by the time any dispute arises. In such a case — a common one where the parties are spouses whose marriage has broken down — it may be possible to infer their common intention from their conduct.

As in so many branches of English law in which legal rights and obligations depend upon the intentions of the parties to a transaction, the relevant intention of each party is the intention which was reasonably understood by the other party to be manifested by that party's words or conduct notwithstanding that he did not consciously formulate that intention in his own mind or even acted with some different intention which he did not communicate to the other party. On the other hand, he is not bound by any inference which the other party draws as to his intention unless that inference is one which can reasonably be drawn from his words or conduct. It is in this sense that in the branch of English law relating to constructive, implied or resulting trusts effect is given to the inferences as to the intentions of parties to a transaction which a reasonable man would draw from their words or conduct and not to any subjective intention or absence of intention which was not made manifest at the time of the transaction itself. It is for the court to determine what those inferences are.

In drawing such an inference, what spouses said and did which led up to the acquisition of a matrimonial home and what they said and did while the acquisition was being carried through is on a different footing from what they said and did after the acquisition was completed. Unless it is alleged that there was some subsequent fresh agreement, acted upon by the parties, to vary the original beneficial interests created when the matrimonial home was acquired, what they said and did after the acquisition was completed is relevant if it is explicable only upon the basis of their having manifested to one another at the time of the acquisition some particular common intention as to how the beneficial interests should be held. But it would in my view be unreasonably legalistic to treat the relevant transaction involved in the acquisition of a matrimonial home as restricted to the actual conveyance of the fee simple into the name of one or other spouse. . . .

. . . Each case must depend upon its own facts but there are a number of factual situations which often recur in the cases.

[After referring to these factual situations, his Lordship continued:] Where . . . contributions, direct or indirect, have been made to the mortgage instalments by the spouse into whose name the matrimonial home has not been conveyed, and the court can infer from their conduct a common intention that the contributing spouse should be entitled to *some* beneficial interest in the matrimonial home, what effect is to be given to that intention if there is no evidence that they in fact reached any express agreement as to what the respective share of each spouse should be?

I take it to be clear that if the court is satisfied that it was the common intention of both spouses that the contributing wife should have a share in the beneficial interest and that her contributions were made upon this understanding, the court in the exercise of its equitable jurisdiction would not permit the husband in whom the legal estate was vested and who had accepted the benefit of the contributions to take the whole beneficial interest merely because at the time the wife made her contributions there had been no express agreement as to how her share in it was to be quantified.

In such a case the court must first do its best to discover from the conduct of the spouses whether any inference can reasonably be drawn as to the probable common understanding about the amount of the share of the contributing spouse upon which each must have acted in doing what each did, even though that understanding was never expressly stated by one spouse to the other or even consciously formulated in words by either of them independently. It is only if no such inference can be drawn that the court is driven to apply as a rule of law, and not as an inference of fact, the maxim 'equality is equity,' and to hold that the beneficial interest belongs to the spouses in equal shares. . . .

Where the wife has made no initial contribution to the cash deposit and legal charges and no direct contribution to the mortgage instalments nor any adjustment to her contribution to other expenses of the household which it can be inferred was referable to the acquisition of the house, there is in the absence of evidence of an express agreement between the parties no material to justify the court in inferring that it was the common intention of the parties that she should have any beneficial interest in a matrimonial home conveyed into the sole name of the husband, merely because she continued to contribute out of her own earnings or private income to other expenses of the household. For such conduct is no less consistent with a common intention to share the day-to-day expenses of the household, while each spouse retains a separate interest in capital assets acquired with their own moneys or obtained by inheritance or gift. There is nothing here to rebut the prima facie inference that a purchaser of land who pays the purchase price and takes a conveyance and grants a mortgage in his own name intends to acquire the sole beneficial interest as well as the legal estate: and the difficult question of the quantum of the wife's share does not arise.

. . . The court is not entitled to infer a common intention to this effect from the mere fact that she provided chattels for joint use in the new matrimonial home; and there is nothing else in the conduct of the parties at the time of the purchase or thereafter which supports such an inference. There is no suggestion that the wife's efforts or her earnings made it possible for the husband to raise the initial loan or the mortgage or that her relieving her husband from the expense of buying clothing for herself and for their son was undertaken in order to enable him the better to meet the mortgage instalments or to repay the loan. The picture presented by the evidence is one of husband and wife retaining their separate proprietary interests in property whether real or personal purchased with their separate savings and is inconsistent with any common intention at the time of the purchase of the matrimonial home that the wife, who neither then nor thereafter contributed anything to its purchase price or assumed any liability for it, should nevertheless be entitled to a beneficial interest in it. . . .

*Note*

Shortly after *Pettitt* and *Gissing* the Matrimonial Proceedings and Property Act 1970 gave the divorce court jurisdiction to adjust the property rights of spouses according to their needs and resources irrespective of their rights of ownership. The 1970 Act was later consolidated with the Divorce Reform Act 1969, containing the grounds for divorce, to become the MCA 1973 (see Chapters 4 and 5).

Lord Bridge's opinion in *Lloyds Bank plc* v *Rosset* is considered to be the approach to be adopted by the courts when a claim is made to a beneficial interest under a constructive trust.

### *Lloyds Bank plc* v *Rosset and another*
### [1991] 1 AC 107
### House of Lords

*Facts*: The matrimonial home, a derelict farmhouse, was purchased in the sole name of the husband, the first defendant. The purchase money had come from the husband's family trust in Switzerland and the trustees had insisted it be purchased in his name. He paid for renovation work. The wife, the second defendant, made no financial contribution to the purchase, but helped with the renovation. Unbeknown to the wife, the husband had charged the house to a bank as security for an overdraft. When he defaulted, the bank sought possession of the home. The wife, by way of defence to the possession action, contended that she was entitled to a half share of the beneficial interest under a constructive trust, which, coupled with her actual occupation of the house, gave her an overriding interest under s. 70(1)(g) of the Land Registration Act 1925, so that the bank was not entitled to possession. The trial judge found in favour of the bank. The Court of Appeal (by a majority) allowed the wife's appeal. The bank appealed to the House of Lords.

*Held*: *inter alia*, and allowing the appeal, that the wife's activities in relation to the house had been insufficient to justify the inference of a common intention that she should have a beneficial interest in it under a constructive trust.

LORD BRIDGE: . . . These considerations lead me to the conclusion that the judge's finding that Mr Rosset held the property as constructive trustee for himself and his wife cannot be supported and it is on this short ground that I would allow the appeal. In the course of the argument your Lordships had the benefit of elaborate submissions as to the test to be applied to determine the circumstances in which the sole legal proprietor of a dwelling house can properly be held to have become a constructive trustee of a share in the beneficial interest in the house for the benefit of the partner with whom he or she has cohabited in the house as their shared home. Having in this case reached a conclusion on the facts which, although at variance with the views of the courts below, does not seem to depend on any nice legal distinction and with which, I understand, all your Lordships agree, I cannot help doubting whether it would contribute anything to the illumination of the law if I were to attempt an elaborate and exhaustive analysis of the relevant law to add to the many already to be found in the authorities to which our attention was directed in the course of the argument. I do, however, draw attention to one critical distinction which any judge required to resolve a dispute between former partners as to the beneficial interest in the home they formerly shared should always have in the forefront of his mind.

The first and fundamental question which must always be resolved is whether, independently of any inference to be drawn from the conduct of the parties in the course of sharing the house as their home and managing their joint affairs, there has at any time prior to acquisition, or exceptionally at some later date, been any agreement, arrangement or understanding reached between them that the property is to be shared beneficially. The finding of an agreement or arrangement to share in this sense can only, I think, be based on evidence of express discussions between the partners, however imperfectly remembered and however imprecise their terms may have been. Once a finding to this effect is made it will only be necessary for the partner asserting a claim to a beneficial interest against the partner entitled to the legal estate to show that he or she has acted to his or her detriment or significantly altered his or her position in reliance on the agreement in order to give rise to a constructive trust or a proprietary estoppel.

In sharp contrast with this situation is the very different one where there is no evidence to support a finding of an agreement or arrangement to share, however reasonable it might have been for the parties to reach such an arrangement if they had applied their minds to the question, and where the court must rely entirely on the conduct of the parties both as the basis from which to infer a common intention to share the property beneficially and as the conduct relied on to give rise to a constructive trust. In this situation direct contributions to the purchase price by the partner who is not the legal owner, whether initially or by payment of mortgage instalments, will readily justify the inference necessary to the creation of a constructive trust. But, as I read the authorities, it is at least extremely doubtful whether anything less will do.

The leading cases in your Lordships' House are *Pettitt* v *Pettitt* [1970] AC 777 and *Gissing* v *Gissing* [1971] AC 886. Both demonstrate situations in the second category to which I have referred and their Lordships discuss at great length the difficulties to which these situations give rise. The effect of these two decisions is very helpfully analysed in the judgment of Lord MacDermott LCJ in *McFarlane* v *McFarlane* [1972] NI 59.

Outstanding examples on the other hand of cases giving rise to situations in the first category are *Eves* v *Eves* [1975] 1 WLR 1338 and *Grant* v *Edwards* [1986] Ch 638. In both these cases, where the parties who had cohabited were unmarried, the female partner had been clearly led by the male partner to believe when they set up home together, that the property would belong to them jointly. In *Eves* v *Eves* the male partner had told the female partner that the only reason why the property was to be acquired in his name alone was because she was under 21 and that, but for her age, he would have had the house put into their joint names. He admitted in evidence that this was simply an 'excuse.' Similarly in *Grant* v *Edwards* the female partner was told by the male partner that the only reason for not acquiring the property in joint names was because she was involved in divorce proceedings and that, if the property were acquired jointly, this might operate to her prejudice in those proceedings. As Nourse LJ put it, at p. 649:

> Just as in *Eves* v *Eves* [1975] 1 WLR 1338, these facts appear to me to raise a clear inference that there was an understanding between the plaintiff and the defendant, or a common intention, that the plaintiff was to have some sort of proprietary interest in the house; otherwise no excuse for not putting her name on to the title would have been needed.

The subsequent conduct of the female partner in each of these cases, which the court rightly held sufficient to give rise to a constructive trust or proprietary estoppel supporting her claim to an interest in the property, fell far short of such conduct as would by itself have supported the claim in the absence of an express representation by the male partner that she was to have such an interest. It is significant to note that the share to which the female partners in *Eves* v *Eves* and *Grant* v *Edwards* were held entitled were one quarter and one half respectively. In no sense could these shares have been regarded as proportionate to what the judge in the instant case described as a 'qualifying contribution' in terms of the indirect contributions to the acquisition or enhancement of the value of the houses made by the female partners.

I cannot help thinking that the judge in the instant case would not have fallen into error if he had kept clearly in mind the distinction between the effect of evidence on the one hand which is capable of establishing an express agreement or an express representation that Mrs Rosset was to have an interest in the property and evidence on the other hand of conduct alone as a basis for an inference of the necessary common intention.

. . .

For the reasons I have indicated I would allow the appeal, set aside the order of the Court of Appeal and, as between Mrs Rosset and the bank, restore the order of the trial judge.

*Questions*
1. Lord Bridge doubted *obiter* whether anything less than a direct contribution to the purchase price would be sufficient to provide evidence of the implied intention needed to give an applicant a beneficial interest under a constructive trust. Is this a correct interpretation of *Gissing* and *Pettitt*? Is there not an implication in those cases that an indirect contribution (i.e. contribution to other household expenses which allows the other partner to pay for the house) might have sufficed? In *McFarlane* v *McFarlane* [1972] NI 59, Lord MacDermott in the Northern Ireland Court of Appeal stated that, as he understood *Pettitt* and *Gissing*, the non-owner might acquire a beneficial interest by virtue of indirect contributions to the purchase price, but only if the indirect contributions were the subject of an agreement or an arrangement by the parties.

2.   The trial judge in *Rosset* was satisfied on the evidence that it was the expressly stated common intention of Mr and Mrs Rosset that the house should be bought in Mr Rosset's name alone because funds for its purchase would not otherwise have been available from Mr Rosset's family trust in Switzerland. The judge was also satisfied that it was their common intention that its restoration should be a joint venture, after which it was to be shared as the family home. Why, then, did Mr and Mrs Rosset lose in the House of Lords?

3.   Are the facts of *Rosset* similar to those of *Eves* v *Eves* and *Grant* v *Edwards* (i.e. but for the Swiss trustees' requirement that the house be bought in Mr Rosset's name, they would both have had an interest)?

4.   Lord Bridge used the words 'agreement, arrangement or understanding'. Are these different concepts? Is it possible to have a common 'understanding'? Can understandings be communicated (see *Springette* v *Defoe*, at 3.3.2.1 *supra*)?

5.   In *Rosset*, Lord Bridge said that the court must consider evidence of express discussions between the parties 'however imperfectly remembered and however imprecise the terms may be'. Is this a satisfactory way of allowing parties to acquire property rights? Might it encourage parties to perjure themselves (see *Hammond* v *Mitchell* below, where Waite J stated that 'both parties were prone to exaggeration' and that 'neither side had the monopoly of truth').

6.   Lord Bridge gave *Eves* v *Eves* and *Grant* v *Edwards* as examples of the first category of cases (i.e. where there was 'an express agreement, arrangement or understanding'). Was there any agreement, arrangement or understanding between the parties in those two 'excuse' cases?

### Gardner, Simon, 'A Woman's Work'
### (1991) 55 MLR 126

. . . *Rosset* joins decisions such as *Murphy* v *Brentwood DC* [[1990] 2 All ER 908] and, albeit somewhat incredibly, *Street* v *Mountford* [[1985] AC 809] in another of the House's contemporary preoccupations: increasing the efficiency of the judicial system by putting the law into concrete 'bright-line' formulæ. Judicial efficiency is no doubt a laudable aim, and such concretisation may be an apt means of promoting it. One can only have misgivings, however, about the way that the House sometimes appears ready to propound its formula without first resolving the underlying doctrinal tensions and incoherences. The lines of the resulting formula may look bright, but the continued fundamental ambiguity means that in practice there remains much uncertainty. *Rosset* typifies this phenomenon. It has its ostensibly clear-cut formula distinguishing between 'express' and 'implied' agreements, with the latter to be inferred only from financial contributions. But as we have seen, this division is actually just a snapshot of the struggle going on between two quite different approaches, a struggle which the formula's newly increased polarisation will only intensify. . . .

Attention will have to be addressed above all to two questions. The first concerns the role of intention. At the moment intention is ostensibly central to these constructive trusts, in the shape of the demand for an agreement. There is certainly a case for attending to intention so as to respect the autonomy of those people who wish to regulate their own affairs. But there still has to be a rule for those who do not give their minds to the matter. At the moment the rule is ostensibly that the paper title prevails — i.e. the house stays with the man. At least some judges seem to regard this as unsatisfactory, though, because they commonly invent the necessary agreement, rather than genuinely discovering or inferring one, so as in reality to predicate shared ownership upon certain other kinds of facts. It would be better to remove the requirement of intention and allow these facts to operate in their own right. The other question would then be what kinds of facts should entail shared ownership in this way. For the adherents of referability the essential matter seems to be the spending (and so the having) of money, whilst other judges evidently have some other qualification in mind, probably centred on playing one's part in the overall business of home-making. The former approach seems invidious: 'to those that have shall be given . . . .' The latter approach seems preferable, as reflecting the nature of the family enterprise: a notion, we are told, that is to become big in the nineties. Other than the fact that their Lordships eschewed it twenty years ago, in *Pettitt* v *Pettitt* and *Gissing* v *Gissing*, is there any reason why this approach should not become the law?

### Detriment
In addition to an agreement, arrangement or understanding, the non-owner must establish a detriment. In *Grant* v *Edwards*, Sir Nicholas Browne-Wilkinson V-C, applying principles analogous to those of proprietary estoppel, referred to the question of detriment.

### Grant v Edwards
[1986] Ch 638
Court of Appeal

*Facts*: The home was bought in the joint names of the male cohabitant and his brother. The male cohabitant told the female cohabitant that the only reason for buying it jointly with his brother was to prevent her being prejudiced in her pending divorce proceedings. When their relationship broke down the female partner claimed that she was entitled to a share in the property under a trust. The male partner admitted in evidence that he had never had any intention of replacing his brother with his female partner once her divorce proceedings were finished.
*Held*: allowing the appeal, that the female partner was entitled to a half share of the beneficial interest.

SIR NICHOLAS BROWNE-WILKINSON V-C: . . . In my judgment, there has been a tendency over the years to distort the principles as laid down in the speech of Lord Diplock in *Gissing* v *Gissing* [1971] AC 886 by concentrating on only part of his reasoning. For present purposes, his speech can be treated as falling into three sections: the first deals with the nature of the substantive right; the second with the proof of the existence of that right; the third with the quantification of that right.

1.  *The nature of the substantive right:* [1971] AC 886, 905B-G
If the legal estate in the joint home is vested in only one of the parties ('the legal owner') the other party ('the claimant'), in order to establish a beneficial interest, has to establish a constructive trust by showing that it would be inequitable for the legal owner to claim sole beneficial ownership. This requires two matters to be demon-

strated: (a) that there was a common intention that both should have a beneficial interest; (b) that the claimant has acted to his or her detriment on the basis of that common intention.

### 2. *The proof of the common intention*
(a)   Direct evidence . . . . It is clear that mere agreement between the parties that both are to have beneficial interests is sufficient to prove the necessary common intention. Other passages in the speech point to the admissibility and relevance of other possible forms of direct evidence of such intention . . . .

(b)   Inferred common intention . . . . Lord Diplock points out that, even where parties have not used express words to communicate their intention (and therefore there is no direct evidence), the court can infer from their actions an intention that they shall both have an interest in the house. This part of his speech concentrates on the types of evidence from which the courts are most often asked to infer such intention viz. contributions (direct and indirect) to the deposit, the mortgage instalments or general housekeeping expenses. In this section of the speech, he analyses what types of expenditure are capable of constituting evidence of such common intention: he does not say that if the intention is proved in some other way such contributions are essential to establish the trust.

Once it has been established that the parties had a common intention that both should have a beneficial interest *and* that the claimant has acted to his detriment, the question may still remain 'what is the extent of the claimant's beneficial interest?' This last section of Lord Diplock's speech shows that here again the direct and indirect contributions made by the parties to the cost of acquisition may be crucially important.

If this analysis is correct, contributions made by the claimant may be relevant for four different purposes, viz.: (1) in the absence of direct evidence of intention, as evidence from which the parties' intentions can be inferred; (2) as corroboration of direct evidence of intention; (3) to show that the claimant has acted to his or her detriment in reliance on the common intention: Lord Diplock's speech does not deal directly with the nature of the detriment to be shown; (4) to quantify the extent of the beneficial interest.

. . .

Applying those principles to the present case, the representation made by the defendant to the plaintiff that the house would have been in the joint names but for the plaintiff's matrimonial disputes is clear direct evidence of a common intention that she was to have an interest in the house: *Eves* v *Eves* [1975] 1 WLR 1338. Such evidence was in my judgment sufficient by itself to establish the common intention: but in any event it is wholly consistent with the contributions made by the plaintiff to the joint household expenses and the fact that the surplus fire insurance moneys were put into a joint account.

But as Lord Diplock's speech in *Gissing* v *Gissing* [1971] AC 886, 905D and the decision in *Midland Bank plc* v *Dobson* [[1986] 1 FLR 171] make clear, mere common intention by itself is not enough: the claimant has also to prove that she has acted to her detriment in the reasonable belief by so acting she was acquiring a beneficial interest.

There is little guidance in the authorities on constructive trusts as to what is necessary to prove that the claimant so acted to her detriment. What 'link' has to be shown between the common intention and the actions relied on? Does there have to be positive evidence that the claimant did the acts in conscious reliance on the common intention? Does the court have to be satisfied that she would not have done the acts relied on but for the common intention, e.g. would not the claimant have contributed to household expenses out of affection for the legal owner and as part of their joint life together even if she had no interest in the house? Do the acts relied on as a detriment have to be inherently referable to the house, e.g. contribution to the purchase or physical labour on the house?

I do not think it is necessary to express any concluded view on these questions in order to decide this case. *Eves* v *Eves* [1975] 1 WLR 1338 indicates that there has to be some 'link' between the common intention and the acts relied on as a detriment. In that case the acts relied on did inherently relate to the house (viz. the work the claimant did to the house) and from this the Court of Appeal felt able to infer that the acts were done in reliance on the common intention. So, in this case, as the analysis of Nourse LJ makes clear, the plaintiff's contributions to the household expenses were essentially linked to the payment of the mortgage instalments by the defendant: without the plaintiff's contributions, the defendant's means were insufficient to keep up the mortgage payments. In my judgment where the claimant has made payments which, whether directly or indirectly, have been used to discharge the mortgage instalments, this is a sufficient link between the detriment suffered by the claimant and the common intention. The court can infer that she would not have made such payments were it not for her belief that she had an interest in the house. On this ground therefore I find that the plaintiff has acted to her detriment in reliance on the common intention that she had a beneficial interest in the house and accordingly that she has established such beneficial interest.

I suggest that in other cases of this kind, useful guidance may in the future be obtained from the principles underlying the law of proprietary estoppel which in my judgment are closely akin to those laid down in *Gissing* v *Gissing* [1971] AC 886. In both, the claimant must to the knowledge of the legal owner have acted in the belief that the claimant has or will obtain an interest in the property. In both, the claimant must have acted to his or her detriment in reliance on such belief. In both, equity acts on the conscience of the legal owner to prevent him from acting in an unconscionable manner by defeating the common intention. The two principles have been developed separately without cross-fertilisation between them: but they rest on the same foundation and have on all other matters reached the same conclusions.

In many cases of the present sort, it is impossible to say whether or not the claimant would have done the acts relied on as a detriment even if she thought she had no interest in the house. Setting up house together, having a baby, making payments to general housekeeping expenses (not strictly necessary to enable the mortgage to be paid) may all be referable to the mutual love and affection of the parties and not specifically referable to the claimant's belief that she has an interest in the house. As at present advised, once it has been shown that there was a common intention that the claimant should have an interest in the house, any act done by her to her detriment relating to the joint lives of the parties is, in my judgment, sufficient detriment to qualify. The acts do not have to be inherently referable to the house: see *Jones (A. E.)* v *Jones (F. W.)* [1977] 1 WLR 438 and *Pascoe* v *Turner* [1979] 1 WLR 431. The holding out to the claimant that she had a beneficial interest in the house is an act of such a nature as to be part of the inducement to her to do the acts relied on. Accordingly, in the absence of evidence to the contrary, the right inference is that the claimant acted in reliance on such holding out and the burden lies on the legal owner to show that she did not do so: see *Greasley* v *Cooke* [1980] 1 WLR 1306.

The possible analogy with proprietary estoppel was raised in argument. However, the point was not fully argued and since the case can be decided without relying on such analogy, it is unsafe for me to rest my judgment on that point. I decide the case on the narrow ground already mentioned.

What then is the extent of the plaintiff's interest? It is clear from *Gissing* v *Gissing* [1971] AC 886 that, once the common intention and the actions to the claimant's detriment have been proved from direct or other evidence, in fixing the quantum of the claimant's beneficial interest the court can take into account indirect contributions by the plaintiff such as the plaintiff's contributions to joint household expenses: see *Gissing* v *Gissing* [1971] AC 886, 909A and D-E. In my judgment, the passage in Lord Diplock's speech at pp. 909G–910A is dealing with a case where there is no evidence of the common intention other than contributions to joint expenditure: in such a case there is insufficient evidence to prove any beneficial interest and the question of the extent of that interest cannot arise.

Where, as in this case, the existence of some beneficial interest in the claimant has been shown, prima facie the interest of the claimant will be that which the parties intended: *Gissing* v *Gissing* [1971] AC 886, 908G. In *Eves* v *Eves* [1975] 1 WLR 1338, 1345G Brightman LJ plainly felt that a common intention that there should be a joint interest pointed to the beneficial interests being equal. However, he felt able to find a lesser beneficial interest in that case without explaining the legal basis on which he did so. With diffidence, I suggest that the law of proprietary estoppel may again provide useful guidance. If proprietary estoppel is established, the court gives effect to it by giving effect to the common intention so far as may fairly be done between the parties. For that purpose, equity is displayed at its most flexible: see *Crabb* v *Arun District Council* [1976] Ch 179. Identifiable contributions to the purchase of the house will of course be an important factor in many cases. But in other cases, contributions by way of the labour or other unquantifiable actions of the claimant will also be relevant.

Taking into account the fact that the house was intended to be the joint property, the contributions to the common expenditure and the payment of the fire insurance moneys into the joint account, I agree that the plaintiff is entitled to a half interest in the house.

*Further reading*
Glover, N., and Todd, P., 'The Myth of Common Intention' (1996) 16 LS 325.
Lawson, A., 'The Things we do for Love: Detrimental Reliance in the Family Home' (1996) 16 LS 218.

*Assessing the claimant's share of the beneficial interest*
Lord Diplock in *Gissing* v *Gissing* [1971] AC 886 at p. 908, dealt with the approach to be adopted by the court when evaluating the proportionate shares of the parties, once it had been established that some beneficial interest was intended (see the paragraph in his opinion at 3.3.2.2 *supra*, beginning 'Where in any of the circumstances described above contributions, direct or indirect, have been made to the mortgage instalments . . .'). These *dicta* were cited and applied by Waite LJ in *Midland Bank* v *Cooke and Another* [1995] 2 FLR 915, CA, at pp. 924 and 925, where his Lordship took the view that once a beneficial interest has been found, the court may undertake a survey of the whole course of dealing between the parties to establish what proportion of the beneficial interest should be granted. Mrs Cooke was granted a half share of the beneficial interest, even though her financial contribution to the purchase represented 6.47 per cent of the value of the property. *Cooke* was criticised by some commentators as being too flexible an application of *Rosset* (e.g., see Wylie, 'Computing Shares in the Family Home' [1995] Fam Law 633). For other comments on *Cooke*, see Oldham, M., 'Quantification of

Beneficial Interests in Land' [1996] CLJ 19 and Gardner, S., 'Fin de Siècle chez *Gissing* v *Gissing*' (1996) 112 LQR 378 at p. 382, who stated that 'with *Midland Bank Plc* v *Cooke*, the point may well have been reached where the classic authorities' approach [i.e. in *Gissing* and *Rosset*] has been so marginalised that it has lost the mass of institutional influence critical for sensible survival'.

*An example of a post-*Rosset *case*
The following case, the facts of which read like a popular novel or the script of a TV soap, provides an example of a post-*Rosset* approach to a property dispute between two cohabitants.

**Hammond v Mitchell**
[1991] 1 WLR 1127
Family Division

*Facts*: Vicky Mitchell and Tom Hammond were cohabitants. When their relationship broke down, Miss Mitchell claimed, *inter alia*, a beneficial interest under s. 30 of the Law of Property Act 1925 in their Essex house and their house in Spain, both owned by Mr Hammond. At the time of the purchase of the Essex house Mr Hammond had told Miss Mitchell that he had put the house in his name for tax reasons and because he was going through a divorce. Soon after completion, he told her: 'Don't worry about the future because when we are married it will be half yours anyway and I'll always look after you and [the boy]'. Miss Mitchell helped him with his English and Spanish businesses and brought up their two children, but made no contribution towards the purchase price.
*Held*: applying *Grant* v *Edwards* and *Rosset, supra*, that Miss Mitchell was entitled to a half share in the English house, but to no interest in the house in Spain.

WAITE J: . . . In the summer of 1977 Mr Tom Hammond, a married man of 40 separated from his wife, was setting off for a ride in Epping Forest when he had a chance encounter with Miss Vicky Mitchell, a 21-year-old girl who had stopped her car to ask the way. Their conversation led to further meetings and within a very short time they were living together. He was a trader, dealing in those days principally in second-hand cars. She was a Bunny Girl employed at a high salary by the Playboy Club in Mayfair as one of their croupiers. They both shared a zest for what each described in evidence as 'the good life,' a concept which for them meant luxury cars rapidly changed, comfortable holidays spent abroad, dining out in restaurants, gaming in casinos and raising and racing greyhounds. They also shared a love of the market-place in the sense of an attachment to dealing for dealing's sake and a mutual delight in bargain hunting. They were, and still are, both highly charged people emotionally, a quality which accounts both for the strength of the relationship which endured for 11 years and produced two children, and also for the intensity of feeling which marked its end. The net value of the assets they were enjoying together at the time of parting and now in dispute between them approaches £450,000. Mr Hammond says that virtually all of it is his; Miss Mitchell claims that a substantial part at least of it is hers.

Had they been married, the issue of ownership would scarcely have been relevant, because the law these days when dealing with the financial consequences of divorce adopts a forward-looking perspective in which questions of ownership yield to the higher demands of relating the means of both to the needs of each, the first consideration given to the welfare of children. Since this couple did not marry, none of that flexibility is available to them, except a limited power to direct capital provision for their children. In general, their financial rights have to be worked out according to their strict entitlements in equity, a process which is anything but forward-looking and involves, on the contrary, a painfully detailed retrospect.

The template for that analysis has recently been restated by the House of Lords and the Court of Appeal in *Lloyds Bank Plc* v *Rosset* [1991] 1 AC 107 and *Grant* v *Edwards* [1986] Ch 638. The court first has to ask itself whether there have at any time prior to acquisition of the disputed property, or exceptionally at some later date, been discussions between the parties leading to any agreement, arrangement or understanding reached between them that the property is to be shared beneficially. Any further investigation carried out by the court will vary in depth according to whether the answer to that initial inquiry is 'Yes' or 'No.' If there have been discussions of that kind and the answer is therefore 'Yes,' the court then proceeds to examine the subsequent course of dealing between the parties for evidence of conduct detrimental to the party without legal title referable to a reliance upon the arrangement in question. If there have been no such discussions and the answer to that initial inquiry is therefore 'No,' the investigation of subsequent events has to take the form of an inferential analysis involving a scrutiny of all events potentially capable of throwing evidential light on the question whether, in the absence of express discussion, a presumed intention can be spelt out of the parties' past course of dealing. This operation was vividly described by Dixon J in Canada as, 'The judicial quest for the fugitive or phantom common intention' (*Pettkus* v *Becker* (1980) 117 DLR (3d) 257), and by Nourse LJ, in *Grant* v *Edwards* [1986] Ch 638, 646, as a 'climb up the familiar ground which slopes down from the twin peaks of *Pettitt* v *Pettitt* [1970] AC 777 and *Gissing* v *Gissing* [1971] AC 886.' The process is detailed, time-consuming and laborious.

The difficulties of applying that formula can be alarming, as this present case has well illustrated. The hearing has occupied no less than 19 days of High Court time and has cost the parties, one of whom is legally aided, more than £125,000 between them in legal fees. Given the mounting pressure on the courts as cases of this kind increase with the growing numbers of the population who choose to live together outside marriage, procedures will clearly have to be worked out to keep such hearings within sensible bounds for the future. This case has been instructive in that respect and at the end of this judgment I shall mention some of the lessons that might be learned from it.

In turning, as I now do, to review the evidence to which the formula has to be applied in the present case, I do not propose to recite everything that was alleged by each party. Neither side had the monopoly of truth. Both were prone to exaggeration. It will be sufficient to say that the findings which now follow represent part-acceptance and part-rejection of the evidence of each party, as well as inferences drawn from their words and actions and the very considerable documentary evidence produced on each side.

[After citing the evidence, Waite J continued: . . .]

That completes the account of the material to which the law requires me in determining beneficial title to apply the principles enunciated in *Lloyds Bank Plc* v *Rosset* [1991] 1 AC 107 and *Grant* v *Edwards* [1986] Ch 638. It will involve asking this question first: is there any, and if so which property which has been the subject of some agreement, arrangement or understanding reached between the parties on the basis of express discussion to the effect that such property is to be shared beneficially; and (if there is) has Miss Mitchell shown herself to have acted to her detriment or significantly altered her position in reliance on the agreement so as to give rise to a constructive trust or proprietary estoppel?

The answer to that question should, in my judgment, in both its parts be 'Yes.' In relation to the bungalow there was express discussion on the occasions I have already described which, although not directed with any precision as to proprietary interests, was sufficient to amount to an understanding at least that the bungalow was to be shared beneficially. It will, of course, be a question of fact and degree in every case where A and B acquire Blackacre in A's sole name with a mutual expectation of a shared beneficial interest, and thereafter enlarge it by extension of existing premises or the purchase in A's sole name of an adjoining property Whiteacre, whether B's beneficial interest was intended to extend to the enlarged hereditament. That can only be determined on a review of the whole course of dealing between the parties. I am satisfied in the present case that the parties intended the bungalow, as it became successively enlarged by addition to its own original structure and by the purchase of the adjoining parcels of land and barns, to be subject to the same understanding as governed the original property. Miss Mitchell, by her participation wholeheartedly in what may loosely be called the commercial activities based on the bungalow, not only acted consistently with that view of the situation but also acted to her detriment in that she gave her full support on two occasions to speculative ventures which, had they turned out unfavourably, might have involved the entire bungalow property being sold up to repay the bank an indebtedness to which the house and land were all committed up to the hilt.

There remains the question in relation to the bungalow of what the proportion of Miss Mitchell's beneficial interest should be held to be. This is not an area where the maxim that 'equality is equity' falls to be applied unthinkingly. That is plain from the lesser proportions awarded in both *Grant* v *Edwards* [1986] Ch 638 and in *Eves* v *Eves* [1975] 1 WLR 1338. Nevertheless, when account is taken of the full circumstances of this unusual case, and when Miss Mitchell's contribution as mother/helper/unpaid assistant and at times financial supporter to the family prosperity generated by Mr Hammond's dealing activities is judged for its proper effect, it seems right to me that her beneficial interest in the bungalow should be held to be one half.

The next question, arising under the *Lloyds Bank Plc* v *Rosset* [1991] 1 AC 107 formula, is whether there is any property in regard to which an intention to share a beneficial ownership should be imputed to the parties in the absence of any express discussion leading to an agreement or understanding to that effect. Miss Mitchell asserts that there is such a property, namely, the Spanish house. She acknowledges that there was no previous discussion remotely touching upon the terms of its ownership, but her counsel . . . claims that when the parties' whole course of dealing is examined (even according to the more rigorous standards which apply when intention has to be inferred from conduct alone) the intention to constitute Mr Hammond a constructive trustee for Miss Mitchell of part of the beneficial interest in the Spanish house becomes manifest. To support that she relies on the cases (both involving married couples and neither of which was cited in *Lloyds Bank Plc* v *Rosset*) of *Nixon* v *Nixon* [1969] 1 WLR 1676, and *Muetzel* v *Muetzel* [1970] 1 WLR 188. I reject that submission. Useful at times though her activities may have been in Spain during the fulfilment of the Soriano venture. Miss Mitchell's activities generally fell a long way short of justifying any inference of intended proprietary interest.

. . .

The fourth [point] relates, finally, to the formulation of the claim to a beneficial interest in more substantial assets such as property or investments. The primary emphasis accorded by the law in cases of this kind to express discussions between the parties ('however imperfectly remembered and however imprecise their terms') means that the tenderest exchanges of a common law courtship may assume an unforeseen significance many years later when they are brought under equity's microscope and subjected to an analysis under which many thousands of pounds of value may be liable to turn on fine questions as to whether the relevant words were spoken in earnest or in dalliance and with or without representational intent. This requires that the express discussions to which the court's initial inquiries will be addressed should be pleaded in the greatest detail, both as to language and as to circumstance. . . .

Particularity will have the further advantage to both sides of enabling the strength of the claim to be assessed by the parties' advisers at an early stage, with sufficient definition to provide a fair basis for reasonable compromise. That will be an especially desirable objective in the case of separating unmarried couples, whose distress or bitterness is often found, paradoxically, to have been increased rather than diminished by their decision not to undertake a commitment to each other in marriage. . . .

*Notes*

1. In this case the proceedings were complex. Mr Hammond brought two actions in the Queen's Bench Division claiming the return of a car and the goods removed from the home by Miss Mitchell. Two days later he began wardship proceedings in the Family Division in respect of their two sons. Shortly after that, Miss Mitchell issued proceedings in the Family Division under s. 30 of the LPA 1925, now replaced by ss. 14 and 15 of the Trusts of Land and Appointment of Trustees Act 1996, and see Baughen, S. [1996] Fam Law 736) to claim a beneficial interest in the bungalow. The husband's actions in the Queen's Bench Division were transferred to the Family Division. Two days before the hearing before Waite J in the Family Division, *supra*, Miss Mitchell applied under s. 12 of the Family Law Reform Act 1987 for secured or lump sum capital provision for the children's maintenance.

2. Waite J laid down guidelines to assist lawyers in cases involving co-habitants, which included, *inter alia*, that in disputes about chattels, cohabitants must expect the court in ordinary cases to adopt 'a robust allegiance' to the maxim that 'equality is equity'.

### Clarke, Linda, and Edmunds, Rod, 'H v M: Equity and the Essex Cohabitant'
[1992] Fam Law 523

. . .

#### WHAT CONSTITUTES AN AGREEMENT, ARRANGEMENT OR UNDERSTANDING?

. . . Together, [two] separate conversations were held to amount to an understanding between the parties that the bungalow was to be held beneficially; an understanding which was found to apply also to the subsequent purchase of adjoining barns and fields. . . .

With respect, this could be seen as an *ex post facto* rationalisation, necessary in order to give the worthy claimant an interest in the property. Strictly speaking, the conduct in the present case (especially the words spoken after the bungalow had been acquired) looks less like a bilateral understanding or agreement and more in the nature of a unilateral assurance by Mr H that once married (an event which never took place) Miss M would have an interest in the bungalow. Such an assurance, like that made to the mistress in *Pascoe* v *Turner* [1978] Fam Law 82, [1979] 1 WLR 431, might then be relied upon to assert a successful proprietary estoppel claim.

In any event, there is something rather odd in basing valuable property rights on informal conversations such as that in *H* v *M*: there will almost always be a conflict of evidence on the point, both as to whether the conversation ever took place, as well as what was said or intended. Had Waite J not accepted Miss M's recollection as to conversations that took place 13 years previously, then she would have been unable to pursue her claim to a beneficial share in the Essex bungalow. The point is vividly reinforced in the court's rejection of Miss M's claim to a share in their Spanish villa, the other major asset acquired solely in Mr H's name during their relationship, precisely because there was no previous discussion between the parties remotely touching upon its ownership. And although Waite J accepted that Miss M had helped Mr H in running a business venture in Spain, her activities 'in no way justified any inference that she is entitled to a proprietary interest'.

## DETRIMENT

For an express agreement to give rise to a common intention constructive trust, detriment is essential. Otherwise the court will be faced solely with a voluntary declaration of trust, which is unenforceable for want of writing. What, then, was the nature of the alleged detriment in the instant case? During the years that they lived together, Miss M did not take a job outside the home; instead, she looked after the children and helped with Mr H's expanding business enterprise in a variety of ways. She also signed a charge executed in favour of Mr H's bank, which postponed any interest that she might have in the property to the claims of the bank. On two occasions Mr H entered into highly speculative business ventures, which, had they failed, would have led to the bank calling in the loan secured on the Essex bungalow. According to Waite J, by encouraging and supporting Mr H in these ventures, Miss M was acting to her detriment because if the ventures had turned out unsuccessfully the bungalow would have been sold to repay the loan.

Where the common intention constructive trust depends upon an express agreement, the courts have found detrimental reliance in a wide range of financial and other contributions which may be measurable in money terms. Doubtless, the categories of detriment are not closed. None the less, the form of the detriment found in the present case is strikingly unusual, and gives the concept a broader interpretation than in previous constructive trusts' cases. Acting to one's detriment usually involves giving something up, forgoing an opportunity, doing some work, or making some payment or contribution that, but for the common understanding between the parties, would not have been made. To extend the concept to supporting a person in a venture which proved successful, and which in any event the person could have taken part in regardless of the claimant's support, is to distort the meaning of the word. In *Grant* v *Edwards* . . . two members of the Court of Appeal differed on the meaning of 'detriment'. Nourse LJ confined detriment to conduct which claimants could not reasonably be expected to embark upon unless they were to have an interest in the house. It is clear from Waite J's judgment that Miss M shared Mr H's love of the good life, as she did his enthusiasm for wheeler-dealing. One might, therefore, have expected Miss M to have behaved exactly as she did, irrespective of her receiving a beneficial interest in the bungalow.

Admittedly, Miss M fares better when reference is made to the more generous description of detriment given in *Grant* v *Edwards* . . . by Browne-Wilkinson V-C:

> any act done by her to her detriment relating to the joint lives of the parties, is in my judgment, sufficient detriment to qualify. The acts do not have to be inherently referable to the house . . .

A difficulty with such a definition is that it gives little by way of practical guidance: in reality, whether or not having children and as a result forgoing employment opportunities and the chance to acquire property in one's own right amounts to detriment may depend upon whether or not the relationship breaks down.

It is submitted that in cases of this kind, the claimant's real detriment is committing many years to the relationship during which they could have been economically active and ensured for themselves a secure financial future. The courts should either recognise this as sufficient to allow a cohabitant to claim property rights; or insist that acting to one's detriment involves something more. The case-law has yet to meet this contention head-on, but the trend of the authorities suggests a reluctance to recognise this form of sacrifice as detriment; see *Coombes* v *Smith* 1 FLR 352 and *Ungurian* v *Lesnoff* [1990] 2 FLR 299.

There is also a circularity of reasoning in finding detriment in Miss M's willingness to postpone her equitable rights to those later created in favour of the bank. For it allows claimants to say that they have acted in reliance upon the agreement and suffered detriment by giving up the very rights that have not yet been shown to exist.

## STATUTORY REFORM

*H* v *M* highlights the absence of legal provision for cohabitants who, having lived together for a number of years, separate. English law does not provide a statutory jurisdiction, of the kind which applies on divorce, for dealing with the property and other financial adjustments between them. Waite J began his judgment by commenting on the contrast between cases involving couples who marry, where the court can take a forward-looking approach, relating the means of the parties to their future needs, and the approach necessary in cases involving cohabitants, where in order to discover the parties' entitlement in equity, the court must engage in a 'painfully detailed retrospect'. As the incidence of cohabitation increases, it may be argued that a thorough review of the need for a broad statutory discretion (akin to, but perhaps broader than, the Matrimonial Causes Act 1973) to sanction the redistribution of the property belonging to cohabitants whose relationship has ended, is long overdue.

. . .

Until such time as statute intervenes, the English courts are left with the substantive equitable principles, including constructive trusts and estoppel. Whatever their combined potential to determine flexibly the rights of cohabitants to specific assets, the jurisdiction falls a long way short of a comprehensive discretionary power to adjust the interests in property by having regard to such contributions 'made in the capacity of homemaker or parent': see [the New South Wales, Australia] De Facto Relationships Act 1984, s. 20(1)(b). Nor are these equitable principles of uncertain application a satisfactory substitute in cases like *H* v *M* for the Scottish proposals which allow for awards to make some provision where one cohabitant has worked without pay to build up the other's business and sacrificed her own career to look after their children.

. . .

## CONCLUSIONS

*H* v *M* is a useful illustration of the chasm opened up by *Lloyds Bank* v *Rosset and Another* . . . between the rights of cohabitants who can establish an express agreement and those who cannot. Once an express agreement is found, *H* v *M* suggests that almost any actions will amount to the detriment necessary to establish a proprietary interest, and that the claimant will then receive whatever share in the property the judge feels is fair. However, without any express agreement, the claimant will receive nothing unless he or she has made direct (or possibly indirect) financial contributions. Thus, Miss M had no claim to the Spanish bungalow. Inevitably, claimants will strive to establish a common express intention, and judges will be tempted to find one in any case where they feel the claimant ought to receive something at the end of a long relationship.

Although there are signs that the courts are gradually assimilating the once distinct equitable principles, proprietary estoppel and the common intention constructive trust, this can at best lead to piecemeal solutions to property disputes between former cohabitants. This is one reason why the better way to help cohabitants like those in the present case lies in a thorough consideration of the merits of introducing a statutory regime and tailor-made procedures to determine such disputes, both in and out of court. . . .

### 3.3.3  Alternatives to constructive trusts

In Canada the constructive trust has been used as a remedy in appropriate cases as a means of compensating for unjust enrichment, which arises where there is 'an enrichment, a corresponding deprivation and absence of any juristic reason for the enrichment' (*Pettkus* v *Becker* (1980) 117 DLR (3d) 257 at p. 274, *per* Dickson J). If unjust enrichment is proved, the court must determine whether in the circumstances a constructive trust is the appropriate remedy to apply to redress the enrichment (see also *Peter* v *Beblow* (1993) 101 DLR (4th) 621 and *Sorochan* v *Sorochan* (1986) 29 DLR (4th) 1).

In Australia, the principle of unconscionability is used to establish whether a claimant should have a share of the beneficial interest (see *Baumgartner* v *Baumgartner* (1987) 164 CLR 137, High Court of Australia), although there have been statutory reforms in some Australian states to give cohabitants a right to apply for property adjustment orders. Hayton ('The Equitable Rights of Cohabitees' [1990] Conv 370) has argued that the distinction between constructive trusts and proprietary estoppel is 'illusory' as both are based on the principle of unconscionability, and has recommended that the Australian approach should be adopted by the English courts. In New Zealand, the approach is based on that of reasonable expectations (see *Gillies* v *Keogh* [1989] 2 NZLR 327, New Zealand Court of Appeal).

Gardner in the following extract considers that the Canadian, Australian and New Zealand approaches are just as problematic as the English approach, for they too are based on the parties' thinking. He argues that doctrines which rely on the parties' thinking are inappropriate, since 'by the nature of the relationship in question, the parties will deal with each other more by trust and collaboration than by organised thinking about their respective rights'. Gardner suggests alternative doctrines and remedies which he considers better suited to the values of trust and collaboration.

## Gardner, Simon, 'Rethinking Family Property'
### (1993) 109 LQR 263

. . . The conclusion is . . . that in all the jurisdictions discussed there is a gap between the articulated doctrines and the manner in which cases are actually decided. On the whole the doctrines do not, when coupled with the true facts, produce remedies as they are claimed to do. The gap lies in the area of the parties' thinking. All the doctrines discussed make reference to the parties' own ideas. Under *Gissing* v *Gissing* there is a search for their common intention. Proprietary estoppel demands an expectation on the part of the plaintiff and at least constructive awareness of that belief on the part of the defendant. Expectation and awareness are similarly required in order to establish unjust enrichment in Canada; to establish that an act was done as part of a joint venture in Australia; and to found the innominate analysis used in New Zealand. In reality, there is very often no such thinking on the part of the parties. According to the articulated analyses, the claim should therefore fail. But the cases frequently proceed to give remedies after all. In most of the jurisdictions the circle is squared by fabricating the necessary facts. In New Zealand the result is achieved by gliding from attention to the parties' own ideas into attention to the views of reasonable persons in the parties' position.

But if the parties' thinking therefore does not generate the claim, what does? A reading suggests that the driving force lies in the relationship itself.

. . . [T]he present treatment of family property cases at common law is unsatisfactory. In broad terms, there seems a measure of agreement as to the desirability of providing relief. However, the doctrines articulated to date are all individualistic, requiring certain thinking on the part of the parties as a precondition for such relief. In reality, the relief is only able to be given by fabricating this thinking, because it is typically absent from the situations with which we are concerned. Its place is taken, as the parties' means of organising their relationship, by trust and collaboration. It has thus been argued that it would be more appropriate to devise a jurisprudence which would provide the desired relief on the foundation of these values instead. Two suggestions have been made.

The first implants trust and collaboration into the familiar framework of unjust enrichment, in place of the individualistic substratum from which there would otherwise arise problems as to voluntariness and subjective devaluation. This approach would provide restitutionary relief. It would be appropriate in cases where the parties trust and collaborate with one another, but on an ad hoc basis. That is, they maintain essentially separate responsibility for their own well-being, but pool efforts and resources on particular matters, which might include the securing of a home. This is in contrast to situations where the parties organise their whole lives collaboratively, so that the wellbeing of each is made dependent on the co-operation of the other. These situations — of communality — are the target of the second suggestion. This recognises a relationship of this kind as in effect a mutually fiduciary relationship, and so gains access to the law's existing learning about fiduciaries. It is thus able to give the parties relief by way of either a half share in, or adequate support from, each other's assets.

Finally, attending to the values inherent in the parties' relationship requires us to observe their thinking where it does exist. It follows that it is open to parties to agree to exclude these obligations. But such agreements would be vitiated if they were procured by oppression, and then the standard relief would arise again.

So how much of a stretch would it be for the law to follow this analysis? At one level, hardly a stretch at all. The guiding principle throughout this article has been to put sustainable doctrinal clothing on the practical *status quo*. The thesis has been that the relief currently being granted or at any rate hankered for is based on certain intuitions about policy, and that these intuitions provide at least a rough working model of the results the law ought to be producing. So the suggestions here would involve comparatively little change as to the practical outcomes of cases. The most notable difference would be to remove English law's 'referability' filter, which discriminates against non-financial contributions: all forms of contribution would count equally well under the modified unjust enrichment analysis, and communality operates independently of contributions. But of course there is already a swell of opinion that this change would be to the good. Beyond that, the change would largely take the form of a more structured pattern of relief. Both restitutionary remedies and ones based on communality are to be found in the existing materials, but the analysis suggested here would provide clarity as to which should lie when.

Doctrinally, of course, the stretch is greater. But the novelty should not be overestimated. The two suggested analyses adopt the existing superstructures of unjust enrichment and fiduciary obligations. The extent of their claim is to be able to base these super-structures on what appear to be new foundations — the values of trust and collaboration — as a substitute for the individualism of the current law of restitution and for the commercial quality of the relationships which are usually characterised as fiduciary. Perhaps even this rebasing would not represent a totally new departure. There are certainly areas of the current law of restitution which cannot well be accounted for within the standard individualistic approach, and in any case restitution might be thought due for a dose of communitarianism, of which the suggestion made here might be thought a specialised manifestation. And it is clear that not all fiduciary relationships are primarily commercial.

In the end, then, much is already in place. Of course, everything advocated here is already standard — though unexplicated — in existing statutory treatments, although the Australian provisions for unmarried couples may be wrong in confining themselves to a restitutionary response, not allowing for the possibility that such relationships might merit a response of communality, as with marriage. At common law, granted a rebasing in trust and collaboration rather than the parties' thinking, *Pettkus* v *Becker* and decisions under it largely provide the model of how the unjust enrichment approach would work. And *Baumgartner* v *Baumgartner*, extending the law as to commercial joint ventures into the domestic context, seems quite close to the fiduciary doctrine used by the communality approach, though the analysis here would suggest that seen in this way, the remedy should definitely be one of equality rather than linked to the claimant's contributions; it is interesting to see the court in that case already leaning in this direction, but apparently mistrusting its instincts.

It is widely perceived that this area of the law needs to be advanced. It is hoped that the re-analysis provided by this article has made some contribution to the work.

*Notes*
1.  Note the '*double entendre*' in Gardner's title.
2.  In *Bernard* v *Josephs* [1982] Ch 391, CA, Griffiths LJ stressed that the nature of the parties' relationship was an important factor when considering what inferences should be drawn from the way they had conducted their affairs.

## 3.4  REFORM OF THE LAW FOR COHABITANTS

The Law Commission is currently looking at the law applicable to the property rights of cohabitants and other home-sharers with a view to making proposals for reform. Item 8 of the Law Commission's Sixth Programme of Law Reform stated that the present rules applicable to the property rights of cohabitants are 'uncertain and difficult to apply and can lead to serious injustice'. If there is to be reform, then the question arises as to what form that reform should take.

In some countries (e.g. in some Australian states) the courts have statutory powers to adjust the property interests of cohabitants. In New South Wales, for instance, the New South Wales De Facto Relationships Act 1984 gives the court power to adjust the property rights of those in a 'de facto relationship' as seems just and equitable, having regard to financial and non-financial contributions made by the parties, which may include any contribution made in the capacity of homemaker or parent to the welfare of the other party or the family (s. 20(1)). A 'de facto relationship' is defined as 'being the relationship of living or having lived together as husband and wife on a bona fide domestic basis although not married to each other' (s. 3(1)). Gardner ((1993) 109 LQR 263) considers that the reference to 'husband and wife' in s. 3(1) is 'rife with problems'. He asks:

Does it render the provision specific to sexual relationships, so as to exclude parent-child cases and so on? If so, is it further specific to heterosexual relationships, so as to exclude homosexual couples? On the other hand, does it exclude those fully committed heterosexual relationships whose parties have deliberately chosen not to marry, thus largely defeating its own purpose?'

What about relationships involving a transsexual?

Other options for reform would be to introduce legislation for cohabitants similar to that governing the divorce court's jurisdiction under s. 24 of the MCA 1973 (see Chapter 5), or to encourage cohabitants to enter into cohabitation contracts (see Barton, C., 'Negotiating Domestic Partnerships' [1989] Fam Law 16) or to apply principles adopted by Lord Denning MR in the 1970s, e.g., as in *Cooke* v *Head* [1972] 1 WLR 518, where his Lordship said that it was not right to approach the case 'by looking at the money contributions of each and dividing up the beneficial interest according to those contributions', but that the 'matter should be looked at more broadly, just as we do in husband and wife cases'.

*Questions*
*1.* Hayton, D., 'The Equitable Rights of Cohabitees' [1990] Conv 370 at p. 387, states:

As things stand, it is up to schools and the media to make it clear to women that, if they do not marry M, then the onus is on them not to move in with M just for love but only on clear financial terms put in writing. Women are becoming more aware of this and are gradually taking steps to protect themselves. In this way the problems . . . should diminish in an area where it seems impractical and undesirable to have paternalistic parliamentary interference.

Do you agree with Hayton, or is 'paternalistic parliamentary interference' needed?

2. Is it satisfactory that principles from House of Lords' cases involving married couples (i.e. *Pettitt*, *Gissing* and *Rosset*, *supra*) should govern the law applicable to property disputes between cohabitants?

3. Is a statutory jurisdiction for property adjustment between cohabitants needed? Should new legislation extend to all forms of partnership? Would new legislation undermine marriage? Would it be better to place more emphasis on encouraging cohabitants to own houses jointly or to sort out their property arrangements contractually?

*Further reading*

Harpum, C., 'Cohabitation Consultation' [1995] Fam Law 657.

Horowitz, M., and Harper, M., 'A Code for Cohabitees — Fairness at Last?' [1995] Fam Law 693.

Parkinson, P., 'The Property Rights of Cohabitees — is Statutory Reform the Answer?', in Pearl, D., and Pickford, R. (eds), *Frontiers of Family Law: Part II*, Chichester: John Wiley, 1995.

## 3.5  PROPRIETARY ESTOPPEL

Instead of using arguments based on trusts, a non-owner spouse or co-habitant (or any other person) may claim an interest in equity under the doctrine of proprietary estoppel. The disadvantage of bringing such a claim is that, once an estoppel has been established, the court must look at the circumstances of the case to decide how the 'equity can be satisfied' (*Plimmer* v *Wellington Corporation* (1884) 9 App Cas 699). In the exercise of its discretion it may merely grant a licence to remain in the property, or award financial compensation for the detriment suffered, rather than give the applicant a right of ownership in equity. Despite Lord Bridge's suggestion in *Rosset*, at 3.3.2.2 *supra*, that proprietary estoppel and the constructive trust are similar concepts, the requirements needed to establish an estoppel are quite different.

### Snell's Principles of Equity (29th edn)
London: Sweet & Maxwell,
1990, pp. 573 and 576

. . . Proprietary estoppel is one of the qualifications to the general rule that a person who spends money on improving the property of another has no claim to reimbursement or to any proprietary interest in the property. Proprietary estoppel is older than promissory estoppel. It is permanent in its effect, and it is also capable of operating positively so as to confer a right of action. The term 'estoppel', though often used, is thus not altogether appropriate. Yet the equity is based on estoppel in that one (A) is encouraged to act to his detriment by the representations or encouragement of another (O) so that it would be unconscionable for (O) to insist on his strict legal rights. . . .

## *Matharu* v *Matharu*
[1994] 2 FLR 597
Court of Appeal

ROCH LJ: . . . Scarman LJ went on to say [in *Crabb* v *Arun District Council* [1976] Ch 179] that the law of equitable estoppel was analysed and spelt out in the judgment of Fry J in *Willmott* v *Barber* (1980) 15 ChD 96. If that is so these are the elements which have to be established by the person claiming the equity:

(1)   that that person has made a mistake as to his or her legal rights;
(2)   that that person has expended some money or done some act on the faith of that mistaken belief;
(3)   the possessor of the legal right must know of the existence of his legal right which is inconsistent with the equity, if it exists;
(4)   the possessor of the legal right must know of the other person's mistaken belief as to his or her rights;
(5)   the possessor of the legal right must have encouraged the other person in his or her expenditure of money or in doing the other acts on which the other person relies, either directly or by abstaining from asserting his legal right. . . .

*Notes*
1.   In *Matharu* v *Matharu*, the Court of Appeal held there was an estoppel, but that the respondent daughter-in-law was not entitled to a beneficial interest in the property but merely to a licence to remain in the property for life or for such shorter period as she might decide. See also *Baker* v *Baker and Another* [1993] 2 FLR 247, CA, and *Maharaj* v *Chand* [1986] AC 898, [1986] 3 All ER 107, PC.
2.   Despite Lord Bridge's apparent merging in *Rosset*, at 3.3.2.2 *supra*, of constructive trusts and estoppel, the following differences exist between the two concepts:

(a)   the constructive trust is based on evidence of a bilateral agreement, arrangement or understanding, whereas estoppel requires unilateral conduct by one party which leads the other party to act to his or her detriment;
(b)   the imposition of a constructive trust gives the claimant equitable rights of ownership, but once an estoppel is proved, the court has a discretion to decide what remedy to grant;
(c)   interests under a constructive trust are retrospective (they are assumed to arise when the claimant acts to his or her detriment), but interests under an estoppel arise from the date of the court decree, for until then the remedy is uncertain.

3.   Hayton ('The Equitable Rights of Cohabitees' [1990] Conv 370) has argued that the distinction between constructive trusts and proprietary estoppel is largely illusory (as both are based on the principle of unconscionability), so that there is no logical justification for maintaining the distinction. Ferguson, ('Constructive Trusts — A Note of Caution' (1993) 109 LQR 114), on the other hand, has warned against eroding the distinction, as

estoppel is 'purely a *remedial* concept centred on the intervention of the court', whereas the constructive trust is 'a *means of creating a proprietary right* which exists independently of the court'. See also Hayton's riposte to Ferguson ('Constructive Trusts of Homes — A Bold Approach' (1993) 109 LQR 485).

*Further reading*
Cooke, E. J., 'Reliance and Estoppel' (1995) 111 LQR 389.

### 3.6  BANKRUPTCY AND THE FAMILY HOME

#### 3.6.1  Ordering a sale of the home

On bankruptcy, the trustee in bankruptcy must realise the bankrupt's assets in order to pay off the creditors. Sometimes the family home must be sold in order to satisfy any debts. This may have drastic consequences for the family, particularly as in an application by the trustee in bankruptcy for an order for sale the court is unlikely to put the family's interests first. The law is weighted in favour of the trustee in bankruptcy and the bankrupt's obligation to the creditors. A spouse or cohabitant who wishes to challenge an order for possession and sale by the trustee in bankruptcy should try to establish a greater beneficial interest in the house than appears to be the case when looking at the legal title, e.g., by seeking a declaration as to the beneficial interest under a resulting or constructive trust (3.3 *supra*).

**Ayton, Lyn, 'Preserving the Family Home in the Face of Bankruptcy'**
[1993] Fam Law 180

. . . If an English man's home is his castle then it needs to be a tightly guarded fortress when the landowner becomes bankrupt! The family home is likely to represent the husband's last remaining asset of any value. All things being equal, he will have disposed of any other assets to avoid the onset of bankruptcy. For the wife, her immediate concern will be to ensure that she and the children do not suddenly find themselves without a roof over their heads. In the long term, she will want to fend off the trustee's claims against the property. The trustee's concern is to realise the husband's interest in the property as quickly as possible.
    . . . Statute and case-law virtually guarantee that the trustee will be able to force a sale where there is an equity to realise — it is only a matter of time. The law in this area is undoubtedly heavily weighted in favour of the trustee. The lesson to be learned from the case-law is that the wife will be well advised to negotiate with the trustee rather than, quite understandably, dismiss her unfortunate circumstances as being the husband's problem for which he should be responsible.
    The wife might even find her negotiations with the husband's trustee to be more advantageous than if she were attempting to purchase her husband's interest directly from him. The trustee has no emotional attachments to the house; it is simply bricks and mortar. Nor will he have the memories of the matrimonial difficulties at the back of his mind. The trustee's priority is to realise sufficient monies to satisfy the husband's creditors and then move on to his next case. He may, therefore, be prepared to accept a lesser sum, thereby avoiding the fees of a sale and the potential

costs and delay of contested possession proceedings, than the husband would have been prepared to accept in the course of the ancillary relief proceedings.

## Insolvency Act 1986

### 336. Rights of occupation etc. of bankrupt's spouse

(2) Where a spouse's rights of occupation under the [Matrimonial Homes Act 1983] are a charge on the estate or interest of the other spouse, or of trustees for the other spouse, and the other spouse is adjudged bankrupt—

(a) the charge continues to subsist notwithstanding the bankruptcy and, subject to the provisions of that Act, binds the trustee of the bankrupt's estate and persons deriving title under that trustee, and

(b) any application for an order under section 1 of that Act shall be made to the court having jurisdiction in relation to the bankruptcy.

(3) Where a person and his spouse or former spouse are trustees for sale of a dwelling house and that person is adjudged bankrupt, any application by the trustee of the bankrupt's estate for an order under section 30 of the Law of Property Act 1925 (powers of court where trustees for sale refuse to act) shall be made to the court having jurisdiction in relation to the bankruptcy.

(4) On such an application as is mentioned in subsection (2) or (3) the court shall make such order under section 1 of the Act of 1983 or section 30 of the Act of 1925 as it thinks just and reasonable having regard to—

(a) the interests of the bankrupt's creditors,

(b) the conduct of the spouse or former spouse, so far as contributing to the bankruptcy,

(c) the needs and financial resources of the spouse or former spouse,

(d) the needs of any children, and

(e) all the circumstances of the case other than the needs of the bankrupt.

(5) Where such an application is made after the end of the period of one year beginning with the first vesting . . . of the bankrupt's estate in a trustee, the court shall assume, unless the circumstances of the case are exceptional, that the interests of the bankrupt's creditors outweigh all other considerations.

*Notes*

1. Section 336 will be amended by sch. 8, para. 57 of the FLA 1996 when Part IV of the FLA 1996 comes into force (expected date 1 October 1997), so that reference is to the 1996 Act and not the Matrimonial Homes Act 1983 (which will be repealed by the FLA 1996).

2. Section 339 of the Insolvency Act 1986 allows the court on the application of the trustee in bankruptcy to set aside a transaction at an undervalue made by the bankrupt within five years preceding the date of presentation of the bankruptcy petition (s. 341(1)(a)). A 'transaction at an undervalue' occurs where a bankrupt makes a gift of property or transfers property in consideration of marriage or for consideration significantly less than its true value (s. 339(3)). See *Re Kumar (A Bankrupt), ex parte Lewis v Kumar* [1993] 2 FLR 382, ChD, where the husband's transfer of the matrimonial home to his wife by consent order on divorce was set aside as it was a transaction at an undervalue.

Case law suggests that it is extremely unlikely on bankruptcy that the court will refuse to order a sale of the matrimonial home, whatever the circumstances. Disruption of the children's education, illness, and lack of alternative accommodation are unlikely to be considered 'exceptional' for the purposes of s. 336(5). The following case involved an application by the trustee in bankruptcy under s. 30 of the Law of Property Act 1925, but the court is likely to adopt a similar approach under s. 336(4) of the Insolvency Act 1986.

### Re Citro (Domenico) (A Bankrupt); Re Citro (Carmine) (A Bankrupt)
[1991] Ch 1342
Court of Appeal

*Facts*: Two brothers in business together were adjudicated bankrupt, each brother's only asset being his half-share in his matrimonial home. One brother was judicially separated. His wife lived in the house with their children, the youngest of whom was 12. The other brother lived in the house with his wife and three children, the youngest of whom was 10. The debts of each brother exceeded the value of his half-share in the beneficial interest. The trustee in bankruptcy sought declarations as to the beneficial interests in the houses and orders for sale and possession under s. 30 of the Law of Property Act 1925. At first instance Hoffmann J declared that the beneficial interest in each house was owned by the bankrupt and the wife in equal shares and made the orders sought, but, in view of the hardship which an immediate order for sale would cause, attached a provision in each case that the order was not to be enforced until the youngest child of each bankrupt reached the age of 16 (i.e. by analogy with a *Mesher* order made on divorce, see Chapter 5). The trustee in bankruptcy appealed seeking the removal of the provisos.
*Held*: allowing the appeal (Sir George Waller dissenting) by deleting the provisos for postponement and substituting short periods of suspension, that the judge had been wrong to refuse an order for immediate sale, and, in exercising his discretion, had failed to give proper weight to the hardship which postponement would cause to the creditors.

NOURSE LJ: In the leading case of *Jones* v *Challenger* [1961] 1 QB 176 it was held by this court that on an application under section 30 of the Law of Property Act 1925 in relation to property acquired jointly as a matrimonial home neither spouse has a right to demand a sale while that purpose still exists. That is now a settled rule of law applicable to property owned jointly by joint occupants, whether married or unmarried. But its application depends on the whole of the beneficial interest being vested in the occupants. If one of them has become bankrupt, so that part of the beneficial interest is vested in his or her trustee, there arises a conflict between the interests of the occupants and the statutory obligation of the trustee to realise the bankrupt's assets for the benefit of the creditors.

In a series of bankruptcy decisions relating to matrimonial homes subsequent to *Jones* v *Challenger* it has been held that the interests of the husband's creditors ought usually to prevail over the interests of the wife and any children and, with one exception, *In re Holliday (A Bankrupt), Ex parte Trustee of the Property of the Bankrupt* v *Holliday* [1981] Ch 405, a sale within a short period has invariably been ordered. It has also been assumed that no distinction ought to be made between a case where the property is still being enjoyed as the matrimonial home and one where it is not. That distinction, if it ought to be made, would be of significance on these appeals, which relate to the matrimonial homes of two bankrupt brothers, one of whom is still living there with his wife and the other of whom has been judicially separated and living elsewhere since 1984. It should be stated at the outset that section 336 of the Insolvency Act 1986 has no application to either case.

. . .

The broad effect of these authorities can be summarised as follows. Where a spouse who has a beneficial interest in the matrimonial home has become bankrupt under debts which cannot be paid without the realisation of that interest, the voice of the creditors will usually prevail over the voice of the other spouse and a sale of the property ordered within a short period. The voice of the other spouse will only prevail in exceptional circumstances. No distinction is to be made between a case where the property is still being enjoyed as the matrimonial home and one where it is not.

What then are exceptional circumstances? As the cases show, it is not uncommon for a wife with young children to be faced with eviction in circumstances where the realisation of her beneficial interest will not produce enough to buy a comparable home in the same neighbourhood, or indeed elsewhere. And, if she has to move elsewhere, there may be problems over schooling and so forth. Such circumstances, while engendering a natural sympathy in all who hear of them, cannot be described as exceptional. They are the melancholy consequences of debt and improvidence with which every civilised society has been familiar. It was only in *In re Holliday* [1981] Ch 405 that they helped the wife's voice to prevail, and then only, as I believe, because of one special feature of that case. One of the reasons for the decision given by Sir David Cairns was that it was highly unlikely that postponement of payment of the debts would cause any great hardship to any of the creditors, a matter of which Buckley LJ no doubt took account as well. . . . without that special feature, I cannot myself see how the circumstances in *In re Holliday* could fairly have been treated as exceptional.

. . .

I am therefore of the opinion that the earlier authorities, as I have summarised them, correctly state the law applicable to the present case. Did Hoffmann J correctly apply it to the facts which were before him? I respectfully think that he did not. First, for the reasons already stated, the personal circumstances of the two wives and their children, although distressing, are not by themselves exceptional. Secondly, I think that the judge erred in fashioning his orders by reference to those which might have been made in the Family Division in a case where bankruptcy had not supervened. That approach, which tends towards treating the home as a source of provision for the children, was effectively disapproved by the earlier and uncontroversial part of the decision of this court in *In re Holliday*. Thirdly, and perhaps most significantly, he did not ask himself the critical question whether a further postponement of payment of their debts would cause hardship to the creditors. It is only necessary to look at the substantial deficiencies referred to earlier in this judgment in order to see that it would. Since then a further 18 months' interest has accrued and the trustee has incurred the costs of these proceedings as well.

In all the circumstances, I think that these cases are clearly distinguishable from *In re Holliday* and ought to have been decided accordingly. . . .

Finally, I refer to section 336 of the Insolvency Act 1986 which, although it does not apply to either of these cases, will apply to such cases in the future. In subsection (5) of that section the court is required, in the circumstances there mentioned, to 'assume, unless the circumstances of the case are exceptional, that the interests of the bankrupt's creditors outweigh all other considerations.' I have no doubt that that section was intended to apply the same test as that which has been evolved in the previous bankruptcy decisions, and it is satisfactory to find that it has. I say that not least because section 336 only applies to the rights of occupation of those who are or have been married. The case law will continue to apply to unmarried couples, who nowadays set up house together in steadily increasing numbers. A difference in the basic tests applicable to the two classes of case would have been most undesirable.

I would allow both appeals by deleting the provisos for postponement from Hoffmann J's orders and substituting short periods of suspension, the length of which can be discussed with counsel.

SIR GEORGE WALLER (dissenting): . . . In this case the judge set out the interests which had to be balanced, the creditors and the two wives and their children who were very much at the critical age for their education, in Mary Citro's case one son wanting to stay at school and to do 'A' levels and another son wanting to start at the same school. In Josephine Citro's case the eldest at school was 14. This can only have been mentioned because the sale of the house in each case would create educational difficulties. He set out fully in his judgment the situation of the families which fell clearly within the situation described in the judgments which I have quoted above. The circumstances relating to the two wives set out by the judge, the housing difficulty, education, difficulties of which were before him and his description of their position as being 'extremely unenviable' in different words describe exactly that which in *In re Holliday* was described as 'hardship' or 'very special circumstances.' That education was a fundamental element of the judge's order is clear from the order itself, namely the sixteenth birthday of the youngest child in each family.

The judge had to exercise his discretion and he followed the decision in *In re Holliday*. . . . I have no difficulty in regarding the circumstances as very special; there has been no similar case with such problems. Although the judge's words may not have precisely followed the words of the judgments in *In re Holliday*, in my opinion he covered exactly the same points and I would dismiss the appeal in both cases.

*Further reading*
Brown, D., 'Insolvency and the Matrimonial Home — The Sins of the Fathers: *In re Citro (A bankrupt)*' (1992) 55 MLR 284.
Cretney, S., 'Women and Children Last?' (1991) 107 LQR 177.
Howell, G., *Family Breakdown and Insolvency*, London: Butterworths, 1993.

### 3.7  HOUSING HOMELESS FAMILIES

Under the Housing Act (HA) 1996 (which came into force on 20 January 1997) a local housing authority (LHA) has statutory duties and powers in respect of homelessness. The scheme of the Act is similar to the scheme which existed under the old law (i.e. under Part III of the Housing Act 1985), but with some important changes. A major change is that a LHA's duty to provide housing is limited to a two-year period, after which it only has a discretion to provide housing. Another major change is in respect of the procedure available for challenging LHA decisions. Under the old law challenges were made by way of judicial review proceedings, but this is no longer the case as the 1996 Act introduces a new system of reviews of LHA decisions and allows appeals on points of law to be heard in the county court. LHAs must comply not only with Part VII of the 1996 Act but also with Part VI, which deals with the allocation of housing accommodation. Under Part VI a LHA must, *inter alia*, establish and maintain a housing register (s. 162) and must maintain an 'allocation scheme' for determining priorities and the procedure to be followed in allocating housing accommodation (s. 167).

# PART VII   HOUSING ACT 1996

### 175.  Homelessness and threatened homelessness
(1)   A person is homeless if he has no accommodation available for his occupation, in the United Kingdom or elsewhere, which he—
    (a)   is entitled to occupy by virtue of an interest in it or by virtue of an order of a court,
    (b)   has an express or implied licence to occupy, or
    (c)   occupies as a residence by virtue of any enactment or rule of law giving him the right to remain in occupation or restricting the right of another person to recover possession.
(2)   A person is also homeless if he has accommodation but—
    (a)   he cannot secure entry to it, or
    (b)   it consists of a moveable structure, vehicle or vessel designed or adapted for human habitation and there is no place where he is entitled or permitted both to place it and to reside in it.
(3)   A person shall not be treated as having accommodation unless it is accommodation which it would be reasonable for him to continue to occupy.
(4)   A person is threatened with homelessness if it is likely that he will become homeless within 28 days.

### 176.  Meaning of accommodation available for occupation
Accommodation shall be regarded as available for a person's occupation only if it is available for occupation by him together with—
    (a)   any other person who normally resides with him as a member of his family, or
    (b)   any other person who might reasonably be expected to reside with him.
References in this Part to securing that accommodation is available for a person's occupation shall be construed accordingly.

### 177.  Whether it is reasonable to continue to occupy accommodation
(1)   It is not reasonable for a person to continue to occupy accommodation if it is probable that this will lead to domestic violence against him, or against—
    (a)   a person who normally resides with him as a member of his family, or
    (b)   any other person who might reasonably be expected to reside with him.
For this purpose 'domestic violence', in relation to a person, means violence from a person with whom he is associated, or threats of violence from such a person which are likely to be carried out.
(2)   In determining whether it should be, or would have been, reasonable for a person to continue to occupy accommodation, regard may be had to the general circumstances prevailing in relation to housing in the district of the local housing authority to whom he has applied for accommodation or for assistance in obtaining accommodation.

(3)   The Secretary of Sate may by order specify—

(a)   other circumstances in which it is to be regarded as reasonable or not reasonable for a person to continue to occupy accommodation, and

(b)   other matters to be taken into account or disregarded in determining whether it would be, or would have been, reasonable for a person to continue to occupy accommodation.

. . .

## 189.   Priority need for accommodation

(1)   The following have a priority need for accommodation—

(a)   a pregnant woman or a person with whom she resides or might reasonably be expected to reside;

(b)   a person with whom dependent children reside or might reasonably be expected to reside;

(c)   a person who is vulnerable as a result of old age, mental illness or handicap or physical disability or other special reason, or with whom such a person resides or might reasonably be expected to reside;

(d)   a person who is homeless or threatened with homelessness as a result of an emergency such as flood, fire or other disaster.

(2)   The Secretary of State may by order—

(a)   specify further descriptions of persons as having a priority need for accommodation, and

(b)   amend or repeal any part of subsection (1).

. . .

## 191.   Becoming homeless intentionally

(1)   A person becomes homeless intentionally if he deliberately does or fails to do anything in consequence of which he ceases to occupy accommodation which is available for his occupation and which it would have been reasonable for him to continue to occupy.

(2)   For the purposes of subsection (1) an act or omission in good faith on the part of a person who was unaware of any relevant fact shall not be treated as deliberate.

(3)   A person shall be treated as becoming homeless intentionally if—

(a)   he enters into an arrangmenet under which he is required to cease to occupy accommodation which it would have been reasonable for him to continue to occupy, and

(b)   the purpose of the arrangement is to enable him to become entitled to assistance under this Part,

and there is no other good reason why he is homeless.

(4)   A person who is given advice or assistance under section 197 (duty where other suitable alternative accommodation available), but fails to secure suitable accommodation in circumstances in which it was reasonably to be expected that he would do so, shall, if he makes a further application under this Part, be treated as having become homeless intentionally.

. . .

## 196.   Becoming threatened with homelessness intentionally

(1)   A person becomes threatened with homelessness intentionally if he deliberately does or fails to do anything the likely result of which is that he will be forced to leave accommodation which is available for his occupation and which it would have been reasonable for him to continue to occupy.

(2)   For the purposes of subsection (1) an act or omission in good faith on the part of a person who was unaware of any relevant fact shall not be treated as deliberate.

(3)   A person shall be treated as becoming threatened with homelessness intentionally if—

(a)   he enters into an arrangement under which he is required to cease to occupy accommodation which it would have been reasonable for him to continue to occupy, and

(b)   the purpose of the arrangement is to enable him to become entitled to assistance under this Part,
and there is no other good reason why he is threatened with homelessness.

(4)   A person who is given advice or assistance under section 197 (duty where other suitable alternative accommodation available), but fails to secure suitable accommodation in circumstances in which it was reasonably to be expected that he would do so, shall, if he makes a further application under this Part, be treated as having become threatened with homelessness intentionally.

. . .


*Notes*

*1.*   The meaning of 'associated persons' for the purposes of Part VII of the HA 1996 is defined in s. 178. The definition is the same as that under Part IV of the FLA 1996 (see Chapter 6 at 6.6).

*2.*   Where a LHA believes an applicant may be homeless or threatened with homelessness, it must make inquiries to establish whether the applicant is eligible for assistance with housing and, if so, whether any duty, and what duty, is owed under Part VII of the Act (s. 184(1)).

*3.*   Where a LHA believes an applicant may be homeless, eligible for assistance with housing and has a priority need, it has an interim duty to provide accommodation pending its decision as to the duty (if any) owed to the applicant (s. 188).

*4.*   Where an applicant is intentionally homeless, a LHA only has a duty to provide appropriate advice and assistance to help the applicant find accommodation (s. 190(3)), except where the applicant has a priority need, when the LHA must provide temporary accommodation and any advice and assistance necessary for the applicant to find accommodation (s. 190).

*5.*   Where an applicant is unintentionally homeless and has no priority need, a LHA must provide appropriate advice and such assistance to enable the applicant to find accommodation (s. 192).

*6.*   Where an applicant is unintentionally homeless and has a priority need the LHA has a full housing duty, i.e. it *must* provide the applicant with accommodation for a minimum period of two years and *may* continue to do so after that period (s. 193).

*7.*   Where an applicant is threatened with homelessness unintentionally and has a priority need, a LHA must take reasonable steps to secure that the accommodation does not cease to be available for his or her occupation (s. 195). Where the applicant is threatened with homelessness intentionally and has no priority need, a LHA must provide appropriate advice and assistance (s. 195(5)).

*8.*   If a LHA has a duty to provide or secure accommodation for the applicant, but other suitable accommodation is available for the applicant in the district, the LHA's duty is to provide only such advice and assistance it considers reasonable to enable the applicant to secure such accommodation (s. 197(1) and (2)).

9. Where an applicant to whom a full housing duty is owed has a local connection with the district of another LHA, the applicant may be referred to that other LHA, except where there is a risk that the applicant or any person who might reasonably be expected to reside with the applicant will suffer any domestic violence in the district of the other LHA (s. 198(1) and (2)). An applicant has a local connection with a LHA district if he or she is or was normally resident there of his or her own choice, or is employed there, or has family associations there, or there are special circumstances (s. 199(1)). Pending a referral a LHA has an interim duty to provide accommodation (s. 200(1)).

10. A LHA must provide advice and information about homelessness (s. 179).

11. An applicant has a right to request a review of a LHA's decision (s. 202), and, if dissatisfied with the decision on a review or if not notified of the decision of the review within the prescribed time limit, may appeal to the county court on any point of law arising from the decision or, as the case may be, the original decision (s. 204).

Local authorities must follow the *Homeless Code of Guidance for Local Authorities* when exercising their statutory duties and powers under Parts VI and VII of the 1996 Act (ss. 169(1) and 182(1)). A new Code is to be drawn up but, as the new law is similar to the old law, the following extracts from the most recent Code provide some idea of the approaches that LHAs must adopt in the exercise of their statutory duties and powers.

**Department of the Environment, Department of Health, and Welsh Office, *Homelessness Code of Guidance for Local Authorities*, 3rd edn (revised), London: HMSO, 1994**

**When is it reasonable to continue to occupy accommodation?**

. . .

5.8 There is no simple rule of reasonableness. Each case must be looked at on its merits. In reaching a decision on whether it is reasonable for an applicant to continue to occupy accommodation authorities should consider the following:

(a) *physical conditions:* Is the property in such a state that it would not be reasonable to expect someone to continue to live there? Is it a short- or long-term problem? How do the physical conditions in the property compare with those in the area generally?

(b) *overcrowding:* How many adults and children are living in the accommodation and, given the housing conditions locally, is it reasonable to expect them to continue living there? . . .

(c) *type of accommodation:* Some types of accommodation, for example bed and breakfast hotels, women's refuges, direct access hostels, and night shelters are not designed to be lived in long-term. Homelessness would therefore have originated in the last settled accommodation before entering these or other types of temporary accommodation.

(d) *violence or threats of violence from outside the home:* The authority will need to consider the seriousness of the violence, or threats of violence, the frequency of occurrence and the likelihood of reoccurrence. Violence or threats of violence could include racial harassment or attacks; violence against a person; sexual abuse or harassment and harassment on the grounds of religious creed.

(e) *cost:* Is it reasonable to expect an applicant to pay the costs of the accommodation given their income? Consideration should be given to whether the applicant can no longer pay the housing costs without being deprived of basic essentials such as food, clothing, heating, transport and other essentials.

(f) *security of tenure:* Has an applicant with no security of tenure left accommodation following receipt of a notice to quit or notice of seeking possession? Should an applicant have gone to court if it was clear to him/her that there was no defence against possession being granted? In these circumstances the authority should start to process the application and make (if appropriate) arrangements to secure accommodation immediately. Authorities will need to be alert to the possibility of collusion between landlords and heads of households. In such cases the assessment of intentionality will be significant.

**Who else is homeless?**

5.9   **The Act (s. 58(3)** [see now HA 1996, s. 175(2)] also defines as homeless someone who has accommodation but cannot use it for one of the following reasons:-

(a) s/he cannot gain entry to it. This includes those who have a legal entitlement to accommodation to which for some practical reason they are unable to gain entry — for example those who have been illegally evicted, or those whose accommodation is being illegally occupied by squatters.

(b) his/her attempt to return to live in the accommodation would be likely to be met with violence or threats of violence likely to be carried out by someone else in it [see now HA 1996, s. 177]. Authorities should respond sympathetically to applications from men and women who are in fear of violence. The fact that violence has not yet occurred does not, on its own, suggest that it is not likely to occur. Injunctions ordering persons not to molest, or enter the home of, the applicant will not necessarily deter people and the applicant should not necessarily be asked to return to their home in this instance. Authorities may inform applicants of the option to take out an injunction, but should make clear that there is no obligation to do so if s/he feels it would be ineffective. This test of homelessness relates only to violence from someone else *within* the home; it does not encompass violence from neighbours.
. . .

**Is the applicant in priority need?**

6.1   **The Act (s. 59)** [see now HA 1996, s. 189] lists those groups of homeless people who have a priority need for accommodation. This chapter discusses how to assess whether applicants fall into one of these groups. It is important that authorities do not fetter their discretion by pre-determining that some groups, e.g. young single people, should never be considered vulnerable. Enquiries must always be carried out where authorities have reason to believe that an applicant is homeless or threatened with homelessness. . . .

**Applicant pregnant?**

6.2   Pregnant women, together with anyone who lives with them, or might reasonably be expected to do so, have a priority need for accommodation. All pregnant women should be included regardless of the length of time they have been pregnant. The normal doctor's letter issued to pregnant women or a midwife's letter ought to be adequate evidence of pregnancy. If a pregnant woman suffers a miscarriage during the assessment process the authority would need to consider whether she continues to be vulnerable.

### Applicant has dependent children?

6.3   An applicant has a priority need for accommodation if s/he has one or more dependent children living with him/her or who might reasonably be expected to do so. . . . **The Act** does not define dependent children, but authorities should normally include all children under 16, and all children aged 16–18 who are in, or are about to begin, full-time education or training or who for other reasons are unable to support themselves and who live at home. Dependants need not necessarily be the applicant's own children. They could be, for example, brothers, sisters, grandchildren, nephews or nieces of the applicant or their partner, or adopted or fostered by the applicant.

6.4   If an applicant is a separated parent, authorities will have to be careful to check that the children do depend on him/her. A child may also be dependent even though s/he does not live with the applicant at all times but divides his/her time between parents or others. . . .

6.5   Authorities should make every effort to avoid splitting families even for short periods because of the personal hardship, the risk of long-term damage to the children, and the social cost. There will, however, be occasions when there are compelling reasons for splitting a family (e.g. where there has been domestic violence or child abuse). Where the children are in care and not living at home, authorities need to look at the terms of the care order and to consider the reasons why they are in care as it may not be reasonable or practicable for them to live with the applicant. The advice of the social services departments or authorities will be essential in cases of this kind.

6.6   In some cases children may be dependent even though they are not actually living with the applicant at the time. The applicant's housing difficulties themselves may be the reason for the children living apart. They may for example be staying with other relatives or may be waiting to join the applicant from abroad. Where children are waiting to join applicants from abroad, and provided that the applicant is not found to be homeless intentionally, authorities should consider allocating permanent accommodation to coincide with their arrival in the country. Refugees' dependants (spouse and children under 18) usually become admissible to the UK as soon as refugee status has been recognised. . . .

. . .

### Other special reasons:

*Young people*

6.13   Local authorities should consider the extent to which a young person is 'at risk' and therefore vulnerable . . . by virtue of being homeless. Young people (16 or over) should not automatically be treated as vulnerable on the basis of age alone. Young people could be 'at risk' in a variety of ways. Risks could arise from violence or sexual abuse at home, the likelihood of drug or alcohol abuse or prostitution. Some groups of young people will be less able to fend for themselves than others, particularly for example: those leaving local authority care; juvenile offenders (including those discharged from young offender institutions); those who have been physically or sexually abused; those with learning difficulties and those who have been the subject of statements of special educational need. These examples are not meant to constitute a complete list. For young people who have not been in care, authorities should always consider the possibility of a reconciliation between the applicant and his/her family.

6.14   Housing authorities will also need to take into account the provisions of **s. 20 of the Children Act 1989** . . . , when assessing the vulnerability of a young person within the terms of the Housing Act 1985. **Subsection (3)** places a duty on a social services authority to provide accommodation to a child in need aged 16 or over whose welfare is otherwise likely to be seriously prejudiced if it does not provide him/her with accommodation; and **subsection (1)** places a duty to provide accommodation for children in need in certain other circumstances. The social services authority may be able to provide such accommodation from its own resources, or those provided by the voluntary or private sector.

6.15 On occasion, however, the social services authority may seek the help of the housing authority. In such a case **s. 27(2) of the Children Act 1989** requires the housing authority to respond to that request provided it is compatible with its own statutory duties and obligations and does not unduly prejudice the discharge of its functions. Thus, while there is no formal correlation between the definition of vulnerability in the Housing Act 1985 and 'serious prejudice' (or 'need') in **s. 20 of the Children Act 1989**, the two might be expected to arise in similar circumstances and housing authorities will need to have regard to a social services authority's or department's assessment that it has an obligation to provide a child with accommodation under **s. 20(1) or (3) of the Children Act 1989**.

6.16   The Secretaries of State are concerned to avoid any possibility that the implementation of the 1989 Act might result in children and young people being sent to and fro between departments or authorities. Each department and authority has a responsibility to those who approach it under its own relevant legislation. However, a corporate policy and clear departmental procedures in respect of collaboration between departments and authorities will help to ensure co-operation at all levels.

*Victims of violence or abuse or sexual and/or racial harassment*
6.17   Authorities should secure wherever possible that accommodation is available for men and women without children who have suffered violence at home or are at risk of further violence if they return home. Authorities should also consider applications from those at risk of harassment or violence on account of their gender, race, colour, ethnic or national origins.
. . .

**Domestic Disputes**
10.23   In some cases, people will be threatened with the loss of their home because of a domestic dispute. Housing authorities should always be alert to the need for quick action where household members are at risk from violence or abuse. Where young people under 18 are involved due to a breakdown in their relationship with their parents, or where they are at risk of abuse, the housing authority must always alert the social services department or authority to the case. In other cases, depending on the severity of the dispute, they may still find it useful to ask the social services department or authority for urgent help. In this respect housing authorities should be aware of the duties of social services departments and authorities under **s. 20 and s.27 of the Children Act 1989**. . . . An approach to a social services department or authority might be directed at relieving tension within the household to enable the members to continue to live together, and social services may be able to offer counselling and support or to advise on other local services and agencies which might provide specialist help.

10.24   Where the housing authority is satisfied that they have a duty to secure accommodation for one or more members of the household, it may be better to give a clear indication of their commitment to do so within a definite period of time rather than to move people out immediately into interim short-term accommodation. Authorities should never, however, put pressure on people to stay in shared accommodation or to return to it where this would cause real distress or physical danger. In particular, someone seeking refuge because of a genuine fear of violence from another member of the household should be found alternative accommodation immediately.
. . .

In the following case young children made applications for housing after their parents had been found to be intentionally homeless.

### R v *Oldham Metropolitan Borough Council, ex parte Garlick and Related Appeals*
[1993] AC 509
House of Lords

*Facts*: The first two appeals concerned applications on behalf of two children aged four who were homeless but whose parents had been refused housing by the LHA on the ground that they were intentionally homeless. The LHA refused to entertain the children's applications on the grounds that such applications were a device to get round the provisions of the Housing Act 1985. Judicial review applications were made on behalf of the children. At first instance and in the Court of Appeal the applications were dismissed. The applicants appealed to the House of Lords.
*Held*: dismissing the first two appeals, that s. 59(1)(c) of the 1985 Act was not intended to confer any rights upon dependent children. It was the intention of the Act that a child's accommodation would be provided by his parents or those looking after him and it was to those persons that the offer of accommodation had to be made.

LORD GRIFFITHS: . . . It is of the first importance to understand the nature of the duty imposed upon local housing authorities by Parliament. It is not a duty to take the homeless off the streets and to place them physically in accommodation. The duty is to give them and their families the first priority in the housing queue. The duty is expressed in section 65(2) as a duty to 'secure that accommodation becomes available for his occupation.' It is a duty to offer a homeless person who applies to them for assistance suitable permanent accommodation to house him and his family: see section 75. It is then up to the applicant to decide whether or not he will accept the accommodation. The local housing authority cannot force the applicant to accept it, but they will have discharged their duty under the Act by finding and offering suitable permanent accommodation.
    The persons to whom this duty is owed are those who are homeless and in priority need and have not disqualified themselves by becoming homeless intentionally. Those in priority need are classified in section 59(1) . . .
    Dependent children are not amongst those classified as in priority need. This is not surprising. Dependent children depend on their parents or those looking after them

to decide where they are to live and the offer of accommodation can only sensibly be made to those in charge of them. There is no definition of a dependent child in the Act but the Homelessness Code of Guidance for Local Authorities, 3rd ed. (1991), to which local authorities must have regard for guidance (see section 71) suggests in paragraph 6.3 that authorities should normally include as dependent all children under 16 and all children aged 16 to 18 who are in, or about to begin, full-time education or training or who for other reasons are unable to support themselves and who live at home. This seems to me to be sensible guidance and likely to result in families being housed together until the children are reasonably mature. There will obviously be the case from time to time when a child leaves home under the age of 16 and ceases to be dependent on the parents or those with whom he or she was living and such a child may be vulnerable and in priority need by virtue of section 59(1)(c): see *Kelly* v *Monklands District Council*, 1986 SLT 169. But however that may be, it cannot possibly be argued that a healthy four-year-old living with parents is other than a dependent child. Such a child is in my opinion owed no duty under this Act for it is the intention of the Act that the child's accommodation will be provided by the parents or those looking after him and it is to those people that the offer of accommodation must be made not to the dependent child.

I cannot accept the argument that extreme youth is a 'special reason' making the child vulnerable and thus giving it a priority need under section 59(1)(c). 'Old age' is mentioned as a cause of vulnerability but 'young age' is not. The reason of course is that already stated, Parliament has provided for dependent children by giving a priority right to accommodation to their parents or those looking after them. Nor can I accept the argument that if a dependent child suffers from some disability it thereby acquires an independent priority right to accommodation. A healthy four-year-old is just as vulnerable as a disabled four-year-old from a housing point of view; neither is capable of looking after himself let alone deciding whether to accept an offer of accommodation. I am satisfied that section 59(1)(c) was not intended to confer any rights upon dependent children.

It is also to be observed that the Act imposes a duty on the authority to give written advice to the applicant and makes it a criminal offence for an applicant not to notify an authority of a change in his circumstances: see sections 64 and 74. This is all part of a pattern that supports the view that the intention of this Act was to create a duty to offer accommodation to those homeless persons in priority need who can decide whether or not to aceept the offer and that this does not include dependent children.

If a family has lost its right to priority treatment through intentional homelessness the parent cannot achieve the same result through the back door by an application in the name of a dependent child; if he could it would mean that the disqualification of intentional homelessness had no application to families with dependent children. If this had been the intention of Parliament it would surely have said so.

For these reasons I would dismiss the first two appeals. I wish however to point out that there are other provisions of our social welfare legislation that provide for the accommodation and care of children and of the duty of co-operation between authorities in the discharge of their duties. [His Lordship drew attention to ss. 20(1) and 27 of the Children Act 1989 .]

*Notes*

*1.* For an attempt to use Part III of the Children Act 1989 (duties of local authorities towards children in need) as a means of obtaining accommodation for children whose parents' applications had failed under Part III of the Housing Act 1985, see Chapter 10.

2.   A person provided with accommodation under the Housing Act 1996 has security of tenure under the Housing Act 1985. Security of tenure may create problems, however, where two persons are joint tenants and the relationship breaks down (see *Hammersmith and Fulham London Borough Council* v *Monk* [1992] 1 AC 478, HL, and *Crawley Borough Council* v *Ure* [1995] 1 FLR 806, CA).

3.   Under Part V of the Housing Act 1985, a secure tenant of two or more years' standing has a right to buy his or her council accommodation at a discount of up to 60 per cent of the market value of the property based on the number of years he or she has rented the property. In many areas the 'right to buy' scheme has severely depleted the public sector housing stock.

*Question*
Fred, an unemployed alcoholic who has been violent to his wife Nora, has been living in a hostel since he was excluded from the matrimonial home under a court order a month ago. Last week he was excluded from the hostel after an allegation of criminal behaviour which he denies. He has no family, other than his wife, and nowhere to live. Does the local housing authority have an obligation to house him?

*Further reading*
Loveland, I., 'The Status of Children as Applicants under the Homelessness Legislation — Judicial Subversion or Legislative Intent?' [1996] 8 CFLQ 89.
Everett and Pawlowski, 'Transfer of Property Orders and Cohabitees' [1995] Fam Law 417.
Gilbert, G., 'Housing for Children' (1993) 5 JCL 166.
Holgate, G., 'Intentional Homelessness, Dependent Children and their Statutory Rights of Occupation' [1994] Fam Law 264.
Holgate, G., 'Homelessness: Application for Accommodation, Priority, Need and Eligibility' [1993] Fam Law 487.

## 3.8   RIGHTS OF INHERITANCE

A spouse, or cohabitant or any family member may make a will leaving his or her property to whomsoever he or she wishes; there is no obligation to leave it to one's partner or children. Thus, for example, a husband with a wife and four dependent children, could leave all his property to a friend or to a charity. In European jurisdictions and in Scotland, the situation is quite different; it is impossible to disinherit one's spouse and children, as by law a reserved share of a deceased spouse's estate must go to the other spouse and any children.

When a spouse fails to make a will, the property is distributed according to the rules of intestate succession. Under the present law, where there are children, the surviving spouse inherits the personal chattels, a statutory legacy of £125,000 of the estate and a life interest in half the residue. Where there are no children but close relatives, the surviving spouse inherits the personal chattels, a statutory legacy of £200,000 and half the balance. In other cases, the surviving spouse inherits the whole estate. On a cohabitant's intestacy, the surviving partner is in a disadvantageous position compared with a surviving spouse because a surviving cohabitant has no automatic right to succeed to the deceased partner's estate. Instead, the estate passes first to the deceased's children, if any, and then to the deceased's parents and then to any other close family members. It is therefore particularly important for cohabitants to make wills, lest the surviving partner be left unprovided for on death.

Where on death a surviving partner (spouse or cohabitant) or any other person who was dependent on the deceased is not provided for, or is insufficiently provided for, an application may be made under the Inheritance (Provision for Family and Dependants) Act 1975 for reasonable financial provision from the deceased's estate. Amendments were made to the 1975 Act by the Law Reform (Succession) Act 1995 in order to improve the position for cohabitants, after recommendations were made by the Law Commission in its report, *Distribution on Intestacy*, Law Com No. 187, London: HMSO, 1989.

## Inheritance (Provision for Family and Dependants) Act 1975

**1.  Application for financial provision from deceased's estate**
   (1)   Where after the commencement of this Act a person dies domiciled in England and Wales and is survived by any of the following persons:—
   (a)   the wife or husband of the deceased;
   (b)   a former wife or former husband of the deceased who has not remarried;
   (ba)   any person (not being a person included in paragraph (a) or (b) above) to whom subsection (1A) below applies;
   (c)   a child of the deceased;
   (d)   any person (not being a child of the deceased) who, in the case of any marriage to which the deceased was at any time a party, was treated by the deceased as a child of the family in relation to that marriage;
   (e)   any person (not being a person included in the foregoing paragraphs of this subsection) who immediately before the death of the deceased was being maintained, either wholly or partly, by the deceased;
that person may apply to the court for an order under section 2 of this Act on the ground that the disposition of the deceased's estate effected by his will or the law relating to intestacy, or the combination of his will and that law, is not such as to make reasonable financial provision for the applicant.
   (1A)   This subsection applies to a person if the deceased died on or after 1st January 1996 and, during the whole of the period of two years ending immediately before the date when the deceased died, the person was living—
   (a)   in the same household as the deceased, and
   (b)   as the husband or wife of the deceased.
   (2)   In this Act 'reasonable financial provision'—
   (a)   in the case of an application made by virtue of subsection (1)(a) above by the husband or wife of the deceased (except where the marriage with the deceased was the subject of a decree of judicial separation and at the date of death the decree was

in force and the separation was continuing), means such financial provision as it would be reasonable in all the circumstances of the case for a husband or wife to receive, whether or not that provision is required for his or her maintenance;

(b)   in the case of any other application made by virtue of subsection (1) above, means such financial provision as it would be reasonable in all the circumstances of the case for the applicant to receive for his maintenance.

(3)   For the purposes of subsection (1)(e) above, a person shall be treated as being maintained by the deceased, either wholly or partly, as the case may be, if the deceased, otherwise than for full valuable consideration, was making a substantial contribution in money or money's worth towards the reasonable needs of that person.

## Notes

1.   Section 2 makes provision for orders. Section 3 lays down matters which must be considered by the court when exercising its powers to make orders. Where an applicant is a cohabitant, the court must take account of: (a) the applicant's age and the length of the period of cohabitation; and (b) the applicant's contribution to the welfare of the deceased's family, including any contribution made by looking after the home or caring for the family (s. 3(2A)). However, despite the new sections added by the Law (Reform) Succession Act 1995, cohabitants are still in a disadvantageous position compared with spouses as unlike an ex-spouse, an ex-cohabitant may not apply by virtue of that status; a cohabitant must have cohabited for two years, whereas a spouse qualifies immediately on marriage; and a cohabitant cannot claim the higher standard of reasonable financial provision available to a spouse, whereby the court must consider what provision the applicant spouse might reasonably have expected to have received if the marriage had been terminated by divorce rather than by death (s. 3(2)(b)).

2.   Minor amendments will be made to the 1975 Act by the Family Law Act 1996 when it comes into force, e.g., so that instead of referring to judicial separation in s. 1(2)(a) *supra*, the provisions refer to a separation order under the 1996 Act.

3.   For cases on the 1975 Act, see *Moody* v *Stevenson* [1992] Ch 486, CA, *Davis* v *Davis* [1993] 1 FLR 54, CA, and *Re Jennings, Deceased* [1994] Ch 286, CA.

## Questions

1.   Should cohabitants be given automatic rights of inheritance on intestacy?

2.   In South Australia a cohabitant who fulfils certain conditions can apply to a court for a declaration that he or she is a 'putative spouse', whereupon he or she is entitled to succeed on intestacy in the same way as a deceased's spouse (but provided that there is no surviving husband or wife of the deceased partner). If there is a surviving spouse, the spouse's share of the deceased cohabitant's estate is divided equally between the lawful spouse and the putative spouse. To qualify as a putative spouse a cohabitant must show that the parties were cohabiting at the date of death of the deceased partner and either that the cohabitation had lasted for at least five years before that

date, or that the parties had a child. Should the concept of a 'putative spouse' be introduced into English law?

*Further reading*
Cretney, S., 'Reform of Intestacy: the Best we can Do?' (1995) 111 LQR 77.

# 4 DIVORCE

This chapter is concerned with the current law and the proposed new law which governs the obtaining of a divorce. The law applicable to financial provision and property arrangements on divorce is dealt with in Chapter 5 and arrangements for children on divorce, including financial provision for children, are dealt with in Chapter 9.

## 4.1 INTRODUCTION

The courts have jurisdiction to grant divorces (and annulments and legal separations) under Part I of the MCA 1973. Orders for finance and property on divorce may be granted under Part II of that Act (see Chapter 5). Rules of divorce procedure are laid down in the Family Proceedings Rules (FPR) 1991. However, fundamental reforms of the law governing the grant of a divorce are due to come into force under Parts I and II of the FLA 1996 on a date to be announced by the Government (expected date is Spring, 1999). When the new law comes into force, the law on finance and property on divorce will continue to be governed by Part II of the MCA 1973 (as amended by the FLA 1996) and child maintenance applications in most cases will continue to be made to the Child Support Agency. Any disputes about children on divorce will continue to be dealt with in family proceedings brought under the Children Act 1989 (as amended by the FLA 1996).

A striking feature of the new divorce law will be an increased emphasis on agreement and settlement, including an increased role for mediation. In fact, a divorce will generally not be available until ancillary matters have been resolved, whether by agreement between the parties or by court order. Under the present law the position is quite different, as most ancillary matters are dealt with after divorce. Mediation during the new divorce process will not be compulsory, but attendance at a private information session will be. At this session, information will be given about opportunities for saving the marriage and for smoothing the path for divorce. The methods for providing information at these sessions are about to be tested in a pilot study conducted under the *aegis* of the Lord Chancellor's Department prior to the implementation of the 1996 Act.

### Lord Hailsham, Debate on the Matrimonial and Family Proceedings Bill (*Hansard*, Lords, 21 November 1983)

Lest anyone should doubt my views on the subject — and some foolish people have — let them now be placed on record. I believe that the family is the solid foundation upon which all human society should be built. I believe that the ideal marriage is one man and one woman during their joint lives. When it occurs, I regard divorce as a misfortune — even a disaster — for both parties, and especially for the children of the marriage. I believe that people flounce out of marriage too often, little recognising and seldom understanding the abiding consequences of dissolution. Marry in haste, they used to say, repent at leisure. Divorce in haste, say I, and the consequences will be with you for the greater part of your life to come.

### Maclean, Mavis, 'Comment: Divorce and the Professionals' [1993] Fam Law 3

. . . Divorce is no longer a strange or deviant activity. We now have some fairly clear idea about how to go about it, but there is a series of complex emotional adjustments and practical arrangements to be made. Many people accomplish the transition without dispute. The minority are less fortunate. Our law-led divorce system dates from the days of the marital offence, and perhaps assumes a higher frequency of disputes than is now the case. The role of the law in divorce may be moving away from dispute resolution towards regulating and formalising the allocation of property and debts in the new post-divorce households. . . .

### McGregor, O. R., *Divorce in England* London: Heinemann, 1957, at p. 199

If the community permits divorce it must be prepared to meet the inevitable consequences of divorce. . . . Rational reform implies modifications in attitudes towards the consequences of divorce. A marriage creates dependencies so also its dissolution may create social casualties which confront responsible people with conflicting obligations that cannot be discharged because there is insufficient money to go round. Such casualties must be accepted at least as the temporary responsibility of social policy.

## 4.2  THE PRESENT LAW: MATRIMONIAL CAUSES ACT 1973, PART I

### 4.2.1  The origins of the present law

**Law Commission, *Facing the Future: A Discussion Paper on the Ground for Divorce*, Law Com No. 170** London: HMSO, 1988

**Origin of the present law**

2.1  Before the Divorce Reform Act 1969, a divorce could only be obtained by proving that the respondent had committed a matrimonial offence (the only material offences were adultery, cruelty and desertion for three years). A petitioner who was himself guilty of such an offence, or had somehow contributed to the offence of the other, or had condoned it, might be refused relief. No divorce could be granted within three years of marriage, unless special leave was given on the ground that the petitioner would suffer exceptional hardship or that the respondent was guilty of exceptional depravity.

2.2   Since the 1950s there had been increasing disillusionment with the operation of the fault-based law. It was clear that there was no real barrier to consensual divorce where both parties wanted it and one was prepared to commit, or perhaps appear to commit, a matrimonial offence to supply the necessary ground. On the other hand, where parties were not prepared to resort to such expedients, there was often no remedy, even though the marriage had irretrievably broken down. It was argued by the proponents of reform that the court was in no position to allocate blame; that in many cases both parties were at fault, and that matrimonial offences were often merely symptomatic of the breakdown of the marriage rather than the cause. However, the majority of the Royal Commission on Marriage and Divorce (the Morton Commission of 1956) affirmed the matrimonial offence as the sole basis of divorce because they saw this as the only means to ensure the stability of the institution of marriage. Three attempts, in Private Members' Bills, to introduce a provision allowing for divorce after long periods of separation were unsuccessful. Finally, the publication in 1966 of the report of the Archbishop of Canterbury's Group, entitled *Putting Asunder — A Divorce Law for Contemporary Society* [SPCK, 1966], paved the way for reform. The report found that the existing law concentrated exclusively on making findings of past delinquencies, whilst ignoring the current viability of the marriage. It therefore recommended that the matrimonial offence be abolished and be replaced by the principle of breakdown as the sole ground for divorce. It was envisaged that the court would determine whether the marriage had broken down after considering all the evidence.

2.3   The Lord Chancellor referred *Putting Asunder* to the Law Commission, whose response was published later in the same year, entitled Reform of the Grounds of Divorce — The Field of Choice (Law Com No. 6, 1966). The Commission agreed with the Archbishop's Group's criticisms of the existing law. In particular, it found that the need to prove a matrimonial offence caused unnecessary bitterness and distress to the parties and their children. The law did not accord with social reality, in that many spouses who could not obtain a divorce simply left the 'empty shells' of their marriages and set up 'stable illicit unions' with new partners. The Commission also agreed that where both parties wanted to end the marriage, divorce was easily available if they were prepared to commit or appear to commit a matrimonial offence. The Commission considered the objectives for a good divorce law to be:

(i)    To buttress, rather than to undermine, the stability of marriage; and

(ii)   When, regrettably, a marriage has irretrievably broken down, to enable the empty legal shell to be destroyed with the maximum fairness, and the minimum bitterness, distress and humiliation [para. 15].

. . .

2.4   Thus, both bodies agreed that the fault principle was unsatisfactory and that the law should be reformed to allow marriages which had irretrievably broken down to be dissolved in a humane fashion. The difficulty, of course, was how to identify those marriages which had irretrievably broken down. The Law Commission did not favour the solution advocated by the Archbishop's Group. First, it considered the proposed inquest impracticable partly because breakdown was not a justiciable issue.

Secondly, it was concerned that such an inquest into the conduct of the parties in order to determine breakdown would cause unnecessary bitterness and humiliation and prevent the marital ties being dissolved with decency and dignity. After consultations between the various interested bodies, a compromise solution was reached whereby breakdown would become the sole ground for divorce, but would be inferred from the existence of one of a number of facts rather than by judicial inquest. This solution was enacted in the Divorce Reform Act 1969.

2.5 The 1969 Act abolished the matrimonial offence principle and with it the bars to relief (of connivance, condonation, collusion and the like). Instead, the sole ground for divorce became irretrievable breakdown of the marriage. However, this breakdown could only be proved by one of five facts, now set out in the Matrimonial Causes Act 1973, section 1(2)(a) to (e). . . .

## Procedure

2.6 The 1969 Act did not alter the procedure by which a divorce was obtained. No divorce could be granted without a court hearing and the statutory duty of the divorce court to inquire into the facts alleged was retained. Research in the early 1970s showed that in undefended cases such judicial hearings, which rarely took more than than ten minutes and often less, served little purpose in that the decree was never refused; they were often unnerving and humiliating for the petitioner; and there was considerable consumer dissatisfaction with the existing procedure. The rise in the divorce rate and the increase in women petitioners, who were more likely to be legally aided, led to a rapid escalation in legal aid expenditure on divorce. In response to this increased cost and to the criticisms of divorce proceedings, the so-called 'special procedure', under which divorces could be obtained without a court hearing, was extended to all undefended divorces in 1977. At the same time, legal aid was withdrawn from the process of obtaining a decree under the new procedure, although legal advice and assistance are available under the green form scheme and full legal aid for contested ancillary proceedings about children, finance and property. Since 1977, nearly all undefended divorces have been obtained under the special procedure. This involves the perusal by the registrar of the petition and a supporting affidavit. If he is satisfied that the contents of the petition have been sufficiently proved and that the petitioner is entitled to a decree, the registrar will make and file a certificate to that effect. The decree nisi is then formally pronounced at a later date by a judge in open court after a list of the case numbers has been read out.

2.7 The savings in legal aid expenditure have not been as great as expected. There has been an increase in legal aid certificates for ancillary proceedings and a shift of expenditure from legal aid to green form scheme. Although parties are technically litigants in person in relation to the divorce, in practice most petitioners and many respondents are advised by solicitors throughout. Clearly, the costs to both public and private resources of returning to a system of divorce by judicial hearing in undefended cases would be very considerable. Nor does the experience of the previous system suggest that there would be any real advantage in doing so. Hence, the Booth Committee on Procedure in Matrimonial Causes (para. 2.8) took the view that 'it is neither desirable nor practicable to try to put the clock back and to revert to former practices' [see *Report of the Matrimonial Causes Procedure Committee* (Chairman: the Hon Mrs Justice Booth DBE), 1985].

2.8 The introduction of the special procedure has undoubtedly had an effect upon the way in which the substantive law operates. The Booth Committee found that:

. . . the ability of the court to carry out its statutory duty to inquire into the facts alleged is greatly circumscribed. In the great majority of cases the court is quite simply in no position to make findings of fact or, in a case based on behaviour, to evaluate the effect of the respondent's behaviour on the petitioner. In reality, the registrar can do no more than read the few documents before him [para. 2.17].

This conclusion would seem to support the view that registrars act as little more than 'rubber stamps'. However, there is a dearth of statistical or other information about the progress of cases through the special procedure; the number of cases in which the registrar refuses his certificate on the basis that he is not satisfied that the petitioner has sufficiently proved the contents of the petition and is entitled to a decree; the number of cases in which the registrar asks for further particulars and which then go before him more than once; or the number of cases which the registrar adjourns to be heard by a judge in open court. A recent small-scale study of solicitors' files suggests that there may be more double handling of cases by registrars than the 'rubber stamp' image might suggest, but that the registrars' queries are more concerned with technical than substantive matters and thus only operate to delay decrees. If this is the case, then such queries and hearings would seem to serve little purpose and their expense difficult to justify. Hence the Booth Committee has recommended that the special duty of inquiry on a divorce court should be removed and the court should merely be required to be satisfied on the evidence, as in other civil cases.

2.9   In the view of some commentators, the procedural changes of the 1970s were 'more radical departures than was the introduction of irretrievable breakdown as the sole ground of divorce' [Ingleby, R. *The Ground for Divorce*, 1986]. In practice, the ability of the court to conduct a proper inquiry in the course of an oral hearing in an undefended case has always been strictly limited. The close interrelationship between substance and procedure in divorce law was stressed in the Booth Report. The Committee clearly felt that the present law, by retaining the fault element, made it more difficult for them to make procedural proposals which would mitigate the intensity of disputes and encourage settlements (as they had been asked to do) and that early review of the ground for divorce would be welcome. Nonetheless, many of their recommendations, if implemented, would have a profound effect on the operation of the substantive law. . . .

### 4.2.2   The grounds for divorce

Until the FLA 1996 comes into force, the 'grounds' for divorce are those laid down in MCA 1973, s. 1.

## MATRIMONIAL CAUSES ACT 1973

### 1.   Divorce on breakdown of marriage

(1)   . . . a petition for divorce may be presented to the court by either party to a marriage on the ground that the marriage has broken down irretrievably.

(2)   The court hearing a petition for divorce shall not hold the marriage to have broken down irretrievably unless the petitioner satisfies the court of one or more of the following facts, that is to say—

(a)   that the respondent has committed adultery and the petitioner finds it intolerable to live with the respondent;

(b)   that the respondent has behaved in such a way that the petitioner cannot reasonably be expected to live with the respondent;

(c)   that the respondent has deserted the petitioner for a continuous period of at least two years immediately preceding the presentation of the petition;

(d)   that the parties of the marriage have lived apart for a continuous period of at least two years immediately preceding the presentation of the petition . . . and the respondent consents to a decree being granted;

(e)   that the parties to the marriage have lived apart for a continuous period of at least five years immediately preceding the presentation of the petition. . . .

## 4.2.2.1   Adultery

**Law Commission, *Facing the Future: A Discussion Paper on the Ground for Divorce*, Law Com No. 170**
London: HMSO, 1988

3.8   . . . The requirement of 'intolerability' was added to the adultery fact with the intention of excluding reliance on a single isolated act of adultery which did not affect the marriage relationship.

. . .

3.17   . . . [T]he adultery fact involves not only a finding that the respondent has committed adultery, but also that the petitioner finds it intolerable to live with the respondent. Again, this requires some finding of incompatibility, although in this case the test is entirely subjective. However, it has been held that there need be no causal link between the two requirements. Thus, the petitioner may find it intolerable to live with the respondent for any reason, not necessarily because he has committed adultery. The court or the registrar is in no position to gainsay the petitioner and there is no requirement that her attitude be reasonable. This could well mean that the petitioner's own behaviour has been much worse than that of the respondent, but the respondent who has admittedly committed adultery has no defence. . . . In any case, if the divorce is undefended, the respondent's apparent fault is generally allowed to form the basis of the divorce without receiving any real judicial scrutiny.

## 4.2.2.2   Behaviour

### *Ash* v *Ash*
[1972] Fam 135
Family Division

BAGNALL J: . . . In order . . . to answer the question whether the petitioner can or cannot reasonably be expected to live with the respondent, in my judgment I have to consider not only the behaviour the respondent has alleged and established in evidence, but the character, personality, disposition and behaviour of the petitioner. The general question may be expanded thus: can this petitioner, with his or her character and personality, with his or her faults and other attributes, good and bad, having regard to his or her behaviour during the marriage, reasonably be expected to live with this respondent. It follows that if a respondent is seeking to resist a petition on the first ground upon which Mr Ash relies, he must in his answer plead and his evidence establish the characteristics, faults, attributes, personality and behaviour on the part of the petitioner upon which he relies. . . . It seems to me that a violent petitioner can reasonably be expected to live with a violent respondent. A petitioner who is addicted to drink can reasonably be expected to live with a respondent who is similarly addicted. . . . If each is equally bad, at any rate in similar respects, each can reasonably be expected to live with the other. . . .

## O'Neill v O'Neill
[1975] 1 WLR 1118
Court of Appeal

ROSKILL LJ: . . . I would respectfully adopt as correct what Dunn J said in *Livingstone-Stallard* [1974] Fam 47 . . . :

> Coming back to my analogy of a direction to a jury, I ask myself the question: Would any right-thinking person come to the conclusion that this husband has behaved in such a way that this wife cannot reasonably be expected to live with him, taking into account the whole of the circumstances and the characters and personalities of the parties?

. . .

## Gollins v Gollins
[1964] AC 644
House of Lords

LORD REID: . . . In matrimonial cases we are not concerned with the reasonable man as we are in cases of negligence. We are dealing with this man and this woman. . . .

### Law Commission, *Facing the Future: A Discussion Paper on the Ground for Divorce*, Law Com No. 170
London: HMSO, 1988

3.17 . . . Behaviour need not be caused by the fault of the respondent at all, as it may be the result of physical or mental illness or injury, even to the extent of being involuntary. Further, the common practice of referring to it as 'unreasonable behaviour' is a complete misnomer and dangerously misleading. What is required is behaviour on the part of the respondent which makes it unreasonable for the petitioner to be expected to live with the respondent. The courts have held that this test involves a subjective element. That is, it might not be reasonable to expect one petitioner to put up with behaviour which it would be reasonable to expect another petitioner to tolerate. This will depend on the sensitivity and disposition of the petitioner. Thus, a finding that the behaviour ground is fulfilled is not necessarily a finding of fault on the part of the respondent, but rather a finding of the petitioner's inability to withstand this behaviour and hence of the incompatibility of the parties. While in many cases reliance will be placed on behaviour which is generally thought wrong, in others the allegations will reflect the differing values and expectations of the parties on matters such as social life, finance or sexual activities.

*Notes*
1.  For a case on unreasonable behaviour, see *Birch v Birch* [1992] 1 FLR 564, CA, where the *dicta* from the cases above were cited to establish that the trial judge had used the incorrect test of behaviour.
2.  About three-quarters of divorces are sought on the 'fault' grounds of adultery and unreasonable behaviour as they provide the only way of obtaining a 'quick' divorce, so that the aim of the 1969 reforms under the

Divorce Reform Act 1969 (later re-enacted as MCA 1973, Part I) to move away from fault has not been achieved in practice — hence the need for reform under the FLA 1996.

3.   Section 10 of the MCA 1973 allows the court (in five- and two-year separation cases) to postpone decree absolute until the petitioner has, if need be, provided reasonable and fair financial provision for the respondent (s. 10(2) and (3)). However, the court may grant the decree absolute if it is desirable to do so without delay and it has obtained a satisfactory undertaking that the petitioner will make appropriate financial provision for the respondent (s. 10(4)). Section 5 (the 'hardship bar') allows the court (in five-year separation cases) to refuse a decree of divorce on the application of the respondent on the ground that the divorce will result in grave or other financial hardship for the respondent, so that it would be wrong to dissolve the marriage (s. 5(1)). Although the s. 5 'hardship bar' is rarely argued and rarely successful, the new divorce law retains it (see FLA 1996, s. 10 and see also the comment by Cretney, S., 'Divorce White Paper — Some Reflections' [1995] Fam Law 302 at p. 303).

### 4.2.3   The 'special procedure' for divorce

Undefended divorces are heard under the 'special procedure'. Defended divorces (virtually non-existent) are heard in open court.

***Pounds* v *Pounds***
[1994] 1 FLR 775
Court of Appeal

WAITE LJ: . . .

*The nature and function of the special procedure for undefended divorce*
In outward form, English divorce law still does its best to emphasise the institutional solemnity of marriage by insisting that it can be ended only by a judicial pronounce-ment, and that the terms of any financial compromise accompanying or following divorce are judicially approved. In practice, procedural corners have had to be cut in the interests of saving time, expense and heartache within a system that has to accommodate more than 150,000 unopposed divorce petitions annually.

One such development has been the enlargement of what began as a 'special' procedure until it became the norm for most unopposed divorces. It still bears the superficial hallmarks of a full-scale judicial process, in that the proceedings are spoken of as a 'cause' and there is reference in the rules to their outcome as a 'trial'. Closer inspection reveals that such descriptions have more pageantry than substance. Al-though the special procedure as now laid down by the Family Proceedings Rules does not greatly differ, I will refer, in summarising it, to the rules which were in operation at the dates in 1990 and 1991 relevant to the present case, namely the former Matrimonial Causes Rules 1977 (as amended), and I will refer to the district judge by his then title of registrar.

Following presentation of the petition, the petitioner's solicitor lodges an applica-tion for 'directions for trial' together with a standard affidavit in the form required to verify the particular ground alleged in the petition. In routine cases (i.e. where no problem of costs or of approving arrangements for the children arises) the registrar gives 'directions for trial' by entering the cause in the special procedure list and thereafter considers the evidence filed by the petitioner If he is satisfied that the petitioner has sufficiently proved the contents of the petition and is entitled to the decree sought and any costs prayed for, he will make and file a certificate to that effect. The court then sends notification to the parties of the date, time and place fixed for the pronouncement of the decree nisi. The parties are also told that their attendance at the pronouncement of decree is not necessary. The actual process of pronouncement of the decree has become reduced to a very brief ceremony of a purely formal character in which decrees are listed together in batches for a collective mention in open court before a judge who speaks (or nods) his assent. The right to a decree absolute 6 weeks thereafter is automatic, on the application of either party (A more detailed summary of the procedure will be found in *Rayden & Jackson on Divorce* (Butterworths, 15th edn, 1991), p. 528.)

The procedures for dissolution of marriage on unopposed petitions in England have thus become truncated over the years to the point that the sole truly judicial function in the entire process is that of the registrar when granting his certificate. Everything that follows is automatic and administrative, and the open court pronouncement of the decree is a pure formality, to which the pronouncing judge (who under current procedures may himself be a district judge) has no option but to consent. If any party attends the ceremony of pronouncement and objects, the judge's powers are accordingly limited to directing that the petition shall be stood out of the pronouncement list, to enable some substantive application to be made to vary or discharge the registrar's certificate, see *Day* v *Day* [1980] Fam 29, (1980) FLR 341, CA.

. . .

*Note*

The 'pronouncing judge' is now the district judge (FPR 1991, r. 2.49(2)).

### Report of the Matrimonial Causes Procedure Committee
(Chairman: The Hon. Mrs Justice Booth DBE)
London: HMSO, 1985

2.8  . . . Procedure governs the application of the substantive law. It cannot of itself alter the law but it is a powerful factor in determining the extent to which it is applied.
. . .

2.9  . . . The general consensus of feeling . . . is that divorce should be truly and not merely artificially based upon a no-fault ground and that the concepts of guilt and innocence which have ruled our divorce laws, and consequently our divorce procedures, since 1857 should no longer have any part to play.

. . .

2.17  . . . [T]he ability of the court to carry out its statutory duty to inquire into the facts alleged is greatly circumscribed. In the great majority of cases the court is quite simply in no position to make findings of fact or, in a case based on behaviour, to evaluate the effect of the respondent's behaviour on the petitioner. Indeed, it has been said that the objectives of the special procedure are simplicity, speed and economy. . . .

*Note*
Many of the 'Booth Report' proposals were incorporated into the divorce reforms.

## 4.3  THE REFORM OF DIVORCE LAW

During the last 20 years or so there has been concern not just about the incidence of divorce and its adverse effects on the parties and their children, but about the grounds for divorce. As a result of a general dissatisfaction with divorce, the Law Commission published a discussion paper, *Facing the Future: A Discussion Paper on the Ground for Divorce*, 1988, Law Com No. 170, in which it criticised the law and made proposals for change. This was followed by a Report, *Family Law: The Ground for Divorce*, 1990, Law Com No. 192, in which it built on its Discussion Paper and made recommendations for divorce over a period of time. The Government subsequently adopted most of the Law Commission's recommendations along with new proposals for an increased role for mediation, and outlined its proposals in a Consultation Paper, *Looking to the Future: Mediation and the Ground for Divorce*, Cm 2424, 1993. After responses to the Consultation Paper were received and processed, the Government published a White Paper, *Looking to the Future: Mediation and the Ground for Divorce: The Government's Proposals*, Cm 2799, 1995, which was followed in November 1995 by the publication of the Family Law Bill, Parts I, II and III of which contained reforms of divorce law and proposals for mediation in family matters. The Bill had a stormy ride through Parliament, with many last-minute amendments made, but on 4 July 1996 the Bill received the Royal Assent. The new Act, the Family Law Act (FLA) 1996, will come into force on a date to be announced by the Government (expected date Spring 1999), although Part IV (family homes and domestic violence) is due to come into force on 1 October 1997 (see Chapter 6).

### 4.3.1  The case for reform

In *Facing the Future: A Discussion Paper on the Ground for Divorce*, 1988, the Law Commission discussed the present law of divorce and made proposals for reform, which, with some amendments, were adopted by the Government as the basis for the new divorce law. In the Discussion Paper, the Law Commission discussed the present law in terms of its original objectives for a good divorce law, which were: '(i) To buttress, rather than to undermine, the stability of marriage; and (ii) When, regrettably, a marriage has irretrievably broken down, to enable the empty legal shell to be destroyed with the maximum fairness, and the minimum bitterness, distress and humiliation.' (see 4.2.1 *supra*). It also considered whether the present law avoided injustice to an economically weak spouse and protected the interests of children on divorce, and whether it was understandable and respected. Much of the discussion centred on the questions of whether marriages are dissolved with maximum fairness and whether the law promotes bitterness, distress and humiliation between the parties.

**Law Commission,** *Facing the Future: A Discussion Paper on the*
*Ground for Divorce,* **Law Com No. 170**
London: HMSO, 1988

. . .

(c)  *Does the law ensure that marriages are dissolved with maximum fairness?*

3.13   One of the criticisms of the old law was that it was unfair for the respondent
to be 'branded as guilty in law though not the more blameworthy in fact'. Despite the
replacement of the matrimonial offence by irretrievable breakdown as the sole ground
for divorce, the original matrimonial offences have been retained in modified form as
the first three of the five facts which evidence breakdown. These each appear to
involve findings of fault. Thus, in reality we now have a dual system with fault-based
divorce alongside the no-fault separation facts and 'the clear concept of the no-fault
irretrievable breakdown of marriage as the only ground for divorce has not been
achieved' [Booth Report *supra*, para. 2.9]. This is highlighted by the cases where a
decree nisi has been refused even though there is no dispute that the marriage has
irretrievably broken down.

. . .

3.15   Experience since the implementation of the 1969 Act has borne out the
predictions made by the Archbishop's Group [in *Putting Asunder*]. The radical
theoretical shift from the offence principle to the breakdown principle has not become
apparent in practice. The law tells the parties, on the one hand, that the sole ground
for divorce is irretrievable breakdown and, on the other hand, that unless they are able
to wait for at least two years after separation, a divorce can only be obtained by
proving fault. Not surprisingly, the subtlety that the facts are not grounds for divorce,
but merely evidence of breakdown, is seldom grasped. The first three facts are still
regarded as matrimonial offences, and the separation facts as last resort grounds for
those who cannot prove fault or prefer to wait for a less acrimonious divorce.

3.16   We are therefore left with much of the unfairness of the old fault-based
system. In petitions based on facts (a), (b) and (c), the parties 'at the outset of
proceedings are required to think in terms of wrongdoing and blameworthiness in a
way which perpetuates the images of the innocent and guilty party' [Booth Report,
para. 2.9]. The fact specified in the petition is seen as the cause of the breakdown for
which the respondent is responsible. Yet the evidence suggests that the fact relied on
is usually rather a symptom of the breakdown which has been caused by the
deterioration in the relationship of the parties for a wide variety of reasons. In most
divorces the spouses will both be 'at fault' in varying degrees and it will be impossible
to apportion responsibility for the breakdown. . . . Thus, the respondent may be
stigmatised as guilty under facts (a), (b) or (c) even where the spouses themselves do
not take such a simplistic view. There is evidence that many respondents resent having
to accept this construction in order to obtain a divorce without waiting tor one of the
separation periods to elapse.

3.17   The unfairness caused by this often unjustified stigmatisation of the respondent is exacerbated by several factors. First, the adultery and behaviour facts as
formulated in the legislation and interpreted by the courts do not necessarily involve
the absolute fault that is suggested by these labels. Behaviour need not be caused by
the fault of the respondent at all as it may be the result of physical or mental illness
or injury, even to the extent of being involuntary. Further, the common practice of
referring to it as 'unreasonable behaviour' is a complete misnomer and dangerously

misleading. What is required is behaviour on the part of the respondent which makes it unreasonable for the petitioner to be expected to live with the respondent. The courts have held that this test involves a subjective element. That is, it might not be reasonable to expect one petitioner to put up with behaviour which it would be reasonable to expect another petitioner to tolerate. This will depend on the sensitivity and disposition of the petitioner. Thus, a finding that the behaviour ground is fulfilled is not necessarily a finding of fault on the part of the respondent, but rather a finding of the petitioner's inability to withstand this behaviour and hence of the incompatibility of the parties. While in many cases reliance will be placed on behaviour which is generally thought wrong, in others the allegations will reflect the differing values and expectations of the parties on matters such as social life, finance or sexual activities. Similarly, the adultery fact involves not only a finding that the respondent has committed adultery, but also that the petitioner finds it intolerable to live with the respondent. Again, this requires some finding of incompatibility, although in this case the test is entirely subjective. However, it has been held that there need be no causal link between the two requirements. Thus, the petitioner may find it intolerable to live with the respondent for any reason, not necessarily because he has committed adultery. . . .

3.18   Secondly, it will often be impracticable for the respondent to challenge the allegations made in the petition, whether or not he is content for the marriage to be ended. The costs of defending are usually prohibitive and legal aid is not generally available for the respondent to defend the petition if it is clear that the marriage has broken down irretrievably. Yet it is thought to be unfair that derogatory allegations made against the respondent should be allowed to form the basis of the divorce without his being given a chance to set the record straight.

3.19   Thirdly, the juxtaposition of fault and no-fault grounds suggests that respondents to petitions based on facts (a), (b) and (c) are at fault whereas respondents in separation cases are blameless. The implication from the existence of statutory safeguards to protect the financial position in separation cases *only* is that the respondents in non-separation cases are blameworthy and do not deserve such protection. . . .

3.20   The fault-based facts may also work capriciously between the parties. A spouse who can present an immediate petition because the other's conduct falls within facts (a) or (b) is in a strong bargaining position if the respondent wants an immediate divorce but has no fact upon which to rely. Similarly, where the parties have been separated for two years, the one who does not need a divorce is afforded a bargaining advantage by having the power to refuse consent. It is unfair that the law should distribute the 'bargaining chips' in this way, when as we have seen, the respondent is not necessarily more blameworthy than the petitioner. This distortion in the relative bargaining power of the parties can affect the negotiations about money and children. The respondent may be prepared to yield in these matters because he wants a divorce. Although all discussions about post-divorce arrangements are conducted in 'the shadow of the law' only *relevant* law should be allowed to influence the parties' decisions.

3.21   Finally, fault is usually not relevant in ancillary matters and where it is, this will be determined in the trial of those matters and not in reliance on the particulars pleaded in the petition. But this is not generally understood and petitioners may choose to use the behaviour fact to cite particular allegations of behaviour specifically because they think that this will help them in proceedings relating to children and financial provision. Similarly, respondents may be induced to defend adultery or behaviour petitions because they are worried that the allegations are damaging to their chances in such proceedings.

(d)  *Does the law promote minimum bitterness, distress and humiliation?*

3.22    In The Field of Choice, the Commission clearly recognised the 'embarrass-ment and bitterness' caused by the need to prove a matrimonial offence under the old law and expressed the hope that parties would prefer to wait to use the separation periods, if introduced, as this would produce less acrimony. Indeed, 693,676 couples, some of whom could no doubt have proven one of the fault-based facts, have done just this. However, the high hopes of the Commission have not been realised and 71 per cent of petitions filed in 1985 relied on one of the fault-based facts. The avoidance of bitterness and hostility between the parties seems even more important today in the light of the modern emphasis on promoting agreement between the parties about the consequences of divorce and the evidence that good post-divorce relations between the parties and between the children and both parents tend to reduce the problems experienced by children as a result of marital breakdown. It must, of course, be remembered that 'it would be unrealistic to expect that such feelings [bitterness and resentment], which are often implicit in the distress which accompanies divorce. could ever wholly be eradicated' [*The Financial Consequences of Divorce: The Basic Policy*, Law Com No. 103, 1980, para. 2.9]. It is unfortunate, however, if the legal process itself is such as to provoke or exacerbate unnecessary antagonism between the parties.

3.23    It has been suggested that much of the bitterness created between parties to fault-based petitions is attributable to the lack of fairness, actual or perceived. A respondent to a fault-based petition will often resent the fact that he is being held responsible for the breakdown, when in his own mind he is no more to blame than the petitioner. This feeling may encourage him either to defend the petition, even if he wants a divorce, simply in order to set the record straight, or at least to be uncooperative in relation to the divorce and any ancillary proceedings. . . . One way of venting his anger is to contest proceedings relating to children and finance. It seems almost paradoxical that the contents of the petition should cause such negative feelings in undefended divorces, when, as we have seen, they are not properly scrutinised and their only relevance to the divorce process is in satisfying the formula required by the legislation.

3.24    The legal process is particularly likely to induce conflict where the parties are still in the matrimonial home and cannot agree upon which should leave. In order to obtain a pre-divorce injunction the petitioner may find it necessary to make more damaging allegations against the respondent than might be sufficient to obtain a decree. So, whatever fact is ultimately relied on, the injunction proceedings themselves will force the parties to adopt hostile and entrenched positions.

3.25    There is evidence that bitterness and hostility between the parties is particu-larly prevalent in behaviour petitions. . . .

3.26    This correlation between hostility and behaviour petitions may be thought simply to reflect the fact that there is more likely to be animosity between the parties already in such cases, either because of the conduct of the respondent, particularly where it has been violent, or because the parties are still living together. However, there is evidence to suggest that the very presentation of a behaviour petition either creates hostility or exacerbates pre-existing antagonism between the parties. Respon-dents to behaviour petitions are more likely to be 'upset' or 'shocked' when they receive the petition and are more likely to feel that the divorce has been more difficult for them because they are respondents. The Booth Report commented that 'Great hostility and resentment may be generated by the recital in the petition of allegations of behaviour, often exaggerated and sometimes stretching back over many years, to the extent that no discussion can take place between the parties or any agreement be reached on any matter relating to their marrriage or to their children' [para. 2.10]. To mitigate this problem, the Committee recommended that incidents of behaviour should not be recited in petitions.

. . .

## Conclusions

3.47    Despite the defects highlighted above, it must be remembered that the present law is a considerable improvement on the previous position. The enactment of irretrievable breakdown as the sole ground for divorce affirms the principle that the law should not require a dead marriage to be kept in existence. Further, the introduction of the two separation facts makes it possible, for all who are prepared to wait, to bury dead marriages with less 'bitterness, distress and humiliation'. Even in behaviour petitions, which are generally the most acrimonious, the bitterness is likely to be less than under a pre-1971 cruelty petition.

3.48    However, the present law falls well short of the objectives it set out to fulfil. It does not, nor could it reasonably be expected to, buttress the stability of marriage by preventing determined parties from obtaining a speedy divorce. Because of the compromise nature of the 1969 Act, the benefits referred to above have been bought at the price of incoherence and increased confusion for litigants. Thus the law is neither understandable nor respected and there is evidence of not inconsiderable consumer dissatisfaction. Attaining the aims of maximum fairness and minimum bitterness has been rendered impossible by the retention of the fault element. The necessity of making allegations in the petition 'draws the battle-lines' at the outset. The ensuing hostility makes the divorce more painful, not only for the parties but also for the children, and destroys any chance of reconciliation and may be detrimental to post-divorce relationships. Underlying all these defects is the fact that whether or not the marriage can be dissolved depends principally upon what the parties have done in the past. In petitions relying on fault-based facts, the petitioner is encouraged to 'dwell on the past' and to recriminate.

3.49    At the same time, the present divorce process may not allow sufficient opportunity for the parties to come to terms with what is happening in their lives. A recent study of the process of 'uncoupling' points out that one party has usually gone far down that path before the other one discovers this, by which time it may be too late. Once the divorce process has been started it may have a 'juggernaut' effect, providing insufficient opportunity for the parties to re-evaluate their positions. Thus, there is little or no scope for reconciliation, conciliation or renegotiation of the relationship. It is clear that both emotionally and financially it is much less costly if ancillary matters can be agreed between the parties. Where antagonism is created or exacerbated by the petition, or their respective bargaining power distorted, the atmosphere is not conducive to calm and sensible negotiations about the future needs of the parties and their children.

3.50    Above all, the present law fails to recognise that divorce is not a final product but part of a massive transition for the parties and their children. It is crucial in the interests of the children (as well as the parties) that the transition is as smooth as possible, since it is clear that their short and long-term adjustment depends to a large extent on their parents' adjustment and in particular on the quality of their post-divorce relationship with each parent. Although divorce law itself can do little actively to this end, it can and should ensure that the divorce process is not positively adverse to this adjustment. . . .

### 4.3.2   Options for reform

The Law Commission in *Facing the Future* discussed various options for reform, in particular separation, mutual consent and unilateral demand.

Law Commission, *Facing the Future: A Discussion Paper on the Ground for Divorce*, Law Com No. 170
London: HMSO, 1988

(b)   *Separation*
4.9   There are a number of obvious advantages to a sole separation ground. Separation is a pure no-fault ground which is morally neutral as between the parties and, unlike actual breakdown, is susceptible to objective proof without undue difficulty. Once the parties have been separated for the requisite length of time, either party can choose to petition and thus the ability to obtain a divorce cannot become a 'bargaining chip'. This is not necessarily an advantage if the parties' bargaining power is otherwise grossly unequal. However, where separation is the sole ground, the divorce law is simple and easily understood and the divorce process can be cheap and unacrimonious.

4.10   There are two main disadvantages of a sole separation ground. First, some find it intolerable that in a case of extreme cruelty the innocent spouse should have to wait for a dissolution. Secondly, the ability of a spouse to obtain a divorce depends on either her ability or her spouse's willingness to effect a separation in the first place. In times or places of housing shortage, particularly in the rented sector, this clearly operates differently as between different socio-economic groups and as between husbands and wives. Thus, spouses with dependent children without alternative accommodation are prejudiced and the ability to separate becomes a 'bargaining chip'. The Australian and New Zealand legislation does address the problem of practical inability to separate by providing for separation under one roof. The case law makes it clear that the criteria to be satisfied are much less stringent than those in the English cases. Although such a provision may alleviate some hardship, it is hardly ideal for parties, or for their children, to be forced to continue to live under the same roof until the separation period has elapsed or for their behaviour towards each other to be conditioned by the requirements of the law.

(c)   *Mutual consent*
4.11   A number of jurisdictions have introduced mutual consent as a ground for divorce. Some countries put limitations on the availability of this ground by restricting its use at the beginning of the marriage and by providing a period of waiting before the decree becomes effective. In Sweden, if there is mutual consent, there is a waiting period of six months where either of the parties has legal custody of a child under 16, unless they have already lived apart for two years. In some countries mutual consent reduces the length of the separation period.

4.12   Although divorce by mutual consent obviates the need for a separation period and enables a divorce to be obtained in a morally neutral way without any adjudication by the court, it is not without its problems. Apart from the difficulty of ensuring that consent is freely given, the party who does not need the divorce can use his right to withhold consent as a 'bargaining chip' in negotiations about finance and children. In some countries, the court must also be satisfied that those matters have been agreed and has very limited powers to supervise such agreements, even in the interests of the children. In any event, it is quite clear that mutual consent cannot be (and is not in any jurisdiction) the only ground for divorce. The use made of consent grounds is therefore crucially influenced by what is available without consent. In France, for example, the alternatives are unilateral demand accepted by the other, fault, and prolonged separation or mental disorder (the last known as 'rupture of community life'), but the financial consequences are different for each. In Sweden, where the other party does not consent or there is a minor child, there is a six month 'reconsideration period' from the date of the application for the divorce, unless the parties have lived apart for two years. At the end of that time, the divorce is obtainable by either party.

(d)  *Unilateral demand*
4.13  Sweden is the only European country which provides for *either* spouse to terminate the marriage at will without proving any ground, albeit after a period of reconsideration in many cases. However, we have seen that divorce on the basis of breakdown is virtually indistinguishable from divorce by unilateral demand where breakdown is proved by the statement of one party that the marriage is no longer viable. Divorce on unilateral demand has the great merits of simplicity, moral neutrality and avoiding bitterness. Swedish lawyers have apparently found that since the reforms there has been less acrimony in relation to the consequences of divorce.
4.14  There are two main criticisms. The first is that it represents the abdication of the State from any responsibility for determining whether a divorce should be granted. Yet, as we have seen, this may be the only logical application of the breakdown principle, which has been so widely accepted as the basis of modern divorce law. If breakdown is not justiciable and any fact chosen to prove breakdown is arbitrary, the only true judges of whether the marriage can continue are the parties themselves. This criticism also fails to address the difficult question of the nature of the State's interest. Once breakdown is accepted as the proper rationale for divorce, it is difficult to devise any logical basis for protecting a spouse who does not wish to be divorced even though the marriage has clearly broken down. The State's real interest may then be in protecting that spouse's financial position (and with it that of the State itself) and the interests of any minor children.
4.15  A second criticism is that if divorce is available immediately on unilateral demand then parties may be tempted to divorce without having considered the implications thoroughly. The mere fact of requiring a court hearing does not necessarily solve this problem, as the court will not always be able to identify a possibility of reconciliation. The Swedish requirement that in cases involving minor children or lack of consent, the divorce is delayed for a six month 'reconsideration period' (unless there has been a two years' separation) is clearly designed to meet the problem of precipitate divorce, although it may be thought too limited. It may, however, be more effective to use the divorce *process*, rather than the ground for divorce, as a means of identifying cases where there is a realistic possibility of reconciliation.
. . .

The Law Commission's preferred option: divorce as a process over time.

**Law Commission, *Facing the Future: A Discussion Paper on the Ground for Divorce*, Law Com No. 170**
**London: HMSO, 1988**

**A process over time**
5.22  We saw earlier that two aspects of the criteria of a good divorce law have been particularly emphasised in recent years. These are, first, the importance of promoting co-operation between the parties and, secondly, the fact that divorce must be seen as a process rather than a single event. Most of the options discussed above treat the actual divorce as separate from its consequences, whereas it would seem preferable to

treat the *process* of divorce with all its repercussions as a whole. This would enable appropriate legal and other support to be given to the parties during the transition from married to non-married life. As others have pointed out, a process which both enables the parties to resolve the practical consequences of their decision before it is made final, and reduces the need for them to make hostile allegations against one another, may increase the chances of a reconciliation between them even though it is not the express objective of the system to do so.

5.23    These aims could be achieved by providing for a period of time (referred to as the transition period) in which this transition can take place and during which the parties would be given every encouragement to reach agreement on all aspects of the divorce, failing which these would be decided judicially. The divorce would not be available until the end of the period. Thus, during the whole transition period the parties would have the opportunity to reflect on whether they really wanted a divorce. This would be particularly valuable as they would be able to reassess their decision as all the repercussions of divorce became clear to them. Under the present system, it is often too late to go back by the time that the full implications have become apparent; issues relating to the children are often resolved, and issues of finance and property can only be resolved, after the divorce nisi has been obtained.

5.24    The underlying principle, which could be stated in the legislation, would remain the irretrievable breakdown of the marriage, but there would be no need to establish any particular basis for the divorce, which would be available as of right at the end of the transition period, subject to a number of possible conditions to be discussed below. Thus, all the negotiations about children, finance and property could take place without any concern as to whether the ground could be made out and without the background of any allegations.

5.25    The main advantage of such a scheme is that it combines the logical position that the only true test of breakdown is that one or both parties consider the marriage at an end, with the need to provide a period for reflection and transition. Once it is accepted that the present system provides neither a real test of breakdown nor any real obstacle to divorce for most people, then the proposed procedure can be seen as an improvement. Because divorce would not be available immediately, it would not be 'too easy'. Attention throughout the process would be focussed on the continuing obligations of the parties in respect of their children and financial arrangements. The object would be to enable both parties to maintain their relationship with their children, while making the necessary arrangements for the future in as civilised a manner and timespan as can be achieved.

*Facing the Future* was followed by the Law Commission's Report, *Family Law: The Ground for Divorce*, Law Com No. 192, 1990, in which it made more detailed proposals about the favoured option, divorce as a process over time. Stephen Cretney in the following extract comments on the Law Commission's proposals.

### Cretney, Stephen M., 'Divorce — A Smooth Transition?'
[1992] Fam Law 472 at p. 473

. . .

### HISTORY REPEATS ITSELF?
Legislative implementation of these proposals would certainly secure benefits — not least the abolition of the 'behaviour' fact with the bitterness and distress which its use

apparently engenders: see Davis and Murch, *The Ground for Divorce* (1988), particularly at pp. 87–99. But, once again, a price would have to be paid for achieving those
benefits and there seems to be a real danger of history repeating itself. Reform is to
be achieved on the basis of expectations which are unlikely to be met.

What are the grounds for taking so pessimistic a view of the likely effect of the
Commission's proposals?

First, it is difficult to avoid the conclusion that the law would remain confusing.
The ground for divorce would, in theory, be irretrievable breakdown but, in fact,
divorce would be available if either party wanted it (irrespective of the wishes of the
other) one year from the filing of a formal notice. It is true that in some circumstances
divorce might be delayed, but the only basis on which it could be refused would be if
the court were satisfied that the divorce would result in grave financial or other grave
hardship to one party and that it would be wrong, in all the circumstances, for the
marriage to be dissolved: see cl. 4 of the Commission's draft Bill. These words are (in
all significant respects) the same as those currently empowering the court to refuse to
grant a decree founded on 5 years' living apart: Matrimonial Causes Act 1973, s. 5.
As the Law Commission candidly admits (see Law Com No. 192, para. 5.75) it would
only be in a 'tiny minority of cases' that divorce could be withheld on this ground.
The awkward truth is that what the Law Commission proposes is, essentially, divorce
by repudiation. Yet that is not how the proposals are presented.

Secondly, the proposed reforms seem unlikely to eliminate the sense of injustice
observed in some of those divorced under the present law. It is true that petitions
containing detailed and, perhaps, unfounded behaviour allegations would no longer
arrive without prior warning to shock the unprepared, but a man or woman who had
behaved cruelly and unreasonably could still insist on divorce against the wishes of
the other spouse. Anger, grief and bitterness might not be assuaged by telling an
ill-used spouse who is unwilling to be divorced that the new law promotes consideration and reflection.

Thirdly, even in less extreme cases, it may be doubted whether the elaborate
court-focused procedure envisaged by the Law Commission in an attempt to ensure that
the period of 'consideration and reflection' be used 'constructively' would, in practice,
achieve that end. This is not only because of the fundamental doubt about whether a
court can realistically be an appropriate forum for the resolution of what are, essentially,
welfare issues (see Walker, 'Divorce — Whose Fault' [1991] Fam Law 234; and the
comments by Professor Freeman in the *International Journal of Family Law Annual
Survey*, 30 JFL 296), but because of the potential implicit in any such procedure for
manipulation and tactical exploitation — the applications to extend the one-year period,
the applications for interim orders, the requests for information and so on, and (as Dr
Clive has asked) does it really make sense to encourage a couple still living together to
value their assets with a view to divorce at the very same time as they are being expected
to reflect seriously on whether the breakdown in their relationship is, indeed, irreparable:
see *The Law of Husband and Wife in Scotland* (1992, 3rd edn) at p. 398?

These reservations can be summed up in a sentence. The Commission's proposals
conceal the reality that marriage will have become terminable at the will of one of the
parties in law (as it always has been in personal terms), behind an elaborate system of
court-led procedures built on assumptions about the aptness of the courts to discharge
a welfare role which experience suggests to be questionable.

**WHY NOT AGREEMENT?**

Is there an alternative? One of the less convincing parts of the Law Commission's
report is the outright dismissal — in the face of the public opinion survey finding that

90 per cent of a representative sample of the population considered such a ground to be acceptable — of mutual consent as one ground for divorce: see Law Com 192, paras 3.13–14. The Commission says that giving or withholding consent could become a powerful weapon in the bargaining between the parties about other matters, such as the home, money, or children. However, that disadvantage — and, as pointed out above, the Commission's own scheme cannot remove the possibility of tactical manoeuvring — must surely be weighed against what might be thought to be the enormous advantage of mutual agreement: it is readily comprehensible. There must be many cases in which a couple, perhaps with the aid of lawyers, mediators or conciliators, are able to achieve a perfectly reasonable agreement without any public intervention at all. Why should we deny that this is the basis on which their divorce is to be granted? The answers which would have been self-evident in the days when dissolution of marriage was seen to be a matter exclusively preserved for the State no longer seem compelling, and refusal to recognise mutual consent as an accepted basis for divorce is inconsistent with the gradual movement of the law away from State control towards private ordering.

## ANOTHER VIEW — THE SCOTTISH LAW COMMISSION
Mutual agreement could not be the sole ground for divorce, and it is to be noted that — whatever the conventional wisdom — 84 per cent of those responding to the Commission's opinion survey believed that divorce for fault remained an acceptable basis for divorce. Against this background, is there not something to be said for the approach of the Scottish Law Commission who, on pragmatic grounds, recommended that reform should involve no more than a reduction of the periods of 'living apart' now required to establish breakdown: see Scot Law Com No. 116 (1989)? The expectation would be that unnecessary recourse to the behaviour 'fact' would be reduced and, perhaps, the offence-based 'facts' would largely wither away. However, it may be thought that there would be considerable attraction in going slightly further than simply reducing the periods, and that mutual agreement by itself should be accepted in substitution for the present 2-year living apart fact. It would, of course, remain for the court to decide (as it does at the moment) whether the arrangements relating to money and the children were such as to require its intervention.

It may be that the evolution of the divorce law — and the gradual shift, traced above, from State involvement in the divorce process — logically points to acceptance of divorce simply by unilateral demand (accompanied of course by procedures designed effectively to protect the financial position of the other spouse and the welfare of any children). As the Law Commission puts it (see *Facing the Future* (Law Com No. 170 (1988), para. 4.13) divorce on unilateral demand has the great merits of simplicity, moral neutrality and avoiding bitterness. But the available evidence (see Scot Law Com No. 116 (1989); Law Com No. 192, p. 183) suggests that such an apparently far-reaching proposal would be unlikely to be acceptable to public opinion (which seems, not yet, to share the view of many family lawyers that the legal basis upon which marriage can be dissolved is irrelevant). Legislative reform in this sensitive area requires a substantial measure of consensus and, perhaps, this influenced the Law Commission to construct a scheme which might, in reality, do little more than increase the confusion now experienced by many ordinary people who find themselves trapped in a system which they do not understand.

## Question
Are you persuaded by the Law Commission's reasons for rejecting other options in favour of the 'process over time'?

### 4.3.3   The Government's proposals

**Government White Paper,** *Looking to the Future: Mediation and the Ground for Divorce. The Government's Proposals*, **Cm** 2799
**Preface and Chapters 3 and 4**
London: HMSO, 1995

## PREFACE

*The key aspects of the Government's proposals are that they will:*

- review present arrangements for marriage preparation;
- examine how couples with marital problems can be encouraged to seek help as early as possible;
- ensure greater integration of Government policies supporting marriage with those on divorce;
- require couples to attend a compulsory information-giving session before starting the divorce process;
- remove the incentive for couples to divorce quickly by making allegations of fault;
- require a 12 month period for reflection on whether the marriage can be saved — better protection for domestic violence victims will be available during this period;
- require couples to think through and face the consequences of divorce before it happens;
- ensure that arrangements for children and other matters are settled before divorce is granted;
- allow divorce to be barred where the dissolution of the marriage would cause grave financial or other grave hardship; and
- introduce comprehensive family mediation as part of the divorce process.

*The benefits of these proposals are that they will:*

- ensure that couples whose marriages are in difficulty will be better informed about the options available to them;
- introduce a system that is better at identifying saveable marriages;
- facilitate referrals to marriage guidance when couples believe there may be some hope for the marriage;
- make available every opportunity to explore reconciliation even after the divorce process has started;
- ensure that there is an adequate period of time to test whether the marriage has genuinely broken down;
- remove the acrimony and hostility inherent in the current divorce process;
- minimise conflict and so reduce the worst effects of separation and divorce on children;
- help and protect children by encouraging parents to focus on their joint responsibility to support and care for their children;
- encourage couples to meet the responsibilities of marriage and parenthood before the marriage is dissolved;
- allow couples to make workable arrangements through family mediation in respect of their children, home and other matters following separation or divorce.

## 3.   WHAT SHOULD DIVORCE LAW AND PROCEDURES SEEK TO DO?

*Divorce Law and Its Relationship with Marriage*

  3.1   Consultees [to the Consultation Paper, *Looking to the Future: Mediation and the Ground for Divorce*] considered that the law and procedures of divorce should reflect the seriousness and permanence of the commitment involved in marriage. Furthermore, the system should require divorcing couples to consider carefully the consequences and implications of divorce before dissolution was finalised. Divorce should not be so easy that the parties have little incentive to make a success of their marriage, and, in particular, to overcome temporary difficulties.

**3.2** Marriage remains the aspiration of most people. Young people today are more likely to postpone marriage in favour of living together. Most will eventually marry with the expectation that the relationship will be for life.

**3.3** Rapid social change in recent decades has had an unparalleled impact on family life to the extent that couples often enter marriage with unrealistic expectations, and little, if any, preparation for the complexities of daily living and the demands of parenting. Sadly, few acknowledge relationship difficulties until problems have become very serious, and many couples postpone seeking professional help until breaking point has been reached.

**3.4** Consultees recognised that marriage involves mutual legal obligations which other relationships do not. This means that there must be mechanisms to enable people who are unhappily married to reorganise their legal obligations when the marriage breaks down. Otherwise, many will simply leave the marriage and set up a second home and family outside marriage. This was a common occurrence, and a major cause for concern, before divorce law was last reformed in 1969. What the law must do effectively is to provide mechanisms to create an opportunity for reflection and reconsideration and to protect the spouses and their children when things go wrong.

*The Government's Objectives*

**3.5** The Consultation Paper put forward Government's objectives for a better divorce process. These were:

- to support the institution of marriage;
- to include practicable steps to prevent the irretrievable breakdown of marriage;
- to ensure that the parties understand the practical consequences of divorce before taking any irreversible decision;
- where divorce is unavoidable, to minimise the bitterness and hostility between the parties and reduce the trauma for the children; and
- to keep to the minimum the cost to the parties and the taxpayer.

. . .

## 4.  OPTIONS FOR CHANGE

*Advantages of the government's proposals*

. . .

**4.31** The Government's proposals will mean that marriages cannot be terminated as precipitously as under the present law.

**4.32** The period of reflection is designed to save saveable marriages where possible, and to provide more convincing proof that the breakdown in the marital relationship is irreparable. In situations where the marriage has obviously and irreparably broken down before the period begins, consideration of the practical consequences will be a much more constructive use of the time spent before the divorce is obtained than is presently the case. Where there remains any doubt as to whether the marriage has broken down at the beginning of the period, a more active preparation for life apart will provide a far more cogent test of whether the parties have a future together.

**4.33** When faced with the problems of dealing with the practical consequences of divorce, some couples may come to realise that they need to re-consider their position, and, perhaps with the help of counselling, find some way of re-negotiating their relationship so that they and their children can have a future together.

**4.34** At the same time, the Government's proposals will help to avoid the major defects in the present law. The damage done by the present encouragement to rely on facts that require allegations of fault irrespective of the real reasons for breakdown will be removed. The couple will, however, be obliged to consider in detail what arrangements should be made for the future before committing themselves irrevocably to divorce. The court will have power to deal with these practical questions before rather than after the divorce, so there will be no rush to obtain a divorce simply in order to be in a position to deal with finance and property. There will be every opportunity to draw back and think again.

**4.35** The period will allow the parties time to consider marriage guidance without prejudice to their position if they subsequently decide to seek a divorce. This will mean that those who initiate the divorce process as a 'cry for help' will be more likely than in the present system to receive the help they need. The period will provide many opportunities to withdraw from the process in the event that parties change their minds, either as a result of attendance at marriage guidance counselling or for some other reason. The removal of the need to make allegations of fault will help to avoid parties becoming polarised at the outset. The period will also create an opportunity for the parties to consider the arrangements for a life apart before the divorce is finalised, in the event that they decide that the marriage is not capable of being saved.

**4.36** The Government's proposals also recognise that divorce can sometimes be a joint decision, responsibly agreed upon between the parties. Many consultees felt strongly that any move towards encouraging and helping couples to take joint responsibility for the breakdown in the marriage, and the consequences that flow from it, would be a positive step.

**4.37** . . . research has demonstrated that children are greatly harmed by conflict between their parents, especially if they are drawn into that conflict as go-betweens or intermediaries, as happens all too often in present divorce cases. A divorce process based on a requirement to reflect rather than recriminate will help to reduce conflict and encourage cooperation, which will in turn minimise the distress caused to children.

**4.38** The Government's proposals for introducing a wider use of family mediation in the divorce process . . . will also assist in that aim. These two reforms are complementary. The process of family mediation is more likely to be effective in the context of a divorce process that does not artificially and unnecessarily heighten conflict between the parties. Conversely, the law of divorce cannot provide the help and support that divorcing couples need when coming to terms with the breakdown in their relationship and in the making of arrangements for a life apart. Mediation would provide that help and support.

## Deech, Ruth, 'Comment: Not Just Marriage Breakdown'
[1994] Fam Law 121

. . . Divorce is sad and painful when it is not the wish of both spouses. It is expensive and it is devastating in many cases to the future of the children, according to long-term studies. Yet every 20 years or so, we ease divorce law, claiming that marital breakdown is attributable to changing social factors and not to the law. Every successive attempt during this century to bring statute law into line with 'reality' has resulted in an increase in the divorce rate. The increased divorce rate results in greater familiarity with divorce as a solution to marital problems, more willingness to use it and to make legislative provision for its aftermath. The resultant pressure on the divorce system leads to a relaxation of practice and procedure (for example, the special procedure), then to a call for a change in the law in order to bring it into line with 'reality', and then to yet another increase in divorce. One can readily predict that if the Lord Chancellor's proposals are enacted, the queue for mediation will soon become so long, and the mediation process so short that it will be labelled a meaningless formality, ripe for reform, and the law will be changed again to remove even this feeble attempt at controlling the breakdown rate.

The 1960s' predictions of the Law Commission concerning divorce can now be seen to have been totally wrong. Today's predictions are unlikely to be any more accurate. The reforms should be recognised for what they are: an attempt to spend even less on the poorest spouses who rely on legal aid, by placing them in the hands of the mediators. The few remaining advantages that wives have in the divorce process will be removed and the divorce rate will rise once again, leading to greater long-term costs and expenditure on broken families. Is this to be England's contribution to the International Year of the Family?

An alternative is the development of a factually based marriage education pro-gramme for schools. Another is to acknowledge the effects of divorce law and re-examine it with a view to restraint, providing, for example, that no decree may be made absolute until at least 12 months have passed from the date of the petition. This small reform would achieve the one sound element of the Green Paper. The current clamour over the Child Support Agency makes clear men's reluctance to support the families they have left behind them. It should also make us reconsider the wisdom of placing even more decisions about broken families in the hands of non-lawyers.

### Cretney, Stephen, 'The Divorce White Paper — Some Reflections' [1995] Fam Law 302

. . . the White Paper seems curiously naive about what is likely to happen during the 'period of reflection'. Far from spending the evenings, as the White Paper, para. 4.16 suggests, 'reflecting on whether their marriage can be saved and, if not, to face up to the consequences of their actions and make arrangements to meet their responsibili-ties' some, at least, of those concerned seem likely to spend the time in the far more pleasurable activity of conceiving — necessarily illegitimate — babies. Some will spend the time exploiting their emotional or financial advantage; others will brood on their grievances. Those who are able to do so will, surely, want to go to the court to exercise pressure to bring matters to a head . . . .

*Question*
Is this a cynical view?

## 4.4   THE NEW LAW: FAMILY LAW ACT 1996

### 4.4.1   Family Law Act 1996, Part I

Part I lays down general principles which apply to Parts II and III of the 1996 Act.

# FAMILY LAW ACT 1996

## 1. The general principles underlying Parts II and III
The court and any person, in exercising functions under or in consequence of Parts II and III, shall have regard to the following general principles—

(a)   that the institution of marriage is to be supported;

(b)   that the parties to a marriage which may have broken down are to be encouraged to take all practicable steps, whether by marriage counselling or otherwise, to save the marriage;

(c)   that a marriage which has irretrievably broken down and is being brought to an end should be brought to an end—

(i)   with minimum distress to the parties and to the children affected;

(ii)   with questions dealt with in a manner designed to promote as good a continuing relationship between the parties and any children affected as is possible in the circumstances; and

(iii)   without costs being unreasonably incurred in connection with the procedures to be followed in bringing the marriage to an end; and

(d)   that any risk to one of the parties to a marriage, and to any children, of violence from the other party should, so far as reasonably practicable, be removed or diminished.

## Lewis, Jane, 'Marriage Saving Revisited'
[1996] Fam Law 423

... The Finer Report [Cmd 5629, London: HMSO, 1974] tackled the larger issue of whether law had any place in trying to control marital behaviour, for example by making marriage and divorce more difficult. It decided that it did not on the grounds that such legislation inevitably imposed a stricter code of familial conduct and sexual morality on one section of society (the poor) than another, and that this was out of keeping in a liberal democratic State. From a right wing perspective just over 20 years later Theresa Gorman argued in the standing committee on the Family Law Bill that such intervention smacked of the 'nanny state' interfering in people's personal lives where it had no business to be. The argument against using divorce law to support marriage can also be made on pragmatic grounds. Martin Richards at [1996] Fam Law 153 has pointed out that, taking the long view, changes in divorce law have had little effect on the extent to which people have sought to end relationships.

Certainly rates of informal separation and cohabitation were probably high at the beginning of this century when access to divorce was extremely restricted, something that the 1912 *Report of the Royal Commission on Divorce and Matrimonial Causes* sought to correct by relaxing the grounds for divorce and thus making remarriage easier. The decades following the second world war were different in that marriage became increasingly the norm and took place at younger and younger ages. There was, in fact, an increase in sexual activity outside marriage and an increased pregnancy rate, but there was still a tendency to marry. A majority of births to women under 20 were conceived out of marriage, but the majority of pre-maritally conceived births took place inside marriage. In addition, divorce rates remained low. The trends in marriage patterns since the beginning of the 1970s have been very different with substantial declines in marriage rates, less marriage and older marriage, the huge rise in divorce rates that plateaued from the 1980s, and the emergence of widespread cohabitation. The growth in cohabitation is signalled by the dramatic rise in extra-marital births since the mid-1980s, together with the fall in the marital birth rate. While the 1960s saw a separation of sex and marriage, the 1980s have seen more of a separation between marriage and parenthood.

This, of course, helps to explain the anxiety expressed by members of Parliament about marriage. However, given the unmistakable trend away from marriage and towards cohabitation, any attempt to make divorce more difficult (which is how many of the Family Law Bill's proposals will be perceived), or indeed to make marriage more difficult, may only succeed in driving up the rate of cohabitation. There is remarkably little research on marriage and we do not know the reasons for its decline, but both greater individualisation and the changing nature of risk in a society in which uncertainty, particularly in terms of employment, has re-emerged, must play a major part. Support for marriage and parenthood is necessary, but the divorce law is not the place for it. Like the Child Support Act 1991 and the Children Act 1989, moves towards making reconciliation a more active component of divorce legislation emphasise individual responsibility. While there is merit in this, it cannot be the whole answer when the number of children living in households with below 50% of average income trebled to 3.9 million between 1979 and 1991. The UK is one of the few European countries not to have taken seriously the problems parents face in combining family and work. In France it is an explicit policy goal to help parents to do this, while in the UK the Government remains officially neutral on the subject, with the result that mothers and fathers, husbands and wives, must work out their own salvation. The UK is bottom of the child-care league and has opposed European Commission proposals in respect of parental leave. There is also increasing evidence as to a lack of investment in children on the part of Government, not only in terms of the increasing levels of child poverty but also in terms of education. Kathleen Kiernan's ('Family Change: Parenthood, Partnership and Policy', in Halpern, Wood, White and Cameron *Options for Britain* (Dartmouth, 1996)) data suggest that a strong predictor of young unmarried motherhood is poor educational attainment. There are definite limits as to what private as opposed to public law can be expected to achieve.

*Questions*
1.   Should marriage saving be one of the main aims of a good divorce law? Will the new law save marriages, or will it deter couples from marrying at all and increase the rate of cohabitation? Would failed marriages be best avoided by making it harder to get married, rather than making it harder to get divorced?
2.   How will the period of consideration and reflection bolster the institution of marriage when the parties will at the same time be being encouraged to settle disputes about property, finance and children?

### 4.4.2   Family Law Act 1996, Part II

Part II of the 1996 Act makes provision in respect of divorce and separation. The rules in respect of separations are almost the same as those for divorce. The law of nullity remains unchanged (see Chapter 2).

## FAMILY LAW ACT 1996

*Court orders*

**2.   Divorce and separation**
   (1)   The court may—
      (a)   by making an order (to be known as a divorce order), dissolve a marriage . . .

(2)   Any such order comes into force on being made.

. . .

### 3.   Circumstances in which orders are made

(1)   If an application for a divorce order . . . is made to the court under this section by one or both of the parties to a marriage, the court shall make the order applied for (but only if)—

(a)   the marriage has broken down irretrievably;

(b)   the requirements of section 8 about information meetings are satisfied;

(c)   the requirements of section 9 about the parties' arrangements for the future are satisfied; and

(d)   the application has not been withdrawn.

(2)   A divorce order may not be made if an order preventing divorce is in force under section 10.

*Notes*

*1.*   Section 8 provides that a party must (except in prescribed circumstances) have attended an information meeting not less than three months before making the statement of marital breakdown (s. 8(2)). At the meeting relevant information must be given to the party or parties, who must be given the opportunity and be encouraged to meet with a marriage counsellor (s. 8(6)). Regulations made under s. 8(6) must in particular provide information about: marriage counselling and support services; the importance of the child's welfare and how children cope with divorce; the nature of financial questions that may arise on divorce; protection against violence; mediation; the availability of independent legal advice; legal aid; and the divorce process (s. 8(9)).

*2.*   Section 9(2) provides that one of the following must be produced to the court as proof that the parties have made arrangements for the future:

(a)   a court order (made by consent or otherwise) dealing with their financial arrangements;

(b)   a negotiated agreement as to their financial arrangements;

(c)   a declaration by both parties that they have made their financial arrangements;

(d)   a declaration by one of the parties (to which no objection has been notified to the court by the other party) that:

(i)   he has no significant assets and does not intend to make an application for financial provision,

(ii)   he believes that the other party has no significant assets and does not intend to make an application for financial provision, and

(iii)   there are therefore no financial arrangements to be made.

If the parties' arrangements for the future include a division of pension assets or rights under s. 25B of the 1973 Act, a statutory declaration is required (s. 9(8)). The court may make a divorce order where the applicant has not provided proof that arrangements have been made for the future (as required by s. 9(2)) if the applicant has taken reasonable steps during the period for reflection and consideration to reach agreement about the parties' financial arrangements but (s. 9(7)):

(a)   the other party has delayed or been obstructive in making financial arrangements (sch. 1, para. 1); or

(b)   the applicant, the other party or a child of the family has suffered ill health, disability or injury and the resulting delay in making a divorce order would be significantly detrimental to the welfare of any child of the family or would be seriously prejudicial to the applicant (sch. 1, para. 2); or

(c)   the applicant has found it impossible to contact the other party (sch. 1, para. 3); or

(d)   an occupation order or non-molestation order is in force and any delay in making a divorce order would be significantly detrimental to the welfare of any child of the family or would be seriously prejudicial to the applicant (sch. 1, para. 4).

3.   An order under s.10 (see s. 3(2), supra) is an order that the marriage not be dissolved (i.e. an 'order preventing divorce'), which the court may make only if it is satisfied that dissolution of the marriage will result in substantial financial or other hardship to the other party or to a child of the family; and that it would be wrong, in all the circumstances (including the conduct of the parties and the interests of any child of the family), for the marriage to be dissolved (s. 10(2)). 'Hardship' includes the loss of a chance to obtain a future benefit (as well as the loss of an existing benefit) (s. 10(6)).

## FAMILY LAW ACT 1996

*Marital breakdown*

### 5.   Marital breakdown

(1)   A marriage is to be taken to have broken down irretrievably if (but only if)—

(a)   a statement has been made by one (or both) of the parties that the maker of the statement (or each of them) believes that the marriage has broken down;

(b)   the statement complies with the requirements of section 6;

(c)   the period for reflection and consideration fixed by section 7 has ended; and

(d)   the application under section 3 is accompanied by a declaration by the party making the application that—

(i)   having reflected on the breakdown, and

(ii)   having considered the requirements of this Part as to the parties' arrangements for the future,

the applicant believes that the marriage cannot be saved.

. . .

### 6.   Statement of marital breakdown

(1)   A statement under section 5(1)(a) is to be known as a statement of marital breakdown; but in this Part it is generally referred to as 'a statement'.

(2)   If a statement is made by one party it must also state that that party—

(a)   is aware of the purpose of the period for reflection and consideration as described in section 7; and

(b)   wishes to make arrangements for the future.

(3)   If a statement is made by both parties it must also state that each of them—

(a)   is aware of the purpose of the period for reflection and consideration as described in section 7; and

(b)   wishes to make arrangements for the future.

. . .

*Note*

The statement and the application made under s. 3 above need not be made by the same party (s. 5(2)). An application for divorce may not be made under s. 3 by reference to a particular statement if:

(a)   the parties have jointly given notice withdrawing the statement; or

(b)   one year (i.e. 'the specified period') has passed since the end of the period for reflection and consideration (s. 5(3)).

## FAMILY LAW ACT 1996

*Reflection and consideration*

### 7.   Period for reflection and consideration

(1)   Where a statement has been made, a period for the parties—

(a)   to reflect on whether the marriage can be saved and to have an opportunity to effect a reconciliation, and

(b)   to consider what arrangements should be made for the future,

must pass before an application for a divorce order . . . may be made by reference to that statement.

(2)   That period is to be known as the period for reflection and consideration.

(3)   The period for reflection and consideration is nine months beginning with the fourteenth day after the day on which the statement is received by the court.

. . .

*Notes*

1.   The period for reflection and consideration lasts for an extra six months (15 months in total) where there are children aged under 16 (s. 7(11) and (13)), except where an occupation order or a non-molestation order is in force (s. 7(12)(a)), or where delaying the divorce order would be significantly detrimental to any child (s. 7(12)(b)). The period of nine months may be extended where there is delay (s. 7(4)), or the possibility of a reconciliation (s. 7(8)) or where a party seeks further time (s. 7(10) and (13)).

2.   Section 11 makes provision for the welfare of children (see Chapter 9). Sections 15–18 deal with financial provision (see Chapter 5). Section 19 provides that the court has jurisdiction to hear divorce proceedings if:

(a)   at least one party was domiciled in England and Wales on the statement date; or

(b)   at least one party was habitually resident in England and Wales throughout the period of one year ending with the statement date; or

(c) nullity proceedings are pending when the divorce proceedings commence.

*Questions*
1.  Is the new law a disguised form of divorce by unilateral demand, or divorce by mutual consent?
2.  Will the new law increase the divorce rate? Will the new law make divorce harder or easier?
3.  What is the purpose of the period for reflection and consideration? Is it the right length? Should there have been a shorter period for divorces where both parties wish to divorce and are in agreement about the consequences? Is there any sense in making the period longer where there are children?
4.  Do the reforms expect too much of human nature?
5.  Under the new law it will be possible for an adulterous husband with dependent children to obtain a divorce, even though his wife has been an exemplary wife and mother. Is this just or satisfactory? How will the law protect such a wife?
6.  Are domestic violence victims adequately protected by the new law? Is the court likely to make more occupation and non-molestation orders under the new law than hitherto? Will the new law encourage violence in the home?
7.  Will the reforms render the marriage contract almost worthless?

## 4.5  MEDIATION AND DIVORCE

(See also Chapter 1 on mediation.)

### 4.5.1  The Government's proposals

**Government White Paper, *Looking to the Future: Mediation and the Ground for Divorce. The Government's Proposals*, Cm 2799**
London: HMSO, 1995

*Family mediation — introduction*
5.1   Separation and divorce constitute a painful process for all the family members concerned, but particularly for children. As well as coping with the emotional stress produced by the breakdown in their marriage, the separating couple have to begin to reorganise significant aspects of their lives. Questions relating to where and with whom the children should live, how contact between the children and the non-resident parent should be organised, how the children are to be financially supported and whether the matrimonial home should be sold or the tenancy transferred, are all questions which have to be resolved. These can be very painful issues.
5.2   The legal process and procedures and the means by which arrangements are concluded can add considerably to the stress and pain suffered by the couple and their children. The way in which these arrangements are negotiated can also affect the financial cost of the divorce whether to the couple concerned or, where one or both parties are legally aided, to the State.
5.3   The Law Commission in its Report recommended the use of mediation as a means of couples negotiating their own arrangements surrounding their separation

and divorce. The Commission saw mediation as a major element in the development of a more constructive approach to the problems of marital breakdown and divorce.

*The Usefulness of Family Mediation*

5.4   Family mediation is a process in which an impartial third person, the mediator, assists couples considering separation or divorce to meet together to deal with the arrangements which need to be made for the future. Because the parties discuss these matters face to face, family mediation is much better able to identify marriages which might be capable of being saved than is the legal process. Family mediation can encourage couples to:

- seek marital counselling if it is appropriate to attempt to save the marriage;
- accept responsibility for the ending of the marriage;
- acknowledge that there may be conflict and hostility, and a strong desire to allege fault and attribute blame;
- deal with their feelings of hurt and anger;
- address issues which may impede their ability to negotiate settlements amicably, particularly the conduct of one spouse;
- focus on the needs of their children rather than on their own personal needs.

5.5   Unlike current legal processes, mediation is a flexible process which can take into account the different needs of families, and differing attitudes and positions of the parties. Since one partner may be more prepared than the other for the ending of the marriage, mediation can enable them to plan for the future at a pace which suits them both and within a timescale which does not push them into making hasty and ill-considered decisions.

5.6   Family mediation has as its primary objectives:

- to help separating and divorcing couples to reach their own agreed joint decisions about future arrangements;
- to improve communications between them; and
- to help couples work together on the practical consequences of divorce with particular emphasis on their joint responsibilities to co-operate as parents in bringing up their children.

Mediators are trained to help couples talk about what they each want for the future and to focus on protecting the best interests of their children, even when talking together may be difficult and painful because they are angry, hurt and confused. They are encouraged to talk about the issues in their own way, using language which is familiar, thus enabling them both to say what they want to each other.

5.7   Under the current system, couples need not resolve painful issues until very late in the divorce process. This usually means after the marriage has been dissolved and, quite often, after at least one party has already remarried and taken on new responsibilities. Use of mediation may not significantly reduce the emotional pain of divorce for the couple or their children, but it can help couples to come to terms with what is happening in their lives. Mediation is likely to ensure that, by the time the divorce is granted by the court, important issues about the welfare of children, accommodation, finance and property have been tackled and resolved in many if not all cases.

5.8   Mediation is an alternative to negotiating matters at arms length through two separate lawyers and to litigating through the courts. It can offer couples a constructive framework for using the period between initiating the divorce process and the making of a final divorce order for profitable reflection and consideration.

**5.9** An increased use of mediation and the development of its potential would mean substantial changes to the divorce process in order to take advantage of the underlying principles and philosophy of mediation. The mediation process is not concerned with allegations but with issues. It encourages the couple to come to terms with the past, look to the future, meet each other on equal terms, and, with the assistance of a neutral third party, reach decisions about the matters they need to address in relation to the future.

. . .

**5.26** The Government recognizes that for the majority of couples whose marriage fails, divorce constitutes a painful and difficult process. It is particularly painful for children. Regrettably no law or procedure connected with separation and divorce can mend marriages or make divorce pleasant, or those going through the divorce process happy. The law, procedures and methods used to deal with the consequences of marriage breakdown can, however, make matters worse.

**5.27** The Government is therefore of the view that a more constructive means of making arrangements for a life apart should be made available to couples in the form of mediation.

*Note*

Part III of the FLA 1996 makes provision for legal aid for mediation in family matters by inserting Part IIIA into the Legal Aid Act 1988 after s. 13. Under s. 13B, any contract entered into by the Legal Aid Board for the provision of mediation must require the mediator to comply with a code of practice, which must require the mediator to have arrangements designed to ensure that:

(a)   the parties participate in mediation only if willing and not influenced by fear of violence or other harm;

(b)   cases where either party may be influenced by fear of violence or other harm are identified as soon as possible;

(c)   the possibility of reconciliation is kept under review throughout mediation; and

(d)   each party is informed about the availability of independent legal advice (Legal Aid Act 1988, s. 13B(7)).

Where there are any children, the code must also require the mediator to have arrangements designed to ensure that the parties are encouraged to consider:

(a)   the welfare, wishes and feelings of each child; and

(b)   whether and to what extent each child should be given the opportunity to express his or her wishes and feelings in the mediation (s. 13B(8)).

Section 15(3F) of the Legal Aid Act 1988 provides that a person shall not be granted representation for the purposes of proceedings relating to family matters unless he has attended a meeting with a mediator to determine whether mediation appears suitable to the dispute, the parties and all the circumstances, and, in particular, whether mediation could take place without either party being influenced by fear of violence or other harm; and, if mediation does appear suitable, to help the person applying for representation to decide whether instead to apply for mediation. Section 15(3F) does not apply to proceedings under Part IV of the FLA 1996, s. 37 of the MCA 1973, and Parts IV or V of the Children Act 1989 (Legal Aid Act 1988, s. 15(3G)).

## Bissett-Johnson, Alastair, and Barton, Chris, 'The Divorce White Paper' [1995] Fam Law 349

. . . The mediation process is not suitable for every spouse, especially the clinically depressed, those not used to negotiating on their own behalf, those dominated by their partner or subjected to violence by their partner. A mediator, however well trained, has limited weapons in the case of inequality of bargaining power.

Mediation is no excuse for a spouse not having good quality, independent legal advice before entering into the mediation process. Mediation's main claim to attention, as Government-sponsored reports indicated in 1989 and 1990, lies in the reduction of acrimony between the parties (quality of life benefits) rather than reduction of expenditure of legal aid (costs-reduction benefits) however desirable these may be.

*Questions*
What is the primary objective of the increased role for mediation? Is settlement always desirable? Is failure to settle necessarily always negative?

*Further reading*
Bainham, A., 'Divorce and the Lord Chancellor: Looking to the Future or Getting Back to Basics?' (1994) 53 CLJ 253.

Bird, R., and Cretney, S., *Divorce: the New Law*, Bristol: Jordans, 1996.

Davies, C., 'Divorce Reform in England and Wales. A Visitor's View' [1993] Fam Law 331.

Davis, G., 'Mediation and the Ground for Divorce: A New Era of Enlightenment or an Orwellian Nightmare?' [1994] Fam Law 103.

Davis, G., 'Divorce Reform — Peering Anxiously into the Future' [1995] Fam Law 564.

Davis, G., and Murch, M., *Grounds for Divorce*, Oxford: Clarendon Press, 1988.

Davis, G., 'Grounds for Divorce and the Law Commission Discussion Paper' [1989] Fam Law 182.

Deech, R., 'Divorce Law and Empirical Studies' (1990) 106 LQR 229.

Eekelaar, J., 'The Family Law Bill: The Politics of Family Law' [1996] Fam Law 46.

Freeman, M., *Divorce: Where Next?*, Aldershot: Dartmouth, 1996.

Grose-Hodge, P., 'Divorce — Development rather than Transition' [1993] Fam Law 419.

Ingleby, R., 'Court Sponsored Mediation: The Case Against Mandatory Participation' (1993) 56 MLR 441.

Kaganas, F., and Piper, C., 'The Divorce Consultation Paper and Domestic Violence' [1994] Fam Law 143.

Mears, M., 'Getting it Wrong Again: Divorce and the Law Commission' [1991] Fam Law 231.
McCarthy, P., and Walker, J., 'Mediation and Divorce Reform — the Lawyer's View' [1995] Fam Law 361.
Pembridge, E., 'Comment: Two-Tier Divorce' [1995] Fam Law 345.
Roberts, S., 'Alternative Dispute Resolution and Civil Justice: An Unresolved Relationship' (1993) 56 MLR 452.
Shepherd, N., 'Green Paper — Red Alert' [1994] Fam Law 65.
Schuz, R., 'Divorce Reform' [1993] Fam Law 580 and 630.
Walker, J., 'Divorce — Whose Fault? Is the Law Commission Getting it Right?' [1991] Fam Law 234.

## 4.6  RECOGNITION OF FOREIGN DIVORCES

Part II of the Family Law Act (FLA) 1986 lays down rules for the recognition in the United Kingdom of foreign divorces (and annulments and separations). It does so by making a distinction between divorces obtained in proceedings (judicial or otherwise) and divorces otherwise obtained. The jurisdictional basis for recognition is much broader for divorces obtained in proceedings.

## FAMILY LAW ACT 1986

**46.  Grounds for recognition**
    (1)  The validity of an overseas divorce . . . obtained by means of proceedings shall be recognised [in the UK] if—
    (a)  the divorce . . . is effective under the law of the country in which it was obtained; and
    (b)  at the relevant date either party to the marriage—
        (i)  was habitually resident in the country in which the divorce . . . was obtained; or
        (ii)  was domiciled in that country; or
        (iii)  was a national of that country.
    (2)  The validity of an overseas divorce . . . obtained otherwise than by means of proceedings shall be recognised [in the UK] if—
    (a)  the divorce . . . is effective under the law of the country in which it was obtained;
    (b)  at the relevant date—
        (i)  each party to the marriage was domiciled in that country; or
        (ii)  either party to the marriage was domiciled in that country and the other party was domiciled in a country under whose law the divorce . . . is recognised as valid; and
    (c)  neither party to the marriage was habitually resident in the United Kingdom throughout the period of one year immediately preceding that date.
    . . .

*Notes*
*1.*  The 'relevant date' for a divorce obtained by proceedings is the date of the commencement of the proceedings; and for other divorces is the date on which the divorce was obtained (s. 46(3)).

2. The court may refuse to recognise an overseas divorce on certain grounds, including refusal on the ground that recognition would be manifestly contrary to public policy (s. 52). In *Eroglu* v *Eroglu* [1994] 2 FLR 287, FD, the wife argued that her Turkish divorce should not be recognised in England and Wales on the ground of public policy since it had been obtained by fraud (they had divorced in Turkey so that her husband could escape Turkish national service). She did so because she wished to petition for divorce in the English courts. Her petition for a divorce in England was dismissed, as her Turkish divorce was held to be valid.

3. In some cases, a divorce may be 'transnational' (i.e., it takes place in two different countries), e.g. the Jewish *get* and the Muslim *talaq*. The English courts have refused to recognise such divorces even though the failure to do so creates a 'limping marriage', i.e. the marriage is recognised as valid in country A but not in country B. The leading authority is *R* v *Secretary of State for the Home Department, ex parte Ghulam Fatima* [1986] AC 527, HL, where a Muslim *talaq* was not recognised. *Fatima* was applied in *Berkovits* v *Grinberg (Attorney-General Intervening)* [1995] Fam 142, FD, where the court refused to recognise a Jewish *get* written by the husband in London but delivered to his wife in Israel.

(For applications for financial relief in England and Wales after a foreign divorce, see Chapter 5.)

*Further reading*
Conway, H., 'New Provisions for Jewish Divorce' [1996] Fam Law 638.
McClean, D., 'The Non-Recognition of Transnational Divorces' (1996) 112 LQR 230.
Reed, A., 'Extra-judicial Divorces since *Berkovits*' [1996] Fam Law 100.

# 5 FINANCE AND PROPERTY ON DIVORCE

## 5.1 INTRODUCTION

On marriage breakdown it will usually be necessary for the parties to make arrangements about the distribution and reallocation of their property and financial assets. Some couples may do so on their own, but others may seek legal advice either because they cannot reach agreement, or because they need professional advice to ensure that their assets are distributed fairly between them. Some couples may seek the assistance of mediators to help facilitate agreement. Where, however, a divorcing couple cannot reach agreement about property and financial matters after mediation or after negotiations between lawyers, a court order may be sought under Part II of the MCA 1973, which, with the Family Proceedings Rules (FPR) 1991, governs the law applicable to finance and property on divorce (and also on nullity and judicial separation). When the new divorce law is implemented under Parts I and II of the FLA 1996 (see Chapter 4), Part II of the 1973 Act will remain in force but with amendments made by sch. 2 of the 1996 Act.

The handling and management of a case will depend on the needs and resources of the parties. At one end of the spectrum, the parties may be living in rented council accommodation and in receipt of welfare benefits. At the other end, the parties may have several houses, substantial income and vast amounts of capital (see, e.g., *Dart* v *Dart* [1996] 2 FLR 286, CA, at 5.3.4 below). The ages of the parties and whether they have any children will also have a significant impact on the outcome of any dispute. A particularly important concern will be future housing needs and the future of the matrimonial home. Another concern, particularly for wives, may be about lost pension entitlement caused by the divorce.

While some cases are litigated in the courts, most are not; litigation is expensive, time-consuming and unpredictable. The following extract provides some idea of the reality of the situation in respect of property and financial matters on divorce.

**Davis, Gwynn, Cretney, Stephen, and Collins, Jean,** *Simple Quarrels*
Oxford: Clarendon Press, 1994, p. 253

The resolution of financial and property disputes on divorce is an identifiable sphere of legal practice and of academic study. Most of what is written on the subject, whether it be aimed at students, academics, or practitioners, is concerned with statute and case law — that is to say, with reports of court decisions which are thought to clarify or refine statue in some way. The focus, then, is upon adjudication. These reported cases offer a guide to practitioners who are attempting to settle cases, and to judges when they have to try them. But these case reports offer comparatively little insight into the routine reality of the divorce process, either for practitioners or the parties. Reading them, one might be tempted to think that divorce is all about getting decisions from a court. This is not so. For most divorcing couples, a decision of the court is as remote a prospect as the summit of Mount Everest viewed from base camp. Divorce, they come to realize, is a process. This may involve attendance at court, but such occasions are seldom decisive. It also involves frequent visits to a solicitor; letters, phone calls, and affidavits; the occasional consultation with a barrister; more letters, phone calls, and affidavits; an application for a penal notice; an application for committal; a hearing on maintenance pending suit — and so on. All this time the divorcing couple may be in direct communication with one another, or they may not. This activity — or, as it might be more accurate to say, the passage of this amount of time — is not represented in any account of court decisions. . . .

*Note*
*Simple Quarrels* was written as the result of a research study in which 80 money and/or property disputes were followed from initial court application to final resolution.

## 5.2   ORDERS THAT CAN BE MADE

Under ss. 23, 24 and 24A of the MCA 1973, the court has jurisdiction to make the following financial provision or property adjustment orders against a party to a marriage on or after a decree nisi of divorce:

- periodical payments (secured or unsecured) and/or lump sum for the other party to the marriage;
- periodical payments (secured or unsecured) and/or lump sum to or for the benefit of a child of the family;
- a transfer of property to the other party and/or to or for the benefit of a child of the family;
- a settlement of property for the benefit of the other party and/or the benefit of the children;
- a variation of any ante-nuptial or post-nuptial settlement for the benefit of one or both of the parties and/or any child of the family, or an order

extinguishing or reducing the interest of either party under such settlement;
- an order for sale of property.

The court also has jurisdiction to make an order for maintenance pending the divorce suit (s. 22), and an order to prevent the dissipation of financial assets pending the outcome of proceedings for finance and property orders (s. 37). The court has jurisdiction to make orders by consent (s. 33A). An order for sale may be made only when or after making a secured periodical payments order, a lump sum order or a property adjustment order (s. 24A). Applications for child support maintenance must in most cases be made to the Child Support Agency under the Child Support Acts 1991 and 1995 (see Chapter 9). Financial provision orders and property orders for children are also available under sch. 1 of the Children Act 1989 (see Chapter 9). A major amendment made to Part II of the MCA 1973 by the FLA 1996 is that orders for finance and property may be made before divorce rather than after as is the case now (FLA 1996, s. 15(2) and sch. 2). The orders will be much the same, except for some changes in detail, in particular as to when they come into effect. During the period for reflection and consideration the court will have jurisdiction, however, to make interim periodical payments and interim lump sum orders, but not property adjustment orders (MCA 1973, s. 22A(4), as amended by the FLA 1996).

*Question*
Is there any coherence in a system where child support is dealt with by administrative procedures and other financial and property matters are dealt with in a discretionary system by lawyers, judges and mediators?

## 5.3   EXERCISE OF JUDICIAL DISCRETION

### 5.3.1   Wide judicial discretion

Under Part II of the MCA 1973, the divorce court has wide discretion to distribute and reallocate property and finance irrespective of ownership, and whether or not there is any relationship between the resource in question and the marriage. In fact '[v]irtually all the economically significant assets of the two spouses are put at the disposition of the court' (Davis *et al.*, *Simple Quarrels*, 1994).

*Gojkovic* v *Gojkovic (No. 2)*
[1992] Fam 40
Court of Appeal

BUTLER-SLOSS LJ: . . . Each case must be decided on its own facts and in accordance with the principles set out in section 25 of the Matrimonial Causes Act

1973, as amended by the Matrimonial and Family Proceedings Act 1984. The wide discretion of the court under section 25 must not be fettered. . . .

## Hanlon v The Law Society
## [1981] AC 124
## Court of Appeal

LORD DENNING MR: . . . The law takes the rights and obligations of the parties all together and puts the pieces into a mixed bag. Such pieces are the right to occupy the matrimonial home or to have a share in it, the obligation to maintain the wife and children, and so forth. The court then takes out the pieces and hands them to the two parties — some to one party and some to the other — so that each can provide for the future with the pieces allotted to him or to her. The court hands them out without paying any too nice a regard to their legal or equitable rights but simply according to what is the fairest provision for the future, for mother and father and the children. . . .

## Maclean, M., and Johnston, J., 'Alimony or Compensation'
## [1990] Fam Law 148

. . . With the British preference for a large element of judicial discretion in deciding the financial arrangements made on divorce, we retain a level of flexibility in seeking the best possible outcome for the largest number of participants, much envied in rule-based jurisdictions. For example, in California the 50/50 property division requirement has the effect of forcing the sale of the matrimonial home. This contrasts with the British system which tries hard to keep the children in the family home while not depriving the husband of his interest in the property. . . .

## Thomas v Thomas
## [1995] 2 FLR 688
## Court of Appeal

WAITE LJ: . . . The discretionary powers conferred on the court by the amended ss 23–25A of the Matrimonial Causes Act 1973 to redistribute the assets of spouses are almost limitless. That represents an acknowledgement by Parliament that if justice is to be achieved between spouses at divorce the court must be equipped, in a society where the forms of wealth-holding are diverse and often sophisticated, to penetrate outer forms and get to the heart of ownership. For their part, the judges who administer this jurisdiction have traditionally accepted the Shakespearean principle that 'it is excellent to have a giant's strength but tyrannous to use it like a giant'. The precise boundaries of that judicial self-restraint have never been rigidly defined nor could they be, if the jurisdiction is to retain its flexibility. But certain principles emerge from the authorities. One is that the court is not obliged to limit its orders exclusively to resources of capital or income which are shown actually to exist. The availability of unidentified resources may, for example, be inferred from a spouse's expenditure or style of living, or from his inability or unwillingness to allow the complexity of his affairs to be penetrated with the precision necessary to ascertain his actual wealth or the degree of liquidity of his assets. Another is that where a spouse enjoys access to wealth but no absolute entitlement to it (as in the case, for example, of a beneficiary under a discretionary trust or someone who is dependent on the generosity of a relative), the court will not act in direct invasion of the rights of, or usurp the discretion exercisable by, a third party. Nor will it put upon a third party undue pressure to act in a way which will enhance the means of the maintaining spouse. This does not, however, mean that the court acts in total disregard of the potential availability of wealth from sources owned or administered by others. . . .

## Jackson, Emily, and Wasoff, Fran, with Maclean, Mavis, and Emerson Dobash, Rebecca, 'Financial Support on Divorce: the Right Mixture of Rules and Discretion' [1993] 7 IJL&F 230

. . . The fundamental financial problem faced by divorcing spouses is that the resources which have sustained one family unit must now support two households. It is clear that families become accustomed to a lifestyle which uses all the available resources, and it will rarely be possible to maintain this standard of living for all family members once their housing costs are effectively doubled. A balance must be struck between competing needs and available resources. This involves a complicated process of deducing needs and expectations, arranging them in a hierarchy, and then attempting to maximize their fulfilment within the limits provided by the brute facts of existing income and capital.

The law has a role in this process. Custodial parents need to know how much they can expect absent parents to contribute so that they can plan family expenditure with some certainty. They need to have the distribution expressed authoritatively by the law so that they can enforce it in the courts in case of default. In turn, absent parents need to be able to know the extent of their obligation to their first family so that they can budget accordingly. The state must know family income and capital levels so that it can calculate welfare entitlements.

The aggregate income will generally be inadequate to meet all the desires and expectations of the former family members. There must be a compromise, and the role of law is to provide a framework of rules and objectives to guide the nature of the settlement, giving strength to legitimate claims and affording some certainty in order to facilitate planning. There is a fundamental tension between the need for certainty and the need to accommodate family expectations. Future circumstances are a crucial factor in determining priorities for expenditure, and these are, by definition, fluid and contingent upon a plethora of variables. There may be new commitments and resources as a result of a second partnership. As the children grow up their needs will vary. The ex-spouses' incomes will be subject to fluctuations in the labour market. It is diffficult for the law to impose certainty on an uncertain situation.

By expressing the problem in this way, we can see the complex nature of the debate surrounding the relative merits of rules and discretion. Rules may delimit entitlement precisely, but in doing so they frustrate the need for flexible responses to individual circumstances. Discretion may seem to provide individualized justice, but at the price of uncertainty and high legal costs.

The rules/discretion dichotomy is at the heart of this dilemma as in many other legal controversies. The Rule of Law dictates that like cases should be treated alike and that the law should be predictable so that individuals are able to foresee the legal consequences of their actions and plan their conduct accordingly. These goals are clearly better secured by the existence of clear, universally applicable rules. At the same time the law has a duty to secure justice and to act fairly to individuals. The law must examine the individual facts of each case in order to ensure that the rule is only applied when the facts are sufficiently analogous. Variation in individual circumstances is thus a good and sufficient reason for the law to distinguish a case and to find an alternative basis for its resolution. There is thus a theoretical basis for some judicial discretion coexisting with a definite rule. . . .

*Note*
Judicial discretion is not, however, totally limitless, as the court must consider the s. 25 criteria (see 5.3.2 below) and must consider whether to effect a 'clean break' between the parties (see 5.5 below). While considerable discretion has advantages, it also has disadvantages, and some critics consider that alternative models for solving property disputes should be adopted (see 5.4 below).

### 5.3.2  The section 25 criteria

### MATRIMONIAL CAUSES ACT 1973

**25.  Matters to which the court is to have regard in deciding how to exercise its powers under sections 23, 24 and 24A**
(1)  It shall be the duty of the court in deciding whether to exercise its powers under section 23, 24, or 24A above and, if so, in what manner, to have regard to all the circumstances of the case, first consideration being given to the welfare while a minor of any child of the family who has not attained the age of eighteen.
(2)  As regards the exercise of the powers of the court under section 23(1)(a), (b) or (c), 24 or 24A above in relation to a party to the marriage, the court shall in particular have regard to the following matters—
(a)  the income, earning capacity, property and other financial resources which each of the parties to the marriage has or is likely to have in the foreseeable future, including in the case of earning capacity any increase in that capacity which it would in the opinion of the court be reasonable to expect a party to the marriage to take steps to acquire;
(b)  the financial needs, obligations and responsibilities which each of the parties to the marriage has or is likely to have in the foreseeable future;
(c)  the standard of living enjoyed by the family before the breakdown of the marriage;
(d)  the age of each party to the marriage and the duration of the marriage;
(e)  any physical or mental disability of either of the parties to the marriage;
(f)  the contributions which each of the parties has made or is likely in the foreseeable future to make to the welfare of the family, including any contribution by looking after the home or caring for the family;
(g)  the conduct of each of the parties, if that conduct is such that it would in the opinion of the court be inequitable to disregard it;
(h)  . . . the value to each of the parties to the marriage of any benefit (for example, a pension) which, by reason of the dissolution . . . of the marriage, that party will lose the chance of acquiring.

*Note*
Sections 25(3) and (4) lay down matters which must be considered by the court when exercising its discretion to make orders for children (see Chapter 9).

### 5.3.3   Conduct

Under MCA 1973, s. 25(2)(g) conduct is taken into account, but only in exceptional circumstances, as the aim of the 1969 divorce reforms was to move away from fault.

### *Wachtel* v *Wachtel*
[1973] Fam 72
Court of Appeal

LORD DENNING MR: . . .

*The conduct of the parties*
When Parliament in 1857 introduced divorce by the courts of law, it based it on the doctrine of the matrimonial offence. This affected all that followed. If a person was the guilty party in a divorce suit, it went hard with him or her. It affected so many things. The custody of the children depended on it. So did the award of maintenance. To say nothing of the standing in society. So serious were the consequences that divorce suits were contested at great length and at much cost.

All that is altered. Parliament has decreed: 'If the marriage has broken down irretrievably, let there be a divorce'. It carries no stigma, but only sympathy. It is a misfortune which befalls both. No longer is one guilty and the other innocent. No longer are there long contested divorce suits. Nearly every case goes uncontested. The parties come to an agreement, if they can, on the things that matter so much to them. They divide up the furniture. They arrange the custody of the children, the financial provision for the wife, and the future of the matrimonial home. If they cannot agree, the matters are referred to a judge in chambers.

When the judge comes to decide these questions, what place has conduct in it? Parliament still says that the court has to have 'regard to their conduct': see s. 5(1) of the 1970 Act. Does this mean that the judge in chambers is to hear their mutual recriminations and go into their petty squabbles for days on end, as he used to do in the old days? Does it mean that, after a marriage has been dissolved, there is to be a post mortem to find out what killed it? We do not think so. In most cases both parties are to blame — or, as we would prefer to say — both parties have contributed to the breakdown.

It has been suggested that there should be a 'discount' or 'reduction' in what the wife is to receive because of her supposed misconduct, guilt or blame (whatever word is used). We cannot accept this argument. In the vast majority of cases it is repugnant to the principles underlying the new legislation, and in particular the 1969 Act. There will be many cases in which a wife (although once considered guilty or blameworthy) will have cared for the home and looked after the family for very many years. Is she to be deprived of the benefit otherwise to be accorded to her by s. 5(1)(f) because she may share responsibility for the breakdown with her husband? There will no doubt be a residue of cases where the conduct of one of the parties is in the judge's words 'both obvious and gross', so much so that to order one party to support another whose conduct falls into this category is repugnant to anyone's sense of justice. In such a case the court remains free to decline to afford financial support or to reduce the support which it would otherwise have ordered. But, short of cases falling into this category, the court should not reduce its order for financial provision merely because of what was formerly regarded as guilt or blame. To do so would be to impose a fine for

supposed misbehaviour in the course of an unhappy married life. Counsel for the husband disputed this and claimed that it was but justice that a wife should suffer for her supposed misbehaviour. We do not agree. Criminal justice often requires the imposition of financial and indeed custodial penalties. But in the financial adjustments consequent on the dissolution of a marriage which has irretrievably broken down, the imposition of financial penalties ought seldom to find a place.
. . .

*Note*
If conduct is taken into account, the court may in the exercise of its discretion decide not to make an order at all or may reduce the amount otherwise payable. In *Kyte* v *Kyte* [1988] Fam 145, *sub nom K* v *K (Financial Provision: Conduct)* [1988] 1 FLR 469, the Court Appeal reduced the wife's lump sum from £14,000 to £5,000 as she had assisted her husband with suicide attempts so that she could set up home with her lover and obtain as much from her husband's estate on his death as possible. See also *A* v *A (Financial Provision: Conduct)* [1995] 1 FLR 345, FD.

*The new s. 25(2)(g)*
After Parliamentary debates in which concern was voiced about insufficient importance being given to conduct in the divorce process, an amendment was made to MCA 1973, s. 25(2)(g) by the FLA 1996, so that the new provision will read as follows (the amendment is in italics):

(g)  the conduct of each of the parties, *whatever the nature of the conduct and whether it occurred during the marriage or after the separation of the parties or (as the case may be) dissolution or annulment of the marriage,* if that conduct is such that it would in the opinion of the court be inequitable to disregard it.

**Bird, Roger, Cretney, Stephen,** *Divorce — The New Law*
Bristol: Jordans, 1996, p. 73

. . . It is difficult to predict the likely impact of this amendment on the approach of the courts. On the one hand, it may be said that the amendment was designed to clarify, rather than change, the law. On the other hand, it may be presumed that Parliament must have intended to change the law in some respects. It seems certain that litigants will be encouraged by these amendments to persist in making allegations of conduct in circumstances in which they would formerly have been advised that to do so would be pointless. . . .

*Questions*
Was the amendment to s. 25(2)(g) made to appease concerns about the move to no-fault divorce? Should conduct be relevant at all when, since the Divorce Reform Act 1969, there has been a retreat from moral judgment?

### 5.3.4  A 'big money case'

In the following case the assets and the cost of litigation were substantial. The wife's costs, for example, were £1,336,400, of which £877,025 was attributable to the English application. The case also provides a useful survey of the development of the law on ancillary relief on divorce.

## *Dart* v *Dart*
[1996] 2 FLR 286
Court of Appeal

*Facts*: The parties were US nationals. The husband's family was extremely wealthy (the Dart family had manufactured foam cups). The parties who had two children, aged 10 and 13 left their home in Michigan and came to live permanently in London. The husband was granted a decree of divorce. In ancillary relief proceedings in England the wife sought an order of £122 million and the house in Michigan. When she sought disclosure of her husband's wealth, he pleaded the 'millionaire's defence' (see *Thyssen-Bornemisza* v *Thyssen-Bornemisza (No. 2)* [1985] Fam 1), i.e. that he would not disclose his assets because he was willing and able to comply with any order the court might make. When the wife's solicitors refused to accept that defence, he served his answer (19 pages of schedules and 7,000 documents in 35 ring binders!). The judge made an order *inter alia* transferring the Michigan house to the wife together with a lump sum of £9 million, and ordering her to pay her husband's costs. The wife appealed.

*Held*: that the appeal be dismissed for the reasons given in the following judgments.

THORPE LJ: . . . [Counsel for the wife] supports with enthusiasm the judgment of this court in *Wachtel* v *Wachtel* [1973] Fam 72 but challenges the entire corpus of subsequent decisions in this court on the application of the s. 25 criteria to what are known as big money cases. Again in my judgment this is a hopeless submission. However, since this judgment may be considered in due course by the courts of Michigan it might be helpful if I demonstrated its elementary failing. According to the law of England and Wales developed from the ecclesiastical law by statute in and after 1857 financial provision for wives after divorce could only be in the form of income payments, variously known as alimony, maintenance or periodical payments, albeit in certain circumstances secured by a charge on some identified capital asset. The power to award a capital sum, labelled a lump sum, was first introduced by statute in 1963. Thus the Matrimonial Proceedings and Property Act 1970 was a most significant landmark in the development of the court's power to make financial provision for an applicant following a decree of divorce, judicial separation, or nullity. By adding to the existing powers a power to order the transfer or settlement of any realty or personalty Parliament introduced a remedy of equitable distribution. The enactment reflected profound social change and met compelling social need. Divorce had become commonplace and equality of rights for men and women had become a reality. Within that reality women were more and more producing wealth as well as children. The manner in which this new power was to be exercised was defined by s. 5 of that statute. That section has developed, with one significant subsequent amendment introduced in 1984, into s. 25 of the Matrimonial Causes Act 1973 which regulates the outcome of this case. The statutory design was to give the judge exercising the power of equitable distribution the widest discretion to do fairness between the parties, reflecting considerations and criteria laid out within the section. Parliament might have opted for a community of property system or some fraction approach. It opted instead for a wide judicial discretion that would produce a bespoke solution to fit the infinite variety of individual cases. The scheme of the Act must also be set in the wider perspective of history and of the general civil law. In this jurisdiction rights of property are not invaded or reduced by statutory powers save for specific and confined purposes. The purpose of this statute was to make fair financial arrangements on or after divorce in the absence of agreement between the former spouses. Beyond that the power was not introduced to reorganise proprietary rights within families. After commencement on 1 January 1971 there was obvious curiosity and speculation amongst practitioners as to how this new power would be interpreted and utilised by the courts. In 1973 Lord Denning MR chose the case of *Wachtel* v *Wachtel* as a vehicle for the pronouncement of guidelines. He proposed a mathematical solution. If the applicant was to have periodical payments her capital share should be one-third. If she were not to have periodical payments then her capital share should be one half. Nearly 25 years later it seems curious that he should have proposed a mathematical application when the statute itself not only did not speak of fractions but had clearly preferred the alternative approach. But practitioners and judges had been used to deciding the level of income support by reference to fractions prior to 1 January 1971. So the language of the Master of the Rolls was familiar if not innovative. Secondly, the approach produced a manifestly fair result on the facts of that case which was not just a typical case but the essentially typical case of a middle class family that had prospered through a long marriage in an inflationary era. Of course the decision was binding on this court and subsequent judgments have acknowledged its application in similarly typical cases. But behind those deferential acknowledgements lies the reality that it has been consistently rejected as an authority of general application. The real interpreter of s. 25 and its predecessor was Ormrod LJ who between 1976 and 1981 demonstrated in a series of judgments in this court how s. 25 should be utilised by practitioners in negotiating or judges in determining the fair result. This was one of his major contributions to the evolution of family law. . . . In *Preston* v *Preston* [1982] Fam 17, (1981) 2 FLR 331 he reviewed the evolution over which he had presided in these terms:

It is only in the rare case where the assets are very large and there is no serious liquidity problem, that it becomes necessary to consider the ultimate limits of the court's discretionary powers under this section.

Hitherto, only three cases involving very large sums have reached this court. [His Lordship then reviewed these three cases, i.e. *O'D* v *O'D* [1976] Fam 83, *Sharpe* v *Sharpe* (unreported), 16 July 1980 and *Page* v *Page* (1981) 2 FLR 198.]

Although the decision in each of these cases depended largely on its individual circumstances, some general propositions can be extracted from them. In the first place the court should approach the problem by following the directions set out [in s. 25(1)], i.e. by considering all the circumstances of the case and, in particular, the factors set out, seriatim in paras (a) to (g) . . .

It is, therefore, wrong in principle to adopt a purely arithmetical approach by considering what proportion of the total assets should be allocated to the wife. The judgments in all three of the cases are agreed on this point. The suggestion in *Wachtel* v *Wachtel* of one half or one-third of the total assets is, therefore, no more than a guide-line, though it may be a useful check on the tentative figure which emerges from working through the considerations set out in the section.

. . . As [counsel for the husband] rightly submitted, in a big money case where the wife has played an equal part in creating the family fortune it would not be unreasonable for her to require what might be even an equal share. Therefore in my judgment the essential function of the judge in the big money case is to declare the boundary between the applicant's reasonable and unreasonable requirements applying all the statutory criteria to the myriad relevant facts of the individual case.
. . .

Accordingly it is my clear conclusion that in all the circumstances of this case it is just that the wife's entitlement to extravagant expenditure should be forfeit or largely curtailed by the costs liabilities that were in Johnson J's contemplation as he composed his judgment and those which subsequently resulted from his determination of the application for costs.

. . . [A]s I have demonstrated, the law in the field of big money cases has been settled for over a decade. That certainty has enabled practitioners to negotiate settlements in a large number of cases. Those that have the misfortune to reach the Court of Appeal are happily only a tiny minority. But manifestly even the greater number that are concluded without substantial litigation are insignificant in number and importance to those who legislate and those who form social policy. The statutory basis upon which the financial affairs of divorcing couples are decided has now been in place for a quarter of a century. It has been well tried, its operation is well understood by practitioners and it has in my estimation served society well. If a fundamental change is to be introduced it is for the legislature and not the judges to introduce it. Not only is the legislative process the democratic process but it enables the route of future change to be surveyed in advance of adoption by extensive research and consultation. That such a process may be in embryo is demonstrated by the Government's response to an amendment laid down to the Family Law Reform Bill currently in Parliament. The amendment sought to replace s. 25 of the Matrimonial Causes Act 1973 with the statutory code currently in force in Scotland. *Hansard* for 16 May 1996 shows that the Lord Chancellor has agreed that he will initiate a consultation process to evaluate the merits of adopting the Scottish system by referring the issue to his Ancillary Relief Advisory Group at the beginning of 1997.

For all these reasons I would dismiss this appeal.

BUTLER-SLOSS LJ: . . . The Matrimonial Causes Act 1973, as amended in 1984, provides the jurisdiction for all applications for ancillary relief from the poverty-stricken to the multimillionaire. It is obvious that a court, in the exercise of the discretion provided by ss. 25 and 25A, will apply the relevant criteria according to the widely differing facts of each case before it. In the low-income cases the assessment of the needs of the parties will lean heavily in favour of the children and the parent with whom they live. If, therefore, the only asset is the house, and the mother is caring for the children, she will get the house and probably outright, even though the effect of that order is to deprive the husband of the whole of the capital accrued during the marriage and directly financed from his resources.

At the other end of the scale, the affluent and the very rich families may have acquired it all during the marriage and by the efforts of both spouses by way of a working as well as a marriage partnership, see for instance *Gojkovic* v *Gojkovic (No. 2)* [1992] Fam 40, [1991] 2 FLR 233. In the case of a wife whose contribution to the marriage is indirect by way of keeping the home and bearing and bringing up the children, the well-known observation of Sir Jocelyn Simon P in a lecture in 1965, and recorded in the judgment of the Court of Appeal in *Wachtel* v *Wachtel* [1973] Fam 72, 92, is apposite. He said:

The cock can feather the nest because he does not have to spend most of his time sitting on it.

It is, however, useful to remember the context in which he said it. Ancillary relief orders prior to the 1960s did not provide for any capital distribution unless there was a trust. In 1963, for the first time, the courts were given the power to award lump sums, which were modest. It was not until the Matrimonial Causes Act 1970, re-enacted in the 1973 Act, that an order for transfer of property was introduced. The President was speaking at a time when the indirect contribution of a wife was not widely recognised and the normal order was a maintenance order for the wife during the joint lives of the former spouses or secured for her life.

Gradually the importance of the different contributions made by the spouses during their marriage has been recognised in a series of cases since the 1970s. The approach of the courts has inevitably reflected the type of case coming before them. Orders vary from the applicant spouse receiving the whole or the larger part of modest assets to receiving a small proportion of a large fortune. The exercise of discretion and the criteria laid down in s. 25 of the 1973 Act as amended have to encompass the enormous variations in the circumstances of each case coming before the courts.

This appeal relates to a 'big money case'. Although such cases do not arise in the English jurisdiction frequently, in the last 20 years or so, side by side with the working out of the principles extracted from the matrimonial financial legislation in cases of moderate or modest available capital, there has grown up, as Thorpe LJ has explained in his judgment, a body of decisions on 'big money' cases which bind this court. [Counsel for the wife] has, with great skill and much ingenuity, sought to set aside those decisions in favour of a broader brush approach which would result in far larger orders being made to spouses of millionaires.

[Counsel for the wife] suggested that the wording of s. 25 implied a starting-point of one half. Not only is it clear from the decided cases that such is not the case, but interestingly it is clear from proposed legislation to which we have been referred in *Hansard* that in Parliamentary debate, at least, such a starting-point was not even contemplated by those arguing from whichever point of view of the existing legislation.

In the process of applying the s. 25(2) criteria to the facts of this case, the needs of the wife are a highly relevant factor. 'Needs' has been defined by Ormrod LJ in *Page* v *Page* (1981) 2 FLR 198, 201 as the 'reasonable requirements' of the spouse seeking an order. Where the resources are great Ormrod LJ in *Preston* v *Preston* [1982] Fam 17, (1981) 2 FLR 331 said at 28 and 339 respectively that there had to be a levelling off or a ceiling on the amounts to be taken into account.
. . .

The court is not bound by any percentage but must have regard to all the relevant criteria in s. 25(2). . . . Within the principles enunciated in the line of cases set out in the judgment of Thorpe LJ there is no ground upon which this appellate court might interfere with [the judge's] exercise of discretion or substitute a higher figure than the award made by the judge in his excellent judgment.

I agree with Thorpe LJ, for the reasons which he has given, that we should not interfere with the effect of costs upon the lump sum awarded.

I would, however, add one further matter. I am glad to see that a consultation process is proposed to reconsider the existing criteria laid down in s. 25. I am sure that any change in the way in which the courts should decide money cases ought to be by legislation. The practice in ancillary relief has become settled. It is well known among practitioners and clear principles are essential in order to assist large numbers of spouses and their legal advisers who make post-divorce financial settlements and apply for consent orders. The Court of Appeal must not set the cat among the pigeons.

I should, however, like to feel that within the consultation process the views expressed by Peter Singer QC in 1992 were carefully considered. I share the doubts raised by Peter Gibson LJ in his judgment. I wonder whether the courts may not have imposed too restrictive an interpretation upon the words of s. 25 and given too great weight to reasonable requirements over other criteria set out in the section. On the present state of the law as interpreted in the authorities Johnson J's order is clearly right. If this appeal was not bound by authority I would not wish to make an order of a kind suggested by [counsel for the wife], but as the sums with which the courts are asked to deal become very large indeed, it may be that we are now perhaps somewhat over-modest in our awards.

On the first issue of discovery, I have no doubt that the *Thyssen* defence to detailed requests for discovery is entirely appropriate even if the award had been substantially greater than £9m. I too would dismiss this appeal.

## Question

What objectives is the court trying to achieve in making orders for financial provision and property adjustment on divorce? Why should the emphasis be on support rather than on the redistribution of assets?

## 5.4   THE PROBLEM WITH DISCRETION

We have seen that the court has considerable discretion to make orders for property and finance on divorce. The question arises whether the discretionary model for allocating property and finance on divorce is satisfactory, and whether other models would provide better solutions.

### Davis, Gwynn, Cretney, Stephen, and Collins, Jean, *Simple Quarrels* Oxford: Clarendon Press, 1994 pp. 255–6

. . . The fact that divorce is a legal process tends to determine its nature, although this varies as between different countries. In the UK the system has a discretionary character. We do not have rules upon which money and property disputes are to be decided. We do not even have one overriding principle. Instead, our statute provides a list of factors which have to be taken into account. Furthermore, one aspect of the parties' financial obligations (say spousal maintenance) may be offset against another (say, the disposition of the matrimonial home). This means that the scope for negotiation is almost infinite. Wherever one looks there is discretion — and not just 'weak' discretion, concerned with an interpretation of the meaning of words or the application of hardship clauses, but 'strong' discretion under which the court and legal advisers are required to weigh competing factors. This is the result of a conscious preference for flexibility — a view that formulas are not appropriate for the determination of ancillary relief issues because the circumstances vary too much. This discretionary system is still vigorously defended. . . . But along with discretion goes *uncertainty; the elevation of professional judgment* (because only lawyers, who deal with these matters all the time, have the necessary knowledge and skill to weigh up the competing factors); *an almost limitless need for information about family finances* (because discretion, if it is to justified at all, has to be based on a minute examination of differing circumstances); and *the demand for large amounts of professional time* (because discretion, if it is not to be exercised arbitrarily, takes time). In practice, of course, there is a limit to the amount of lawyer-time which divorcing couples can purchase, and also a limit to the amount which the State is prepared to support. Court-time is likewise expensive and has, somehow, to be rationed. This means that we have all the trappings of discretionary justice, underpinned by procedures whose complexity is designed to cope with major disputes, and yet very little court-time and very little solicitor-time.

[After discussing the drawbacks of settlement as an alternative to discretion, the authors continue: . . .]

A more likely alternative direction, recently given legislative form in the Child Support Act 1991, is that we move to a system of administrative decision-making in respect of some, if not all, of the financial issues which arise on divorce. This might be considered a logical step in view of much of the evidence presented in this book. One possible conclusion to draw from our research is that a discretionary system is not geared to mass proceedings such as we have in divorce these days. The proposal that outcomes be determined by the application of a formula, and usually by an administrative authority, can certainly be supported in relation to the relatively straightforward cases which comprised the bulk of our sample. Of course there is room for discretion in administrative systems as well as in judicial ones, but one would have thought it possible to design a formula-based system for dealing with *income* which would achieve greater certainty than is available at the moment. There might also be other benefits, not least that the outcome would no longer depend on the nuances of the power-play between professional advocates and negotiators. It is likely furthermore that formulas would be easier for the divorcing couple to understand — there would be clear guidelines which they could consult. This is quite unlike the position which we have described, with the parties all too often being surprised at the outcome of their own case. In that sense formulas would be more democratic. . . .

[In the Preface to *Simple Quarrels*:] . . . It is possible to conclude from the study that the attempt to provide individualised justice through the courts . . . does not work well in divorce. . . . Our research would appear to reinforce the case — powerfully argued some twenty years ago by the Finer Committee — for the support obligation following divorce to be assessed by administrative process. Clearly something needed to be done to produce a simple, stream-lined mechanism for determining the outcome of the relatively straightforward issues arising on marital breakdown. . . .

### 5.4.1  Marriage contracts?

Marriage contracts would provide one way of avoiding the need for wide judicial discretion, as in addition to creating certainty, they would encourage the parties to make their own plans for the future and to realise their responsibilities and obligations on marriage. A major problem with marriage contracts, however, is that they would not cope well with changing circumstances (e.g., the birth of children, illness or redundancy) and they might be considered unromantic and a disincentive to marriage. Another problem is the extent to which the State should interfere with the terms of such contracts. Should it interfere to protect a vulnerable party or the children of the relationship? Should there be safeguards to deal with undue influence, misrepresentation, lack of disclosure, fraud, and inequality of bargaining power?

The Law Society mooted the possibility of marriage contracts as well as other alternatives to discretion in its *Memorandum* (see below), para. 1.1 of which reads as follows:

1.1 Over recent years the Family Law Committee has given a great deal of thought to possible reforms of the law on maintenance and capital provision on divorce. This has been prompted by widespread dissatisfaction among both practitioners and the public at the current discretionary system which, although embodying sufficient flexibility to deal with the circumstances of each case, is seen by many as being arbitrary, inconsistent and lacking in certainty. It also does not assist the increasing numbers of divorcing couples who wish to resolve their financial position by negotiation and settlement, not litigation.

### Legal Practice Directorate, The Law Society, *Memorandum: Maintenance and Capital Provision on Divorce — Recommendations for Reform of the Law and Procedure made by the Family Law Committee*, 1991

. . .

(a) **Advantages of marriage contracts**

3.33 Perhaps the greatest advantage of marriage contracts and the reason for the current high level of interest in them is the fact that they provide a means whereby the parties can decide for themselves how their property should be divided between them. This reduces or removes the possibility of court involvement and the imposition of a solution by the court which may be completely contrary to the parties' wishes. This would further the current trend, as demonstrated in the Children Act 1989, of reducing court interference in family life, wherever possible, and encouraging the parties to accept responsibility themselves. This would mean that both the parties' privacy and their freedom to arrange their own lives in the way that they wish would be enhanced.

3.34 Many of the problems which arise in relation to finance and property on divorce arise because the parties have little or no idea about how they regarded these issues during the course of the marriage — having at best had only limited discussions on how their financial affairs are to be organised. An awareness of the individual needs, resources and obligations of the parties at the time of the marriage would undoubtedly assist in the analysis of who should get what on divorce. The 1989 figures from the Office of Population Censuses and Surveys show that 12.7 out of every 1000 married couples in England and Wales got divorced and in view of this it is submitted that the philosophy of a marriage contract is not dissimilar to that of making a will: it is a wise precaution. Moreover, it is thought that it is better for a couple to consider their financial position *before* they get involved in the emotional trauma of marriage breakdown and divorce.

3.35 It is implicit in what is said above that the use of marriage contracts will lead to increased certainty for those couples who decide to use them without producing an overly rigid system — a major criticism of the community property system.

3.36 The discussion necessary for drawing up a contract would be a good means of identifying any potential areas of conflict between the parties. To clarify the couple's expectations and sort out any problems before the marriage could, it is submitted, only be beneficial in ensuring a viable relationship based on mutual understanding, rather than encourage a 'throw away attitude' to marriage. Contracts may therefore have a role in contributing to marital longevity.

(b)  **Disadvantages of marriage contracts**

3.37  They are thought to be unromantic and a threat to marriage. It is true that the concept of a marriage contract is not very romantic. However, the arguments set out at paragraphs 3.34 and 3.36 can be used to counter this.

3.38  Can two adults engaged in a sexual relationship make a contract? The Family Law Committee does not believe that a sexual relationship per se prevents a rational discussion of financial affairs. However, a fear has been expressed about the danger that may exist of one party (usually a woman) being forced to enter a contract against her will which does not provide favourably enough for her. Clearly there is a danger that one party to the marriage could force the other to enter into a contract or defraud them. However, the more likely danger is that the dominant partner in a relationship would have greater bargaining power and may seek to take advantage of this. Two points can be made about this. First, this inequality in the relationship would exist whether or not a contract was drawn up and at least if a contract is drawn up the weaker party will know what he or she is letting him or herself in for before he or she actually gets married. Secondly, the Family Law Committee's procedural proposals . . . relating to marriage contracts will, it is submitted, in most cases prove sufficient to counteract this and provide the nearest thing to equality of bargaining power that is possible between any couple. Indeed, in requiring each party to have legal representation at the time of making the contract they may benefit from advice which they may not otherwise receive.

3.39  The most fundamental objection to marriage contracts is that a contract which may have been perfectly fair and freely entered into does not remain so in the face of changing circumstances. The Committee recognises that this argument has force and seeks to deal with this issue below (see paragraph 3.50 et seq.).

(c)  **The Family Law Committee's Proposals**

3.40  The Family Law Committee proposes that the law should be changed so that marriage contracts are recognised and enforceable in this country. Clearly, if this is accepted a number of procedural safeguards will be necessary and the issue of the status of these contracts within the current system will need to be clarified. . . .

3.41  The Committee recommends that the contents of marriage contracts in this country should not reflect either those in Sweden or America but should steer a middle course. . . .

. . .

3.50  The Committee is . . . of the view that any legislation should provide a number of triggers that should have the effect of revoking a contract or triggering a review (subject to any contrary intention shown in the document itself). For example, the birth of a first or subsequent child, the onset of permanent disability or long-term unemployment. If such an event did take place and the contract was then revoked (as opposed to being reviewed) this would not prevent the parties drawing up a new contract to reflect their changed circumstances.

3.51  Unfortunately, no such list of triggers could ever be completely comprehensive and this, therefore, means that the risk would still exist that the contract could become unrealistic or unfair. The Committee therefore recommends that terms relating to a periodic review should be included in all contracts and the possible effects of a failure to include such a term should be pointed out to the couple involved. For instance, a provision could be included stating that a review must take place at least every five years. Each such review should be carried out with legal assistance to ensure the continuance of procedural safeguards. If a contract is not reviewed according to its terms this would mean that it would be unenforceable although the court could presumably take its terms into account.

3.52 A system of regular reviews should limit the incidence of ad hoc arrangements developing. If, despite this, they do exist the Committee believes that they should be resolved in accordance with the principles of contract law e.g. estoppel.
. . .

3.54 It must be recognised that a couple cannot have an absolute freedom to contract — it will not, for example, be possible to contract out of statutory obligations to pay tax and child maintenance. . . .

3.55 The Committee accepts that the proposal to recognise marriage contracts is controversial and not completely problem free. However, it is clear, having considered the advantages and disadvantages identified above, that the introduction of marriage contracts would be a worthwhile reform — particularly if coupled with the procedural safeguards which the Family Law Committee has proposed.
. . .

### Note

Marriage contracts are recognised in many European and other common law countries, but they are usually made before marriage in order to opt out of a State-imposed regime of community of property (i.e. whereby a spouse on divorce or on the death of the other party is entitled to a fixed share of any property assets acquired during marriage).

### 5.4.2 A set of principles?

Would a set of principles help, such as those which exist in Scotland under the Family Law (Scotland) Act 1985?

## FAMILY LAW (SCOTLAND) ACT 1985

**9. Principles to be applied**
(1) The principles which the court shall apply in deciding what order for financial provision, if any, to make are that—
(a) the net value of the matrimonial home should be shared fairly between the parties to the marriage;
(b) fair account should be taken of any economic advantage derived by either party from contributions by the other, and of any economic disadvantages suffered by either party in the interests of the other party or of the family;
(c) any economic burden of caring, after divorce, for a child of the marriage under the age of 16 years should be shared fairly between the parties;
(d) a party who has been dependent to a substantial degree on the financial support of the other party should be awarded such financial provision as is reasonable to enable him to adjust, over a period of not more than three years from the date of the decree of divorce, to the loss of that support on divorce;
(e) a party who at the time of the divorce seems likely to suffer serious financial hardship as a result of the divorce should be awarded such financial provision as is reasonable to relieve him of hardship over a reasonable period.
(2) In subsection (1)(b) above and section 11(2) of the Act—
'economic advantage' means advantage gained whether before or during the marriage and includes gains in capital, in income and in earning capacity, and 'economic disadvantage' shall be construed accordingly;

'contributions' means contributions made whether before or during the marriage; and includes indirect and non-financial contributions and, in particular, any such contribution made by looking after the family home or caring for the family.

### 5.4.3  Community of property?

Under a system of community of property, matrimonial property is divided equally between the parties on divorce, subject to certain statutory exceptions or subject to a marital, or more usually a pre-marital, agreement to the contrary. Community of property regimes are common in European countries and in some states of the USA. This possibility was also mooted by the Family Law Committee of the Law Society.

**Legal Practice Directorate, The Law Society,** *Memorandum: Maintenance and Capital Provision on Divorce — Recommendations for Reform of the Law and Procedure made by the Family Law Committee,* **1991**

. . .

2.3  Systems of community property can take a number of different forms. The Swedish model involves an automatic fifty/fifty split of all assets owned by the parties however or whenever acquired. Any couple wishing to opt out of this system in whole or in part has to do so by means of a marriage contract. Alternatively, community property can be limited to a community of acquests system as in Germany and Quebec. This means that only property acquired during the marriage, other than by gift or inheritance, falls into the community. All other property remains the separate property of the spouse who owns it.

. . .

2.9  A system of community property would be likely to produce certainty by ensuring that the rights of each party over property would be set out and known to them both. However, the system would not completely preclude court intervention as . . . a residual discretion would need to be retained to deal with unusual cases. A system of community property also has the advantage that it promotes a view of marriage as being a partnership between equals.

2.10  The Law Commission in their paper *'Family Law, Matrimonial Property'* *(1988) Law Com No. 175* considered the question of which spouse owns what property during marriage. The Law Commission rejected a system of community property as, in countries where it is used, it was felt to be too restrictive and did not alleviate the poverty experienced by former wives. It can also have unfortunate consequences in cases where a marriage has only been of very short duration.

2.11  Prior to the enactment of the Family Law (Scotland) Act 1985 the Scottish Law Commission in its report *'Family Law, Report on Matrimonial Property'* *((1984) Scot Law Com No. 86)* also considered whether to recommend the introduction of a community of acquests system. The Law Commission rejected this option on the following grounds:—

One of these disadvantages would be excessive legal complexity. If a community of acquests system were introduced there would have to be rules enabling spouses to opt out by marriage contract . . . It would not always be easy to decide what should or should not be excluded and framing suitably precise rules would add considerably to the complexity of any scheme. As there would, in many marriages, be three separate lots of property — the husband's, and wife's and the community property — there would have to be rules on the allocation of property to each category (including, probably, rules for 'tracing' property if, for example, an asset is acquired during the marriage with funds owned by one spouse before the marriage) and rules on the reimbursement of one fund by the other where, for example, the first has borne an expense which should properly have been borne by the other. We think that the legal complexity involved in introducing a community of acquests system should not be underestimated.

The other main disadvantage of a community of acquests system is its rigidity. It is easier for couples to opt into voluntary sharing under a separate property system than it is for them to opt out of a community property system. The former involves no more, in relation to many types of assets, than taking a title in joint names: the latter involves employing a lawyer to draw up a marriage contract. Moreover, in so far as a community of acquests system involves a fixed rule of equal sharing of certain property on the dissolution of a marriage by divorce, it imposes too rigid a solution to suit the circumstances of all cases. Even those commentators who favoured the introduction of a community of acquests system generally favoured the conferring of some discretion to depart from equal sharing on divorce. Yet, if such a discretion is conferred, the system offers no advantages, on divorce, over a separate property system with (rules for adjusting property on divorce).

2.12   It is interesting to note that these problems have led to a limited departure from community properly in both Sweden and Quebec. . . .

2.13   Although the Committee thinks that the adoption of a community property system would be consistent with its aim of increasing certainty and consistency it is clear that it does not satisfy the needs of the families involved due to its complexity and rigidity. For these reasons, the Committee does not feel that the advantages of such a system outweigh the disadvantages. It would therefore be inappropriate to recommend the introduction of such a system in this country.

*Notes*

1.   The Family Law Committee rejected a complete reform of the substantive law relating to maintenance and capital provision on divorce and concluded that, although it recognised the problems inherent in the current law, it did 'not consider that the wholesale adoption of any of the alternative systems discussed would embody sufficient advantages over the current system such as to justify a departure from it' (para. 2.39).

2.   The Family Law Committee in its *Memorandum* stated that research had shown that the Scottish principles did not seem to be 'a universal panacea' (para. 2.22), and that, while being a 'a useful tool', they did not represent the complete answer (para. 2.25). They also had the 'the potential to produce arbitrary results' (para. 2.20).

*Questions*

1.   In Scotland the divorce court may only allocate and redistribute 'matrimonial property' (defined by s. 10 of the Family Law (Scotland) Act 1995 as property acquired, other than by way of gift or succession from a third party). Is it fair that the English divorce court may in the exercise of its discretion take account of any resources, whether or not the resource has much

connection with the marriage (see, e.g., *Schuller* v *Schuller* [1990] 2 FLR 193, CA, where the court took into account the husband's inheritance)?
2.   What are the advantages and disadvantages of the courts having wide discretion to make finance and property orders on divorce? Do any of the other options have significant enough advantages to justify reform? Would a statutory definition of matrimonial property help with the problem of discretion? Would the introduction of a mathematical formula help, like that for calculating child maintenance (see Chapter 9)? Would a greater emphasis on reaching agreement help, or are there pitfalls with agreement?

## 5.5   THE CLEAN BREAK

Part II of the MCA 1973, as a result of amendments made by Part II of the Matrimonial and Family Proceedings Act 1984, makes provision for a concept known as the 'clean break', a catch-phrase which incorporates the notion that divorced spouses should not remain under a long-term obligation to one another after divorce. Different considerations, however, apply to child maintenance, where 'the on-going responsibility of the parents has remained a basic factor to which the clean break principle has never applied' (Booth J in *Crozier* v *Crozier* [1994] Fam 114, FD, at p. 122).

### MATRIMONIAL CAUSES ACT 1973

**25A.   Exercise of court's powers in favour of party to marriage on decree of divorce or nullity of marriage**
(1)   Where on or after the grant of a decree of divorce . . . the court decides to exercise its powers under section 23(1)(a), (b) , or (c), 24 or 24A . . . in favour of a party to the marriage, it shall be the duty of the court to consider whether it would be appropriate so to exercise those powers that the financial obligations of each party towards the other will be terminated as soon after the grant of the decree as the court considers just and reasonable.
(2)   Where the court decides in such a case to make a periodical payments or secured periodical payments order in favour of a party to the marriage, the court shall in particular consider whether it would be appropriate to require those payments to be made or secured only for such term as would in the opinion of the court be sufficient to enable the party in whose favour the order is made to adjust without undue hardship to the termination of his or her financial dependence on the other party.
(3)   Where on or after the grant of a decree of divorce . . . an application is made by a party to the marriage for a periodical payments or secured periodical payments order in his or her favour, then, if the court considers that no continuing obligation should be imposed on either party to make or secure periodical payments in favour of the other, the court may dismiss the application with a direction that the applicant shall not be entitled to make any future application in relation to that marriage for an order under section 23(1)(a) or (b) above.

*Notes*
1.   There are other clean break provisions in the MCA 1973 (see ss. 28(1A) and 31(7)). Furthermore, s. 15(1) of the Inheritance (Provision for Family

and Dependants) Act 1975 (see Chapter 3) gives the court power on the grant of a decree of divorce to order that one party may not apply under the 1975 Act against the other party's estate on death.

2.   A clean break (by court order or by agreement) is easier to arrange if substantial assets are available for distribution, as a capital sum can be transferred which can be invested to produce an income, if necessary for life (Diana, Princess of Wales, received a capital sum of between £15 to £17 million on her divorce from HRH The Prince of Wales to give her an income suitable for her needs for life).

3.   Except for minor changes in detail, the clean break provisions of Part II of the MCA 1973 will remain the same when the divorce reforms under the FLA 1996 come into force.

4.   The Child Support Act 1995 allows the Child Support Agency to take account of clean break settlements made before the Child Support Act 1991 came into effect (see Chapter 9).

Balcombe LJ's dissenting judgment in the following case, which concerned an application for a clean break in s. 31 variation proceedings, contains a useful survey of the law and background to the clean break.

### *Whiting* v **Whiting**
[1988] 1 WLR 565
Court of Appeal

*Facts*: A consent order was made on divorce in which the wife, a school teacher, was granted, *inter alia*, nominal maintenance of 5p per annum. Later, after the husband's earnings had dropped significantly, he applied under s. 31(7) of the MCA 1973 to have the nominal maintenance order discharged, with a direction that his wife should not be entitled to make any further application for maintenance. He also applied for an order under s. 15 of the Inheritance (Provision for Family and Dependants) Act 1975 that she should not be entitled on his death to apply under that Act for provision against his estate. Their three children were financially independent. The wife's earnings were £10,500 per annum. The husband's were £4,358 per annum. The trial judge dismissed the husband's application on the ground that the nominal maintenance order should continue as a 'last backstop' for the wife. The husband appealed.

*Held*: dismissing the appeal (Balcombe LJ dissenting) that as the court had a discretion under s. 31(7) to direct that the original order continue on a nominal basis as a backstop for the payee, the judge had been entitled on the facts to take the view that the nominal maintenance order should be kept alive lest unforeseen circumstances (e.g. illness or redundancy) would deprive the wife of her ability to provide for herself. The three judges were unanimous in holding that the court could not make an order under s. 15(1) of the 1975 Act unless it had before it some idea of the nature of the estate and details of those persons who might have a prior claim to it.

BALCOMBE LJ (dissenting): . . . I now turn to consider the relevant law. The policy reasons which underlie the principle of the 'clean break' were clearly stated by Lord Scarman in *Minton v Minton* [1979] AC 593, 608:

> There are two principles which inform the modern legislation. One is the public interest that spouses, to the extent that their means permit, should provide for themselves and their children. But the other — of equal importance — is the principle of 'the clean break.' The law now encourages spouses to avoid bitterness after family break-down and to settle their money and property problems. An object of the modern law is to encourage each to put the past behind them and to begin a new life which is not over-shadowed by the relationship which has broken down.

However, it was held by this court in *Dipper v Dipper* [1981] Fam 31 that the court had no power to impose a 'clean break' by dismissing a wife's claim for periodical payments, unless she agreed to that being done. Without such an agreement, the court had at least to make a nominal order in favour of the wife.

In October 1980 the Law Commission published a Discussion Paper entitled 'The Financial Consequences of Divorce: The Basic Policy' (Cmnd 8041). As a result of this paper, and the many comments made on it, the Law Commission in 1981 published a report No. 112 H/C 68 entitled 'The Financial Consequences of Divorce' making a number of recommendations for a change in the law. The following passages from this report are relevant:

> VII. (ii) *Greater weight to be given to a divorced wife's earning capacity; and to the desirability of both parties becoming self-sufficient*
> 26. The existing law requires the court to consider the income and earning capacity of both husband and wife, and (as reported cases indicate) the courts do take account of a wife's earning potential. There was, however, a widespread feeling amongst those who commented on the discussion paper that greater weight should be given to the importance of each party doing everything possible to become self-sufficient, so far as this is consistent with the interests of the children; and we believe that the statutory provisions should contain a positive assertion of this principle.
> 27. The court has, under the existing law, power to make orders for a limited term, and this power is sometimes exercised when it is felt that a spouse (usually the wife) needs some time to readjust to her new situation but could not or should not expect to rely on continuing support from her husband. We think that it would be desirable to require the court specifically to consider whether an order for a limited term would not be appropriate in all the circumstances of the case, given the increased weight which we believe should be attached to the desirability of the parties becoming self-sufficient.
> (iii) *Imposing a 'clean break' where practicable and appropriate*
> 28. It is true, as Ormrod LJ has pointed out, that the expression 'a clean break' is in danger of being indiscriminately used to express different and sometimes contradictory ideas. Moreover, it must be accepted that the occasions on which it is possible for the parties to arrive at a final, once for all settlement, on the occasion of their divorce will be comparatively few, and almost non-existent where there are young children. To seek to attain a 'clean break' in many — perhaps the majority of cases — would simply be to drive divorced wives on to supplementary benefit. That (it has been said) is not the policy of the present legislation; nor (in our view) should it become the policy of the reformed legislation which we now envisage.

Nevertheless, the response to the Discussion Paper showed strong support for the view (with which we agree) that such finality should be achieved wherever possible, as for example where there is a childless marriage of comparatively short duration between a husband and a wife who has income, or an earning capacity, or in cases of a longer marriage, where there is an adequate measure of capital available for division.

29. At the moment, there is a technical difficulty in imposing such a 'clean break,' even in those cases where the court would wish to do so because the Court of Appeal has held that the court has no jurisdiction to dismiss a wife's claim for periodical payments without her agreement. We believe (and in this we are supported by the judges of the Family Division) that the court should have such a power available for use in those, perhaps rare, cases where to use it would be appropriate. It is in our view desirable that this fetter on the court's power should be removed; and that this should be done whether or not any other change in the substance of the law is made in the near future.

30. The response to the discussion paper indicated wide support for the view that the courts should be more clearly directed to the desirability of promoting a severance of financial obligations between the parties at the time of divorce; and to give greater weight to the view that in the appropriate case any periodical financial provision ordered in favour of one spouse (usually the wife) for her own benefit — as distinct from periodical payments made to her to enable her to care for the children — should be primarily directed to secure wherever possible a smooth transition from marriage to the status of independence. We believe that this general objective should be embodied in the legislation.

As a result of this report Part II of the Matrimonial and Family Proceedings Act 1984 made a number of significant amendments to those provisions of the Matrimonial Causes Act 1973 concerned with financial relief in matrimonial proceedings.

[After citing ss. 25A, 28(1A) and 31(7) of the MCA 1973 and s. 15(1) of the Inheritance (Provision for Family and Dependants) Act 1975, his Lordship continued: . . .]

It will be seen that these provisions of the Act of 1984 were clearly intended to enable the court to impose a 'clean break,' where that was appropriate. The effect of the legislation was well expressed by Waite J, giving the leading judgment of this court in *Tandy* v *Tandy* (unreported) 24 October 1986; Court of Appeal (Civil Division) Transcript No. 929, in the following terms:

The effect of the legislation, as now amended, is thus to give effect, whether upon the making of an original order or on a subsequent application to vary it, to what has become loosely known as 'the clean break' — a term which is perhaps now used in a wider context than when it first appeared. The legislative purpose, that is to say, is to enable the parties to a failed marriage, wherever fairness allows, to go their separate ways without the running irritant of financial interdependence or dispute. For better off families that can and will normally be achieved by a capital lump sum paid in satisfaction or commutation of the right to be maintained on a periodic basis. The legislation clearly contemplates, however (and there is no dispute as to this), that there will be circumstances in which fairness to one side demands, and to the other side permits, a severance of the maintenance tie in cases where no capital resources are available.

. . .

The reason for the judge's decision is to be found in the following passage from her judgment:

There is no imminent likelihood that the wife would need or wish to make any financial call on the husband, it is however at last backstop. The order was made by consent in January 1979 and I see no reason to disturb it.

It was common ground that the statutory obligation upon the judge was to

consider whether in all the circumstances . . . it would be appropriate to vary the [1979] order so that payments under the order are required to be made . . . only for such further period as will . . . be sufficient to enable the [wife] . . . to adjust without undue hardship to the termination of those payments; . . .

It was also common ground that such consideration had to be a real consideration, and not just a payment of lip service to the words of the subsection. But, provided that the judge did give proper consideration to the provisions of section 31(7), it is clear that she had a discretion whether or not to accede to the husband's application to discharge the 1979 order for nominal periodical payments in favour of the wife.

The principles upon which an appellate court will interfere with the exercise of a judicial discretion by a judge of first instance are well known. The following passage from the judgment of Asquith LJ in *Bellenden (formerly Satterthwaite) v Satterthwaite* [1948] 1 All ER 343, 345 was cited with approval by Lord Fraser of Tullybelton in *G v G (Minors: Custody Appeal)* [1985] 1 WLR 647, 651–652:

It is, of course, not enough for the wife to establish that this court might, or would, have made a different order. We are here concerned with a judicial discretion, and it is of the essence of such a discretion that on the same evidence two different minds might reach widely different decisions without either being appealable. It is only where the decision exceeds the generous ambit within which reasonable disagreement is possible, and is, in fact, plainly wrong, that an appellate body is entitled to interfere.

In the same speech Lord Fraser also cited with approval the following passage from the speech of Lord Scarman in *B v W (Wardship: Appeal)* [1979] 1 WLR 1041, 1055:

But at the end of the day the court may not intervene unless it is satisfied either that the judge exercised his discretion upon a wrong principle or that, the judge's decision being so plainly wrong, he must have exercised his discretion wrongly.

I have already drawn attention to certain errors in the judge's judgment, and to certain irrelevant matters which she appears to have taken into account. However, I believe that it would be intellectually dishonest to seize upon these errors and matters, and to say that therefore she exercised her discretion upon a wrong principle by taking into account matters that she should not have taken into account. In my judgment, however, the judge was plainly wrong in her decision.
. . .

Accordingly, for the reasons I have endeavoured to give, I would allow this appeal to the extent of discharging the nominal periodical payments order made on 22 January 1979 in favour of the wife and by declaring that the wife shall not be entitled to make any further application in respect of periodical payments or secured periodical payments for herself.

*Further reading*
Mears, M., 'The Clean Break v the Courts: the Illogical Backstop' [1989] Fam Law 398.
Walsh, B., '*Whiting* v *Whiting*: Whither the Clean Break Principle?' [1989] Fam Law 157.

## 5.6 THE DUTY OF FULL AND FRANK DISCLOSURE

A cardinal principle in proceedings brought under Part II of the MCA 1973 is that the parties must make full and frank disclosure of their financial circumstances, for without complete, accurate and up-to-date information, the court is unable properly to exercise its discretion and lawyers cannot properly give advice. Each party must swear an affidavit of means giving full particulars of his or her property and income, and parties who wish the court to make a 'consent order' must provide the court with prescribed information (see 5.9.2 below). Non-disclosure is a serious problem on divorce. The following is the leading case on the duty of full and frank disclosure.

### *Livesey (formerly Jenkins)* v *Jenkins*
[1985] AC 424
House of Lords

*Facts*: The parties agreed on divorce that the husband would transfer his half share in the matrimonial home to his wife expressly to provide a home for her and the children, in consideration of her agreeing to relinquish all her claims for periodical payments. Six days later, the wife became engaged to another man but did not disclose this fact to her husband or to their solicitors. Three weeks after the consent order was made the wife remarried and two months later put the matrimonial home up for sale. When the husband learned of his wife's remarriage, he appealed against the consent order asking for it to be set aside on the ground that he had been induced to agree to its being made by the wife's misrepresentation as to her true position. At first instance and on appeal his application was dismissed, the Court of Appeal holding that the wife had been under no duty to disclose her engagement. The husband appealed to the House of Lords.
*Held*: allowing the appeal, setting aside the order and remitting the case for a rehearing, that there was a duty in contested and consent proceedings to make full and frank disclosure to the court and the other party of all material facts, including matters which the court was statutorily to have regard to under s. 25 of the MCA 1973.

LORD BRANDON: My Lords, this appeal arises in the field of family law and concerns the making by the court of consent orders for financial provision and property adjustment following a divorce.
  On the facts of the present case two important questions of principle require to be decided by your Lordships. The first question is this. Where a compromise in respect

of claims for financial provision and property adjustment made by either or both of the former spouses has been reached by two firms of solicitors acting on their respective behalf, with the intention that the terms of such compromise shall subsequently be given effect to by a consent order of the court, is each of the former spouses under a remaining duty to disclose to the other, or to the other's solicitors, the occurrence of a material change in his or her situation, which has taken place after the compromise has been reached, but before effect has been given to it by the making of a consent order by the court? The second question is this. Assuming that the remaining duty referred to above exists, and is not complied with by one of the two former spouses, so that a consent order is made by the court without such material change having been taken into account, is the other former spouse entitled, in proceedings before a judge of first instance, to have the order so made set aside?

. . .

In considering the questions from the point of view of principle, there are four matters which I think that it is necessary to state and emphasise from the beginning. The first matter is that the powers of a judge of the Family Division of the High Court, or of a judge of a divorce county court, to make orders for financial provision and property adjustment following a divorce are conferred on them, and conferred on them solely, by statute, the relevant statute at the time of the proceedings out of which this appeal arises being the Matrimonial Causes Act 1973. The second matter is that there is no difference in this respect between a judge's powers to make such orders after a disputed hearing involving evidence on both sides, and his powers to make such orders by the consent of the parties without having heard any evidence at all. The third matter is that the powers of registrars to make such orders, when delegated to them by rules of court, are exactly the same as those of judges, whether the proceedings concerned are in the principal registry of the Family Division, or in the registry of a divorce county court. The fourth matter is that, when parties agree the provisions of a consent order, and the court subsequently gives effect to such agreement by approving the provisions concerned and embodying them in an order of the court, the legal effect of those provisions is derived from the court order itself, and does not depend any longer on the agreement between the parties: *de Lasala* v *de Lasala* [1980] AC 546, 560 *per* Lord Diplock.

. . .

My Lords, the terms of section 25(1) of the Act of 1973 . . . are, in my opinion, of crucial importance in relation to the questions raised by this appeal. The scheme which the legislature enacted by sections 23, 24 and 25 of the Act of 1973 was a scheme under which the court would be bound, before deciding whether to exercise its powers under sections 23 and 24, and, if so, in what manner, to have regard to all the circumstances of the case, including, *inter alia*, the particular matters specified in paragraphs (a) and (b) of section 25(1). It follows that, in proceedings in which parties invoke the exercise of the court's powers under sections 23 and 24, they must provide the court with information about all the circumstances of the case, including, *inter alia*, the particular matters so specified. Unless they do so, directly or indirectly, and ensure that the information provided is correct, complete and up to date, the court is not equipped to exercise, and cannot therefore lawfully and properly exercise, its discretion in the manner ordained by section 25(1).

In contested cases relating to the exercise of the court's powers under sections 23 and 24 the requirement that it should have the prescribed information is met by rules of court with which both parties must comply.

. . . [U]nless a court is provided with correct, complete and up-to-date information on the matters to which, under section 25(1), it is required to have regard, it cannot lawfully or properly exercise its discretion in the manner ordained by that subsection. It follows necessarily from this that each party concerned in claims for financial provision and property adjustment (or other forms of ancillary relief not material in the present case) owes a duty to the court to make full and frank disclosure of all material facts to the other party and the court. This principle of full and frank disclosure in proceedings of this kind has long been recognised and enforced as a matter of practice. The legal basis of that principle, and the justification for it, are to be found in the statutory provisions to which I have referred.

. . .

My Lords, once it is accepted that this principle of full and frank disclosure exists, it is obvious that it must apply not only to contested proceedings heard with full evidence adduced before the court, but also to exchanges of information between parties and their solicitors leading to the making of consent orders without further inquiry by the court. If that were not so, it would be impossible for a court to have any assurance that the requirements of section 25(1) were complied with before it made such consent orders.

[After referring to *Wadham* v *Wadham* [1977] 1 WLR 199, *Tommey* v *Tommey* [1983] Fam 15, and *Robinson* v *Robinson* [1982] 1 WLR 786n., Lord Brandon concluded: . . .]

Both on principle and on authority, therefore, I am of opinion that the wife was in this case under a duty to disclose the fact of her engagement as soon as it took place, and that her failure to do so is relevant to the validity of the consent order. I am further of the opinion that, since the fact which was not disclosed undermined, as it were, the whole basis on which the consent order was agreed, that order should be set aside and the proceedings for financial provision and property adjustment remitted to the Family Division of the High Court for rehearing by a judge of that division. I would, therefore, allow the appeal and remit the case in the manner indicated.

I would end with an emphatic word of warning. It is not every failure of frank and full disclosure which would justify a court in setting aside an order of the kind concerned in this appeal. On the contrary, it will only be in cases when the absence of full and frank disclosure has led to the court making, either in contested proceedings or by consent, an order which is substantially different from the order which it would have made if such disclosure had taken place that a case for setting aside can possibly be made good. Parties who apply to set aside orders on the ground of failure to disclose some relatively minor matter or matters, the disclosure of which would not have made any substantial difference to the order which the court would have made or approved, are likely to find their applications being summarily dismissed, with costs against them, or, if they are legally aided, against the legal aid fund.

*Notes*

1.   If an action for non-disclosure is by way of appeal rather than by an action to set the order aside, it may be necessary to seek leave to appeal out of time (see 5.10.2 below).

2.   Where one party knows or suspects that the other party may be failing to disclose relevant evidence, an application may be made to the High Court for an *Anton Piller* order which, if granted, will enable the applicant to enter premises and take away documents which can be used as evidence in court proceedings. However, because of the their Draconian nature, such orders are granted only in exceptional circumstances (see, e.g., *Emanuel* v *Emanuel* [1982] 1 WLR 669).

3.   An exception to the principle of full and frank disclosure is the 'million-aire's defence', whereby detailed discovery is not required of a spouse who accepts that there are sufficient assets available to satisfy any court order (see *Thyssen-Bornemisza* v *Thyssen-Bornemisza* [1985] FLR 1069, CA at 5.3.4, and *B* v *B* *(Discovery: Financial Provision)* [1990] 2 FLR 180, FD).

*Question*
Will the increased role for mediation under the divorce reforms lead to more divorcing spouses failing to disclose their assets?

## 5.7   THE MATRIMONIAL HOME ON DIVORCE

The future of the matrimonial home on divorce will be an important matter for both parties not only because it provides accommodation, but also because it is often the couple's most valuable asset. The future of the home will depend on the parties' needs and resources. Under Part II of the MCA 1973 the court has wide discretionary powers to make various property adjustment orders. It may order a sale under s. 24A, or may under s. 24 order that the house be transferred to one spouse with or without a lump sum being paid to the transferor by way of compensation. Sometimes, the court will make an order under s. 24 postponing sale of the home until a later date, e.g., until the children have grown up and/or until the other party remarries or cohabits. Two orders enable sale to be postponed: a '*Mesher*' order and a '*Martin* order'. The relative merits of these two orders, as well as outright transfers of the home, were considered in the following case. Another option is to give the transferor a charge on the house for a certain amount.

***Clutton* v *Clutton***
[1991] 1 WLR 359
Court of Appeal

*Facts*: On divorce the matrimonial home (worth approx. £50,000) was the parties' only substantial asset. The husband had remarried and was earning about £20,000 a year, but had substantial debts. The wife had a small income of her own. The husband had wished for a *Martin* order, but the wife preferred a clean break as she did not wish to be under the constant supervision of her husband. At first instance the husband was ordered to transfer the house to his wife subject to a charge in his favour for £7,000, but on appeal the judge ordered the house to be transferred to the wife absolutely as there ought to be a clean break. The husband appealed.
*Held*: allowing the appeal, that the court did not have to strive for a clean break regardless of other considerations. Here the matrimonial home had been acquired by the joint efforts of the spouses and the courts should ensure that if possible the asset should eventually be shared. The court made a *Martin* order, under which sale of the house would be postponed until the wife's death, remarriage or cohabitation, whereupon the proceeds

of sale would be divided on the basis of two-thirds to the wife and one-third to the husband.

LLOYD LJ: . . . An order whereby the sale of the matrimonial home is postponed until the youngest child of the family is 18, or some other age, is usually known as a *Mesher* order: see *Mesher v Mesher and Hall (Note)* [1980] 1 All ER 126. An order whereby the sale is postponed until the wife dies, remarries or cohabits with another man, is usually known as a *Martin* order: see *Martin (B.H.) v Martin (D.)* [1978] Fam 12. It will be seen that while, in 1984, the wife was asking for an out-and-out transfer of the matrimonial home, she would have been content, in the alternative, with a *Martin* order.

. . . [T]he husband asked for a *Martin* order, on terms that he should have one third of the proceeds of sale, should the wife remarry or cohabit. Otherwise she would be entitled to live in the matrimonial home for the rest of her life. The wife asked for a clean break. It was said on her behalf that this had been a long marriage, that she had limited income and earning capacity compared to her husband, and that she had a genuine fear of 'perpetual supervision' by the husband for the purpose of establishing cohabitation.

. . .

Where the judge went wrong, and plainly wrong in my opinion, was in refusing to make a *Martin* order. As I have pointed out, that is what the wife was orignally content to accept. It is also what the husband was asking for. Why then did the judge not make a *Martin* order? We cannot tell, because we do not know his reasons. It cannot surely have been because a *Martin* order would offend against the principle of the clean break. A charge which does not take effect until death or remarriage could only be said to offend against the principle of the clean break in the most extended sense of that term. The only clue we have is the argument on behalf of the wife that she did not want to be spied on.

I see some force in that argument, although it was scarcely pressed before us. Indeed it was not mentioned at all until it was raised by the court. Whatever the force of the argument, it is far outweighed by the resentment which the husband will naturally feel if the wife remarries within a year or two and continues thereafter to occupy the matrimonial home. She says she has no intention of marrying Mr Davidson. But it remains a distinct possibility. . . .

It is true that, in the present case, the husband's earning capacity is very much greater than that of the wife. In due course, when he has paid off his debts, he will be able to get back on to the property ladder without insuperable difficulty. . . . The question is whether the difference in earning capacity, and the severance of the maintenance tie, justified an out-and-out transfer of the sole capital asset to the wife. In my judgment it did not. The very least which the judge should have done was to order a charge in favour of the husband in the event of the wife's death or remarriage.

Cohabitation raises a separate problem. But if, as Lord Scarman said in *Minton v Minton* [1979] AC 593, the reason underlying the principle of the clean break is the avoidance of bitterness, then the bitterness felt by the husband when he sees the former matrimonial home occupied by the wife's cohabitee must surely be greater than the bitterness felt by the wife being subject, as she fears, to perpetual supervision.

Not to have made a *Martin* order in this case was therefore in my opinion manifestly unfair to the husband. It deprived him forever of any share in the sole capital asset of the marriage, without any sufficient corresponding benefit to the wife.

I am, of course, aware of the limited function of this court in these cases, a limitation which is well illustrated by the majority judgment in the recent case of

*Whiting* v *Whiting* [1988] 1 WLR 565. But I am emboldened to interfere in the present case, first because the judge did not give any reasons for his judgment, and secondly because I consider that his conclusion was in any event plainly wrong.

I would be happy to leave the matter there. But [counsel for the husband] is not now content with a *Martin* order, as was his instructing solicitor, who appeared in this case in the court below. He asks us to consider making a *Mesher* order so that the charge would become effective on [their daughter] attaining the age of 18 or some other age.

The rise and fall of the *Mesher* order has been charted in many previous decisions of this court. Though decided in 1973, the case was not reported until 1980: *Mesher* v *Mesher and Hall (Note)* [1980] 1 All ER 126. It caught on very quickly, so much so that by the time of *Martin (B.H)* v *Martin (D.)* [1978] Fam 12 Ormrod LJ felt it necessary to say that the *Mesher* order was never intended to be a general practice:

> There is no magic in the fact that there are children to be considered. All it means is that the interests of the children take priority in these cases, so that often there can be no question of sale while the children are young. But the situation that will arise when the children reach the age of 18 requires to be carefully considered. Otherwise a great deal of hardship may be stored up in these cases by treating it as a rule of thumb that the matrimonial home should then be sold. It is not a rule of thumb.

Ormrod LJ went on to say, however, that in some cases a *Mesher* order might be the only way of dealing with the situation.

The dangers of the *Mesher* order were emphasised in a number of cases in the early 1980s. In *Mortimer* v *Mortimer-Griffin* [1986] 2 FLR 315 Sir John Donaldson MR said, at pp. 318–319:

> It does seem to me that both orders suffer from the defects to which Ormrod LJ drew attention, that 'chickens come home to roost' at an unpredictable time and in unpredictable circumstances; and that while an adjustment based on percentages seems attractive at the time, experience shows that it is subject to all kinds of difficulties and objections when it is worked out in the event.

Parker LJ said, at p. 319:

> I would also add that I wholly endorse what my Lord, the Master of the Rolls, has said with regard to what is known as a *Mesher* order. It has been criticised since its birth; it is an order which is likely to produce harsh and unsatisfactory results. For my part, I hope that that criticism, if it has not got rid of it, will at least ensure that it is no longer regarded as the 'bible'.

It seems to me, with respect to Parker LJ, that there are still cases where, if only by way of exception, the *Mesher* order provides the best solution. Such a case might be where the family assets are amply sufficient to provide both parties with a roof over their heads if the matrimonial home were sold, but nevertheless the interests of the children require that they remain in the matrimonial home. In such a case it may be just and sensible to postpone the sale until the children have left home, since, ex hypothesi, the proceeds of sale will then be sufficient to enable the wife to rehouse herself. In such a case the wife is 'relatively secure': see the judgment of Ormrod LJ in *McDonnell* v *McDonnell* (1976) 6 Fam Law 220.

But where there is doubt as to the wife's ability to rehouse herself, on the charge taking effect, then a *Mesher* order should not be made. That is, as I see it, the position here. The split suggested by the husband would give the wife two thirds of £50,000. It must be very uncertain whether this would be sufficient to enable the wife to rehouse herself in a few years' time when [their daughter] leaves home. That is no doubt the reason why the registrar declined to make a *Mesher* order. I would agree with him. But the *Martin* order does not suffer from the same disadvantages.

In conclusion I would reject [counsel for the husband's] submission that we should make a *Mesher* order, but accept his submission that we should make a *Martin* order. The split which he suggests seems about right. Accordingly, I would grant leave and allow the appeal to that extent.

In *Clutton*, the *Martin* order postponed sale *inter alia* until the wife's remarriage or cohabitation. The following extract considers whether such 'cohabitation clauses' are appropriate.

### Hayes, Mary, ' "Cohabitation Clauses" in Financial Provision and Property Adjustment Orders — Law, Policy and Justice' (1994) 110 LQR 124

. . . It seems likely that the majority of cohabitation clauses will be found in consent orders rather than in orders externally imposed by a court. While the private ordering of affairs on the breakdown of marriage is generally to be applauded, it is suggested that there are strong policy reasons why the insertion of such a clause should be regarded as inappropriate and strongly discouraged by scrutinising district judges. Cohabitation clauses in orders for periodical payments take the parties outside the comprehensive statutory code provided by the statutory framework, with its in-built checks and balances designed to promote fairness between the parties. These clauses take automatic effect and . . . it is unlikely that an ex-wife would be in the position to make either a fresh application or a variation application for periodical payments whatever her personal circumstances. But to terminate an order solely because an ex-wife is cohabiting is to respond crudely to what is often a complex situation. It makes no allowance for the reasons why a periodical payments order was made in the first instance and why the ex-wife was then in a state of financial dependency on her husband. It makes no allowance for the reasons why such dependency may be continuing. It makes no allowance for the impact termination of the ex-wife's order might have on any children of the family, who must be a court's first consideration in any court proceedings. It assumes not only that the cohabitant is currently providing the ex-wife with financial support but also that he will continue to do so, since the wife is deprived for all time from making any further claim against her ex-husband. By contrast the courts' discretionary jurisdiction can give weight to all of these factors and respond appropriately. Similar points can be made about the practice of inserting cohahitation clauses into property adjustment orders. Their objectionable character-istic is that entitlement to sale of the property occurs automatically by operation of law and, consequently, a court has no opportunity to consider either the spouses' respective needs and resources, or the needs of any children, when the time for sale arrives.

. . . In *Clutton* v *Clutton*, the wife resisted the insertion of a cohabitation clause into the court's order because she feared 'perpetual supervision' by her ex-husband for the purposes of establishing that she was living with another man. The Court of Appeal was dismissive of her fear. However, she may have had good cause to be apprehensive. It is not unknown for an ex-husband to employ inquiry agents to observe his ex-wife's

home early in the morning and late at night and for these inquiry agents to provide evidence for a court in which they describe such matters as the times when the ex-wife and the man with whom she is alleged to be cohabiting have gone in and out of the house together, the number of lights in bedroom windows, whether the man's car is parked in the drive over night, and the occasion when the man is observed leaving the house first thing in the morning. When parties are married, it is generally accepted that they owe one another an obligation of sexual fidelity, so the gathering of this type of evidence to prove that a wife is having an intimate relationship with another man may have occasional justification for divorce purposes. Nonetheless, this sort of unseemly inquiry is reminiscent of some of the worst aspects of the divorce law which preceded the reforms of 1969, when observations of this nature took place for the purposes of proving adultery. When parties have divorced, any obligation of fidelity comes to an end, and it is submitted that there can be no justification for engaging third parties to take note of how an ex-wife is conducting her personal life. Observations of this kind are prurient and menacing, and amount to a serious invasion of the ex-wife's privacy.
. . .

*Note*
*Mesher* and *Martin* orders became increasingly unpopular because of the problems they stored up until a later date (see, e.g., *Carson v Carson* [1983] 1 WLR 285, CA, and *Thompson v Thompson* [1986] Fam 38, CA) but with uncertainties about the amount of child maintenance to be paid after the creation of the Child Support Agency under the Child Support Act 1991, some divorcing spouses who are absent parents may prefer to postpone sale of the home on divorce rather than agree to its transfer.

## 5.8  PENSIONS ON DIVORCE

Under the current law the court may take into account future or lost pension entitlement under s. 25(2) of the MCA 1973 (particularly under subsections (a), (b) and (h)) and may delay or refuse to grant a divorce under ss. 5 and 10 of the 1973 Act in two- or five-year separation cases, so that the petitioner may make provision for the respondent's lost pension entitlement (see, e.g., *K v K (Financial Relief: Widow's Pension)* [1997] 1 FLR 35, FD). However, after growing concern about the inadequacy of the court's powers to deal with pensions on divorce, which caused injustice to divorced wives in particular, ss. 25B, 25C and 25D were inserted into the MCA 1973 by the Pensions Act 1995, giving the court jurisdiction to 'earmark' pensions on divorce so as to enable income to be paid to a divorced spouse at the time of retirement. These provisions came into force on 1 August 1996.

'Earmarking' to allow payment at retirement is not, however, an ideal solution because of uncertainties in the future (e.g., the husband may become ill, or may be made redundant or may make new pension arrangements); and after concern voiced in the Parliamentary debates on the Family Law Bill during the 1995–96 session of Parliament, s. 16 of the FLA 1996 was enacted which amends ss. 25B and 25C of the MCA 1973 to allow pension splitting at the time of divorce. In July 1996 the Government published a Consultation

Paper on pensions, *The Treatment of Pension Rights on Divorce* (Cm 3345, 1996). A White Paper, *Pension Rights on Divorce* (Cm 3564), was published on 26 February 1997. It is unlikely, however, that pension splitting at divorce will come into effect until the next century.

The unitalicised part of the following provisions came into force on 1 August 1996 in respect of divorces granted after 1 July 1996. The parts in italics were inserted by the FLA 1996, but at the time of writing are not in force.

## MATRIMONIAL CAUSES ACT 1973

**25B. Pensions**
(1) The matters to which the court is to have regard under section 25(2) above include—
(a) in the case of paragraph (a), any benefits under a pension scheme which a party to the marriage has or is likely to have, and
(b) in the case of paragraph (h), any benefits under a pension scheme which, by reason of the dissolution or annulment of the marriage, a party to the marriage will lose the chance of acquring,
and, accordingly, in relation to benefits under a pension scheme, section 25(2)(a) above shall have effect as if 'in the foreseeable future' were omitted.
(2) In any proceedings for a financial provision order under section 23 [*section 22A or 23*] above in a case where a party to the marriage has, or is likely to have, any benefit under a pension scheme, the court shall, in addition to considering any other matter which it is required to consider apart from this subsection, consider—
(a) whether, having regard to any matter to which it is required to have regard in the proceedings by virtue of subsection (1) above, such an order (whether deferred or not) should be made,
(b) where the court determines to make such an order, how the terms of the order should be affected, having regard to any such matter, and
(c) *in particular, where the court determines to make such an order, whether the order should provide for the accrued rights of the party with pension rights ('the pension rights') to be divided between that party and the other party in such a way as to reduce the pension rights to the party with those rights and to create pension rights for the other party.*
. . .

**25C. Pensions: Lump sums**
(1) The power of the court under section 23 [*section 22A or 23*] above to order a party to the marriage to pay a lump sum to the other party includes, where the benefits to which the party with pension rights has or is likely to have under a pension scheme include any lump sum payable in respect of his death, power to make any of the following provision by the order.
(2) The court may—
(a) if the trustees or managers of the pension scheme in question have power to determine the person to whom the sum, or any part of it, is to be paid, require them to pay the whole or part of that sum, when it becomes due, to the other party,
(b) if the party with pension rights has power to nominate the person to whom the sum, or any part of it, is to be paid, require the party with pension rights to nominate the other party in respect of the whole or part of that sum,
(c) in any other case, require the trustees or managers of the pension scheme in question to pay the whole or part of that sum, when it becomes due, for the benefit

of the other party instead of to the person to whom, apart from the order, it would be paid.

(3)   Any payment by the trustees or managers under an order made under section 23 [section 22A or 23] above by virtue of this section shall discharge so much of the trustees', or managers', liability in respect of the party with pension rights as corresponds to the amount of the payment.

## Joshi, H., and Davies, H., 'Pensions, Divorce and Wives' Double Burden'
### (1992) 6 IJL&F 289

Pension after divorce is a growing problem in Britain, with increasing numbers of women losing access to their spouse's benefits and likely to be inadequately covered in their own right. Part of the problem is that existing law makes it difficult to divide pension rights. Another is that married women are still unlikely to be earning much of a pension in their own right. A third aspect is the low level of information, about pensions among the public at large and many law practitioners, and, in the pensions world, about divorce. . . .

. . . Pensions are far into the future of most divorces, and ignoring them is in some ways part of the spirit of the clean break, putting the failed marriage in the past. Yet while the marriage lasted, one or both parties may have been making tax-privileged arrangements for financial provisions in old age on which both could have expected to draw had the marriage survived. By the time women who are now at the peak age for risk of divorce become pensioners, there are likely to be about a million elderly divorced women in England and Wales. Many of these will have small pensions; most of them will have pensions inferior to those of their ex-husbands, or to those they would have shared in had they remained married or remarried, or indeed to those of the new wives their husbands may replace them with. For women whose own earnings are reduced in the domestic division of labour, to share a husband's pension rights contingent on the marriage lasting into old age is to give a hostage to fortune. The calculations reported above suggest that for those lucky enough to gain access to an interest in a good pension, pension-splitting could be useful as well as equitable, but for parties mainly relying on SERPS, there are not enough pension resources to make an effective transfer. Pension-splitting would be rather a capricious vehicle for bringing extra support to a vulnerable group. Neither is it the ideal way of pooling the pension costs of childrearing; some would be undercompensated; others, including the childless, would be overcompensated.

Women's advances in the labour market have meant that they will be able to 'earn their own pensions': but only up to a point. The limitations on women's economic gains mean that most are still partially financially dependent on their husbands. Under these circumstances it would not be right to condemn pension-splitting as perpetuating dependency within marriage. Rather it recognizes that dependency has not completely disappeared and helps to prevent inequity arising when pooling ceases. Where domestic responsibilities have not been divided, it is not equal treatment to expect women to carry the double burden of society's unpaid work and earn themselves, as individuals, the pension rights that their husbands and ex-husbands managed to earn, freed from the need to run the unpaid side of life. We have attempted to weigh this burden. Pension-splitting could help to relieve it, especially where an ex-husband has a good pension, but it is not a panacea. Divorced or not, women fare badly from earnings-linked pensions, because they fare badly in the labour market. There is a case for establishing procedures to deal with the assignment of pension rights on divorce, but to protect women from hardship, it would be better to improve the Basic Pension.

. . .

*Note*

In *Brooks* v *Brooks* [1995] 2 FLR 13, the House of Lords held that the court had jurisdiction to vary the terms of a pension scheme, as the particular pension arrangement could be construed as a post-nuptial settlement and thereby capable of adjustment under s. 24(1)(c) of the MCA 1973. The impact of *Brooks* was limited due to the special nature of the pension arrangement (a small, company-run scheme where the husband was marginally the majority shareholder), but it did highlight the need for reform.

*Further reading*
Chatterton, D., 'Pension Rights on Divorce: The Implications of *Brooks* v *Brooks*' [1993] Fam Law 423.
Martin, A., 'Pensions and Divorce' [1996] Fam Law 432.
Salter, D., 'Pensions after *Brooks*' [1994] Fam Law 520.

## 5.9   THE EMPHASIS ON AGREEMENT AND SETTLEMENT

### 5.9.1   The danger of reaching an agreement

Parties to a divorce are encouraged to reach agreement about property and financial matters on divorce, because agreements are cheaper and more predictable than court orders and they reduce hostility between the parties, thereby making it less traumatic for themselves and their children. Most solicitors adopt a conciliatory approach to ancillary matters and encourage agreements to be reached (see the Code of Practice of the Solicitors' Family Law Association in Chapter 1). Parties may reach agreement in various ways, either formally or informally, and with or without the assistance of mediation and/or legal advice. Agreements may be incorporated into a court order known as a 'consent order'. Despite the emphasis on agreement, however, the parties can never have the final say, as the court is always the final arbiter. It is thus not possible by agreement to oust the jurisdiction of the court or of the Child Support Agency.

Despite the advantages of agreement, there may be dangers as the following case demonstrates.

*Edgar* **v** *Edgar*
[1980] 1 WLR 1410
Court of Appeal

*Facts*: After lengthy negotiations, the parties executed a deed of separation, in which the wife, despite legal advice that she would do better in ancillary relief proceedings, agreed that she would not claim lump sum or property transfer orders on divorce. Her husband had neither pressurised her to accept the terms of the deed nor exploited his position as a wealthy man. The husband performed his obligations under the deed. Subsequently the wife applied in divorce proceedings for a lump sum, but the husband argued that the court should refuse to order a lump sum as his wife had agreed not to seek such an order. The trial judge found for the wife and ordered the husband to pay her a lump sum of £67,000, a sum substantially larger than the amount paid under the agreement. The husband appealed.

*Held*: allowing the appeal, that when exercising its discretion to order a lump sum, the court was required to give effect to a prior agreement by the wife not to claim a lump sum by treating that agreement as conduct of the parties under s. 25(2)(g) of the MCA 1973.

OLIVER LJ: . . . The principles to be applied are not seriously in dispute. After a review of the relevant authorities the judge stated them in the five propositions which have already been referred to in the judgment of Ormrod LJ and I accept them subject to the same reservations as those which he has stated and in particular as regards the reference which the judge made to 'equal bargaining power' and 'disparity of bargaining power.' If, by these references, Eastham J meant no more than that one must look in every case at all the circumstances to see whether there was some unfair or unconscionable advantage taken of some factor or of some relationship between the parties which enables the court to say that an agreement was not truly entered into by one party or the other as a free agent, then I have no quarrel with them. If, however, he meant that the court must engage in an exercise of dissecting the contract and weighing the relative advantages and bargaining position on each side in order to ascertain whether there is some precise or approximate equilibrium, then I respectfully disagree. Men and women of full age, education and understanding, acting with competent advice available to them, must be assumed to know and appreciate what they are doing and their actual respective bargaining strengths will in fact depend in every case upon a subjective evaluation of their motives for doing it. One may, of course, find that some unfair advantage has been taken of a judgment impaired by emotion, or that one party is motivated by fear induced by some conduct of the other or by some misapprehension of a factual or legal position, but in the absence of some such consideration as that — and these are examples only — the mere strength of one party's desire for a particular result or the mere fact that one party has greater wealth than the other cannot, I think, affect the weight to be attributed to a freely negotiated bargain.

Having said that, I do not, of course, quarrel for one moment with the proposition that the court in every case must — indeed is enjoined by statute to — look at all the circumstances in exercising its powers under section 25(1) of the Act of 1973 to produce the result directed by that section. That is not in issue here, but the extent to which the court is directed and is able to produce the result of placing all the parties in the financial position in which they would have been if the marriage had not broken down is controlled first by practicability and secondly by the consideration of what is just having regard to their conduct. In that consideration the existence of a freely negotiated bargain entered into at the instance of one of the parties and affording to him or her everything for which he or she has stipulated must be a most important element of conduct which cannot be lightly ignored. Essentially therefore what is in issue in the instant case is whether, in exercising the jurisdiction which the statute required him to exercise, Eastham J was right to decline to hold the wife to a particular term of the agreement into which she had entered four years earlier. I say 'a particular term' because there is really no dispute between the parties that, if the wife makes out a proper case for additional income payments beyond those specified in the deed of separation, the husband is willing to provide them. There may be a lively dispute both about the necessity and the quantum, but there is, if I understand Mr Jackson right, no dispute in principle. What is in dispute is whether, having regard to clause 8 of the deed, to which Ormrod LJ has already referred, the judge was right to award to the wife the very large capital sum which he did award.

[After referring to the facts, his Lordship continued: . . .]

In the last analysis the attack upon the agreement centres, as Eastham J recognised, not upon any unfair pressure or leverage, but simply upon the disparity in bargaining power between the parties, that is to say the inequality in the weapons which were available to them if they chose to use them and not in the use of them or even threats of use of them which they actually made. That does not, in my judgment, constitute any ground for going behind this agreement in the circumstances of this case, where it was, throughout, the wife who, for her own convenience, was pressing for it and threatening proceedings if it was not concluded and implemented. By its terms she achieved the independence she desired, she obtained the home of her own choosing, and she obtained a not insubstantial income for the support of herself and her children. It was a result which commended itself to her at the time and it does not become an unjust result merely because she could have done better if she had taken the professional advice which she was given. Clearly it did not give her the standard of life which she had enjoyed in the company of a husband with whom she was no longer prepared to live, but in a consideration of what is just to be done in the exercise of the court's powers under the Act of 1973 in the light of the conduct of the parties, the court must, I think, start from the position that a solemn and freely negotiated bargain by which a party defines her own requirements ought to be adhered to unless some clear and compelling reason, such as, for instance, a drastic change of circumstances, is shown to the contrary. No such compelling reason has been demonstrated in the evidence placed before this court. The wife's reasons for seeking to resile from the agreement, as they emerge from her affidavit, appear to be that she feels unable to offer her children amenities comparable to those which her husband is able to offer and that she would like to buy a farm and to have a house in London. I find myself wholly unpersuaded that such considerations furnish any ground for relieving her of the bargain into which she freely entered and I would hold her to that bargain. I agree therefore that the appeal should be allowed and I concur in the course proposed by Ormrod LJ.

*Note*

For cases where the *Edgar* principle was departed from, see *Richardson* v *Richardson (No. 2)* [1994] 2 FLR 1051, FD, *N* v *N (Consent Order: Variation)* [1993] 2 FLR 868, CA, and *Camm* v *Camm* (1983) 4 FLR 577, CA.

### 5.9.2   Consent orders

Under s. 33A of the MCA 1973, the court has jurisdiction to make consent orders for financial provision and property adjustment, provided that the parties have furnished the court with information prescribed by the FPR 1991, r. 2.61 (i.e. the duration of the marriage, the age of the parties and any minor or dependent children, an estimate of the approximate value of the capital resources and net income of each party and of any minor child, the intended arrangements for accommodation for the parties and minor children, whether either party has remarried or has any intention to marry or to cohabit, and any other especially significant matter). The reason for the requirements in s. 33A of the MCA 1973 and r. 2.61 of the 1991 Rules is to give effect to the principle of full and frank disclosure (see 5.6).

In practice, consent orders are routinely made. Their advantage over informal or formal agreements is that the court can scrutinise the agreement and variation can be sought under s. 31 of the 1973 Act should circumstances change.

### *Pounds* v *Pounds*
### [1994] 1 FLR 775
### Court of Appeal

WAITE LJ: . . . The effect of section 33A and the rules and directions made under it is thus to confine the paternal function of the court when approving financial consent orders to a broad appraisal of the parties' financial circumstances as disclosed to it in summary form, without descent into the valley of detail. It is only if that survey puts the court on inquiry as to whether there are other circumstances into which it ought to probe more deeply that any further investigation is required of the judge before approving the bargain that the spouses have made for themselves. . . .

*Example of a consent order*
The following is an example of a consent order (taken from *Crozier* v *Crozier* [1994] 1 FLR 126 at pp. 130 and 131):

By consent it is ordered that:

(1)   The respondent do pay or cause to be paid to the petitioner for the benefit of the child . . . (born 31 October 1984), maintenance pending suit and thereafter periodical payments at the rate of £0.05 pa until the said child shall attain the age of 17 years or until further order.

(2)   The petitioner's claim for maintenance for herself be dismissed.

(3)   The respondent do transfer to the petitioner absolutely all his legal and equitable estate in the property . . . subject to the mortgage in favour of the . . . Building Society, and it is recorded that the petitioner will use her best endeavours to obtain the release of the respondent from his obligations under the said mortgage. All rights of occupation of the property by the respondent shall then be terminated.

(4)   That the contents of the former matrimonial home shall be hereby declared to be the property of the petitioner absolutely.

(5)   And it is hereby agreed and declared between the parties that the respondent is transferring all his estate, share and interest in the matrimonial home to the petitioner absolutely on the basis that there is to be a nominal order for maintenance for the child only and that the petitioner will have the full responsibility of maintaining the said child in future.

(6)   It is recorded that this order is intended to effect a full and final settlement of all financial and property claims arising between the parties from the breakdown of

the marriage whether present or future, save for child maintenance, and upon compliance with paras 1–7 herein the respective claims of the parties under ss. 23, 24, and 24A of the Matrimonial Causes Act 1973 do stand dismissed and neither party shall make any application under the Married Women's Property Act 1882.

(7)   Without prejudice to the generality of the foregoing it is directed:

(a)   neither party shall make any further application for an order under s. 23(1)(a) or (b) of the Matrimonial Causes Act 1973;

(b)   neither party shall upon the death of the other apply for an order under s. 2 of the Inheritance (Provision for Family and Dependants) Act 1975.

(8)   No order for costs save that the costs of the petitioner be taxed on a standard basis in accordance with the provisions of the Second Schedule to the Legal Aid Act 1974.

### 5.9.3   Problems with agreement

**Davis, Gwynn, Cretney, Stephen, and Collins, Jean, *Simple Quarrels***
Oxford: Clarendon Press, 1994, at pp. 2 and 261–63

. . . There is inevitably some ambiguity about the court's function when presented with an agreement; and the balance between acting as a rubber stamp and a 'forensic ferret' [*per* Ward J in *BT* v *BT* [1990] 2 FLR 1, at p. 17] is not easy to strike. . . .

. . . [I]t is apparent from this research, as it is from previous studies . . . , that there are problems with settlement. First, to settle cases, when applying the individual justice or 'discretionary' model, requires full knowledge of the parties' financial circumstances; but, as we have seen, settlement is often negotiated in the absence of full knowledge. Second, settlement negotiated 'in the shadow of the court' (and the fore-shadowing of an adjudicative outcome is usually quite explicit) requires predictability; but agreement is often reached in a climate of great uncertainty. Third, settlement is generally portrayed as short-circuiting the legal process; but the settled cases which we observed lasted, on average, as long as those which were adjudicated, suggesting that many 'settlements' are a product of fatigue and domination. Fourth, settlement is portrayed as cost-saving; but that depends on the lawyer-time that goes into it — in several of our 'continuous monitoring' cases, settlement proved exceedingly expensive. It is not surprising therefore that preoccupation with securing a legal settlement is a lawyers' preoccupation; it is not something to which the parties are committed, or to which they attach importance — indeed, in most cases they see no prospect of reaching agreement. The applicant (if not the respondent) is concerned with bringing the matter to a conclusion and achieving a satisfactory result. In these circumstances the solicitor may become an apologist for the court system with all its inertia and built-in frustrations; he may also act as a kind of fifth columnist, employing his position of influence in order to overcome his client's resistance to whatever solution is proposed.

. . .

We have found, in the divorce context, that the pressures which bear on the parties in the course of ancillary relief negotiation apply unequally to men and women. Inequality in terms of the ability and commitment of legal advisers, to which we have already referred, is paralleled by an inequality of bargaining power between the parties — principally reflected in their ability to tolerate a postponed resolution. The fact that, in most cases, one party (usually the woman) needs an order, whilst the other (usually the man) is content for the stalemate to continue, has considerable influence upon the terms of any settlement. This particular bargaining 'chip' is rendered more potent by the failure to impose any effective sanction when faced with one party's failure to meet a court-imposed timetable.

That delay and lack of full disclosure produce rewards for one side but costs for the other provides — or should provide — the basis for a feminist critique of the present method of dealing with ancillary relief. Inequality of bargaining power includes the ability to frustrate — not to reach any agreement — and the present system colludes with this. It favours whichever party has the greater capacity to withhold information and tolerate delay. There developed in the early 1980s feminist criticism of the emerging conciliation services on the basis that these failed to protect the rights of the more vulnerable spouse; this critique emphasized the protection afforded by 'due process'. . . . Diversion from trial is a dominant theme in matrimonial proceedings. We have seen that again in the course of this research. Women do better — or at least feel they do better — with trials. This was also our impression, based on the failure to protect the woman's interests in the course of some of the negotiations which we observed. 'Settlement' in some of these cases reflected fatigue, lawyer pressure, and anxiety about rising costs. This observation is diametrically opposed to the view expressed by the Law Society (1991). The Law Society Committee charged with considering these matters had 'suggested that a negotiated settlement would be more in their (female) clients' interests than the strict application of the principles [enshrined in the 1973 Matrimonial Causes Act]'. Our evidence invites a contrary conclusion.

The other important point to make about settlement is that, at least in those cases which involved an application to the court (what we have termed 'the procedural route'), there seemed no obvious relationship between complexity of case (assessed in terms of the parties' wealth) and time taken to reach a conclusion. Indeed, we strongly suspect that, in general, the more meagre the assets, the longer it takes. . . .

We would conclude, therefore that effective progress is seldom achieved by the procedural route. Instead, the system is characterized by procedural complexity, often in circumstances where the final outcome will make no difference to the woman and children's net income because they are bound to remain dependent upon Income Support. This has profound consequences in terms of financial cost, both to the parties and the State, and in terms of the stress, amounting in many instances to despair, which it generates. Delay, then, is a major component in eventual abandonment, but also in eventual settlement, with many litigants simply giving up under lawyer pressure following years of stagnation.
. . .

*Notes*
1.   For a feminist critique of the pressure to reach agreement, see Bottomley, A., 'Resolving Family Disputes: A Critical View' in Freeman, M. (ed.), *State, Law and the Family*, London: Tavistock, 1984.
2.   The reference to the Law Society in the above extract is to its 1991 *Memorandum* (see 5.3).

*Question*
One of the main themes of the research conducted by Davis *et al.* on ancillary relief and reported in *Simple Quarrels*, at pp. 2 and 3, concerned the pressure brought to bear on the parties to come to an agreement and the question of

whether the present procedures in practice met the declared objectives of protecting economically vulnerable people and upholding the public interest. Why is there pressure on the parties to reach agreement? Is there too much pressure? Are there any dangers in exerting such pressure?

## 5.10  CHANGES OF CIRCUMSTANCES AFTER AN ORDER HAS BEEN MADE

Periodical payments orders may be varied or discharged in MCA 1973, s. 31 variation proceedings. Property adjustment orders and lump sum orders (except for the instalments) cannot be varied, so that the only way to challenge such an order is to appeal against it or to apply to have it set aside, on the grounds, e.g. of non-disclosure, mistake, fraud, misrepresentation or duress. Where the time for lodging an appeal has passed, leave to appeal will be needed, which the court will grant only if the '*Barder* principles' are satisfied (see 5.10.2 below). Sometimes an application for leave to appeal out of time will be combined with an application to have the original order set aside, so that new terms can be negotiated and a different order made.

### 5.10.1  Variation

Under s. 31 of the MCA 1973 the court has jurisdiction to vary an order for maintenance pending suit, any interim maintenance order, any periodical payments order, and an order for the sale of property. Lump sum orders (except the instalments) and property adjustment orders may not be varied.

## MATRIMONIAL CAUSES ACT 1973

**31.  Variation, discharge, etc., of certain orders for financial relief**
    (7)   In exercising the powers conferred by this section the court shall have regard to all the circumstances of the case, first consideration being given to the welfare while a minor of any child of the family who has not attained the age of eighteen, and the circumstances of the case shall include any change in any of the matters to which the court was required to have regard when making the order to which the application relates, and—
    (a)   in the case of a periodical payments or secured periodical payments order made on or after the grant of a decree of divorce . . . the court shall consider whether in all the circumstances and after having regard to any such change it would be appropriate to vary the order so that payments under the order are required to be made or secured only for such further period as will in the opinion of the court be sufficient to enable the party in whose favour the order was made to adjust without undue hardship to the termination of those payments;
    . . .

*Note*
The FLA 1996 leaves s. 31 unchanged, except for changes in detail, but inserts s. 31A into the 1973 Act to give the court power to vary or discharge lump sum and/or property adjustment orders on the joint application of the

parties made before the grant of a divorce order (FLA 1996, sch. 2, para. 8). Schedule 8 of the FLA 1996 inserts new subsections (7A) to (7F) into s. 31(7) of the 1973 Act to allow the court, *inter alia*, to order the payment of a lump sum or one or more property adjustment orders when it discharges a periodical payments order (secured or unsecured) in favour of a party to a marriage or makes such an order for a limited term.

### 5.10.2    Appeals out of time: the '*Barder* principles'

Not every application for leave to appeal out of time will be granted. The '*Barder* principles' must be satisfied.

#### *Barder* v *Barder* (*Caluori intervening*)
#### [1988] 1 AC 20
#### House of Lords

*Facts*: A consent order was made on divorce in which the husband agreed to transfer his interest in the matrimonial home to his wife; but before the transfer had been executed the wife killed the children and committed suicide. The husband appealed out of time against the order, on the ground that it had been based on a fundamental assumption that the wife and children would, for a substantial period of time, require a suitable home and that the assumption had been totally invalidated by their deaths. His mother-in-law obtained leave to intervene to oppose the application. The trial judge granted the husband's application and set aside the order on the ground that it had been vitiated by a fundamental mistake, namely that it had been considered that the wife and children would continue to live and benefit from the terms of the order for an appreciable time after it had been made. The Court of Appeal allowed the mother-in-law's appeal. The husband appealed to the House of Lords.

*Held*: allowing the appeal and setting aside the order, that leave to appeal out of time against an order for ancillary relief would be granted only if certain conditions were satisfied. On the facts the fundamental assumption (i.e. that the wife and children would have need of a suitable home for a substantial period of time) had been totally invalidated by their deaths.

LORD BRANDON: . . .

*The question of leave to appeal*
My Lords, the question whether leave to appeal out of time should be given on the ground that assumptions or estimates made at the time of the hearing of a cause or matter have been invalidated or falsified by subsequent events is a difficult one. The reason why the question is difficult is that it involves a conflict between two important legal principles and a decision as to which of them is to prevail over the other. The first principle is that it is in the public interest that there should be finality in litigation. The second principle is that justice requires cases to be decided, so far as practicable, on the true facts relating to them, and not on assumptions or estimates with regard to those facts which are conclusively shown by later events to have been erroneous.
. . .

My Lords, the result of the two lines of authority to which I have referred appears to me to be this. A court may properly exercise its discretion to grant leave to appeal out of time from an order for financial provision or property transfer made after a divorce on the ground of new events, provided that certain conditions are satisfied. The first condition is that new events have occurred since the making of the order which invalidate the basis, or fundamental assumption, upon which the order was made, so that, if leave to appeal out of time were to be given, the appeal would be certain, or very likely, to succeed. The second condition is that the new events should have occurred within a relatively short time of the order having been made. While the length of time cannot be laid down precisely, I should regard it as extremely unlikely that it could be as much as a year, and that in most cases it will be no more than a few months. The third condition is that the application for leave to appeal out of time should be made reasonably promptly in the circumstances of the case. To these three conditions, which can be seen from the authorities as requiring to be satisfied, I would add a fourth, which it does not appear has needed to be considered so far, but which it may be necessary to consider in future cases. That fourth condition is that the grant of leave to appeal out of time should not prejudice third parties who have acquired, in good faith and for valuable consideration, interests in property which is the subject matter of the relevant order.

It is because I consider that the first condition set out above must be satisfied that I cannot agree with the view of Woolf LJ that consideration of the question of leave to appeal out of time can or should be treated separately from the question of the merits of the appeal if leave is granted.

### Conclusion

My Lords, I have now given my answers to the three questions which I said earlier it was necessary to examine in this appeal. In answer to the first question, that of abatement, I have held that Judge Smithies had jurisdiction to entertain the husband's application for leave to appeal out of time, and, having done so, to entertain his appeal, notwithstanding that the wife had died. To the second question, that of merits on appeal, I have expressed the view that, on the hypothesis that leave to appeal out of time is given, the appeal succeeds and the order of Judge Smithies should be restored. In answer to the third question, that of leave to appeal, I have held that an appellate court may properly exercise its discretion to grant leave to appeal out of time, provided that four conditions, which I have specified, are satisfied.

Judge Smithies was the appellate court in this case and it was a matter for his discretion whether leave to appeal out of time should be granted or not. In my opinion, on the facts of the present case, all the four conditions for the grant of leave to appeal out of time which I have specified were satisfied. Judge Smithies was, accordingly, entitled to exercise his discretion by granting leave to appeal out of time, and there is no ground on which that exercise of discretion by him could properly be reversed by the Court of Appeal. Judge Smithies was further right, having granted leave to appeal out of time, to allow the appeal on the merits.

My Lords, for the reasons which I have given, I would allow the appeal, set aside the order of the Court of Appeal dated 9 May 1986 and restore the order of Judge Smithies dated 15 November 1985, save in so far as it directed that costs be reserved.

### Notes

*1.* The 'two lines of authority' referred to by Lord Brandon were those in the field of actions for death or personal injuries and those involving orders for financial provision or property transfers after divorce.

*2.* For an excellent survey of the law on setting aside and appealing against financial provision and property adjustment orders, see Hale J in *Cornick* v *Cornick* [1994] 2 FLR 530, FD.

*3.* In *Smith* v *Smith (Smith and others intervening)* [1992] Fam 69, the Court of Appeal held that where an order was reconsidered after changed circumstances which invalidated the basis of the order, the court should take account of the facts as known at the date of the reassessment and reach a fresh decision having regard to all the criteria in s. 25 of the MCA 1973.

*4.* Appeals out of time on the basis of changes of circumstances are common in the law reports: see, e.g., *Penrose* v *Penrose* [1994] 2 FLR 621, CA, (husband's unforeseen increased tax liability), *Heard* v *Heard* [1995] 1 FLR 970, CA, (inaccurate valuation of the matrimonial home), and *Crozier* v *Crozier* [1994] Fam 114, FD (new and unexpected obligations under the Child Support Act 1991). See also *Benson* v *Benson (Deceased)* [1996] 1 FLR 692, FD, for 'a fascinating conflation' (Burrows [1996] Fam Law 426) of *Barder* and *Edgar* principles.

*Question*
What is the rationale of the *Barder* principles?

## 5.11 PREVENTING THE DISSIPATION OF ASSETS

Imagine the following scenario. The husband owns a villa in Portugal, a business in London and has substantial investments and capital in a bank account. His wife has told him she is going to apply for divorce. He does not wish her to get hold of any of his money. He therefore takes immediate steps to sell the Portuguese house and his business in London, and to transfer his investments and capital to a Swiss bank account. What can his wife do?

## MATRIMONIAL CAUSES ACT 1973

**37. Avoidance of transactions intended to prevent or reduce financial relief**
(1) . . .
(2) Where proceedings for financial relief are brought by one person against another, the court may, on the application of the first-mentioned person—
 (a) if it is satisfied that the other party to the proceedings is, with the intention of defeating the claim for financial relief, about to make any disposition or to transfer out of the jurisdiction or otherwise deal with any property, make such order as it thinks fit for restraining the other party from so doing or otherwise for protecting the claim;
 (b) if it is satisfied that the other party has, with that intention, made a reviewable disposition and that if the disposition were set aside financial relief or different financial relief would be granted to the applicant, make an order setting aside the disposition;
 (c) if it is satisfied, in a case where an order has been obtained under any of the provisions mentioned in subsection (1) above by the applicant against the other party, that the other party has, with that intention, made a reviewable disposition, make an order setting aside the disposition;

and an application for the purposes of paragraph (b) above shall be made in the proceedings for the financial relief in question.

*Notes*
1.   'Financial relief' is defined in MCA 1973, s. 37(1).
2.   Instead of using s. 37, a party may apply *ex parte* to the High Court for a *Mareva* injunction under the court's inherent jurisdiction (e.g., where the necessary intention under s. 37 cannot be proved). The courts have held that the *Mareva* injunction is a Draconian remedy of last resort existing at the limit of the court's powers (see e.g. *Ghoth* v *Ghoth* [1992] 2 All ER 920 and *Shipman* v *Shipman* [1991] 1 FLR 250).

## 5.12   APPLICATION FOR FINANCIAL PROVISION AND PROPERTY ADJUSTMENT ORDERS AFTER A FOREIGN DIVORCE

Under Part III of the Matrimonial and Family Proceedings Act 1984, the English High Court and specially designated divorce county courts have jurisdiction to make finance and property orders where the parties have been divorced abroad, provided that the foreign divorce is recognised in England and Wales (s. 12) and provided that leave has been granted to make the application (ss. 13, 15, and 16). Once leave has been granted, s. 17 imports into the 1984 Act the provisions of Part II of the MCA 1973, and by s. 18 the court in exercising its discretion must apply the factors listed in s. 25 of the 1973 Act.

## MATRIMONIAL AND FAMILY PROCEEDINGS ACT 1984

**12.   Applications for financial relief after overseas divorce etc.**
   (1)   Where—
      (a)   a marriage has been dissolved . . . in an overseas country, and
      (b)   the divorce . . . is entitled to be recognised as valid in England and Wales, either party to the marriage may apply to the court . . . for an order for financial relief.
   . . .

**13.   Leave of the court required for applications for financial relief**
   (1)   No application for an order for financial relief shall be made under this Part . . . unless the leave of the court has been obtained in accordance with rules of court; and the court shall not grant leave unless it considers that there is substantial ground for the making of an application for such an order.
      . . .

**16.   Duty of the court to consider whether England and Wales is appropriate venue for application**
   (1)   Before making an order for financial relief the court shall consider whether in all the circumstances of the case it would be appropriate for such an order to be made by a court in England and Wales, and if the court is not satisfied that it would be appropriate, the court shall dismiss the application.
      . . .

*Notes*
1.  'Overseas country' in s. 12(1) is a country or territory outside the British Isles (s. 27 of the 1984 Act).
2.  When considering whether to grant leave, the court must in particular consider, *inter alia* (s. 16(2)): (a) the parties' connection with England and Wales, the country where the marriage was dissolved and any other country; (b) any financial benefit the applicant or any child of the family has received, or is likely to receive, as a result of the divorce, either by virtue of any agreement or under the law of a foreign country; (c) any right to apply for financial relief in a foreign country and any reason for omitting to do so; (d) the availability of any property in England and Wales; (e) the likely enforceability of any English order if made; and (f) the length of time since the divorce.

### Hewitson v Hewitson
[1995] Fam 100
Court of Appeal

*Facts*: The parties, an Irish wife and an American husband, were divorced in California, where the Californian court made a clean break final order between them based on a negotiated and comprehensive agreement made by the parties. They came to England where they cohabited for a few years, but when they finally parted the wife applied under s. 13 of the Matrimonial and Family Proceedings Act 1984 for leave to apply for financial relief in the English courts. Leave was granted. The husband appealed.
*Held*: allowing the appeal, that the mischief that the 1984 Act was designed to address was a narrow one and did not include the case of a foreign court of competent jurisdiction making an order which had been neither appealed nor impugned. Since there was no prospect of the English courts making an order for financial relief, the grant of leave would be set aside.

BUTLER-SLOSS LJ: . . . [Counsel] for the former wife has submitted that the words of the Act of 1984 are wide enough to give the courts jurisdiction and the effect is to enable a former spouse after a foreign divorce to have the opportunity to come back to court even in circumstances in which an English court would refuse to intervene after an English financial order. He suggested that the remedies available under our domestic matrimonial jurisdiction were inadequate and those applying under the Act should not be penalised by a refusal to grant leave when Parliament has passed legislation in terms wider than the domestic law. He relied on two decisions of first instance which do not, in my view, assist us. By not referring to *M v M (Financial Provision after Foreign Divorce)* [1994] 1 FLR 399, I should not like it to be assumed that I necessarily agree with it. The decision in *S v S (Financial Provision: Post-Divorce Cohabitation)* [1994] 2 FLR 288 is, however one in respect of which I have the gravest reservations.

[Counsel for the wife] accepted that the present case was not one contemplated either by the Law Commission or by Parliament. That concession for me is crucial since I can see no reason to give to those in the position of this wife a benefit which was not intended by the passing of the Act of 1984 and is unavailable under the domestic matrimonial legislation. The objective of the Act was to mitigate disadvantage, not to give extra advantages to a particular group of applicants.

I respectfully agree with Russell LJ in his judgment in *Holmes v Holmes* [1989] Fam 47, 59 when he said: 'Prima facie the order of the foreign court should prevail save in exceptional circumstances . . .' In my judgment it would be wrong in principle and contrary to public policy to extend the narrow compass of an Act designed to meet limited objectives to cover a wider and unintended situation. The facts of this case vividly illustrate my conclusion. A court of competent jurisdiction in California has made a consent order negotiated by lawyers. That order was not appealed or successfully criticised. It was designed to be comprehensive and final, embodying all the ancillary matters following on the dissolution of a failed marriage. The husband complied with the order. It is inconsistent with the comity existing between courts of comparable jurisdiction for an English court to review or seek to supplement the foreign order on the basis of the subsequent relationship of the former spouses. It is all the more so when an applicant in similar circumstances seeking to vary a final order under our matrimonial jurisdiction would by statute be precluded from doing so. In 1984, the same year as the Act with which we are concerned, there were major amendments to the Matrimonial Causes Act 1973 in its ancillary relief provisions, but significantly not to give rights to former spouses within England and Wales similar to those now claimed for applicants after foreign divorces.

There has to be finality and an end to litigation. In my view the umbrella of the dissolved marriage which covers the post-divorce period cannot remain open for ever. On the making and implementing of a 'clean break' order between spouses with no children, that umbrella has to be shut. Thereafter the relationship which may develop between former spouses is to be dealt with under civil law. The rights of one who enters into cohabition without marriage are manifestly less satisfactory than under our matrimonial legislation but that deficiency is not a reason to extend the provisions of the Act of 1984 to cover a situation neither referred to by the Law Commission nor in the contemplation of the legislature. Nothing I have said however is intended to affect that group of cases which properly fall within the ambit of Part III of the Act of 1984.

The prospects of success of this application under section 13 are nil and consequently I do not consider that there was substantial ground for the making of the application. . . .

### Holmes v Holmes
[1989] Fam 47
Court of Appeal

PURCHAS LJ: . . . the purpose of [the 1984 Act] is . . . to remit hardships which have been experienced in the past in the presence of a failure in a foreign jurisdiction to afford appropriate financial relief. The obvious cases are those jurisdictions where there simply are not any provisions to grant financial relief to wives or children or, maybe, husbands and children. In such cases, although the dissolution of the marriage has taken place in a foreign jurisdiction according to foreign laws, then the courts in this country are empowered by Parliament to step in and fill the gap. For my part I do not believe that the intention of Parliament in passing this Act was in any way to vest in the English courts any powers of review or even correction of orders made in a foreign forum by a competent court in which the whole matter has been examined

in a way exactly equivalent to the examination which would have taken place if the application had been made in the first instance in the courts here. That is not the object of this legislation at all.
. . .

*Notes*
1.   See also *M v M (Financial Provision after Foreign Divorce)* [1994] 1 FLR 399, FD, which involved a scenario which is all too easy to imagine happening: an English dream of setting up home in France which was shattered. It also involved a mother-in-law. The wife's application for ancillary relief in England after a French divorce was set aside, as she had pursued her financial rights in France fully and, as the French court was a court of competent jurisdiction in a friendly neighbouring jurisdiction, the principles of comity required that its orders be recognised and respected. In *Lamagni v Lamagni* [1995] 2 FLR 452, the Court of Appeal, distinguishing earlier cases, granted leave under s. 13 of the 1984 Act to the wife after she had been divorced by her Italian husband in Belgium, even though her application for leave had been made 12 years after her divorce. The delay had partly been caused by her making fruitless attempts to enforce Belgian maintenance pending suit orders.
2.   In international divorce cases it may be necessary for the English court to stay ancillary proceedings in this country if proceedings relating to the same matter have already commenced in the other country or would be better dealt with there (see FLA 1986, s. 5).

## 5.13   FINANCIAL DISPUTE RESOLUTION: A PILOT SCHEME

A new procedure for ancillary relief cases is currently being tested in certain courts under a Pilot Scheme set up as a result of recommendations made by the Lord Chancellor's Advisory Group on Ancillary Relief Procedure. The following Practice Direction explains the scheme.

### *Practice Direction (Ancillary Relief Procedure: Pilot Scheme)*
[1996] 2 FLR 368

(1)   Pursuant to this Direction, in certain specified courts a new procedure will apply to all applications for ancillary relief commenced on and after 1 October 1996. The new procedure has been formulated by the Lord Chancellor's Advisory Group on Ancillary Relief Procedure in the form of a new rule ('the new rule'), the text of which appears in Annex I to this Direction. Application of the new rule to specified courts only is by way of a 'pilot scheme' so as to enable the procedure to be monitored and an evaluation made of the operation of the rule and the extent to which it achieves the objectives for which it has been devised. The procedure under the draft rule is intended to reduce delay, facilitate settlements, limit costs incurred by parties to the proceedings and provide the court with much greater control over the conduct of proceedings than exists at present.

*Application and extent*

(2)   The procedure under the new rule will apply to all ancillary relief applications (including applications under s. 10(2) of the Matrimonial Causes Act 1973) where notice of the application or notice of intention to proceed with the application for ancillary relief made in the petition or answer is filed on or after 1 October 1996 in matrimonial proceedings pending or commenced in the courts which are listed in the column headed 'Pilot' in Annex 2 to this Direction.

(3)   The new rule provides for an early first directions appointment at which directions will be given with the objective of defining the issues and saving costs. Provision is made for there to be a financial dispute resolution ('FDR') appointment where proposals for resolving the application can be discussed in circumstances of privilege. The extent of discovery will be limited. Written estimates of costs will be required to be provided at each hearing so that the parties are fully aware of the costs that are being incurred in the proceedings.

*Legal representation*

(4)   Where legal representatives attend the first appointment or the FDR appointment they will be required to have full knowledge of the case.

*Judiciary*

(5)   The district judge or judge before whom the FDR appointment is held will have no further involvement with the application other than to conduct any further FDR appointment. Where possible all appointments (other than the FDR appointment) should be before the same district judge.

*Application of Family Proceedings Rules*

(6)   In the proceedings to which this Direction applies, the Family Proceedings Rules 1991 shall apply with the modifications . . .

*Note*

Under the 'new rule' referred to above an intention to apply for ancillary relief made in the petition or answer or an application for ancillary relief must be made on Form A. Not less than 35 days before the first appointment each party must file with the court and simultaneously exchange with each other a statement on Form E, which must be signed and sworn to be true, and which must contain specified information about the parties and their children including concise statements, e.g., of each party's means, earning capacity, present and future reasonable needs, standard of living during the marriage etc. Both parties must personally attend every appointment unless the court orders otherwise.

## Singer, L., 'FDR and the Holy Grail'
### [1996] Fam Law 751

*A new option*

First we had conciliation, then alternative dispute resolution (ADR), then mediation, then comprehensive mediation, then all issues mediation, and now we have the financial dispute resolution (FDR) appointment in selected county courts. The purpose of this item is to analyse what FDR is, how it relates to mediation, and what the role of mediation is in the new court process.

## What is FDR?

The FDR is now part of a new system of ancillary relief procedure made pursuant to *Practice Direction: Ancillary Relief Procedure: Pilot Scheme* (25 July 1996) [1996] 2 FLR 368 which became effective as a one-year pilot scheme in certain courts on 7 October 1996. The district judge has a discretion to arrange for FDR on the first directions appointment. He has other options, for example to refer the parties to out-of-court mediation or proceed with the case to a contested trial in due course. However, it is intended that 'the vast majority of cases' will proceed to FDR.

## Similarities with mediation

(1)  FDR is an attempt to reach a negotiated settlement through the intervention of a facilitator (in this case usually the district judge) who has no formal power to impose a result on the parties.

(2)  FDR is generally confidential and without prejudice to either party's rights.

(3)  It is expected that the parties will put their 'cards on the table' about financial disclosure, and other relevant matters. In particular, detailed financial statements must be exchanged in advance.

(4)  Any 'agreement' arrived at only becomes enforceable if there is a further agreement that such should be so.

(5)  Both parties are encouraged to have independent legal advice.

## Differences from mediation

(1)  A judge may order FDR without the consent of the parties, whereas no one is forced to go to mediation.

(2)  The judge may also compel personal attendance by parties to FDR. It is unlikely to be permitted for parties who do not wish to sit in the same room merely to send their legal representatives.

(3)  FDR will include legal representatives, be held at court premises, and before a judge (in complicated cases a circuit or even High Court judge). Mediation takes place away from the court, and mediators have no authority other than to keep the parties in a fair process of negotiation as long as it seems mutually worthwhile.

(4)  The 'applicant' in FDR (why not both parties?) must give details of any prior 'offers, proposals or responses thereto' (this includes 'pillow talk'). At present, this is not required in mediation, although such matters arise frequently.

(5)  Rule 8(e) provides that parties attending FDR 'shall use their best endeavours to reach agreement on relevant matters in issue between them'. This would appear to place a great burden on them. 'Use their best endeavours' has been judicially defined as 'leaving no stone unturned'. In mediation, no one is pressurised into reaching an agreement.

(6)  The structure of the FDR process means that there is bound to be a high regard for what might be a court imposed solution, particularly because of the standing of the judge. It is very easy to treat the judge as an oracle. Although mediators might know, through experience, what a 'court imposed' solution might be, the parties are free to come to their own arrangement. Unfair agreements arise out of an unfair process, and mediators can and will withdraw from a mediation without giving reasons, and before the 'agreement is reached' (usually saying 'you had better both seek further legal advice before going further').

(7)  There are different rules between FDR and mediation about what is 'privileged'. In FDR nothing said is admissible in evidence 'save upon the trial of a person for an offence committed at the appointment'. In mediation it is made clear that any

financial disclosures made at an appointment are not privileged, and anything said which discloses serious harm to a child is not privileged.

(8)   In FDR parties are expected to be legally represented. In mediation, negotiation is usually away from lawyers, who operate in a supportive role only.

*How will it work in practice?*
It is said that FDR will not be a 'banging heads together' session. However, one's general experience of district judges, who are used to wielding authority in their own court and on their own territory, makes it difficult to believe that a forceful district judge will not have a considerable effect on the outcome of FDR.

How far will district judges go in applying current mediation thinking? For example, will options be generated, where possible, by the parties themselves and not imposed on them from above? Will agreements, if reached, emerge from the nature of the negotiating process? Will they use flip charts? Will they explore other matters which may be making agreement difficult, for example problems about children or new partners? Will they be prepared to use shuttle mediation, and if so will they refuse to be confidants? Will they be able to discern when the process is going 'off the rails' through power imbalancing, or a party is about to walk out in distress?

What is not known, of course, is what the clients' expectation of their respective roles would be at FDR. How far will parties be actively involved in the negotiation process and 'own' an agreement? Will they be consigned only to a secondary role? In child-related 'in court' mediation sessions with a court welfare officer, in most courts only the clients attend. There are a few courts, however, where the practice is for lawyers to accompany their clients to these sessions. Usually, the lawyers take a 'back seat' and are not much more than observers and occasional clarifiers of facts.

It is not clear what the relationship of lawyer/client/judge at FDR will be, and it may be that each court will develop its own style. Lawyers tend to accept a more passive role when it comes to mediating about children, but they are inclined to perceive themselves as wiser in the ways of finance than their clients and are therefore more likely to be 'in charge' during FDR. Will judges still make comments like, 'please do not say anything Mr Smith, that is what your lawyer is here for'? Lawyers are unlikely to resist the temptation to keep the process for themselves, and to treat the clients as mute observers of their negotiating skills.

How much time will be allotted for FDR? A succession of appointments may be necessary before an agreement is reached, but will pressure on court time panic parties into reaching 'unfair' agreements? To what extent will parties be able to reach limited agreements, or no agreement at all, without feeling they are total failures? What may happen after a 'failed' FDR? It has been suggested that if the judge has given a strong 'suggestion' which was not accepted by one party, a *Calderbank* letter would be likely to follow by the other, and the case might settle anyway. Mediation might still be considered. For example, a less formal atmosphere might relax the parties, who may need time to consider matters further, particularly if the court has run out of time. Finally, parties might choose to let the court impose a solution. This is just as much a choice as reaching an agreement. Parties should be allowed to make that choice with dignity. If so, they would best be able to cope with any outcome.

*Referrals to mediation*
The court has power to refer to mediation. It is not clear at what point in the process this would be appropriate. When the draft rules were discussed during the Solicitors Family Law Association annual conference in February 1996, one delegate commented 'sotto voce' that a judge may refer couples to mediation when the lawyers were

impossible. However, it seems that if out-of-court mediation as we know it has any place in the grand scheme of things it should be before rather than after FDR. Judges and lawyers need to understand the very real differences between FDR and mediation, and their own limitations, as otherwise they will not appreciate in what circumstances parties might benefit from out-of-court mediation.

*Further reading*
Coleridge, P., Simpson, J., Mostyn, N., and Rae, M., 'FDR — The Pilot Scheme' [1996] Fam Law 746.

# 6  DOMESTIC VIOLENCE

This chapter deals with the civil remedies available to protect family victims of domestic violence. In many cases, however, police intervention will be needed and criminal proceedings will be taken against the perpetrator of violence.

The following 'family law' statutes give the court jurisdiction to grant injunctions to protect the victims of violence: the Domestic Violence and Matrimonial Proceedings Act (DVMPA) 1976; the Domestic Proceedings and Magistrates' Courts Act (DPMCA) 1978; and the Matrimonial Homes Act (MHA) 1983. However, after much criticism of the law (notably that the remedies were complex and confusing and lacked integration), Part IV of the Family Law Act (FLA) 1996 was enacted making major changes to the law. Part IV is due to come into force on 1 October 1997. This chapter considers both the 'old' and the 'new' law.

## 6.1  THE NATURE AND CAUSES OF DOMESTIC VIOLENCE

**Law Commission, *Domestic Violence and Occupation of the Family Home*, Law Com No. 207**
London: HMSO, 1992

**The social context**

. . .

2.1  A large literature has developed over the past 20 years upon the problems of domestic violence, its nature, causes and extent and the effectiveness of various responses to it. Domestic violence is generally thought of as taking place between husband and wife or cohabiting partners but, although this is the most common situation, violence can and not infrequently does extend also to children or others living in the same household. Whilst the phenomenon is by no means new, its recognition as a major social problem dates only from the early 1970s. There can be no doubt of the extent of the problem. It has been summarised thus:

all studies that exist indicate that wife abuse is a common and pervasive problem and that men from practically all countries, cultures, classes and income groups indulge in the behaviour. The issue has serious implications from both a short-term and long-term perspective and from an individual and societal perspective. Many victims suffer serious physical and psychological injury, sometimes even death, while the economic and social costs to the community are enormous and the implications for future generations impossible to estimate.

[*Violence against Women in the Family*, UN Centre for Social Development and Humanitarian Afairs, 1989, p. 7.]

*(a)   Nature*

. . .

2.3   Domestic violence can take many forms. The term 'violence' itself is often used in two senses. In its narrower meaning it describes the use of threat of physical force against a victim in the form of an assault or battery. But in the context of the family, there is also a wider meaning which extends to abuse beyond the more typical instances of physical assaults to include any form of physical, sexual or psychological molestation or harassment which has a serious detrimental effect upon the health and well-being of the victim, albeit that there is no 'violence' involved in the sense of physical force. Examples of such 'non-violent' harassment or molestation cover a very wide range of behaviour. Common instances include persistent pestering and intimidation through shouting, denigration, threats or argument, nuisance telephone calls, damaging property, following the applicant about and repeatedly calling at her home or place of work. Installing a mistress into the matrimonial home with a wife and three children, filling car locks with superglue, writing anonymous letters and pressing one's face against a window whilst brandishing papers have all been held to amount to molestation. The degree of severity of such behaviour depends less upon its intrinsic nature than upon it being part of a pattern and upon its effect on the victim. Acts of molestation often follow upon previous behaviour which has been violent or otherwise offensive. Calling at the applicant's house on one occasion may not be objectionable. Calling frequently and unexpectedly at unsocial hours when the victim is known to be afraid certainly is. Such forms of abuse may in some circumstances be just as harmful, vicious and distressing as physical injuries. Other forms of 'non-violent' abuse, such as the sexual abuse of a child, may in the long term be more harmful.

*(b)   Extent*

2.4   The true extent of domestic violence is impossible to assess. It is possible only to build up a fragmented picture from a number of different sources of information, each of which has its own limitations. However, it is clear from the information which is available that it is a widespread problem which takes up a significant amount of court time. There is also good reason to think that a considerable amount of such violence is never brought to the courts' attention at all. . . .

*(c)   Causes*

2.6   There is no generally accepted explanation of the reasons for domestic violence and abuse, although a number of different theories have been put forward. However, none of these alone satisfactorily explains why violence occurs in one family and not in another. Given the range of situations in which violence occurs and the variety of people involved it would be surprising if there were a simple explanation. We think, however, that the various theories put forward in the literature are of relevance in giving an additional perspective to the problem. It must always be emphasised that, whatever the causes of domestic violence, the law should be concerned with its consequences and in particular with the need to supply adequate protection for its victims. The law should also provide an affirmation that victims do not have to put up with violence, whatever the reason for its occurrence in the particular case.

2.7   Aspects of all these theories are controversial and leave parts of what is a very intricate problem unexplained. Also, other factors such as the use of drugs and alcohol may play a part, although they are not causes of domestic violence as such. The theories can be divided into three broad groups, outlined briefly below:

*(i)   Psychopathological theories*
These theories argue that the violent person is ill or has an inadequate or defective personality, being typically aggressive, jealous and over possessive. Sometimes it is argued that the victim is masochistic or excessively dependent and insecure, or that the violence is a result of the interaction of two personalities with such traits. This has been developed to suggest that domestic violence is 'learned behaviour' following a pattern copied from childhood experiences in a violent home and leading to cycles of violence in subsequent generations.

*(ii)   Social and economic deprivation theories*
These theories see domestic violence as a symptom of personal desperation, stress and frustration caused by blocked goals and problems such as financial difficulties, poor housing, unemployment, isolation or cultural differences.

*(iii)   Theories about the position of women in society*
These theories see domestic violence as having its roots in the very structure of the social and legal system. Although a husband's formal right to chastise his wife has long been abolished, it has left a legacy of unequal power relationships between the sexes. Feminist theories thus see violence against women as typical rather than rare behaviour and as a manifestation of this endemic patriarchal bias and a reflection of the subordinate status of wives and mothers.

*Note*
The above Report made recommendations for reform of the various discretionary remedies which exist in family law for dealing with protection against violence and regulating occupation of the family home. These recommendations were partially adopted by the Government and became Part IV of the FLA 1996 (see 6.4 and 6.5 below).

*Further reading*
Edwards, S., *Sex and Gender in the Legal Process*, London: Blackstone Press, 1996, Chapter 5.

## 6.2   THE CURRENT LAW

**Law Commission, *Domestic Violence and Occupation of the Family Home*, Law Com No. 207**
London: HMSO, 1992

. . .

2.8   Domestic violence is not simply a legal problem which can be eradicated by the appropriate legal remedies. It is also a social and psychological problem which can be eliminated only by fundamental changes in society and in attitudes to women and children. While legal remedies are an attempt to alleviate the symptoms of domestic violence, they can do little to tackle the causes. Also, their effectiveness can be hampered by various factors. First, they have to operate in an area where there is a constant tension between the need for instant protection to be given to the victim and the need to observe due process in the conduct of proceedings against the alleged perpetrator. A balance has to be struck between the victim's need and the rights of other people, although there is, of course, room for argument about what the correct balance should be. Also, legal remedies can be undermined by the gap which exists between the letter and spirit of the law and the law in practice. It has been said that those who work in this area, including solicitors, barristers, police, court staff and judiciary, can, perhaps unconsciously, deter applicants from pursuing their proceedings or prevent the law operating as effectively as it might, if their reactions are affected by particular perceptions of male and female roles or an ambivalence about the propriety of legal or police intervention within the family. As a recent study has concluded 'whatever legal reforms may be made, and whatever changes may be made to court procedures, without effective enforcement by police officers and by courts, injunctions and protection orders will continue to be "not worth the paper they are written on"'. [Barron, J., *Not Worth the Paper: the Effectiveness of Legal Protection for Women and Children Experiencing Domestic Violence*, 1990, p. 136.]

2.9   Remedies against domestic violence are provided not only by family law, but also by criminal law and the law of tort. An incident of domestic violence will often amount to an assault or battery and to an offence against the person. But, although parts of the law of tort and the criminal law are specifically designed to deal with violence and the risk of harm (and have therefore developed useful machinery for this purpose such as arrest and remand), they remain blunt instruments in the context of domestic violence because of the relationship between the parties. Criminal law is primarily intended to punish the offender and actions in assault and battery to compensate the victim. However, most victims of domestic violence are not primarily interested in punishment or compensation. They want the violence to stop and they want protection. Sometimes they want the relationship to end or at least be suspended, but sometimes they do not. The first aim of the civil domestic violence legislation should be to provide this protection in a flexible way which enables account to be taken of different victims' differing needs and of the many special considerations which apply in this area of the law. . . .

2.10   The possible responses to domestic violence lie along a continuum at one end of which is the use of criminal penalties and at the other, referral to therapy or counselling. The two extremes reflect a philosophical difference of opinion upon the correct approach to the problem. On the one hand, there is the view that those who beat their partners should be treated just like any other criminal and should be routinely arrested and prosecuted. . . . On the other hand, it can be argued that, particularly where the parties are still living together and the violence is a symptom of difficulties in a relationship rather than the cause, 'automatic' prosecution can do more harm than good and may precipitate the final breakdown of the family. In some cases, a final separation may be the right course, but in others it may not. Imprisonment usually leads to loss of employment and to consequent financial hardship for the victim and children. It may exacerbate the problem by inciting further violence, and the children may suffer as a result of separation from their father. Unless the defendant has independent financial resources, fines or compensation are counter-productive as they simply reduce the finances available to maintain the family. It is not possible to say that either approach is the 'correct' one. There is something to be said for both,

and one is certainly likely to be more appropriate than the other in any particular case.
. . .

2.11    The civil domestic violence remedies approach the problems from a perspective which has a number of important differences from the approach of the criminal law. The emphasis is more upon the needs of the victim: she can choose to apply for the remedy she wants. Although the remedies are discretionary, the facts have to be proved only upon the balance of probabilities and not beyond reasonable doubt and issues of intention and *mens rea* are not relevant. Civil remedies are prospective and positive: their main aim is to regulate and improve matters for the future, rather than to make judgments upon or punish past behaviour. Unlike criminal proceedings, they can also provide an immediate means of evicting the perpetrator from the home. This is often the only effective method of stopping abuse and molestation, as when the parties live together there are unique opportunities for it to continue. . . . Although domestic cases are now taken much more seriously than they used to be by police, prosecutors and the courts, the consequences bear no relation to the future needs of the victim. In civil proceedings, on the other hand, it may be possible to obtain an immediate ouster order which can continue until she is able to take divorce proceedings and obtain a property transfer order or find alternative accommodation. Thus although civil proceedings do not result in a criminal record, their practical consequences may sometimes be more serious for the respondent in other respects.

2.12    But, although civil proceedings have certain advantages, civil remedies are not in general designed to handle violence and other forms of extreme behaviour normally dealt with under the criminal law. To make the remedies properly effective for the purposes they are intended to serve within this particular context, it has been found necessary to develop certain specialised quasi-criminal machinery, principally powers of remand and arrest. Attaching a power of arrest to an injunction is a serious step as it places the respondent at risk of losing his liberty, at least for a short time without a court deciding that the respondent has breached the injunction. However, the power will often be the only effective means of deterring the respondent from a breach, or of protecting the victim should it occur. . . .

2.13    Disputes about the occupation of the family home and applications for ouster or exclusion orders can arise in a variety of circumstances. In a common case, an ouster order may be souɡht to evict a man from the house where a non-molestation injunction is felt to be insufficient protection against his violence. Alternatively one party may be inflicting an intolerable degree of non-violent harassment upon the other, or there may be no particular violence or harassment, but the parties' relationship has broken down and the tensions and strains of living in the same house have become too great for them or their children to bear.

2.14    Different policy considerations may apply to cases where an ouster order is sought for protection and those in which it is sought to resolve disputes over the occupation of the home during or following relationship breakdown, although in practice the dividing line between them may be difficult to draw. The former needs a clear and urgent response, whereas in the latter immediate relief and protection are not required to secure personal safety, however desperate the applicant may be to live apart from her partner. There is often, however, a need for a practical solution to the family's problem for the sake of all concerned, particularly if there are children. There may also be a difference in the time span for which relief is needed. Short term relief may provide sufficient protection in some cases, simply by creating a breathing space to allow the applicant to find alternative accommodation or the respondent time to come to terms with the changed situation. But in cases where the relationship has permanently broken down, a medium term solution will often be needed until the question of occupation of the property can be permanently settled, usually by an application under section 24 of the Matrimonial Causes Act 1973 or under the ordinary law of property. In a few cases, for example where a married couple do not want to divorce or to dispose of the property, a long term solution may be needed.

### 6.2.1   The 'family law' statutes

The following 'family law' statutes give the civil courts jurisdiction to grant injunctions to protect spouses, cohabitants and their children from domestic violence. These provisions will, however, be repealed by Part IV of the FLA 1996 when it comes into force. In addition to the following statutes, the High Court and county court have jurisdiction to grant injunctions ancillary to legal proceedings (see 6.2.3 below).

## DOMESTIC VIOLENCE AND MATRIMONIAL PROCEEDINGS ACT 1976

**1.   Matrimonial injunctions in the county court**
(1)   Without prejudice to the jurisdiction of the High Court, on an application by a party to a marriage a county court shall have jurisdiction to grant an injunction containing one or more of the following provisions, namely,—
    (a)   a provision restraining the other party to the marriage from molesting the applicant;
    (b)   a provision restraining the other party from molesting a child living with the applicant;
    (c)   a provision excluding the other party from the matrimonial home or a part of the matrimonial home or from a specified area in which the matrimonial home is included;
    (d)   a provision requiring the other party to permit the applicant to enter and remain in the matrimonial home or a part of the matrimonial home;
whether or not any other relief is sought in the proceedings.
(2)   Subsection (1) above shall apply to a man and a woman who are living with each other in the same household as husband and wife as it applies to the parties to a marriage and any reference to the matrimonial home shall be construed accordingly.

*Note*
The court has jurisdiction to make an order under s. 1 of the DVMPA 1976 whether or not the applicant has a proprietary interest in the home (*Davis* v *Johnson* [1979] AC 264, HL).

## DOMESTIC PROCEEDINGS AND MAGISTRATES' COURTS ACT 1978

**16.   Powers of court to make orders for the protection of a party to a marriage or a child of the family**
(1)   Either party to a marriage may . . . apply to a magistrates' court for an order under this section.
(2)   Where on an application for an order under this section the court is satisfied that the respondent has used, or threatened to use, violence against the person of the applicant or a child of the family and that it is necessary for the protection of the

applicant or a child of the family that an order should be made under this subsection, the court may make one or both of the following orders, that is to say—

(a)   an order that the respondent shall not use, or threaten to use, violence against the person of the applicant;

(b)   an order that the respondent shall not use, or threaten to use, violence against the person of a child of the family.

(3)   Where on an application for an order under this section the court is satisfied—

(a)   that the respondent has used violence against the person of the applicant or a child of the family, or

(b)   that the respondent has threatened to use violence against the person of the applicant or a child of the family and has used violence against some other person, or

(c)   that the respondent has in contravention of an order made under subsection (2) above threatened to use violence against the person of the applicant or a child of the family,

and that the applicant or a child of the family is in danger of being physically injured by the respondent (or would be in such danger if the applicant or child were to enter the matrimonial home) the court may make one or both of the following orders, that is to say—

(i)   an order requiring the respondent to leave the matrimonial home;

(ii)   an order prohibiting the respondent from entering the matrimonial home.

. . .

## MATRIMONIAL HOMES ACT 1983

**1.   Rights concerning matrimonial home where one spouse has no estate, etc.**

(1)   [defines 'rights of occupation', see chapter 3]

(2)   So long as one spouse has rights of occupation, either of the spouses may apply to the court for an order—

(a)   declaring, enforcing, restricting or terminating those rights, or

(b)   prohibiting, suspending or restricting the exercise by either spouse of the right to occupy the dwelling house, or

(c)   requiring either spouse to permit the exercise by the other of that right.

(3)   On an application for an order under this section, the court may make such order as it thinks just and reasonable having regard to the conduct of the spouses in relation to each other and otherwise, to their respective needs and financial resources, to the needs of any children and to all the circumstances of the case.

. . .

*Notes*

Proceedings under the DVMPA 1976, the DPMCA 1978 and the MHA 1983 above are 'family proceedings' for the purposes of the Children Act 1989 (see Chapter 7), as will be proceedings under Part IV of the FLA 1996 when it comes into force.

*Questions*

1.   What differences are there between s. 1 of the DVMPA 1976 and s. 16 of the DPMCA 1978? Is the law confusing?

2.   How do the criteria for making an ouster order laid down in s. 1(3) of the MHA 1983 differ from the criteria applicable under the new law?

## 6.2.2    Ouster orders are 'Draconian' orders

Although an ouster order may be granted without there having been any violence, the courts have consistently held that an ouster order is a 'Draconian' order because of the severity of removing a person from his or her home, particularly where he or she has a proprietary interest. Such orders are therefore orders of last resort. It is likely that the court will adopt a similar approach under Part IV of the FLA 1996.

*Wiseman* v *Simpson*
[1988] 1 WLR 35
Court of Appeal

*Facts*: When their relationship broke down the wife evicted her husband from the flat of which they were joint tenants telling him she was 'taking over the flat from now on'. He went to live with his parents, while she remained in the flat with their young child. The husband applied under s. 1 of the DVMPA 1976 for an order that he be permitted to return home. The county court judge found that the husband 'was not a bad man and was not violent' and that 'two very young people had ceased to be in love with each other', but as the wife and child had no alternative accommodation and the husband had a home with his parents, he granted an injunction restraining the husband from returning to the flat. The husband appealed on the ground that no order can properly be made under s. 1(1)(c) of the DVMPA 1976 without proof of violence or serious molestation.
*Held*: allowing the appeal and ordering a retrial, that the ouster order was not just and reasonable.

RALPH GIBSON LJ: . . . The submission that in the present case the judge failed to consider the Draconian nature of an ouster order was based on the decision of *Summers* v *Summers* [[1986] 1 FLR 343]. In that case May LJ noted that the judge had apparently regarded as relevant the possibility that a separation, enforced by the ouster order 'might ease a reconciliation' and said that that was not an approach which the statute required the court to take. May LJ continued, at p. 347:

> In addition, it does seem to me that the judge failed to include in the balance of the exercise of his discretion what in this and in many cases is an important consideration, namely the Draconian nature of such an ouster order and the effect that it has upon the party against whom it is made.

Kerr LJ in that case said, at p. 348, that the judge's 'findings concerning conduct, needs and children led me to doubt whether this is a case in which a Draconian order ousting the husband was in any event appropriate.' This court in *Summers*' case was not, of course, laying down a requirement that the judge in ouster cases must recite some direction to himself as to the Draconian nature of the ouster order if he is to escape a ruling that he has failed to direct himself properly. As I understand the judgment and ruling of Kerr and May LJJ in *Summers*' case, they were in substance considering the basic requirement of an order made under the Act of 1976 by reference to section 1(3) of the Matrimonial Homes Act 1983 that any order made must be as the court thinks 'just and reasonable.' Although the judge has duly considered the conduct of the spouses in relation to each other and otherwise, and their respective needs and financial resources, and the needs of the child, and all the circumstances of the case, as listed in section 1(3) of the Act of 1983, he cannot properly make an ouster order merely because the case of one party is in his view on those matters stronger than the case of the other. It can only be 'just and reasonable' to make an ouster order if the case of the party claiming the order is not only stronger on those matters than the other party's case but is such as to justify making an order that a man or woman be ousted from his or her home. It must be very rare for a judge not to have in mind this nature of an ouster order and the effect on the party against whom the order is made. It seems to me that the court is driven to question whether a judge has had proper regard to the Draconian nature of an ouster order where the findings of the judge concerning conduct, needs and children cause the court to doubt whether an ouster order could properly be made at all. . . .

It was essential that the judge, having considered as he did the conduct of the parties, and their respective needs and financial resources and the needs of the child, and having concluded as he did that the need of the respondent and the child for the flat was greater than the need of the applicant, go on to consider whether in all the circumstances of the case the respondent had proved that it was just and reasonable to make an ouster order against the applicant having regard to all the circumstances and to the nature and purpose of such an order. Lloyd LJ in *Burke* v *Burke* (unreported), 24 November 1986; Court of Appeal (Civil Division) Transcript No. 1047 of 1986 said:

It must never be forgotten that an ouster order is a very serious order to make. It is described by Ormrod LJ in a case to which we were referred, as a 'drastic order' and an order which should only be made in cases of real necessity. It must not be allowed to become a routine stepping stone on the road to divorce on the ground that the marriage has already broken down and that the atmosphere in the matrimonial home is one of tension.

That passage was cited by this court (Kerr and Neill LJJ) in *Summers* v *Summers (No. 2), The Times,* 19 May 1987. In the first *Summers* v *Summers* case [1986] 1 FLR 343, referred to above, this court, in a case not unlike the present case, was driven from the terms of the judgment and the facts of the case to consider that the judge had failed to include in the balance of the exercise of his discretion what in that case, and in this, is an important consideration, namely, the Draconian nature of such an ouster order and the effect that it has on the party against whom it is made. I have fully in mind the fact that the circumstances of this young man, the applicant, are such that the effect on him of this order must have been less than would have been caused to many men in different circumstances, and the judge would have been aware of that. But to order a man who has done no wrong out of his home is without question drastic. When it is to be done I would prefer to see the expression of the reasons why it is necessary to take that step. On the facts of this case, I find it hard to know how the order can be justified, I would therefore take the same course as this court took in *Summers* v *Summers* [1986] 1 FLR 343. I would set aside the order made. For the reasons I have given, however, I would not dismiss the respondent's application and make an order in favour of the applicant because I do not think it is possible to say that the respondent made out no prima facie case on her allegations at the hearing and, in the words used by Kerr LJ in *Summers'* case, at p. 348:

> I do not feel that this court is in a position to substitute its own conclusion on the balancing exercise for that of the judge, who has seen the parties and may only have expressed himself in a way which is open to criticism.

. . .

### Hayes, Mary, 'The Law Commission and the Family Home'
### (1990) 53 MLR 222

. . . [I]t is a dangerous social policy which regulates the right to occupy the matrimonial home only where there is proof of violence. Such an approach has been developing since *Richards* v *Richards* [[1989] AC 174], and there appears to be no reported case in the Court of Appeal since *Richards* of ouster in circumstances other than violence. Such a rigid approach could provoke a wife, desperate to live apart from her husband, but needing to stay in the family home (perhaps because of the children) either falsely to accuse him of violence or, in an extreme case, to precipitate an act of violence against herself. The disadvantages of this in terms of risk to the wife, damage to an already estranged relationship and potential for criminalisation of the husband do not need elaboration.

*Notes*
1.  Draconian: 'extremely severe', i.e. like the laws of Draco, an archon (a chief magistrate) in Athens, 621 BC.
2.  Due to its Draconian nature, an ouster order should not be made where there is conflicting affidavit evidence, unless there has been a proper opportunity for oral evidence and cross-examination (see *Shipp* v *Shipp* [1988] 1 FLR 345, CA, and *Whitlock* v *Whitlock* [1989] 1 FLR 208, CA).
3.  The court has no jurisdiction to make a specific issue or prohibited steps order under the Children Act 1989 (see Chapter 7) to oust someone from the home (see *Pearson* v *Franklin (Parental Home: Ouster)* [1994] 1 FLR 246, CA), but the FLA 1996 will amend the 1989 Act to enable an abusing parent to be removed from the home when an interim care or emergency protection order is made (see Chapter 10).

### 6.2.3   Injunctive protection ancillary to other proceedings

Under the following provisions, injunctive relief providing protection against violence and molestation and/or protecting occupation rights may be sought ancillary to other proceedings brought in the High Court or county court.

### SUPREME COURT ACT 1981

**37.   Powers of High Court with respect to injunctions and receivers**
   (1)   The High Court may by order (whether interlocutory or final) grant an injunction . . . in all cases in which it appears to the court to be just and convenient to do so.

# COUNTY COURTS ACT 1984

### 38.  General ancillary jurisdiction

(1)  Subject to what follows, in any proceedings in a county court the court may make any order which could be made by the High Court if the proceedings were in the High Court.

*Note*

Section 38, CCA 1984 is as substituted by the Courts and Legal Services Act 1990.

In the following case the plaintiff sought injunctive protection in tort proceedings.

*Khorasandjian v Bush*
[1993] QB 727
Court of Appeal

*Facts*: The parties had been friends, but had never cohabited. When the plaintiff terminated their relationship, the defendant, who was unable to accept it, assaulted her, threatened her with violence, verbally abused and persecuted her, and pestered her mother and her boyfriend with telephone calls. The plaintiff was granted an interlocutory injunction restraining the defendant from 'using violence to, harassing, pestering or communicating with' the plaintiff. The defendant appealed submitting that the judge had no jurisdiction to grant an injunction in those terms as those words did not reflect any tort known to the law.

*Held*: dismissing the appeal, that the injunction was in principle justified in law. Threats of violence, being threats to commit a tort, could be restrained by injunction. Harassment by unwanted telephone calls amounted to interference with the enjoyment of property where the plaintiff was lawfully present, and could be restrained by an injunction *quia timet* as a private nuisance. Harassment likely to cause physical or psychological illness could also be restrained by an injunction *quia timet*. Peter Gibson J, on the other hand, held that harassment was not an actionable wrong and that it was wrong in law to give the plaintiff, as a mere licensee, a right to sue in private nuisance.

DILLON LJ: . . . The defendant was born on 13 August 1969 and thus is now a young man of 23. The plaintiff was born on 28 March 1974 and is thus now a girl of 18. They are not, and have never been, married to each other and they have never cohabited with each other. Thus there is no jurisdiction in this case to grant an injunction against 'molestation' under section 1 of the Domestic Violence and Matrimonial Proceedings Act 1976, nor has the plaintiff sought to invoke that Act.

The power of the county court to grant injunctions, whether interlocutory or final, in cases where the county court has jurisdiction, is the same as the power of the High Court. The statutory authority is now section 37(1) of the Supreme Court Act 1981, which provides that the High Court may by order (whether interlocutory or final) grant an injunction 'in all cases in which it appears to the court to be just and convenient to do so.' It is well understood, however, despite the apparent width of those words, that, as Lord Diplock put it in relation to the predecessor of section 37(1) in *Siskina (Owners of cargo lately laden on board)* v *Distos Compania Naviera SA* [1979] AC 210, 254:

> That subsection, speaking as it does of interlocutory orders, presupposes the existence of an action, actual or potential, claiming substantive relief which the High Court has jurisdiction to grant and to which the interlocutory orders referred to are but ancillary.

Therefore it is necessary to consider what claims for substantive relief, or causes of action, the plaintiff has against the defendant. I say 'has' against the defendant rather than 'is asserting against the defendant by her pleadings' because it is conceded on behalf of the defendant that at this stage in this particular case the plaintiff should not be limited to her actual particulars of claim, which are in informal language and were issued in a hurry when the first application to the county court for an injunction was made. The pleadings can be amended, or, if technically necessary, a further action can be started and the two can be consolidated. It is therefore appropriate to consider the whole of the plaintiff's evidence, to determine what cause of action she appears to have on that evidence, and to consider what interlocutory injunctions the court has power to grant on that evidence. It is fair to the defendant to say that he has sworn affidavits disputing the plaintiff's account of events, but the immediate question is what causes of action the plaintiff has if she is right as to what has happened.

It is, of course, not in dispute that an interlocutory injunction can, in an appropriate case, be granted quia timet before an actual tort has been committed against a plaintiff. It is also clear that the form of an interlocutory injunction does not have to follow slavishly the form of the substantive relief which would be likely to be granted at the trial if the plaintiff succeeds. . . . But [counsel for the defendant] submits, in reliance on the decision of this court in *Malone* v *Laskey* [1907] 2 KB 141, that the basis of the tort of private nuisance is interference with the enjoyment of a person's property, and therefore the plaintiff, as in law a mere licensee in her mother's property with no proprietary interest, cannot invoke the tort of private nuisance or complain of unwanted and harassing telephone calls made to her in her mother's home.

To my mind, it is ridiculous if in this present age the law is that the making of deliberately harassing and pestering telephone calls to a person is only actionable in the civil courts if the recipient of the calls happens to have the freehold or a leasehold proprietary interest in the premises in which he or she has received the calls. [Counsel for the defendant] submits, however, that English law does not recognise any tort of harassment or invasion of privacy or, save in the different context of such a case as *Rookes* v *Barnard* [1964] AC 1129, intimidation. Therefore, she says that, save as expressly conceded as set out above, the defendant's conduct to the plaintiff is, even on the plaintiff's version of it, under the English civil law, legitimate conduct of which the plaintiff has no power or right to complain. I apprehend that it is correct, historically, that the tort of private nuisance, which originated as an action on the case, was developed in the beginning to protect private property or rights of property, in relation to the use or enjoyment of land. It is stated in *Clerk & Lindsell on Torts*, 16th ed. (1989), p. 1354, para. 24–01 that 'the essence of nuisance is a condition or activity which unduly interferes with the use or enjoyment of land.'

That a legal owner of property can obtain an injunction, on the ground of private nuisance, to restrain persistent harassment by unwanted telephone calls to his home was decided by the Appellate Division of the Alberta Supreme Court in *Motherwell* v *Motherwell* (1976) 73 DLR (3d) 62. . . .

I respectfully agree [with the decision in *Motherwell*] and in my judgment this court is entitled to adopt the same approach. The court has at times to reconsider earlier decisions in the light of changed social conditions; in this court we saw an example of that only the day before the hearing of this appeal began, when we were referred to *Dyson Holdings Ltd* v *Fox* [1976] QB 503. If the wife of the owner is entitled to sue in respect of harassing telephone calls, then I do not see why that should not also apply to a child living at home with her parents.

[After referring to *Burnett* v *George* [1992] 1 FLR 525 (CA), *Pidduck* v *Molloy* [1992] 2 FLR 202 (CA), and *Patel* v *Patel* [1988] 2 FLR 179 (CA), his Lordship continued: . . .]

I should next refer to the decision of Scott J in *Thomas* v *National Union of Mineworkers (South Wales Area)* [1986] Ch 20, to which we were referred. That case arose out of the miners' strike of 1984. In the course of a fairly long and careful reserved judgment. Scott J held that miners who wanted to return to work were entitled to use the public highway to enter the colliery where they worked without unreasonable harassment and, in particular, without having abuse shouted at them by some 50 to 70 striking miners who were picketing the colliery. The actions of the striking miners were therefore actionable in nuisance. The relevant part of the judgment of Scott J was criticised in argument in *News Group Newspapers Ltd* v *Society of Graphical and Allied Trades 1982 (No. 2)* [1987] ICR 181, a case about another industrial dispute which came before Stuart-Smith J. The criticism, in which Stuart-Smith J saw force (see p. 206D–F), seems to have been to the effect that mere interference with a person's right to use the public highway could not per se be a new tort, when an action by an individual for obstruction of the public highway as a nuisance only lay on proof of special damage: see *Clerk & Lindsell on Torts*, 16th ed., pp. 1402–1404, para. 24–68. I do not find it necessary for the determination of this appeal to examine the correctness of the decision of Scott J.

For the reasons I have endeavoured to indicate. I regard the injunction granted by Judge Stockdale as in principle justified in law as an interlocutory injunction on the facts of this case as they were before him. I turn to consider the question of the choice of words, and the wording of any continuing injunction.

The word 'molest' is well known to, and well understood by, lawyers in its context in section 1 of the Domestic Violence and Matrimonial Proceedings Act 1976, and, therefore, the enforcement of an injunction against 'molestation' under that Act presents little difficulty. It was said by Ormrod LJ in *Horner* v *Horner* [1982] Fam 90, 93, that the word 'molesting' in section 1 of the Act of 1976:

> does not imply necessarily either violence or threats of violence. It applies to any conduct which can properly be regarded as such a degree of harassment as to call for the intervention of the court.

In *Johnson* v *Walton* [1990] 1 FLR 350, 352H Lord Donaldson of Lymington MR held, with the concurrence of the other members of the court, that the word 'molestation' has that meaning whenever it is used, regardless of whether the particular proceedings are or are not brought under the Act of 1976. It follows, in my judgment, that in the circumstances of the present case there could have been no objection if the judge had granted an injunction to restrain the defendant from 'molesting' the plaintiff.

. . .

PETER GIBSON J: . . . This is not a case to which the Domestic Violence and Matrimonial Proceedings Act 1976 applies, the parties being neither married to, nor cohabiting with, each other, nor are there children to protect. Although there have been calls for the extension of the domestic violence legislation so that the wide remedies under it (including the grant of injunctions to restrain any form of molestation, the exclusion of a party from a home or from a specified area including the home and the attachment of a power of arrest to certain injunctions) would become available in proceedings between parties whose relationships are not limited by reference to marriage and cohabitation (see, in particular, the Law Commission's Report on Family Law: Domestic Violence and Occupation of the Family Home (1992) (Law Com. No. 207)), no such extension has yet been enacted; and even if the Law Commission's recommendations were implemented, a person in the plaintiff's position would probably still be unable to invoke such remedies. Such a person must therefore look to the common law in order to obtain protection.

The particulars of claim contain allegations of actual and threatened violence by the defendant against the plaintiff causing her 'great fear and distress;' she is said to be 'very scared and feels very frightened by the [defendant's] abnormal and irrational obsession,' and his behaviour is said to have caused her 'mental anguish.' She seeks, *inter alia*, damages for assault, trespass (which in the circumstances pleaded must be trespass to the person) and nuisance. Further details supporting these allegations and containing other allegations of intimidatory behaviour by the defendant are contained in the affidavit evidence. The plaintiff is still only 18 and there is evidence that her life has been threatened on several occasions by the defendant, who has written to her that his thoughts and actions are based on pure hatred and always have been. It is hardly surprising that she claims to be frightened and under stress.

. . .

The correct approach in a case like this is, in my judgment, that adopted in this court in *Burnett* v *George* [1992] 1 FLR 525, decided in 1986 but only recently reported. In that case the female plaintiff and the defendant, after living together for a period, parted in circumstances which left the defendant with a burning resentment against the plaintiff. She was subjected to assaults and molestation including telephone threats. She was granted an injunction restraining the defendant from assaulting, molesting or otherwise interfering with her. Sir John Arnold P, with whom Sir Roualeyn Cumming-Bruce agreed, said, at pp. 527–528:

The foundation of the appeal is that the formula of it being just and convenient to grant injunctive relief in these circumstances, which is the statutory formula under which the High Court and the county court both act, upon its proper interpretation requires justice to be in the form of an identifiable and protectable legal interest, and convenience to be something which is indicated by the circumstances of the case. There is much authority which supports that position. . . . It is said, and in my judgment said with some force, that molestation and interference are not, in the circumstances of this case, in which no question of matrimonial nexus arises and where there are no children to protect, actionable wrongs, and therefore it is not just to grant an injunction to restrain them. For my part, I regard that as a conclusive argument, unless there be evidence that the health of the plaintiff is being impaired by molestation or interference calculated to create such impairment, in which case relief would be granted by way of an injunction to the extent that it would be necessary to avoid that impairment of health. That exception is, in my judgment, validly grounded on *Wilkinson* v *Downton* [1987] 2 QB 57 at first instance, which was adopted and confirmed in this court in *Janvier v Sweeney* [1919] 2 KB 316. . . .

The order made by this court in *Burnett v George*, as appears from the headnote, restrained the defendant from 'assaulting, molesting or otherwise interfering with the plaintiff by doing acts calculated to cause her harm.'
. . .

To the limited extent, therefore, that I would qualify the conduct restrained by the addition of a coda to limit that conduct to actionable wrongs, I would allow the appeal.

## Noble, Margaret, 'Harassment — a Recognised Tort?' (1993) 143 NLJ 1685

. . . Many of us were surprised when the plaintiff in *Khorasandjian v Bush* succeeded, as her road to success in nuisance was beset with pitfalls. . . .

Private nuisance is defined as an unlawful interference with the use and enjoyment of land. In *Khorasandjian* there was substantial interference with the enjoyment of land as the telephone calls were persistent. However, private nuisance protects land interests. Therefore, it is logical to expect the owner or occupier to sue. In order to make a claim it has long been held that one requires an interest in land, which Miss Khorasandjian manifestly had not. . . .

. . . When the conduct of the tortfeasor is intentional rather than unintentional, as in *Khorasandjian v Bush*, it could be argued that the action should lie in trespass rather than in nuisance.

*Notes*
1.   For other cases where injunctions were granted in tort proceedings, see *Patel v Patel* [1988] 2 FLR 179, CA, *Pidduck v Molloy* [1992] 2 FLR 202, CA, *Burris v Azadani* [1996] 1 FLR 266, CA and *Burnett v George* [1992] 1 FLR 525, CA (heard in 1986).
2.   The divorce court has jurisdiction under s. 38(1) of the County Courts Act 1984 and s. 37(1) of the Supreme Court Act 1981 to grant injunctions ancillary to divorce proceedings, e.g., to protect the parties and their children, and to grant an order excluding, if necessary, a party from the home pending the divorce suit.
3.   The Government has recently made proposals (see the Protection from Harassment Bill 1996) to introduce two new criminal offences of harassment and 'putting people in fear of violence'.

*Questions*
Did Miss Khorasandjian want protection or compensation? What are the likely drawbacks of bringing tort proceedings? Would she have had a remedy under Part IV of the FLA 1996, had it been in force?

*Further reading*
Cretney, S., 'Being a Nuisance' (1993) 109 LQR 361.

Murphy, J., 'The Emergence of Harassment as a Recognised Tort' (1993) 143 NLJ 926.

## 6.3  THE NEW LAW — THE NEED FOR REFORM

Part IV of the FLA 1996 will reform the civil law of domestic violence by giving the court jurisdiction to make 'occupation orders' and 'non-molestation orders' for a much larger class of applicants than under the present law. Part IV also makes provision for certain persons to be granted 'matrimonial home rights' (see Chapter 3), and makes provision for transfer of tenancies, including new provisions for the transfer of tenancies between cohabitants. It also amends the Children Act 1989 to enable the court to oust the abuser when making an emergency protection or interim care order (see Chapter 10).

Proposals for reform were originally put forward by the Law Commission in a report, *Domestic Violence and Occupation of the Family Home*, Law Com No. 207, which was published in May 1992. The Report contained a draft Bill which was initially adopted almost in its entirety by the Government, and was published in February 1995 as the Family Homes and Domestic Violence Bill. However, due to problems during its Parliamentary progress, the Bill was abandoned at the end of 1995, but reappeared later in a much amended form as Part IV of the Family Law Bill. The Bill was given the Royal Assent in July 1996. Part IV of the FLA 1996 is due to to come into force on 1 October 1997. The provisions are not as far-reaching and radical as the Law Commission's proposals, which had recommended provision for protection for a much wider class of applicants.

**Law Commission: *Domestic Violence and Occupation
of the Family Home*, 1992, Law Com No. 207**
London: HMSO, 1992

**The range and aims of this project**

1.1   This report makes recommendations for reform of the various discretionary remedies which exist in family law to deal with two distinct but inseparable problems: providing protection for one member of a family against molestation or violence by another and regulating the occupation of the family home where the relationship has broken down whether temporarily or permanently. . . .

1.2   The existing civil remedies in this area have been the source of much complaint. They are complex, confusing and lack integration. Lord Scarman has described the statutory provisions as 'a hotchpot of enactments of limited scope passed into law to meet specific situations or to strengthen the powers of specified courts. The sooner the range, scope and effect of these powers are rationalised into a coherent and comprehensive body of statute law, the better' [*Richards v Richards* [1984] AC 174 at 206–7]. Our aims in undertaking this project have therefore been threefold. The first is to remove the gaps, anomalies and inconsistencies in the existing remedies, with a view to synthesising them, so far as possible, into a clear, simple and comprehensive code. Secondly, we have taken it for granted that any reform should not reduce the level of protection which is available at present and might wish to improve it. Thirdly, however, it is desirable, and consistent with our work on children and divorce, to seek to avoid exacerbating hostilities between the adults involved, so far as this is compatible with providing proper and effective protection both for adults and for children.

1.3   The major proposal in the working paper was that there should be a single consistent set of remedies which would be available in all courts having jurisdiction in family matters, although perhaps with some specific limitations on the magistrates' courts' powers. All the respondents who commented specifically upon this issue were in favour of such a code and no-one argued against it. Accordingly, a recommendation for a comprehensive code forms the basis of this report.

. . .

2.23   There are many inconsistencies and anomalies in the present law. These have arisen largely as a result of piecemeal statutory development and the adoption or adaptation of a remedy developed for a particular purpose in one context for different purposes in another. The existing remedies have been developed in response to a variety of needs. Those under the Matrimonial Homes Act 1983 were first introduced in 1967 in order to ensure that deserted wives were not left without a roof over their heads, by giving them rights of occupation in the matrimonial home which could be registered and enforced against third parties, and by giving the court power to regulate occupation of the matrimonial home in the long or short term. To this was later added a power to prohibit the exercise by the property-owning spouse of his right to occupy the home. The remedies provided in sections 16–18 of the Domestic Proceedings and Magistrates' Courts Act 1978 and the Domestic Violence and Matrimonial Proceedings Act 1976 have protection against violence and molestation as their primary objective and were designed to provide an urgent legal response to this, which could include an exclusion order where the circumstances justified it. The principles applicable to regulating occupation of the home in the short or long term and to providing protection from violence and molestation are not necessarily the same. But it is impossible to treat them separately because, very often, the removal of one party from the house is the only effective protection which can be provided in cases of violence.

. . .

2.25   The criteria applicable under the different Acts are also diverse and, in many ways, unsatisfactory in themselves. Neither the general powers under which the Courts grant injunctions in pending proceedings or the 1976 Act lay down any criteria for the exercise of the court's discretion. But, despite the fact that the courts had developed their own principles to govern the exercise of this jurisdiction, in *Richards* v *Richards* [[1989] AC 174], the House of Lords decided that the criteria set out in section 1(3) of the 1983 Act should be applied in any case where an ouster order is sought between spouses, whether under that Act, the 1976 Act or in pending matrimonial proceedings. These criteria are not, however, applied in applications for exclusion orders under the Domestic Proceedings and Magistrates' Courts Act 1978. This Act has its own criteria based mainly on the use or threat of violence and danger of injury.

2.26   A number of possible criticisms of the present law, and in particular the application of the Matrimonial Homes Act criteria, were put forward in the working paper and were generally approved by those who responded to it. These can be summarised as follows:

(i)   the criteria are now out-dated, having first been enacted in 1967 for the purpose of identifying those non-owning spouses (usually wives) who were sufficiently deserving of long term accommodation in the matrimonial home to entitle them to resist dispositions to third parties; this was before most of the significant developments in this field;

(ii)    by requiring the parties' conduct to be balanced against the other factors, the criteria may suggest that an ouster order is in effect punishment for bad behaviour, so that the court should be asking itself whether the respondent's conduct is serious enough to justify an order, rather than whether the effect upon the other people in the household is serious enough to do so;

(iii)    these criteria with their concentration upon the conduct of the parties are applied to the whole range of very different situations: the need to provide immediate protection against violence or other forms of abuse; the need to resolve short term problems of accommodation when a relationship is or may be breaking down; and the need to resolve longer term problems where the relationship has already broken down;

(iv)    where divorce proceedings have already begun, there may well be a need to resolve disputes about who should live in the matrimonial home in the short term, and if possible this should be done without either prejudging issues which may be in dispute in the proceedings or forcing upon the parties a procedure that is based on language relying on conduct and fault whether or not they wish to pursue the disputes between them in those terms;

(v)    there is a risk that the children's welfare will be given insufficient weight, contrary to the general trend towards giving increased, if not predominating, weight to their interests even in relation to matters of finance and property;

(vi)    a general assumption that the effects of an exclusion order are invariably so severe as to merit the terms drastic or even Draconian, while obviously warranted in many cases, may obscure the considerable differences between the circumstances of the individual parties and in which the remedy is sought; in combination with a requirement that the respondent's conduct be bad enough to merit such a step, this may impede the sensible and practical resolution of the particular problem presented;

(vii)    the Matrimonial Homes Act criteria are not easily applicable to unmarried couples, for example because they do not give any indication of the relevance, if any, of respective property rights.

2.27    A further difficulty is that the present remedies available in the magistrates' courts are much more limited than those in the superior courts. The Domestic Proceedings and Magistrates' Courts Act 1978 applies only to spouses, not to cohabitants, and the remedies it provides are limited to cases of actual or threatened violence. There is thus no remedy in the magistrates' court for non-violent harassment.

2.28    The present law can also be criticised on the ground that it provides no protection for a number of people who have the misfortune to fall outside the specific categories of people covered by the different Acts, but may nevertheless have a clear need for such protection. Thus, many remedies are unavailable once the spouses are divorced. A former spouse cannot apply to a magistrates' court under the 1978 Act, nor can she apply under the 1976 Act unless she and her former husband are still living together as husband and wife after the decree. Rights of occupation under the Matrimonial Homes Act 1983 also end on decree absolute unless the court has ordered otherwise. Although it may be possible to obtain a non-molestation order and perhaps an ouster order in the divorce proceedings, there is no general power to adjust the parties' rights of occupation pending the conclusion of the ancillary relief application, and because the parties are no longer husband and wife, the court cannot attach a power of arrest to injunctions against violence under section 2 of the Domestic Violence and Matrimonial Proceedings Act 1976. Similarly, in the case of cohabitants, there is no power to provide protection once the relationship has ended. The only alternative is to proceed in tort, but this is a more cumbersome procedure, and is unlikely to be as effective because of difficulties over the precise scope of the protection available against molestation. Yet protection is often very necessary against former cohabitants or spouses who find it impossible to accept that the relationship is over.

. . .

*Notes*

*1.* A major reason for reform is that the DVMPA 1976, DPMCA 1978 and MHA 1983 (see 6.2) provide remedies for spouses and cohabitants only during the subsistence of the relationship. Former spouses and cohabitants must seek injunctive protection ancillary to other proceedings (e.g., in tort or divorce). Where children are involved, the position is slightly better, as the court *may* have an inherent jurisdiction to grant injunctions in order to protect children (but see the conflicting Court of Appeal decisions of *Wilde* v *Wilde* [1988] 2 FLR 83 and *M* v *M (Custody Application)* [1988] 1 FLR 225). Even where there are children, the court may be unwilling to remove the respondent from the home, particularly where the applicant has no proprietary interest in the home and is a cohabitant (see *Ainsbury* v *Millington* [1986] 1 All ER 73, CA, and *Pearson* v *Franklin (Parental Home: Ouster)* [1994] 1 FLR 246, CA).

*2.* In *Adeoso* v *Adeoso* [1981] 2 All ER 107, CA, 'living together in the same household as husband and wife' for the purposes of s. 1 of the DVMPA 1976 was given a liberal construction to give the female cohabitant a remedy even though she and her partner had no communal life under the same roof.

*3.* Where the court has no jurisdiction to make an injunction in respect of occupation, a victim of violence with children may apply for an order under the Children Act 1989, sch. 1, para. 1(2)(e)(i), which would give him or her, as against the respondent, an exclusive right of occupation (*per* Thorpe J in *Pearson* v *Franklin (Parental Home: Ouster)* [1994] 1 FLR 246, CA).

### 6.4   THE NEW LAW — OCCUPATION ORDERS

Under the FLA 1996, Part IV, ss. 33–41, the court has jurisdiction to make occupation orders. The court also has other powers, e.g., to impose repair and maintenance obligations on either party, order payment of rent, and to order that reasonable steps be taken to keep the house and its contents secure (see s. 40). An order under s. 33 may last for a specified period, until the occurrence of a specified event or until further order (s. 33(10)), but orders under ss. 35–38 may only last for a maximum of six months (although on a further application the order may be extended for up to one more maximum six-month period (ss. 35(10), 36(10), 37(5) and 38(6))). Occupation orders may be made *ex parte* (s. 45) and the court may accept an undertaking from any party to the proceedings instead of making an order (s. 46). It also has the power to attach a power of arrest to an order (s. 47).

Applicants for occupation orders fall into two categories: 'entitled' applicants; and 'non-entitled' applicants.

### 6.4.1 'Entitled' applicants

## FAMILY LAW ACT 1996

**33. Occupation orders where applicant has estate or interest etc. or has matrimonial home rights**

(1)  If—

(a)  a person ('the person entitled')—

(i)  is entitled to occupy a dwelling-house by virtue of a beneficial estate or interest or contract or by virtue of any enactment giving him the right to remain in occupation, or

(ii)  has matrimonial home rights in relation to a dwelling-house, and

(b)  the dwelling-house—

(i)  is or at any time has been the home of the person entitled and of another person with whom he is associated, or

(ii)  was at any time intended by the person entitled and any such other person to be their home,

the person entitled may apply to the court for an order containing any of the provisions specified in subsections (3), (4) and (5).

(2)  . . .

(3)  An order under this section may—

(a)  enforce the applicant's entitlement to remain in occupation as against the other person ('the respondent');

(b)  require the respondent to permit the applicant to enter and remain in the dwelling-house or part of the dwelling-house;

(c)  regulate the occupation of the dwelling-house by either or both parties;

(d)  if the respondent is entitled as mentioned in subsection (1)(a)(i), prohibit, suspend or restrict the exercise by him of his right to occupy the dwelling-house;

(e)  if the respondent has matrimonial home rights in relation to the dwelling-house and the applicant is the other spouse, restrict or terminate those rights;

(f)  require the respondent to leave the dwelling-house or part of the dwelling-house; or

(g)  exclude the respondent from a defined area in which the dwelling-house is included.

. . .

(6)  In deciding whether to exercise its powers under subsection (3) and (if so) in what manner, the court shall have regard to all the circumstances including—

(a)  the housing needs and housing resources of each of the parties and of any relevant child;

(b)  the financial resources of each of the parties;

(c)  the likely effect of any order, or of any decision by the court not to exercise its powers under subsection (3), on the health, safety or well-being of the parties and of any relevant child; and

(d)  the conduct of the parties in relation to each other and otherwise.

(7)  If it appears to the court that the applicant or any relevant child is likely to suffer significant harm attributable to conduct of the respondent if an order under this section containing one or more of the provisions mentioned in subsection (3) is not made, the court shall make the order unless it appears to it that—

(a)  the respondent or any relevant child is likely to suffer significant harm if the order is made; and

(b) the harm likely to be suffered by the respondent or child in that event is as great as, or greater than, the harm attributable to conduct of the respondent which is likely to be suffered by the applicant or child if the order is not made.

*Notes*
1. For the definition of 'associated persons' etc., see 6.6 below.
2. 'Matrimonial home rights' are defined by s. 30(1) (see Chapter 3).

### 6.4.2 'Non-entitled' applicants

Under .the FLA 1996, ss. 35–38, spouses, former spouses, cohabitants and former cohabitant with no entitlement to occupy a dwelling-house under s. 33(1) may apply for an occupation order by virtue of their status, whether or not the respondent is entitled.

### 6.4.2.1 Non-entitled former spouse applicant and entitled respondent

## FAMILY LAW ACT 1996

**35. One former spouse with no existing right to occupy**
(1) This section applies if—
(a) one former spouse is entitled to occupy a dwelling-house by virtue of a beneficial estate or interest or contract, or by virtue of any enactment giving him the right to remain in occupation;
(b) the other former spouse is not so entitled; and
(c) the dwelling-house was at any time their matrimonial home or was at any time intended by them to be their matrimonial home.
(2) The spouse not so entitled may apply to the court for an order under this section against the other former spouse ('the respondent'). . . .

*Notes*
1. The order must give an applicant in occupation the right not to be evicted or excluded from the house or part of it by the respondent for a specified period and must prohibit the respondent from evicting or excluding the applicant during that period (s. 35(3)). The order must give an applicant not in occupation the right to enter and occupy the house for a specified period and require the respondent to permit the exercise of that right (s. 35(4)).
2. The remaining subsections of s. 35 are virtually identical to those in s. 33 (see 6.4.1), except that the court must take into account the following additional factors when deciding whether to make an order and (if so) in what manner (s. 35(6)):
(e) the length of time that has elapsed since the parties ceased to live together;
(f) the length of time that has elapsed since the marriage was dissolved or annulled; and
(g) the existence of any pending proceedings between the parties—
(i) for an order under section 23A or 24 of the Matrimonial Causes Act 1973 (property adjustment orders in connection with divorce proceedings etc.);

(ii)    for an order under paragraph 1(2)(d) or (e) of Schedule 1 to the Children Act 1989 (orders for financial relief against parents); or

(iii)   relating to the legal or beneficial ownership of the dwelling-house.

## 6.4.2.2   Non-entitled cohabitant or former cohabitant applicant and entitled respondent

## FAMILY LAW ACT 1996

**36.   One cohabitant or former cohabitant with no existing right to occupy**

(1)   This section applies if—

(a)   one cohabitant or former cohabitant is entitled to occupy a dwelling-house by virtue of a beneficial estate or interest or contract or by virtue of any enactment giving him the right to remain in occupation;

(b)   the other cohabitant or former cohabitant is not so entitled; and

(c)   that dwelling-house is the home in which they live together as husband and wife or a home in which they at any time so lived together or intended so to live together.

(2)   The cohabitant or former cohabitant not so entitled may apply to the court for an order under this section against the other cohabitant or former cohabitant ('the respondent') . . .

*Notes*

*1.*   The remaining provisions of s. 36 are virtually identical to those in s. 33 (see 6.4.1), except that the following additional factors must be taken into account by the court when deciding whether and (if so) in what manner to make an order (s. 36(6)):

(e)   the nature of the parties' relationship;

(f)   the length of time during which they have lived together as husband and wife;

(g)   whether there are or have been any children who are children of both parties or for whom both parties have or have had parental responsibility;

(h)   the length of time that has elapsed since the parties ceased to live together; and

(i)   the existence of any pending proceedings between the parties—

(i)   for an order under paragraph 1(2)(d) of Schedule 1 to the Children Act 1989 (orders for financial relief against parents); or

(ii)   relating to the legal or beneficial ownership of the dwelling-house.

## 6.4.2.3   Neither spouse or former spouse entitled to occupy

## FAMILY LAW ACT 1996

**37.   Neither spouse entitled to occupy**

(1)   This section applies if—

(a)   one spouse or former spouse and the other spouse or former spouse occupy a dwelling-house which is or was the matrimonial home; but

(b)   neither of them is entitled to remain in occupation—

(i)   by virtue of a beneficial estate or interest or contract; or

(ii)   by virtue of any enactment giving him the right to remain in occupation.

(2)   Either of the parties may apply to the court for an order against the other under this section.

*Note*
The order may allow re-entry to the house or part of it, regulate its occupation, require the respondent to leave the house or exclude the respondent from a defined area in which the dwelling-house is included (s. 37(3)). Subsections 33(6) and (7) (see 6.4.1) govern the exercise of the court's powers (s. 37(4)).

### 6.4.2.4   Neither cohabitant or former cohabitant entitled to occupy

## FAMILY LAW ACT 1996

**38.   Neither cohabitant or former cohabitant entitled to occupy**
   (1)   This section applies if—
      (a)   one cohabitant or former cohabitant and the other cohabitant or former cohabitant occupy a dwelling-house which is the home in which they live or lived together as husband and wife; but
      (b)   neither of them is entitled to remain in occupation—
         (i)   by virtue of a beneficial estate or interest or contract; or
         (ii)   by virtue of any enactment giving him the right to remain in occupation.
   (2)   Either of the parties may apply to the court for an order against the other under this section.

*Notes*
1.   The order may allow re-entry to the house or part of it, regulate its occupation, require the respondent to leave the house or exclude the respondent from a defined area in which the dwelling-house is included (s. 38(3)). When exercising its power to make an order, the court must have regard to all the circumstances including factors in s. 38(4) which are the same as those in s. 33(6) (see 6.4.1). The court must also apply a balance of harm test (s. 38(5)) and must take account of the fact that the parties have not given each other the commitment involved in marriage (s. 41).
2.   For definitions of 'cohabitants' and 'former cohabitants' etc., see 6.6 below.

## 6.5   THE NEW LAW — NON-MOLESTATION ORDERS

## FAMILY LAW ACT 1996

**42.   Non-molestation orders**
   (1)   In [Part IV of the Act] a 'non-molestation order' means an order containing either or both of the following provisions—
      (a)   provision prohibiting a person ('the respondent') from molesting another person who is associated with the respondent;

(b)   provision prohibiting the respondent from molesting a relevant child.

(2)   The court may make a non-molestation order—

(a)   if an application for the order has been made (whether in other family proceedings or without any other family proceedings being instituted) by a person who is associated with the respondent; or

(b)   if in any family proceedings to which the respondent is a party the court considers that the order should be made for the benefit of any other party to the proceedings or any relevant child even though no such application has been made.

(3)   In subsection (2) 'family proceedings' includes proceedings in which the court has made an emergency protection order under section 44 of the Children Act 1989 which includes an exclusion requirement (as defined in section 44A(3) of that Act).

(4)   Where an agreement to marry is terminated, no application under subsection (2)(a) may be made by virtue of section 62(3)(e) by reference to that agreement after the end of the period of three years beginning with the day on which it is terminated.

(5)   In deciding whether to exercise its powers under this section and, if so, in what manner, the court shall have regard to all the circumstances including the need to secure the health, safety and well-being—

(a)   of the applicant or, in a case falling within subsection (2)(b), the person for whose benefit the order would be made; and

(b)   of any relevant child.

(6)   A non-molestation order may be expressed so as to refer to molestation in general, to particular acts of molestation, or to both.

(7)   A non-molestation order may be made for a specified period or until further order.

(8)   A non-molestation order which is made in other family proceedings ceases to have effect if those proceedings are withdrawn or dismissed.

*Notes*

1.   The court may make an *ex parte* order (s. 45), accept an undertaking (i.e. a promise to do or not to do something) from any party to the proceedings (s. 46), and may attach a power of arrest to an order (s. 47).

2.   A child under 16 may apply for an order with leave of the court (s. 43(1)), but leave may be granted only if the child has sufficient understanding to make the proposed application (s. 43(2)). Regulations will be made for the separate representation of children (s. 64(1)).

## 6.6   THE NEW LAW — DEFINITIONS

Sections 62 and 63 of the FLA 1996 contain some definitions which are crucial to an understanding of the new law. These definitions are relevant to applications for occupation orders and non-molestation orders.

## FAMILY LAW ACT 1996

**62.   Meaning of 'cohabitants', 'relevant child' and 'associated persons'**

(1)   For the purposes of [Part IV of the Act sections 62 and 63 of the Family Law Act 1996 contain some definitions]—

(a) 'cohabitants' are a man and a woman who, although not married to each other, are living together as husband and wife; and

(b) 'former cohabitants' is to be read accordingly, but does not include cohabitants who have subsequently married each other.

(2) In [Part IV of the Act], 'relevant child', in relation to any proceedings under this Part, means—

(a) any child who is living with or might reasonably be expected to live with either party to the proceedings;

(b) any child in relation to whom an order under the Adoption Act 1976 or the Children Act 1989 is in question in the proceedings; and

(c) any other child whose interests the court considers relevant.

(3) For the purposes of [Part IV of the Act], a person is associated with another person if—

(a) they are or have been married to each other;

(b) they are cohabitants or former cohabitants;

(c) they live or have lived in the same household, otherwise than merely by reason of one of them being the other's employee, tenant, lodger or boarder;

(d) they are relatives;

(e) they have agreed to marry one another (whether or not that agreement has been terminated);

(f) in relation to any child, they are both persons falling within subsection (4); or

(g) they are parties to the same family proceedings (other than proceedings under this Part).

(4) A person falls within this subsection in relation to a child if—

(a) he is a parent of the child; or

(b) he has or has had parental responsibility for the child.

(5) If a child has been adopted or has been freed for adoption by virtue of any of the enactments mentioned in section 16(1) of the Adoption Act 1976, two persons are also associated with each other for the purposes of [Part IV] if—

(a) one is a natural parent of the child or a parent of such a natural parent; and

(b) the other is the child or any person—

(i) who has become a parent of the child by virtue of an adoption order or has applied for an adoption order, or

(ii) with whom the child has at any time been placed for adoption.

. . .

### 63. Interpretation of Part IV

(1) In this Part—

. . .

'relative in relation to a person, means:

(a) the father, mother, stepfather, stepmother, son, daughter, stepson, step-daughter, grandmother, grandfather, grandson or granddaughter of that person or of that person's spouse or former spouse; or

(b) the brother, sister, uncle, aunt, niece or nephew (whether of the full blood or of the half blood or by affinity) of that person or of that person's spouse or former spouse,

and includes in relation to a person who is living or has lived with another person as husband and wife, any person who would fall within paragraph (a) or (b) if the parties were married to each other.

. . .

(2)   The enactments referred to in the definition of 'family proceedings' are:
    (a)   Part II [of the FLA 1996];
    (b)   this Part;
    (c)   the Matrimonial Causes Act 1973;
    (d)   the Adoption Act 1976;
    (e)   the Domestic Proceedings and Magistrates' Courts Act 1978;
    (f)   Part III of the Matrimonial and Family Proceedings Act 1984.
    (g)   Parts, I, II and IV of the Children Act 1989;
    (h)   section 30 of the Human Fertilisation and Embryology Act 1990.
. . .

*Questions*

1.   The Law Commission, in its Report, *Domestic Violence and Occupation of the Family Home*, Law Com No. 207, recommended that remedies in respect of domestic violence and occupation of the home should be available to a wider class of applicants (i.e. where there was something resembling a family relationship or where there was a sexual relationship between the parties), but these recommendations were rejected by the Government. Why do you think they were?

2.   How would you advise the following, applying both the 'old' law and the 'new' law?

(a)   Sue is divorced and lives in the former matrimonial home with the children. Her ex-husband David keeps telephoning her all night and banging on the door and annoying her in the street.

(b)   After years of violence, Jenny ended her relationship with Mark three months ago and moved out of the house with their three young children and went to live with a friend. Jenny wishes to move back into the home, which they own jointly.

(c)   Last year Ann met Fred at a night club and went out for him for a few weeks. Recently, Fred has been pestering her non-stop to go out with him again and has been telephoning her at all hours of the night.

(d)   Norma is 80 years old and incontinent. Her husband Fred sometimes treats her very roughly and bruises her because he gets impatient and frustrated.

(e)   Tom, aged 14, is regularly punched by his alcoholic father.

(f)   Linda is often beaten up by her 15-year-old nephew who lives with her.

(g)   John and Jim are homosexuals who jointly own the house they share. John has been violent to Jim for several months. Jim moved out, but John keeps following him and pestering him at work. Jim wishes to stop the harassment and to move back into the house as he has just been diagnosed as having AIDS.

*Further reading*
Bird, R., *Domestic Violence: the New Law, Part IV of the Family Law Act 1996*, Bristol: Jordans, 1996.

His Honour Judge N. Fricker, 'Inherent Jurisdiction, Ouster and Exclusion' [1994] Fam Law 629.
Brazier, M., 'Personal Injury by Molestation — An Emergent or Established Tort' [1992] Fam Law 346.

# 7 CHILDREN

This chapter deals with children's rights, the Children Act 1989 and wardship.

## 7.1 CHILDREN'S RIGHTS

**Freeman, Michael D. A., 'The Limits of Children's Rights',
in Freeman, Michael D. A., and Veerman, P., (eds)
*The Ideologies of Children's Rights*,**
Dordrecht: Martinus Nijhoff and Kluwer International, 1992, p. 29

*The Importance of Children's Rights*

There are still those who argue that, however important rights are, it is not necessary to recognise as such children's rights. Where such arguments are put, they tend to employ one of two myths.

One . . . idealises adult-child relations: it emphasises that adults (and parents in particular) have the best interests of children at heart. Those who argue in this way tend, like Goldstein, Freud and Solnit or indeed the British government which was recently responsible for major children's legislation, to adopt a *laissez-faire* attitude towards the family. Thus, the only right for children which Goldstein *et al.* would appear to accept is the child's right to autonomous parents. A policy of minimum coercive intervention by the state accords, they maintain, with their 'firm belief as citizens in individual freedom and human dignity'. But *whose* freedom and *what* dignity does this uphold? It certainly would not appear to be those of the child. The recent English Children Act of 1989 very much reflects this philosophy. It is somewhat unfortunate that in an age when so much abuse is being uncovered that governments and writers should cling to the 'cereal packet' image of the family.

The second myth can be captured more succinctly. It sees childhood as a golden age, as the best years of our life. Childhood is synonymous with innocence. It is a time when we are spared the rigours of adult life; it is a time of freedom, of joy, of play. The argument runs that, just as we avoid the responsibilities and adversities of adult life in childhood, so there should be no necessity to think in terms of children's rights. Whether or not the premise underlying this is correct or not (and I think that the carefree nature of a child's life can be exaggerated), it represents an ideal state of affairs, and one which ill-reflects the lives of many of to-day's children and adolescents.

There are countries which to-day are systematically exterminating children as if they were vermin (Brazil and Guatemala are two well-documented examples). Poverty, disease, exploitation are rife in every part of the globe: the briefest of glances at the annual *State of the World's Children* publication soon reveals that.

Even in the developed world the lives of children are fraught with deprivation. Thus, the latest data to 'emerge' from Britain reveals that, in a decade in which awareness of children's rights has heightened, child poverty numbers have nearly doubled. In a report just published (written by Jonathan Bradshaw for the National Children's Bureau) the conclusion is drawn that during the 1980s 'children have borne the brunt of the changes that have occurred in the economic conditions, demographic structure and social policies of the United Kingdom'. Three million children in Britain (that is 28 per cent of the total number) live on state benefits which force them to exist at or below (depending upon definition and interpretation) subsistence level. For contrast the percentage in 1979 was 17 per cent.

The case posited to attack those who espouse children's rights does not, therefore, command respect. Rights are important because possession of them is part of what is necessary to constitute persònality. Those who lack rights are like slaves, means to others' ends, and never their own sovereigns. It is surely significant that when we wish to deny rights to those who have attained chronological adulthood we label them (blacks in South Africa, the mentally retarded) children. To be a child, one does not have to be young. . . . Childhood is, of course, a social construct, a man-made phenomenon: those in authority determine who is a child. That they have not done so with any consistency or, it would seem, coherent thought can not detain us here.

To say that rights are important, and important also for children, is not to gainsay the crucial part which other morally significant values, such as love, friendship and compassion, have and play in life's relationships. . . . But, short of a cultural revolution beyond our wildest dreams, rights will remain important.

And, it will remain important to recognise children's rights. . . . It is generally agreed that denial of rights is a bad thing, so that something should be done about it. 'Rights' enables one to talk in terms of 'entitlements'.
. . .

## Eekelaar, John, 'The Emergence of Children's Rights'
### (1986) 6 *Oxford J Legal Stud* 161 at p. 66

*Interests and rights*
Joseph Raz has argued that 'a law creates a right if it is based on and expresses the view that someone has an interest which is sufficient ground for holding another to be subject to a duty'; and, again, that 'to be a rule conferring a right it has to be motivated by a belief in the fact that someone's (the rightholder's) interest should be protected by the imposition of duties on others' ['Legal Rights' (1984) 4 *Oxford J Legal Stud* 1, at pp. 13–14].

The reference to the 'beliefs motivating' the rule-creators requires, in this context at any rate, a subtle examination of the public perception of the purpose of the law. Blackstone may indeed have appreciated the 'interests' of children in this context, but when we look at the private law, we see that it makes no direct attempt to protect them. Rather, it is the interest of the father to which the legal remedies are related. It is true that their enforcement may *incidentally* benefit the children, but that is not their aim and purpose. This distinction is even clearer when we look at public law. The first *legal* expression of a father's duty to support his children can be found in the poor laws of the sixteenth century. Here the law would step in and indirectly enforce the father's obligation to educate his children by putting them out to apprenticeship. . . .

We might usefully at this point reflect on how we might characterize the position thus reached in terms of children's rights. We may accept that the *social perception* that an individual or class of individuals has certain interests is a precondition to the conceptualization of rights. But these interests must be capable of isolation from the interests of others. I might believe that it is in my infant daughter's interests that I (and not she) take decisions concerning her medical welfare. This may even be supportable by objective evidence. But my interest, or right, to take such decisions is not identical with her interests. I might make stupid or even malicious decisions. Her interest is that I should make the best decisions for her. I am no more than the agent for fulfilling her interests. Hence we should be careful to understand that when we talk about rights as protecting interests, we conceive as interests only those benefits which the subject himself or herself might plausibly claim in themselves. This point is of great importance in the context of modern assertions of the right to parental autonomy. This has been advanced as a fuller enhancement of children's rights. Goldstein, Freud and Solnit [*Before the Best Interests of the Child*, 1979, p. 9] construct the concept of 'family integrity' which is a combination of 'the three liberty interests of direct concern to children, parental autonomy, the right to autonomous parents and privacy'. But can we say the children might plausibly claim any of these things in themselves? If they are claimed (which they may be) it will be because they are believed to advance other desirable ends (perhaps material and emotional stability) which are the true objects of the claims. Observe that the formulation refers to claims children might plausibly make. Not, be it noted, what they actually claim. We here meet the problem that children often lack the information or ability to appreciate what will serve them best. It is necessary therefore to make some kind of imaginative leap and guess what a child might retrospectively have wanted once it reaches a position of maturity. In doing this, values of the adult world and of individual adults will inevitably enter. This is not to be deplored, but openly accepted. It encourages debate about these values. There are, however, some broad propositions which might reasonably be advanced as forming the foundation of any child's (retrospective) claims. General physical, emotional and intellectual care within the social capabilities of his or her immediate caregivers would seem a minimal expectation. We may call this the 'basic' interest. What a child should expect from the wider community must be stated more tentatively. I have elsewhere suggested the formulation that, within certain overriding constraints created by the economic and social structure of society (whose extent must be open to debate), all children should have an equal opportunity to maximize the resources available to them during their childhood (including their own inherent abilities) so as to minimize the degree to which they enter adult life affected by avoidable prejudices incurred during childhood. In short, their capacities are to be developed to their best advantage. We may call this the 'developmental' interest. The concept requires some elaboration.

It seems plausible that a child may expect society at large, no less than his parents, to ensure that he is no worse off than most other children in his opportunities to realize his life-chances. Could a child also plausibly claim that he should be given a *better* chance than other children, for example, by exploitation of his superior talents or a favoured social position? As an expectation addressed to the child's parents, such a claim might have some weight. A child of rich parents might retrospectively feel aggrieved if those resources were not used to provide him with a better chance in life than other children. On the other hand, such an expectation is less plausibly addressed to society at large, except perhaps with respect to the cultivation of singular talents. But from the point of view of a theory of rights, it does not much matter whether we decide that a privileged child has an interest in inequality favourable to himself. For, if the interest is to become a right it must be acknowledged in the public domain as demanding protection for its own sake. As far as the 'developmental' interest is concerned, therefore, societies may choose to actualize it in harmony with their overall social goals, which may (but not necessarily) involve creating equality of opportunity and reducing socially determined inequalities, but encouraging diversity of achievement related to individual talent.

There is a third type of interest which children may, retrospectively, claim. A child may argue for the freedom to choose his own lifestyle and to enter social relations according to his own inclinations uncontrolled by the authority of the adult world, whether parents or institutions. Claims of this kind have been put forward on behalf of children by Holt [*Escape from Childhood*, 1975] and by Farson [*Birthrights*, 1973]. We may call them the 'autonomy' interest. Freeman [*The Rights and Wrongs of Children*, 1983] has argued that such interests might be abridged insofar as children also have a right to be protected against their own inclinations if their satisfaction would rob them of the opportunity 'to mature to a rationally autonomous adulthood . . . capable of deciding on [their] own system of ends as free and rational beings'. This may be no more than a version of the developmental interest defined earlier. The problem is that a child's autonomy interest may conflict with the developmental interest and even the basic interest. While it is possible that some adults retrospectively approve that they were, when children, allowed the exercise of their autonomy at the price of putting them at a disadvantage as against other children in realizing their life-chances in adulthood, it seems improbable that this would be a common view. We may therefore rank the autonomy interests subordinate to the basic and the developmental interests. However, where they may be exercised without threatening these two interests, the claim for their satisfaction must be high.
. . .

### Eekelaar, John, 'The Importance of Thinking that Children have Rights', in Alston, P., Parker, S. and Seymour, J. (eds), *Children, Rights and the Law*, Oxford: Clarendon Press, 1992, p. 221

. . . The starting-off point, then, of any rights-based approach to social policy is to have regard to claims which people make and to provide opportunities for claims to be made. What these claims actually are is an empirical matter. This is not simply a theoretical point. It involves the process, so easy for politicians, welfare professionals and even academics to forget: *listening to people*. No social organization can hope to be built on the rights of its members unless there are mechanisms whereby those members may express themselves and wherein those expressions are taken seriously. *Hearing what children say* must therefore lie at the root of any elaboration of children's rights. No society will have begun to perceive its children as rightholders until adults' attitudes and social structures are seriously adjusted towards making it possible for children to express views, and towards addressing them with respect.

We now confront the problem faced by all children's rights theorists: children may be too young to say anything. Even if they are not, their opinions may be coloured by ignorance or parental influence. Yet they surely have rights. We may be tempted, then, to abandon the claim theory entirely. But we should remember the example given above where rights are conferred on or held by an ignorant population. They take their force as rights only to the extent that it can reasonably be assumed that, when fully informed, the people will wish to exercise them. If this is implausible (for example, a 'right' granted to a rebellious populace to serve in the army) we cannot sensibly think that a right has been conferred at all. So adults' duties towards young children cannot be convincingly perceived as reflecting rights held by the children unless it can be plausibly assumed that, if fully informed of the relevant factors and of mature judgement, the children would want such duties to be exercised towards them.

This hypothetical judgement is necessary in order to maintain theoretical coherence with the central character of rights asserted here. As a construct, it is partly an artefact constrained by the assumptions of full information and maturity. This precludes contemplating the conditioning of children so as to ensure that when they reach adulthood they will always approve of whatever was done to them during their childhood. The assumptions of information and maturity incorporate into rights-based decision-making regarding young children the requirement that such decisions promote the goal of maturity, which is taken to be the ability to confront the truth and exercise self-determination. Maturity opens up options; it does not close them down.

Despite these external constraints, the hypothetical judgement does not abstract the child from his or her context. On the contrary, it stipulates a *process* which requires serious attention to be given to what *the child in question*, of his or her gender, ethnicity and other personal and social characteristics, is likely to have wanted if fully informed and mature. This has important consequences. General theories of what comprises children's best interests will not in themselves suffice as grounds for decision-making. Also, since children mature gradually, it will always be necessary to observe the child closely for indications of what is important *for that child*, and why. This is in direct opposition to the devastating neglect of children's own opinions which has character-ized much of the welfarist approach hitherto. Finally, the process looks forward to the future adult. It is easy (though not inevitable) that the welfarist approach should emphasize short-term effects over potential long-term consequences. A child's im-mediate contentment is of course important to the development of an integrated adult personality. But the hypothetical viewpoint demands serious attention to be paid also to the social and cultural environment into which the child is likely to grow. What is important about this is not so much the particular answer given in a particular case, but in the territory which this process opens up. Decisions which are taken about children will need to be justified by articulating how they may plausibly relate to the child's hypothesized viewpoint. This carries with it the discipline of precise specifica-tion. It could never be enough to assert simply that an action will be in the child's welfare. We now need to think how the action could be one which the child might plausibly want. We need to consider closely the child's individual circumstances, to separate the child's claims from competing claims and relate the proposed action to both.

Since the reference to the hypothetical viewpoint is a process and not an end-result (as in the welfarist model) it will not always reveal a clear-cut conclusion. On such occasions we can assume only that the child would expect adults to make their best assessment of his or her welfare according to their own lights. But the process could lead to a re-evaluation of some current assumptions of welfarist thinking. For example, the concealment from a child of information about its birth by artificial insemination is usually justified on the ground that this is in the child's best interests. But the rights perspective poses the question: would that child, as an adult, be likely to choose to live his or her life on the basis of a deliberate deception about his or her origins? It would also ask: would a child born as a result of embryo donation choose to be brought up into the family of its gestational or its genetic parents? Similar re-framing could have significant consequences in the context of inter-racial adoption or fostering placements. It could be important also in decisions about secular and religious education and the exposure of children to literature and ideas.

. . .

*Question*
O'Neill, O., 'Children's Rights and Children's Lives', in Alston *et al.* (eds), *Children, Rights and the Law,* argues at p. 25 that 'taking rights as fundamental in ethical deliberations about children has neither theoretical nor political advantages' and that a more 'perspicuous and complete view' of ethical aspects of children's lives 'can be obtained by taking obligations as fundamental'. Do you agree?

*Further reading*
Freeman, M., *The Rights and Wrongs of Children,* London: Frances Pinter, 1983.
Roche, J., 'Children's Rights: In the Name of the Child' [1995] JSWFL 281.
The Children's Legal Centre, University of Essex, Colchester CO4 3SQ, publishes useful booklets and leaflets about children and their legal rights, as well as a monthly magazine, *Childright.*

## 7.2   THE UN CONVENTION ON THE RIGHTS OF THE CHILD 1989

### King, Michael, 'Children's Rights as Communication: Reflections on Autopoietic Theory and the United Nations Convention',
(1994) 57 MLR 385

. . . Children's physical and economic vulnerability and dependence on adult protection means that all too easily they become the innocent victims of wars, famines, economic mismanagement, social policies driven by political dogma, austerity measures, or religious or customary practices. Some notorious exceptions apart, it is extremely difficult to attribute direct responsibility for most of the large-scale suffering experienced by children throughout the world. Even what seem to be at first sight the most straightforward acts of the mistreatment of a child by a culpable adult or culpable adults as in sexual abuse and physical neglect, have a tendency on closer examination to relate to a complex range of interpersonal and social factors.

. . .

### Asquith, Stewart, and Hill, Malcolm (eds),
*Justice for Children,*
Dordrecht: Martinus Nijhoff and Kluwer International, 1994,
Editorial Introduction at pp. 13–15

UN CONVENTION ON THE RIGHTS OF THE CHILD
The rapid social and demographic changes which children have experienced in the last decade have been accompanied by gradual but continuing alteration to their social

and political status. In particular, the United Nations Convention on the Rights of the Child embodies a whole new philosophy which will influence current and future developments relating to children.

By ratifying the Convention, governments are committed to the full implementation of the rights set out in the Convention and which can be grouped into three broad categories:

*Protection:*     children have a right to protection from cruelty, abuse, neglect and exploitation
*Participation:*  children have a right to play an active role in society and to have a say in their own lives
*Provision:*      children have a right to have their basic needs met

By granting children (all those under 18) universal rights, the convention at the same time places children's issues on the political agenda and also puts them in an international context. Moreover, the universality of the rights granted through the convention means that children should not be discriminated against on grounds of age, gender, ethnicity, religious affiliation or class.

The Convention is based on the philosophy that children are equals and that they have the same value as adults. But they are also at the same time vulnerable because of their age and because of the ways in which their lives are subject to the decisions and behaviour of adults. Herein lies a tension, not just for the Convention but for adults either as parents or as members of agencies responsible for children — how best to treat children as equals but at the same time recognise their vulnerability. Two articles in the convention are crucial in this respect. Article 3.1 states:

⁂ In all actions concerning children, whether undertaken by public or private social welfare institutions, courts of law, administrative authorities or legislative bodies, the best interests of the child shall be a primary consideration.

Thus, the interests of others including parents and social work, education or health agencies are less important than those of the child. . . .

Moreover, the child should also have a say in decisions about his or her future. Article 12.1 states that:

States Parties shall assure to the child who is capable of forming his or her own views the right to express these views freely in all matters affecting the child, the views of the child being given due weight in accordance with the age and maturity of the child.

What these articles reflect is the view that the protection of children has to be balanced with a concern for their growth to independence and respect for their rights as individuals. The Convention, far from establishing a framework which would allow children to do simply what they wanted, relates rights to responsibilities. Children are to be offered protection when needed but are also to be given greater opportunities for participation in and exercising responsibility over decisions affecting their lives as and when appropriate. The right of children to their childhood, particularly younger children, is protected against excessive demands imposed by the expectation that they should behave as adults.

One of the main implications of the Convention is that developments in child care and child law will increasingly give children the right to be involved in decisions in all situations in which they find themselves whether these involve their parents or other adults in key agencies such as health, social work or education.

Though the Convention is child centred it should not be seen as only commenting on the rights of children. It also states the rights, responsibilities and duties of parents and legal guardians. The right of parents and legal guardians to provide 'appropriate direction' in the exercise of rights by children is qualified again by the need to recognise the importance of children's interests and the evolving capacities of the child. In fact the Convention embodies the principle that separation of the parents in no way absolves either parent from the responsibility of parenting. Parents and the family are to be given support and assistance but when it is clear that children are not being given sufficient protection or help to express their wishes then the state has to intervene, with the child's interests a primary consideration.

Moreover, the Convention imposes obligations and duties on states to provide material and other wherewithal necessary for children to realise their physical and intellectual potential. For example, Article 27 states that:

States Parties recognise the right of every child to a standard of living adequate for the child's physical, mental, spiritual, moral and social development.

States Parties . . . shall take appropriate measures to assist parents others and others responsible for the child to implement this right and shall in case of need provide material assistance and support programmes, particularly with regard to nutrition, clothing and housing.

Broadly speaking what the Convention does is not simply set up a list of rights for children and impose a correlate set of duties on others such as parents and the state. It goes further than that in presenting a framework whereby the very social and political status of children, their relationship to their parents and adults in general may be viewed very differently. It alters the balance of power between children and adults in such a way that children generally can play a more active part in democratic social life. It also imposes duties on states to provide the necessary resources with which children can grow to realise their potential and can themselves contribute to social and political change throughout the world.

Ultimately, a concern with justice for children says something about how they are conceived of as members of society and also mirrors the very notion of justice we as adults employ. Perez de Cuellar put it neatly when he said

The way a society treats its children reflects not only its qualities of compassion and protective caring, but also its sense of justice, its commitment to the future and its urge to enhance the human condition for coming generations. This is as indisputably true of the community of nations as it is of nations individually . . .

. . .

**Eekelaar, John, 'The Importance of Thinking that Children Have Rights', in Alston, P., Parker, S., and Seymour, J. (eds),**
***Children, Rights and the Law,***
Oxford: Clarendon Press 1992, p. 221 at p. 234

. . . It would be logically possible to have framed the Convention on the Rights of the Child as a list of duties owed by adults to children. But that would have revealed a negative, suspicious, view of human nature; it would have seen people as servile, responding best to restraint and control. The strength of the rights formulation is its recognition of humans as individuals worthy of development and fulfilment. This is not an appeal to narrow self-interest. On the contrary, it recognizes the insight that people can contribute positively to others only when they are respected and fulfilled.

And to recognize people as having rights from the moment of their birth continuously into adulthood could turn out, politically, to be the most radical step of all. If all *young people* are secured all the physical, social and economic rights proclaimed in the Convention, the lives of millions of adults of the next generation would be transformed. It would be a grievous mistake to see the Convention as applying to childhood alone. Childhood is not an end in itself, but part of the process of forming the adults of the next generation. The Convention is for all *people*. It could influence their entire lives. If its aims can be realized, the Convention can truly be said to be laying the foundations for a better world.

Some of the key provisions of the UN Convention on the Rights of the Child 1989 are as follows:

## UNITED NATIONS CONVENTION ON THE RIGHTS OF THE CHILD 1989

**Article 2**

1. States Parties shall respect and ensure the rights set forth in the present Convention to each child within their jurisdiction without discrimination of any kind, irrespective of the child's or his or her parent's or legal guardian's race, colour, sex, language, religion, political or other opinion, national, ethnic or social origin, property, disability, birth or other status.

2. States Parties shall take all appropriate measures to ensure that the child is protected against all forms of discrimination or punishment on the basis of the status, activities, expressed opinions, or beliefs of the child's parents, legal guardians, or family members.

**Article 3**

1. In all actions concerning children, whether undertaken by public or private social welfare institutions, courts of law, administrative authorities or legislative bodies, the best interests of the child shall be a primary consideration.

. . .

**Article 6**

1. States Parties recognize that every child has the inherent right to life.

2. States Parties shall ensure to the maximum extent possible the survival and development of the child.

**Article 9**

1. States Parties shall ensure that a child shall not be separated from his or her parents against their will, except when competent authorities subject to judicial review determine, in accordance with applicable law and procedures, that such separation is necessary for the best interests of the child. . . .

**Article 11**

1. States Parties shall take measures to combat the illicit transfer and non-return of children abroad.

. . .

**Article 12**

1. States Parties shall assure to the child who is capable of forming his or her own views the right to express those views freely in all matters affecting the child, the views of the child being given due weight in accordance with the age and maturity of the child.

2.  For this purpose, the child shall in particular be provided the opportunity to be heard in any judicial and administrative proceedings affecting the child, either directly, or through a representative or an appropriate body, in a manner consistent with the procedural rules of national law.

### Article 16
1.  No child shall be subjected to arbitrary or unlawful interference with his or her privacy, family, home or correspondence, nor to unlawful attacks on his or her honour and reputation.
2.  The child has the right to the protection of the law against such interference or attacks.

### Article 27
1.  States Parties recognize the right of every child to a standard of living adequate for the child's physical, mental, spiritual, moral and social development.
    . . .

*Notes*
1.  Other rights for children include: freedom of expression (art. 13); freedom of thought, conscience and religion (art. 14); freedom of association and freedom of peaceful assembly (art. 15); enjoyment of minority rights (art. 30); education (art. 28); rest and leisure and to engage in play and recreational activities (art. 31); protection from economic exploitation and from performing work which will interfere with the child's education or harm the child's health or development (art. 32).
2.  There is no international court to punish violations of the UN Convention (*cf.* the position under the European Convention for the Protection of Human Rights), but the UN Committee on the Rights of the Child (established under art. 43 of the Convention) monitors the implementation of the Convention in countries which have ratified it. In addition to the monitoring powers of the UN Committee, abuses of children's rights may be brought before the European Court of Human Rights under the European Convention for the Protection of Human Rights.

*Questions*
1.  Is it surprising that children were given no opportunity to voice their views on the content and drafting of the UN Convention?
2.  During the deliberations of the UN Convention on the Rights of the Child, Senegal introduced a new article: 'The child has a duty to respect his parents and give them assistance in case of need.' Although such a duty was a cultural value in Africa and Asia, it was voted against, some UN delegates arguing that it was tantamount to child labour (but see art. 29(1)(c)). Do children have any duties or responsibilities?

*Further reading*
Hamilton, C., and Standley, K. (eds), *Family Law in Europe*, London: Butterworths, 1995.
Kilkelly, U., 'The UN Committee on the Rights of the Child — An Evaluation in the Light of Recent UK Experience' [1996] 8 CFLQ 105.

Landsdown, G., 'Implementing the UN Convention on the Rights of the Child in the UK' [1995] 7 CFLQ 122.

McGoldrick, D., 'The United Nations Convention on the Rights of the Child' (1991) 5 IJL&F 132.

Olsen, F., 'Children's Rights: Some Feminist Approaches to the United Nations Convention on the Rights of the Child', in Alston, P., et al. (eds), *Children, Rights and the Law*, Oxford: Clarendon Press, 1992.

Van Bueren, G., 'Protecting Children's Rights in Europe — A Test Case Strategy' (1996) 2 *European Human Rights Law Review* 171.

Van Bueren, G., 'Child-Oriented Justice — An International Challenge for Europe' (1992) 6 IJL&F 381.

Walsh, B., 'The United Nations Convention on the Rights of the Child: A British View' (1991) 5 IJL&F 170.

## 7.3   CHILDREN'S AUTONOMY RIGHTS

**Freeman, Michael, 'Taking Children's Rights More Seriously' in Alston, P., Parker, S., and Seymour, J. (eds),**
***Children, Rights and the Law,***
Oxford: Clarendon Press, 1992, p. 52 at p. 53

To respect a child's autonomy is to treat that child as a person and as a rights-holder. It is clear that we can do so to a much greater extent than we have assumed hitherto. But is also clear that the exercising of autonomy by a child can have a deleterious impact on that child's life-chances. It is true that adults make mistakes too (and also make mistakes when interfering with a child's autonomy). Having rights, means being allowed to take risks and make choices. There is a reluctance to interfere with an adult's project. This reluctance is tempered when the project pursuer is a child by the sense that choice now may harm choice later. . . .

. . .

   To take children's rights more seriously requires us to take seriously nurturance and self-determination. It demands of us that we adopt policies, practices, structures and laws which both protect children and their rights. . . .

### 7.3.1   The *Gillick* case

The landmark case on children's autonomy rights is the *Gillick* case, in which the central issue for the House of Lords was whether a doctor could in any circumstances lawfully give contraceptive treatment to a girl under the age of 16 without parental consent.

*Gillick* v *West Norfolk and Wisbech Area Health Authority and Another*
. [1986] AC 112
House of Lords

*Facts*: A Memorandum of Guidance issued by the Department of Health and Social Security (DHSS) provided that health authorities, doctors and

others involved in family planning services could in exceptional circumstances give contraceptive advice and treatment to girls under the age of 16
without parental consent. Mrs Gillick, a Roman Catholic with five daughters under the age of 16, sought a declaration that the Memorandum was
unlawful, and a declaration against the Area Health Authority that no
contraceptive or abortion advice and treatment should be offered to any
child under 16 without parental consent. She submitted: (i) that parental
rights should be protected from any unauthorised invasion or interference;
(ii) that the provision of contraceptive treatment to girls under 16 constituted criminal conduct, or was so closely analogous thereto as to be
contrary to public policy; and (iii) that a girl under 16 was incapable in law
of giving a valid consent to medical treatment, particularly contraceptive or
abortion treatment. Mrs Gillick failed at first instance but succeeded before
a unanimous Court of Appeal. The DHSS appealed to the House of Lords.
*Held*: allowing the appeal, that: (i) the law did not recognise a rule of
absolute parental authority; (ii) a doctor who gave contraceptive advice and
treatment did not commit a criminal offence; and (iii) the doctor therefore
had a discretion to give contraceptive advice or treatment to a girl under
16 without parental knowledge or consent provided that the girl had
reached an age where she had sufficient understanding and intelligence to
enable her to understand fully what was proposed.

LORD FRASER: . . . It seems to me verging on the absurd to suggest that a girl or
a boy aged 15 could not effectively consent, for example, to have a medical
examination of some trivial injury to his body or even to have a broken arm set. Of
course the consent of the parents should normally be asked, but they may not be
immediately available. Provided the patient, whether a boy or a girl, is capable of
understanding what is proposed, and of expressing his or her own wishes, I see no
good reason for holding that he or she lacks the capacity to express them validly and
effectively and to authorise the medical man to make the examination or give the
treatment which he advises. After all, a minor under the age of 16 can, within certain
limits, enter into a contract. He or she can also sue and be sued, and can give evidence
on oath. Moreover, a girl under 16 can give sufficiently effective consent to sexual
intercourse to lead to the legal result that the man involved does not commit the crime
of rape — see *Reg* v *Howard* [1966] 1 WLR 13, 15. . . . Accordingly, I am not disposed
to hold now, for the first time, that a girl aged less than 16 lacks the power to give
valid consent to contraceptive advice or treatment, merely on account of her age.
. . .
   It was, I think, accepted both by Mrs Gillick and by the DHSS, and in any event I
hold, that parental rights to control a child do not exist for the benefit of the parent.
They exist for the benefit of the child and they are justified only in so far as they enable
the parent to perform his duties towards the child, and towards other children in the
family. If necessary, this proposition can be supported by reference to *Blackstone
Commentaries*, 17th ed. (1830), vol. 1, p. 452, where he wrote 'The power of parents
over their children is derived from . . . their duty.' . . .
   In times gone by the father had almost absolute authority over his children until
they attained majority. A rather remarkable example of such authority being upheld
by the court was *In re Agar-Ellis* (1883) 24 ChD 317 which was much relied on by
the Court of Appeal. The father in that case restricted the communication which his

daughter aged 17 was allowed to have with her mother, against whose moral character nothing was alleged, to an extent that would be universally condemned today as quite unreasonable. The case has been much criticised in recent years and, in my opinion, with good reason. . . .

Once the rule of the parents' absolute authority over minor children is abandoned, the solution to the problem in this appeal can no longer be found by referring to rigid parental rights at any particular age. The solution depends upon a judgment of what is best for the welfare of the particular child. Nobody doubts, certainly I do not doubt, that in the overwhelming majority of cases the best judges of a child's welfare are his or her parents. Nor do I doubt that any important medical treatment of a child under 16 would normally only be carried out with the parents' approval. That is why it would and should be 'most unusual' for a doctor to advise a child without the knowledge and consent of the parents on contraceptive matters. But, as I have already pointed out, Mrs Gillick has to go further if she is to obtain the first declaration that she seeks. She has to justify the absolute right of veto in a parent. But there may be circumstances in which a doctor is a better judge of the medical advice and treatment which will conduce to a girl's welfare than her parents. . . .

The only practicable course is to entrust the doctor with a discretion to act in accordance with his view of what is best in the interests of the girl who is his patient. He should, of course, always seek to persuade her to tell her parents that she is seeking contraceptive advice, and the nature of the advice that she receives. At least he should seek to persuade her to agree to the doctor's informing the parents. But there may well be cases, and I think there will be some cases, where the girl refuses either to tell the parents herself or to permit the doctor to do so and in such cases, the doctor will, in my opinion, be justified in proceeding without the parents' consent or even knowledge provided he is satisfied on the following matters: (1) that the girl (although under 16 years of age) will understand his advice; (2) that he cannot persuade her to inform her parents or to allow him to inform the parents that she is seeking contraceptive advice; (3) that she is very likely to begin or to continue having sexual intercourse with or without contraceptive treatment; (4) that unless she receives contraceptive advice or treatment her physical or mental health or both are likely to suffer; (5) that her best interests require him to give her contraceptive advice, treatment or both without the parental consent.

That result ought not to be regarded as a licence for doctors to disregard the wishes of parents on this matter whenever they find it convenient to do so. Any doctor who behaves in such a way would be failing to discharge his professional responsibilities, and I would expect him to be disciplined by his own professional body accordingly. The medical profession have in modern times come to be entrusted with very wide discretionary powers going beyond the strict limits of clinical judgment and there is nothing strange about entrusting them with this further responsibility which they alone are in a position to discharge satisfactorily.
. . .

LORD SCARMAN: . . .

*Parental right and the age of consent*
Mrs Gillick relies on both the statute law and the case law to establish her proposition that parental consent is in all other circumstances necessary. The only statutory provision directly in point is section 8 of the Family Law Reform Act 1969. Subsection (1) of the section provides that the consent of a minor who has attained the age of 16 to any surgical, mental, or dental treatment which in the absence of consent would constitute a trespass to his person shall be as effective as if he were of

full age and that the consent of his parent or guardian need not be obtained. Subsection (3) of the section provides:

Nothing in this section shall be construed as making ineffective any consent which would have been effective if this section had not been enacted.

I cannot accept the submission made on Mrs Gillick's behalf that subsection (1) necessarily implies that prior to its enactment the consent of a minor to medical treatment could not be effective in law. Subsection (3) leaves open the question whether the consent of a minor under 16 could be an effective consent. Like my noble and learned friend, Lord Fraser of Tullybelton, I read the section as clarifying the law without conveying any indication as to what the law was before it was enacted. So far as minors under 16 are concerned, the law today is as it was before the enactment of the section.

Nor do I find in the provisions of the statute law to which Parker LJ refers in his judgment in the Court of Appeal . . . any encouragement, let alone any compelling reasons, for holding that Parliament has accepted that a child under 16 cannot consent to medical treatment. I respectfully agree with the reasoning and conclusion of my noble and learned friend, Lord Fraser of Tullybelton, on this point.

The law has, therefore, to be found by a search in the judge-made law for the true principle. The legal difficulty is that in our search we find ourselves in a field of medical practice where parental right and a doctor's duty may point us in different directions. This is not surprising. Three features have emerged in today's society which were not known to our predecessors: (1) contraception as a subject for medical advice and treatment; (2) the increasing independence of young people; and (3) the changed status of woman. . . .

. . .

The law ignores these developments at its peril. . . .

In this appeal, therefore, there is much in the earlier case law which the House must discard — almost everything I would say but its principle. For example, the horrendous *Agar-Ellis* decisions, 10 ChD 49; 24 ChD 317 of the late 19th century asserting the power of the father over his child were rightly remaindered to the history books by the Court of Appeal in *Hewer* v *Bryant* [1970] 1 QB 357 an important case to which I shall return later. . . .

Approaching the earlier law . . . , one finds plenty of indications as to the principles governing the law's approach to parental right and the child's right to make his or her own decision. Parental rights clearly do exist, and they do not wholly disappear until the age of majority. Parental rights relate to both the person and the property of the child — custody, care, and control of the person and guardianship of the property of the child. But the common law has never treated such rights as sovereign or beyond review and control. Nor has our law ever treated the child as other than a person with capacities and rights recognised by law. The principle of the law, as I shall endeavour to show, is that parental rights are derived from parental duty and exist only so long as they are needed for the protection of the person and property of the child. The principle has been subjected to certain age limits set by statute for certain purposes: and in some cases the courts have declared an age of discretion at which a child acquires before the age of majority the right to make his (or her) own decision. But these limitations in no way undermine the principle of the law, and should not be allowed to obscure it.

. . .

Let me make good, quite shortly, the proposition of principle.

First, the guardianship legislation. Section 5 of the Guardianship of Infants Act 1886 began the process which is now complete of establishing the equal rights of mother and father. In doing so the legislation, which is currently embodied in section 1 of the Guardianship of Minors Act 1971 [repealed by the Children Act 1989], took over from the Chancery courts a rule which they had long followed (it was certainly applied by Lord Eldon, during his quarter of a century as Lord Chancellor, as Parker LJ, quoting Heilbron J in *In re D (A Minor) (Wardship: Sterilisation)* [1976] Fam 185, 2 193–194, reminds us) that when a court has before it a question as to the care and upbringing of a child it must treat the welfare of the child as the paramount consideration in determining the order to be made [see now CA 1989, s. 1]. There is here a principle which limits and governs the exercise of parental rights of custody, care, and control. It is a principle perfectly consistent with the law's recognition of the parent as the natural guardian of the child; but it is also a warning that parental right must be exercised in accordance with the welfare principle and can be challenged, even overridden, if it be not.

Secondly, there is the common law's understanding of the nature of parental right. We are not concerned in this appeal to catalogue all that is contained in what Sachs LJ has felicitously described as the 'bundle of rights' (*Hewer v Bryant* [1970] 1 QB 357, 373) which together constitute the rights of custody, care, and control. It is abundantly plain that the law recognises that there is a right and a duty of parents to determine whether or not to seek medical advice in respect of their child, and, having received advice, to give or withhold consent to medical treatment. The question in the appeal is as to the extent, and duration, of the right and the circumstances in which outside the two admitted exceptions to which I have earlier referred it can be overridden by the exercise of medical judgment.

. . . A most illuminating discussion of parental right is to be found in *Blackstone's Commentaries,* 17th ed. (1830), vol. 1, chs. 16 and 17. He analyses the duty of the parent as the 'maintenance . . . protection, and . . . education' of the child: p. 446. He declares that the power of parents over their children is derived from their duty and exists 'to enable the parent more effectually to perform his duty, and partly as a recompense for his care and trouble in the faithful discharge of it:' op. cit., p. 452. . . .

The two chapters provide a valuable insight into the principle and flexibility of the common law. The principle is that parental right or power of control of the person and property of his child exists primarily to enable the parent to discharge his duty of maintenance, protection, and education until he reaches such an age as to be able to look after himself and make his own decisions. . . .

Although statute has intervened in respect of a child's capacity to consent to medical treatment from the age of 16 onwards, neither statute nor the case law has ruled on the extent and duration of parental right in respect of children under the age of 16. More specifically, there is no rule yet applied to contraceptive treatment, which has special problems of its own and is a late-comer in medical practice. It is open, therefore, to the House to formulate a rule. The Court of Appeal favoured a fixed age limit of 16, basing themselves on a view of the statute law which I do not share and upon their view of the effect of the older case law which for the reasons already given I cannot accept. They sought to justify the limit by the public interest in the law being certain. Certainty is always an advantage in the law, and in some branches of the law it is a necessity. But it brings with it an inflexibility and a rigidity which in some branches of the law can obstruct justice, impede the law's development, and stamp upon the law the mark of obsolescence where what is needed is the capacity for development. The law relating to parent and child is concerned with the problems of the growth and maturity of the human personality. If the law should impose upon the process of 'growing up' fixed limits where nature knows only a continuous process, the price would be artificiality and a lack of realism in an area where the law must be sensitive to human development and social change. If certainty be thought desirable, it is better that the rigid demarcations necessary to achieve it should be laid down by legislation after a full consideration of all the relevant factors than by the courts confined as they are by the forensic process to the evidence adduced by the parties and to whatever may properly fall within the judicial notice of judges. Unless and until Parliament should think fit to intervene, the courts should establish a principle flexible enough to enable justice to be achieved by its application to the particular circumstances proved by the evidence placed before them.

The underlying principle of the law was exposed by Blackstone and can be seen to have been acknowledged in the case law. It is that parental right yields to the child's right to make his own decisions when he reaches a sufficient understanding and intelligence to be capable of making up his own mind on the matter requiring decision. Lord Denning MR captured the spirit and principle of the law when he said in *Hewer v Bryant* [1970] 1 QB 357, 369:

> I would get rid of the rule in *In re Agar-Ellis*, 24 ChD 317 and of the suggested exceptions to it. That case was decided in the year 1883. It reflects the attitude of a Victorian parent towards his children. He expected unquestioning obedience to his commands. If a son disobeyed, his father would cut him off with a shilling. If a daughter had an illegitimate child, he would turn her out of the house. His power only ceased when the child became 21. I decline to accept a view so much out of date. The common law can, and should, keep pace with the times. It should declare, in conformity with the recent Report of the Committee on the Age of Majority [Cmnd. 3342, 1967], that the legal right of a parent to the custody of a child ends at the 18th birthday: and even up till then, it is a dwindling right which the courts will hesitate to enforce against the wishes of the child, and the more so the older he is. It starts with a right of control and ends with little more than advice.

. . .

For the reasons which I have endeavoured to develop much of the case law of the 19th and earlier centuries is no guide to the application of the law in the conditions of today. The *Agar-Ellis* cases, 10 ChD 49; 24 ChD 317 (the power of the father) cannot live with the modern statute law. . . .

The modern law governing parental right and a child's capacity to make his own decisions was considered in *Reg* v *D* [1984] AC 778. The House must, in my view, be understood as having in that case accepted that, save where statute otherwise provides, a minor's capacity to make his or her own decision depends upon the minor having sufficient understanding and intelligence to make the decision and is not to be determined by reference to any judicially fixed age limit. . . .

In the light of the foregoing I would hold that as a matter of law the parental right to determine whether or not their minor child below the age of 16 will have medical treatment terminates if and when the child achieves a sufficient understanding and intelligence to enable him or her to understand fully what is proposed. It will be a question of fact whether a child seeking advice has sufficient understanding of what is involved to give a consent valid in law. Until the child achieves the capacity to consent, the parental right to make the decision continues save only in exceptional circumstances. Emergency, parental neglect, abandonment of the child, or inability to find the parent are examples of exceptional situations justifying the doctor proceeding to treat the child without parental knowledge and consent: but there will arise, no doubt, other exceptional situations in which it will be reasonable for the doctor to proceed without the parent's consent.

When applying these conclusions to contraceptive advice and treatment it has to be borne in mind that there is much that has to be understood by a girl under the age of 16 if she is to have legal capacity to consent to such treatment. It is not enough that she should understand the nature of the advice which is being given: she must also have a sufficient maturity to understand what is involved. There are moral and family questions, especially her relationship with her parents; long-term problems associated with the emotional impact of pregnancy and its termination; and there are the risks to health of sexual intercourse at her age, risks which contraception may diminish but cannot eliminate. It follows that a doctor will have to satisfy himself that she is able to appraise these factors before he can safely proceed upon the basis that she has at law capacity to consent to contraceptive treatment. And it further follows that ordinarily the proper course will be for him, as the guidance lays down, first to seek to persuade the girl to bring her parents into consultation, and if she refuses, not to prescribe contraceptive treatment unless he is satisfied that her circumstances are such that he ought to proceed without parental knowledge and consent.
. . .

I am, therefore, satisfied that the department's guidance can be followed without involving the doctor in any infringement of parental right. Unless, therefore, to prescribe contraceptive treatment for a girl under the age of 16 is either a criminal offence or so close to one that to prescribe such treatment is contrary to public policy, the department's appeal must succeed.

### Eekelaar, John, 'The Eclipse of Parental Rights'
(1986) 102 LQR 4 at pp. 8 and 9

. . . even if the result [in *Gillick*] enhances the legal status of children against the adult world, it must be tempered with realism. Both Lord Scarman and Lord Fraser stressed that full capacity was no simple matter. There will undoubtedly be a temptation to believe that unless a child takes the same view of its interests as an adult (or a court) holds, it falls short of maturity . . .

### Eekelaar, John, 'The Emergence of Children's Rights'
(1986) 6 *Oxford J Legal Stud* 161 at p. 178

. . . Both Lord Scarman and Lord Fraser adopted the major premise that once a child had attained sufficient understanding and maturity, he had full capacity to enter legal relationships without the consent of his parents. The consistency of this position with authority and principle has already been demonstrated. Lord Scarman then concluded that as soon as a child reached this position, any parental right within the relevant area, terminated. The parental right 'yielded' to the child's right. Lord Fraser, however, was less clear about this. In the medical context, he seemed to say that a doctor would only be 'justified' in treating a child without parental consent if this was in the child's best interests, and, as far as contraceptive treatment was concerned, this would normally entail involvement of the parents, although this could be avoided if the child refused to permit it, and the protection of (her) physical and mental health required such treatment despite lack of parental knowledge and consent. This might mean that, in certain situations, the parental right survives the minor child's acquisition of capacity and, with judicial support, could prevent such a child from acting according to her wishes if her interests demanded such restriction. But an alternative interpretation of the speech is possible. This would permit anyone to deal lawfully with a minor child who had acquired capacity, and restrict the requirement to consult parents (outside exceptional situations) to a rule of good practice applicable only in medical matters and enforceable only through professional discipline. No help is obtained from Lord Bridge, who simply agreed with both Lord Scarman and Lord Fraser. Lord Templeman, who dissented on the issue as far as it related to *contraceptive* treatment, seemed to express a view close to that of Lord Scarman as far as other medical matters were concerned.

The significance of Lord Scarman's opinion with respect to children's autonomy interests cannot be over-rated. It follows from his reasoning that, where a child has reached capacity, there is no room for a parent to impose a contrary view, *even if this is more in accord with the child's best interests.* For its legal superiority to the child's decision can rest only on its status as a parental right. But this is extinguished when the child reaches full capacity. More importantly, the argument catches the court itself. Should the child be warded, custody of the child vests in the court. The inherent jurisdiction of the High Court to intervene in the lives of children rests on the doctrine of the Crown's role as *parens patriae.* But on what principle can the Crown retain the parental jurisdiction when the parent himself has lost it, not through deprivation, but due to the superior right of the child? The primary question in wardship cases involving older children can no longer be: what is in the best interest of the child? It must be, has the child capacity to make his own decisions?

This recognition of the autonomy interests of children can be reconciled with their basic and developmental interests only through the empirical application of the concept of the acquisition of full capacity. This, as Lord Scarman made clear, may be no simple matter. The child must not only understand the nature of the transaction, but be able to evaluate its implications. Intellectual understanding must be supplemented by emotional maturity. It is easy to see how adults can conclude that a child's decision which seems, to the adult, to be contrary to his interests, is lacking in sufficient maturity. In this respect, the provision of the simple test of age to provide an upper limit to the scope of a supervisory, paternalistic power has advantages. We cannot know for certain whether, retrospectively, a person may not regret that some control was not exercised over his immature judgment by persons with greater experience. But could we not say that it is on balance better to subject all persons to this potential inhibition up to a defined age, in case the failure to exercise the restraint unduly prejudices a person's basic or developmental interests? It avoids judgments in which questions of fact and value will be impenetrably mixed. But the decision, it seems, has been taken. Children will now have, in wider measure than ever before, that most dangerous but most precious of rights: the right to make their own mistakes.

### Burrows, David, 'A Child's Understanding'
[1994] Fam Law 579

It remains the case that the issue of assessment of a child's understanding is among the most difficult that the 1989 Act has thrown up. . . .

### *In re S (A Minor) (Independent Representation)*
[1994] Fam 263
Court of Appeal

SIR THOMAS BINGHAM MR: . . . Different children have differing levels of understanding at the same age. And understanding is not an absolute. It has to be assessed relatively to the issues in the proceedings. Where any sound judgment on these issues calls for insight and imagination which only maturity and experience can bring, both the court and the solicitor will be slow to conclude that the child's understanding is sufficient. . . .

*Questions*
1.  What was the *ratio decidendi* of *Gillick*?
2.  Is it satisfactory that, despite the impact of *Gillick*, there are no references to children's rights in the Children Act 1989?
3.  There has recently been a discussion about installing in schools machines selling contraceptives. Is this a good idea or does it further undermine any rights that parents might have?

*Further reading*
Bainham, A., 'The Balance of Power in Family Decisions' [1986] CLJ 262.
Cretney, S., 'Gillick and the Concept of Legal Capacity' (1989) 105 LQR 356.
De Cruz, S., 'Parents, Doctors and Children: the *Gillick* Case and Beyond' [1987] JSWL 93.
Parkinson, P., 'The *Gillick* Case — Just what has it Decided?' [1986] Fam Law 11.

### 7.3.2  'Gillick competency' and medical decisions

*Prince* v *Massachusetts*
(1944) 321 US Reports 158
The Supreme Court of the United States

JUSTICE HOLMES: . . . Parents may be free to become martyrs themselves, but it does not follow that they are free in identical circumstances to make martyrs of their children before they have reached the age of full and legal discretion when they can make choices for themselves.

*Note*
Justice Holmes' *dicta* were by Ward J in *Re E (A Minor) (Wardship: Medical Treatment)* [1993] 1 FLR 386, at p. 394.

In a series of cases where children have *refused* to consent to medical treatment (*Gillick* was about consent, not refusal), the court has had to decide whether the wishes of a '*Gillick* competent' child (i.e. a child with sufficient intelligence and maturity to make an informed decision) should be overridden. In addition to judge-made principles, the following statutory provision is relevant.

### FAMILY LAW REFORM ACT 1969

**8.   Consent by persons over 16 to surgical, medical and dental treatment**
    (1)  The consent of a minor who has attained the age of sixteen years to any surgical, medical or dental treatment which, in the absence of consent, would

constitute a trespass to his person, shall be as effective as it would be if he were of full age; and where a minor has by virtue of this section given an effective consent to any treatment it shall not be necessary to obtain any consent for it from his parent or guardian.

(2)   In this section 'surgical, medical or dental treatment' includes any procedure undertaken for the purposes of diagnosis, and this section applies to any procedure (including, in particular, the administration of an anaesthetic) which is ancillary to any treatment as it applies to that treatment.

(3)   Nothing in this section shall be construed as making ineffective any consent which would have been effective if this section had not been enacted.

*Note*
Subsection 8(3) leaves it open for courts to override the consent of a child aged over 16.

### In Re R (A Minor) (Wardship: Medical Treatment)
[1992] Fam 11
Court of Appeal

*Facts*: A mentally ill 15-year-old girl in care of the local authority was transferred to an adolescent psychiatric unit, where the issue of consent to treatment arose. The unit was not prepared to retain her as a patient unless it was given authority to use appropriate medication to control her. The local authority applied in wardship proceedings, with the girl and her parents as defendants, for leave for the unit to administer the necessary medication without the girl's consent. Waite J in the Family Division held that if a child was *Gillick* competent, the court had no power to substitute its own view for that of the child, but as the girl did not have the necessary capacity, granted the application. The Official Solicitor appealed.
*Held*: dismissing the application, that (i) as *Gillick* competency required there to be full understanding on a lasting basis in order to refuse medical treatment, Waite J had been right to find that the girl lacked the necessary capacity to refuse treatment and to hold that the court could authorise medication; and (ii) irrespective of whether a child was *Gillick* competent, the wardship court, whose powers were wider than parental powers, had jurisdiction to override a ward's decision to refuse medical treatment in any case in the interests of the child's welfare.

LORD DONALDSON MR: . . . The guidance afforded by the speeches in *Gillick's* case needs, as always, to be considered in context. The Gillick children were not wards of court and the wardship jurisdiction of the court was not in issue. None of Mrs Gillick's daughters aged 13, 12, 10 and 5 contemplated engaging in sexual intercourse in the immediate future or had sought or were likely independently to seek contraceptive advice or treatment. . . . Mrs Gillick's concern was not the immediate protection of her daughters or of any specific children, but to challenge the legality of a 'Memorandum of Guidance' issued by the Department of Health and Social Security . . .

. . . [Mrs Gillick] was asserting an absolute right of veto on the part of parents generally, and herself in particular, on medical advice and treatment of the nature specified in relation to their children under the age of 16: see [1986] AC 112, 173F. She was not challenging the right of a wardship court to exercise its parens patriae jurisdiction. Indeed she accepted it in her printed case. . . . Nor was she concerned with how that jurisdiction should be exercised.

It is trite law that in general a doctor is not entitled to treat a patient without the consent of someone who is authorised to give that consent. If he does so, he will be liable in damages for trespass to the person and may be guilty of a criminal assault. This is subject to the necessary exception that in cases of emergency a doctor may treat the patient notwithstanding the absence of consent, if the patient is unconscious or otherwise incapable of giving or refusing consent and there is no one else sufficiently immediately available with authority to consent on behalf of the patient. However consent by itself creates no obligation to treat. It is merely a key which unlocks a door. Furthermore, whilst in the case of an adult of full capacity there will usually only be one keyholder, namely the patient, in the ordinary family unit where a young child is the patient there will be two keyholders, namely the parents, with a several as well as a joint right to turn the key and unlock the door. If the parents disagree, one consenting and the other refusing, the doctor will be presented with a professional and ethical, but not with a legal, problem because, if he has the consent of one authorised person, treatment will not without more constitute a trespass or a criminal assault.
. . .

In the instant appeal [counsel], appearing for the Official Solicitor, submits that (a) if the child has the right to give consent to medical treatment, the parents' right to give or refuse consent is terminated and (b) the court in the exercise of its wardship jurisdiction is only entitled to step into the shoes of the parents and thus itself has no right to give or refuse consent. Whilst it is true that he seeks to modify the effect of this rather startling submission by suggesting that, if the child's consent or refusal of consent is irrational or misguided, the court will readily infer that in the particular context that individual child is not competent to give or withhold consent, it is necessary to look very carefully at the *Gillick* decision to see whether it supports his argument and, if it does, whether it is binding upon this court.

The key passages upon which [counsel] relies are to be found in the speech of Lord Scarman, at pp. 188–189:

as a matter of law the parental right to determine whether or not their minor child below the age of 16 will have medical treatment terminates if and when the child achieves a sufficient understanding and intelligence to enable him or her to understand fully what is proposed. It will be a question of fact whether a child seeking advice has sufficient understanding of what is involved to give a consent valid in law. Until the child achieves the capacity to consent, the parental right to make the decision continues save only in exceptional circumstances. Emergency, parental neglect, abandonment of the child, or inability to find the parent are examples of exceptional situations justifying the doctor proceeding to treat the child without parental knowledge and consent: but there will arise, no doubt, other exceptional situations in which it will be reasonable for the doctor to proceed without the parent's consent.

And, at p. 186:

The underlying principle of the law was exposed by Blackstone and can be seen to have been acknowledged in the case law. It is that parental right yields to the child's right to make his own decisions when he reaches a sufficient understanding and intelligence to be capable of making up his own mind on the matter requiring decision.

What [counsel's] argument overlooks is that Lord Scarman was discussing the parents' right '*to determine* whether or not their minor child below the age of 16 will have medical treatment' (my emphasis) and this is the 'parental right' to which he was referring at p. 186D. A right of determination is wider than a right to consent. The parents can only have a right of determination if *either* the child has no right to consent, that is, is not a keyholder, *or* the parents hold a master key which could nullify the child's consent. I do not understand Lord Scarman to be saying that, if a child was '*Gillick* competent,' to adopt the convenient phrase used in argument, the parents ceased to have an independent right of consent as contrasted with ceasing to have a right of determination, that is, a veto. In a case in which the '*Gillick* competent' child refuses treatment, but the parents consent, that consent *enables* treatment to be undertaken lawfully, but in no way determines that the child shall be so treated. In a case in which the positions are reversed, it is the child's consent which is the enabling factor and again the parents' refusal of consent is not determinative. If Lord Scarman intended to go further than this and to say that in the case of a '*Gillick* competent' child, a parent has no right either to consent or to refuse consent, his remarks were obiter, because the only question in issue was Mrs Gillick's alleged right of veto. Furthermore I consider that they would have been wrong.

One glance at the consequences suffices to show that Lord Scarman cannot have been intending to say that the parental right to consent terminates with the achievement by the child of '*Gillick* competence.' It is fundamental to the speeches of the majority that the capacity to consent will vary from child to child and according to the treatment under consideration, depending upon the sufficiency of his or her intelligence and understanding of that treatment. If the position in law is that upon the achievement of '*Gillick* competence' there is a transfer of the right of consent from parents to child and there can never be a concurrent right in both, doctors would be faced with an intolerable dilemma, particularly when the child was nearing the age of 16, if the parents consented, but the child did not. On pain, if they got it wrong, of being sued for trespass to the person or possibly being charged with a criminal assault, they would have to determine as a matter of law in whom the right of consent resided at the particular time in relation to the particular treatment. I do not believe that that is the law.

I referred to a child who is nearing the age of 16, because at that age a new dimension is added by section 8 of the Family Law Reform Act 1969 to which Lord Fraser of Tullybelton referred. . . .

[After citing s. 8 of the Family Law Reform Act 1969, his Lordship continued: . . .]

[Counsel for the Official Solicitor] submits, rightly as I think, that consent by a child between the ages of 16 and 18 is no more effective than that of an adult if, due to mental disability, the child is incapable of consenting. That is, however, immaterial for present purposes. What is material is that the section is inconsistent with [counsel's] argument. If [counsel's] interpretation of Lord Scarman's speech were correct, where a child over the age of 16 gave effective consent to treatment, not only would it 'not be necessary' to obtain the consent of the parent or guardian, it would be legally impossible because the parent or guardian would have no power to give consent and the section would, or at least should, have so provided. Furthermore subsection (3) would create problems since, if the section had not been enacted, a parent's consent would undoubtedly have been effective *as a consent.*

Both in this case and in *In re E* the judges treated *Gillick v West Norfolk and Wisbech Area Health Authority* [1986] AC 112 as deciding that a '*Gillick* competent' child has a right to refuse treatment. In this I consider that they were in error. Such a child can consent, but if he or she declines to do so or refuses, consent can be given by someone else who has parental rights or responsibilities. The failure or refusal of the 'Gillick competent' child is a very important factor in the doctor's decision whether or not to treat, but does not prevent the necessary consent being obtained from another competent source.

. . .

### 'Gillick competence'

The test of 'Gillick competence,' although not decisive in this case, is nevertheless of general importance and the evidence of Dr R suggests that it is capable of being misunderstood. The House of Lords in that case was quite clearly considering the staged development of a normal child. For example, at one age it will be quite incapable of deciding whether or not to consent to a dental examination, let alone treatment. At a later stage it will be quite capable of both, but incapable of deciding whether to consent to more serious treatment. But there is no suggestion that the extent of this competence can fluctuate upon a day to day or week to week basis. What is really being looked at is an assessment of mental and emotional age, as contrasted with chronological age, but even this test needs to be modified in the case of fluctuating mental disability to take account of that misfortune. It should be added that in any event what is involved is not merely an ability to understand the nature of the proposed treatment — in this case compulsory medication — but a full understanding and appreciation of the consequences both of the treatment in terms of intended and possible side effects and, equally important, the anticipated consequences of a failure to treat.

On the evidence in the present case it is far from certain that Dr R was saying that R understood the implications of treatment being withheld, as distinct from understanding what was proposed to be done by way of treatment — 'the nature of the proposal' which I take to have been intended as a paraphrase of Lord Scarman's 'to understand fully what is proposed.' But, even if she was capable on a good day of a sufficient degree of understanding to meet the Gillick criteria, her mental disability, to the cure or amelioration of which the proposed treatment was directed, was such that on other days she was not only 'Gillick incompetent,' but actually sectionable. No child in that situation can be regarded as 'Gillick competent' and the judge was wholly right in so finding in relation to R.

### Conclusion

1.  No doctor can be required to treat a child, whether by the court in the exercise of its wardship jurisdiction, by the parents, by the child or anyone else. The decision whether to treat is dependent upon an exercise of his own professional judgment, subject only to the threshold requirement that, save in exceptional cases usually of emergency, he has the consent of someone who has authority to give that consent. In forming that judgment the views and wishes of the child are a factor whose importance increases with the increase in the child's intelligence and understanding.

2.  There can be concurrent powers to consent. If more than one body or person has a power to consent, only a failure to, or refusal of, consent by all having that power will create a veto.

3.  A 'Gillick competent' child or one over the age of 16 will have a power to consent, but this will be concurrent with that of a parent or guardian.

4.  'Gillick competence' is a developmental concept and will not be lost or acquired on a day to day or week to week basis. In the case of mental disability, that disability must also be taken into account, particularly where it is fluctuating in its effect.

5.   The court in the exercise of its wardship or statutory jurisdiction has power to override the decisions of a 'Gillick competent' child as much as those of parents or guardians.

6.   Waite J was right to hold that R was not 'Gillick competent' and, even if R had been, was right to consent to her undergoing treatment which might involve compulsory medication.

### Bainham, Andrew, 'The Judge and the Competent Minor'
### (1992) 108 LQR 194

. . . The decision on the facts, that R had not achieved *Gillick* competence, is unexceptional. Any other conclusion could have made it impossible for the unit to retain realistic managerial control of her case. So also is the view that a young person suffering from a significant mental illness, albeit mitigated by lucid intervals, was not really within the contemplation of House of Lords in *Gillick*. But the decision also confirms the suspicion that the acquisition of capacity by children is capable of manipulation by adults. The test propounded by the Court of Appeal is sufficiently exacting that many adults might fail it. We ought perhaps to question whether the law should demand a greater level of appreciation and understanding of the implications of decisions from children than it appears to require of adults who are *assumed* to have, but not required to demonstrate, emotional or intellectual maturity. Yet, in this respect at least, *Re R* is easily squared with Lord Scarman's opinion in *Gillick*. On the contraception question Lord Scarman had emphasised that a *Gillick* competent child would need to understand the 'moral and family' questions involved as well as the medical issues surrounding the treatment itself. Where any adult decision-maker disagrees strongly with a child the temptation to deem him or her incompetent must be almost irresistible. While this is a temptation from which the judiciary are not immune, it can at least be hoped that the involvement of the courts will inject a measure of detachment and objectivity into these assessments.

### *In Re W (A Minor) (Consent to Medical Treatment)*
### [1993] Fam 64
### Court of Appeal

*Facts*: A 16-year-old girl in local authority care suffered from anorexia nervosa. Her condition deteriorated so that she had to be admitted to a clinic to be fed by a nasogastric tube and to have her arms encased in plaster to prevent her picking her skin. The local authority, thinking it might be necessary to give her medical treatment against her will, applied under s. 100(3) of the Children Act 1989 seeking leave of the court in the exercise of its inherent jurisdiction to allow the child to be moved to a new treatment unit and for her to receive medical treatment without her consent. Thorpe J in the High Court granted leave and authorised the proposed treatment. The child appealed. By this time she weighed only 5 stone 7lb (35kg) and had refused solid food for 10 days.
*Held*: dismissing her appeal, that neither common law (*Gillick*) nor statute (i.e. the Family Law Reform Act 1969, s. 8) had conferred on a 16- to 18-year-old child complete autonomy in the area of medical treatment, so

that there was no overriding limitation to prevent the court exercising its inherent jurisdiction to act in a child's best interests.

LORD DONALDSON MR: . . .

*Is section 8 ambiguous?*
The wording of subsection (1) shows quite clearly that it is addressed to the legal purpose and legal effect of consent to treatment, namely, to prevent such treatment constituting in law a trespass to the person, and that it does so by making the consent of a 16- or 17-year-old as effective as if he were 'of full age.' No question of '*Gillick* competence' in common law terms arises. The 16- or 17-year-old is conclusively presumed to be '*Gillick* competent' or, alternatively, the test of '*Gillick* competence' is bypassed and has no relevance. The argument that W, or any other 16- or 17-year-old, can by refusing to consent to treatment veto the treatment notwithstanding that the doctor has the consent of someone who has parental responsibilities, involves the proposition that section 8 has the further effect of depriving such a person of the power to consent. It certainly does not say so. Indeed if this were its intended effect, it is difficult to see why the subsection goes on to say that it is not *necessary* to obtain the parents' consent, rather than providing that such consent, if obtained, should be ineffective. Furthermore such a construction does not sit easily with subsection (3) which preserves the common law as it existed immediately before the Act which undoubtedly gave parents an effective power of consent for all children up to the age of 21, the then existing age of consent: see *Gillick's* case [1986] AC 112, 167c, *per* Lord Fraser of Tullybelton, and at p. 182E, *per* Lord Scarman.

The most promising argument in favour of W having an exclusive right to consent to treatment and thus, by refusing consent, to attract the protection of the law on trespass to the person, lies in concentrating upon the words 'as effective as it would be if he were of full age.' If she were of full age her ability to consent would have two separate effects. First, her consent would be fully effective as such. Second, a failure or refusal to give consent would be fully effective as a veto, but only *because no one else would be in a position to consent*. If it is a possible view that section 8 is intended to put a 16- or 17-year-old in exactly the same position as an adult and there is thus some ambiguity, although I do not think that there is, it is a permissible aid to construction to seek to ascertain the mischief at which the section is directed.
. . .

I have no doubt that the wishes of a 16- or 17-year-old child or indeed of a younger child who is '*Gillick* competent' are of the greatest importance both legally and clinically, but I do doubt whether Thorpe J was right to conclude that W was of sufficient understanding to make an informed decision. I do not say this on the basis that I consider her approach irrational. I personally consider that religious or other beliefs which bar any medical treatment or treatment of particular kinds are irrational, but that does not make minors who hold those beliefs any the less '*Gillick* competent.' They may well have sufficient intelligence and understanding fully to appreciate the treatment proposed and the consequences of their refusal to accept that treatment. What distinguishes W from them, and what with all respect I do not think that Thorpe J took sufficiently into account (perhaps because the point did not emerge as clearly before him as it did before us), is that it is a feature of anorexia nervosa that it is capable of destroying the ability to make an informed choice. It creates a compulsion to refuse treatment or only to accept treatment which is likely to be ineffective. This attitude is part and parcel of the disease and the more advanced the illness, the more compelling it may become. Where the wishes of the minor are themselves something which the doctors reasonably consider need to be treated in the minor's own best interests, those wishes clearly have a much reduced significance.

There is ample authority for the proposition that the inherent powers of the court under its parens patriae jurisdiction are theoretically limitless and that they certainly extend beyond the powers of a natural parent: see for example *In re R (A Minor) (Wardship: Consent to Treatment)* [1992] Fam 11, 25B, 28G. There can therefore be no doubt that it has power to override the refusal of a minor, whether over the age of 16 or under that age but '*Gillick* competent.' It does not do so by ordering the doctors to treat which, even if within the court's powers, would be an abuse of them or by ordering the minor to accept treatment, but by authorising the doctors to treat the minor in accordance with their clinical judgment, subject to any restrictions which the court may impose.

The remaining issue is how this power should be exercised in the context of a case in which a minor is refusing treatment or, whilst consenting to one form of treatment, is refusing to consent to another. [Counsel], appearing as amicus curiae, in his most helpful skeleton argument approached the matter as if 16- and 17-year-olds were in a special category. In a sense, of course, they are because section 8 applies to them. But [counsel] so treated them because, in his submission, section 8 conferred complete autonomy on such minors, thus enabling them effectively to refuse medical treatment irrespective of how parental responsibilities might be sought to be exercised. That submission I have already rejected. This is not, however, to say that the wishes of 16- and 17-year-olds are to be treated as no different from those of 14- and 15-year-olds. Far from it. Adolescence is a period of progressive transition from childhood to adulthood and as experience of life is acquired and intelligence and understanding grow, so will the scope of the decision-making which should be left to the minor, for it is only by making decisions and experiencing the consequences that decision-making skills will be acquired. As I put it in the course of the argument, and as I sincerely believe, 'good parenting involves giving minors as much rope as they can handle without an unacceptable risk that they will hang themselves.' As Lord Hailsham of St Marylebone LC put it in *In re B (A Minor) (Wardship: Sterilisation)* [1988] AC 199, 202, the 'first and paramount consideration [of the court] is the well being, welfare or interests [of the minor]' and I regard it as self-evident that this involves giving them the maximum degree of decision-making which is prudent. Prudence does not involve avoiding all risk, but it does involve avoiding taking risks which, if they eventuate, may have irreparable consequences or which are disproportionate to the benefits which could accrue from taking them. I regard this approach as wholly consistent with the philosophy of section 1 of the Children Act 1989, and, in particular, subsection (3)(a). It was submitted that whilst this might be correct, such an approach is inconsistent with sections 38(6), 43(8) and 44(7) of that Act and with paragraphs 4 and 5 of Schedule 3. Here I disagree. These provisions all concern interim or supervision orders and do not impinge upon the jurisdiction of the court to make prohibited steps or specific issue orders under section 8 of the Act of 1989 in the context of which the minor has no right of veto, unless it is to be found in section 8 of the Act of 1969.

. . .

*Summary*

1.  No question of a minor consenting to or refusing medical treatment arises unless and until a medical or dental practitioner advises such treatment and is willing to undertake it.

2.  Regardless of whether the minor or anyone else with authority to do so consents to the treatment, that practitioner will be liable to the minor in negligence if he fails

to advise with reasonable skill and care and to have due regard to the best interests of his patient.

3. This appeal has been concerned with the treatment of anorexia nervosa. It is a peculiarity of this disease that the disease itself creates a wish not to be cured or only to be cured if and when the patient decides to cure himself or herself, which may well be too late. Treatment has to be directed at this state of mind as much as to restoring body weight.

4. Section 8 of the Family Law Reform Act 1969 gives minors who have attained the age of 16 a right to consent to surgical, medical or dental treatment Such a consent cannot be overridden by those with parental responsibility for the minor. It can, however, be overridden by the court. This statutory right does not extend to consent to the donation of blood or organs.

5. A minor of any age who is 'Gillick competent' in the context of particular treatment has a right to consent to that treatment which again cannot be overridden by those with parental responsibility, but can be overridden by the court. Unlike the statutory right this common law right extends to the donation of blood or organs.

6. No minor of whatever age has power by refusing consent to treatment to override a consent to treatment by someone who has parental responsibility for the minor and a fortiori a consent by the court. Nevertheless such a refusal is a very important consideration in making clinical judgments and for parents and the court in deciding whether themselves to give consent. Its importance increases with the age and maturity of the minor.

7. The effect of consent to treatment by the minor or someone else with authority to give it is limited to protecting the medical or dental practitioner from claims for damages for trespass to the person.

I would allow the appeal only to such extent as may be necessary to enable the order which, in a changed situation, this court made on 30 June to be substituted for that made by Thorpe J.

BALCOMBE LJ: . . . The issue in *Gillick's* case was stated by Lord Fraser of Tullybelton in the following terms [1986] AC 112, 165:

> The central issue in the appeal is whether a doctor can ever, in any circumstances, lawfully give contraceptive advice or treatment to a girl under the age of 16 without her parents' consent.

To the like effect was Lord Scarman, at p. 181F. To that issue the construction of section 8 was at best peripheral.

The section was mentioned by both Parker and Fox LJJ in the Court of Appeal [1986] AC 112, 123, 144–145, but neither attempted to give any definitive construction. In the House of Lords Lord Fraser of Tullybelton mentioned the section, but also did not attempt to define its meaning. Lord Bridge of Harwich, Lord Brandon of Oakbrook and Lord Templeman did not even mention the section. Lord Scarman did, however, mention the section at several points in the course of his speech, and after a consideration of its provisions and other matters said, at pp. 188–189:

> In the light of the foregoing I would hold that as a matter of law the parental right to determine whether or not their minor child below the age of 16 will have medical treatment terminates if and when the child achieves a sufficient understanding and intelligence to enable him or her to understand fully what is proposed.

I accept that the words 'or not' in this passage suggest that Lord Scarman considered that the right to refuse treatment was co-existent with the right to consent to treatment. I also accept that if a *'Gillick* competent' child under 16 has a right to refuse treatment, so too has a child over the age of 16. Nevertheless I share the doubts of Lord Donaldson of Lymington MR whether Lord Scarman was intending to mean that the parents of a *'Gillick* competent' child had no right at all to consent to medical treatment of the child as opposed to no exclusive right to such consent. If he did so intend then, in the case of a child over the age of 16, his interpretation of the law was inconsistent with the express words of section 8(3) of the Act of 1969. It is also clear that Lord Scarman was only considering the position of the child vis-à-vis its parents: he was not considering the position of the child vis-à-vis the court whose powers, as I have already said, are wider than the parents'.

I am therefore satisfied that there is no interpretation of section 8 of the Act of 1969 — and certainly no 'settled' interpretation — which persuades me that my view of the clear meaning of the section is wrong. I express no view on the question whether a young person, whether over the age of 16 or under that age if *'Gillick* competent,' should have complete autonomy in the field of medical treatment. That is a matter of social policy with which Parliament can deal by appropriate legislation if it wishes to do so. What I am clear about is that Parliament has not conferred such autonomy on a 16- to 18-year-old child by virtue of section 8 of the Act of 1969, and that the common law, as interpreted by the House of Lords in *Gillick's* case does not do so either.

Since Parliament has not conferred complete autonomy on a 16-year-old in the field of medical treatment, there is no overriding limitation to preclude the exercise by the court of its inherent jurisdiction and the matter becomes one for the exercise by the court of its discretion. Nevertheless the discretion is not to be exercised in a moral vacuum. Undoubtedly the philosophy behind section 8 of the Act of 1969, as well as behind the decision of the House of Lords in *Gillick's* case is that, as children approach the age of majority, they are increasingly able to take their own decisions concerning their medical treatment. In logic there can be no difference between an ability to consent to treatment and an ability to refuse treatment. This philosophy is also reflected by some provisions of the Children Act 1989 which give a child, of sufficient understanding to make an informed decision, the right to refuse 'medical or psychiatric examination or other assessment' or 'psychiatric and medical treatment' in certain defined circumstances: see sections 38(6), 43(8), 44(7) and Schedule 3, paragraphs 4(4)(a) and 5(5)(a). Accordingly the older the child concerned the greater the weight the court should give to its wishes, certainly in the field of medical treatment. In a sense this is merely one aspect of the application of the test that the welfare of the child is the paramount consideration. It will normally be in the best interests of a child of sufficient age and understanding to make an informed decision that the court should respect its integrity as a human being and not lightly override its decision on such a personal matter as medical treatment, all the more so if that treatment is invasive. In my judgment, therefore, the court exercising the inherent jurisdiction in relation to a 16- or 17-year-old child who is not mentally incompetent will, as a matter of course, ascertain the wishes of the child and will approach its decision with a strong predilection to give effect to the child's wishes. (The case of a mentally incompetent child will present different considerations, although even there the child's wishes, if known, must be a very material factor.) Nevertheless, if the court's powers are to be meaningful, there must come a point at which the court, while not disregarding the child's wishes, can override them in the child's own best interests, objectively considered. Clearly such a point will have come if the child is seeking to refuse treatment in circumstances which will in all probability lead to the death of the child or to severe permanent injury. An example of such a case was in *In re E (A Minor)* (unreported), which came before Ward J on 21 September 1990. There a 15-year-old Jehovah's Witness, and his parents of the same faith, were refusing to allow doctors to give the boy a blood transfusion without which there was a strong risk (on the medical evidence) that the boy would die. Ward J authorised the blood transfusion. In my judgment he was right to do so. In the course of his judgment he said:

> There is compelling and overwhelming force in the submission of the Official Solicitor that this court, exercising its prerogative of protection, should be very slow to allow an infant to martyr himself.

I agree.

. . .

## Lowe, Nigel, and Juss, Sarvinder, 'Medical Treatment — Pragmatism and the Search for Principle' (1993) 56 MLR 865

. . . *Re W* is a pragmatic remedies approach well-suited to the common law tradition. It takes a case-by-case approach to individual problems without showing an excessive desire to formulate legal principles. *Gillick*, however, was a rights-based approach where the court advocated a view of rights that was broad and general in terms. That approach has now had its wings clipped. Whether one uses Lord Donaldson MR's 'keyholder analogy' or his 'flak jacket' approach, the effect is the same. It enables the court to prevent, in the words of the Latey Committee, 'permanent disability' or 'unnecessary pain and suffering.'

In our view, the decision in *Re W* should not be reversed by the House of Lords. Similarly, we would support the outcome in *Re R* and in *Re E*. In the former case, a 15-year-old girl, having suffered emotional abuse, became suicidal and she was put under drugs at an adolescent psychiatric unit. During a lucid period, she indicated that she would refuse such treatment. In the latter case, a 15-year-old boy suffering from leukaemia refused an urgently required blood transfusion as a life-saving measure because of his religious beliefs. In the former case, the child was perhaps controversially ruled to lack *Gillick* competence, while in the latter, as in *Re W* the court simply overrode the child's competently held views on the basis of the child's interests. Collectively, these decisions establish two grounds upon which a child's refusal can be overridden; namely, (1) the inability to make an informed judgment, in which case the refusal carries no weight; and (2) where the child *is* capable of making an informed view, that preference is balanced against the harm to the child's welfare which will ensue if these wishes are observed.

We would support the decisions on either basis because it seems to us wrong for the court to allow a child to refuse treatment that would do him or her irreparable harm. After all, it is perhaps all too easily forgotten that, in the final analysis, a child is still only a child. Moreover, the entire thesis based on the premise of Lord Scarman's child of 'sufficient understanding and intelligence' who is able 'to understand fully what is proposed' is, it is submitted, in one sense open to question. Is a child of sufficient understanding and intelligence if he or she acts irrationally? Is autonomy meaningful if it is irrational? The point is well illustrated by *Re W* itself. At first instance, Thorpe J, with support from W's consultant psychiatrist who specialised in anorexia nervosa, had 'no doubt at all' that she was '*Gillick* competent.' Lord Donaldson MR, however, had serious doubts contending, 'it is a feature of anorexia nervosa that it is capable of destroying the ability to make an informed choice' being 'an illness which is not the fault of the sufferer' but which in its clinical manifestations

contains 'a firm wish not to be cured.' Balcombe LJ recognised that if W's refusal not
to take solid food was not shortly reversed 'she would be likely to suffer permanent
damage to her brain and reproductive organs' and not be able to bear children. Can
it humanely be argued, in these circumstances, that the court ought not to have
intervened? We agree with Ward J that a court should be slow to let a child martyr
himself. To those who question how a child can be held able to give a valid consent
yet be unable to exercise a power of veto, we would reply that there *is* a rational
distinction to be made between giving consent and withholding it. We must start with
the assumption that a doctor will act in the best interests of his patient. Hence, if the
doctor believes that a particular treatment is necessary for his patient, it is perfectly
rational for the law to facilitate this as easily as possible and hence allow a '*Gillick*
competent' child to give a valid consent, and also to protect the child against parents
opposed to what is professionally considered to be in its best medical interests. In
contrast, it is surely right for the law to be reluctant to allow a *child* of whatever age
to be able to veto treatment designed for his or her benefit particularly if a refusal
would lead to the child's death or permanent damage. In other words, the clear and
consistent policy of the law is to protect the child against wrong-headed parents and
against itself with the final safeguard, as *Re W* unequivocally establishes, of giving the
court the last word in cases of dispute.

## Brazier, Margaret, and Bridge, Caroline, 'Coercion or Caring: Analysing Adolescent Autonomy' (1996) 16 LS 84

. . . Anorexia is most common in adolescents but recognises no age barrier at 18. A
subsequent judgment has classified anorexia as a mental disorder, so why was W not
treated within the provisions made by the Mental Health Act? The Mental Health Act
is summarily dismissed by Lord Donaldson.

> Probably (the Mental Health Acts) would have had no application to W, but even
> where they are applicable it may be in the long term interests of the minor that if
> the same treatment can be secured on some other basis, this shall be done. Although
> mental illness should not be regarded as any different from physical illness, it is not
> always so viewed by the uninformed and the fact that later in life it might become
> known that a minor had been treated under the Acts might rebound to his or her
> disadvantage.

Is that brief statement the key to *Re R* and *Re W*? Both were very sick young women.
Both suffered from illness which distorted their judgment, deprived them of the
capacity to make a choice. In neither instance was their condition unique to their age.
Their minority was fortuitous. What their age allowed was for the courts to avoid the
'stigma' of the Mental Health Acts. Farquharson LJ in *Re R* stated openly that *Gillick*
'was concerned with mentally normal children'. The Court of Appeal used child
welfare law to avoid the detriment which they perceived as flowing from mental health
law. In doing so they undermined the principles pertinent to 'normal' children and
re-inforced stigmatisation of mental illness.
. . .

*Conclusion*
The judicial retreat from *Gillick* and the consequent attack on adolescent autonomy
was motivated by diverse concerns. Misunderstanding of what constitutes maximally

autonomous choice resulted in judges apparently overruling 'competent' choices which analysis shows to be in no real sense autonomous choice. Anxiety about the impact of invoking Mental Health Act procedures to protect minors caused judges to seek means to attain that Act's ends by different means. Many difficult cases relating to minors could be properly resolved once the law comprehends more fully the concept of autonomy and overcomes fears of stigmatisation in relation to mental illness. One problem however defies any neat solution. If an adolescent has made an autonomous choice, if he suffers from no mental disability, can society bring itself to endorse an outcome the vast majority of the community reject? Eekelaar offers a model of dynamic self-determinism which reconciles best interests and autonomy in many, many instances. He imposes a final *caveat*. An apparently autonomous choice by a minor may be overridden where such a choice threatens the child's *self-interest*. His proposition begs the question of who defines that self-interest. The young Jehovah's Witness in *Re E* would have defined his self-interest as his immortal life. If society is not prepared to allow adolescents to court unfavourable outcomes in judgments relating to medical treatment, we should say so openly. The law should not pretend to apply a 'functional' test of autonomy to every patient when younger patients are in fact subjected to an 'outcome' test.
. . .

*Notes*
1. The references to *Re E* in the extracts above are to *Re E (A Minor) (Wardship: Medical Treatment)* [1993] 1 FLR 386, FD (15-year-old Jehovah's Witness refused consent to a blood transfusion).
2. *Re R* was applied in *Re K, W and H (Minors) (Medical Treatment)* [1993] 1 FLR 854, FD, where Thorpe J held that the children concerned, who were in secure accommodation, were not *Gillick* competent. See also *Re O (A Minor) (Medical Treatment)* [1993] 2 FLR 149, FD, and *Re R (A Minor) (Blood Transfusion)* [1993] 2 FLR 757, FD, which involved applications by local authorities for leave to allow children of Jehovah's Witnesses to have blood transfusions despite parental objections.

*Questions*
1. Is is possible to give children rights of self-determination while at the same time affording them the necessary protection?
2. What about the 'rights' of the following children: Tom, aged 10, who wishes to have more contact with his father; Sue, aged 12, who does not wish to move house and leave her friends and wishes to move in with her best friend's family; David, aged 11, who does not wish to go to bed at 8 pm every night; Linda, aged 14, who wishes to stop her mother smoking as it makes her asthma worse; Carol aged 15 (or alternatively aged 17), a strict Roman Catholic with heart trouble who refuses to consent to an abortion even though the continuation of pregnancy will threaten her life?
3. Brazier, M., and Bridge, C., 'Coercion or Caring — Analysing Adolescent Autonomy' (1996) 16 LS 84, state at p. 93:

. . . Marriage is permitted at 16. Heterosexual teenagers can legally consent to sexual intercourse at 16. At 16 the law permits the purchase of cigarettes, a lethal substance.

Criminal responsibility is imposed at 10, providing that the child is found capable of knowing right from wrong. The law affirms several choices made at a time of perceived instability. Is patient autonomy so totally different in nature?'

What do you think?

*Further reading*
Bainham, A., 'The Judge and the Competent Minor' (1992) 108 LQR 194.
Bainham, A., 'Growing Up in Britain: Adolescence in the Post-*Gillick* Era', in Eekelaar, J., and Šarčević, P. (eds), *Parenthood in Modern Society, Legal and Social Issues for the Twenty-First Century*, Dordrecht: Martinus Nijhoff, 1993 p. 501.
Douglas, G., 'The Retreat from *Gillick*' (1992) 55 MLR 569.
Eekelaar, J., 'White Coats or Flak Jackets? Doctors, Children and the Courts — Again?' (1993) 109 LQR 182.
Eekelaar, J., 'The Interests of the Child and the Child's Wishes: The Role of Dynamic Self-Determinism' (1994) 8 IJL&F 42.
Houghton-James, H., 'The Child's Right to Die' [1992] Fam Law 550.
Houghton-James, H., 'Children Divorcing their Parents [1994] JSWFL 185.
Murphy, J., 'W(h)ither Adolescent Autonomy?' [1992] JSWFL 529.
Nicholls, N., 'Keyholders and Flak Jackets — Consent to Medical Treatment for Children' [1994] Fam Law 81.
Plomer, A., 'Parental Consent and Children's Medical Treatment' [1996] Fam Law 739.
Seymour J., 'An "Uncontrollable" Child: A Case Study in Children's and Parents' Rights', in Alston, P., *et al.* (eds), *Children, Rights and the Law*, Oxford: Clarendon Press, 1992, p. 98.
Thornton, R., 'Multiple Keyholders — Wardship and Consent to Medical Treatment' [1992] CLJ 34.
Thornton, R., 'Minors and Medical Treatment — Who Decides?' [1993] CLJ 33.

## 7.4   THE CHILDREN ACT 1989

The Children Act 1989 came into force on 14 October 1991. The following was *The Times* editorial for that day.

### *The Times*
### 14 October 1991, Editorial

### BORN UNDER ONE LAW

The Children Act 1989, which comes into force today, may well change more lives more profoundly than any other new law for many years. Yet the consensus in its favour is such that the Act has generated little controversy. This is a pity. Too few families know how it might affect them. Too few grandparents will make use of their right under the Act to seek regular contact with their grandchildren while the parents are separated, as one couple in Avon is doing today. Too few voters will notice whether their council is carrying out its new duties.

This statute transforms the legal status of children themselves. It also redefines the rights and duties of parents, other relatives and local authorities. Its laudable aim is to use the authority of the law to conciliate rather than to compel, adapting law to take account of the latest metamorphoses of 'the subversive family'.

Divorce, which now ends one marriage in three, will no longer have winners and losers but rather a new form of 'parental responsibility' applying equally to both partners. Out go 'custody' and 'access'. In comes a broader palette of legal options, all of which place the onus on the parents, rather than the court, to decide on the best solution for their child's welfare. For the first time, parents who separate will be forced to consider the interests of the chief casualties of any divorce: the children.

The most controversial area covered by the Act concerns care orders and child abuse. It seeks to mitigate the power of the state — as in the disturbing cases in Cleveland, Rochdale and Orkney — while safeguarding the interests of the child. No longer may the authorities override parental rights by resorting to wardship proceedings or 28-day place of safety orders; many more children who may not need to be in care should remain at home. Instead of months passing before the parents' objections are heard, the new eight-day emergency protection orders can be challenged within 72 hours. Parents will have a statutory right of access. Wherever they are affected by the Act, the wishes of children must be taken into account, and not as an afterthought.

Finally, by codifying and uniting disparate public and private law, thereby forcing judges, lawyers and social workers to retrain, the Act will virtually create specialised family courts. . . .

Within some local authorities, on the other hand, there are worries about the cost of helping children in need to stay with their families. The government says that it has provided for these costs, but it cannot prevent councils from diverting the extra money to other things. Children have no votes, and they cannot always make their voices heard above the cacophony of lobbyists. It is right that the government should leave spending priorities to local authorities' discretion. But it would be unforgivable for councils to deny the most vulnerable citizens the support which this Act requires.

### Bainham, Andrew, 'The Privatisation of the Public Interest in Children'
### (1990) 53 MLR 206 at p. 219

. . . One of the central aims of the [Children Act] is to bring together and collect in one statute as much as possible of the public and private law affecting children. It is hoped that this will make for a more coherent and comprehensible system. An important element in this process is the intended harmonisation of public and private law at both the substantive and procedural level. A total fusion would be out of the question since State intervention in family life is of its nature quite different from private disputes between individual family members. The process which will be brought about by the 1989 Act is probably more accurately described as one of confluence. The detailed aspects of public and private law will remain distinct but the two streams are intended to run together through the equal application of the fundamental principles enshrined in Part I of the Act in public and private proceedings. Both types of proceedings will be 'family proceedings' for the purpose of the Act. . . .

## In re S (Independent Representation)
[1993] Fam 263
Court of Appeal

SIR THOMAS BINGHAM MR: . . .

*The background to the legislation*
The Children Act 1989 was a statute with many purposes. A complete code was to be provided for social work intervention in the care of children, incorporating the lessons learned from the Cleveland Inquiry and other cases which had attracted national concern. The extent to which that would be subject to supervision and control by the courts would be prescribed in detail; thus putting an end to the tensions created by co-existence of statutory powers vested in local authorities with prerogative powers of the sovereign parens patriae vested in the judges of the High Court: see *A v Liverpool City Council* [1982] AC 363. The opportunity would be taken at the same time of codifying in one statute the numerous enactments into which child care law had become confusingly fragmented.

The purposes of the Act were not, however, solely legislative. They were in part declaratory of the attitudes and purposes that were to inform and direct the courts and other agencies in dealing with children. The child's welfare was to be treated uniformly as the paramount consideration. Delay was to be avoided. Basic freedoms were to be emphasised and officiousness discouraged, through application of the rubric that no order should be made in respect of a child unless the court considered that to do so would be better for the child than making no order at all. Every opportunity was to be afforded for the child's own views to be communicated and, where appropriate, explained through independent representation.

. . .

## The Children Act 1989 Guidance and Regulations: Vol. 1, Court Orders
London: HMSO, 1991

1.1    The Children Act 1989 brings together in a single coherent legislative framework the private and public law relating to children. It aims to strike a balance between the rights of children to express their views on decisions made about their lives, the rights of parents to exercise their responsibilities towards the child and the duty of the State to intervene where the child's welfare requires it.

. . .

1.5    The Children Act rests on the belief that children are generally best looked after within the family with both parents playing a full part and without resort to legal proceedings. That belief . . . is reflected in:

(a)    the new concept of parental responsibility;
(b)    the ability of unmarried fathers to share that responsibility by agreement with the mother;
(c)    the local authority's duty to give support to children and their families;
(d)    the local authority's duty to return a child looked after by them to his family unless this is against his interests;
(e)    the local authority's duty to ensure contact with his parents whenever possible for a child looked after by them away from home.

### 7.4.1    The section 1 welfare principles

Section 1 of the CA 1989 lays down certain fundamental principles which apply to both private and public law proceedings brought under the Act.

### 7.4.1.1    The welfare principle

## CHILDREN ACT 1989

**1.  Welfare of the child**
(1)   When a court determines any question with respect to—
  (a)  the upbringing of a child; or
  (b)  the administration of a child's property or the application of any income arising from it,
the child's welfare shall be the court's paramount consideration.

*Notes*
1.   See art. 3(1) of the UN Convention on the Rights of the Child 1989 *supra*.
2.   The welfare principle applies to public law proceedings (i.e. care and emergency protection) and to private law proceedings (e.g. an application for a s. 8 order), but it does not apply to applications for financial relief for children under sch. 1 of the CA 1989 (see CA 1989, s. 105, which defines 'upbringing' in s. 1(1) as including the care of the child, but not his maintenance).

### 7.4.1.2    The 'no delay' principle

## CHILDREN ACT 1989

**1.  Welfare of the child**
(2)   In any proceedings in which any question with respect to the upbringing of a child arises, the court shall have regard to the general principle that any delay in determining the question is likely to prejudice the welfare of the child.

*Note*
Progress of a case is controlled by the court, not by the parties. In s. 8 order proceedings, the court must draw up a timetable with a view to determining the question without delay (s. 11(1)(a)) and must give appropriate directions for ensuring that, as far as is reasonably practicable, the timetable is adhered to (s. 11(1)(b)). Rules of court must also make provision for the avoidance of delay (s. 11(2)). Despite these provisions, children's cases are taking longer than they did before the 1989 Act (see the Booth Report, *Avoiding Delay*, 1996). Other problems under the Act include the relationship between the courts and local authorities, the lack of independent representation for children in private law proceedings, and the difficult relationship between family and criminal proceedings in child abuse cases (see Levy, A., 'Children Still in Need' [1996] *The Times*, 12 November).

### 7.4.1.3   The welfare checklist

## CHILDREN ACT 1989

**1.   Welfare of the child**

(3)   In the circumstances mentioned in subsection (4), a court shall have regard in particular to—

(a)   the ascertainable wishes and feelings of the child concerned (considered in the light of his age and understanding);

(b)   his physical, emotional and educational needs;

(c)   the likely effect on him of any change in his circumstances;

(d)   his age, sex, background and any characteristics of his which the court considers relevant;

(e)   any harm which he has suffered or is at risk of suffering;

(f)   how capable each of his parents, and any other person in relation to whom the court considers the question to be relevant, is of meeting his needs;

(g)   the range of powers available to the court under this Act in the proceedings in question.

(4)   The circumstances are that—

(a)   the court is considering whether to make, vary or discharge a section 8 order, and the making, variation or discharge of the order is opposed by any party to the proceedings; or

(b)   the court is considering whether to make, vary or discharge an order under Part IV.

### *H* v *H (Residence Order: Leave to Remove from Jurisdiction)*
[1995] 1 FLR 529
Court of Appeal

STAUGHTON LJ: . . . [Section 1(3)] is usefully called a 'checklist' by judges and practitioners, although not by the statute. Perhaps one should remember, that when one calls it a checklist, that it is not like the list of checks which an airline pilot had to make with his co-pilot, aloud one to the other before he takes off. The statute does not say that the judge had to read out the seven items in s. 1(3) and pronounce his conclusion on each. Sometimes judges will do that, maybe more often than not; but it is not mandatory. . . .

### 7.4.1.4   The no-order presumption

## CHILDREN ACT 1989

**1.   Welfare of the child**

(5)   Where a court is considering whether or not to make one or more orders under this Act with respect to a child, it shall not make the order or any of the orders unless it considers that doing so would be better for the child than making no order at all.

### *The Children Act 1989 Guidance and Regulations: Vol. 1,*
### *Court Orders*
London: HMSO, 1991

1.12   . . . The first [aim of the 'no order' principle] is to discourage unnecessary court orders being made, for example as part of a standard package of orders. If orders are restricted to those cases where they are necessary to resolve a specific problem this should reduce conflict and promote parental agreement and co-operation. The second aim is to ensure that the order is granted only where it will positively improve the child's welfare and not simply because the grounds for making the order are made out as, for example, in care proceedings where the court may decide that it would be better for a particular child not to be in local authority care.

*Further reading*
Bainham, A., 'The Children Act 1989: Welfare and Non-interventionism' [1990] Fam Law 143.
Bennett, S., and Armstrong Walsh, S., 'The No Order Principle, Parental Responsibility and the Child's Wishes' [1994] Fam Law 91.

### 7.4.2   Section 8 orders

Section 8 of the CA 1989 lists and defines four orders, which can be used for a wide range of different matters involving children. These orders can be made on an application, or by the court in any family proceedings even though no such application has been made. The principles in s. 1, *supra*, apply.

## CHILDREN ACT 1989

**8.   Residence, contact and other orders with respect to children**
    (1)   In this Act—
    'a contact order' means an order requiring the person with whom a child lives, or is to live, to allow the child to visit or stay with the person named in the order, or for that person and the child otherwise to have contact with each other;
    'a prohibited steps order' means an order that no step which could be taken by a parent in meeting his parental responsibility for a child, and which is of a kind specified in the order, shall be taken by any person without the consent of the court;
    'a residence order' means an order settling the arrangements to be made as to the person with whom a child is to live; and
    'a specific issue order' means an order giving directions for the purpose of determining a specific question which has arisen, or which may arise, in connection with any aspect of parental responsibility for a child.
    (2)   In this Act 'a section 8 order' means any of the orders mentioned in subsection (1) and any order varying or discharging such an order.
    . . .

*Notes*
1.   The most common use of residence and contact orders is to settle disputes about residence and contact on family breakdown (see Chapter 9).
2.   A residence order gives a person without parental responsibility such responsibility for the duration of the order (s. 12(2)). Persons other than a parent or guardian may seek a residence order, but they need leave to make the application and special restrictions apply to local authority foster-parents (s. 9(3) and (4)). If a residence order is made in favour of a father without parental responsibility, the court must make a s. 4 order giving him parental responsibility (s. 12(1)). While the order is in force there are restrictions on changing the child's surname and removing the child from the UK (s. 13).

The residence order is the only s. 8 order which may be made in respect of a child in local authority care (s. 9(1)). A residence order may be made *ex parte* in an emergency, e.g., in a case of threatened child abduction (see Chapter 12) or where the children are at risk (see, e.g., *Re G (Minors) (Ex Parte Interim Residence Order)* [1993] 1 FLR 910, CA, where an *ex parte* residence order was made in favour of the father where the mother was on drugs).

3. For cases where applications were made for a specific issue order, see, e.g., *Re F (A Minor) (Blood Transfusion)* [1993] 2 FLR 757, FD (specific issue order granted to a local authority so that medical treatment, including blood transfusions, could be given to a 10-month-old child with leukaemia whose parents were Jehovah's Witnesses) and *Re HG (Specific Issue Order: Sterilisation)* [1993] 1 FLR 587, FD (17-year-old girl with severe epilepsy and low mental age applied by her father as next friend for specific issue order to authorise her own sterilisation).

### 7.4.3  What are 'family proceedings' for the purposes of the Children Act?

Section 8 orders can be made by the court on an application or of its own motion in any 'family proceedings'. It is therefore important to know what sorts of proceedings are classified as 'family proceedings'.

## CHILDREN ACT 1989

**8.  Residence, contact and other orders with respect to children**
   (3)  For the purposes of this Act 'family proceedings' means any proceedings—
      (a)  under the inherent jurisdiction of the High Court in relation to children; and
      (b)  under the enactments mentioned in subsection (4),
but does not include proceedings in an application for leave under section 100(3).
   (4)  The enactments are—
      (a)  Parts I, II and IV of this Act;
      (b)  the Matrimonial Causes Act 1973;
      (c)  the Domestic Violence and Matrimonial Proceedings Act 1976;
      (d)  the Adoption Act 1976;
      (e)  the Domestic Proceedings and Magistrates' Courts Act 1978;
      (f)  sections 1 and 9 of the Matrimonial Homes Act 1983;
      (g)  Part III of the Matrimonial and Family Proceedings Act 1984.

*Note*
As the DVMPA 1976 and the MHA 1983 will be repealed when Part IV of the FLA 1996 comes into force, the FLA 1996, sch. 8, para. 60(1) amends s. 8(4) of the 1989 Act by omitting paras (c) and (f) and by inserting after (g) the words '(h) the Family Law Act 1996'.

### *Re SW (A Minor) (Care Proceedings)*
[1993] 2 FLR 609
Family Division

BOOTH J: . . . . it would be wise for legal advisers to ensure that their clients are made well aware of the power of the court in family proceedings to make a wide range of orders under the Act of its own motion. For example, not only may the court make an order under section 34 of the Act in relation to contact with the child in care, but by virtue of section 10(1)(b) it may also make any s. 8 order even though no application for such an order has been made. In each and every case the court is not constrained by the applications before it but will act in accordance with what it finds to be in the child's welfare, which is its paramount consideration, and in accordance with those matters to which it must have regard under section 1 of the Act. . . .

### 7.4.4  Power of the court to make section 8 orders

The court has jurisdiction to make any s. 8 order in family proceedings on the application of a parent or guardian, a person with a residence order in his or her favour, or a person who has been granted leave to apply; or if the court considers it should make such an order even though no such application has been made (s. 10(1)). However, in respect of s. 8 residence and contact orders the following may apply without leave: a step-parent; a person with whom the child has lived for at least three years; a person who has the consent of all those persons with a residence order in their favour; a person who has the consent of all those with parental responsibility for the child; and a person who has the consent of the local authority where the child is in care (s. 10(5)). Other persons need leave of the court.

## CHILDREN ACT 1989

**10.  Power of court to make section 8 orders**
   (9)  Where the person applying for leave to make an application for a section 8 order is not the child concerned, the court shall, in deciding whether or not to grant leave, have particular regard to—
   (a)  the nature of the proposed application for the section 8 order;
   (b)  the applicant's connection with the child;
   (c)  any risk there might be of that proposed application disrupting the child's life to such an extent that he would be harmed by it; and
   (d)  where the child is being looked after by a local authority—
      (i)  the authority's plans for the child's future; and
      (ii)  the wishes and feelings of the child's parents.

*Note*
In *Re A and W (Minors) (Residence Order: Leave to Apply)* [1992] Fam 182, the Court of Appeal held, *inter alia*, that the child's welfare was not the paramount consideration in applications for leave. Where the child applies for leave to apply for a s. 8 order, the court may grant leave only if the child has sufficient understanding to make the proposed application (s. 10(8)).

### 7.4.5  'Hybrid' orders

The following orders are described here as 'hybrid' orders because they cross the boundaries between private and public law.

*W v Wakefield City Council*
[1995] 1 FLR 170
Family Division

WALL J: . . . The Children Act has specifically divided proceedings into categories of public and private law. Family life does not divide itself so neatly or conveniently. . . .

### 7.4.5.1 The family assistance order

## CHILDREN ACT 1989

**16. Family assistance orders**

(1) Where, in any family proceedings, the court has power to make an order under this Part with respect to any child, it may (whether or not it makes such an order) make an order requiring—

(a) a probation officer to be made available; or

(b) a local authority to make an officer of the authority available,

to advise, assist and (where appropriate) befriend any person named in the order.

(2) The persons who may be named in an order under this section ('a family assistance order') are—

(a) any parent or guardian of the child;

(b) any person with whom the child is living or in whose favour a contact order is in force with respect to the child;

(c) the child himself.

(3) No court may make a family assistance order unless—

(a) it is satisfied that the circumstances of the case are exceptional; and

(b) it has obtained the consent of every person to be named in the order other than the child.

(4) A family assistance order may direct—

(a) the person named in the order; or

(b) such of the persons named in the order as may be specified in the order,

to take such steps as may be so specified with a view to enabling the officer concerned to be kept informed of the address of any person named in the order and to be allowed to visit any such person.

. . .

*Note*

Unless otherwise specified, a family assistance order is effective for up to six months (s. 16(5)), but it may be varied or discharged (s. 16(6)).

### 7.4.5.2 The section 37 direction

## CHILDREN ACT 1989

**37. Powers of court in certain family proceedings**

(1) Where in any family proceedings in which a question arises with respect to the welfare of any child, it appears to the court that it may be appropriate for a care or supervision order to be made with respect to him, the court may direct the appropriate authority to undertake an investigation of the child's circumstances.

(2) Where the court gives a direction under this section the local authority concerned shall, when undertaking the investigation, consider whether they should—

(a) apply for a care order or for a supervision order with respect to the child;

(b) provide services or assistance for the child or his family; or

(c) take any other action with respect to the child.

(3) Where a local authority undertake an investigation under this section, and decide not to apply for a care order or supervision order with respect to the child concerned, they shall inform the court of—

(a)   their reasons for so deciding;
(b)   any service or assistance which they have provided, or intend to provide, for the child and his family; and
(c)   any other action which they have taken, or propose to take, with respect to the child.
. . .

*Notes*
1.   See *Re H (A Minor) (Section 37 Direction)* [1993] 2 FLR 541, FD, for an example of a situation where a s. 37 direction might be useful. The case also illustrates the flexibility of the range of orders available to the court under the CA 1989.
2.   In *Re CE (Section 37 Direction)* [1995] 1 FLR 26, FD, Ward J held, *per curiam*, that the court should not order a local authority to conduct a s. 37 investigation unless it appeared that it might be appropriate to make a public law order.

### 7.4.5.3   Asking for a welfare report

## CHILDREN ACT 1989

**7.   Welfare reports**
(1)   A court considering any question with respect to a child under this Act may—
(a)   ask a probation officer; or
(b)   ask a local authority to arrange for—
(i)   an officer of the authority; or
(ii)   such other person (other than a probation officer) as the authority considers appropriate,
to report to the court on such matters relating to the welfare of that child as are required to be dealt with in the report.
(3)   The report may be made in writing, or orally, as the court requires.

*Note*
Wall J in *W v Wakefield City Council* [1995] 1 FLR 170, FD, at p. 175 described s. 7 as 'an underused section' and stated at p. 176:

. . . [Section 7] goes a long way to bridge the gulf between private and public law proceedings. In a private law case where a local authority has been involved, and evidence from the local authority is relevant, the proper course is for an application to be made to the court hearing the private law proceedings for a report under s. 7, which the local authority is duty-bound to provide.

(For public law orders, e.g., care and supervision orders, see Chapter 10.)

*Further reading*
Bainham, A., with Cretney, S., *Children — The Modern Law*, Bristol: Jordans, 1993.
Crook, H., 'Grandparents and the Children Act 1989' [1994] Fam Law 135.
Moxon, C., 'Prohibited Steps Orders' [1994] Fam Law 271.

## 7.5  WARDSHIP AND THE INHERENT JURISDICTION

## SUPREME COURT ACT 1981

#### 41.  Wards of court

(1)  . . . no minor shall be made a ward of court except by virtue of an order to that effect made by the High Court.

(2)  Where an application is made for such an order in respect of a minor, the minor shall become a ward of court on the making of the application, but shall cease to be a ward of court at the end of such period as may be prescribed [i.e. 21 days] unless within that period an order has been made in accordance with the application.

(2A)  Subsection (2) does not apply with respect to a child who is the subject of a care order (as defined by section 105 of the Children Act 1989).

(3)  The High Court may, either upon an application in that behalf or without such an application, order that any minor who is for the time being a ward of court shall cease to be a ward of court.

### Re Z (Freedom of Publication)
[1996] 1 FLR 191
Court of Appeal

WARD LJ: . . .

(1)  *Wardship*
The origins of wardship are buried deep in the murky history of feudal times. It was an incident of tenure by which, upon a tenant's death, the lord became guardian of the surviving infant's land and body. Although the entitlement to the profits of the land carried with it the reciprocal duty of maintaining and educating the ward according to his station, a cynical historian may well take the view that this valuable source of revenue to the Crown, which in about 1540 was transferred from the officials of the Royal Household to the Court of Wards and Liveries, was more concerned to protect the rights of the guardian rather than those of the ward. When that entitlement and that court were abolished in 1660 wardship did not wither away. *Cary (Lord Falkland)* v *Bertie* (1696) 2 Vern 333 at p. 342 saw the jurisdiction transferred to the Court of Chancery. There it became substantively and procedurally assimilated to the parens patriae jurisdiction and as it increasingly lost its close connection with property, it became more protective in nature. Emphasising wardship's shift away from being an incident of property to an essentially parental jurisdiction where the court would do what in the circumstances a wise parent acting for the true interests of the child would or ought to do, the Law Reform (Miscellaneous Provisions) Act 1949 simplified the procedure for making a child a ward. Wardship became even more accessible when legal aid became available in 1949, and on its transfer to the Family Division in 1971, its popularity soared. In 1951 only 74 originating summonses were issued, rising to 622 in 1971 and 4791 in 1991, and reducing dramatically to 492 in 1992 after the Children Act 1989 had come into effect. Although the Children Act curtailed the use of wardship, it did not affect the court's inherent jurisdiction:

> Wardship was the result of, and not the ground for, the exercise of the jurisdiction and I am bound to say that in view of the cases to which I have referred . . . , I find considerable difficulty in accepting the view . . . that the effect of the 1949 Act is

to destroy the inherent jurisdiction of this court over infants in this country' (*per* Stamp J in *Re N (Infants)* [1967]1 Ch 512 at p. 531).

In *Re L (An Infant)* [1968] P 119, at p. 156, Lord Denning MR referred to the jurisdiction of the Court of Chancery which:

. . . derives from the right and duty of the Crown as parens patriae to take care of those who are not able to take care of themselves . . . The child was usually made a ward of court, and thereafter no important step in the child's life could be taken without the court's consent; but that was only machinery. Even if there was no property and the child was not a ward of court, nevertheless the Court of Chancery had the power to interfere for the protection of the infant by making whatever order might be appropriate.

In *Re C (A Minor) (Wardship: Medical Treatment) (No. 2)* [1990] Fam 39, sub nom *Re C (A Minor) (No. 2) (Wardship: Publication of Information)* [1990] 1 FLR 263, Lord Donaldson of Lymington MR said at pp. 46 and 266 respectively:

The origin of the wardship jurisdiction is the duty of the Crown to protect its subjects and particularly children who are the generations of the future. It is exercised by the courts on behalf of the Crown: see *Re A (A Minor) (Wardship: Jurisdiction)* [1975] Fam 47 at p. 52, per Latey J. The machinery for its exercise is an application to make the child a ward of court. Thereafter, the court is entitled and bound in appropriate cases to make decisions in the interests of the child which override the rights of its parents.

The result of a somewhat reluctant realisation of this by the profession has been that practitioners are now more frequently issuing proceedings entitled as is the case before us, 'In the Matter of the Inherent Jurisdiction'. For all practical purposes the jurisdiction in wardship and the inherent jurisdiction over children is one and the same and I shall, therefore, consider them together.

(2)   *The inherent jurisdiction*
(i)   *Its nature*
The first question is what is the nature of this jurisdiction? The answer was given in 1827 by Lord Eldon LC who was able to declare in *Wellesley v Duke of Beaufort* (1827) 2 Russ 1 at p. 20 that:

It belongs to the King, as parens patriae, having the care of those who are not able to take care of themselves, and is founded on the obvious necessity that the law should place somewhere the care of individuals who cannot take care of themselves, particularly in cases where it is clear that some care should be thrown around.

On appeal to the House of Lords as *Wellesley v Wellesley* (1828) 2 Bli NS 124, Lord Redesdale said at p. 130:

Now, upon what does Lord Somers, upon what does Lord Nottingham, upon what does Lord Hardwicke, upon what ground does every Chancellor who has been sitting on the bench, in the Court of Chancery since that time, place the jurisdiction? They all say that it is a right which devolves to the Crown, as parens patriae, and that it is the duty of the Crown to see that the child is properly taken care of.

Twenty years later Lord Cottenham LC said in *Re Spence* (1847) 2 Ph 247 at p. 251:

I have no doubt about the jurisdiction. The cases in which [the Court of Chancery] interferes on behalf of infants are not confined to those in which there is property . . . This Court interferes for the protection of infants, qua infants, by virtue of the prerogative which belongs to the Crown as parens patriae, and the exercise of which is delegated to the Great Seal.

. . .

## Mrs R v Central Independent Television plc
### [1994] Fam 192
### Court of Appeal

WAITE LJ: . . . The prerogative jurisdiction has shown a striking versatility, throughout its long history, in adapting its powers to the protective needs of children in all kinds of different situations. Although the jurisdiction is theoretically boundless, the courts have nevertheless found it necessary to set self-imposed limits upon its exercise for the sake of clarity and consistency, and of avoiding conflict between child welfare and other public advantages. . . .

*Notes*
1. In *Re Z (Freedom of Publication)*, *supra*, an injunction was granted to restrain the media from publishing information which would lead to the ward's identity. (For a note on *Re Z*, see Moriarty, J., 'Publicity, Parents and Performing Children' [1996] CLJ 212.)
2. A ward's welfare sometimes takes second place to other public interests, e.g., to freedom of speech and freedom of publication (see *Re Z, supra* and *R (Mrs) v Central Independent Television plc* [1994] Fam 192, [1994] 2 FLR 151) or to immigration policy (see, e.g., *Re F (A Minor) (Wardship: Immigration)* [1989] 1 FLR 233, CA).
3. The wardship jurisdiction has become a residual jurisdiction because of the introduction of specific issue and prohibited steps orders (see 7.4.2), which give the family proceedings court power to make orders similar to those that were available in wardship. Wardship remains useful for sensitive and difficult cases, e.g., surrogacy (*Re C (A Minor) (Wardship: Surrogacy)* [1985] FLR 846) and consent to medical treatment (*Re B (A Minor) (Wardship: Sterilisation)* [1988] 1 AC 199 and *Re D (A Minor) (Wardship: Sterilisation)* [1976] Fam 185). Wardship is also important in child abduction cases, particularly in non-Convention cases (see Chapter 12).

(For local authorities and wardship, see Chapter 10.)

*Further reading*
Seymour, J., '*Parens Patriae* and Wardship Powers: Their Nature and Origins' (1994) 14 *Oxford J Legal Stud* 159.

# 8 PARENTS

## 8.1 PARENTAL RIGHTS OR RESPONSIBILITIES?

### United Nations Convention on the Rights of the Child 1989

**Article 5**
States Parties shall respect the responsibilities, rights and duties of parents or, where applicable, the members of the extended family or community as provided for by local custom, legal guardians or other persons legally responsible for the child . . .

**Article 14**
1. States Parties shall respect the right of the child to freedom of thought, conscience and religion.
2. States Parties shall respect the rights and duties of the parents . . . to provide direction to the child in the exercise of his or her right in a manner consistent with the evolving capacities of the child.
. . .

**Article 18**
1. States Parties shall use their best efforts to ensure recognition of the principle that both parents have common responsibilities for the upbringing and development of the child. Parents or, as the case may be, legal guardians, have the primary responsibility for the upbringing and development of the child. The best interests of the child will be their basic concern.
2. For the purpose of guaranteeing and promoting the rights set forth in the present Convention, States Parties shall render appropriate assistance to parents and legal guardians in the performance of their child-rearing responsibilities and shall ensure the development of institutions, facilities and services for the care of children.
3. States Parties shall take all appropriate measures to ensure that children of working parents have the right to benefit from child-care services and facilities for which they are eligible.

**Article 27**

1. States Parties recognize the right of every child to a standard of living adequate for the child's physical, mental, spiritual, moral and social development.

2. The parent(s) or others responsible for the child have the primary responsibility to secure, within their abilities and financial capacities, the conditions of living necessary for the child's development.

. . .

## 8.1.1 Do parents have rights?

### *Gillick* v *West Norfolk and Wisbech Area Health Authority and Another*
[1986] AC 112
House of Lords

LORD SCARMAN: . . . The principle of the law, as I shall endeavour to show, is that parental rights are derived from parental duty and exist only so long as they are needed for the protection of the person and the property of the child.

### Montgomery, Jonathan, 'Children as Property?'
(1988) 51 MLR 323 at pp. 323 and 341

One of the consequences of the ascendancy of the welfare principle has been a reduced emphasis on the nature and extent of parental rights.

. . . Parental rights protect the interests of children not parents.

### Dickens, Bernard M., 'The Modern Function and Limits of Parental Rights',
(1981) 97 LQR 462

. . . The modern function of parental rights, it is proposed, is not to enforce duties children owe their parents, or simply to enforce against third parties powers of custody and control parents enjoy over their children. It is to permit parents to discharge their duties to their children. These duties are not positively to do good, but to avoid harm. It is obvious that to the extent that ill-health and, for instance, illiteracy are considered harm, parents are bound by positive duties to provide health care and education. This proposition may be derived from an abundance of case law and legislation. The duty to avoid harm is more elastic, however, since it affords license to control a child not for its benefit, but in non-beneficial or non-therapeutic ways falling short of causing or risking harm. The issue to be critically addressed is the point at which an exercise of parental choice over a child's management and future is so potentially harmful to the welfare or interests of the child as to require state intervention and possibly a countermanding of parental choice.

Principles may be derived from a position of extremity. Where parents leave a child at risk of avoidable death, intervention is clearly justifiable. Legal doctrines of necessity to save human life and the quality of life, meaning physical and mental health, supersede laws prohibiting unauthorised surgical or other physical interventions, and prohibiting unauthorised entry upon land, such as where the endangered child is in custody. The focus of the law is upon preservation of life and health, to enable the child to grow into maturity and consequent autonomy. The law protects the present child, in order to protect the future adult the child is intended to survive to become. This indicates another means of expressing the modern function of parental rights. They exist to preserve and to prepare children for adulthood and emerging autonomy. A parental decision to take immediate non-emergency action which may deny the child an option to be exercised later by the child upon gaining maturity, may violate this function of parenthood. As such, it may not be a legitimate exercise of parental authority, and may present a limitation of parental rights. This is clearly demonstrated where a parental decision is concerned which may result in avoidable or premature termination of the child's life, but is equally true at a less extreme level concerning decisions affecting the child's future options in life and life-style. The principle would apply to parental decisions on such matters as contraceptive or eugenic sterilisation, and, for instance, on committal to detention in a psychiatric facility. . . .

The modern function of parental rights is to prepare children and adolescents for maturity, and as minors come to achieve maturity and to exercise autonomy, this may be seen not as a limitation or defeat of parental control, but as a successful discharge of parental responsibility. It is not accidental that a common manifestation of maturity in minors lies in the area of fertility control and family planning, since this is the link through which they themselves decide to become parents, and to acquire the rights and responsibilities which attend upon that status. Where parents exercise choice over their children's survival, and over the quality of the lives they will grow up to lead, a need exists to have a means of public monitoring. Without questioning parental good intentions, one can see that cases exist which show that the latest proposals of Goldstein, Freud and Solnit, strongly favouring parental autonomy, should not drown other and opposing views giving emphasis to the rights of children themselves. The book *Before the Best Interests of the Child* offers a helpful first word to assist judicial and administrative analysis. It cannot necessarily serve, however, as the last word.

The following case, a pre-Children Act 1989 case, contains some interesting *dicta* on parental rights.

### Re KD (A Minor) (Ward: Termination of Access)
[1988] AC 806
House of Lords

*Facts*: A mother whose access to her four-year-old son, a ward of court, had been terminated so that the local authority could place him for adoption, appealed to the House of Lords submitting that a natural parent has a legal right to access, and that, although that right could be overborne by considerations of the welfare of the child, it must prevail when there is no positive evidence that access would be damaging to the child.
*Held*: dismissing the appeal and applying the welfare principle, that the judge at first instance was entitled on the evidence to reach the conclusion that continued access would be harmful to the child.

LORD OLIVER: . . . Thus, it is argued, not only is support to be found for the existence of a legal right of access in statute and in some at least of the English authorities but the right is one recognised by the European Court of Human Rights as a fundamental element of family life protected by a convention to which the United Kingdom is a party. In the light of this, your Lordships have heen invited to reconsider the approach to such cases as it emerges from the speech of Lord MacDermott in *J* v *C* [1970] AC 668 to which reference has already heen made. My Lords I do not, for my part, discern any conflict between the propositions laid down by your Lordships' House in *J* v *C* and the pronouncements of the European Court of Human Rights in relation to the natural parent's right of access to her child. Such conflict as exists, is, I think, semantic only and lies only in differing ways of giving expression to the single common concept that the natural bond and relationship between parent and child gives rise to universally recognised norms which ought not to be gratuitously interfered with and which, if interfered with at all, ought to be so only if the welfare of the child dictates it. The word 'right' is used in a variety of different senses, both popular and jurisprudential. It may be used as importing a positive duty in some other individual for the non-performance of which the law will provide an appropriate remedy, as in the case of a right to the performance of a contract. It may signify merely a privilege conferring no corresponding duty on any one save that of non-interference, such as the right to walk on the public highway. It may signify no more than the hope of or aspiration to a social order which will permit the exercise of that which is perceived as an essential liberty, such as, for instance, the so-called 'right to work' or a 'right' of personal privacy. Parenthood, in most civilised societies, is generally conceived of as conferring upon parents the exclusive privilege of ordering, within the family, the upbringing of children of tender age, with all that that entails. That is a privilege which, if interfered with without authority, would be protected by the courts, but it is a privilege circumscribed by many limitations imposed both by the general law and, where the circumstances demand, by the courts or by the authorities upon whom the legislature has imposed the duty of supervising the welfare of children and young persons. When the jurisdiction of the court is invoked for the protection of the child the parental privileges do not terminate. They do, however, become immediately subservient to the paramount consideration which the court has always in mind, that is to say, the welfare of the child. That is the basis of the decision of your Lordships' House in *J* v *C* [1970] AC 668 and I see nothing in *R* v *United Kingdom* (Case 6/1986/104/152) which contradicts or casts any doubt upon that decision or which calls now for any reappraisal of it by your Lordships. In particular, the description of those familial rights and privileges enjoyed by parents in relation to their children as 'fundamental' or 'basic' does nothing, in my judgment, to clarify either the nature or the extent of the concept which it is sought to describe. Willmer LJ's reference in *S* v *S* [1962] 1 WLR 445, 448 to access as a 'basic right of any parent' has not received universal acceptance. Thus, for instance, in *M* v *M* *(Child: Access)* [1973] 2 All ER 81, 88, Latey J commented that to speak of a 'basic right of access' meant

> not that a parent has any proprietorial right to access but that save in exceptional circumstances to deprive a parent of access is to deprive a child of an important contribution to his emotional and material growing up in the long term.

In that case he spoke of access as being more naturally the right of the child than that of the parent. Later cases have emphasised the ephemeral nature of any parental 'right' to access. Thus in *A* v *C* [1985] FLR 445, 455, in considering a statement by the trial judge that 'prima facie . . . a parent should have access to his child,' Ormrod LJ, at p. 456, regarded it as dangerous to

> talk in terms of presumption and burden of proof. . . . It is simply a statement of common sense that in the ordinary way, as society today is constituted, both parents

should be in contact with their children, even if they have parted. It is no more than that and I would deprecate any idea that there is a presumption either way in these matters or an onus either way.

He had previously considered the trial judge's observation that, in relation to access, it was a mistake to talk in terms of rights. He said, at p. 455:

The word 'rights' is a highly confusing word which leads to a great deal of trouble if it is used loosely, particularly when it is used loosely in a court of law. So far as access to a child is concerned, there are no rights in the sense in which lawyers understand the word. It is a matter to be decided always entirely on the footing of the best interests of the child, either by agreement between the parties or by the court if there is no agreement. The judge very properly directed himself in accordance with the law, particularly as it is laid down in *J* v *C* [1970] AC 668 in the House of Lords, that the first paramount consideration was the welfare of the child, bearing in mind, of course, the wishes and feelings and so on of the respective parents and other people concerned with the child, but always bearing in mind that the decision must rest in terms of the best interests of the child, having taken all these other factors into account.

. . .

[Counsel for the appellant] suggests that these cases display an erroneous approach and invites your Lordships to accept and pronounce that the starting point in every case should be that a parent has a right of access which should be given effect to by the court and curtailed and inhibited only if the court is satisfied that the exercise of the right will be positively inimical to the interests of the child. My Lords, for my part, I think that this is an invitation which your Lordships should decline. I say this not solely because it is, as I think, out of line with an approach which has been universally acted upon ever since the decision of your Lordships' House in *J* v *C* [1970] AC 668 but also because I believe the debate to be one without content. It is, I suppose, possible to envisage circumstances in which, perhaps as a result of an accident, a child's consciousness of the world about him might be such as to suggest that access to him by his parent could have no effect at all on him either for good or for ill. But aside from such a case, where the question of access could hardly be a live issue in any event, I do not find it possible to conceive of any circumstances which could occur in practice in which the paramount consideration of the welfare of the child would not indicate one way or the other whether access should be had or should continue. Whatever the position of the parent may be as a matter of law — and it matters not whether he or she is described as having a 'right' in law or a 'claim' by the law of nature or as a matter of common sense — it is perfectly clear that any 'right' vested in him or her must yield to the dictates of the welfare of the child. If the child's welfare dictates that there be access, it adds nothing to say that the parent has also a right to have it subject to considerations of the child's welfare. If the child's welfare dictates that there should be no access, then it is equally fruitless to ask whether that is because there is no right to access or because the right is overborne by considerations of the child's welfare. For my part, I think that the President's analysis in *Hereford and Worcester County Council* v *J.A.H.* [1985] FLR 530 places the emphasis perhaps too much upon the necessity of finding a positive benefit to the child from parental access. As a general proposition a natural parent has a claim to access to his or her child to which the court will pay regard and it would not I think be inappropriate to describe such a claim as a 'right.' Equally, a normal assumption is, as Latey J observed to *M* v *M* *(Child: Access)* [1973] 2 All ER 81, that a child will benefit from continued contact with his natural parent. But both the 'right' and the assumption will always be displaced if the interests of the child indicate otherwise and I find nothing in the decision in *R v United Kingdom* which suggests otherwise. . . .

## Thompson, J. M., 'A Right of Access?'
### (1989) 105 LQR 6

. . . The welfare principle is fast becoming an overworked concept. While the decision in *Re KD (A Minor)* might appear to support the concept of a parental right of access, it is a right without substance in that all access disputes are to be decided according to the welfare principle . . . Yet, as the events in Cleveland have shown, family autonomy can seriously be undermined by the purported exercise of the welfare principle. Parents as well as children have rights. The House of Lords in *Re KD (a Minor)* had the opportunity to buttress these rights by accepting that a parent's right of access should be given effect unless it was clearly established by the party disputing the exercise of the right that it was against the child's interest to have contact with the parent. However, the House of Lords chose not to do so. It remains to be seen how many parents — and children — will suffer as a consequence.

## CONSTITUTION OF IRELAND 1937

**Article 42**
1. The State acknowledges that the primary and natural educator of the child is the Family and guarantees to respect the inalienable right and duty of parents to provide, according to their means, for the religious and moral, intellectual, physical and social education of their children.

*Notes and questions*
1. Duncan, W., 'The Constitutional Protection of Parental Rights', in Eekelaar, J., and Šarčević, P. (eds) *Parenthood in Modern Society — Legal and Social Issues for the Twenty-First Century*, Dordrecht: Martinus Nijhoff, 1993, Chapter 29, states that Irish constitutional guarantees in respect of parental rights have had an influence on the legal system and on legislation.
2. There is no list of parental rights, but parents are considered to have, *inter alia*, the following rights: a right to possession of the child; a right to make decisions about the child's education, medical treatment, and place of residence; a right to choose the child's name; a right to consent to a minor child's marriage; a right to consent to the child's adoption; a right to administer the child's property; a right to represent the child in legal proceedings; a right to enter into contracts on the child's behalf; a right to appoint a guardian; and a right to apply for orders under the CA 1989. However, these rights are not absolute, in that they may be overruled by the court. Would it be a good idea to have a list of parental rights and responsibilities? Are rights the same as responsibilities? Do parents have a right to smack their children?
3. In *F v Wirral Metropolitan Borough Council* [1991] Fam 69, the Court of Appeal held that parents have no right of action for damages arising out of any interference with their parental rights, as any parental right stems from

parental duty towards the child and is subservient to the welfare of the child (see Bainham, A., 'Interfering with Parental Responsibility — A New Challenge for the Law of Torts' (1990) 2 JCL 3).

### 8.1.2 Parental decisions about medical treatment for the child

Although parents have a right to consent to the child's medical treatment, they do not have an absolute right as the child's best interests may prevail over their wishes. Parents do not have complete autonomy, and in some cases the court has overridden the wishes of parents in respect of their child's medical treatment (as it did in *Gillick*, see Chapter 7). In the following case, the parents did not wish their child to have a life-saving operation, but the court decided differently.

*Re B (A Minor) (Wardship: Medical Treatment)*
[1981] 1 WLR 1421
Court of Appeal

*Facts*: The child, born with Down's syndrome, was also born with an intestinal blockage. Without surgery the child would die, but with surgery there was a good chance of the blockage being removed and the child living for 20 or 30 years. The child's parents refused to consent to the operation, genuinely believing that it was in the best interests of the child that the operation should not be performed and that she be allowed to die. The local authority made the child a ward of court and sought an order authorising the operation to be carried out. Ewbank J in the High Court refused to make the order. The local authority appealed.

*Held*: allowing the appeal and making the order, that the question for the court was whether it was in the best interests of the child that she should have the operation, and not whether the parents' wishes should be respected.

TEMPLEMAN LJ: . . . The question which this court has to determine is whether it is in the interests of this child to be allowed to die within the next week or to have the operation in which case if she lives she will be a mongoloid child, but no one can say to what extent her mental or physical defects will be apparent. No one can say whether she will suffer or whether she will be happy in part. On the one hand the probability is that she will not be a cabbage as it is called when people's faculties are entirely destroyed. On the other hand it is certain that she will be very severely mentally and physically handicapped.

On behalf of the parents [Counsel] has submitted very movingly, if I may say so, that this is a case where nature has made its own arrangements to terminate a life which would not be fruitful and nature should not be interfered with. He has also submitted that in this kind of decision the views of responsible and caring parents, as these are, should be respected and that their decision that it is better for the child to be allowed to die should be respected. Fortunately or unfortunately, in this particular case the decision no longer lies with the parents or with the doctors, but lies with the court. It is a decision which of course must be made in the light of the evidence and views expressed by the parents and the doctors, but at the end of the day it devolves on this court in this particular instance to decide whether the life of this child is demonstrably going to be so awful that in effect the child must be condemned to die, or whether the life of this child is still so imponderable that it would be wrong for her to be condemned to die. There may be cases, I know not, of severe proved damage where the future is so certain and where the life of the child is so bound to be full of pain and suffering that the court might be driven to a different conclusion, but in the present case the choice which lies before the court is this: whether to allow an operation to take place which may result in the child living for 20 or 30 years as a mongoloid or whether (and I think this must be brutally the result) to terminate the life of a mongoloid child because she also has an intestinal complaint. Faced with that choice I have no doubt that it is the duty of this court to decide that the child must live. The judge was much affected by the reasons given by the parents and came to the conclusion that their wishes ought to be respected. In my judgment he erred in that the duty of the court is to decide whether it is in the interests of the child that an operation should take place. The evidence in this case only goes to show that if the operation takes place and is successful then the child may live the normal span of a mongoloid child with the handicaps and defects and life of a mongol child, and it is not for this court to say that life of that description ought to be extinguished.

Accordingly the appeal must be allowed and the local authority must be authorised themselves to authorise and direct the operation to be carried out on the little girl.

*Notes and questions*
1. In *Re T (A Minor) (Wardship: Medical Treatment)* [1996] *The Times*, 28 October, a baby suffered from a life-threatening liver defect and without a transplant would not live beyond the age of two and a half. Although the chances of the transplant's success were good, the parents did not wish the operation to take place. The question for the Court of Appeal was whether it should overrule the parents' wishes. The Court of Appeal allowed the mother's appeal against the decision of Connell J in the Family Division, whereby he directed that the mother present the baby at a hospital for assessment for transplant surgery, holding that Connell J did not weigh in the balance the reasons which a reasonable parent might have for not wishing the transplant to take place. If the welfare of the child is the paramount consideration, not the wishes of parents, why did the Court of Appeal decide as it did? Is there a danger in the court making such a decision? Should such decisions be left to doctors or an ethics committee rather than to judges?
2. See also *Re R (A Minor) (Blood Transfusion)* [1993] 2 FLR 757, FD, where the parents, who were Jehovah's Witnesses, refused to consent to their 10-month-old daughter receiving medical treatment for her leukaemia. Booth J made a specific issue order that the child should receive blood products in any imminently life-threatening situation without parental consent. How is this situation any different from that in *Re T supra*?

(For parental autonomy and State intervention by local authorities, see Chapter 10.)

## 8.2 PARENTAL RESPONSIBILITY

### 8.2.1 Parental responsibility: a key concept in the Children Act 1989

Parental responsibility, rather than rights, is the concept used in the CA 1989. The Law Commission in its Reports on *Illegitimacy* and *Guardianship and Custody* provided arguments in favour of the need for responsibility, not rights.

### Law Commission, *Report on Guardianship and Custody*, Law Com No. 172 London: HMSO, 1988

2.4   Scattered throughout the statute book at present are such terms as 'parental rights and duties' or the 'powers and duties', or the 'rights and authority' of a parent. However, in our first Report on Illegitimacy [Law Com No. 118, 1982, para. 4.18], we expressed the view that 'to talk of parental "rights" is not only inaccurate as a matter of juristic analysis but also a misleading use of ordinary language.' The House of Lords, in *Gillick* v *West Norfolk and Wisbech Area Health Authority* [[1986] AC 112, see Chapter 7] has held that the powers which parents have to control or make decisions for their children are simply the necessary concomitant of their parental duties. To refer to the concept of 'right' in the relationship between parent and child is therefore likely to produce confusion, as that case itself demonstrated. As against third parties, parents clearly have a prior claim to look after or have contact with their child, but as the House of Lords has recently pointed out in *Re KD (A Minor) (Ward: Termination of Access)* [1988] AC 806, [1988] 1 All ER 577, HL, that claim will always be displaced if the interests of the child indicate to the contrary. The parental claim can be recognised in the rules governing the allocation of parental responsibilities, but the content of their status would be more accurately reflected if a new concept of 'parental responsibility' were to replace the ambiguous and confusing terms used at present. Such a change would make little difference in substance but it would reflect the everyday reality of being a parent and emphasise the responsibilities of all who are in that position. . . .
2.5   One further advantage is that the same concept could then be employed to define the status of local authorities when children have been compulsorily committed to their care. The reports of the inquiries into the deaths of Jasmine Beckford and Tyra Henry indicate how helpful it would be in emphasising the continuing parental responsibility of the local authority even if the child has been allowed to live at home.

*Question*
Do you agree with the words in para. 2.4 above that '[s]uch a change would make little difference in substance but it would reflect the everyday reality of being a parent'?

## CHILDREN ACT 1989

**2.   Parental responsibility for children**
   (1)   Where a child's father and mother were married to each other at the time of his birth, they shall each have parental responsibility for the child.
   (2)   Where a child's father and mother were not married to each other at the time of his birth—
      (a)   the mother shall have parental responsibility for the child;
      (b)   the father shall not have parental responsibility for the child, unless he acquires it in accordance with the provisions of this Act.
      . . .

### 3. Meaning of 'parental responsibility'

(1) In this Act 'parental responsibility' means all the rights, duties, powers, responsibilities and authority which by law a parent of a child has in relation to the child and his property.

. . .

## Department of Health, *Introduction to the Children Act 1989*
### London: HMSO, 1989

1.4   The Act uses the phrase *'parental responsibility'* to sum up the collection of duties, rights and authority which a parent has in respect to his child. That choice of words emphasises that the duty to take care of the child and to raise him to moral, physical and emotional health is the fundamental task of parenthood and the only justification for the authority it confers.

1.5   The importance of parental responsibility is emphasised in the Act by the fact that not only is it unaffected by the separation of parents but even when courts make orders in private proceedings such as divorce, that responsibility continues and is limited only to the extent that any order settles certain concrete issues between the parties. That arrangement aims to emphasise that interventions by the courts where there is family breakdown should not be regarded as lessening the duty on both parents to continue to play a full part in the child's upbringing.

## Edwards, Susan, and Halpern, Ann, 'Parental Responsibility — An Instrument of Social Policy'
### [1992] Fam Law 113

**Introduction**
The concept of parental responsibility is a central theme underpinning much of recent legislation affecting children's welfare, financial support and the control of criminality. On one level the idea of parental responsibility functions to create a more cohesive family form where parents take more responsibility for the emotional and financial care, discipline and control of their children. Whilst any move towards making parents more responsible for child welfare cannot on the surface be criticised, we . . . argue that this concept is being used as a mechanism to legitimate the withdrawal of the State from financial responsibility to families and also as an ideological mechanism to restructure thinking on family stability and juvenile delinquency. In place of the benevolent State the hope is that parents will be able to provide both financial support and, through financial liability, also take on a 'policing' function. . . .

**The Child Support Act 1991**
The concept of parental responsibility has been used as the justification for recouping public expenditure on the support of children in single-parent families, a principle endorsed by the Lord Chancellor, when he said on the publication of the White Paper, *Children Come First* that '. . . its aim is to give priority to the welfare of children and to highlight their parents' responsibility for ensuring it. . . . The payment of child maintenance is one important way in which parents fulfil those responsibilities' . . . .

In emphasising the financial responsibility of parents in this Act, the aspects of responsibility which relate more to emotional and physical security are ignored. There is still an intense debate about ensuring that children know both their parents and deciding how this can best be assured. Fathers who pay maintenance are generally more likely to insist on keeping contact with their children. Fathers who failed to pay have largely been those who have lost contact with their children. The requirement that absent fathers will have to pay under this new scheme may well encourage them to keep contact with their children. How this will turn out in practice, given that often demand will be met with denial, has yet to be considered.

[The authors, having considered parental responsibility under the Criminal Justice Act 1991, conclude: . . .]

**Conclusion**

It is apparent that we understand parental responsibility in these specific legal provisions to contain three major but not always consistent or complementary threads. One thread is represented by a notion of responsibility which emphasises the emotional and psychological commitment parents owe to their children, whilst the second thread specifically emphasises the financial responsibility owed by parents to the State for the child, and the third blames parents for any failure to exercise parental responsibility which contributes to the delinquency of their children. Throughout, we have examined the way in which parental responsibility is used as a powerful instrument of social policy in shaping the family.

The legal requirement that parents honour their parental responsibility serves several functions and is predicated on certain ideologies involved in the provision of State welfare. First, it functions as a psychological device which assumes that any damage caused to children, either by commission or omission, is regarded, both in the public mind and internalised by individual parents themselves, as their own fault. Such psychological strategies have often been employed to bring about change in human conduct and also to foster a particular form of analysis of and explanation for human problems. These psychological devices have frequently been used to explain the causes of family breakdown which, it is argued, results from individual pathologies, bad genes and bad families, rather than from social or economic factors or from government policy.

Secondly, it functions so as to positively promote parental responsibility in the place of State responsibility when, previously, family and State co-existed as distinct and polarised approaches. The recent emphasis given to parental responsibility seems to be firmly supported by the fundamental principles of *laissez-faire* individualism and self-sufficiency, the twin guiding tenets of recent Conservative governments. There is also a financial imperative of reduction in State expenditure which results in the transference of financial liability on to the parent. In examining the concept of 'parental responsibility' in the Children Act 1989, John Eekelaar ((1991) JSWL 37) argues that what it represents is a reduction of State power and control over the family and a lessening of State intervention in the family. This is clearly the case in the context of the Children Act 1989. Yet it can equally well be argued that the psychological device of parental responsibility is used in cases where parents fail in their responsibility as a mechanism which allows the State to exercise greater control over the individual than before by more determinedly enforcing that responsibility. Such mechanisms are therefore designed to give the appearance of a new family, independent of the State, whilst for many the reality is more likely to be a new State, independent of the family.

*Notes and questions*

1. More than one person may have parental responsibility (CA 1989, s. 2(5)), which does not cease if someone else acquires it (s. 2(6)). Persons with parental responsibility may act independently of each other in meeting their responsibility, except where any statute requires the consent of more than one person in a matter affecting the child (s. 2(7)). A person

with parental responsibility is not entitled to act incompatibly with any order made under the CA 1989 (s. 2(8)). Parental responsibility may not be surrendered or transferred, but a person with such responsibility may delegate parental responsibility to some other person whether or not that person has parental responsibility; but such delegation does not exclude the person delegating responsibility from being liable for any failure to meet any part of his or her parental responsibility (s. 2(9), (10) and (11)).

2. Eekelaar ('Parental Responsibility, State of Nature or Nature of the State?' [1991] JSWL 37) considers that parental responsibility represents two ideas ('one that parents must behave dutifully towards their children; the other, that responsibility for child care belongs to parents, not the state') and demonstrates how the second idea came to replace the first during the development of the CA 1989. He asks whether the promotion of the second sort of responsibility will encourage parents to act more responsibly. What do you think? Are there any dangers in the second sort of responsibility prevailing? What sort of responsibility is 'parental responsibility'? Are parental duties different from parental responsibilities? If so, how?

3. Parental responsibility, rather than rights, was the concept recommended by the Committee of Ministers of the Council of Europe (Recommendation No. R(84)4, 28 February 1984).

### 8.2.2 Parental responsibility and unmarried fathers

### CHILDREN ACT 1989

**4. Acquisition of parental responsibility by father**
(1)  Where a child's father and mother were not married to each other at the time of his birth—
(a)  the court may, on the application of the father, order that he shall have parental responsibility for the child; or
(b)  the father and mother may by agreement ('a parental responsibility agreement') provide for the father to have parental responsibility for the child.
(2)  . . .
(3)  Subject to section 12(4), an order under subsection (1)(a), or a parental responsibility agreement, may only be brought to an end by an order of the court made on the application—
(a)  of any person who has parental responsibility for the child; or
(b)  with leave of the court, of the child himself.
(4)  The court may only grant leave under subsection (3)(b) if it is satisfied that the child has sufficient understanding to make the proposed application.

*Notes*
1.  A parental responsibility agreement is effective only if made on a prescribed form and recorded in the Principal Registry of the Family Division of the High Court (see CA 1989, s. 4(2)).
2.  A parental rights order may be made even though such rights are not enforceable or exerciseable (*Re C (Minors) (Parental Rights)* [1992] 1 FLR 1, CA).

3.   For cases where parental responsibility orders were refused because of the behaviour of the unmarried father, see *Re T (A Minor) (Parental Responsibility: Contact)* [1993] 2 FLR 450, CA, and *Re G (A Minor) (Parental Responsibility Order)* [1994] 1 FLR 504, CA.

An excellent survey of the law on acquiring parental responsibility under s. 4 by court order is to be found in the judgment of Wall LJ in the following case.

**Re S (A Minor) (Parental Responsibility)**
[1995] 2 FLR 648
Court of Appeal

*Facts*: After the breakdown of her parents' cohabiting relationship, the child (aged about 7 at the time of the hearing) remained with her mother in the former home with the father paying for the mortgage and for maintenance and nursery fees for the child. Contact between the father and the child was severed by the mother after he was convicted for offences of possession of obscene literature, but was resumed due to the child's distress and behaviour and eventually developed into staying contact. The father applied for a parental responsibility order which the mother opposed because of his unreliability about money and his criminal conviction. The judge refused the application because of the conviction, holding that for the father to have the power to interfere with present arrangements would be contrary to the child's best interests. The father appealed.
*Held*: allowing the appeal, that there was no reason to refuse the order.

WALL LJ: . . . At the risk of being tedious, it may be necessary for me to recite some of the principles on which these applications ought to be judged. The case of *D v Hereford and Worcester County Council* [1991] Fam 14, [1991] 1 FLR 205 was, I believe, the first of this kind of application and it happened to come before me. I endeavoured to explain my understanding of the precursor to s. 4 of the Children Act, namely s. 4 of the Family Law Reform Act 1987 which gave the power to grant parental rights, as it was phrased, in the language of the day. I endeavoured to explain how the Law Commission had wrestled over a number of years and in a number of reports, with the dilemmas that the question posed seen against the background that it was right and proper in this day and age to sweep aside those distinctions between legitimacy and illegitimacy which bore unfavourably upon the children.

The logic would have suggested that one should also sweep away any disability that remained vested in the father of the illegitimate child. Since science could conclusively determine the fact of fatherhood the concept of filius nullius was no longer one which could command respect. But there are obvious difficulties, which the Law Commission recognised, in giving a total equality of status to the father who has married the mother, and to the putative father who had not. At its most emotive, but none the less pertinent point of distinction it would cause offence to right-thinking people that the rapist should claim parental rights or parental responsibilities over the child which that criminal act produced. That led to the Commission entertaining the debate as to whether or not they should do what I believe may have been done in Scotland, that is to say, to confer parental responsibility on the father but with a right upon the mother to apply to disenfranchise him. [The Children (Scotland) Act 1995 does not in fact contain such a provision, but follows the English approach]. They grappled with the concept of defining an irresponsible father who should not be afforded this status and eventually they left it to the court to decide. In the language of the Act, s. 4 provides that:

> Where a child's father and mother were not married to each other at the time of his birth—
> (a)   the court may, on the application of the father, order that he shall have parental responsibility for the child; . . .

No guidance is given as to how the court should approach the exercise of that broad discretion given to it. My puny efforts to provide that guidance in the case of *D* v *Hereford and Worcester* were distilled and approved by the Court of Appeal in the first important case on this subject. It is *Re H (Minors) (Local Authority: Parental Rights) (No. 3)* [1991] Fam 151, sub nom *Re H (Illegitimate Children: Father: Parental Rights) (No. 2)* [1991] 1 FLR 214. Balcombe LJ described the effect of the law and the reforms that the Family Law Reform Act 1987 had made in these terms: the whole purpose of the 1977 Act, which as was stated in its preamble was to reform the law relating to the consequences of birth outside marriage, had as its undoubted aim in an *appropriate* case to equate the position of the father of the child born out of wedlock to that of the father of a legitimate child.

He suggested, and most helpfully, this test at pp. 158D and 218F respectively:

> In considering whether to make an order under s. 4 of the 1987 Act, the court will have to take into account a number of factors of which the following will undoubtedly be material (although there may well be others, as the list is not intended to be exhaustive):
>
> (1)   the degree of commitment which the father has shown towards the child;
> (2)   the degree of attachment which exists between the father and the child; and
> (3)   the reasons of the father for applying for the order.

There followed the case of *Re C (Minors) (Parental Rights)* [1992] 1 FLR 1. This is another judgment often cited for the eloquent words of Waite J, as he then was. He was there dealing with the problem of how parental rights were to be enforced and what would happen if it was not possible fully to enforce them. He said at p. 3F:

> Given, therefore, that the prospective enforceability of parental rights is a relevant consideration for a judge deciding whether or not to grant them, there is, in our judgment, nothing in the Act to suggest that it should be an overriding consideration. It would be quite wrong, in our view, to assume that just because few or none of the parental rights happen to be enforceable under conditions prevailing at the date of the application, it would necessarily follow as a matter of course that a PRO [parental rights order] would be refused. That can be illustrated by looking — as the legislation clearly requires one to look — at the position of a lawful father in analogous circumstances. Conditions may arise (for example in cases of mental illness) where a married father has, regretfully, to be ordered, in effect, to step out of his children's lives altogether. In such a case, his legal status as a parent remains wholly unaffected, and he retains all his rights in law, although none of them may be exercisable in practice. This does not mean that his parental status becomes a dead letter or a mere paper title. It will have real and tangible value, not only as

something he can cherish for the sake of his own peace of mind, but also as a status carrying with it rights in waiting, which it may be possible to call into play when circumstances change with the passage of time. It is not difficult to imagine situations in which similar considerations would apply in the case of a natural father. Though existing circumstances may demand that his children see or hear nothing of him, and that he should have no influence upon the course of their lives for the time being, their welfare may require that if circumstances change he should be reintroduced as a presence, or at least as an influence, in their lives. In such a case a PRO, notwithstanding that only a few or even none of the rights under it may currently be exercisable, may be of value to him and also of potential value to the children.

He set out, later at p. 8G, his test in similar terms to that of Balcombe LJ in these words:

> . . . was the association between the parties sufficiently enduring, and has the father by his conduct during and since the application shown sufficient commitment to the children, to justify giving the father a legal status equivalent to that which he would have enjoyed if the parties had been married, due attention being paid to the fact that a number of his parental rights would, if conferred on him by a PRO, be unenforceable under current conditions?

It is, therefore, important to observe the interrelation between the rights and the status and the exercise of those rights and, of course, the restrictions upon the exercise of those rights. *Re H (A Minor) (Parental Responsibility)* [1993] 1 FLR 484 was another case where, although contact had been denied yet the question posed by Waite J, in the passage I have just read, was answered affirmatively by the court and parental responsibility was granted. Waite J gave more guidance in *Re CB (A Minor) (Parental Responsibility Order)* [1993] 1 FLR 920, where he allowed an appeal from justices who fell into error in subordinating any independent assessment of the father's parental responsibility application on its merits to the demands of ensuring, in that case, the successful rehabilitation of the child to the mother which was so crucially important for that particular child. He said at p. 930B:

> Whether this natural father should or should not be given a status equivalent to that of a marital parent is one question. Whether this child should be the subject of a phased programme of rehabilitation to her mother is another. The two questions are not, of course, wholly irrelevant to each other, and each has to be answered according to the best interests of [the child] as the paramount consideration. They are, however, entirely separate and distinct questions, to be examined from quite different perspectives. By failing to appreciate that, the magistrates disabled themselves from giving a proper consideration to the merits of granting the father a lawful father's status here and now, regardless of what the future might be intended to hold for any eventual return of the child to her mother.

*Re T (A Minor) (Parental Responsibility: Contact)* [1993] 2 FLR 450 was one of the few cases where a refusal of the parental responsibility order was upheld. It is instructive to take some note of the facts of that particular case. There the mother and father separated during the mother's pregnancy. The cause of the separation was a totally violent assault by the father on the mother, so severe that he had to take her to hospital. He was utterly feckless in his payment of maintenance. He was a man of unbridled hostility, who head-butted the mother on another occasion when one of the few attempts to arrange contact dissolved into this violence. He abducted the little girl from the mother for a period of days, which was an act rightly described by my Lady, Butler-Sloss LJ, as cruel and callous behaviour in respect of a young child, with no thought for her welfare.

It is not surprising, in those circumstances, that the judge below, Ewbank J, found that he had no worthwhile part whatever to play in the life of this child and declined to afford him parental rights. Later Eastham J denied him all his contact and debarred him under s. 91(4) from making any further application. That gives a clue to the nature of the beast in that particular case.

Another case where parental responsibility was refused was *W v Ealing London Borough Council* [1993] 2 FLR 7888 in which my Lord, Simon Brown LJ, was a member of the court giving the judgment of the court. In that case the father's conduct was so outrageous that his attempt to apply for a residence order, in respect of the child in care, was dismissed without being heard on its merits. The application he made for parental responsibility was one which was also dismissed because at that stage the children were prepared for a termination of their contact to their parents, the introductions to their prospective adopters were imminent and to change that would have left the children in limbo and confused. The Court of Appeal found that, in truth (at p. 796C):

> . . . the only real reason he could have for making the application under the Children Act was the hope that he might thereby thwart the making of an adoption order.

That seems to me, as I understand that judgment, to strike at the heart of his bona fides and to the genuineness of his commitment to that child. The decision is wholly right, if I may respectfully say so.

In *Re G (A Minor) (Parental Responsibility Order)* [1994] 1 FLR 504, again a decision of the Court of Appeal, Balcombe LJ at p. 508A said this, endorsing observations of my Lady, Butler-Sloss LJ in *Re T*, which I have already referred to:

> . . . I am quite prepared to accept that the making of a parental responsibility order requires the judge to adopt the welfare principle as the paramount consideration. But having said that, I should add that, of course, it is well established by authority that, other things being equal, it is always to a child's welfare to know and, wherever possible, to have contact with both its parents, including the parent with whom it is not normally resident, if the parents have separated.
>
> Therefore, prima facie, it must necessarily also be for the child's benefit or welfare that it has an absent parent sufficiently concerned and interested to want to have a parental responsibility order. In other words, I approach this question on the basis that where you have a concerned although absent father, who fulfils the other test about which I spoke in *Re H*, namely having shown a degree of commitment towards the child, it being established that there is a degree of attachment between the father and the child, and that his reasons for applying for the order are not demonstrably improper or wrong, then prima facie it would be for the welfare of the child that such an order should be made.

The next in this long litany is a judgment of first instance, a judgment of Wilson J in *Re P (A Minor) (Parental Responsibility Order)* [1994] 1 FLR 578. There the justices had decided that a parental responsibility order might be used by the father to question aspects of the child's upbringing which would normally remain in the domain solely of the person with day-to-day care. As to that Wilson J said this at pp. 584G–585D:

It is important to be quite clear that an order for parental responsibility to the father does not give him a right to interfere in matters within the day-to-day management of the child's life.

. . .

It is to be noted that on any view an order for parental responsibility gives the father no power to override the decision of the mother, who already has such responsibility: in the event of disagreement between them on a specific issue relating to the child, the court will have to resolve it. If the father were to seek to misuse the rights given him under s. 4 such misuse could, as a second to last resort, be controlled by the court under a prohibited steps order against him and/or a specific issue order. The very last resort of all would presumably be the discharge of the parental responsibility order. But, on the evidence before the magistrates, and indeed on the basis of their conclusion as to the father's fitness to continue to care responsibly for the child during regular and extensive periods of contact in the future, there seems to be no basis for such extremely pessimistic hypotheses, which I mention only for the sake of completeness.

The final case is that *Re E (Parental Responsibility: Blood Tests)* [1995] 1 FLR 392. The Court of Appeal there held in the judgment of Balcombe LJ at pp. 398G–400C:

I would certainly approach any application for a parental responsibility order under the Children Act 1989 by a father who has shown the degree of attachment and commitment to his child as this father has shown to [the child] on the basis that such an order would be prima facie for the welfare of the child. I would require to be convinced by cogent evidence that the child's welfare would be adversely affected by the making of such an order.

. . .

It does seem to me that there was here no valid ground whatsoever for refusing the parental responsibility order, bearing in mind the approach which I believe is the correct one, namely that in a case such as the present, where there has been constant commitment by the father to [the child] since her birth; regular contact; and, I should add, financial provision made as well — although the precise amount of that is subsequently to be considered by the court, nevertheless there is no suggestion that the father has failed to make financial provision for [the child] — it must be prima facie in [the child's] welfare that a parental responsibility order be made in favour of this committed father, and certainly the matters which the judge referred to do not provide anything like the contra-indication which would be necessary, in my view, to show that such an order is contrary to her welfare.

I have engaged in this laborious review of the authorities because it is my increasing concern, both from the very fact that there are so many reported cases on this topic and from my experience when dealing with the innumerable appeals from justices to the Family Division, that applications under s. 4 have become one of these little growth industries born of misunderstanding. Misunderstanding arises from a failure to appreciate that, in essence, the granting of a parental responsibility order is the granting of status. It is unfortunate that the notion of 'parental responsibility' has still to be defined by s. 3 of the Children Act to mean '. . . all the rights, duties, powers, responsibilities and authority which by law a parent . . . has in relation to the child and his property', which gives outmoded pre-eminence to the 'rights' which are conferred. That it is unfortunate is demonstrated by the very fact that, when pressed in this case to define the nature ·and effect of the order which was so vigorously opposed, counsel for the mother was driven to say that her rooted objection was to the rights to which it would entitle the father and the power that it would give to him. That is a most unfortunate failure to appreciate the significant change that the Act has brought about where the emphasis is to move away from rights and to concentrate on responsibilities. She did not doubt that if by unhappy chance this child fell ill whilst she was abroad, his father, if then enjoying contact, would not deal responsibly with her welfare.

It would, therefore, be helpful if the mother could think calmly about the limited circumstances when the exercise of true parental responsibility is likely to be of practical significance. It is wrong to place undue and therefore false emphasis on the rights and duties and the powers comprised in 'parental responsibility' and not to concentrate on the fact that what is at issue is conferring upon a committed father the status of parenthood for which nature has already ordained that he must bear responsibility. There seems to me to be all too frequently a failure to appreciate that the wide exercise of s. 8 orders can control the abuse, if any, of the exercise of parental responsibility which is adverse to the welfare of the child. Those interferences with the day-to-day management of the child's life have nothing to do with whether or not this order should be allowed.

There is another important emphasis I would wish to make. I have heard, up and down the land, psychiatrists tell me how important it is that children grow up with good self-esteem and how much they need to have a favourable positive image of the absent parent. It seems to me important, therefore, wherever possible, to ensure that the law confers upon a committed father that stamp of approval, lest the child grow up with some belief that he is in some way disqualified from fulfilling his role and that the reason for the disqualification is something inherent which will be inherited by the child, making her struggle to find her own identity all the more fraught.

Trying, therefore, to apply those principles to this case, at the heart of it lies the finding by the judge that in terms of commitment, attachment and bone fides this father passed the test. She rightly stated that that was not the conclusive list of requirements, and she rightly had regard to the fact of his conviction. But it seems to me that however disreputable the conviction, it was not one which demonstrably and directly affected the child in her day-to-day life. . . .

In my judgment the judge has failed to appreciate that the scope to interfere, as Waite LJ and Wilson J have explained, is not material to the issue here, especially since there is, it seems, a paucity of evidence to justify that finding. Moreover, the judge, in looking at the contact, has failed to appreciate that the contact application had been before the court and no conditions of supervision were imposed upon the exercise of it by the father. The liability to increase proceedings and to unsettle the child arises not from the grant or refusal of parental responsibility and the conferring of the status on the father, but the mother's anxieties arising out of contact, and s. 8 and conditions that may be imposed under s. 11 deal with those difficulties. When the judge dealt with welfare she dealt with it in a way that leaves me uncertain how she, in fact, approached that important question. . . .

I find it difficult to see how the little child's freedom to invite her friends to her father's house is adverse to her best interests. I do not, I confess, understand what she finds to be adverse to the best interests in those arrangements and I fear she has wholly failed to appreciate the emphasis that Balcombe LJ placed upon children growing up in the knowledge that their father is committed enough to wish to have parental responsibility conferred upon him. Given the commitment, the attachment, the affection that is plain and uncontroverted in this case, it seems to me that this is, indeed, the case where the father, who has the burden of proof upon him, has abundantly satisfied it and where there is no cogent reason, and, in my judgment, little reason at all, for refusing the order which he seeks. I would therefore allow the appeal.

## Bainham, Andrew, 'The Privatisation of the Public Interest in Children'
### (1990) 53 MLR 206 at p. 219

. . . The attempt in the 1989 Act to distinguish between different fathers (i.e. married or unmarried) is a particularly glaring example of legislative discrimination, both between men and women and between different categories of men in their role as parents. . . . [T]he failure to assimilate the legal position of unmarried fathers with that of other parents is an impediment to the intended establishment of parenthood as a primary legal concept and to the abolition of legitimacy. . . .

## Eekelaar, John, 'Parental Responsibility — A New Legal Status?'
### (1996) 112 LQR 233

. . . The Re S cases were right . . . to hold that the grant of parental responsibility would not in itself give the fathers any greater rights against the mothers. However, whether the fathers would be encouraged by the orders to attempt to intermeddle (say, by trying to deal directly with the child's school) would be a question of fact, which neither trial court adequately addressed. It is suggested that this is an eminently sensible position. We are left, however, with the puzzle as to why a parental responsibility order should be important for an unmarried, absent, father who is not bent on intermeddling. Certainly, should the child be accommodated by a local authority, he will acquire the right to remove it (Children Act 1989, s. 20(7), (8)), and his consent will be necessary for its adoption, but these are rare events. If the child spends a good deal of time with him, he may often be in a practical position to make 'parental' decisions with respect to the child. But it is clear that parental responsibility may be granted even if contact is not: Re C (Minors: Parental Rights) [1992] 1 FLR 1; Re H (A Minor: Parental Responsibility) [1993] 1 FLR 484; Re G (A Minor: Parental Responsibility Order) [1994] 1 FLR 504. On one reading of Ward LJ's analysis, and following that of Butler-Sloss LJ, the order does little more than affirm the duties the father already owes to the child. But that seems a very weak version of the concept: why should a father invoke a legal procedure to confirm his existing responsibilities?

Ward LJ, however, added a further justification for granting parental responsibility.

I have heard, up and down the land, psychiatrists tell me how important it is that children grow up with good self-esteem, and how much they need to have a favourable positive image of the absent parent. It seems to me important, therefore, wherever possible, to ensure that the law confers upon a committed father that stamp of approval, lest the child grow up with some belief that he is in some way disqualified from fulfilling his role and that the reason for the disqualification is something inherent which will be inherited by the children, making her struggle to find her own identity all the more fraught.

Whether or not judicial approval of the moral character of the father has such effects on children, it is suggested that this passage hints at the true nature and purpose of the concept. Parental responsibility can best be understood as legal recognition of the *exercise* of social parenthood. It thus comprises a factual (recognition of a state of affairs) and a normative (giving the state of affairs the 'stamp of approval') element. It is conferred automatically on all mothers, and on all married fathers, because it is assumed that they will in fact exercise social parenthood, and that it is normally appropriate that they (in preference to other individuals, or the state) should do so. This assumption is not made in the case of unmarried fathers, partly because it is not clear how far they do exercise social parenthood and partly because of doubts as to whether it is always appropriate for them to do so. We do not know how valid these reservations are. Slightly over half of unmarried couples having a child are recorded as living at the same address when the child is born, and probably many fathers who are not living with the mother adopt a parental role. But although the reluctance to assume that unmarried fathers normally exercise social parenthood may be questioned, as long as the assumption is not made it is consistent with the concept of parental responsibility as a legitimated form of social parenthood that it should be withheld from them until its exercise (or potential exercise) and its appropriateness is demonstrated through their attachment and commitment to the child.

Naturally, the social parenthood a father who is living apart from a child can exercise is more limited than that of the other parent, but it is social parenthood nonetheless. In the cases where parental responsibility has been granted while contact is still denied, it is clear that the father's commitment and attachment have created the expectation that he will exercise a form of social parenthood later. So parental responsibility may be granted as a signal of approval of such actual or expected parental actions as can be *practically* exercised by the absent parent, subject to any judicial restraint. Parental responsibility may be described as a legal status, but it is one which, perhaps uniquely, for a large part consists in and is co-extensive with practical action.

*Note*
See also *Re S (A Minor) (Parental Responsibility: Contract)* [1995] 3 FCR 564.

*Questions*
1.   Does the fact that unmarried fathers have no automatic parental responsibility discriminate against them and their children? Does it make any difference that unmarried fathers, like married fathers, have a duty to pay child maintenance whether or not they have parental responsibility (see Chapter 9)? In *Re P (Terminating Parental Responsibility)* [1995] 1 FLR 1048, FD, an unmarried father was deprived of his parental responsibility because he had brutally injured his young child. Why should unmarried fathers be singled out in this way? Would it be a good idea to deprive other parents of their parental responsibility? If not, why not?
2.   Is it bizarre to define responsibilities in terms of rights?
3.   Did the House of Lords in *Gillick* say that parents have no rights?
4.   Have the following persons acted unlawfully: a chef who engages a schoolgirl as a waitress each night against her parents' wishes; a preacher at the local Baptist church who prepares the son of Roman Catholic parents for baptism; an aunt who accepts a child into her home against the wishes of the child's parents? What sort of parental right has been broken, if any? What sort of remedy is, or should be, available?

## 8.3  ESTABLISHING A CHILD'S PARENTAGE

In some cases it may be important to establish who is the child's parent, e.g., for the purposes of inheritance, or because a father wishes to obtain parental responsibility for or have contact with his child, or to establish whether a person has an obligation to pay maintenance. Although it is a rebuttable presumption of law that the mother's husband is her child's father (except in child support cases under the Child Support Act 1991) and entry of a particular man's name as the child's father in the register of births is *prima facie* evidence that he is the father (Births and Deaths Registration Act 1953, s. 34(2), developments in forensic science (particularly DNA profiling) have made it easier to establish parentage with certainty.

Certain legal procedures exist for determining parentage. Under s. 56 of the Family Law Act (FLA) 1986 the court has jurisdiction to make a declaration of paternity or legitimacy, and under s. 20(1) of the Family Law Reform (FLRA) 1969, the court in any civil proceedings may direct that a blood test be carried out, whether or not an application has been made for such a test. Although the court may in the exercise of its discretion under s. 20(1) refuse a blood test (e.g., because it is contrary to the child's best interests or because it may destabilise the family unit), the court generally considers that a child's interests are best served by knowing the truth. Directions under s. 20(1) for a blood test are often made in the context of child support as many fathers deny paternity in order to escape paying maintenance under the Child Support Act (CSA) 1991 (see 9.5.1.1). Where an absent father denies parentage for the purposes of child support, the DSS or the person with care may apply to the court for a declaration as to whether or not the alleged parent is the child's parent (CSA 1991, s. 27) and the court under FLRA 1969, s. 20(1) may order a blood test.

In the following case the applicant wished to have contact with the child and claimed that he, not the mother's husband, was the natural father of the child.

### Re H (Paternity: Blood Test)
[1996] 2 FLR 65
Court of Appeal

*Facts*: The mother had had a sexual relationship with Mr B and with her husband. A child was born, and his birth was registered in the husband's name. A month after the child's birth Mr B applied *inter alia* for contact and, if paternity was disputed, for a blood test for DNA profiling. Despite the mother's opposition, the judge made a direction that blood samples be provided to establish paternity. The mother appealed.

*Held*: dismissing the appeal, for the reasons given in the following judgment.

WARD LJ: . . .The following issues arise in this appeal:

(1) Is refusal to undergo blood testing determinative of the application for a direction under s. 20(1) of the Family Law Reform Act 1969?

(2) Can an inference adverse to the refusing party be drawn only if refusal is made after the court has directed the use of blood testing?

(3) How does the child's welfare influence the decision?

(4) How do the prospects of success in the proceedings influence the decision?

(5) What are this child's best interests?

*(1)   Is the refusal determinative?*
In *Re F (A Minor) (Blood Tests: Parental Rights), sub nom Re F (A Minor: Paternity Test)* [[1993] Fam 314] the Court of Appeal posed the question but may not have given a clear answer. In *Re G (A Minor) (Blood Test)* [[1994] 1 FLR 495] Mr Michael Horowitz QC sitting as a deputy judge of the High Court answered the question, 'No'; but in *Re CB (A Minor) (Blood Tests)* [[1994] 2 FLR 762] Wall J said, 'Yes'. His Honour Judge Coningsby QC declined to follow Wall J. Did he misdirect himself? The answer necessitates a somewhat semantic review of the authorities.

The Family Law Reform Act 1969 was passed after the Commission's Report No. 16 on *Blood Tests and the Proof of Paternity in Civil Proceedings. . . .*

The scheme of the Act is as follows:

**20.   Power of court to require use of blood tests**
(1)   In any civil proceedings in which the paternity of any person falls to be determined by the court hearing the proceedings, the court may on an application by any party to the proceedings, give a direction for the use of blood tests to ascertain whether such tests show that a party to proceedings is or is not thereby excluded from being the father of that person . . .

**21.   Consents etc required for taking of blood samples**
(1)   Subject to the provisions of subsections (3) and (4) of this section, a blood sample which is required to be taken from any person for the purpose of giving effect to a direction under section 20 of this Act shall not be taken from that person except with his consent.

. . .

(3)   A blood sample may be taken from a person under the age of sixteen years . . . if the person who has the care and control of him consents.

**23.   Failure to comply with directions for taking blood tests**
(1)   Where a court gives a direction under section 20 of this Act and any person fails to take any step required of him for the purpose of giving effect to the direction, the court may draw such inferences, if any, from that fact as appear proper in the circumstances.

. . .

[After referring to *S v McC (otherwise S) and M (DS Intervener), W v W* [1972] AC 24, HL, and *Re F, supra,* his Lordship continued:]

Section 23(1) expressly provides that indirect means, namely, the ability to draw such inference as may be proper from the refusal to take any step required of the party for the purpose of giving effect to the court's direction.

I conclude, therefore, that whereas refusal is a factor to take into account (and, for example, in the case of a haemophiliac, it may be a very powerful factor), it cannot be determinative of the application and I disagree with Wall J's conclusion in *Re CB* at [1994] 2 FLR 762, 773H. In my judgment his Honour Judge Coningsby QC did not misdirect himself.

*(2) Can an inference be drawn only if the refusal to give blood samples is made after the court's direction?*
[Counsel for the applicant] supports the judge's conclusion that, 'because of the of the statutory provision it must be only in the circumstances in which an adverse inference may be drawn as laid down in the Act that any such inference can be drawn and this cannot happen outside the Act'. I see the force of that and was at first inclined to accept the submission thatif there is a statutory scheme, then the statutory scheme is the only operative scheme. [Counsel for the applicant] submitted that the Act permitted an inference to be drawn which until then the court had not been able to do. I do not agree that this introduced a change to the law of evidence. In *Re L (An Infant)* [1968] P 119, 159 Lord Denning MR had said:

> If an adult unreasonably refuses to have a blood test, or to allow a child to have one, I think it is open to the court in any civil proceedings . . . to treat his refusal as evidence against him, and may draw an inference therefrom adverse to him. This is simply common sense.

That common sense drove Wall J to a similar conclusion in *Re CB*.
Within the criminal law a refusal without reasonable excuse to supply hair samples for scientific examination has been held capable of amounting to corroboration. In *R v Smith (Robert William)* (1985) 81 Cr App R 286 the court said at 292:

> . . . we have come to the conclusion that the . . . judge was entitled to leave the appellant's refusal to give the sample, and the circumstance refusal, as material which was capable of corroborating the evidence of the accomplice. . . .
> . . .

The question seems to me to be not so much whether the court is entitled to draw an adverse inference but what, if any, inference can be drawn from a refusal. . . .
It should be remembered that at that time blood testing served only to exclude paternity: it did not establish it. It seems to me that a refusal to comply after the solemnity of the court's decision is more eloquent testimony of an attempt at hiding a truth than intransigent objection made as a forensic tactic. Science has now advanced. The whole truth can now be known. As Waite LJ said in *Re A (A Minor) (Paternity: Refusal of Blood Test)* [1994] 2 FLR 463, 473B:

> Against that background of law and scientific advance, it seems to me to follow, both in justice and in common sense, that if a mother makes a claim against one of the possible fathers, and he chooses to exercise his right not to submit to be tested, the inference that he is the father of the child should be virtually inescapable. He would certainly have to very clear and cogent reasons for this refusal to be tested — reasons which it would be just and fair and reasonable for him to be allowed to maintain.

Although that was a case of a refusal being made after a direction had been given, I, like Wall J, 'see no intellectual difference between situations'. Common sense seems to me to dictate that if the truth can be established with certainty, a refusal to produce the certainty justifies some inference that the refusal is made to hide the truth, even if the inference is not as strong as when the court's direction is flouted.
Although, therefore, his Honour Judge Coningsby QC was wrong, I do not see this to be such a fundamental misdirection as ineluctably to undermine his decision. It is not enough by itself to allow the appeal.

*(3)   How do considerations of the child's welfare influence the decision?*
The judge correctly directed himself that he should 'refuse the test if satisfied it would
be against the child's interests to order it'. This is wholly in accordance with *S* v *McC.*
There Lord Reid said at [1972] AC 24, 45D:

> I would, therefore, hold that the court ought to permit a blood test of a young child
> to be taken unless satisfied that that would be against the child's interests.

Lord Hodson said at 58G:

> The court in ordering a blood test in the case of an infant has, of course, a discretion
> and may make or refuse an order for a test in the exercise of its discretion, but the
> interests of other persons than the infant are involved in ordinary litigation. The
> infant needs protection but that is no justification for making his rights superior to
> those of others.

It is clear, therefore, that whereas welfare is the paramount consideration in deciding
the applications for parental responsibility and contact orders, welfare does not
dominate this decision.

*(4)   How do the prospects of success in the proceedings influence the decision?*
In *Re F* it was held at [1993] Fam 314, 320A and [1993] 1 FLR 598, 603C
respectively that:

> If the probable outcome of those proceedings will be the same whoever may be the
> natural father of E, then there can be no point in exposing the possible disadvan-
> tages of a blood test.

The speeches in *S* v *McC* in the House of Lords seem to take a somewhat different
view. Lord MacDermott, at [1972] AC 24, 48E, says:

> . . . if the court had reason to believe that the application for a blood test was of a
> fishing nature, designed for some ulterior motive to call in question the legitimacy,
> otherwise unimpeached, of a child who had enjoyed a legitimate status, it may well
> be that the court, acting under its protective rather than its ancillary jurisdiction,
> would be justified in refusing the application. I need not, however, pursue such
> instances as they do not arise on these appeals.

. . .

Reading those authorities together, it seems to me that the correct approach must
be:
  (1)   The paternity issue must be judged as a free-standing application entitled to
consideration on its own.
  (2)   The outcome of the proceedings in which the paternity issue has been raised,
insofar as it bears on the welfare of child, must be taken into account.
  (3)   Any gain to the child from preventing any disturbance to his security must be
balanced against the loss to him of the certainty of who he is.
  (4)   The terms of s. 10(4) of the Children Act 1989 are explicit in giving a parent
a right to apply for contact because they provide:

> The following persons *are entitled to apply* to the court for any section 8 order with
> respect to a child—
>   (a)   any parent . . . of the child; . . .

There is no statutory justification for transforming the paternity issue into a disguised application for leave to apply and judging the paternity issue by the criteria set out in s. 10(9).

(5) Accordingly, whilst the outcome of the s. 8 proceedings and the risk of disruption to the child's life both by the continuance of the paternity issue as well as the pursuit of the s. 8 order are obviously factors which impinge on the child's welfare, they are not, in my judgment, determinative of the blood-testing question.

In this case the judge's conclusion was that 'it would be rather unlikely that the court would make an order for contact'. That is a conclusion he was plainly entitled to reach, and one which I would support. He did not however, expressly deal with the parental responsibility order. We were told from the Bar that both counsel treated them as standing or falling together. Whilst that may or may not be a correct view of this case, parental responsibility orders and contact orders embrace quite different concepts. The parental responsibility order grants the status of paternity but it does not deal with the actual exercise of the parental responsibility there by conferred onto the father: see *Re S (A Minor) (Parental Responsibility)* [1995] 2 FLR 648. Features of this case are that at one time the mother undoubtedly intended to make her future life with the applicant and the judge found him to have 'quite a strong case for wanting to play a part in the life of this child'. If that is the true measure of his commitment, if his reasons for making the application are genuine, and if the child has a right to know who his father is, the application for parental responsibility may not be as hopeless as his case for contact.

*(5)    What are the child's best interests?*

The mother submits that 'pursuing contact would be to destabilise her own marriage which has only recently been put together again to the disadvantage of the child'. [Counsel for the mother] submits accordingly that the case is indistinguishable from *Re F*.

I do not agree. The argument is of course similar and what won the day in that case undoubtedly was 'the interests of the child not to be disturbed in its present status or its position as a child of, or residence in, the family of [Mr and Mrs F] in the particular circumstances of this case' — see his Honour Judge Callman's judgment at [1993] Fam 314, 319 and [1993] 1 FLR 598, 603. It is seldom useful in a case which depends on the exercise of judicial discretion to attempt to draw factual similarities between cases. The report facts of *Re F* are sparse and I am totally unpersuaded that there is such a similarity between them as to compel the same conclusion. . . .

. . . In my judgment every child has a right to know the truth unless his welfare clearly justifies the cover-up. The right to know is acknowledged in the UN Convention on the Rights of the Child 1989 (Cm 1976) which has been ratified by the UK and in particular Art. 7 which provides 'that a child has, as far as possible, the right to know and be cared for by his or her parents'. In *Re F* the putative father submitted that the child's welfare included her right to know under this Article. Balcombe LJ said at [1993] Fam 314, 321A and [1993] 1 FLR 598, 604C respectively:

> Whether or not Mr B is included in this definition of a parent within the meaning of this article, it is not in fact possible for E to be cared for by both her parents (if Mr B is such). No family unit exists, or has ever existed, between Mr B and Mrs F, and if Mr B were able to assert his claims to have a share in E's upbringing it would inevitably risk damaging her right to be cared for by her mother, Mrs F.

That passage concentrates on the child's right to be cared for by his or her parents. I do not read it as refuting what to me seems the clear intent of the Article that there are two separate rights, the one to know, and the other to be cared for by, one's parents. As Balcombe LJ has himself observed in *Re G (A Minor) (Parental Responsibility Order)* [1994] 1 FLR 504, 508B:

> . . . it is well established by authority that, other things being equal, it is always to a child's welfare to know and, wherever possible, to have contact with both its parents, including the parent with whom it is not normally resident, if the parents have separated.

. . . This is the whole tenor of the speeches in *S v McC* in the House of Lords. Lord Reid (and Lord Guest) said at [1972] AC 24, 45D:

> The court must protect the child, but it is not really protecting the child to ban a blood test on some vague and shadowy conjecture that it may turn out to be to its disadvantage: it may equally well turn out to be for its advantage or at least do it no harm.

. . . Given the real risk bordering on inevitability that H will at some time question his paternity, then I do not see how this case is not concluded by the unassailable wisdom expressed by Lord Hodson in *S v McC* at 57H:

> The interests of justice in the abstract are best served by the ascertainment of the truth and there must be few cases where the interests of children can be shown to be best served by the suppression of truth.

If, as she should, this mother is to bring up her children to believe in and to act by the maxim, which it is her duty to teach them at her knee, that honesty is the best policy, then she should not sabotage that lesson by living a lie.
. . . If the child has the right to know, then the sooner it is told the better. The issue of biological parentage should be divorced from psychological parentage. Acknowledging Mr B's parental responsibility should not dent Mr H's social responsibility for a child whom he is so admirably prepared to care for and love irrespective of whether or not he is the father. If the cracks in the H marriage are so wide that they will be rent asunder by the truth then the piece of paper which dismisses the application hardly seems adhesive enough to bind them together.
. . . If H grows up knowing the truth, that will not undermine his attachment to his father-figure and he will cope with knowing he has two fathers. Better that than a time bomb ticking away.

*(6) Conclusions*
The judge concluded that it was not within his power to prevent this father pursuing his application. I agree. Short of striking out the applications for being frivolous and vexatious or an abuse of the process of the court (and assuming there is the power, this is not a striking out case on the findings of the judge) the proceedings have to be heard.
. . .
Accordingly I would dismiss the appeal, but, for the technical reasons I have indicated, the order should be varied and the following direction substituted: . . .

*Note and questions*
In *Re F (A Minor: Paternity Test)* [1993] 1 FLR 598, CA, a case with similar facts, the Court of Appeal exercising its discretion under FLRA 1969, s. 20(1), refused to order that blood tests be carried out to establish the child's paternity on the grounds, *inter alia*, that it would not order a blood

test against the will of a parent who had sole parental responsibility for the child since birth and where it would disturb the stability of the family relationship (see Fortin, J., 'Re F: "The Goosberry Bush Approach"' (1994) 57 MLR 296). Do you think the decision in Re F was justifiable when art. 7 of the UN Convention on the Rights of the Child 1989 provides that a child, as far as possible, has a right to know who his or her parents are? Do you prefer the decision in Re H, supra?

*Further reading*
Bainham, A., 'When is a Parent not a Parent? Reflections on the Unmarried Father and his Child in English Law' (1989) 3 IJL&F 208.
Barton, C., and Douglas, G., *Law and Parenthood*, London: Butterworths, 1995.
Deech, R., 'The Rights of Fathers: Social and Biological Concepts of Parenthood', in Eekelaar, J., and Šarčević, P. (eds), *Parenthood and Modern Society: Legal and Social Issues for the Twenty-First Century*, Dordrecht: Martinus Nijhoff, 1993, Chapter 2.
Douglas, G., *Law, Fertility and Reproduction*, London: Sweet & Maxwell, 1991.
Douglas, G., 'The Intention to be a Parent and the Making of Mothers' (1994) 57 MLR 636.
Douglas, G., and Lowe, N., 'Becoming a Parent in English Law' (1992) 108 LQR 414.
Eekelaar, J., 'What are Parental Rights?' (1973) 89 LQR 210.
Eekelaar, J., 'The Eclipse of Parental Rights' (1986) 102 LQR 4.
Eekelaar, J., 'Are Parents Morally Obliged to Care for their Children?' (1991) 11 *Oxford J Legal Stud* 51.
Eekelaar, J., and Šarčević, P. (eds), *Parenthood and Modern Society: Legal and Social Issues for the Twenty-First Century*, Dordrecht: Martinus Nijhoff, 1993.
Grand, A., 'What is This Thing called Parental Responsibility?' [1994] Fam Law 586.
Hall, J., 'The Waning of Parental Rights' [1972B] CLJ 248.
Kaganas, F., 'Responsible or Feckless Fathers? Re S (Parental Responsibility)' [1996] 8 CFLQ 165.
McCall Smith, A., 'Is Anything Left of Parental Rights?' in Sutherland, E., and McCall Smith, A. (eds), *Family Rights: Family Law and Medical Advance*, Edinburgh: University Press, 1990.
Montgomery, J., 'Children as Property' (1988) 51 MLR 323.
Morgan, D., 'A Surrogacy Issue: Who is the Other Mother?' (1994) 8 IJL&F 386.

# 9 CHILDREN ON FAMILY BREAKDOWN

This chapter deals with children on the breakdown of their parents' relationship, whether their parents are married or unmarried. It considers the trauma of divorce and separation, residence and contact arrangements for children, and financial provision for children.

## 9.1 THE TRAUMA OF DIVORCE AND SEPARATION

### Hewitt, Patricia, 'Family Values'
[1994] Fam Law 160

. . .

*The Children*
Cohabitation, divorce, remarriage and step-parenting will not go away, because adults do not want them to go away, but what may be good for adults is not necessarily good for children, and the evidence is quite clear. The absence in the home of a second parent, usually the father, condemns the majority of lone parents and their children to low incomes. As a result of that economic deprivation, the children of lone parents, on average, tend to do less well at school and subsequently than the children of two-parent families. There are many steps which could and should be taken to enable lone parent and other low-income families to make a better living for themselves. But the emotional difficulties which children face in rapidly changing family circumstances must be stressed.

Children, and their parents, urgently need a legal framework which promotes conciliation rather than conflict. A divorce law that encourages parents to think and say the worst about each other, and to fight it out in the courts, makes the price of divorce even higher for children. The work of National Family Mediation and others is invaluable, not least because it provides an alternative model for the resolution of disputes between couples — a model which could and should be used as the basis for divorce law reform. For children themselves, one of the great benefits of mediation and conciliation is that it may help the parents arrive at an understanding that where there are children there can be no 'clean break' — that children need both parents, even if the parents no longer need each other. The skills of mediation and conciliation must be available far more widely than at the point of separation or divorce. . . .

## The Fathers

Many children are having problems with their fathers, rather than their mothers. There is an urgent need to shift the focus of the family debate away from mothers and towards fathers. Surveys and child developmental psychology show that children need 'good enough fathers' as well as 'good enough mothers'. What is a 'good enough father' in the 1990s? Clearly, with women already making up half the workforce, a 'good enough father' is not simply the family breadwinner: in the majority of families where there are two parents, the breadwinner role is shared with the woman. Women are used to juggling the roles of breadwinner and nurturer: indeed, all that most lone mothers ask is that they should be given a chance to be breadwinners as well as nurturers. The complaint which so many women, women who are living with men as well as those on their own, make about men is that the men have not adapted to a new role in the home at anything like the speed with which women have adapted to their new role in the economy. Nor is this surprising when public policy, employers' arrangements, social and cultural expectations generally still assume that women will carry the main responsibilities of looking after children, of meeting the emotional needs of the family. The Government, grudgingly, requires employers to give women paid maternity leave but there is no equivalent for men who become fathers. Employers, recognising that they cannot succeed without female talent, are developing 'family-friendly' working practices: but 'family-friendly' almost always means helping women to combine employment and family, not men, and the Child Support Act, right in principle, but wrong in its practical details, risks confirming the view that the most important contribution men can make is monetary.

There is also a sense in which many women themselves underestimate the importance of fathers to their children. It is not surprising that women should be impatient with men who do not pull their emotional weight; how many married women say, 'Officially I've got two children, but really I've got three' — or lone parents, 'I've already got two children, what do I want with another?'. Many lone mothers put a great deal of effort into trying to maintain contact between their former partners and their children but many women find it much easier, for themselves and also, they believe, for their children, to end contact with the father, in some cases to try and start afresh with a new partner who will also be a new father to the children. One of the objections made to the Child Support Agency is that, by chasing up men for money, it encourages men to demand contact with their children. But unless the child is at risk of abuse from the father, do we have any right to object to fathers demanding contact with their children? Quite the reverse, we ought to be encouraging them. The interests of the mother do not always coincide with the interests of the child. If parents are to be enabled to overcome that conflict, we need, as parents and as prospective parents, to develop a much better understanding of the needs of children and the importance of fathers as well as mothers. That, of course, comes back to the emotional education which schools should provide, to young men as well as to young women, and to the need to extend counselling and other forms of support to parents when they first become parents and throughout their parenting, and not simply when they separate or divorce.

Richards, Martin, 'Divorcing Children: Roles for Parents and
the State', in Maclean, Mavis, and Kurczewski, Jacek (eds.),
*Families, Politics and the Law*
Oxford: Clarendon Press, 1994, Chapter 17, pp. 306–8

. . .

### Consequences of parental divorce for children

Children of divorcing parents tend to show a period of disturbed behaviour — either
acting-out disruptive behaviour or depressive and anxious patterns. This may last
through the whole process of divorce beginning months or years before a separation
and continuing some time after this. School work often shows some falling-off around
the time of separation and, as effects for educational attainment may be cumulative,
children are likely to leave school with fewer qualifications and have a reduced chance
of going on to a university . . .

Some effects may persist into adulthood and studies in Britain and the United
States have found lower occupational status and earnings, earlier marriage and
divorce, and increased frequency of psychological and psychiatric problems. . . . In
short, parental divorce may be associated with downward social mobility for the
children.

Of course, effects of divorce are very variable depending on many aspects of the
particular circumstances and such things as the age of the children, the social position
of the family, and the living arrangements after the separation. Not all children show
significant persistent effects. However, these are sufficiently common and of such
importance — we are talking of effects which, in some cases, influence the life-long
chances for adults — that it seems reasonable that we should regard these as the prime
concern which we need to consider when discussing interventions at divorce. . . .

Why should parental divorce have these long term effects? Clearly, this is a very
complex question and there are no simple answers. . . . But the significance of the
divorce effect is variable depending on both individual and social factors. The analysis
of the follow-up study of the cohort of children born in 1958, for example, suggests
that girls from middle-class homes show the strongest effects in early adulthood while
boys from working-class backgrounds are least affected. . . . Moreover, the links are
certainly complex. Nevertheless, we can point to a number of crucial effects of
parental divorce. So, for instance, a child that does badly at school is more likely to
leave at the minimum age with few or no qualifications and is less likely to proceed
to further education or training and so has reduced job prospects. Children who have
left education are more likely to leave home and live independently. Marriage and
cohabitation are more probable for those living independently and, associated with
these, are earlier reproduction, which in turn may further reduce employment
possibilities, especially for women. . . . The association between leaving home,
marriage, and cohabitation is probably the end result of two different processes;
leaving home because a decision has been taken to get married, and because those
living independently may be more likely to form relationships that develop more
rapidly into cohabitation or marriages. Where relationships are difficult or strained at
home a young person may choose to leave earlier than otherwise. A poor relationship
with a step-parent is a significant factor for some. Social-class differences are very
important here, not least because of the need for financial resources to find independent accommodation. . . .

Divorce is associated with a sharp drop in income for homes with children. In
Britain, a majority of households containing divorced women and their children
become dependent on state benefits for at least a period of time . . . and some remain

caught in the poverty trap. Inadequate income reduces children's educational attainment and in many other ways has adverse effects on·their life chances. While parental remarriage, and probably cohabitation, may improve incomes, the levels are seldom restored to those preceding the divorce. Even if these events have beneficial effects for household income, they may lead to further psychological and social disruptions for children. Follow up studies . . . tend to show small but consistently negative effects for children from remarriage homes as compared with those where a mother remained on her own after the divorce.

After divorce most children live with their mothers, and fathers become, at best, occasional visitors in their lives. Research in Britain and the USA suggests that within a short time of separation many children cease to have a relationship with their father. . . . The breaking of established relationships with fathers and other family members may have significant effects on a child's social development and their capacity to form and sustain relationships with others. When a father disappears from a child's life that child often feels a persistent sense of abandonment and loss which damages their self esteem and sense of worth. Lack of self esteem, in turn, has many psychological and social consequences. The loss of a parent and kin could also have economic and social effects for children which may continue into adult life. Fathers who are in contact with their children are more likely to be contributing towards their support and, though there seems to be no direct evidence to make the point, other transfers of money and practical support are likely to be reduced or cease where divorce ends effective contact. . . .

Conflict between parents before and after divorce is associated with poorer outcome for children. Where parents are living together, if the conflict is conducted in such a way that children are not directly involved, they seem to be protected from some of its consequences. . . . An important point here is that the effects of inter-parent conflict for children may be relatively benign if the children are able to see their parents settle their differences and restore good relationships. Conflict in the closing stages of a marriage or after separation may be more serious because it is less likely that this happens and because children, and the arrangements for their care, are more likely to be the subject of disputes. Conflict between parents will often erode parent-child relationships or end them.

Separating and divorced adults tend to have higher rates of psychological and physical illness. . . . Parents who are ill, depressed, preoccupied, and generally under stress are less effective as parents and their children may lack sustained support and emotional engagement. Such parental difficulties may further exacerbate the psychological problems of the children of divorce.

These problems may also be increased by moves which may mean a change of school and loss of friends and familiar peers. Changes of school tend to be associated with poorer educational attainment. Divorce may not simply lead to a single move but, for some, is the beginning of continued changes as a lone parent moves in and out of further relationships (and households).

The analysis I have sketched out provides a set of clear issues which could become goals for policies related to divorce and children. Such policies should aim to encourage the maintenance of a child's existing relationships with parents and the wider family and kin, ensure an adequate income to post-divorce households with children, reduce as far as possible conflict between divorcing parents or, at least, encourage its expression in areas that do not involve children, encourage the provision of emotional and practical support for divorcing parents who have the care of children and, finally, avoid as far as possible moves of house or school. . . .

## *In re Re D (Minors) (Conciliation: Disclosure of Information)*
[1993] Fam 231
Court of Appeal

SIR THOMAS BINGHAM MR: . . . It is notorious that when marriages break down
the victims include not only the spouses themselves but also, and particularly, their
children, who are swept into the vortex of their parents' embittered emotions at the
cost of much unhappiness and, not infrequently, lasting psychological damage. It is
also notorious that when marriages break down and problems arise affecting the
children, resolution of these problems through the ordinary processes of adversarial
litigation often leads to exaggerated accusations and counter-accusations with, in
consequence, an exacerbation of feelings and a heightening of tension. In the interests
of the children there is everything to be gained and nothing lost if the parents can be
induced, through the good offices of an intermediary, to compose their differences so
as to achieve a working compromise which may be wholly welcome to neither parent
but acceptable to each. This interest is shared by the public at large, which not only
wishes to spare children unnecessary suffering but also to reduce the great burden of
cost and delay which contested litigation of this kind necessarily imposes on an already
overloaded legal system.

  . . .

*Recent practice*
The benefits of resolving disputes about children by conciliation wherever possible
have been increasingly recognised in recent years by those professionally concerned in
this field. In the last 10 years or so schemes have been set up round the country both
independent of (out-of-court conciliation) and connected with (in-court conciliation)
local divorce court centres. One of the first was Bristol which has operated both
schemes. Many other county courts, for example, in Newcastle, Birmingham, Mid-
Glamorgan, Croydon, have set up court-based conciliation arrangements. In 1982 the
Principal Registry of the Family Division at Somerset House set up a pilot scheme
referred to in a *Practice Direction (Family Division: Conciliation Procedure)* [1982] 1
WLR 1420. The scheme originally applied only to custody and access cases arising
out of matrimonial disputes. But it was extended in 1984 by a *Practice Direction
(Family Division: Conciliation Procedure) (No. 2)* [1984] 1 WLR 1326, to wardship and
guardianship. Under the latest *Practice Direction (Family Division: Conciliation)* [1992]
1 WLR 147, reflecting the changes brought about by the Children Act 1989, in
applications for residence or contact the district judge *shall* refer the application for
conciliation. There has been within the Principal Registry a marked progression from
the pilot scheme in 1982 to a mandatory referral in 1992 for conciliation of all
contested residence and contact applications. In the 1992 *Practice Direction* the
discussions in the Principal Registry are stated to be privileged.
  The concept of conciliation was defined and given approval by the Report of the
Committee on One-Parent Families (1974) (Cmnd. 5629). The Report of the
Inter-departmental Committee on Conciliation (1983) supported the concept of
conciliation in disputes over children and recommended the establishment of a
Conciliation Project Unit ('CPU') to monitor the operation of a number of different
types of in-court conciliation schemes. The CPU was initiated by the Lord Chancel-
lor's Department and based on Newcastle University. The CPU Report entitled 'The
Costs and Effectiveness of Family Conciliation' was published in March 1989. Its

research indicated that conciliation, particularly of certain categories of dispute, generates important social benefits.

The increasing importance attached to conciliation is also reflected in the thinking of the Matrimonial Causes Procedure Committee and the Law Commission. The use of conciliation formed a significant part of the recommendations of the Report of the Matrimonial Causes Procedure Committee (1985). They proposed that conciliation should form a recognised part of the legal procedure and should be made available to parties to matrimonial litigation: see paragraphs 3.10 to 3.13.

The Law Commission Report, Family Law: The Ground for Divorce (1990) (Law Com. No. 192), considered various types of conciliation in paragraphs 5.29 to 5.48 and made specific recommendations supporting voluntary conciliation with encouragement from the court in paragraphs 7.24 to 7.28. The Law Commission recommended, at paragraphs 7.29 and 7.30, that there should be a statutory privilege conferred on statements made during conciliation procedures. Statements made during conciliation which indicate a risk of harm to a child should be privileged but not confidential.

The National Association of Probation Officers ('NAPO') issued a policy document which was set out in (1990) 20 Fam Law 85. In it they supported voluntary conciliation schemes and drew the distinction between their members acting as conciliators and as reporters to the court: see p. 86. This followed a practice direction, *Registrar's Direction (Children: Inquiry and Report by a Welfare Officer)* [1986] 2 FLR 171, setting out a registrar's direction that, where a court welfare officer has acted as a conciliator, if conciliation fails any report ordered by the court must be undertaken by another court welfare officer, thus preserving the privilege of the attempts at conciliation. NAPO set a limit on confidentiality in respect of suspicion of child abuse.

The National Family Conciliation Council, now renamed the National Association of Family Mediation and Conciliation Services, brings together 56 conciliation services under its umbrella. It issued a code of practice in 1986 which emphasised the importance of the meetings being without prejudice, with the reservation of reporting any matter relating to substantial danger to a child.

The practice of conciliation has grown and evolved in various ways over the last 10 years, in court and out of court, voluntary or directed, and extends over many parts of the country. Resolution of disputes over children by parents locked in acrimony and controversy has gradually but perceptibly taken over from efforts to preserve the state of the marriage of the parents. Conciliation of parental or matrimonial disputes does not form part of the legal process but as a matter of practice is becoming an important and valuable tool in the procedures of many family courts. . . .

*Note*

In *In Re D (Minors) (Conciliation: Disclosure of Information)*, *supra* the Court of Appeal held that statements made in conciliation (or mediation) discussions could not be used as evidence in court proceedings, except where the maker of the statement had caused harm to the child or would be likely to do so in the future.

*Questions*

*1.* If the welfare of children is of the utmost concern, does the State discriminate against non-marital children by failing to consider arrangements for them on their parents' relationship breakdown? Should the State adopt a

more paternalistic and interventionist role on divorce to consider arrangements for children of divorcing parents?
2.   What can be done to encourage the importance of the continuing relationship between the child and the non-residential parent?

*Further reading*
Bainham, A., 'The Privatisation of the Public Interest in Children' (1990) 53 MLR 206.
Douglas, G., Murch, M., and Perry, A., 'Supporting Children When Parents Separate — A Neglected Family Justice or Mental Health Issue?' [1996] 8 CFLQ 121.
Elliott, B., and Richards, M., 'Children and Divorce: Educational Behaviour, Before and After Parental Separation' (1991) 5 IJL&F 258.
Elliott, J. *et al.*, 'Divorce and Children: A British Challenge to the Wallerstein View' [1990] Fam Law 309.
Kelly, J., 'Children's Post-Divorce Adjustment: Effects of Conflict, Parent Adjustment and Custody Arrangement' [1991] Fam Law 52.
Richards, M., 'Children and Parents and Divorce', in Eekelaar, J., and Šarčević, P. (eds), *Parenthood in Modern Society — Legal and Social Issues for the Twenty-First Century*, Dordrecht: Martinus Nijhoff, 1993, Chapter 21.
Richards, M., 'Private Worlds and Public Intentions — the Role of the State at Divorce', in Pearl, D., and Pickford, R. (eds), *Frontiers of Family Law*, Part I, Chichester: John Wiley, 1995, Chapter 1.
Wallerstein, J. and Kelly, J., *Surviving the Breakup: How Children and Parents Cope with Divorce*, New York: Basic Books Inc., 1980.

## 9.2   CHILDREN AND THE DIVORCE PROCESS

### 9.2.1   Introduction

A divorcing parent must complete a form containing a statement of the proposed living and educational arrangements for the children after divorce. The district judge must look at the form and consider whether to exercise any of the powers laid down in s. 41 of the MCA 1973.

## MATRIMONIAL CAUSES ACT 1973

**41.   Restrictions on decrees for dissolution, annulment or separation affecting children**
    (1)   In any proceedings for a decree of divorce or nullity of marriage, or a decree of judicial separation, the court shall consider—
        (a)   whether there are any children of the family to whom this section applies; and
        (b)   where there are any such children, whether (in the light of the arrangements which have been, or are proposed to be, made for their upbringing and welfare) it should exercise any of its powers under the Children Act 1989 with respect to any of them.

(2) Where, in any case to which this section applies, it appears to the court that—

(a) the circumstances of the case require it, or are likely to require it, to exercise any of its powers under the Act of 1989 with respect to any such child;

(b) it is not in a position to exercise the power or (as the case may be) those powers without giving further consideration to the case; and

(c) there are exceptional circumstances which make it desirable in the interests of the child that the court should give a direction under this section,

it may direct that the decree of divorce or nullity is not to be made absolute, or that the decree of judicial separation is not to be granted, until the court orders otherwise.

*Note*

Section 41 applies to any child of the family under the age of 16 (MCA 1973, s. 41(3)) and includes a non-marital child of one or both parties and any other child treated by the parties as a child of the family (but not a foster-child placed with the parties by a local authority) (MCA 1973, s. 52). Powers under the CA 1989 which could be exercised under s. 41 would be: to ask for a welfare report on the child (s. 7); to make a residence, contact, specific issue or prohibited steps order (s. 8); or to direct a local authority to investigate the child's circumstances (s. 37).

### 9.2.2  Does the present law protect the interests of children involved in divorce?

**Law Commission, *Facing the Future — A Discussion Paper on the Ground for Divorce*, Law Com No. 170**
London: HMSO, 1988

3.37   The need for the law to protect the interests of children whose security and stability is threatened by their parents' divorce has long been recognised. This was one of the reasons why the Morton Commission did not recommend relaxation of divorce laws. However by the 1960s the 'general orthodoxy' among social scientists was that 'a bad marriage was worse for children than a divorce' [Richards, M., and Dyson, M., *Separation, Divorce and the Development of Children: A Review*, DHSS, 1982, p. 77]. The Law Commission in The Field of Choice was careful to reject any generalisation on this point and to conclude that in some cases it would be better for the children if their parents were to stay together and in other cases if they were to divorce. It was recognised, however, that restrictive divorce laws did not make the parents stay together and that it was the separation rather than the divorce which was usually damaging to the children. So to prohibit or make divorce more difficult for those with children would serve little purpose and would cause resentment in the parents who would see the children as the obstacle to their divorce. . . . Thus, restrictive grounds for divorce do not necessarily safeguard the interests of the children of the parties.

3.38   However, it may be possible to use the divorce process to do so. Since 1958, divorce courts have had to consider the arrangements made for the couple's children before the divorce can be made absolute. The 1969 Act added nothing to this. Since then, the findings of a number of studies and the huge increase in the number of children who witness the divorce of their parents have focussed attention on the plight of the children of divorced parents. This increased concern for such children can be seen, for example, from the recent provision giving priority to their interests in financial provision proceedings between their parents. Also, the report of the Booth Committee, whose terms of reference included making recommendations 'to provide further for the welfare of the children of the family' [para. 1(c)] states at the outset that 'The welfare of the children is a matter of the utmost concern. We do not think that it can be doubted that society generally has an interest in ensuring the security and stability of the minor children of divorcing or separating parents' [para. 2.22]. The difficulty is in identifying *how* the law can promote the interests of the children.

3.39   Several studies have indicated that most children whose parents have separated would have preferred them to have stayed together. Children of parents who have separated are more likely to suffer from at least temporary social and behavioural problems during and in the aftermath of the separation. Although the findings are less clear, research has also linked marital separation with various longer-term problems. As marital separation frequently leads to downward social mobility and economic hardship such findings are not surprising, but once again may be attributed to the consequences of separation rather than divorce as such. Perhaps the most significant research finding is that adjustment to separation depends on the quality of the relationships with and between both parents *after* the separation. Thus good continuing relationships with both parents seem to be protective against the problems associated with children from broken marriages. Conversely, post-divorce conflict between the parents is more damaging than marital conflict.

3.40   The implications from this research are that, although divorce law is powerless to prevent prejudice to the children caused by marital breakdown, it can help to minimise that prejudice in two ways. First, since the children are most vulnerable in the immediate aftermath of the separation which often coincides with the timing of the divorce process, nothing should be involved in that process which makes it more difficult for the children to cope with the separation. Secondly, every effort should be made to encourage good post-divorce relationships with both parents and between the parents themselves. The Booth Committee, expressing the view that divorcing or separating parents should be encouraged and advised to maintain their joint responsibility for the children and to co-operate in this respect, recommended that provision should be made for joint statement of arrangements to be filed. Such co-operation may only be possible where there has not been irretrievable harm to the spouses' own relationship.

3.41   Unfortunately the present law would not seem to satisfy either of these requirements. First, the divorce process itself *is* likely to exacerbate the trauma of the parental separation for the children. Perceived lack of fairness and the exacerbation of bitterness and hostility will make the divorce more difficult for the children as well as the parents. The more stressful the divorce process is for the parents the less time and ability they will have to provide emotional support for the children. If there is conflict between the parents, the children may be encouraged to take sides, which may be very distressing for them particularly if arrangements for their future are in issue. Contested custody proceedings increase uncertainty and increase the insecurity felt by many children following marital breakdown. Secondly, a likely effect of perceived unfairness and the conflict and hostility engendered by the system is to poison post-divorce relationships. Parents who have been further alienated from each other by the divorce process will be less likely to be able to exercise their parental responsibilities jointly. The non-custodial parent may feel so resentful that he wants to cut himself off entirely from what has happened and so loses contact with his children. Where children have been encouraged to take sides, their relationship with both parents may be impaired as a result of the conflict of loyalties.

. . .

### 9.2.3   The impact of the new divorce law on children
### FAMILY LAW ACT 1996

**11.  Welfare of children**

(1)  In any proceedings for a divorce order or a separation order, the court shall consider—

(a)  whether there are any children of the family to whom this section applies; and

(b)  where there are any such children, whether (in the light of the arrangements which have been, or are proposed to be, made for their upbringing and welfare) it should exercise any of its powers under the Children Act 1989 with respect to any of them.

(2)  Where, in any case to which this section applies, it appears to the court that—

(a)  the circumstances of the case require it, or are likely to require it, to exercise any of its powers under the Children Act 1989 with respect to any such child,

(b)  it is not in a position to exercise the power, or (as the case may be) those powers, without giving further consideration to the case, and

(c)  there are exceptional circumstances which make it desirable in the interests of the child that the court should give a direction under this section,
it may direct that the divorce order or separation order is not to be made until the court orders otherwise.

(3)  In deciding whether the circumstances are as mentioned in subsection (2)(a), the court shall treat the welfare of the child as paramount.

(4)  In making that decision, the court shall also have particular regard, on the evidence before it, to—

(a)  the wishes and feelings of the child considered in the light of his age and understanding and the circumstances in which those wishes were expressed;

(b)  the conduct of the parties in relation to the upbringing of the child;

(c)  the general principle that, in the absence of evidence to the contrary, the welfare of the child will be best served by—

(i)  his having regular contact with those who have parental responsibility for him and with other members of his family; and

(ii)  the maintenance of as good a continuing relationship with his parents as is possible; and

(d)  any risk to the child attributable to—

(i)  where the person with whom the child will reside is living or proposes to live;

(ii)  any person with whom that person is living or with whom he proposes to live; or

(iii)  any other arrangements for his care and upbringing.

(5)  This section applies to—

(a)  any child of the family who has not reached the age of sixteen at the date when the court considers the case in accordance with the requirements of this section; and

(b)  any child of the family who has reached that age at that date and in relation to whom the court directs that this section shall apply.

### Richards, Martin, 'But what about the Children? Some Reflections on the Divorce White Paper'
### [1995] 7 CFLQ 223

. . . [T]he Children Act 1989 and now the White Paper proposals represent a continuing retreat into private ordering. While some in the field welcome this trend, there are causes for concern. Courts will be involved primarily in settling disputes between parents. Otherwise, they will play no direct part in encouraging parents to make appropriate arrangements for children. The White Paper proposes that we should safeguard the interests of children by providing information about their needs to the initiating parent, presumably the mother in the large majority of cases, through reducing conflict by not requiring any statement from spouses about what may have happened during the marriage, and the abolition of the notion of fault, and by encouraging the use of mediation where there may be a dispute. However, there is no requirement, or encouragement, nor could there be in the context of the Children Act 1989, to seek orders concerning children, but simply for a parent to tell the court what plans have been made for them.

. . .

If there is a dispute between the parents, whether about money (and the CSA is not involved), property, or the children the couple will be encouraged to go to mediation. Indeed they may have little choice if they hope to receive any assistance with legal expenses. The White Paper argues at paragraph 5.17 that mediation will help to reduce the trauma for the children because it will minimise conflict between parents and encourage them to communicate over arrangements. Insofar as mediation may achieve these ends, the White Paper proposals should be welcomed. However, in its discussion, the White Paper glosses over the central dilemma of mediation in relation to disputes over children — who is to protect their interests? The reason why parental divorce is such a powerful disruption of the lives of children is because the interests of parents and children often diverge. Parents may do things and make arrangements that children do not want and which may not be in their best interests — for example, a child is likely to want to see her parents stay together, and failing that, to stay in the family home. The divorcing parents cannot offer the former, and may be divided about the latter. Children often feel that their interests are being ignored. For them to see their own parents do this is deeply disturbing. No intervention can remove this central conflict of interest, but we can, and should, attempt to protect the interests of the weaker party.

The White Paper states correctly at paragraph 5.33 that thinking in relation to the involvement of children in mediation is developing rapidly, but however it develops it cannot square a circle. Currently very few mediators see children. Almost everyone is agreed that children should not be directly included in the mediation process itself. To do so would be to expose them to impossible emotional pressures and conflicts. Children are sometimes invited to a final session held after an agreement has been reached to hear what is proposed from both parents together. This is a helpful procedure, especially in the light of the evidence of how little many parents talk to children about what may happen to them at divorce. It may also have a powerful symbolic effect as the children can see their parents together planning for their future and this allows them to feel that their voice has been heard. . . . Mediation is adult business and, although adults may be bargaining in the shadow of their children's needs as they perceive them, children cannot be party to it. The children simply have to live with whatever arrangements emerge from the process and their own under-standing of the process that has led to the arrangements.

Therefore, while mediation may do much to help parents reach agreements and set up workable arrangements for children, it cannot protect children's interests. It must rely on the information about the children which the parties bring to the sessions. Necessarily this information will be presented in the light of parental perceptions, hopes, fears, anxieties, and guilt. In most cases this will serve children's interests well enough, but it cannot be termed *protection*, as it is not based on an independent view.

If parents continue to disagree about arrangements for children the case will ultimately go to court. At that point there is a possibility of an independent view of the children's interests through a court welfare report, but even then such reports are not mandatory and children are not necessarily safe-guarded by independent representation (as would be quite consistent with the general thrust of the Children Act 1989). Apart from the tiny proportion of cases that reach the courts, how will children's interests be protected? Should we leave this to the good sense of parents supported and encouraged by what they may learn in the information appointment, together with whatever mediation can do in the cases where it is used? Will the requirement to make arrangements for the children before a divorce can be granted be helpful, or possibly will the time pressures increase the likelihood of children becoming bargaining chips in the divorce process?

A major concern with the new proposals is that nothing is suggested which will support or encourage fathers to remain significant figures in the lives of their children. The information appointment can offer encouragement but what proportion of fathers will choose to attend? There are many reasons why a father may disappear from the lives of children after a divorce. A father may be simply repeating the pattern he followed in the marriage when his relationship with his children was effectively managed and arranged by a partner who may be unable or unwilling to continue this role after a separation. If he has moved into a new relationship there may be pressures from the new partner to end links with the original family. For others there may be a belief that cutting ties with their children may best serve the interests of the children and leave the field clear for a stepfather, or that by avoiding contact he may avoid support payments. We cannot be precise about the relative importance of these and other motives because we lack systematic research on the topic, but what is certain is that currently after separation many, if not most, fathers cease to have effective relationships with their children. This may be the cause of great hurt to their children. Given this, there is a very strong case for fathers to attend this information appointment but as the new proposals stand it would seem likely that a majority would not do this. The obvious remedy would be to require *both* parents to attend. That does, however, create the consequent difficulty that a reluctant spouse could use nonattendance to block an unwelcome divorce, but it should be possible to devise a procedure to prevent this.

The key question is whether a system based on the group information appointment, mediation and the courts as the long stop for persistent disputes, can provide sufficient protection for children. . . .

What of children whose parents chose not to marry? . . . One-third of children are born to parents who are not married to each other. This proportion is rising rapidly and trends elsewhere in Europe suggest that this group may become the majority in the not too distant future. A major proportion of these non-marital children are born to cohabiting parents. There is no reason to think that, from a children's point of view, the separation of cohabiting parents is any more benign than that of married ones. Yet it is not clear that the needs of this very significant group of children are being adequately addressed, although the Children Act 1989 does give the cohabiting mother the possibility of a claim on the family home until the children become independent. The law, like many other institutions, is still struggling to catch up with one of the major demographic changes of the last couple of decades. Will separating cohabiting couples be able to use the information appointment system or the State-financed mediation system that is now proposed? However, even if this were the case there would still be a two-track system as there would be no requirement for unmarried parents to make arrangements before separation or, indeed, publicly to record their arrangements for their children if they separate. From the perspective of these children this seems very unsatisfactory.

This report article has raised a number of concerns about the implications of further privatisation of the divorce process from the perspective of children. As the separation and divorce process is placed more firmly in the hands of the separating parties, a move which has much to recommend it from an adult perspective, we must consider carefully the needs of those whose bargaining chips do not even reach the table. While endorsing the moves towards emphasising the continuation of parental responsibility through marriage, divorce, to repartnering and beyond, we may wish to think more about the way in which we safeguard the position of children. . . .

*Questions*
1. Should the State intervene more in the divorce process with respect to children, or would this be a threat to family autonomy?
2. Freeman, M. in *Rights and Wrongs of Children*, London: Pinter Press, 1983 stated that 'Divorce is an adult solution to an adult problem'. Should children be given a greater opportunity to participate in the divorce process? Should there be separate representation for children on their parents' divorce as there is in care and supervision proceedings? With the divorce reforms under the FLA 1996 (see Chapter 4) mediation will play a greater role in divorce. Should children be involved in mediation sessions?
3. John and Sue agree on divorce that David, their son aged 12, is to live with John and have monthly contact with Sue. David is adamant that he would rather live with his mother. What can David do?
4. How, if at all, are the divorce reforms (see Chapter 4) likely to affect children involved in the divorce process?

### 9.3   LIVING ARRANGEMENTS FOR CHILDREN ON FAMILY BREAKDOWN

#### 9.3.1   A residence order

#### CHILDREN ACT 1989

**8.   Residence, contract and other orders with respect to children**
  (1)   In this Act—
    . . . 'a residence order' means an order settling the arrangements to be made as to the person with whom a child is to live. . . .

Where parents, married or unmarried, cannot agree about living arrangements for their children on relationship breakdown, either parent may apply to the court for a s. 8 residence order (see Chapter 7). Parents must be advised, however, that the court in family proceedings has a discretion to do what is best for the child's welfare, and consequently may not make the order applied for (s. 1(5)), or may make a different s. 8 order (s. 10(1)(b)). Furthermore, it may direct that a welfare report on the child be carried out (s. 7), or direct that a local authority investigate the child's circumstances

(s. 37). Persons other than parents and guardians may apply for a residence order with leave of the court (see Chapter 7). When a residence order is in force, there are restrictions on changing the child's surname and taking the child out of the UK (s. 13).

The s. 1 welfare principles of the CA 1989 govern the application (see Chapter 7), but judge-made principles are sometimes applied, even from cases decided before the 1989 Act, e.g., that siblings should not be separated, that children (particularly very young children) are better with their mothers, that maintaining the *status quo* is usually beneficial for children. However, whether the court will make a residence order will depend on the circumstances of the case.

### *Brixey* v *Lynas*
### [1996] 2 FLR 499
### House of Lords (Scotland)

*Facts*: The father of a young child appealed to the House of Lords against a decision of the Scottish Court of Session (First Division) which had allowed the mother's appeal and granted her custody, on the basis that it was better for a young child to be cared for by its mother (the 'maternal preference' principle) and because of the advantage of maintaining the status quo which had successfully existed since the child's birth. The father appealed to the House of Lords, his main ground of appeal being that the court had erred in accepting a principle of maternal preference, with the sexual discrimination which that was said to involve.

*Held*: dismissing the appeal, that as the mother's care could not be criticised, the court had not erred in considering the status quo and the advantage to a very young child of being cared for by its mother.

LORD JAUNCEY: . . . [Counsel for the father] referred to two English cases in support of his attack on maternal preference. In *Re S (A Minor) (Custody)* [1991] 2 FLR 388, Butler-Sloss LJ in the Court of Appeal said at 390F:

There are dicta of this court to the effect that it is likely that a young child, particularly perhaps a little girl, would be expected to be with her mother, but that is subject to the overriding factor that the welfare of the child is the paramount consideration.

She later stated, at 390H:

I would just add that it is natural for young children to be with mothers but, but where it is in dispute, it is a consideration but not a presumption.

In *Re A (A Minor) (Custody)* [1991] 2 FLR 394 Butler-Sloss LJ also stated, at 400A:

In cases where the child has remained throughout with the mother and is young, particularly when a baby or a toddler, the unbroken relationship of the mother and child is one which it would be very difficult to displace unless the mother was unsuitable to care for the child. But where the mother and child have been separated, and the mother seeks the return of the child, other considerations apply, and there is no starting-point that the mother should be preferred to the father and only displaced by a preponderance of evidence to the contrary.

My Lords in my view these cases do nothing to support Mr Mitchell's argument. Butler-Sloss LJ with her great experience of family cases accepts that it is natural for young children to be with their mothers and in the above passage in *Re A* which is particularly relevant to this case she points to the difficulty of displacing an unbroken relationship between a mother and a very young child unless the mother is unsuitable to have care.

The paramount consideration in any dispute as to custody is the welfare of the child (s. 3(2) of the Law Reform (Parent and Child) (Scotland) Act 1986). To determine what is in the best interests of a very young child regard must necessarily be had to its relationship with the mother with whom it is living. To suggest that any recognition of the normal mother's natural ability to look after a very young child amounts to sexual discrimination is absurd. Nature has endowed men and women with very different attributes and it so happens that mothers are generally better fitted than fathers to provide for the needs of very young children. This is no more discriminatory than the fact that only women can give birth. Every case must be considered on its own facts. There will be cases where the mother is wholly unfitted to care for even the youngest child and the court will proceed accordingly. There will be other cases where the child is older and the matter is finely balanced. However, here the child is very young, has never been separated from its mother or half-sister for any significant length of time and it is not suggested that the mother is unsuitable to care for her. In that situation the advantage of continued care with the mother without disturbance of the status quo must be an important factor to be taken into account.

. . .

My Lords, to summarise, the advantage to a very young child of being with its mother is a consideration which must be taken into account in deciding where lie its best interests in custody proceedings in which the mother is involved. It is neither a presumption nor a principle but rather recognition of a widely held belief based on practical experience and the workings of nature. Its importance will vary according to the age of the child and to the other circumstances of each individual case such as whether the child has been living with or apart from the mother and whether she is or is not capable of providing proper care. Circumstances may be such that it has no importance at all. Furthermore it will always yield to other competing advantages which more effectively promote the welfare of the child. However, where a very young child has been with its mother since birth and there is no criticism of her ability to care for the child only the strongest competing advantages are likely to prevail. Such is not this case.

For the foregoing reasons I would dismiss the appeal. . . .

## Questions

*1.* Peter has divorced Jane because she is having a lesbian relationship with Stella. Jane is an excellent mother to the two young children of the marriage who are living with her, but Peter considers that they should live with him because Jane's lesbian relationship will damage the children now and permanently. What do you think the court is likely to decide and what factors might be important? (See *B v B (Minors) (Custody, Care and Control)* [1991] 1 FLR 402, FD, and *C v C (A Minor) (Custody: Appeal)* [1991] 1 FLR 223, CA.)

*2.* Would the courts allow homosexuals or transsexuals to obtain residence or contact orders?

*Further reading*
Barton, C., 'The Homosexual in the Family' [1996] Fam Law 626.
Beresford, S., 'Lesbians in Residence and Parental Responsibility Cases' [1994] Fam Law 643.
Boyd, S., 'What is a "Normal" Family? *C* v *C* (*A Minor*) (*Custody Appeal*)' (1992) 55 MLR 269.
Standley, K., 'Children and Lesbian Mothers: *B* v *B* and *C* v *C*' (1991) 3 JCL 134.
Tasker, F., and Golombok, S., 'Children Raised by Lesbian Mothers: the Empirical Evidence' [1991] Fam Law 184.

### 9.3.2   Shared residence

### CHILDREN ACT 1989

**11.   General principles and supplementary provisions**
. . .
   (4)   Where a residence order is made in favour of two or more persons who do not themselves all live together, the order may specify the periods during which the child is to live in the different households concerned.

*The Children Act 1989 Guidance and Regulations: Vol. 1,*
*Court Orders*
London: HMSO, 1991

. . . A residence order may be made in favour of more than one person at the same time even though they do not live together, in which case the order may specify the periods during which the child is to live in the different households concerned. A shared residence order could therefore be made where the child is to spend, for example, weekdays with one parent and weekends with the other or term time with one parent and school holidays with the other, or where the child is to spend large amounts of time with each parent. This latter arrangement was disapproved of by the Court of Appeal in *Riley* v *Riley* [[1986] 2 FLR 429] which must now be taken to have been overruled by s. 11(4). But it is not expected that it would become a common form of order, partly because most children will still need the stability of a single home, and partly because in the cases where shared care is appropriate there is less likely to be a need for the court to make any order at all. However, a shared care order has the advantage of being more realistic in those cases where the child is to spend considerable amounts of time with those parents, brings with it certain other benefits (including the right to remove the child from accommodation provided by a local authority under s. 20), and removes any impression that one parent is good and responsible whereas the other parent is not. . . .

*A* v *A* (*Minors*) (*Shared Residence Order*)
[1994] 1 FLR 669
Court of Appeal

*Facts*: The parties were divorced. The father was granted a shared residence order under s. 11(4) of the CA 1989 in respect of the two children of the marriage. The mother appealed, arguing that the facts of the case were not exceptional, and relied on the judgment of Purchas LJ in *Re H (A Minor) (Shared Residence)* [1994] 1 FLR 717 where on the facts the Court of Appeal refused to make a shared residence order in respect of a 14-year-old boy who had been looked after by both cohabiting parents under a shared care arrangement.

*Held*: dismissing the appeal, that a shared residence order should be granted.

BUTLER-SLOSS LJ: I agree with the judgment Connell J has just given. On the test adopted by the judge, he had evidence upon which he could exercise his discretion to come to the conclusion to which he came. It is not for this court to substitute its own discretion. He was entitled to come to the conclusion that a shared residence order was the correct order in this case.

[After referring to ss. 11(4) and 8 of the Children Act 1989, her Ladyship continued: . . .]

Consequently, the Children Act specifically contemplated, as part of the statutory framework, that a child might have a residence with more than one person.

As my Lord has already said, there is guidance in *The Children Act 1989 Guidance and Regulations* (HMSO, 1991), *vol. 1: Court Orders*, para. 2.28. We, in this court, are not bound by that guidance, but none the less it is helpful. In the light of the statutory framework of s. 8 and s. 11(4) the disapproval of a joint custody order stated in the decision of this court in *Riley* v *Riley* [1986] 2 FLR 429 can no longer be good law and has, as the guidance suggested, been overruled by the statute.

The effect of the Children Act is to provide a wider and more flexible approach to the care of children and to those who are the carers. The traditional approach of judges before the Children Act must give way to the statutory framework which we are bound to apply. We are, at this moment, still feeling our way through the implications of the Children Act. But we must none the less do so in the light of the wisdom of the past distilled in many cases, and the fact that children's problems have not changed and the emotions of parents equally have not changed. Although we no longer can rely upon the view of a joint custody order in *Riley* v *Riley*, the wisdom expressed by May LJ, and reported and cited by Purchas LJ in *Re H (A Minor) (Shared Residence)* [1994] 1 FLR 717 at p. 728, that a child should have one home and the other place of spending time, including overnight, is not the home but a place where visits may regularly and frequently be made, and that competing homes lead to confusion and stress, is likely to be the case in many of the situations which arise in the courts. As I have said, the problems still arise although this court is now bound by statute.

[Counsel for] the father, accepts that the conventional order still is that there would be residence to one parent with contact to the other parent. It must be demonstrated that there is positive benefit to the child concerned for a s. 11(4) order to be made, and such positive benefit must be demonstrated in the light of the s. 1 checklist, to which my Lord has already referred. The usual order that would be made in any case where it is necessary to make an order is that there will be residence to one parent and a contact order to the other parent. Consequently, it will be unusual to make a shared residence order. But the decision whether to make such a shared residence order is always in the discretion of the judge on the special facts of the individual case. It is for him alone to make that decision. However, a shared residence order would, in my view, be unlikely to be made if there were concrete issues still arising between the parties which had not been resolved, such as the amount of contact, whether it should be staying or visiting contact or another issue such as education, which were muddying the waters and which were creating difficulties between the parties which reflected the way in which the children were moving from one parent to the other in the contact period.

If a child, on the other hand, has a settled home with one parent and substantial staying contact with the other parent, which has been settled, long-standing and working well, or if there are future plans for sharing the time of the children between two parents where all the parties agree and where there is no possibility of confusion in the mind of the child as to where the child will be and the circumstances of the child at any time, this may be, bearing in mind all the other circumstances, a possible basis for a shared residence order, if it can be demonstrated that there is a positive benefit to the child. It does not mean it will be; it may be. In this case, the children stay with the father for approximately one-third of the year and a very substantial portion of their free time. He plays a particularly important part in their life. The judge found that his relationship with them was exceptional. The type and quantum of contact, the fact that it is staying and for long periods at any time, has never been, for a considerable period at least, in dispute.

The judge followed the decision of this court in *Re H*, to which I have already referred, and imposed upon himself the test of exceptional circumstances which was referred to by Purchas LJ at p. 728B. Having set out the fact that s. 11(4) provides for a shared residence order, Purchas LJ said:

> But at the same time it must be an order which would rarely be made and would depend upon exceptional circumstances.

In the case in which he made those observations, it was plain as a pikestaff that a shared residence order ought not to have been made. But insofar as the Lord Justice imported a general test of exceptional circumstances into the interpretation of s. 11(4) of the Children Act, his observations appear to me to have been obiter. I respectfully disagree with him. The section does not import such a constraint. Having said that, I would like to reiterate what I have already said, that the usual order would be a sole residence order, and that there has to be positive benefit to the children in making an order which is not the conventional order. Consequently, a shared residence order is an unusual order which should only be made in unusual circumstances. Each case, as I have said, must be decided on its own facts. A judge will exercise his discretion in accordance with the sections of the Children Act and in accordance with the checklist in s. 1. The judge will decide which order, if any, is to be made and whether it is better to make an order than not to make one.

For those reasons, as well as the reasons given in the judgment of Connell J, I agree that this appeal should be dismissed.

## Notes

1. In *Riley v Riley* [1986] 2 FLR 429, a pre-CA 1989 case, the Court of Appeal refused to make a joint custody order in respect of a 9-year-old girl, despite the fact that for a considerable period of time she had spent alternate weeks at each parent's house (they were a mile apart) and with no obvious detrimental effect.

2. In *Re H (A Minor) (Shared Residence)* [1994] 1 FLR 717, the Court of Appeal refused to make a shared residence order, stressing the exceptional

nature of such an order. Purchas LJ stated (at p. 728) that the 'establishment
. . . of two competing homes only leads to confusion and stress'.

*Further reading*
Bridge, C., 'Shared Residence in England and New Zealand — a Comparative Analysis' [1996] 8 CFLQ 12.
Hoggett, B., 'Joint Parenting Systems: the English Experiment' (1994) 6 JCL 8.

## 9.4   CONTACT ARRANGEMENTS ON FAMILY BREAKDOWN

### 9.4.1   Contact

### UNITED NATIONS CONVENTION ON THE RIGHTS OF THE CHILD 1989

**Article 9**
. . .
   (3)   States Parties shall respect the right of the child who is separated from one or both parents to maintain personal relations and direct contact with both parents on a regular basis, except if it is contrary to the child's best interests. . . .

### *Re A (A Minor) (Contact)*
[1993] 2 FLR 762
Court of Appeal

BUTLER-SLOSS LJ: . . . It is the right of a child to have a relationship with both parents wherever possible. This principle has been stated again and again in the appellate courts. It is underlined in the United Nations Convention on the Rights of the Child and endorsed in the Children Act 1989. When parents divorce, in general the parent with whom the child does not live has a continuing role to play, which is recognised by s. 2(1) of the Children Act 1989. It does no harm to repeat it from time to time:

   Where a child's father and mother were married to each other at the time of his birth, they shall each have parental responsibility for the child.

As Balcombe LJ said in *Re H (Minors) (Access)* [1992] 1 FLR 148 at p. 152C — this was, I think, cited to the judge — the judge should have asked himself the question:

   Are there here any cogent reasons why this father should be denied access to his children; or putting it another way: are there any cogent reasons why these two children should be denied the opportunity of access to their natural father?

The judge in this case did direct himself on that matter. But it is the starting-point of any test where, as used to be called, a non-custodial parent wishes to retain contact with his or her child.
   . . .

## Murch, Mervyn, *Justice and Welfare in Divorce*
London: Sweet & Maxwell, 1980, p. 92

. . . [T]hese parents expressed strong and sometimes ambivalent views about access.
Here are three illustrations: Mother of a three-year-old girl:

> There's no arrangement about access at all. After we split up he came and saw her
> a couple of times. Then he didn't see her for seven months. Since then he has never
> made any effort to see her or enquire how she is. I think now because of his attitude
> it's best for her not to see him because just seeing him occasionally for five minutes
> will be perhaps more upsetting to her as she gets older and begins to realise who he
> is. Obviously she is going to wonder as she gets older. Well then it will be up to her
> whether to see him. But I worry about it. You see my own parents were separated
> and I didn't see my father for nine years. I know what she'll perhaps feel.

A mother of a five-year-old boy told us:

> I'm lucky his father doesn't seem to take any interest in him. If he did I would do
> anything to prevent him seeing the child until he is 15. You see from my own
> experience I've been lucky because my own father protected me until I was 15 from
> seeing my mother. Even then I wasn't ready for it and it has sort of hurt. I don't
> get on with her maybe because of not seeing her all those years. If my little boy
> misbehaves what I try to avoid is to say 'You're just like your father.' When my own
> father was disappointed in me he used to say 'You're just like your mother' and that
> used to hurt me so.

A mother of four children who was letting the children decide about access despite a
bitterly contested custody dispute remarked:

> I resent what happened to me, not being allowed to see my father. My mother
> would *not* let me see him. And yet she left us on our own in a convent for three
> years in Wales so that she could go to London and work.

Interviewer:

'What were your feelings about not seeing your father?'

'The divorce was over and about a fortnight later Dad came to the house. I'll never
forget it. I remember we had a glass door. I remember trying to push past it. I broke
the glass. But she wouldn't let me go to him. They had a terrible row about it and
I can never remember my parents arguing like that before. I was nine at the time.'

Interviewer:

'How had you got on with your father?'
'Oh, very well. I thought he was marvellous. He had a lovely voice and was always
very good to me. Being a soldier he was a disciplinarian and we were brought up
to respect authority but I didn't mind.'

Interviewer:

'Have you ever tried to contact him since?'

'No, we moved and then we went to the convent. He went away with the regiment
and we never saw him again. I promised my mother I would never see him or try
to see him. I've no idea where he is and it's nearly 20 years. . . . Anyhow you can

see why I'm happy that in our case the children should decide when they want to see their father.'

. . .

The general conclusion to be drawn from all these illustrations is that access problems are often symptomatic of a fundamental dilemma facing divorcing parents. This is how to disengage from the broken marriage while preserving a sense of being a parent with a part to play in the children's future. Some can not resolve it and give up their parental role, others strike an amicable balance between these conflicting demands, and yet others argue and fight. . . .

### 9.4.2   A contact order

Parents, married or unmarried, who cannot agree about contact may apply under the CA 1989 for a contact order. The s. 1 principles govern the application (see Chapter 7). A contact order requiring contact with the other parent automatically ceases to be effective if the parents live together for a continuous period of more than six months (s. 11(6)). An application may be made by a person other than a parent and guardian, and the child may also apply (see Chapter 7).

## CHILDREN ACT 1989

**8.   Residence, contact and other orders with respect to children**
   (1)   In this Act—
      a 'contact order' means an order requiring the person with whom a child lives, or is to live, to allow the child to visit or stay with the person named in the order, or for that person and the child otherwise to have contact with each other; . . .

### Re D (Contact: Interim Order)
[1995] 1 FLR 495
Family Division

WALL J: . . .

*The underlying law as to contact generally*
There is now a plethora of authority on contact questions. It is, therefore in my view necessary to remind oneself of some fundamental propositions. Above all, of course, the welfare test under s. 1 of the Children Act 1989 applies in every case. . . .
   In *Re M (A Minor) (Contact: Conditions)* [1994] 1 FLR 272 at p. 279G, I accepted a submission that the law in relation to the principle of re-establishing or maintaining contact was summarised by the following propositions:

   (1)   Wherever possible, a child should get to know his estranged parent, and cogent reasons should be given for denying contact (*Re R (A Minor) (Contact)* [1993] 2 FLR 762).
   (2)   No court should deprive a child of contact to a natural parent unless wholly satisfied that it is in the interests of the child that contact should cease and that is a conclusion at which a court should be extremely slow to arrive (*Re KD (A Minor) (Access: Principles)* [1988] AC 806, [1988] 2 FLR 139 and *Re H (Minors) (Access)* [1992] 1 FLR 148 at p. 150C, following *M v M (Child: Access)* [1973] 2 All ER 81).

(3) It is the normal assumption that a child would benefit from continued contact with a natural parent (*Re B (Minors) (Access)* [1992] 1 FLR 140 at p. 142A). Moreover, as the Court of Appeal made clear in the case of *Re H* (above) the same principles apply whether one is deciding whether or not contact between a child and his absent parent should cease, or whether it should be reintroduced.

. . .

*Note*

See also *Re H (Contact: Principles)* [1994] 2 FLR 969, CA.

In some cases, the court has had to consider whether hostility to contact by the residential parent should justify a refusal of contact.

## Re O (Contact: Imposition of Conditions)
### [1995] 2 FLR 124
### Court of Appeal

*Facts*: The parents were never married and separated before the child was born. The mother did not wish the father to have contact. After direct contact orders were made, the mother would not allow the father to have contact, whereupon a further contact order was made with conditions attached. The mother applied to have one of the conditions discharged as she did not wish to come into contact with the father herself, but her application was dismissed. The mother appealed.

*Held*: dismissing the appeal, that s. 11(7) of the CA 1989 conferred wide and comprehensive powers on the court to ensure contact between the child and the non-custodial parent, where it promoted the welfare of the child.

SIR THOMAS BINGHAM MR: . . . [Section 11(7)] in my judgment confers a wide and comprehensive power to make orders which will be effective to ensure contact between the child and the non-custodial parent where to do so is judged to promote the welfare of the child. . . .

It may perhaps be worth stating in a reasonably compendious way some very familiar but none the less fundamental principles. First of all, and overriding all else as provided in s. 1(1) of the 1989 Act, the welfare of the child is the paramount consideration of any court concerned to make an order relating to the upbringing of a child. It cannot be emphasised too strongly that the court is concerned with the interests of the mother and the father only insofar as they bear on the welfare of the child.

Secondly, where parents of a child are separated and the child is in the day-to-day care of one of them, it is almost always in the interests of the child that he or she should have contact with the other parent. The reason for this scarcely needs spelling out. It is of course that the separation of parents involves a loss to the child and it is desirable that that loss should so far as possible be made good by contact with the non-custodial parent that is the parent in whose day-to-day care the child is not. This has been said on a very great number of occasions and I cite only two of them. In *Re*

*H (Minors) (Access)* [1992] 1 FLR 148 at p. 151A, Balcombe LJ quoted, endorsing as fully as he could, an earlier passage in a judgment of Latey J in which that judge had said:

> . . . where the parents have separated and one has the care of the child, access by the other often results in some upset in the child. Those upsets are usually minor and superficial. They are heavily outweighed by the long-term advantages to the child of keeping in touch with the parent concerned so that they do not become strangers, so that the child later in life does not resent the deprivation and turn against the parent who the child thinks, rightly or wrongly, has deprived him, and so that the deprived parent loses interest in the child and therefore does not make the material and emotional contribution to the child's development which that parent by its companionship and otherwise would make.

My second citation is from *Re J (A Minor) (Contact)* [1994] 1 FLR 729 at p. 736B–C, where Balcombe LJ said:

> But before concluding this judgment I would like to make three general points. The first is that judges should be very reluctant to allow the implacable hostility of one parent (usually the parent who has a residence order in his or her favour), to deter them from making a contact order where they believe the child's welfare requires it. The danger of allowing the implacable hostility of the residential parent (usually the mother) to frustrate the court's decision is too obvious to require repetition on my part.

Thirdly, the court has power to enforce orders for contact, which it should not hesitate to exercise where it judges that it will overall promote the welfare of the child to do so. I refer in this context to the judgment of the President of the Family Division in *Re W (A Minor) (Contact)* [1994] 2 FLR 441 at p. 447H, where the President said:

> However, I am quite clear that a court cannot allow a mother, in such circumstances, simply to defy the order of the court which was, and is, in force, that is to say that there should be reasonable contact with the father. That was indeed made by consent as I have already observed. Some constructive step must be taken to permit and encourage the boy to resume contact with his father.

At p. 449A the President added:

> I wish to make it very clear to the mother that this is an order of the court. The court cannot be put in a position where it is told. 'I shall not obey an order of the court'.

Fourthly, cases do, unhappily and infrequently but occasionally, arise in which a court is compelled to conclude that in existing circumstances an order for immediate direct contact should not be ordered, because so to order would injure the welfare of the child. In *Re D (A Minor) (Contact: Mother's Hostility)* [1993] 2 FLR 1 at p. 7G, Waite LJ said:

> It is now well settled that the implacable hostility of a mother towards access or contact is a factor which is capable, according to the circumstances of each particular case, of supplying a cogent reason for departing from the general principle that a child should grow up in the knowledge of both his parents. I see no reason to think that the judge fell into any error of principle in deciding, as he clearly did on the plain interpretation of his judgment, that the mother's present attitude

towards contact puts D at serious risk of major emotional harm if she were to be compelled to accept a degree of contact to the natural father against her will.

I simply draw attention to the judge's reference to a serious risk of major emotional harm. The courts should not at all readily accept that the child's welfare will be injured by direct contact. Judging that question the court should take a medium-term and long-term view of the child's development and not accord excessive weight to what appear likely to be short-term or transient problems. Neither parent should be encouraged or permitted to think that the more intransigent, the more unreasonable, the more obdurate and the more unco-operative they are, the more likely they are to get their own way. Courts should remember that in these cases they are dealing with parents who are adults, who must be treated as rational adults, who must be assumed to have the welfare of the child at heart, and who have once been close enough to each other to have produced the child. It would be as well if parents also were to bear these points in mind.

Fifthly, in cases in which, for whatever reason, direct contact cannot for the time being be ordered, it is ordinarily highly desirable that there should be indirect contact so that the child grows up knowing of the love and interest of the absent parent with whom, in due course, direct contact should be established. This calls for a measure of restraint, common sense and unselfishness on the part of both parents. If the absent parent deluges the child with presents or writes long and obsessive screeds to the child, or if he or she uses his or her right to correspond to criticise or insult the other parent, then inevitably those rights will be curtailed. The object of indirect contact is to build up a relationship between the absent parent and the child, not to enable the absent parent to pursue a feud with the caring parent in a manner not conducive to the welfare of the child.

The caring parent also has reciprocal obligations. If the caring parent puts difficulties in the way of indirect contact by withholding presents or letters or failing to read letters to a child who cannot read, then such parent must understand that the court can compel compliance with its orders; it has sanctions available and no residence order is to be regarded as irrevocable. It is entirely reasonable that the parent with the care of the child should be obliged to report on the progress of the child to the absent parent, for the obvious reason that an absent parent cannot correspond in a meaningful way if unaware of the child's concerns, or of where the child goes to school, or what it does when it gets there, or what games it plays, and so on. Of course judges must not impose duties which parents cannot realistically be expected to perform, and it would accordingly be absurd to expect, in a case where this was the case, a semi-literate parent to write monthly reports. But some means of communication, directly or indirectly, is essential if indirect contact is to be meaningful, and if the welfare of the child is not to suffer.

. . .

Reviewing this matter overall, I find no fault in the judge's direction on the law, nor in any conclusion of fact, nor in any exercise of discretion. It appears to me that he has handled this case with a high degree of sensitivity, understanding and wisdom, and I would dismiss the appeal.

### Re H (A Minor) (Contact)
[1994] 2 FLR 776
Court of Appeal

BUTLER-SLOSS LJ: . . . It is important that there should not be . . . 'a selfish parents' charter'; that if you do not want your child to see the other parent, then you can make so much fuss that you can prevent the court ordering it. That is not the way the courts see these cases. If it is right for the child to see the husband, then that order is there to be obeyed.

*Notes*
1.   In *Re J (A Minor) (Contact)* [1994] 1 FLR 729, the Court of Appeal refused to make a contact order because of the mother's implacable hostility to contact, but Balcombe LJ emphasised that the case was exceptional and said that 'judges should be very reluctant to allow the implacable hostility of one parent (usually the parent who has a residence order in his or her favour), to deter them from making a contact order where they believe the child's welfare requires it'.
2.   Where there is hostility, indirect contact or a contact order with conditions imposed under CA 1989, s. 11(7) may provide a solution (see *Re O (Contact: Imposition of Conditions), supra*).
3.   Contact is a right of the child, not a parent: see Thompson, J., 'A Right of Access?' (1989) 105 LQR 6 and *Re KD (A minor) (Ward: Termination of Access)* [1988] AC 806 (both referred to in Chapter 7).

*Question*
Many men lose touch with their children when their relationship breaks down. Why do they? Is there anything that could be done about it?

*Further reading*
Ingman, T., 'Contact and the Obdurate Parent' [1996] Fam Law 615.
Jolly, S., 'Implacable Hostility, Contact, and the Limits of the Law' [1995] 7 CFLQ 228.

## 9.5   FINANCE AND PROPERTY ARRANGEMENTS FOR CHILDREN ON FAMILY BREAKDOWN

When parental relationships break down, some parents will agree about financial and property arrangements for their children by reaching agreement themselves or with the help of a solicitor and/or mediator. Where a parent fails to agree about or to cooperate in paying child maintenance, an application may be made to the Child Support Agency under the Child Support Act 1991. In some cases, however, an application for maintenance may be made to the court (e.g., where the child is disabled, or in school fees cases, or where the parents are particularly wealthy). Applications may be made to the divorce court for periodical payments and lump sums for children under Part II of the MCA 1973 and to the family proceedings court under s. 15, and sch. 1 of the CA 1989. The magistrates' court also has jurisdiction under the Domestic Proceedings and Magistrates' Courts Act 1978 to make periodical payments orders and lump sum orders for children, but not property orders.

### 9.5.1 Maintenance

## UNITED NATIONS CONVENTION ON THE RIGHTS OF THE CHILD 1989

**Article 27**

1. States Parties recognize the right of every child to a standard of living adequate for the child's physical, mental, spiritual, moral and social development.

2. The parent(s) or others responsible for the child have the primary responsibility to secure, within their abilities and financial capacities, the conditions of living necessary for the child's development.

3.   . . .

4. States Parties shall take all appropriate measures to secure the recovery of maintenance for the child from the parents or other persons having financial responsibility for the child, both within the State Party and from abroad. In particular, where the person having financial responsibility for the child lives in a State different from that of the child, States Parties shall promote the accession to international agreements or the conclusion of such agreements, as well as the making of other appropriate arrangements.

### 9.5.1.1 Maintenance applications under the Child Support Act 1991

The Child Support Act (CSA) 1991 came into force on 5 April 1993. Before that date any dispute about child maintenance was determined by the courts, which used a discretionary approach to the calculation of maintenance. Dissatisfaction with the discretionary court-based system led to the publication of a Government White Paper, *Children Come First*, which set out the Government's proposals for a new system of child maintenance.

*Children Come First*, **The Government's Proposals on the Maintenance of Children, Cm. 1264**
London: HMSO, vol. 1, 1990

#### FOREWORD

Every child has a right to care from his or her parents. Parents generally have a legal and moral obligation to care for their children until the children are old enough to look after themselves.

The parents of a child may separate. In some instances the parents may not have lived together as a family at all. Although events may change the relationship between the parents — for example, when they divorce — those events cannot in any way change their responsibilities towards their children.

The payment of child maintenance is one crucial way in which parents fulfil their responsibilities towards their children. . . .

The proposals in this White Paper are . . . aimed at . . . the . . . objective of giving priority to the child's welfare if his family breaks up and clarifying and highlighting parental responsibility for securing that welfare.

Government cannot ensure that families stay together. But we can and should ensure that proper financial provision for children is made by their parents whenever it can reasonably be expected.

While many absent parents make regular payments, 70 per cent regrettably do not. The inevitable result is that more and more caring parents and their children have become dependent on Income Support. This makes it more difficult for them to achieve greater independence through working. And, at the same time, it places the responsibility for maintaining the children on other taxpayers, many of whom are raising families of their own.

It is indeed in everyone's interests that the sytem should be reformed. It is in the interests of the children that they should be maintained by their parents. Maintenance provides them with a reliable source of income and they learn about the responsibilities which family members owe to each other.

It is in the interests of their caring parent if they have maintenance for their children. Maintenance provides an invaluable bridge from reliance on Income Support into the world of work.

Many caring parents wish to help provide for their own children by going to work. We believe that Government should help those who are making efforts to do so. So this White Paper also contains proposals to provide further assistance to working parents by amending the rules for paying social security benefits to them.

The measures set out in this White Paper will secure many advantages. Most important of all, they will serve to advance the welfare of children. . . .

## THE SYSTEM NOW — THE CASE FOR CHANGE

. . .

### The case for change

1.5   A number of problems arise in the present system:

- decisions about how much maintenance is to be paid are based largely on discretion and are made in hundreds of courts and hundreds of social security offices. There is inconsistency in the decisions reached even where the circumstances of the people involved appear to be very similar. For example, recent research identified two fathers each with one child to maintain, each earning £150 per week net. One was required to pay £5 per week in maintenance; the other £50 per week;
- some patterns are observable despite this inconsistency. One such pattern is that the 'going rate' for maintenance of one child is about £18 per week. There may be some overlap with awards of spousal maintenance but it plainly costs more than this to care for a child as well as providing food, clothing and other necessities;
- in some instances, the comparatively low level of the maintenance award reflects accurately the ability of the absent parent to pay. Absent parents as a group have a lower average income than the working population at large. But there is nevertheless evidence that higher payments could be afforded in other cases. Maintenance awards represent only about 11% of the total net income of absent parents on above average incomes;
- there is no automatic way in which awards can be reviewed. The period over which a parent may be liable to pay maintenance can extend for many years. The median age of the youngest child at the time maintenance is first assessed is 3 years. Maintenance will be payable for that child for at least another 13 years. During that time many things can change. As they get older, children cost more to feed and clothe; the income of one or both of the parents may change; prices change;
- in 1989 only 30% of lone mothers and 3% of lone fathers received regular child maintenance;
- in 1989 only 23% of lone parents receiving Income Support received child maintenance payments. In 1979 this figure was 50%;

- more than 750,000 lone parents — about two thirds of the total number — are dependent on Income Support to meet the day to day expenses of their children and themselves. Income Support payments represent 45% of the income of all lone parents. The cost in real terms to the taxpayer of income related benefits for lone parents and their children has risen from £1.4 billion in 1981/82 to £3.2 billion in 1988/89;
- while many awards are made promptly, others take weeks or months. The median time to produce a maintenance award varies from 48 days in the magistrates' courts to 131 days in the county courts. Even if the maintenance is part of a divorce settlement, this is a long time, though county courts may make interim awards;
- in a high proportion of cases, payment of the awards made falls into arrears. When payment falls into arrears, the caring parent has to ask the court to take action and it can take weeks to re-establish payment. The full amount of the arrears is recovered in only 23% of cases where DSS takes action. This is equivalent to only 5% of the total value of the arrears;
- 40% of lone mothers work. This compares to 54% of married women with dependent children. Yet three quarters of the lone mothers who are not working and are receiving Income Support express a wish to work now or at some time in the near future;
- the system requires considerable effort on the part of the caring parent to pursue maintenance for her children at the same time as coping with the stress of family break-up.

1.6   There are signs that the system at large is searching for a pattern. The outcomes are not entirely random, but they are not consistent either. There are many actors involved, and each has wide discretion. Consistency, and the perceived fairness which consistency produces, will emerge only by chance. In the interests of the children, a single system is needed and that system needs a structure of consistent and rational principles and clearly established priorities.

## 2.   THE SYSTEM IN THE FUTURE: THE PROPOSALS FOR CHANGE

2.1   The Government proposes to establish a system of child maintenance which will be equally available to any person seeking maintenance for the benefit of a child and which will:

- ensure that parents honour their legal and moral responsibility to maintain their own children whenever they can afford to do so. It is right that other taxpayers should help to maintain children when the children's own parents, despite their own best efforts, do not have enough resources to do so themselves. That will continue to be the case. But it is not right that taxpayers, who include other families, should shoulder that responsibility instead of parents who are able to do it themselves;
- recognise that where a liable parent has formed a second family and has further natural children, he is liable to maintain all his own children. A fair and reasonable balance has to be struck between the interests of the children of a first family and the children of a second;
- produce consistent and predictable results so that people in similar financial circumstances will pay similar amounts of maintenance, and so that people will know in advance what their maintenance obligations are going to be;

- enable maintenance to be decided in a fair and reasonable way which reduces the scope for its becoming a contest between the parents to the detriment of the interests of the children;
- produce maintenance payments which are realistically related to the costs of caring for a child;
- allow for maintenance payments to be reviewed regularly so that changes in circumstances can be taken into account automatically;
- recognise that both parents have a legal responsibility to maintain their children;
- ensure that parents meet the cost of their children's maintenance whenever they can without removing the parents' own incentives to work, and to go on working;
- enable caring parents who wish to work to do so as soon as they feel ready and able;
- provide an efficient and effective service to the public which ensures that:

    (a) maintenance is paid regularly and on time so that it provides a reliable income for the caring parent and the children and
    (b) produces maintenance quickly so that the habit of payment is established early and is not compromised by early arrears;

- avoid the children and their caring parent becoming dependent on Income Support whenever this is possible and, where it is not possible, to minimise the period of dependence.

. . .

# CHILD SUPPORT ACT 1991

## 1. The duty to maintain
(1) For the purposes of this Act, each parent of a qualifying child is responsible for maintaining him.

(2) For the purposes of this Act, an absent parent shall be taken to have met his responsibility to maintain any qualifying child of his by making periodical payments of maintenance with respect to the child of such amount, and at such intervals, as may be determined in accordance with the provisions of this Act.

(3) Where a maintenance assessment made under this Act requires the making of periodical payments, it shall be the duty of the absent parent with respect to whom the assessment was made to make those payments.

## 2. Welfare of children: the general principle
Where, in any case which falls to be dealt with under this Act, the Secretary of State or any child support officer is considering the exercise of any discretionary power conferred by this Act, he shall have regard to the welfare of any child likely to be affected by his decision.

## 3. Meaning of certain terms used in this Act
(1) A child is a 'qualifying child' if—
    (a) one of his parents is, in relation to him, an absent parent; or
    (b) both of his parents are, in relation to him, absent parents.
(2) The parent of any child is an 'absent parent', in relation to him, if—
    (a) that parent is not living in the same household with the child; and
    (b) the child has his home with a person who is, in relation to him, a person with care.

(3)  A person is a 'person with care', in relation to any child, if he is a person—

(a)  with whom the child has his home;

(b)  who usually provides day to day care for the child (whether exclusively or in conjunction with any other person); and

(c)  who does not fall within a prescribed category of person.

(4)  . . .

(5)  For the purposes of this Act there may be more than one person with care in relation to the same qualifying child.

. . .

## 6. Applications by those receiving benefits

(1)  Where income support, family credit or any other benefit of a prescribed kind is claimed by or in respect of, or paid to or in respect of, the parent of a qualifying child she shall, if—

(a)  she is a person with care of the child; and

(b)  she is required to do so by the Secretary of State,

authorise the Secretary of State to take action under this Act to recover child support maintenance from the absent parent.

(2)  The Secretary of State shall not require a person ('the parent') to give him the authorisation mentioned in subsection (1) if he considers that there are reasonable grounds for believing that—

(a)  if the parent were to be required to give that authorisation; or

(b)  if she were to give it,

there would be a risk of her, or of any child living with her, suffering harm or undue distress as a result.

. . .

## 9. Agreements about maintenance

. . .

(2)  Nothing in this Act shall be taken to prevent any person from entering into a maintenance agreement.

(3)  The existence of a maintenance agreement shall not prevent any party to the agreement, or any other person, from applying for a maintenance assessment with respect to any child to or for whose benefit periodical payments are to be made or secured under the agreement.

(4)  Where any agreement contains a provision which purports to restrict the right of any person to apply for a maintenance assessment, that provision shall be void.

. . .

## 44. Jurisdiction

(1)  A child support officer shall have jurisdiction to make a maintenance assessment with respect to a person who is—

(a)  a person with care;

(b)  an absent parent; or

(c)  a qualifying child,

only if that person is habitually resident in the United Kingdom.

. . .

## 55. Meaning of 'child'

(1)  For the purposes of this Act a person is a child if—

(a)  he is under the age of 16;

(b)   he is under the age of 19 and receiving full-time education (which is not advanced education)—
    (i)   by attendance at a recognised educational establishment; or
    (ii)  elsewhere, if the education is recognised by the Secretary of State; or
(c)   he does not fall within paragraph (a) or (b) but—
    (i)   he is under the age of 18, and
    (ii)  prescribed conditions are satisfied with respect to him.
(2)   A person is not a child for the purposes of this Act if he—
(a)   is or has been married;
(b)   has celebrated a marriage which is void; or
(c)   has celebrated a marriage in respect of which a decree of nullity has been granted.
. . .

## Notes

*1.*   A 'qualifying child' includes an adopted child and also a child born to a couple by artificial insemination by donor, unless it is proved that the husband did not consent to the insemination. Under the Human Fertilisation and Embryology Act 1990, a man who signs a fertility clinic consent form is legally the father of the child.
*2.*   The CSA 1991 is backed up by a vast body of secondary legislation.

### 9.5.1.2   Assessing maintenance
Appendix B to the White Paper, *Improving Child Support*, explains how the formula for assessing the maintenance payable works.

**Government White Paper, *Improving Child Support*, Cm 2745**
London: HMSO, 1995, Appendix B

**General principle**
The formula is designed to reflect the ability of *both* parents to contribute to the maintenance of their children. Consequently, the circumstances of each of them are considered when maintenance payable by the absent parent is assessed. In the majority of cases, the parent with care may be in receipt of Income Support or may otherwise have a low income and so cannot normally afford to contribute. However, where a parent with care does have sufficient income, she is assessed to contribute to the cost of maintaining her children on the same basis as the absent parent, and this has the effect of reducing the amount of maintenance the absent parent is required to pay.

**The formula**
The maintenance formula consists of several component parts, as follows:

* The **maintenance requirement** for the children, which is based on Income Support rates and is the amount all parents should pay if they can afford it.
* The **assessable income** of each parent, derived from a calculation of the net income of each parent less an allowance for expenses (known as exempt income). Maintenance is paid at the rate of 50p in each £1 of assessable income until the maintenance requirement is met.

- An **additional element** payable by parents who can pay more than the maintenance requirement, up to a maximum amount.
- A safeguard — **protected income** — which reduces the maintenance payable by absent parents in certain circumstances, to ensure their income remains well above Income Support level.

## The maintenance requirement

This is the amount needed to provide for the basic day-to-day needs of the child or children for whom a maintenance assessment is being made. It is based on the Income Support rates for personal and other needs. Because a child needs to be looked after, as well as fed and clothed, the maintenance requirement includes an amount equal to the Income Support personal allowance for a person aged 25 or over. This is for the care needed by the child and does *not* represent maintenance for the parent with care — spousal maintenance remains a matter for the courts to decide. This allowance is reduced when the youngest child reaches 11 and again at 14, to reflect the fact that the level of day-to-day care needed by children lessens as they grow older. It is omitted where there is no child aged under 16 to be maintained.

## Calculating income

After calculating the maintenance requirement the formula looks at parents' ability to pay. The first stage is to calculate net income, which includes income from other sources as well as earnings from employment. The net earnings from employment are calculated by deducting tax, national insurance and half of any contributions to a pension, from the gross amount. The allowance of half of the pension contribution follows the general pattern adopted in the assessment of income-related benefits, achieving roughly equal treatment between those contracted into and those contracted out of the state pension scheme. This approach also provides a balance between the need to make provision for retirement and a child's need for basic maintenance.

The calculation of earnings for the self-employed is intended to reflect the flow of cash through the business and the money available to the absent parent for payment of maintenance. The calculation reflects the difference between the gross receipts from the business and expenses wholly, exclusively and necessarily incurred in *running*, but not in *expanding*, the business. This means that a very wide range of expenses is allowed. Although there is no allowance for capital expenditure, the interest payments on a loan reasonably taken out for the purposes of the business are allowed. In addition, capital repayments may be allowed where the loan is for the replacement of equipment or machinery. These provisions are designed to strike a balance between the needs of the business and a child's right to basic maintenance.

## Exempt income

The next step is to calculate an allowance known as exempt income. This represents the basic personal expenditure of the parents and any children of their own who live with them, again based on Income Support rates. It includes a personal allowance for the parent and the parent's housing costs. It also includes allowances and housing costs for any children of that parent living with him or her.

## Cases where the absent parent has a new partner

An absent parent's new partner has no liability for the maintenance of children from the absent parent's previous relationship. Her income is ignored in the assessment of his net income. She is, however, expected to contribute equally to the support of her own children from the new relationship, if she has sufficient income.

Additionally, the housing costs included in his exempt income are allowed only for himself and any of his own children who live with him. When he has a new partner, or a second family, the costs are apportioned, the absent parent being allowed only the share for himself and any of his own children in the exempt income calculation.

### Calculating the amount of maintenance payable

When the exempt income has been calculated, it is subtracted from net income to leave an element of the formula known as assessable income. A deduction rate of 50 per cent is applied to the assessable income until the maintenance requirement is met. Where the absent parent has assessable income left after he has met the basic maintenance requirement, the formula provides for an additional element of maintenance to be calculated. The deduction rate applied is 15 per cent where there is only one child, 20 per cent where there are two children, and 25 per cent where there are three or more. The principle behind the additional element is that, as a parent's income increases, it is right that his children should share in his prosperity as they would if they continued to live with him. The lower deduction rates reflect the fact that, in general, as income rises, a greater proportion is kept by parents for their own use.

### Protected income

The maintenance formula includes an important safeguard known as protected income. A calculation is made in all cases to ensure that the absent parent (and his second family if he has one) retains significantly more income after he has paid maintenance, than he would receive if he were unemployed and claiming Income Support. When calculating protected income, the needs of all members of the second family are considered, with allowances for the new partner and any step-children as well as for the absent parent and any of his children who live with him. This amount is then compared with the family's total income.

Overall, the level of protection is set at a minimum of £30 above the appropriate Income Support level. An additional level of protection, set at 15 per cent of the difference between this amount and the family's net income, is then added to that basic amount.

The protected income calculation shows whether the absent parent can afford to pay the full amount of maintenance which has been assessed, or whether it needs to be reduced so that he and his new family keep more of his income. It ensures that, where absent parents have insufficient income, the interests of second families are protected and placed before those of the first. In particular, the allowances for step-children safeguard their interests where their own absent parent is not paying maintenance.

### Phasing in payments

There are also provisions for phasing in the new amounts of maintenance where absent parents have previously been paying under a court order or written maintenance agreement, and have responsibility for children. These provisions were extended considerably in February 1994, and absent parents now have up to 18 months to adjust to the new levels.

### Shared care

Where two parents each care for a child at least 104 nights a year (that is, two nights a week on average), the parent who provides the lesser amount of care is treated as the absent parent. The maintenance assessment in these cases differs from the standard formula. The allowances made against the absent parent's net income for basic expenditure include amounts for the child, based on the time spent with the parent. The maintenance payment for the child is then worked out in the normal way, but is reduced pro rata to the number of nights the child stays with him.

These provisions mean that an absent parent's maintenance liability will be reduced where he is providing a significant amount of care for a child. Basing the provision on nights of care recognises the additional costs involved in providing overnight accommodation.

**Absent parent required to pay maintenance for children in more than one family**
Where there are applications to the Agency in respect of children in two or more families, the maintenance requirement for the children in each family is assessed in the normal way. The absent parent's assessable income is then divided pro rata to each maintenance requirement before maintenance is deducted.

*Notes*
1.  Applications for child maintenance may be made to the court where:

*   the absent parent's income is substantial and it is appropriate to apply for an order to 'top up' the Agency assessment (s. 8(6));
*   maintenance is required for the child's instruction or training while at an educational establishment or while undergoing training for a trade, profession or vocation (s. 8(7));
*   maintenance is required to provide expenses for a child in receipt of disability allowance or who is disabled (s. 8(8)); or
*   where maintenance is required against the person with care of the child (s. 8(10)).

2.  There is nothing in the 1991 Act to prevent parents making private agreements and consent orders (see Chapter 5) about child maintenance, but the agreement or order cannot oust the jurisdiction of the Agency (see CSA 1991, ss. 9 and 8(5)).

The following were some of the reactions to the creation of the Child Support Agency.

### *Independent on Sunday*, 20 February 1994

A hate campaign involving death threats, bomb hoaxes and abuse is being waged against staff at the government agency designed to track down absent parents. . . . In one case, a man said he would use a shotgun to kill himself and a member of staff. General abuse occurs daily.

### *The Sunday Telegraph*, 27 March 1994

The CSA began life with the aim of catching 'deadbeat dads' and slashing the social security bill. But . . . it metamorphosed into an engine of state power that has provoked outrage, farce and tragedy.

### Ann Chant, Director of the Child Support Agency, at the Commons Select Committee on the Parliamentary Commissioner for Administration, as reported in *The Times*, 2 February 1995

I have never seen in 30 years in social security such an orchestrated and organised attempt to avoid legal liability. That was unprecedented and I don't think it could reasonably have been foreseen.

### Maggie Rae, reviewing the Child Support Agency's First Annual Report
### (1994) 144 NLJ 970

. . . Supporters of the Child Support Agency are few and far between these days and we tend to keep ourselves carefully hidden from view. Unhappily, the First Annual Report of the operations of the Agency gives more ammunition to those who call for repeal than those of us who still want reform. . . .

### Bispham, Jennifer, and Greaney, Angeline, 'Child Support Act: Contra-indications for Ancillary Relief and Contact'
### [1993] Fam Law 525

. . . It is a matter of much regret that the Child Support Act 1991, rather than complementing the operation and effectiveness of the Children Act 1989, runs contrary to the Children Act philosophy of non-intervention, trust, support and partnership approach wherever possible. It is, in essence, a taxing statute. . . .

*Further reading*
Maclean, M., and Eekelaar, J., 'Child Support: The British Solution' (1993) 7 IJL&F 205.
Stone, P., 'Discrimination in Child Maintenance', in Dine, J., and Watt, R. (eds), *Justifying Discrimination*, London: Longman, 1996, Chapter 7.

### 9.5.1.3 Improving child support

### Debates on the Child Support Bill 1995
*Hansard*, HL vol. 564, col. 1190

LORD SIMON OF GLAISDALE: . . . [The 1991 Act] has been an unprecedented legislative disaster. It has caused injustice; it has caused hardship; it has caused enormous public expense resulting in administrative chaos.

After considerable public criticism of the 1991 Act, the Government published a White Paper (*Improving Child Support*) in 1995, in which it outlined proposals to improve the child maintenance system existing under the CSA 1991. Criticisms had been made, in particular, about the Act's detrimental effect on step-children (see, e.g., *R v Secretary of State for Social Security, ex parte Biggin* [1995] 1 FLR 851, QBD) and its unjust impact on divorce 'clean break' settlements made prior to the Act coming into force (see, e.g., *Crozier* v *Crozier* [1994] Fam 114).

## Government White Paper, *Improving Child Support*, Cm. 2745
### London: HMSO, 1995

**Introduction and summary**

**1.** This White Paper sets out proposals for changes to the child support maintenance scheme.

**2.** The regular receipt of maintenance can transform the lives of parents with care and their children, because it widens the choices available to them and enables them to work if they wish to do so, improving the standard of living of their children. . . . The proposals in this White Paper are intended to ensure that many more children are supported by their own parents whenever they can afford to maintain them, and that absent parents are not able wilfully to avoid their responsibilities. The Government believes that changes are needed to the system to ensure that it is more widely acceptable to absent parents and that more maintenance is actually paid to parents with care.

**3.** The Government believes that the principles underlying the child support system are right. They command support from both the general public and Parliament, and have been endorsed by the Social Security Select Committee on each occasion it has examined the scheme. The Government believes also that a formula approach to the assessment of child support maintenance is appropriate for the great majority of separated parents. The Government has always recognised, however, that the Child Support Act was a major change in the law with significant social implications and has repeatedly stressed its intention to examine the effects of the child support system. The Secretary of State for Social Security has accordingly monitored the child support arrangements and has taken careful note of the helpful and constructive advice of the Social Security Select Committee in its recent second report on the scheme [*The Operation of the Child Support Act: Proposals for Change,* Session 1993–94 (Fifth Report)]. The Government has decided that changes are needed to prevent undue hardship and to enable the Child Support Agency to operate effectively. In framing its proposals for change, the Government has taken care to ensure that the interests of all the parties — the absent parent, the parent with care and the children, and the taxpayer — are taken fully into account and that a sound balance has been maintained throughout.

**4.** The changes proposed are summarised below.

**a.** The introduction during 1996/7, following primary legislation, of some discretion to depart from the maintenance formula assessment in cases where the absent parent would otherwise face hardship or where certain property or capital transfers took place before April 1993. There will be closely specified grounds for the special circumstances that will be considered, and limits on the extent of the departure. Either parent will be able to apply for a departure, and both will be entitled to make representations.

**b.** Changes to the maintenance formula from April 1995:

- no absent parent will be assessed to pay more than 30 per cent of his normal net income in current child maintenance, or more than 33 per cent in a combination of current maintenance and start-up arrears;

- a broad-brush adjustment will be provided in the maintenance formula to take account of property and capital settlements;
- an allowance will be made towards high travel-to-work costs;
- housing costs will be allowed for a new partner or step-children;
- the maximum level of maintenance payable under the formula will be reduced.

**c.** From April 1997, parents with care in receipt of Income Support or Jobseeker's Allowance will be able to build up a maintenance credit which will be paid as a lump sum when the recipient starts work of at least 16 hours a week.

**d.** Family Credit and Disability Working Allowance recipients will receive some compensation for loss of maintenance where the changes in **b.** above result in a reduction in their assessment during an award of benefit.

**e.** Fees will be suspended for a period of two years until April 1997; and interest payments will also be suspended, to be replaced after two years with a penalty for late payment.

**f.** Changes will also be made to improve the administration of the scheme including:

- the deferment of the take-on by the Child Support Agency in 1996/7 of cases not in receipt of Income Support, Family Credit or Disability Working Allowance where there was a court order or written maintenance agreement before April 1993. These cases will continue to be able to use the courts;
- where the Agency causes a delay in setting maintenance, consideration will be given to not enforcing more than six months' worth of arrears, provided the absent parent gives a commitment to meet his on-going liability;
- a simpler way of dealing with change of circumstances reports;
- periodic reviews every two years;
- deferral of liability by eight weeks when the absent parent provides certain relevant information within four weeks of the date the maintenance enquiry form is issued to him;
- changes to simplify the definitions of housing costs and earnings;
- changes to the interim maintenance assessment rules including:

  — the introduction of an interim assessment for self-employed absent parents;
  — the introduction of a protected income provision when deduction from earnings orders are applied in interim maintenance assessment cases;

. . .

**Experience to date**

**1.3** The child support system represents a substantial improvement compared with the old fragmented and uncertain system which preceded it. However, it has faced a great deal of opposition, mainly from absent parents who were unwilling to pay any maintenance or higher amounts of maintenance than in the past. Some of them have deliberately obstructed the work of the Agency. This matches experience in other countries that have introduced similar schemes and demonstrates the magnitude of the changes in attitude and practice needed if parents are to recognise that the primary responsibility for supporting their children rests with them rather than the state. Again, experience in other countries is that parents' attitudes do change over time, as child support schemes gain wider public acceptance. The Government has consistently promised to keep the scheme under review and to make any necessary changes in the light of experience.

**1.4** The Government introduced measures in February 1994 which met many of the early criticisms of the scheme. In particular, the changes aimed to ease the transition to higher payments for some pre-1993 cases, and to moderate maintenance payments for absent parents with low incomes or substantial second family commitments.

**1.5** As the Child Support Agency's case-load has increased, the Government has continued to look carefully at the whole system in the light of experience and criticism of it, bearing in mind the following principles:

- parents should maintain their own children to the extent that they can afford to do so;
- the scheme should be perceived to be fair in its treatment of both parents and of the children;
- child maintenance should be paid at an appropriate amount, regularly and on time;
- the Child Support Agency should deliver an efficient and effective service;
- some protection should be afforded to parents with care on benefit who are affected by the changes;
- incentives for parents with care who wish to work should be improved;
- recognition should be given to formal child maintenance arrangements involving transfers of assets, made before the Child Support Act was implemented in April 1993;
- absent parents should be able to support themselves after paying maintenance.

. . .

### Introduction of discretion

**1.7** The Government continues to believe that the principles underlying the child support system are best realised, in the main, through maintenance assessments based on an objective formula. There is no wish in Government or in Parliament to see a return to a discretion-based system, with its attendant problems of inconsistency and unfairness. But the Government recognises that there is a small minority of cases where there are special circumstances which it would be right to take into account but which cannot be reflected in a universal formula.

**1.8** The Government therefore proposes to introduce a Bill to provide for a limited discretion to depart from the strict formula assessment in appropriate cases. This should provide a safety valve for the genuine hard case. It is important, however, that discretion does not undermine the whole basis of the Act. The Bill will therefore provide for discretion to be exercised only in tightly specified circumstances: generally that the absent parent has necessary expenses not allowed for in the formula and that failure to take them into account would result in hardship. This will not be an automatic process: each case will be thoroughly examined, and departure will be allowed only where this is fair, taking account of the circumstances of both parents and the interests of the children. Parents with care will also be able to apply for a departure from the formula. The system of departures will also deal with property or capital settlements in certain cases.

**1.9** Discretion will be exercised by the Child Support Agency in the first instance, but there will be a right for either party to ask that the issues be looked at afresh by an independent Child Support Appeal Tribunal. . . .

**1.10** The Government intends to bring forward the necessary legislation in the current session of Parliament and to introduce the new departures system during 1996/7, the earliest possible date in view of the need for legislation.

## Property or capital transfers
**1.11** A major source of criticism has been the lack of specific recognition for cases where, as part of a settlement between parents made prior to April 1993, there was a transfer of property or capital from one parent to the other. Settlements of this kind have been labelled 'clean break settlements'. In relation to children, this terminology is incorrect, since it is not possible for parents to terminate their financial obligations to their children. Where there was a property or capital settlement between the parents, it was always open to the parent with care to return to court for increased child maintenance and for the Secretary of State for Social Security to seek maintenance to recover Income Support paid for the children. The practical consequences of these settlements are often reflected in the maintenance formula. For example, an absent parent's maintenance payment will be lower if handing over his share of the equity in the former home means he then has less capital to spend on his new home and has taken out a larger mortgage on it (which is taken into account under the formula). However, the effects of such a settlement are not all directly taken into account in the formula. The Government intends, therefore, that either party should be able to ask for the consequences of a settlement to be taken into account.
**1.12** The system for departures from the formula will eventually be able to deal with these cases on an individual basis. But the need for primary legislation means that departure arrangements cannot be introduced until well into 1996. The Government proposes, therefore, to introduce from April 1995 a broad-brush adjustment in the formula to provide some recognition of these settlements. Once the system for departures is established, either parent will be able to ask for their case to be considered individually, if they believe the broad-brush provision under the formula is inappropriate. . . .

## Changes to the formula
**1.13** The Government believes the formula approach is right in the majority of cases, but, in the light of experience, it proposes to make some modifications to the formula to take account of particular concerns that have been raised. The Government intends to bring the changes described below into effect in April 1995. . . .

## A limit to maintenance as a proportion of net income
**1.14** The original expectation, based on detailed modelling using the best available information before the scheme was introduced, was that only a very small number of cases would involve maintenance payments of more than 30 per cent of net income. Experience has shown that a significant minority of absent parents is assessed to pay more than 30 per cent. The Government intends, therefore, to introduce a cap on the amount of maintenance payable under the formula, so that normally no one is assessed to pay more than 30 per cent of net income in current maintenance. In cases where there are also arrears which have accumulated in the period before maintenance was assessed, payments will generally be limited to no more than 33 per cent of net income.

## Costs of travel to work
**1.15** The net income remaining after maintenance is paid should in most cases be sufficient to enable absent parents to meet their travel-to-work costs amongst other expenses, but the Government recognises that, in some cases, the costs of travel to work will be unusually high. It is therefore proposed to introduce into the formula some provision for those who commute long distances based on the distance between the parent's home and workplace. The allowance will not apply to self-employed people or to those who do not incur an actual cost. People facing exceptional travel

costs not covered by this allowance in the formula will be able to seek a departure from the formula.

**Second families**
**1.16** Many parents have argued that the formula does not treat their second family fairly compared with the first family. In fact, the needs of natural children of a second relationship have always taken precedence over maintenance for a first family, and in many cases the protected income provision in the formula ensures that the needs of step-children take precedence too. But at present, where an absent parent does not benefit from the protected income provision, no allowance is made for the housing costs of his new partner or step-children. The Government proposes to remedy this by allowing the new partner's housing costs, and those of any step-children living with the parent, in the calculation of exempt income.

**Maximum payable under the formula**
**1.17** Where an absent parent is able to pay the full amount of the basic maintenance requirement and still has assessable income above that level, he is required to pay an 'additional element' until he reaches the maximum payable under the formula. The maximum varies from case to case and can be very high indeed where there are several children. The Government has decided to halve the maximum additional element.
. . .

The proposals in the White Paper were enacted in the Child Support Act 1995, the main feature of which has been to introduce a 'departures' system, whereby the Secretary of State is able to issue a direction modifying the application of the formula in certain prescribed cases. The Act should not, however, be seen as a return to a discretionary system.

Section 1 of the Child Support Act 1995 inserts, *inter alia*, the following new provision, s. 28A, after s. 28 of the 1991 Act, to deal with applications for a departure direction, i.e. a departure from the usual rules for determining maintenance assessments.

## CHILD SUPPORT ACT 1991

**28A. Application for a departure decision**
(1) Where a maintenance assessment ('the current assessment') is in force—
    (a) the person with care, or absent parent, with respect to whom it was made, or
    (b) where the application for the current assessment was made under section 7, either of those persons or the child concerned,
may apply to the Secretary of State for a direction under section 28F (a 'departure direction').
(2) An application for a departure direction shall state in writing the grounds on which it is made and shall, in particular, state whether it is based on—
    (a) the effect of the current assessment; or
    (b) a material change in the circumstances of the case since the current assessment was made.
(3) In other respects, an application for a departure direction shall be made in such manner as may be prescribed.
. . .

*Questions*
1.   What are the advantages of a discretionary system of calculating maintenance? What are the advantages of a formulaic approach? Which is more just?
2.   Maintenance is an important part of parental responsibility for children,
but the unmarried father with no parental responsibility (see Chapter 8) also
has an obligation to pay maintenance. Is this justifiable?
3.   Was the main aim of the CSA 1991 to cut down on the social security
costs consequent on family breakdown or to promote the welfare of children?
4.   Is there any logical or rational coherence in a system which devolves child
maintenance to an administrative agency, while lawyers, judges and mediators retain responsibility for dealing with property and capital issues both for
parents and for children?
5.   Why should biological parenthood rather than social parenthood provide
the basis for the support obligation towards children?
6.   Are the terms 'caring parent' and 'absent parent' satisfactory terms or are
they somewhat derogatory?

*Further reading*
Abbott, D., 'Child Support and the Clean Break: Once a Parent . . .' (1994)
144 NLJ 244.
Bird, R., 'Child Support: Reform or Tinkering' [1995] Fam Law 112.
Collier, R., 'The Campaign against the Child Support Act; "Errant Fathers"
and "Family Men"' [1994] Fam Law 384.
Eekelaar, J., 'A Child Support Scheme for the UK — an Analysis of the
White Paper' [1991] Fam Law 15.
Eekelaar, J., 'Third Thoughts on Child Support' [1994] Fam Law 99.
Elly, C., 'Comment: Policy or Politics?' [1994] Fam Law 361.
Gillespie, G., 'The Child Support Act — the Hand that Rocks the Cradle'
[1996] Fam Law 162.
Hilaire, B., 'Reflections on the Child Support Act 1991' (1993) 5 JCL 77.
Jackson, E., and Wasoff, F. with Maclean, M., and Emerson Dobash, R.,
'Financial Support on Divorce: the Right Mixture of Rules and Discretion?'
(1993) 7 IJL&F 230.
Leigh, J., 'Child Maintenance: a View from the Law Society' (1991) 3 JCL
41.
Meadows, H., 'Child Maintenance after the 1991 Act. The Residual Func-
tions of the Court' [1994] Fam Law 96.
Rae, M., 'The Future of the Child Support Act' (1993) 143 NLJ 1600.
Rae, M., 'Caring Parents and Absent Parents' (1993) 143 NLJ 513.
*Child Support Handbook*, 4th edn, London: Child Poverty Action Group,
1996.

### 9.5.2   Finance and property orders for children in divorce
proceedings

The divorce court has jurisdiction under Part II of the MCA 1973 to make
financial provision orders (maintenance and lump sums) and property adjust-

ment orders for children, although applications for child maintenance must be made to the Child Support Agency under the CSA 1991 and 1995 (see 9.5.1) unless the child is a special case.

The divorce court must consider the following matters when exercising its jurisdiction to make periodical payments, lump sums and property orders for children (see 5.2 for more detail).

## MATRIMONIAL CAUSES ACT 1973

**25. Matters to which court is to have regard in deciding how to exercise its powers under sections 23, 24 and 24A**

(1)   It shall be the duty of the court in deciding whether to exercise its powers under section 23, 24 or 24A . . . and, if so, in what manner, to have regard to all the circumstances of the case, first consideration being given to the welfare while a minor of any child of the family who has not attained the age of eighteen.

(2)   . . .

(3)   As regards the exercise of the powers of the court . . . in relation to a child of the family, the court shall in particular have regard to the following matters—

(a)   the financial needs of the child;

(b)   the income, earning capacity (if any), property and other financial resources of the child;

(c)   any physical or mental disability of the child;

(d)   the manner in which he was being and in which the parties to the marriage expected him to be educated or trained;

(e)   the considerations mentioned in relation to the parties to the marriage in paragraphs (a), (b), (c) and (e) of subsection (2) above [see 5.3.2].

(4)   As regards the exercise of the powers of the court . . . above against a party to a marriage in favour of a child of the family who is not the child of that party, the court shall also have regard—

(a)   to whether that party assumed any responsibility for the child's maintenance, and, if so, to the extent to which, and the basis upon which, that party assumed such responsibility and to the length of time for which that party discharged such responsibility;

(b)   to whether in assuming and discharging such responsibility that party did so knowing that the child was not his or her own;

(c)   to the liability of any other person to maintain the child.

### 9.5.3   Finance and property orders under the Children Act 1989, sch. 1

Under sch. 1 to the CA 1989, the court has jurisdiction to make orders for financial relief for children against their parents. Under para. 1, the court, on the application of a parent or guardian, or of a person with a residence order in his or her favour in respect of the child, has jurisdiction to make the following orders for children:

- periodical payments (unsecured and secured);
- a lump sum;
- a settlement of property;
- a transfer of property.

These powers may be exercised at any time (sch. 1, para. 1(3)). The magistrates' family proceedings court has only jurisdiction to make periodical payments and lump sum orders, not property orders (sch. 1, para. 1(1)(b)).

Under para. 2, the court has jurisdiction to make periodical payments and lump sum orders against one or both parents on the application of a 'child' aged over 18, who will or (if an order were made under para. 2) would be receiving instruction at an educational establishment or undergoing training for a trade, profession or vocation (whether or not in gainful employment), or where special circumstances justify the making of an order.

Schedule 1, para. 4 lays down the matters which the court must consider when exercising its powers under paras 1 and 2.

## CHILDREN ACT 1989

### SCHEDULE 1
### FINANCIAL PROVISION FOR CHILDREN

. . .

4.—(1)   In deciding whether to exercise its powers under paragraph 1 or 2, and if so in what manner, the court shall have regard to all the circumstances, including—

(a)   the income, earning capacity, property and other financial resources which each person mentioned in sub-paragraph (4) has or is likely to have in the foreseeable future;

(b)   the financial needs, obligations and responsibilities which each person mentioned in sub-paragraph (4) has or is likely to have in the foreseeable future;

(c)   the financial needs of the child;

(d)   the income, earning capacity (if any), property and other financial resources of the child;

(e)   any physical or mental disability of the child;

(f)   the manner in which the child was being, or was expected to be, educated or trained.

(2)   In deciding whether to exercise its powers under paragraph 1 against a person who is not the mother or father of the child, and if so in what manner, the court shall in addition have regard to—

(a)   whether that person has assumed responsibility for the maintenance of the child and, if so, the extent to which and basis on which he assumed that responsibility and the length of the period during which he met that responsibility;

(b)   whether he did so knowing that the child was not his child;

(c)   the liability of any other person to maintain the child.

(3)   Where the court makes an order under paragraph 1 against a person who is not the father of the child, it shall record in the order that the order is made on the basis that the person against whom the order is made is not the child's father.

(4)   The persons mentioned in sub-paragraph (1) are—

(a)   in relation to a decision whether to exercise its powers under paragraph 1, any parent of the child;

(b)   in relation to a decision whether to exercise its powers under paragraph 2, the mother and father of the child;

(c)   the applicant for the order;

(d)   any other person in whose favour the court proposes to make the order.

. . .

*Notes*
1.   Schedule 1 to the CA 1989 has been given a narrow construction to emphasise that the aim of applications is to provide financial provision during a child's dependency (except where the child has special needs or is receiving full-time education or vocational training) (see *T* v *S (Financial Provision for Children)* [1994] 2 FLR 883, FD, and *A* v *A (A Minor: Financial Provision)* [1994] 1 FLR 657, FD).
2.   As sch. 1 proceedings are 'family proceedings' (CA 1989, s. 8(4)), the court may make any s. 8 order (see Chapter 7) on an application or of its own motion in the proceedings.
3.   The welfare principle in CA 1989, s. 1(1) does not apply to applications for financial provision under sch. 1 (see CA 1989, s. 105(1), which defines the term 'upbringing' in s. 1(1) as including the care of the child but not his or her maintenance).
4.   For a case involving a property transfer to a child for the child's benefit, see *K* v *K (Minors: Property Transfer)* [1992] 2 FLR 220, CA (a case brought under the Guardianship of Minors Act 1971 (repealed by the CA 1989), but the provisions of which are not materially different from the CA 1989, sch. 1). See also *H* v *P (Illegitimate Child: Capital Provision)* [1993] Fam 515.

*Further reading*
Wingert, R., 'Capital Provision for Children of Unmarried Parents' [1994] Fam Law 194.

# 10 CHILDREN: PUBLIC LAW PROTECTION

This chapter looks at the public law provisions of the Children Act (CA) 1989 which afford support and protection for children in need, or those who are suffering or at risk of suffering harm.

## 10.1 INTRODUCTION

### UNITED NATIONS CONVENTION ON THE RIGHTS OF THE CHILD 1989

**Article 9**

1. States Parties shall ensure that a child shall not be separated from his or her parents against their will, except when competent authorities subject to judicial review determine, in accordance with applicable law and procedures, that such separation is necessary for the best interests of the child. Such determination may be necessary in a particular case such as one involving abuse or neglect of the child by the parents, or one where the parents are living separately and a decision must be made as to the child's place of residence.

2. In any proceedings pursuant to paragraph 1 of the present article, all interested parties shall be given an opportunity to participate in the proceedings and make their views known.

3. States Parties shall respect the right of the child who is separated from one or both parents to maintain personal relations and direct contact with both parents on a regular basis, except if it is contrary to the child's best interests.

. . .

**Article 19**

1. States Parties shall take all appropriate legislative, administrative, social and educational measures to protect the child from all forms of physical or mental

violence, injury or abuse, neglect or negligent treatment, maltreatment or exploitation, including sexual abuse, while in the care of parent(s), legal guardian(s) or any other person who has the care of the child.

. . .

**Article 20**
1.   A child temporarily or permanently deprived of his or her family environment, or in whose own best interests cannot be allowed to remain in that environment, shall be entitled to special protection and assistance provided by the State.
2.   States Parties shall in accordance with their national laws ensure alternative care for such a child.
3.   Such care could include, *inter alia*, foster placement, *kafalah* of Islamic law, adoption or if necessary placement in suitable institutions for the care of children. When considering solutions, due regard shall be paid to the desirability of continuity in a child's upbringing and to the child's ethnic, religious, cultural and linguistic background.

. . .

**Article 25**
States Parties recognize the right of a child who has been placed by the competent authorities for the purposes of care, protection or treatment of his or her physical or mental health, to a periodic review of the treatment provided to the child and all other circumstances relevant to his or her placement.

'Samantha's story' in the following extract provides an horrific example of one child's experience of child abuse.

**Report of the Inquiry into Child Abuse in Cleveland 1987, Cm 412**
London: HMSO, 1987, pp. 9 and 10

. . .

**Samantha's Story**
34.   During his investigations into the children in Cleveland the Official Solicitor interviewed a girl of 19 from the Cleveland area and her story provides a most helpful insight into many problems and issues raised by child sexual abuse. She chose to call herself Samantha and the Inquiry is grateful to her for allowing her story to be made public.
Samantha's mother died when she was very young and her father brought up her younger brother and herself singlehanded. He began to abuse her when she was 4. When she was little he covered her head and top half with a blanket and interfered with her vagina. By the age of 10 it was regular sexual intercourse and thereafter it included buggery and oral intercourse. 'He made me say that I enjoyed it, that I wanted it. He wouldn't like any disagreement.' As she got older she began to realise that this did not happen to other girls. She said that:— 'it got to the stage that if I wanted a favour, to go out with a friend, or buy a new pair of shoes, I had to let him do it first.'
She had no-one to confide in, no-one to turn to: — 'I thought any adult would not believe me — they would think I was making up a story. . . . I didn't know what might happen. For my brother's sake I didn't want my family split up. . . . I loved my father so much. I respected him as a father. But I was confused, didn't understand. I wanted it to stop. I hated that part of it so much.'
The abuse continued several times a week. The father told her when she was 14 that many years earlier he had been to prison for a sexual offence with a minor. He

also told her that he had been having sexual intercourse with her best friend who was also under 16:— 'After that, I thought that if I told anyone he would hit me.'

She did well in exams at school. She did not mix much with other girls. Her father did not like her going out. He was:— 'extremely possessive, jealous of me.' She had no boy friends when she left school at 16. Her father would not let her. She also dreaded the idea.

She left school and went to college and there met a boy she called Andrew and became very fond of him. She found it very difficult to respond to the boyfriend's sexual advances and:— 'The first time I was petrified, just shaking. He had realised from early on there was something wrong, something deeply worrying me. I wouldn't tell him. I could open up part of me, like lifting a curtain, but I couldn't tell him.' Samantha was asked by her father if she had been to bed with Andrew and he threatened to throw her out of the house and beat her. He continued to abuse her sexually until 1985.

Eventually Samantha told Andrew and with his help and the help of a member of his family she went to the police. Her father was arrested. She went into care. Her father was tried and convicted.

. . .

Her father was convicted and sentenced to 2 years' imprisonment. He was released on parole after 8 months:— 'That really cracked me up, after what I had had to go through for 12 years.'

## 10.2  LOCAL AUTHORITIES: INTERVENTION OR NON-INTERVENTION

Local authorities through their social services departments are entrusted with statutory duties and powers under the CA 1989 to provide a range of services for children and to protect them from harm. Social services departments are in a difficult position for they must tread a fine line between taking sufficient steps to protect children, while ensuring that they are not over-zealous in their protection and thereby too intrusive into family life.

### EUROPEAN CONVENTION FOR THE PROTECTION OF HUMAN RIGHTS AND FUNDAMENTAL FREEDOMS 1950

**Article 8   Right to respect for family and private life**
1.   Everyone has the right to respect for his private and family life, his home and his correspondence.
2.   There shall be no interference by a public authority with the exercise of this right except such as is in accordance with the law and is necessary . . . for the prevention of disorder or crime, for the protection of health or morals, or for the protection of the rights and freedoms of others.

### *In Re KD (A Minor) (Ward: Termination of Access)*
[1988] AC 806
House of Lords

LORD TEMPLEMAN: My Lords, English common law and statute require that in all matters concerning the upbringing of an infant the welfare of the child shall be the first and paramount consideration. [His Lordship quoted art. 8 of the Convention and

continued: . . .] The English rule was evolved against an historical background of conflict between parents over the upbringing of their children. The Convention rule was evolved against an historical background of claims by the state to control the private lives of individuals. Since the last war interference by public authorities with families for the protection of children has greatly increased in this country. In my opinion there is no inconsistency of principle or application between the English rule and the Convention rule. The best person to bring up a child is the natural parent. It matters not whether the parent is wise or foolish, rich or poor, educated or illiterate, provided the child's moral and physical health are not endangered. Public authorities cannot improve on nature. Public authorities exercise a supervisory role and interfere to rescue a child when the parental tie is broken by abuse or separation. In terms of the English rule the court decides whether and to what extent the welfare of the child requires that the child shall be protected against harm caused by the parent, including harm which could be caused by the resumption of parental care after separation has broken the parental tie. In terms of the Convention rule the court decides whether and to what extent the child's health or morals require protection from the parent and whether and to what extent the family life of parent and child has been supplanted by some other relationship which has become the essential family life for the child.
. . .

## Barton, Chris, and Douglas, Gillian, *Law and Parenthood*
London: Butterworths, 1995, pp. 305 and 306

. . . The dilemma for the law and policy makers is to provide a range of powers available to social workers to facilitate investigation of the problem and protection of the child, while at the same time to preserve the family from 'unwarranted' interference. The difficulty is that one person's 'unwarranted interference' is another's 'necessary investigation'. The retrenchment since Cleveland has ostensibly redressed the balance in favour of parental autonomy and privacy, but there is still scope to invoke compulsion. . . .

## Morris, Allison, Giller, Henri H., Szwed, Elizabeth, and Geach, Hugh, *Justice for Children*
London: Macmillan, 1980, p. 128

. . . Every child must have the basic right of remaining in his own family unless there are compelling reasons which justify his removal. This presumption in favour of parental autonomy should only be rebutted on proof of some *specific* harm to the child or of the disruption or absence of parental ties. Even where this is proved, however, there should be a presumption against removal of the child from his home; such intervention should be a last resort. Removal should require a thorough survey of alternative ways of dealing with the situation (for example, by voluntary services and support) and evidence that such measures are inadequate.

## Goldstein, Joseph, Freud, Anna, and Solnit, Albert J., *Before the Best Interests of the Child*
London: Burnett Books, 1980, Chapter 1, pp. 3 ff

. . . When and why should a child's relationship to his parents become a matter of State concern? What must have happened to or in the life of a child before the State should be authorized to investigate, modify, or terminate an individual child's relationship with his parents, with his family? Considering what a child loses when he passes, even temporarily, from the personal authority of parents to the impersonal authority of the law, what grounds for placing a family under State scrutiny are reasonable? What can justify overcoming the presumption in law that parents are free to determine what is 'best' for their children in accord with their own beliefs, preferences, and life-styles?

. . .

Two purposes underlie the parents' right to be free of State intrusion. The first is to provide parents with an uninterrupted *opportunity* to meet the developing physical and emotional needs of their child so as to establish the familial bonds critical to every child's healthy growth and development. The second purpose, and the one on which the parental right must ultimately rest, is to safeguard the *continuing maintenance* of these family ties — of psychological parent–child relationships — once they have been established. . . .

Beyond these biological and psychological justifications for protecting parent–child relationships and promoting each child's entitlement to a permanent place in a family of his own, there is a further justification for a policy of minimum State intervention. It is that the law does not have the capacity to supervise the fragile, complex interpersonal bonds between child and parent. As *parens patriae* the State is too crude an instrument to become an adequate substitute for flesh and blood parents. . . .

### Dingwall, Robert, and Eekelaar, John, 'Rethinking Child Protection', in Michael D. A. Freeman, *The State, the Law and the Family*
London: Tavistock Publications, with Sweet & Maxwell, 1984, pp. 104 and 105

. . . There is a central dilemma within western liberalism over the relative priority to be afforded to individual freedoms, social justice, and civil or moral order.

The 'family autonomy' position is an attempt to evade this dilemma by reformulating children's rights in terms of adult freedoms. . . . Children's rights are identified with a parental right to freedom from State supervision on the basis of an assertion that children have a right to develop and maintain unconstrained psychological ties with their parents.

In fact, this is not a theory of children's rights at all so much as a political theory about the proper relationship between families and the State. A theory of children's rights would actually need to express claims that enhanced their interests as a matter of principle rather than coincidence. An uninterrupted parent/child relationship can damage the child: it cannot, therefore, be said to be a right in itself. . . .

The equation of children's rights with family autonomy rests on a political theory that actually denies the possibility of independent rights for children and on a series of contingent judgements about the present condition of developmental psychology that are inconsistent and self-contradictory. There can be no escape from the fact that the recognition of children's interests necessarily entails the abridgement of family autonomy. The trade-off between these objectives is a political decision.

. . .

### DHSS, *Review of Child Care Law — Report to Ministers of an Interdepartmental Working Party*
London: HMSO, 1985

**Children and parents**

2.8  A distinction is often drawn between the interests of children and the interests of their parents. In the great majority of families, including those who are for one reason or another in need of social services, this distinction does not exist. The interests of the children are best served by their remaining with their families and the interests of their parents are best served by allowing them to undertake their natural and legal responsibility to care for their own children. Hence the focus of effort should be to enable and assist parents to discharge those responsibilities. Even where a child has to spend some time away from home, every effort should be made to maintain and foster links between the child and his family, to care for the child in partnership with rather than in opposition to his parents, and to work towards his return to them. . . .

2.9    Nevertheless, we agree with the Select Committee that the 'rights [of parents] have no absolute validity; they derive from the exercise of responsibilities'. There must come a point at which the parents are, for whatever reason, so unable to exercise their responsibilities for the good of their children that action must be taken to remove them. Clearly the process by which such action is taken must give fair protection to the interests of parents, fairer protection than is given by the present procedures. . . .

### Nottingham County Council v P
### [1993] 1 FLR 514
### Family Division

WARD J: . . . In my judgment Parliament by the Children Act 1989 clearly determined that the sanctity of the family should be preserved and protected. It is an expression of the underlying purpose of the Act that organs of the State, be they the local authority or the courts, shall not interfere with the independence and integrity of the family save in limited circumstances. Those limited circumstances which justify intervention by the local authority are where there is, or where there is fear of significant harm being occasioned to the children. The whole tenor of Parts IV and V of the Children Act 1989 is that the local authority may not intervene in family life unless and until that threshold has been crossed. It is only when significant harm is established that the local authority can seek to interfere in where the child is to live and with whom the child is to have contact. . . .

### 10.2.1    Too little intervention: the death of Maria Colwell

Maria Colwell, aged 7, was taken into care after her father's death because her mother could not cope, and was placed with her aunt and uncle as foster-parents, with whom she thrived. Later, the social services department transferred her back to her mother, despite Maria's extreme resistance and severe distress and despite evidence of physical abuse. Maria eventually suffered horrendous physical abuse at the hands of her mother and step-father which ultimately led to her death. Both the social services department and the NSPCC failed to remove Maria from her mother and step-father despite being informed by neighbours and others that Maria was suffering extreme physical abuse. The social worker involved had failed to recognise Maria's suffering, and instead of listening to Maria and people who knew her, had listened only to Maria's mother and step-father. Furthermore, at no stage had Maria been referred to a doctor or psychologist. After her death, a public inquiry was held, and the following Report was published. The last few paragraphs demonstrate the tragedy of the social services department's failure to act.

*Report of the Committee of Inquiry into the Care and Supervision*
*Provided in Relation to Maria Colwell* 1974 (Chairman:
T. G. Field-Fisher QC)
DHSS, London: HMSO, 1974

. . .

147.    The following morning the Kepples took Maria in the pram to the hospital where she was found to be dead. The post mortem carried out by Professor Cameron on 11 January showed that she was severely bruised all over the body and head and had sustained severe internal injuries to the stomach. There was a healing fracture of one rib. The bruising, which was described by Professor Cameron as the worst he had ever seen, was of variable age up to 10 to 14 days at most, which was the longest period that bruising might be expected to last, but the majority dated from within 48 hours. The majority of the injuries he described as the result of extreme violence. The stomach was empty and the body weighed 36 lbs, whereas the medical evidence in the case generally showed that she should for her age and height have weighed anything between 46 and 50 lbs or thereabouts. She had in fact grown one inch and lost over 5 lbs since her last medical examination on 4 August 1971, 17 months before her death.

148.    To conclude the narrative of events, when the 'scenes of crime' police officer visited Maria's bedroom at number 119 on the 7 January he found that the door handle was removable so that when the door was closed from the outside anyone inside the room was shut in. Mrs Kepple in the course of her lengthy interviews with the police subsequently admitted that Maria was from time to time so confined because she was afraid she would run away as she had done before in 1971. Although she denied this admission in her written statement to us we are satisfied that Maria was so confined on occasions.

[The stepfather, William Kepple, was found guilty of Maria's murder in April 1973. Three months later an appeals court substituted a verdict of manslaughter for that of murder and sentenced him to eight years' imprisonment. Mr Kepple had had a minor criminal record at the time of Maria's transfer — unknown to the caseworkers at the time — which included four cases of violence on two separate occasions.]

*Notes*
1.    Maria's wishes were not heard and no one had a duty to express her wishes to the court independently of the social services department or of her mother and step-father. Guardians *ad litem* were introduced as a result of Maria's death in order to put the child's view before the court.
2.    For other inquiries where local authorities have been criticised for failing to take steps to protect children, see Department of Health, *Child Abuse — A Study of Inquiry Reports 1980–1989*, London: HMSO, 1991.

### 10.2.2    Too much intervention: the 'Cleveland affair'

In the 'Cleveland affair', a social services department was criticised for its over-zealous intrusion into family life, when between 1 January and 31 July 1987, 276 place of safety orders (pre-CA 1989 orders) were applied for by social services to remove children from their homes after they had been diagnosed as having been sexually abused. It later transpired that the diagnosis, which had been made by two paediatricians without consulting other persons, was faulty. As a result of enormous public concern, an inquiry was ordered by the Secretary of State for Social Services. The findings of the inquiry, which was chaired by Lady Butler-Sloss, were published in the following Report. Some of the inquiry's recommendations were incorporated into the CA 1989, particularly in respect of emergency protection of children and of a new emphasis on the need for all professionals involved with children to work together to protect them (see *Working Together*, below).

### *Report of the Inquiry into Child Abuse in Cleveland 1987*, Cm. 412
### London: HMSO, 1987

#### PART 3

#### Final Conclusions

1.  We have learned during the Inquiry that sexual abuse occurs in children of all ages, including the very young, to boys as well as girls, in all classes of society and frequently within the privacy of the family. The sexual abuse can be very serious and on occasions includes vaginal, anal and oral intercourse. The problems of child sexual abuse have been recognised to an increasing extent over the past few years by professionals in different disciplines. This presents new and particularly difficult problems for the agencies concerned in child protection. In Cleveland an honest attempt was made to address these problems by the agencies. In Spring 1987 it went wrong.

2.  The reasons for the crisis are complex. In essence they included:

— lack of a proper understanding by the main agencies of each others' functions in relation to child sexual abuse;

— a lack of communication between the agencies;

— differences of views at middle management level which were not recognised by senior staff. These eventually affected those working on the ground.

. . .

14. It is unacceptable that the disagreements and failure of communication of adults should be allowed to obscure the needs of children both long term and short term in so sensitive, difficult and important a field. The children had unhappy experiences which should not be allowed to happen again.

15. It is however important to bear in mind that those who have a responsibility to protect children at risk, such as social workers, health visitors, police and doctors have in the past been criticised for failure to act in sufficient time and to take adequate steps to protect children who are being damaged. In Cleveland the general criticism by the public has been of over-enthusiasm and zeal in the actions taken. It is difficult for professionals to balance the conflicting interests and needs in the enormously important and delicate field of child sexual abuse. We hope that professionals will not as a result of the Cleveland experience stand back and hesitate to act to protect the children.

16. In many Inquiries it is social workers who are under scrutiny for their failure to act in time. We are concerned that in advising a calm, measured and considered approach to the problem of child sexual abuse, we are not seen to imply either that there are never occasions when immediate action may need to be taken or that there

is not a problem to be faced and children to be protected. It is a delicate and difficult line to tread between taking action too soon and not taking it soon enough. Social Services whilst putting the needs of the child first must respect the rights of the parents; they also must work if possible with the parents for the benefit of the children. These parents themselves are often in need of help. Inevitably a degree of conflict develops between those objectives.

. . .

## Recommendations
### 1. Recognition of sexual abuse
There is a need:

    a.   To recognise and describe the extent of the problem of child sexual abuse;

    b.   To receive more accurate data of the abuse which is identified.

### 2. Children
There is a danger that in looking to the welfare of the children believed to be the victims of sexual abuse the children themselves may be overlooked. The child is a person and not an object of concern.

We recommend that:

    a.   Professionals recognise the need for adults to explain to children what is going on. Children are entitled to a proper explanation appropriate to their age, to be told why they are being taken away from home and given some idea of what is going to happen to them.

    b.   Professionals should not make promises which cannot be kept to a child, and in the light of possible court proceedings should not promise a child that what is said in confidence can be kept in confidence.

    c.   Professionals should always listen carefully to what the child has to say and take seriously what is said.

    d.   Throughout the proceedings the views and the wishes of the child, particularily as to what should happen to him/her, should be taken into consideration by the professionals involved with their problems.

    e.   The views and the wishes of the child should be placed before whichever court deals with the case. We do not however, suggest that those wishes should predominate.

    f.   Children should not be subjected to repeated medical examinations solely for evidential purposes. Where appropriate, according to age and understanding, the consent of the child should be obtained before any medical examination or photography.

    g.   Children should not be subjected to repeated interviews nor to the probing and confrontational type of 'disclosure' interview for the same purpose, for it in itself can be damaging and harmful to them. The consent of the child should where possible be obtained before the interviews are recorded on video.

    h.   The child should be medically examined and interviewed in a suitable and sensitive environment, where there are suitably trained staff available.

    i.   When a child is moved from home or between hospital and foster home it is important that those responsible for the day to day care of the child not only understand the child's legal status but also have sufficient information to look after the child properly.

    j.   Those involved in investigation of child sexual abuse should make a conscious effort to ensure that they act throughout in the best interests of the child.

### 3. Parents

We recommend:

a. The parents should be given the same courtesy as the family of any other referred child. This applies to all aspects of the investigation into the suspicion of child sexual abuse, and should be recognised by all professionals concerned with the family.

b. Parents should be informed and where appropriate consulted at each stage of the investigation by the professional dealing with the child, whether medical, police or social worker. Parents are entitled to know what is going on, and to be helped to understand the steps that are being taken.

c. We discuss below the position of parents in case conferences.

d. Social Services should confirm all important decisions to parents in writing. Parents may not understand the implications of decisions made and they should have the opportunity to give the written decision to their lawyers.

e. Parents should always be advised of their rights of appeal or complaint in relation to any decisions made about them or their children.

f. Social Services should always seek to provide support to the family during the investigation. Parents should not be left isolated and bewildered at this difficult time.

g. The service of the place of safety order on parents should include a written explanation of the meaning of the order, the position of the parents, their continuing responsibilities and rights and advice to seek legal advice.

*Further reading*

Bainham, A., 'The Children Act 1989: the State and the Family' [1990] Fam Law 231.

*Children Act Advisory Committee — Annual Reports*, London: HMSO.

Department of Health, *Child Protection — Messages from Research*, London: HMSO, 1995.

Harris, R., 'A Matter of Balance: Power and Resistance in Child Protection Policy' [1990] JSWL 332.

King, M., and Trowell, J., *Children's Welfare and the Law: The Limits of Legal Intervention*, London: Sage, 1992.

Levy, A. (ed.), *Re-Focus on Child Abuse*, London: Hawksmere, 1994.

Parton, N., 'The Contemporary Politics of Child Protection' [1992] JSWFL 100.

Thoburn, J., Lewis, A., and Shemmings, D., *Paternalism or Partnership? Family Involvement in the Child Protection Process*, London: HMSO, 1995.

Timms, J., 'The Tension Between Welfare and Justice' [1997] Fam Law 38.

## 10.3  THE PRACTICE OF CHILD PROTECTION

### 10.3.1  Guiding principles

The CA 1989 lays down the following guiding principles which govern the practice of those working together to protect and support children:

- the welfare of the child is the paramount consideration;
- children should be brought up within their own families where possible;
- where children are in need, parents should be provided with support to help them bring them up themselves;

- children should be protected by effective intervention where they are suffering or are likely to suffer significant harm;
- courts should ensure that delay is avoided;
- courts should make an order only if it is better than making no order at all;
- children should be informed about plans for them, and should be given the opportunity to participate in decisions about them;
- parents continue to have parental responsibility when a child is in local authority care and should be kept informed about and participate in decisions about their children.

### 10.3.2   The importance of partnership and participation

**Department of Health, *The Children Act 1989 Guidance and Regulations, Vol. 3,***
***Family Placements***
London: HMSO, 1991, Chapter 2

. . .

2.10   One of the key principles of the Children Act is that responsible authorities should work in partnership with the parents of a child who is being looked after and also with the child himself, where he is of sufficient understanding, provided that this approach will not jeopardise his welfare. A second, closely related principle is that parents and children should participate actively in the decision-making process. Partnership will only be achieved if parents are advised about and given explanations of the local authority's power and duties and the actions the local authority may need to take, for example exchanges of information between relevant agencies. The general duties of responsible authorities in sections 22, 61 and 64 of the Children Act are primarily based on these principles. These duties require responsible authorities to consult parents and others and the child (where he is of sufficient understanding) before any decision is made affecting a child who is about to be or is already being looked after by a local authority, or who is accommodated in a voluntary home or registered children's home. This new approach reflects the fact that parents always retain their parental responsibility. A local authority may limit parents' exercise of that responsibility when a child is looked after by a local authority as a result of a court order, but only if it is necessary to do so to safeguard and promote the child's welfare (section 33(3)(b) and (4)).

2.11   Planning and review of a child's case with the involvement of parents will provide the basis of partnership between the responsible authorities and parents and child. The development of a successful working partnership between the responsible authorities and the parents and the child, where he is of sufficient understanding, should enable the placement to proceed positively so that the child's welfare is safeguarded and promoted.

2.12   The successful development of partnership with parents should in most cases avoid the need for care proceedings or emergency action. Although genuine partnership will be easier to achieve in the absence of compulsory measures, the same kind of approach should be taken in cases where a child is in the care of the local authority as a result of a court order. This will be achieved by:

  (a)   consulting and notifying the parents about decisions affecting the child;

  (b)   promoting contact between the child and his parents and family where it is reasonably practicable and consistent with the child's welfare; and

(c)   by seeking to work with the parents to achieve a safe and stable environment for the child to return to (where this is judged feasible) or by finding a satisfactory alternative placement for the child.

. . .

### 10.3.3   The importance of inter-agency cooperation

**Department of Health,** *Working Together Under the Children Act 1989*
*— A Guide to Arrangements for Inter-agency Cooperation for the Protection of Children from Abuse*
London: HMSO, 1991, Preface

. . . It is well established that good child protection work requires good inter-agency co-operation. It is important for all professionals to combine an open-minded attitude to alleged concerns about a child with decisive action when this is clearly indicated. Intervention in a family, particularly if court action is necessary, will have major implications for them even if the assessment eventually leads to a decision that no further action is required. Public confidence in the child protection system can only be maintained if a proper balance is struck avoiding unnecessary intrusion in families while protecting children at risk of significant harm.

. . .

*Note*
*Working Together* is to be revised in the light of a new focus on the way in which local authorities provide services for children and families (see Timms, J. [1997] Fam Law 38 at p. 39).

### 10.3.4   The child protection conference

**Department of Health,** *Working Together Under the Children Act 1989*
*— A Guide to Arrangements for Inter-agency Cooperation for the Protection of Children from Abuse*
London: HMSO, 1991

. . .

6.1   The child protection conference is central to child protection procedures. It is *not* a forum for a formal decision that a person has abused a child. That is a matter for the courts. It brings together the family and the professionals concerned with child protection and provides them with the opportunity to exchange information and plan together. The conference symbolises the inter-agency nature of assessment, treatment and the management of child protection. Throughout the child protection process, the work is conducted on an inter-agency basis and the conference is the prime forum for sharing information and concerns, analysing risk and recommending responsibility for action. It draws together the staff from all the agencies with specific responsibilities in the child protection process (health, social services, police, schools and probation), and other staff who can offer relevant specialist advice, for example psychiatrists, psychologists, lawyers, and provides them with the forum for conducting and agreeing their joint approach to work with the child and family.

6.2   There are two kinds of child protection conference:

• the initial child protection conference

and
* the child protection review.

. . .

### The Responsibility to Convene a Child Protection Conference

6.3   A child protection conference will be convened by the agency with statutory powers (the SSD or the NSPCC) [Social Services Director or the National Society for the Protection of Cruelty to Children] following an investigation and indication that a decision has to be made about further action under the child protection procedures. At the time of the initial conference, it will be agreed if and when a child protection review will be needed. In addition, any concerned professional may ask the agency with statutory powers to convene a child protection review when he or she believes that the child is not adequately protected or when there is a need for a change to the child protection plan. If a child's name is placed on the child protection register, a review conference should be held at a time agreed at the initial conference and the intervening period should be no more than six months. For the first review it will be less, unless the initial conference had before it enough material to assess fully the risk to the child.

### Purpose of the Initial Child Protection Conference

6.4   An initial child protection conference should be called only after an investigation under Section 47 of the Children Act has been made into the incident or suspicion of abuse which has been referred. . . . it is emphasised that it should not be convened until relevant information and reports are available to inform the decisions of the conference. All initial conferences should normally take place within eight working days of referral except where there are particular reasons for delay such as the need to get far enough with the assessment to plan for the future needs of the child, provided the court process does not entail an earlier date.

6.5   The initial child protection conference brings together family members and professionals from the agencies which are concerned with child care and child protection to share and evaluate the information gathered during the investigation, to make decisions about the level of risk to the child(ren), to decide on the need for registration and to make plans for the future. If a decision to register is made, it will be necessary to appoint a named key worker and make recommendations for a core group of professionals to carry out the inter-agency work.

. . .

6.7   The key worker has two main tasks. He or she must fulfil the statutory responsibilities of his or her agency which will include the development of a multi-agency, multi-disciplinary plan for the protection of the child. The key worker also has a responsibility to act as lead worker for the inter-agency work in this case. In this role he or she will provide a focus for communication between professionals involved and will co-ordinate the inter-agency contributions to the assessment, planning and review of this case. The key worker must also ensure that parents and children are fully engaged in the implementation of the child protection plan.

6.8   The only decision for an initial child protection conference is whether or not to register the child. It discusses and records a proposed plan of action and it is for each agency representative to decide whether to accept the recommendations for action and their part in the plain. There should be a locally agreed procedure for confirming that these recommendations will be acted upon. It is essential that parents, and children where appropriate, should be fully involved in the discussions about what should constitute a plan. Agreement should be striven for between the professionals, the family and the child. Making a formal agreement is in itself a useful way to record plans. Authorities may find it helpful to consider the Family Right, Group model agreement.

*Purpose of the Child Protection Review*
6.9 . . . The purpose [of the child protection review] is to review the arrangements for the protection of the child, examine the current level of risk and ensure that he or she continues to be adequately protected, consider whether the inter-agency co-ordination is functioning effectively and to review the protection plan. Every child protection review should consider whether registration should be continued or ended. The first review conference may be the occasion for the production of the full child protection plan, based on the compehensive assessment.
. . .

*The Involvement of Children, Parents, and Carers in Child Protection Conferences*
6.11   This Guide stresses the need to ensue that the welfare of the child is the overriding factor guiding child protection work. It also emphasises the importance of professionals working in partnership with parents and other family members or carers and the concept of parental responsibility. These principles must underpin all child protection work. . . . However, it cannot be emphasised too strongly that involvement of children and adults in child protection conferences will not be effective unless they are fully involved from the outset in all stages of the child protection process, and unless from the time of referral there is as much openness and honesty as possible between families and professionals.
. . .

## 10.3.5   The child protection register

**Department of Health, *Working Together Under the Children Act 1989***
*— A Guide to Arrangements for Inter-agency Cooperation for the Protection of Children from Abuse*
London: HMSO, 1991

. . .
*The Child Protection Register*
6.36   In each area covered by a social services department, a central register must be maintained which lists all the children in the area who are considered to be suffering from or likely to suffer significant harm and for whom there is a child protection plan. This is not a register of children who have been abused but of children for whom there are currently unresolved child protection issues and for whom there is an inter-agency protection plan. The registers should include children who are recognised to be at risk and who are placed in the local authority's area by another local authority or agency. Registration does not of itself provide any protection and it must lead to an inter-agency protection plan. Registration should not be used to obtain resources which might otherwise not be available to the family.

*The purpose of the Register*
6.37   The purpose of the register is to provide a record of all children in the area for whom there are unresolved child protection issues and who are currently the subject of an inter-agency protection plan and to ensure that the plans are formally reviewed every six months. The register will provide a central point of speedy inquiry for professional staff who are worried about a child and want to know whether the child is the subject of an inter-agency protection plan. The register will also provide

useful information for the individual child protection agencies and for the ACPC [Area Child Protection Conference] in its policy development work and strategic planning.

*Criteria for Registration*

6.38   The inclusion of a child's name on the child protection register will only occur following a child protection conference. The exception is when a child on another register moves into the area. Such children will be registered immediately pending the first child protection conference in the new area.

*Requirements for Registration*

6.39   Before a child is registered the conference must decide that there is, or is a likelihood of, significant harm leading to the need for a child protection plan. One of the following requirements needs to be satisfied:

   (i)    There must be one or more identifiable incidents which can be described as having adversely affected the child. They may be acts of commission or omission. They can be either physical, sexual, emotional or neglectful. It is important to identify a specific occasion or occasions when the incident has occurred. Professional judgement is that further incidents are likely; or

   (ii)   Significant harm is expected on the basis of professional judgement of findings of the investigation in this individual case or on research evidence.

The conference will need to establish so far as they can a cause of the harm or likelihood of harm. This cause could also be applied to siblings or other children living in the same household so as to justify registration of them. Such children should be categorised according to the area of concern.

*Categories of Abuse for Registration*

6.40   The following categories should be used for the register and for statistical purposes. They are intended to provide definitions as a guide for those using the register. In some instances, more than one category of registration may be appropriate. This needs to be dealt with in the protection plan. The statistical returns will allow for this. Multiple abuse registration should not be used just to cover all eventualities.

**Neglect:** The persistent or severe neglect of a child, or the failure to protect a child from exposure to any kind of danger, including cold or starvation, or extreme failure to carry out important aspects of care, resulting in the significant impairment of the child's health or development, including non-organic failure to thrive.

**Physical Injury:** Actual or likely physical injury to a child, or failure to prevent physical injury (or suffering) to a child including deliberate poisoning, suffocation and Munchausen's syndrome by proxy.

**Sexual Abuse:** Actual or likely sexual exploitation of a child or adolescent. The child may be dependent and/or developmentally immature.

**Emotional Abuse:** Actual or likely severe adverse effect on the emotional and behavioural development of a child caused by persistent or severe emotional ill-treatment or rejection. All abuse involves some emotional ill-treatment. This category should be used where it is the main or sole form of abuse.

6.41   These categories for child protection register purposes do not tie in precisely with the definition of 'significant harm' in Section 31 of the Children Act which will be relevant if Court proceedings are initiated. For example, with a case of neglect it will be necessary to consider whether it involves actual or likely 'significant harm', and whether it involves 'ill treatment' or 'impairment of health or development' (in each case as defined by the Act). The Courts may well provide an interpretation of 'sexual abuse' (which is not defined in the Act) which is different from that used above in particular cases, in which case their definition should be used in relation to those cases.

*Pre-birth Child protection Conferences*
6.42  On occasions there will be sufficient concern about the future risk to an unborn child to warrant the implementation of child protection procedures and the calling of a child protection conference to consider the need for registration and the need for a child protection plan. Such a conference should have the same status and be conducted in the same manner as an initial child protection conference. Those who would normally attend an initial child protection conference should be invited. Parents or carers should be invited as to other child protection conferences and should be fully involved in plans for the child's future. If a decision is made that the child's name needs to go on the child protection register, the main cause for concern should determine the category of registration.

*Criteria for De-registration*
6.43  De-registration should be considered at every child protection review. Additionally any of the agencies involved with the child may request that a conference is convened to consider the possibility of de-registration.
6.44  For de-registration to occur all the members of the review conference must be satisfied that the abuse or risk of abuse (either the original type or any other) is no longer present or is no longer of a level to warrant registration. Their decision must be based on a careful and thorough analysis of current risk.
    . . .

*Removal of Names from Register*
6.47  If the child protection conference agrees that the child's name should be removed from the child protection register this must be recorded in the minutes. Dissenting views or failure to agree must be recorded. . . .
6.48  De-registration should not lead to automatic cessation of services, and the professionals involved should discuss with the parents and the child what services might be needed following de-registration. With a young person approaching the age of 18 it would be good practice to consult with the young person in advance about the inevitable de-registration to establish what help he or she would find useful. The decision of the review and future plans should be confirmed in writing as usual with all those present.
    . . .

*Note*
*Working Together* does not have the full force of statute, but must be complied with 'unless local circumstances indicate exceptional reasons which justify a variation' (Preface to *Working Together*).

*Further reading*
Thomson, P., 'Parents at Case Conferences — a Legal Advisor's Viewpoint' (1992) 4 JCL 15.

## 10.4  LOCAL AUTHORITY SUPPORT FOR CHILDREN IN NEED

Under Part III of the CA 1989, local authorities have wide-ranging duties of support for children in need and their families. These duties include the provision of services (ss. 17 to 19) and accommodation (ss. 20 and 21). Local authorities also have duties to children 'looked after' by them (ss. 22 and 23) and must provide advice and assistance (s. 24), and in some cases provide secure accommodation (s. 25). Local authorities must hold case reviews, must cooperate with each other and must consult education authorities (ss. 26 to 30). Schedule 2 to the Act lists the services which might be helpful to parents and to children in need, e.g., counselling, home-help, day care centres, assistance with travelling and holidays.

### 10.4.1  The general duty towards children

### CHILDREN ACT 1989

**17.  Provision of services for children in need, their families and others**
    (1)   It shall be the general duty of every local authority (in addition to the other duties imposed on them by [Part III of the Act])—
        (a)   to safeguard and promote the welfare of children within their area who are in need; and
        (b)   so far as is consistent with that duty, to promote the upbringing of such children by their families,
by providing a range and level of services appropriate to those children's needs.
    (2)   For the purpose principally of facilitating the discharge of their general duty under this section, every local authority shall have the specific duties and powers set out in Part I of Schedule 2.
    . . .

### 10.4.2  Who is a 'child in need'?

### CHILDREN ACT 1989

**17.  Provision of services for children in need, their families and others**
    . . .
    (10)   For the purposes of [Part III of the Act] a child shall be taken to be in need if—
        (a)   he is unlikely to achieve or maintain, or to have the opportunity of achieving or maintaining, a reasonable standard of health or development without the provision for him of services by a local authority under [Part III];
        (b)   his health or development is likely to be significantly impaired, or further impaired, without the provision for him of such services; or
        (c)   he is disabled,
and 'family', in relation to such a child, includes any person who has parental responsibility for the child and any other person with whom he has been living.
    (11)   . . . a child is disabled if he is blind, deaf or dumb or suffers from mental disorder of any kind or is substantially and permanently handicapped by illness, injury or congenital deformity or such other disability as may be prescribed; and . . .
    'development' means physical, intellectual, emotional, social or behavioural development; and
    'health' means physical or mental health.

### 10.4.3  The duty to provide accommodation

An important duty under Part III of the Children Act is the duty to provide accommodation for children in need.

# CHILDREN ACT 1989

## 20.  Provision of accommodation for children: general

(1)  Every local authority shall provide accommodation for any child in need within their area who appears to them to require accommodation as a result of—

(a)  there being no person who has parental responsibility for him;

(b)  his being lost or having been abandoned; or

(c)  the person who has been caring for him being prevented (whether or not permanently, and for whatever reason) from providing him with suitable accommodation or care.

. . .

*Note*

Before providing accommodation, a local authority must, so far as is reasonably practicable and consistent with the child's welfare, ascertain the child's wishes about the provision of accommodation and give due consideration (having regard to the child's age and understanding) to the wishes of the child (s. 20(6)). A local authority must not provide accommodation if any person with parental responsibility objects, and that person is willing and able to provide accommodation or able to arrange it (s. 20(7)) (except where a person with a residence order or who has care of the child under a court order agrees to the child being accommodated by the local authority, s. 20(9)). Any person with parental responsibility for the child may at any time remove the child from local authority accommodation (s. 20(8)), except where a person with a residence order or who has care of the child under a court order agrees to the child being accommodated by the local authority (s. 20(9)).

# CHILDREN ACT 1989

## 27.  Co-operation between authorities

(1)  Where it appears to a local authority that any authority or other person mentioned in subsection (3) [i.e. any local authority or housing authority] could, by taking any specific action, help in the exercise of any of their functions under this Part, they may request the help of that other authority or person . . ..

(2)  An authority whose help is so requested shall comply with the request if it is compatible with their own statutory or other duties and obligations and does not unduly prejudice the discharge of any of their functions.

. . .

## *Smith v Northavon DC*
[1994] 2 AC 402
House of Lords

*Facts*: The husband and wife and their five young children moved into housing accommodation when their gypsy caravan became uninhabitable, but later moved into a relative's caravan because of local antipathy to gypsies. The husband's application to Northavon DC for accommodation under Part III of the Housing Act 1985 [now the Housing Act 1996] was rejected on the ground that, although they were in priority need, they were intentionally homeless. The social services department of Avon CC decided that the children were in need and made a request under s. 27 of the CA 1989 that Northavon DC provide accommodation for them. Northavon refused on the ground that it had already fulfilled its duty under the 1985 Act. The husband sought judicial review of Northavon's refusal. The High Court dismissed the application, but the Court of Appeal, allowing the appeal, directed Northavon to reconsider the request. Sir Thomas Bingham MR stated that the duty to provide or secure accommodation or assistance with accommodation must rest somewhere, and that if children in need did not command protection under one statutory code they must command it under another. Northavon DC appealed.

*Held*: allowing the appeal, that there was nothing in s. 27(2) of the CA 1989 which enlarged or otherwise amended the powers and duties of the requested authority under the Housing Act 1985.

LORD TEMPLEMAN: . . . The question to be determined is whether the housing authority's letter dated 19 January 1993 was an unlawful response to the request made by the social services authority under section 27 of the Children Act 1989. Several arguments were advanced in support of the order made by the Court of Appeal quashing the decisions contained in the letter. First, it was said that the housing authority were under a duty to provide permanent accommodation for the family of Mr Smith at the request of the social services authority. Secondly, it was said that following that request, the housing authority should at least have given further consideration to the possibility of providing permanent accommodation for the Smith family. Thirdly, it was said that the housing authority should at least have provided and paid or considered the provision and payment for temporary accommodation. Fourthly, it was said that the letter dated 19 January 1993 did not give adequate reasons for refusing to comply with the request made by the social services authority for permanent accommodation and did not give any reason at all for refusing to comply with the request made by the social services authority for temporary accommodation. My Lords, these arguments demonstrate the need to prevent the functions of a housing authority and the functions of a social services authority becoming blurred. If any of these arguments were accepted, every social services authority will understandably seek to exercise their powers under section 27 in order to transfer the burden of the children of a person intentionally homeless from the social services authority to the housing authority. Every refusal by a housing authority to comply with a request under section 27 will be scrutinised and construed with the object of discovering grounds for judicial review. The welfare of the children involved, the welfare of children generally and the interests of the public cannot be advanced by such litigation.

. . .

The housing authority were not under a duty to Mr Smith or any member of his family to provide permanent accommodation or to provide temporary accommodation beyond the period which they thought appropriate under section 65(3)(a) of the Housing Act 1985. . . .

The provisions of section 27 of the Children Act of 1989 which . . . required the housing authority to co-operate with the social services authority, imposed on the housing authority a duty to ascertain whether the housing authority could, without unduly prejudicing the discharge of their functions, provide a solution or co-operate in securing a solution to the problems of the Smith family to the extent necessary to prevent the children from suffering from lack of accommodation.

Following such consideration the result might have been that no solution was obtainable with the reasonable co-operation of the housing authority. There might have been no available accommodation which the housing authority could provide without unduly prejudicing the discharge of any of their functions. There might have been no solution which did not impose on the housing authority a financial burden which they considered unduly prejudicial to the discharge of their functions. Mr Smith might have been an unacceptable tenant. Failing any acceptable solution, it would have been the duty of the social services authority to protect the children of Mr Smith by providing financial assistance towards the accommodation of the family or by exercising the other powers available to the social services authority under the Children Act 1989.

In the event the housing authority were able, without in their view unduly prejudicing the discharge of any of their functions, to co-operate in arrangements whereby the children of Mr Smith did not suffer from lack of accommodation. The social services authority are responsible for children and the housing authority are responsible for housing. The two authorities must co-operate. Judicial review is not the way to obtain co-operation. The court cannot decide what form co-operation should take. Both forms of authority have difficult tasks which are of great importance and for which they may feel their resources are not wholly adequate. The authorities must together do the best they can.

In this case the housing authority were entitled to respond to the social services authority as they did. I would accordingly allow the appeal and restore the order of [the trial judge]. . . .

*Note*
For an application for housing by a child under Part III of the Housing Act 1985 (now HA 1996), see *R v Oldham Metropolitan Borough Council, ex parte Garlick* [1993] AC 509, HL, in Chapter 3.

*Further reading*
Gilbert, G., 'Housing for Children' (1993) 5 JCL 166.
Thoburn, J., 'The Children Act 1989 and Children "In Need"', in Pearl, D., and Pickford, R. (eds), *Frontiers of Family Law*, 2nd edn, Chichester: John Wiley, 1995.

## 10.5   CARE AND SUPERVISION OF CHILDREN

Under Part IV of the CA 1989 the court has power to make care and supervision orders to protect children.

### Department of Health, *The Children Act 1989 Guidance and Regulations: Vol. 1, Court Orders*
London: HMSO, 1991, Chapter 3

3.2.   . . . [A] care or supervision order will be sought only when there appears to be no better way of safeguarding and promoting the welfare of the child suffering, or likely to suffer significant harm. The local authority has a general duty to promote the upbringing of children in need by their families so far as this is consistent with its duty to promote children's welfare and to avoid the need for proceedings where possible; it should have regard to the court's presumption against making an order in section 1(5) while at the same time giving paramount consideration to the child's welfare. This means that voluntary arrangements through the provision of services to the child and his family should always be fully explored. Where a care or supervision order is the appropriate remedy because control of the child's circumstances is necessary to promote his welfare, applications in such proceedings should be part of a carefully planned process. The new scheme imposes strict conditions which have to be met but does not place unnecessary obstacles in the way of action that is necessary to protect the child. It also increases opportunities to apply for discharge and variation of care orders and supervision orders.

. . .

## 10.5.1 The 'threshold conditions'
## CHILDREN ACT 1989

### 31. Care and supervision orders

(1) On the application of any local authority or authorised person, the court may make an order—

(a) placing the child with respect to whom the application is made in the care of a designated local authority; or

(b) putting him under the supervision of a designated local authority or of a probation officer.

(2) A court may only make a care order or supervision order if it is satisfied—

(a) that the child concerned is suffering, or is likely to suffer, significant harm; and

(b) that the harm, or likelihood of harm, is attributable to—

(i) the care given to the child, or likely to be given to him if the order were not made, not being what it would be reasonable to expect a parent to give him; or

(ii) the child's being beyond parental control.

(3) . . .

(4) An application under this section may be made on its own or in any other family proceedings.

. . .

(9) In this section—

. . .

'harm' means ill-treatment or the impairment of health or development;

'development' means physical, intellectual, emotional, social or behavioural development;

'health' means physical or mental health; and

'ill-treatment' includes sexual abuse and forms of ill-treatment which are not physical.

(10) Where the question of whether harm suffered by a child is significant turns on the child's health or development, his health and development shall be compared with that which could reasonably be expected of a similar child.

. . .

## DHSS, *Review of Child Care Law — Report to Ministers of an Interdepartmental Working Party*
### London: HMSO, 1985

. . .

15.15 We consider that, having set an acceptable standard of upbringing for the child, it should be necessary to show some *substantial* deficit in that standard. Minor

short-comings in the health care provided or minor deficits in physical, psychological or social development should not give rise to compulsory intervention unless they are having, or are likely to have, serious and lasting effects upon the child. The courts are used to assessing degrees of harm, for example in the context of prosecution for assaults, and we consider that they could also do so here.
. . .

*Notes*

1. 'Significant harm' is an important concept in the CA 1989 (see ss. 31, 43, and 44). While 'harm' is defined in s. 31 above, 'significant' is not. The Department of Health's *Guidance*, vol. 3, suggests that harm may be 'significant' if it is likely to have a 'serious and lasting' effect on the child.

2. The court must perform a two-stage test when deciding whether to make a care or supervision order. It must first decide whether the 'threshold' criteria in s. 31(2) are met. If they are, it must then apply the s. 1 principles (see Chapter 7) to decide whether to make an order. As Part IV proceedings are 'family proceedings', the court may make a s. 8 order (see Chapter 7) instead of a care or supervision order.

3. When hearing an application for a care or supervision order, the court must scrutinise the local authority's care plan (*Re T (A Minor) (Care Order: Conditions)* [1994] 2 FLR 423, CA). If it does not agree with the plan, it may refuse to make a care order (*Re J (Minors) (Care: Care Plan)* [1994] 1 FLR 253). Before making a care order the court must consider the arrangements the local authority has made, or proposes to make, for affording any person contact with a child to whom s. 34 applies (see 10.6 below) and invite the parties to the proceedings to comment on those arrangements (s. 34(11)).

4. A care order, other than an interim order, remains in force until the child reaches 18 'unless brought to an end earlier' (s. 91(12)).

5. A care order gives the local authority parental responsibility for the child, but does not terminate the parental responsibility of parents (ss. 2(8) and 33(3)(b)). The effect of a supervision order is for the child to be advised, assisted and befriended by a supervisor (see s. 35(1) and Parts I and II of sch. 3).

6. The court has jurisdiction to make interim care or supervision orders where it has reasonable grounds to believe the conditions in s. 31(2) *supra* are satisfied (see s. 38). Where the court makes an interim order, it may give directions in respect of medical or psychiatric examination or other assessment of the child, but a child with sufficient understanding to make an informed decision may refuse to be examined or assessed (s. 38(6)) (but see *South Glamorgan County Council* v *W and B* [1993] FLR 574, FD, where the children's wishes were overriden, despite the statutory provision). In *Re C (Interim Care Order: Residential Assessment)* [1997] 1 FLR 1 an interim care order was made with a direction attached under s. 38(6) that an assessment involving the child and his parents take place at a specified venue. This was ordered despite the contrary wishes of the local authority who objected, largely because of financial constraints. The House of Lords, allowing the appeal and overruling *Re M (Interim Care Order: Assessment)* 2 FLR 464, CA,

held that the phrase 'other assessment' in ss. 38(6) and (7) was not to be interpreted as restricting assessments to those which were similar to medical or psychiatric examinations, nor was it to be construed as applying to assessments only restricted to the child, as it was impossible to assess a child separate and apart from his or her environment. Although the interaction between the child and those caring for the child was an essential element in assessing a child, the court could not compel parents to take part in an assessment against their wishes or compel a child to do so if he or she were capable of making an informed decision. Thus, the court could override the powers of a local authority which the latter would otherwise have under an interim order, and a direction that a residential assessment should take place at a particular venue did not interfere with a local authority's power under CA, s. 23 to determine a child's place of residence under a care order.

7.   The court may discharge a care order (see s. 39), or substitute it with a supervision order or may discharge the care order and make a s. 8 order instead.

### 10.5.2   When do the threshold conditions have to be satisfied?

#### In Re M (A Minor) (Care Order: Threshold Conditions)
[1994] 2 AC 424
House of Lords

*Facts*: When M was four months old his mother was murdered by his father in his presence and that of his older brothers and sisters. Emergency protection proceedings were taken by the police. Later Bracewell J made residence orders in respect of the three older children in favour of Mrs W, a cousin of M's mother, and made a care order in respect of M with a view to his being adopted. Bracewell J held that the relevant date for the words 'is suffering' in s. 31(2)(a) of the CA 1989 was the period immediately before the process of protecting the child had been put in motion. On appeal, the Court of Appeal substituted the care order with a residence order in respect of M in favour of Mrs W, holding that the threshold criteria had not been satisfied on the relevant date, namely the date when the case came before the court for disposal. M's father appealed to the House of Lords.

*Held*: allowing the appeal, restoring the care order and reversing the decision of the Court of Appeal, that nothing in s. 31(2) required that the satisfaction of the threshold principles was to be disassociated from the time when the local authority made the application.

LORD MACKAY LC: . . . In my opinion the opening words of s. 31 link the making of an order by the court very closely with the application to the court by a local authority or authorised person. Section 31(2) then goes on to specify the conditions which are necessary to be satisfied before the court can make a care order or supervision order, but it is plain from this and the statute as a whole that even if these conditions are satisfied the court is not bound to make an order but must go through the full procedure particularly set out in s. 1 of the statute. It is also clear that

Parliament expected these cases to proceed with reasonable expedition and in particular I refer to s. 32 in which the hearing by the court is not regarded only as taking place at the time when the applications are disposed of. Indeed, I think there is much to be said for the view that the hearing that Parliament contemplated was one which extended from the time the jurisdiction of the court is first invoked until the case is disposed of and that was required to be done in the light of the general principle that any delay in determining the question is likely to prejudice the welfare of the child. There is nothing in s. 31(2) which in my opinion requires that the conditions to be satisfied are disassociated from the time of the making of the application by the local authority. I would conclude that the natural construction of the conditions in s. 31(2) is that where, at the time the application is to be disposed of, there are in place arrangements for the protection of the child by the local authority on an interim basis which protection has been continuously in place for some time, the relevant date with respect to which the court must be satisfied is the date at which the local authority initiated the procedure for protection under the Act from which these arrangements followed. If after a local authority had initiated protective arrangements the need for these had terminated, because the child's welfare had been satisfactorily provided for otherwise, in any subsequent proceedings, it would not be possible to found jurisdiction on the situation at the time of initiation of these arrangements. It is permissible only to look back from the date of disposal to the date of initiation of protection as a result of which local authority arrangements had been continuously in place thereafter to the date of disposal.

It has to be borne in mind that this in no way precludes the court from taking account at the date of the hearing of all relevant circumstances. The conditions in subs. (2) are in the nature of conditions conferring jurisdiction upon the court to consider whether or not a care order or supervision order should be made. Conditions of that kind would in my view normally have to be satisfied at the date on which the order was first applied for. It would in my opinion be odd if the jurisdiction of the court to make an order depended on how long the court took before it finally disposed of the case.

However, I believe that help in the construction of this provision is obtained from the judgment of your Lordships' House in Re D (A Minor) [1987] AC 317, [1987] 1 FLR 422. That was concerned with the provisions of the Children and Young Persons Act 1969 as later amended. . . .

Accordingly, I am of the opinion that the decision of this House [in Re D] which I take to have been unanimous on this point, provides cogent support for the view which I have taken on a reading of the language of the current provision.

It is true that an important change has been made in the statutory provisions in respect that it is now permissible under the second branch of s. 31(2)(a) to look to the future even if no harm has already occurred in the past. This is an important difference from the previous legislation but in my opinion to read the present legislation as the Court of Appeal has done is substantially to deprive the first branch of s. 31(2)(a) of effect, as in the argument before your Lordships became very apparent. It is also clear that while Parliament added the new provisions looking to the future without any necessary connection with harm already suffered, it wished to retain the first branch in respect of harm which the child is suffering.

In my opinion the provisions of s. 31(2) must be considered before the question of any competing order under the provisions of Part II of the Act are decided upon. The scheme of s. 1(3) and (4) and in particular s. 1(3)(g) appears to me to require that the court decides whether or not it has power available to it to make a care order or a supervision order before it decides whether or not to make an order at all and in particular whether or not to consider a s. 8 order.

I have only to add that in my opinion the approach taken by Ewbank J in *Northamptonshire County Council* v *S and Others* [1993] Fam 136 at p. 140, [1993] 1 FLR 554 at p. 557 in the passage quoted by the Court of Appeal is correct. I also consider that the decision of this House in *Re W (An Infant)* [1971] AC 682, where the question was whether the time at which the court decides whether consent is being withheld unreasonably is the time of the hearing, referred to an entirely different subject matter from the present and therefore is not helpful in this context.

It follows that in my opinion the decision of the Court of Appeal in the present case was wrong and that the court did have jurisdiction to make a care order in the present case. This decision means that the basis on which the Court of Appeal in *Oldham Metropolitan Police Council* v *E* [1994] 1 FLR 568 intervened to overturn the decision at first instance following as it was bound to do the decision of the Court of Appeal in the present case can no longer be regarded as sound.

. . .

LORD TEMPLEMAN: My Lords, this appeal is an illustration of the tyranny of language and the importance of ascertaining and giving effect to the intentions of Parliament by construing a statute in accordance with the spirit rather than the letter of the Act.

. . .

Balcombe LJ said [in the Court of Appeal]:

> . . . use of the present tense . . . 'is suffering' — makes it clear that the harm must be being suffered at the relevant time, which is when the court . . . decides whether or not to make a care order.

This preoccupation with the present tense involves the proposition that if a child suffers harm and is rescued by a local authority, a care order cannot be made in favour of the local authority because it can no longer be said that the child is suffering harm and if the parent who has caused the child harm is dead or in prison or disclaims any further interest it cannot be said that the child is likely to suffer harm. I cannot accept this approach. Restrictions on the right of a local authority to apply for a care order were imposed by s. 31 to prevent a local authority interfering too readily with the rights and responsibility of parents. A local authority cannot apply for a care order unless at the date of the application the child is suffering or is likely to suffer significant harm. Once the local authority has grounds for making an application, the court has jurisdiction to grant that application. If between the date of the application and the date of the judgment of the court, circumstances arise which make a care order unnecessary or undesirable, the local authority can withdraw its application for a care order or the court can refuse to make a care order. If the court is faced with an application for a residence order and an application for a care order then the court must decide, as Bracewell J decided, whether the welfare of the child will be best safeguarded by making a residence order under s. 8 or a care order under s. 31.

I would therefore allow the appeal and restore the care order made by Bracewell J.

. . .

*Note*
Lord Mackay LC referred to *Re D (A Minor)* [1987] AC 317, HL, to assist with the construction of CA 1989, s. 31(2). In *Re D*, which concerned a baby born with drug withdrawal symptoms after the mother had taken drugs during pregnancy, the House of Lords had to construe the old ground for

making a care order under s. 1 of the Children and Young Persons Act 1969. The problem with s. 1 of the 1969 Act was that it was phrased in the present tense only, which made it difficult for social workers to apply for care orders when they considered the child was likely to suffer harm in the future. This problem was remedied by s. 31(2) of the CA 1989, which refers both to present harm and likelihood of harm.

### 10.5.3   Standard of proof of child abuse

*In re H (Minor) (Sexual Abuse: Standard of Proof)*
[1996] AC 563
House of Lords

*Facts*: The local authority applied for care orders in respect of three girls aged 13, 8 and 2, after allegations had been made by the eldest daughter, aged 14, that she had been sexually abused by her mother's cohabitant. He was charged with rape but acquitted. The applications for care orders were dismissed as the judge could not be sure 'to the requisite high standard of proof' that the 14-year-old daughter's allegations were true, in order to satisfy the threshold conditions of s. 31(2). The local authority's appeal to the Court of Appeal was dismissed (see [1995] 1 FLR 643), whereupon it appealed to the House of Lords.

*Held*: dismissing the appeal (Lords Browne-Wilkinson and Lloyd dissenting), that the conditions of s. 31(2) had not been satisfied.

LORD NICHOLLS: . . .

*'Likely' to suffer harm*

I shall consider first the meaning of 'likely' in the expression 'likely to suffer significant harm' in section 31. In your Lordships' House [counsel for the local authority] advanced an argument not open in the courts below. He submitted that likely means probable, and that the decision of the Court of Appeal to the contrary in *Newham London Borough Council v A.G.* [1993] 1 FLR 281 was wrong. I cannot accept this contention.

In everyday usage one meaning of the word likely, perhaps its primary meaning, is probable, in the sense of more likely than not. This is not its only meaning. If I am going walking on Kinder Scout and ask whether it is likely to rain, I am using likely in a different sense. I am inquiring whether there is a real risk of rain, a risk that ought not to be ignored. In which sense is likely being used in this subsection?

In section 31(2) Parliament has stated the prerequisites which must exist before the court has power to make a care order. These prerequisites mark the boundary line drawn by Parliament between the differing interests. On one side are the interests of parents in caring for their own child, a course which prima facie is also in the interests of the child. On the other side there will be circumstances in which the interests of the child may dictate a need for his care to be entrusted to others. In section 31(2) Parliament has stated the minimum conditions which must be present before the court can look more widely at all the circumstances and decide whether the child's welfare requires that a local authority shall receive the child into their care and have parental responsibility for him. The court must be satisfied that the child is already suffering significant harm. Or the court must be satisfied that, looking ahead, although the child may not yet be suffering such harm, he or she is likely to do so in the future. The court may make a care order if, but only, if, it is satisfied in one or other of these respects.

In this context Parliament cannot have been using likely in the sense of more likely than not. If the word likely were given this meaning, it would have the effect of leaving outside the scope of care and supervision orders cases where the court is satisfied there is a real possibility of significant harm to the child in the future but that possibility falls short of being more likely than not. Strictly, if this were the correct reading of the Act, a care or supervision order would not be available even in a case where the risk of significant harm is as likely as not. Nothing would suffice short of proof that the child will probably suffer significant harm.

The difficulty with this interpretation of section 31(2)(a) is that it would draw the boundary line at an altogether inapposite point. What is in issue is the prospect, or risk, of the child suffering significant harm. When exposed to this risk a child may need protection just as much when the risk is considered to be less than 50–50 as when the risk is of a higher order. Conversely, so far as the parents are concerned, there is no particular magic in a threshold test based on a probability of significant harm as distinct from a real possibility. It is otherwise if there is no real possibility. It is eminently understandable that Parliament should provide that where there is no real possibility of significant harm, parental responsibility should remain solely with the parents. That makes sense as a threshold in the interests of the parents and the child in a way that a higher threshold, based on probability, would not.

In my view, therefore, the context shows that in section 31(2)(a) likely is being used in the sense of a real possibility, a possibility that cannot sensibly be ignored having regard to the nature and gravity of the feared harm in the particular case. By parity of reasoning the expression likely to suffer significant harm bears the same meaning elsewhere in the Act; for instance, in sections 43, 44 and 46. Likely also bears a similar meaning, for a similar reason, in the requirement in section 31(2)(h) that the harm or likelihood of harm must be attributable to the care given to the child or 'likely' to be given him if the order were not made.

. . .

*The standard of proof*

Where the matters in issue are facts the standard of proof required in non-criminal proceedings is the preponderance of probability, usually referred to as the balance of probability. This is the established general principle. There are exceptions such as contempt of court applications, but I can see no reason for thinking that family proceedings are, or should be, an exception. By family proceedings I mean proceedings so described in the Act of 1989, sections 105 and 8(3). Despite their special features, family proceedings remain essentially a form of civil proceedings. Family proceedings often raise very serious issues, but so do other forms of civil proceedings.

The balance of probability standard means that a court is satisfied an event occurred if the court considers that, on the evidence, the occurrence of the event was more likely than not. When assessing the probabilities the court will have in mind as a factor, to whatever extent is appropriate in the particular case, that the more serious the allegation the less likely it is that the event occurred and, hence, the stronger should be the evidence before the court concludes that the allegation is established on the balance of probability. Fraud is usually less likely than negligence. Deliberate physical injury is usually less likely than accidental physical injury. A step-father is usually less likely to have repeatedly raped and had non-consensual oral sex with his under age stepdaughter than on some occasion to have lost his temper and slapped her. Built into the preponderance of probability standard is a generous degree of flexibility in respect of the seriousness of the allegation.

Although the result is much the same, this does not mean that where a serious allegation is in issue the standard of proof required is higher. It means only that the inherent probability or improbability of an event is itself a matter to be taken into account when weighing the probabilities and deciding whether, on balance, the event occurred. The more improbable the event, the stronger must be the evidence that it did occur before, on the balance of probability, its occurrence will be established. . . .

I . . . agree with the recent decisions of the Court of Appeal in several cases involving the care of children, to the effect that the standard of proof is the ordinary civil standard of balance of probability: see *H v H (Minors) (Child Abuse: Evidence)* [1990] Fam 86, 94, 100, *In re M (A Minor) (Appeal) (No. 2)* [1994] 1 FLR 59, 67 and *In re W (Minors) (Sexual Abuse: Standard of Proof)* [1994] 1 FLR 419, 424, *per* Balcombe LJ. The Court of Appeal were of the same view in the present case. It follows that the contrary observations already mentioned, in *In re G (A Minor) (Child Abuse: Standard of Proof)* [1987] 1 WLR 1461, 1466 and *In re W (Minors) (Sexual Abuse: Standard of Proof)* [1994] 1 FLR 419, 429, are not an accurate statement of the law.

. . .

*A conclusion based on facts*

The starting point here is that courts act on evidence. They reach their decisions on the basis of the evidence before them. When considering whether an applicant for a care order has shown that the child is suffering harm or is likely to do so, a court will have regard to the undisputed evidence. The judge will attach to that evidence such weight, or importance, as he considers appropriate. Likewise with regard to disputed evidence which the judge accepts as reliable. None of that is controversial. But the rejection of a disputed allegation as not proved on the balance of probability leaves scope for the possibility that the non-proven allegation may be true after all. There remains room for the judge to have doubts and suspicions on this score. This is the area of controversy.

In my view these unresolved judicial doubts and suspicions can no more form the basis of a conclusion that the second threshold condition in section 31(2)(a) has been established than they can form the basis of a conclusion that the first has been established. My reasons are as follows.

Evidence is the means whereby relevant facts are proved in court. What the evidence is required to establish depends upon the issue the court has to decide. . . .

At trials, however, the court normally has to resolve disputed issues of relevant fact before it can reach its conclusion on the issue it has to decide. . . . A decision by a court on the likelihood of a future happening must be founded on a basis of present facts and the inferences fairly to be drawn therefrom.

The same, familiar approach is applicable when a court is considering whether the threshold conditions in section 31(2)(a) are established. Here, as much as anywhere else, the court's conclusion must be founded on a factual base. The court must have before it facts on which its conclusion can properly be based. That is clearly so in the case of the first limb of section 31(2)(a). There must be facts, proved to the court's satisfaction if disputed, on which the court can properly conclude that the child is suffering harm. An alleged but non-proven fact is not a fact for this purpose. Similarly with the second limb: there must be facts from which the court can properly conclude there is a real possibility that the child will suffer harm in the future. Here also, if the facts are disputed, the court must resolve the dispute so far as necessary to reach a proper conclusion on the issue it has to decide.

There are several indications in the Act that when considering the threshold conditions the court is to apply the ordinary approach, of founding its conclusion on facts, and that nothing less will do. The first pointer is the difference in the statutory language when dealing with earlier stages in the procedures which may culminate in a care order. Under Part V of the Act a local authority are under a duty to investigate where they have 'reasonable cause to suspect' that a child is suffering or is likely to suffer harm. The court may make a child assessment order if satisfied that the applicant has 'reasonable cause to suspect' that the child is suffering or is likely to suffer harm. The police may take steps to remove or prevent the removal of a child where a constable has 'reasonable cause to believe' that the child would otherwise be likely to suffer harm. The court may make an emergency protection order only if satisfied there is 'reasonable cause to believe' that the child is likely to suffer harm in certain eventualities. Under section 38 the court may make an interim care order or an interim supervision order if satisfied there are 'reasonable grounds for believing' that the section 31(2) circumstances exist.

In marked contrast is the wording of section 31(2). The earlier stages are concerned with preliminary or interim steps or orders. Reasonable cause to believe or suspect provides the test. At those stages, as in my example of an application for an interlocutory injunction, there will usually not have been a full court hearing. But when the stage is reached of making a care order, with the far-reaching consequences this may have for the child and the parents, Parliament prescribed a different and higher test: 'a court may only make a care order or supervision order if it is satisfied . . . that . . . the child . . . is suffering, or is likely to suffer, significant harm; . . .'

This is the language of proof, not suspicion. At this stage more is required than suspicion, however reasonably based.

The next pointer is that the second threshold condition in paragraph (a) is cheek by jowl with the first. Take a case where a care order is sought in respect of a child on the ground that for some time his parents have been maltreating him. Having heard the evidence, the court finds the allegation is not proved. No maltreatment has been established. The evidence is rejected as insufficient. That being so, the first condition is not made out, because there is no factual basis from which the court could conclude that the child is suffering significant harm attributable to the care being given to him. Suspicion that there may have been maltreatment clearly will not do. It would be odd if, in respect of the self-same non-proven allegations, the self-same insufficient evidence could nonetheless be regarded as a sufficient factual basis for satisfying the court there is a real possibility of harm to the child in the future.

The third pointer is that if indeed this were the position, this would effectively reverse the burden of proof in an important respect. It would mean that once apparently credible evidence of misconduct has been given, those against whom the allegations are made must disprove them. Otherwise it would be open to a court to hold that, although the misconduct has not been proved, it has not been disproved and there is a real possibility that the misconduct did occur. Accordingly there is a real possibility that the child will suffer harm in the future and, hence, the threshold criteria are met. I do not believe Parliament intended that section 31(2) should work in this way.

Thus far I have concentrated on explaining that a court's conclusion that the threshold conditions are satisfied must have a factual base, and that an alleged but unproved fact, serious or trivial, is not a fact for this purpose. Nor is judicial suspicion, because there is no more than a judicial state of uncertainty about whether or not an event happened.

I must now put this into perspective by noting, and emphasising, the width of the range of facts which may be relevant when the court is considering the threshold conditions. The range of facts which may properly be taken into account is infinite. Facts include the history of members of the family, the state of relationships within a family, proposed changes within the membership of a family, parental attitudes, and omissions which might not reasonably have been expected, just as much as actual physical assaults. They include threats, and abnormal behaviour by a child, and unsatisfactory parental responses to complaints or allegations. And facts, which are minor or even trivial if considered in isolation, when taken together may suffice to satisfy the court of the likelihood of future harm. The court will attach to all the relevant facts the appropriate weight when coming to an overall conclusion on the crucial issue.

I must emphasise a further point. I have indicated that unproved allegations of maltreatment cannot form the basis for a finding by the court that either limb of section 31(2)(a) is established. It is, of course, open to a court to conclude there is a real possibility that the child will suffer harm in the future although harm in the past has not been established. There will be cases where, although the alleged maltreatment itself is not proved, the evidence does establish a combination of profoundly worrying features affecting the care of the child within the family. In such cases it would be open to a court in appropriate circumstances to find that, although not satisfied the child is yet suffering significant harm, on the basis of such facts as are proved there is a likelihood that he will do so in the future.

That is not the present case. The three younger girls are not at risk unless D1 was abused by Mr R in the past. If she was not abused, there is no reason for thinking the others may be. This is not a case where Mr R has a history of abuse. Thus the one and only relevant fact is whether D1 was abused by Mr R as she says. The other surrounding facts, such as the fact that D1 made a complaint and the fact that her mother responded unsatisfactorily, lead nowhere relevant in this case if they do not lead to the conclusion that D1 was abused. To decide that the others are at risk because there is a possibility that D1 was abused would be to base the decision, not on fact, but on suspicion that D1 may have been abused. That would be to lower the threshold prescribed by Parliament.

*Conclusion*

I am very conscious of the difficulties confronting social workers and others in obtaining hard evidence, which will stand up when challenged in court, of the maltreatment meted out to children behind closed doors. Cruelty and physical abuse are notoriously difficult to prove. The task of social workers is usually anxious and often thankless. They are criticised for not having taken action in response to warning signs which are obvious enough when seen in the clear light of hindsight. Or they are criticised for making applications based on serious allegations which, in the event, are not established in court. Sometimes, whatever they do, they cannot do right.

I am also conscious of the difficulties facing judges when there is conflicting testimony on serious allegations. On some occasions judges are left deeply anxious at the end of a case. There may be an understandable inclination to 'play safe' in the interests of the child. Sometimes judges wish to safeguard a child whom they fear may be at risk without at the same time having to fasten a label of very serious misconduct on to one of the parents.

These are among the difficulties and considerations Parliament addressed in the Children Act 1989 when deciding how, to use the fashionable terminology, the balance should be struck between the various interests. As I read the Act, Parliament decided that the threshold for a care order should be that the child is suffering significant harm, or there is a real possibility that he will do so. In the latter regard the threshold is comparatively low. Therein lies the protection for children. But, as I read the Act, Parliament also decided that proof of the relevant facts is needed if this threshold is to be surmounted. Before the section 1 welfare test and the welfare 'checklist' can be applied, the threshold has to be crossed. Therein lies the protection for parents. They are not to be at risk of having their child taken from them and removed into the care of the local authority on the basis only of suspicions, whether of the judge or of the local authority or anyone else. A conclusion that the child is suffering or is likely to suffer harm must be based on facts, not just suspicion.

It follows that I would dismiss this appeal. In his judgment, when deciding that the alleged sexual abuse was not proved, the judge referred to the headnote in *In re W (Minors) (Sexual Abuse: Standard of Proof)* [1994] 1 FLR 419 and the need for a higher than ordinary standard of proof. Despite these references the Court of Appeal were satisfied that the judge applied the right test. I agree. Reading his judgment overall, I am not persuaded he adopted a materially different standard of proof from the standard I have mentioned above. Sexual abuse not having been proved, there were no facts upon which the judge could properly conclude there was a likelihood of harm to the three younger girls.

. . .

LORD BROWNE-WILKINSON (dissenting): My Lords, I have the misfortune to disagree with the view reached by the majority of your Lordships. Although the area of disagreement is small, it is crucial both to the outcome of this appeal and to the extent to which children at risk can be protected by the courts.

. . .

Where I part company is in thinking that the facts relevant to an assessment of risk ('is likely to suffer . . . harm') are not the same as the facts relevant to a decision that harm is in fact being suffered. In order to be satisfied that an event has occurred or is occurring the evidence has to show on balance of probabilities that such event did occur or is occurring. But in order to be satisfied that there is a risk of such an occurrence, the ambit of the relevant facts is in my view wider. The combined effect of a number of factors which suggest that a state of affairs, though not proved to exist, may well exist is the normal basis for the assessment of future risk. To be satisfied of the existence of a risk does not require proof of the occurrence of past historical events but proof of facts which are relevant to the making of a prognosis.

Let me give an example, albeit a dated one. Say that in 1940 those responsible for giving air-raid warnings had received five unconfirmed sightings of approaching aircraft which might be enemy bombers. They could not, on balance of probabilities, have reached a conclusion that any one of those sightings was of an enemy aircraft: nor could they logically have put together five non-proven sightings so as to be satisfied that enemy aircraft were in fact approaching. But their task was not simply to decide whether enemy aircraft were approaching but whether there was a risk of an air-raid. The facts relevant to the assessment of such risk were the reports that unconfirmed sightings had been made, not the truth of such reports. They could well, on the basis of those unconfirmed reports, have been satisfied that there was a real possibility of an air-raid and given warning accordinglly.

So in the present case, the major issue was whether D1 had been sexually abused (the macro-fact). In the course of the hearing before the judge a number of other facts (the micro-facts) were established to the judge's satisfaction by the evidence. The judge in his careful judgment summarised these micro-facts: that D1 had been consistent in her story from the time of her first complaint; that her statement was full and detailed showing 'a classic unfolding relevation of progressively worse abuse'; that

there were opportunities for such abuse by Mr R and that he had been lying in denying
that he had ever been alone either with D1 or with any of the other children; that D2
had made statements which indicated that she had witnessed 'inappropriate' behaviour between Mr R and D1; that the mother (contrary to her evidence) also suspected
that something had been going on between Mr R and D1 and had sought to dissuade
D2 from saying anything to the social workers. The judge also found a number of
micro facts pointing the other way. Having summarised all these micro facts pointing
each way, he reached his conclusion on the macro fact: 'I cannot be sure to the
requisite high standard of proof that [D1's] allegations are true.' But he also made
further findings (which he thought to be irrelevant in law) on the basis of the
micro-facts:

> This is far from saying that I am satisfied the child's complaints are untrue. I do
> not brush them aside as the jury seem to have done. I am, at the least, more than
> a little suspicious that [Mr R] has abused her as she says. If it were relevant, I would
> be prepared to hold that there is a real possibility that her statement and her
> evidence are true, nor has [Mr R] by his evidence and demeanour, not only
> throughout the hearing but the whole of this matter, done anything to dispel those
> suspicions . . .

That conclusion that there was a real possibility that the evidence of D1 was true was
a finding based on evidence and the micro-facts that he had found. It was not a mere
suspicion as to the risk that Mr R was an abuser: it was a finding of risk based on facts.

My Lords, I am anxious that the decision of the House in this case may establish
the law in an unworkable form to the detriment of many children at risk. Child abuse,
particularly sex abuse, is notoriously difficult to prove in a court of law. The relevant
facts are extremely sensitive and emotive. They are often known only to the child and
to the alleged abuser. If legal proof of actual abuse is a prerequisite to a finding that
a child is at risk of abuse, the court will be powerless to intervene to protect children
in relation to whom there are the gravest suspicions of actual abuse but the necessary
evidence legally to prove such abuse is lacking. Take the present case. Say that the
proceedings had related to D1, the complainant, herself. After a long hearing a judge
has reached the conclusion on evidence that there is a 'real possibility' that her
evidence is true, i.e. that she has in fact been gravely abused. Can Parliament really
have intended that neither the court nor anyone else should have jurisdiction to
intervene so as to protect D1 from any abuse which she may well have been enduring?
I venture to think not.

My Lords, for those reasons and those given by my noble and learned friend, Lord
Lloyd of Berwick, I would allow the appeal.

## Bainham, Andrew, 'Sexual Abuse in the Lords'
### [1996] CLJ 209

. . . The recognition by the House that in the child protection context 'likely' does
not mean 'probable' is sensible and welcome, yet this is a decision which itself has
some 'profoundly worrying features' highlighted in part in the dissenting speeches of
Lords Lloyd and Browne-Wilkinson. The idea that because something is serious it is
less likely is an odd notion but also a dangerous one. As Lord Lloyd points out, it
'would be a bizarre result if the more serious the anticipated injury, whether physical
or sexual, the more difficult it became for the authority to . . . secure protection for
the child'. There is, he convincingly argues, surely a case for *lowering* the threshold

here rather than raising it, or at least applying a simple test of balance of probabilities without the gloss.

. . .

At heart these issues are a question of balancing the rights of parents to 'due process' with the welfarist concerns of child protection. Yet, if mistakes are to be made in marginal cases, it is surely better that the rights of parents are eroded than that children be exposed to danger. As the nation mourns the children of Dunblane, many there will be who will share the sentiment that those charged with the unenviable task of protecting children should be able to act on substantial suspicion.

### Keating, Heather, 'Shifting Standards in the House of Lords: Re H and Others (Minors) (Sexual Abuse: Standard of Proof)' [1996] 8 CFLQ 157

. . . The path of reasoning adopted by Lord Nicholls seems logical but, arguably, he both starts and finishes at strange locations. His argument is premised on the very broad assertion that serious abuse is less likely than minor abuse by, for example, stating that a stepfather is usually less likely to have repeatedly raped his stepdaughter than to have slapped her. But do we know this? Even if true, does it follow that we should be more sceptical of serious allegations when made? One could take the opposite view that the very seriousness of them means that they are less likely to be made unless true. Of course, neither of the assertions can be proved. Each case has to be considered on its own merits in the light of all the available evidence, and a bald generalisation about levels of abuse in society is not evidence from which the credibility of a particular allegation can be judged. More fundamentally, the outcome is that in serious cases of abuse — which are notoriously difficult to prove — we are making the task harder. Lord Lloyd is right to describe this result as bizarre. The absence of argument by counsel on what is the most important aspect of the appeal is truly unfortunate. One accepts, of course, the weight of authority prior to Re H on the issue but given Kennedy LJ's strong dissent in the Court of Appeal there was still a case to be argued. Given that the threshold is only the starting-point in the decision-making process, a simple balance of probabilities standard is both more workable and less dangerous. It does not amount to an unwarranted intervention into family life and does not leave local authorities powerless to protect children. In practical terms this decision may not only leave children exposed to risks which cannot be proved to the high standard being required, but will exacerbate the trend towards legalism in the work of social workers.

. . .

Nobody would wish to see applications for care orders being brought on the basis of hunches or suspicions. However, in pursuit of their entirely proper objective of protecting families from unwarranted intervention the House of Lords may well have reduced the law to almost Delphic opaqueness. Worse than that, however, is the fear that this decision will deprive some vulnerable children of the protection which, on the facts, they deserve.

### 10.5.4  A local authority's discretion to bring care or supervision proceedings

The court has no power to compel a local authority to institute proceedings for a care or supervision order, but may make a direction under s. 37 of the

CA 1989 that a local authority investigate the child's circumstances (see Chapter 7). Judicial concern at the court's lack of jurisdiction to compel a local authority to take action was expressed by Stephen Brown P in the following case, in which the Court of Appeal held that the court had no jurisdiction to grant a local authority a s. 8 prohibited steps order to exclude the father from the home, as such an application was excluded by s. 9(2) of the CA 1989.

### Nottinghamshire County Council v P
[1994] Fam 18
Court of Appeal

STEPHEN BROWN P: . . . This court is deeply concerned at the absence of any power to direct this authority to take steps to protect the children. In the former wardship jurisdiction it might well have been able to do so. The operation of the Children Act 1989 is entirely dependent upon the full co-operation of all those involved. This includes the courts, local authorities, social workers, and all who have to deal with children. Unfortunately, as appears from this case, if a local authority doggedly resists taking the steps which are appropriate to the case of children at risk of suffering significant harm it appears that the court is powerless. The authority may perhaps lay itself open to an application for judicial review but in a case such as this the question arises, at whose instance? The position is one which it is to be hoped will not recur and that lessons will be learnt from this unhappy catalogue of errors.
 . . .

*Note*
Before the CA 1989, the court in divorce, nullity or judicial separation proceedings and the High Court in wardship could make a care or supervision order in exceptional circumstances even though no such order had been applied for. These provisions were repealed by the 1989 Act.

*Questions*
1.   'The question of the threshold criteria and the standard of proof by which they are to be judged goes to the very heart of the issue of State intervention in family life. Clearly the case strikes a balance between the State's interest in protecting vulnerable children and the family's right to privacy, but which of their Lordships strikes the better balance?' (Keating, *op. cit.* at 10.5.3, at pp. 159 and 160). What do you think?
2.   The Interdepartmental Working Group on Child Care considered whether it would be better to have a broad welfare test as a ground for compulsory intervention rather than specific threshold conditions (*Review of Child Care Law*, at 10.5.1, para. 5.10). Would this have been a good idea?
3.   The court in any family proceedings may of its own motion make any s. 8 order. Is it satisfactory that the court has no similar power to make care or supervision orders? What do you think were the reasons for removing this power from the court?

*Further reading*
Brasse, G., 'The Section 31 Monopoly' [1993] Fam Law 691.
Smith, V., 'Significant Harm' [1994] Fam Law 197.

## 10.6   CONTACT IN CARE

*Re J (A Minor) (Contact)*
[1994] 1 FLR 729
Court of Appeal

BALCOMBE LJ: . . . Contact with the parent with whom the child is not resident is a right of the child, and very cogent reasons are required for terminating such contact.

. . .

The CA 1989, s. 34 and sch. 2, para. 15, radically improved the situation in respect of parental contact with children in care. There is a presumption of continuing contact, so that the onus is on the local authority to apply to the court for an order authorising it to refuse or terminate contact.

**Department of Health, *Children Act 1989 Guidance and Regulations, Vol. 1, Court Orders***
London: HMSO, 1991, Chapter 4

. . .

3.76   Section 34 introduces major new provisions on contact with children in care. It establishes that a local authority must allow reasonable contact with his parents and certain other people, unless directed otherwise by a court order, or the local authority temporarily suspend contact in urgent circumstances. It requires the court to consider contact arrangements before making a care order and gives it wide powers to deal with problems. The underlying principle is that the authority, child and other persons concerned should as far as possible agree reasonable arrangements before the care order is made, but should be able to seek the court's assistance if agreement cannot be reached or the authority want to deny contact to a person who is entitled to it under the Act. These provisions substantially improve the position of parents and others seeking contact compared with previous legislation, and limit the authority's power to control and deny contact. However, it should be recognised that there will be cases where contact will be detrimental to the child's welfare. This possibility should be considered at the pre-court proceedings stage, when plans for contact are being drawn up. . . .

3.77   The presumption that contract is allowed for certain named people, and the pro-active role given to the court reflect the importance of this subject. Regular contact with parents, relatives and friends will usually be an important part of the child's upbringing in his new environment and is essential to successful rehabilitation. Lack of contact can, over a period, have vital consequences for the rights of parents and children; it can be a major factor in deciding whether to discharge a care order or to dispense with parental agreement to adoption. This is too important to be regarded as simply a matter of management within the sole control of the local authority. The new scheme is intended to provide a basis for good practice and remove the perceived unfairness in previous arrangements. It is separate from the contact provisions in Part II of the Act; a section 8 contact order cannot be made when a child is in local authority care (section 9(1)), and an existing order is automatically discharged on the making of a care order (section 91(2)).

3.78    The authority is required to allow the child reasonable contact with his parents, any guardian, and any person having the benefit of a residence order or care of the child under wardship immediately before the care order was made (on the making of which the residence order or wardship lapses). The parent includes an unmarried father. Subject to any court order, it is for the authority to decide what is reasonable contact in the circumstances. The degree of contact should not necessarily remain static; the local authority may plan for the frequency or duration of contact to increase or decrease over time. Again this should be specified in the plan which is prepared and submitted to the court prior to the making of an order. Where possible, the plan should have been discussed with the child and his parents; any disagreements can be resolved by the court making an order as to the degree of contact.

. . .

# CHILDREN ACT 1989

### 34.  Parental contract etc. with children in care

(1)   Where a child is in the care of a local authority, the authority shall (subject to the provisions of this section) allow the child reasonable contact with—

(a)   his parents;

(b)   any guardian of his;

(c)   where there was a residence order in force with respect to the child immediately before the care order was made, the person in whose favour the order was made; and

(d)   where, immediately before the care order was made, a person had care of the child by virtue of an order made in the exercise of the High Court's inherent jurisdiction with respect to children, that person.

(2)   On the application made by the authority or the child, the court may make such order as it considers appropriate with respect to the contact which is to be allowed between the child and any named person.

(3)   On an application made by—

(a)   any person mentioned in paragraphs (a) to (d) of subsection (1); or

(b)   any person who has obtained the leave of the court to make the application,

the court may make such order as it considers appropriate with respect to the contact which is to be allowed between the child and that person.

(4)   On an application made by the authority or the child, the court may make an order authorising the authority to refuse to allow contact between the child and any person who is mentioned in paragraphs (a) to (d) of subsection (1) and named in the order.

(5)   When making a care order with respect to a child, or in any family proceedings in connection with a child who is in the care of a local authority, the court may make an order under this section, even though no application for such an order has been made with respect to the child, if it considers that the order should be made.

(6)   An authority may refuse to allow the contact that would otherwise be required by virtue of subsection (1) or an order under this section if—

(a)   they are satisfied that it is necessary to do so in order to safeguard or promote the child's welfare; and

(b)   the refusal—

(i)    is decided upon as a matter of urgency; and

(ii)   does not last for more than seven days.

. . .

*Note*

A s. 34 order may impose conditions (s. 34(7)). It may be varied or discharged (s. 34(9)). It may be made when the care order is made or subsquently (s. 34(10)).

### In re B (Minor) (Termination of Contact: Paramount Consideration)
[1993] Fam 301
Court of Appeal

*Facts*: The local authority obtained care orders in respect of two little girls. The mother gave birth to a boy and had successful contact with the girls. The local authority applied under CA 1989, s. 34(4) for an order authorising it to refuse contact between the girls and their mother, so that the girls could be placed with prospective adopters. The mother opposed the application, but the application was granted. The guardian *ad litem* appealed.

*Held*: allowing the appeal and applying the welfare principle, that the judge had erred by failing to investigate the mother's potential as the future carer of all three children before reaching the decision to terminate contact.

BUTLER-SLOSS LJ: . . . My understanding of the Act of 1989 is that it aims to incorporate the best of the wardship jurisdiction within the statutory framework without any of the perceived disadvantages of judicial monitoring of administrative plans. It provides for the court a wide range of options and the possibility of its own motion to set in train a line of investigation not contemplated or asked for by the parties. Like wardship, however, these wide powers are to be sparingly used.

The present position of a child whose welfare is being considered under Part IV of the Act appears to me to be that he will not be placed in care unless a court has been satisfied that the threshold conditions in section 31 have been met and that it is better to make a care order than not to do so. After the care order is made, the court has no continuing role in the future welfare of the child. The local authority has parental responsibility for the child by section 33(3). However, issues relating to the child may come before the court, for instance on applications for contact or leave to refuse contact, to discharge the care order or by an application for a section 8 residence order. The making of a residence order discharges the care order: section 91(1). At the moment that an application comes before the court, at whichever tier, the court has a duty to apply section 1, which states that when a court determines any question with respect to the upbringing of a child, the child's welfare shall be the court's paramount consideration. The court has to have regard to the prejudicial effect of delay, to the checklist including the range of orders available to the court and whether to make an order. On a section 34 application, therefore, the court has a duty to consider and apply the welfare section.

Contact applications generally fall into two main categories: those which ask for contact as such, and those which are attempts to set aside the care order itself. In the first category there is no suggestion that the applicant wishes to take over the care of the child and the issue of contact often depends on whether contact would frustrate long-term plans for the child in a substitute home, such as adoption, where continuing contact may not be for the long-term welfare of the child. The presumption of contact, which has to be for the benefit of the child, has always to be balanced against the long-term welfare of the child and, particularly, where he will live in the future. Contact must not be allowed to destabilise or endanger the arrangements for the child and in many cases the plans for the child will be decisive of the contact application. There may also be cases where the parent is having satisfactory contact with the child and there are no long-term plans or those plans do not appear to the court to preclude some future contact. The proposals of the local authority, based on their appreciation of the best interests of the child, must command the greatest respect and consideration from the court, but Parliament has given to the court, and not to the local authority, the duty to decide on contact between the child and those named in section 34(1). Consequently, the court may have the task of requiring the local authority to justify their long-term plans to the extent only that those plans exclude contact between parent and child. In the second category, contact applications may be made by parents by way of another attempt to obtain the return of the children. In such a case the court is obviously entitled to take into account the failure to apply to discharge the care order, and in the majority of cases the court will have little difficulty in coming to the conclusion that the applicant cannot demonstrate that contact with a view to rehabilitation with the parent is a viable proposition at that stage, particularly if it had already been rejected at the earlier hearing when the child was placed in care. The task for the parents will be too great and the court would be entitled to assume that the plans of the local authority to terminate contact are for the welfare of the child and are not to be frustrated by inappropriate contact with a view to the remote possibility, at some future date, of rehabilitation.

But in all cases the welfare section has to be considered, and the local authority have the task of justifying the cessation of contact. There may also be unusual cases where either the local authority have not made effective plans or there has been considerable delay in implementing them and a parent, who has previously been found by a court unable or unwilling to care for the child so that a care order has been made, comes back upon the scene as a possible future primary carer. If the local authority with a care order decide not to consider that parent on the new facts, [counsel for the guardian *ad litem*] argued that it is for the court, with the enhanced jurisdiction of the Act of 1989, to consider whether even at this late stage there should be some investigation of the proposals of the parent, with the possibility of reconsidering the local authority plans. [Counsel for the local authority] argued that the court cannot go behind the long-term plans of the local authority unless they were acting capriciously or were otherwise open to scrutiny by way of judicial review.

I unhesitatingly reject the local authority argument. As I have already said, their plan has to be given the greatest possible consideration by the court and it is only in the unusual case that a parent will be able to convince the court, the onus being firmly on the parent, that there has been such a change of circumstances as to require further investigation and reconsideration of the local authority plan. If, however, a court were unable to intervene, it would make a nonsense of the paramountcy of the welfare of the child which is the bedrock of the Act, and would subordinate it to the administrative decision of the local authority in a situation where the court is seized of the contact issue. That cannot be right.

But I would emphasise that this is not an open door to courts reviewing the plans of local authorities. Generally, where parties choose not to pursue applications, they are well advised not to do so. But there is now a flexibility in the approach of the court to the problems of the child before it, and occasionally the court may wish to invoke section 10(1)(b), which provides that a court may, in any family proceedings, which includes care proceedings, make a section 8 order with respect to a child if 'the court considers that the order should be made even though no application has been made.'

A court may also make a contact or an interim contact order and impose such conditions as it considers appropriate section 34(7).

In my view the judge was in error in not appreciating that he was able, if he thought it right, to have another look at the mother as a possible future carer and give appropriate directions for assessments to be made. He did look at the relevant issues of possible rehabilitation and delay and came to conclusions adverse to the mother But those conclusions were very much influenced by his belief that he had no right to interfere in any way with the plans put forward by the local authority. His conclusion that his hands were tied, in my view, vitiated his exercise of discretion and his decision cannot stand.

This court, therefore, has to decide whether the mother should be assessed as the potential carer of all three children. There is a large question mark over the wisdom of straining the placement for S by the possibility of putting all three children together in the care of a relatively untried mother. But the guardian ad litem and the social worker saw a real possibility that she might become an adequate mother for all three children. The decision requires consideration of the competing factors that on the one side there is the prospect that the mother may come up trumps and, if so, the enormous advantage for these three children to be brought up together by their own mother in preference to a substitute family, however suitable. On the other side there is the real danger that the problems would be too great, that the assessment would be disappointing and, most worrying of all, the danger that this attempt might imperil the relationship between the mother and S, who would be devastated by losing his mother at this stage. We must add to those factors the need to settle these children and the fragility of their present placement from which they will have to move in any event, and the question of delay is very important. However, I have come to the clear conclusion that the mother's potential must be investigated and not to do so would be unfair to the children and, if the prospective adoption application were to be made, might create a serious obstacle on the special facts of this case.

Since there is some urgency to have these matters looked at as soon as possible, we allowed the appeal last week for reasons which we are now giving, and invited counsel to agree an order. The appeal will be allowed on the terms of the order handed in.

*Notes*

1.   For a case on contact and care plans, see *Re E (A Minor) (Care Order: Contact)* [1994] 1 FLR 146, CA, in which *Re B, supra,* was approved. Butler-Sloss LJ's *dicta* in *Re B* were also adopted in *Re M (Care: Contact: Grandmother's Application for Leave)* [1995] 2 FLR 86, CA.

2.   In *Re D and H (Minors) (Children in Care: Termination of Contact)* (1997) *The Times,* 19 February, the Court of Appeal held that it was wrong for a judge in the course of family proceedings to make an order under CA 1989, s. 34(2) or (5) phasing out contact between a mother and her children where such an order was inconsistent with the local authority's recommendations for the children set out in its care plan.

*Further reading*

Brasse, G., 'Section 34: a Trojan Horse? The Assault on Plans for Children in Care?' [1993] Fam Law 55.

Jolly, S., 'Cutting Ties — the Termination of Contact in Care' [1994] JSWFL 299.

## 10.7  PROTECTION OF CHILDREN

Part V of the CA 1989 provides the legal framework for dealing with children needing protection, whether in an emergency or otherwise, by making provision *inter alia* for child assessment orders (s. 43) and emergency protection orders (ss. 44 and 45). As Part V proceedings are not family proceedings (see Chapter 7), the court cannot make a s. 8 order in the proceedings. When deciding whether or not to make a Part V order, the court must apply the welfare principle (s. 1(1)) and the no order presumption (s. 1(5)), but not the statutory checklist (s. 1(3)), as information would not be available to the court in a situation of emergency in order for it to conduct the s. 1(3) exercise.

### 10.7.1  Child assessment orders

Section 43 of the 1989 Act enables a medical or psychiatric assessment of the child to be carried out *without removing the child from home*. For this reason, it is less Draconian than an emergency protection order. The child assessment order was introduced as a result of the criticisms made of the now repealed place of safety order (see the 'Cleveland affair' at 10.2.2).

### CHILDREN ACT 1989

**43.  Child assessment orders**
    (1)   On the application of a local authority or authorised person . . . the court may make [a child assessment] order if, but only if, it is satisfied that—
    (a)   the applicant has reasonable cause to suspect that the child is suffering, or is likely to suffer, significant harm;
    (b)   an assessment of the state of the child's health or development, or of the way in which he has been treated, is required to enable the applicant to determine whether or not the child is suffering, or is likely to suffer, significant harm; and
    (c)   it is unlikely that such an assessment will be made, or be satisfactory, in the absence of an order under this section.
    . . .

*Note*
The application may be treated as an application for an emergency protection order (s. 43(3)). The court must not make a child assessment order if it is satisfied that there are grounds for making an emergency protection order with respect to the child, and that it ought to make an emergency protection order rather than a child assessment order (s. 43(4)). The child assessment order authorises any person carrying out the assessment, or any part of the assessment, to do so in accordance with the terms of the order; but a child of sufficient understanding to make an informed decision may refuse to submit to a medical or psychiatric examination or other assessment (s. 43(7) and (8), but see *South Glamorgan County Council* v *W and B* [1993] FLR 574, FD).

*Further reading*
Lavery, Ruth, 'The Child Assessment Order — A Reassessment' [1996] 8 CFLQ 41.

Dickens, J., 'Assessment and the Control of Social Work: Analysis of the Reasons for the Non-use of the Child Assessment Order' [1993] JSWFL 88.

## 10.7.2 Emergency protection orders

## CHILDREN ACT 1989

**44. Orders for emergency protection of children**

(1) Where any person ('the applicant') applies to the court for [an emergency protection order], the court may make the order if, but only if, it is satisfied that—

(a) there is reasonable cause to believe that the child is likely to suffer significant harm if—

(i) he is not removed to accommodation provided by or on behalf of the applicant; or

(ii) he does not remain in the place in which he is then being accommodated;

(b) in the case of an application made by a local authority—

(i) enquiries are being made with respect to a child under section 47(1)(b); and

(ii) those enquiries are being frustrated by access to the child being unreasonably refused to a person authorised to seek access and that the applicant has reasonable cause to believe that access to the child is required as a matter of urgency; or

(c) in the case of an application made by an authorised person—

(i) the applicant has reasonable cause to suspect that a child is suffering, or is likely to suffer, significant harm;

(ii) the applicant is making enquiries with respect to the child's welfare; and

(iii) those enquiries are being frustrated by access to the child being unreasonably refused to a person authorised to seek access and the applicant has reasonable cause to believe that access to the child is required as a matter of urgency.

. . .

*Notes*

1. While the order is in force it operates as a direction to any person who is in a position to do so to comply with any request to produce the child to the applicant and (i) authorises the removal of the child at any time to accommodation provided by or on behalf of the applicant and his being kept there, or (ii) prevents the child's removal from any hospital, or other place, in which the child was being accommodated immediately before the order was made (s. 44(4)(a) and (b)). The order gives the applicant parental responsibility for the child (s. 44(4)(c)), but other persons with parental responsibility do not lose it.

2. Section 45 of the CA 1989 makes provision in respect of the duration and discharge of emergency protection orders.

3. For cases where emergency protection orders were sought, see, e.g., *Re O (A Minor) (Medical Treatment)* [1993] 2 FLR 149, FD (premature baby of Jehovah's Witnesses requiring blood transfusion) and *Re P (Emergency Protection Order)* [1996] 1 FLR 482 (paediatrician suspecting the mother of attempting to suffocate the child).

## 10.8   EXCLUDING THE ABUSER FROM THE HOME

There are no provisions in the CA 1989 to remove the abuser rather than the child victim from the home when the child needs protection. If a family environment is generally considered to be the best place in which to bring up a child, then it would make sense if in some cases the abuser, rather than the child, were removed from the home. Removing the child will not always be in the child's best interests. As a result of recommendations made by the Law Commission in its Report *Domestic Violence and Occupation of the Family Home* (Law Com No. 207, 1992) and by the Government, s. 52 and sch. 6 of the FLA 1996 amend the 1989 Act to give the court jurisdiction to include an exclusion requirement in an interim care order (s. 38A) and an emergency protection order (s. 44A), so that the abuser, rather than the child, is removed from the home. Part IV of the FLA 1996 is expected to come into force on 1 October 1997.

### Law Commission, *Domestic Violence and Occupation of the Family Home*, Law Com No. 207
### London: HMSO, 1992

### CHILDREN ACT 1989

**Ouster orders for the protection of children**
6.15   During the debates in Parliament which led to the passage of the Children Act 1989, considerable support was given to the possibility of ousting an abuser or suspected abuser from the home instead of having to remove the child, but the question was not finally resolved. . . .
6.16   However, a power to oust an abuser or suspected abuser received much support in principle on consultation. There are obviously cases where a child needs immediate and guaranteed protection from risk of serious harm which can only be given by removal from home. There are other cases where instant removal is not obviously the answer, but there are serious concerns and it is difficult to know whether the trauma to the child of a hasty or unjustified removal will be greater than the hazards of leaving him at home pending further investigations. Sudden removal from home, whatever its deficiencies, always carries some risk to the child's welfare, varying with the age of the child and how the removal is done. In a few cases, there may be a good reason to believe that the child can be properly safeguarded from harm if one of the adults is removed, at least until the matter can be properly investigated and the facts discovered. A further advantage of legislating is that it appears that some local authorities are already inducing suspected abusers to leave, rather than have the children removed, and this would provide a way of regularising and controlling the practice. . . .

### CHILDREN ACT 1989

**38A.   Power to include exclusion requirement in interim care order**
   (1)   Where—
      (a)   on being satisfied that there are reasonable grounds for believing that the circumstances with respect to a child are as mentioned in section 31(2)(a) and (b)(i), the court makes an interim care order with respect to a child, and

(b)   the conditions mentioned in subsection (2) are satisfied,
the court may include an exclusion requirement in the interim care order.

(2)   The conditions are—

(a)   that there is reasonable cause to believe that, if a person ('the relevant person') is excluded from a dwelling-house in which the child lives, the child will cease to suffer, or cease to be likely to suffer, significant harm, and

(b)   that another person living in the dwelling-house (whether a parent of the child or some other person)—

(i)   is able and willing to give the child the care which it would be reasonable to expect a parent to give him, and

(ii)   consents to the inclusion of the exclusion requirement.

(3)   For the purposes of this section an exclusion requirement is any one or more of the following—

(a)   a provision requiring the relevant person to leave a dwelling-house in which he is living with the child,

(b)   a provision prohibiting the relevant person from entering a dwelling-house in which the child lives, and

(c)   a provision excluding the relevant person from a defined area in which a dwelling-house in which the child lives is situated.

. . .

*Notes*

1.   Similar provisions exist in respect of an emergency protection order (see CA 1989, s. 44A, as inserted by the FLA 1996, sch. 6).

2.   A power of arrest may be attached to an exclusion requirement (s. 38A(5)). The court may accept an undertaking from the 'relevant person', instead of inserting an exclusion requirement into the interim care order (s. 38B). Similar provisions exist in respect of emergency protection orders (see ss. 44A(5) and 44B).

3.   A parent may be removed from the house for the sake of the children where there is domestic violence (see Chapter 6).

4.   For attempts to remove the abuser from the house under the present law, see, e.g., *Re H (Prohibited Steps Order)* [1995] 1 FLR 638, CA, and *Nottinghamshire County Council* v *P* [1994] Fam 18, where the Court of Appeal allowed a father's appeal against a prohibited steps order preventing him returning to the home where he had sexually abused his daughter.

*Further reading*
Cobley, C., and Lowe, N., 'Ousting Abusers — Public or Private Law Solutions?' (1994) 10 LQR 38.
Dewar, J., 'Local Authorities, Ouster Orders and the Inherent Jurisdiction — *Re S (Minors) (Inherent Jurisdiction: Ouster)*' (1995) 7 JCL 64.
Roberts, M., 'Ousting abusers — Children Act 1989 or Inherent Jurisdiction? *Re H (Prohibited Steps Order)*' [1995] 7 CFLQ 243.

## 10.9   LOCAL AUTHORITIES: WARDSHIP OR THE INHERENT JURISDICTION?

A major concern before the CA 1989 was the excessive use of wardship by local authorities as a means of taking children into care, despite the existence of statutory grounds in the Children and Young Persons Act 1969 (repealed by the CA 1989) for making care and supervision orders. The use of wardship was expensive and time-consuming and there were huge delays in the courts, which was particularly traumatic for children. One of the main reforms of the CA 1989 was to restrict the use of wardship by local authorities. (For wardship generally, see Chapter 7.)

## Department of Health, *Children Act 1989 Guidance and Regulations: Vol. 1, Court Orders*
London: HMSO, 1991, Chapter 3

. . .

3.98    The impact of the Children Act on the inherent jurisdiction of the High Court will be considerable. By incorporating many of the beneficial aspects of wardship, such as the 'open door' policy, and a flexible range of orders, the Act will substantially reduce the need to have recourse to the High Court. But in addition there is a specific prohibition against using the inherent jurisdiction in general, and wardship in particular, as an alternative to public law orders. Without this prohibition, the threshold criteria which have been carefully designed as the minimum circumstances justifying state intervention would be undermined, as too would any directions attached to these orders (such as to their duration or other effects). Where a wardship court thinks that a care or supervision order may be needed, it may direct a local authority to investigate the child's circumstances and, if the statutory conditions are satisfied, make an interim care or supervision order. These are the same powers that are available to any court in family proceedings. Similarly, since proceedings under the inherent jurisdiction are family proceedings it is open to the court to make a section 8 order.

3.99    The Act also affects the relationship between wardship and local authority care. Under the old law it was possible for a child in compulsory care also to be a ward of court. Wardship in these circumstances could only be invoked with the local authority's agreement. An exception arose where a ward of court was committed to care under section 7(2) of the Family Law Reform Act 1969 and the court retained the power to give directions to the local authority on the application of others such as the child's parents. While the child was a ward of court, the local authority's powers were uncertain because, in wardship, the court is said to be the child's guardian. The local authority's powers were restricted by the rule which required major decisions in the child's life to be referred to the court. Where the child is in care this division of responsibility should not occur. The local authority has parental responsibility for the child and should be able to take whatever decisions are necessary. The Act therefore makes wardship and care incompatible. If a ward of court is committed to care the wardship ceases to have effect (section 91(4)). While a child is in care he cannot be made a ward of court (section 100(2) and section 41 of the Supreme Court Act 1981 as amended by paragraph 45 of schedule 13).

3.100    The inherent jurisdiction remains available as a remedy of last resort where a local authority seeks the resolution of a specific issue concerning the future of a child in its care. But there are restrictions: The first is that the local authority must have the High Court's leave to apply for the exercise of its inherent jurisdiction (section 100(3)). Leave may only be granted where the court is satisfied that the local authority could not achieve the desired result through the making of any order other than one under the inherent jurisdiction. Where there are statutory remedies within the Act, the local authority will be expected to pursue those. In particular, where a child is not in local authority care, the local authority will rarely be granted leave since they could otherwise obtain a specific issue or prohibited steps order under section 8. An exception might be where the local authority seek to restrain publicity about the child. Second, even where there is no other statutory remedy within the Act, there must be reasonable cause to believe that the child is likely to suffer significant harm if the inherent jurisdiction is not exercised.

3.101   Since the local authority will have parental responsibility for children in their care they should make decisions themselves in consultation with the parents as appropriate and after taking the child's views into account. Nevertheless there may be occasions where recourse to the High Court is appropriate as the decisions to be taken are highly contentious, and/or fall far outside the normal scope of decision-making for children in care. An example might be the sterilisation of a child in care. Other less extreme situations may also merit High Court intervention, for example, to restrain harmful publicity about the child. In such cases when the inherent jurisdiction is the only means of obtaining the remedy, it should not be too difficult to satisfy the leave criteria.

3.102   The Act further prevents the High Court from exercising its inherent jurisdiction 'for the purposes of conferring on any local authority power to determine any question which has arisen, or which may arise in connection with any aspect of parental responsibility'. Thus, in making an order under its inherent jurisdiction, the court cannot confer on the local authority any degree of parental responsibility it does not already have (section 100(2)).

. . .

# CHILDREN ACT 1989

## 100.   Restrictions on use of wardship jurisdiction

. . .

(2)   No court shall exercise the High Court's inherent jurisdiction with respect to children—

(a)   so as to require a child to be placed in the care, or put under the supervision, of a local authority;

(b)   so as to require a child to be accommodated by or on behalf of a local authority; or

(c)   so as to make a child who is the subject of a care order a ward of court; or

(d)   for the purpose of conferring on any local authority power to determine any question which has arisen, or which may arise, in connection with any aspect of parental responsibility for a child.

(3)   No application for any exercise of the court's inherent jurisdiction with respect to children may be made by a local authority unless the authority have obtained the leave of the court.

(4)   The court may only grant leave if it is satisfied that—

(a)   the result which the authority wish to achieve could not be achieved through the making of any order of a kind to which subsection (5) applies; and

(b)   there is reasonable cause to believe that if the court's inherent jurisdiction is not exercised with respect to the child he is likely to suffer significant harm.

(5)   This subsection applies to any order—

(a)   made otherwise than in the exercise of the court's inherent jurisdiction; and

(b)   which the local authority is entitled to apply for (assuming, in the case of any application which may only be made with leave, that leave is granted).

*Note*
For examples of local authority applications under the inherent jurisdiction, see *Re S (A Minor) (Medical Treatment)* [1993] 1 FLR 376 (local authority applied for leave to permit a blood transfusion to be given to a child suffering from leukaemia as his parents were Jehovah's Witnesses); *Re J (A Minor) (Medical Treatment)* [1992] 2 FLR 165 (local authority applied for guidance for the treatment of a severely handicapped child); *Re M (Care: Leave to Interview Child)* [1995] 1 FLR 825 (local authority used the inherent jurisdiction to ask the court whether it should permit a solicitor to interview two boys in care concerning a rape). See also the cases in Chapter 7.

*Further reading*
Bainham, A., 'The Children Act 1989: the Future of Wardship' [1990] Fam Law 270.
Parry, M., 'The Children Act 1989: Local Authorities, Wardship and the Removal of the Inherent Jurisdiction' [1993] JSWL 212.

## 10.10   THE PRELIMINARY DRAFT HAGUE CONVENTION ON THE PROTECTION OF CHILDREN

In some cases, it may be necessary to invoke the assistance of social services agencies in other countries in order to protect children. In such cases, it will be necessary to establish which law applies and to encourage cooperation between the States involved. The draft Hague Convention on the Protection of Children (adopted by the Special Commission of the Hague Conference on Private International Law on 22 September 1995) aims to do this. It will replace the Hague Convention on the Protection of Minors 1961 (to which the UK is not a party).

## THE PRELIMINARY DRAFT HAGUE CONVENTION ON THE PROTECTION OF MINORS

**Article 1**
1.   The objects of this Convention are—
    (a)   to determine which State's authorities have jurisdiction to take measures directed to the protection of the person or property of the child;
    (b)   to determine which law is to be applied by such authorities in exercising their jurisdiction;
    (c)   to determine the law applicable to parental responsibility;
    (d)   to provide for the recognition and enforcement of such measures in all Contracting States;
    (e)   to establish such co-operation between the authorities of the Contracting States as may be necessary in order to achieve the purposes of this Convention.

2. For the purposes of this Convention, the term 'parental responsibility' includes parental authority, or any analogous responsibility or authority in relation to the person or the property of the child.

*Note*
A Consultation Paper on the Draft Convention was published by the Lord Chancellor's Department and Scottish Court Administration in April 1996.

## 10.11  REMEDIES AGAINST LOCAL AUTHORITIES

A person wishing to challenge a public law order made under the CA 1989 may appeal against the order or apply for its variation or discharge. Where Part III powers and duties of local authorities are involved, a complaint may be made under the complaints procedure which every local authority must establish (see CA 1989, s. 26, and the Representations Procedure (Children) Regulations 1991). Another way of challenging a decision of a local authority is to use the public law remedy of judicial review (see, e.g., *R v Royal Borough of Kingston upon Thames, ex parte T* [1994] 1 FLR 798, QBD). Other options are to apply to the ombudsman or local ombudsman.

Attempts have been made to bring private law actions against local authorities (e.g., for damages for negligence or breach of statutory duty), but such actions have failed, largely for reasons of public policy, as the following case shows.

### *X (Minors)* v *Bedfordshire County Council and Related Appeals*
[1995] 2 AC 633
House of Lords

*Facts*: The plaintiffs brought related appeals in two child abuse cases and three special educational needs cases, alleging they had been injured by public authorities in the carrying out of their statutory functions. In the first child abuse case, the local authority had failed to take steps in respect of children despite reports that they were being abused and neglected. In the second abuse case, the mistaken identity of the alleged abuser had resulted in the child being unnecessarily separated from her mother for one year. The children in the first abuse case and the mother in the second made claims in damages against the local authority for breach of statutory duty and breach of the common-law duty of care. The proceedings were struck out and their appeals to the Court of Appeal were dismissed. The plaintiffs appealed.
*Held*: *inter alia*, that in respect of the abuse cases the claims for breach of statutory duty had been rightly struck out; and that the courts should proceed with great care before holding liable in negligence those charged by Parliament with the task of protecting society from the wrongdoing of others.

LORD BROWNE-WILKINSON:    . . . Is it, then, just and reasonable to superimpose a common law duty of care on the local authority in relation to the performance of its statutory duties to protect children? In my judgment it is not. Sir Thomas Bingham MR took the view, with which I agree, that the public policy consideration which has first claim on the loyalty of the law is that wrongs should be remedied and that very potent counter considerations are required to override that policy. . . . However, in my judgment there are such considerations in this case.

First, in my judgment a common law duty of care would cut across the whole statutory system set up for the protection of children at risk. As a result of the ministerial directions contained in 'Working Together' the protection of such children is not the exclusive territory of the local authority's social services. The system is inter-disciplinary, involving the participation of the police, educational bodies, doctors and others. At all stages the system involves joint discussions, joint recommendations and joint decisions. The key organisation is the Child Protection Conference, a multi-disciplinary body which decides whether to place the child on the Child Protection Register. This procedure by way of joint action takes place, not merely because it is good practice but because it is required by guidance having statutory force binding on the local authority. The guidance is extemely detailed and extensive: the current edition of 'Working Together' runs to 126 pages. To introduce into such a system a common law duty of care enforceable against only one of the participant bodies would be manifestly unfair. To impose such liability on all the participant bodies would lead to almost impossible problems of disentangling as between the respective bodies the liability, both primary and by way of contribution, of each for reaching a decision found to be negligent.

Second, the task of the local authority and its servants in dealing with children at risk is extraordinarily delicate. Legislation requires the local authority to have regard not only to the physical wellbeing of the child but also to the advantages of not disrupting the child's family environment: see, for example, section 17 of the Act of 1989. In one of the child abuse cases, the local authority is blamed for removing the child precipitately: in the other, for failing to remove the children from their mother. As the Report of the Inquiry into Child Abuse in Cleveland 1987 (Cm. 412) said, at p. 244:

It is a delicate and difficult line to tread between taking action too soon and not taking it soon enough. Social services whilst putting the needs of the child first must respect the rights of the parents; they also must work if possible with the parents for the benefit of the children. These parents themselves are often in need of help. Inevitably a degree of conflict develops between those objectives.

Next, if a liability in damages were to be imposed, it might well be that local authorities would adopt a more cautious and defensive approach to their duties. For example, as the Cleveland Report makes clear, on occasions the speedy decision to remove the child is sometimes vital. If the authority is to be made liable in damages for a negligent decision to remove a child (such negligence lying in the failure properly first to investigate the allegations) there would be a substantial temptation to postpone making such a decision until further inquiries have been made in the hope of getting more concrete facts. Not only would the child in fact being abused be prejudiced by such delay: the increased workload inherent in making such investigations would reduce the time available to deal with other cases and other children.

The relationship between the social worker and the child's parents is frequently one of conflict, the parent wishing to retain care of the child, the social worker having to consider whether to remove it. This is fertile ground in which to breed ill feeling and litigation, often hopeless, the cost of which both in terms of money and human resources will be diverted from the performance of the social service for which they were provided. The spectre of vexatious and costly litigation is often urged as a reason for not imposing a legal duty. But the circumstances surrounding cases of child abuse make the risk a very high one which cannot be ignored.

If there were no other remedy for maladministration of the statutory system for the protection of children, it would provide substantial argument for imposing a duty of care. But the statutory complaints procedures available under the Act of 1989 provide a means to have grievances investigated, though not to recover compensation. Further, it was submitted (and not controverted) that the local authorities Ombudsman would have power to investigate cases such as these.

Finally, your Lordships' decision in [*Caparo Industries plc v Dickman* [1990] 2 AC 605] lays down that, in deciding whether to develop novel categories of negligence the court should proceed incrementally and by analogy with decided categories. We were not referred to any category of case in which a duty of care has been held to exist which is in any way analogous to the present cases. Here, for the first time, the plaintiffs are seeking to erect a common law duty of care in relation to the administration of a statutory social welfare scheme. Such a scheme is designed to protect weaker members of society (children) from harm done to them by others. The scheme involves the administrators in exercising discretions and powers which could not exist in the private sector and which in many cases bring them into conflict with those who, under the general law, are responsible for the child's welfare. To my mind, the nearest analogies are the cases where a common law duty of care has been sought to be imposed upon the police (in seeking to protect vulnerable members of society from wrongs done to them by others) or statutory regulators of financial dealings who are seeking to protect investors from dishonesty. In neither of those cases has it been thought appropriate to superimpose on the statutory regime a common law duty of care giving rise to a claim in damages for failure to protect the weak against the wrongdoer: see *Hill v Chief Constable of West Yorkshire* [1989] AC 53 and *Yuen Kun Yeu v Attorney-General of Hong Kong* [1988] AC 175. In the latter case, the Privy Council whilst not deciding the point said, at p. 198, that there was much force in the argument that if the regulators had been held liable in that case the principles leading to such liability 'would surely be equally applicable to a wide range of regulatory agencies, not only in the financial field, but also, for example, to the factory inspectorate and social workers, to name only a few.' In my judgment, the courts should proceed with great care before holding liable in negligence those who have been charged by Parliament with the task of protecting society from the wrongdoings of others.

. . .

## Cane, Peter, 'Suing Public Authorities in Tort'
### (1996) 112 LQR 13

. . . The decision in *X v Bedfordshire CC* is of enormous practical significance to social workers, psychiatrists, educational psychologists, and social welfare and education authorities. The chance of successful litigation against them in respect of the exercise of the statutory functions of such authorities is now very small. At the conceptual level, it seems clear that the courts will not entertain negligence actions in respect of the exercise of statutory discretions where the imposition of a common law duty of care would be incompatible with the scheme of the relevant statute or where the judgment of whether the challenged decision or action was unreasonable (and, therefore, negligent) would require the court to pronounce upon matters which it thinks are beyond its competence or the proper scope of its concerns. In other words, there will be some decisions of public authorities which may be challengeable by way of judicial review but not in a tort action for damages. In this respect, although the decision does not seem significantly to alter the law as it was understood prior to this litigation, it should be welcomed for the additional clarification it gives on some thorny issues. The ways in which the decision does appear to break fresh ground are, first, by suggesting that the exercise of a statutory discretion can be challenged in a negligence action only if it is *Wednesbury* unreasonable; and secondly by introducing a novel distinction between liability for breach of direct duties of care and vicarious liability. It also contains important statements about the scope of the judicial process immunity of witnesses. It remains to be seen how these various strands of reasoning will develop in contexts other than that of applications for striking-out.

## Question
As a general principle, it can be said that the right to challenge the actions or inactions of local authorities, whether by public law or private law remedies, is severely circumscribed. Is this satisfactory?

## Further reading
Fleming, D., 'Damages for Neglecting Neglect' [1996] CLJ 29.
Lindsay, M., 'Complaints Procedures and their Limitations' [1991] JSWL 432.

# 11 ADOPTION

## 11.1 INTRODUCTION

### UNITED NATIONS CONVENTION ON THE RIGHTS OF THE CHILD 1989

**Article 21**
States Parties that recognize and/or permit the system of adoption shall ensure that the best interests of the child shall be the paramount consideration and they shall:

(a)   ensure that the adoption of a child is authorized only by competent authorities who determine, in accordance with applicable law and procedures and on the basis of all pertinent and reliable information, that the adoption is permissible in view of the child's status concerning parents, relatives and legal guardians and that, if required, the persons concerned have given their informed consent to the adoption on the basis of such counselling as may be necessary;

(b)   recognize that inter-country adoption may be considered as an alternative means of child's care, if the child cannot be placed in a foster or an adoptive family or cannot in any suitable manner be cared for in the child's country of origin;

. . .

Adoption law in England and Wales is governed by the Adoption Act 1976 (as amended by the CA 1989) which was enacted after recommendations were made by the Houghton Committee, which between 1969 and 1971 undertook a review of adoption law. Significant changes made by the 1976 Act were that the power to arrange adoptions was limited to local authorities and approved adoption societies, and that local authorities were placed under a duty to provide a comprehensive adoption service. In the last few years, however, proposals for the reform of adoption law have been made in order to keep pace with changes in adoption practice. After conducting a review of adoption law and publishing a consultation document in 1992 (*Review of Adoption Law, Report to Ministers of an Interdepartmental Working Group*), the

Government published a White Paper (*Adoption: The Future*, Cm. 2288) in 1993. In March 1996 it published a Consultation Paper and draft Adoption Bill (*Adoption — A Service for Children*).
The following extract highlights some of the changes in adoption practice.

**Department of Health and Welsh Office, *Review of Adoption Law*, Report to Ministers of an Interdepartmental Working Group, 1992**

1.4    Since the Houghton Report, adoption practice has developed in response to the new obligations placed upon agencies and courts by implementation of the 1975 [Children] Act; to changing social trends; and to changes in professional and public conceptions of the needs of children, birth families and adoptive families. In particular, there has continued to be a steady fall in the numbers of babies needing adoptive families and an increasing emphasis on placing older children, children in care and children with special needs. There has been growing recognition of the need to involve birth parents in the adoption process; the need felt by some adopted people to learn about their origins and/or make contact with members of birth families; and the importance of a child's needs arising from racial and cultural background and the need to seek adoptive families from minority ethnic groups. The number of voluntary adoption societies has fallen, and many of the remaining societies have developed specialised 'family finding' services, especially for children with special needs. Inter-agency working arrangements and partnerships between agencies have been developed. And there has been a growth in the number and range of other voluntary organisations and self-help groups to meet the needs of people involved in adoption, especially in connection with post-adoption services.

Due to changes in adoption practice, as well as a need to bring adoption law into line with the Children Act 1989, the following consultative document, which included a draft Bill, was published by the Government. The Foreword outlines the proposals for reform.

**Department of Health and Welsh Office, *Adoption — A Service for Children*, 1996**

**1. FOREWORD**
1.1    We very much endorse the title of this consultative document: adoption is essentially a service to meet the needs of children who, for whatever reason, are no longer able to live with their own families. The provisions in this draft Bill are designed to improve the quality and efficiency of that service.
1.2    Although the Bill provides a separate code for adoption, its principles are firmly embedded in the Children Act 1989. In any decision about the adoption of a child, the interests of the child will be paramount. A welfare check list is to apply. Courts and adoption agencies are to have greater regard to the general principle that any delay in reaching a decision is likely to prejudice the welfare of the child.
1.3    Provisions include the introduction of new procedures for the placement of children for adoption — placement by consent and placement orders; the right of an adopted child on reaching the age of 18 to obtain information about his background (which will not identify his birth family); a new procedure will be established to deal with representations, including complaints; a duty on adoption agencies to make known more widely the facilities they provide as part of the adoption service and

encourage more families to consider adoption, particularly families from ethnic communities.

1.4 Specific provisions regulating intercountry adoption are to be welcomed in the light of occasional adverse publicity where children have been removed from their country of origin without authority. The Bill makes it clear that local authorities have a duty to provide a service for those who wish to adopt a child from abroad. Approved adoption societies will be able to provide a specialist intercountry adoption service, giving prospective adopters a choice as to whom they may approach if they wish to adopt a child from overseas.

1.5 Provisions relating to intercountry adoption reflect a number of important international agreements since 1976, including the 1989 UN Convention on the Rights of the Child; they will also enable the United Kingdom to ratify the 1993 Hague Convention on Protection of Children and Co-operation in respect of Intercountry Adoption. The Bill therefore gives force to the Government's commitment to uphold these agreements whose principal objective is the protection of vulnerable children.

1.6 The draft Bill reflects the Government's policy on adoption announced in November 1993 in the White Paper 'Adoption — The Future'. Publication of the Bill in advance of its introduction into Parliament provides a further opportunity for those involved in the adoption service — practitioners, parents, adopters and adopted persons as well as the general public — to consider these provisions and comment.

## 11.2 THE WELFARE OF CHILDREN IN THE ADOPTION PROCESS

## ADOPTION ACT 1976

### 6. Duty to promote welfare of child
In reaching any decision relating to the adoption of a child a court or adoption agency shall have regard to all the circumstances, first consideration being given to the need to safeguard and promote the welfare of the child throughout his childhood; and shall so far as practicable ascertain the wishes and feelings of the child regarding the decision and give due consideration to them, having regard to his age and understanding.

*Note*
The welfare test must be satisfied before the court considers the question of consent to the adoption (see Balcombe LJ in *Re E (A Minor) (Adoption)* [1989] 1 FLR 126, CA, and Butler-Sloss LJ in *Re D (A Minor) (Adoption: Freeing Order)* [1991] 1 FLR 48, CA).

The Adoption Bill makes changes to the adoption welfare principle and introduces a statutory checklist similar to that in s. 1(3) of the CA 1989 (see 7.4.1.3).

## DRAFT ADOPTION BILL 1996

### 1. Considerations applicable to the exercise of powers
(1) This section applies whenever a court or adoption agency is coming to a decision relating to the adoption of a child.

(2)   The paramount consideration of the court or adoption agency must be the child's welfare, in childhood and later.

(3)   The court or adoption agency must at all times bear in mind that any delay in coming to a decision is likely to prejudice the child's welfare.

(4)   The court or adoption agency must have regard to the following matters (among others)—

(a)   the child's ascertainable wishes and feelings regarding the decision (considered in the light of the child's age and understanding),

(b)   the child's particular needs,

(c)   the likely effect on the child (during childhood or later) of having ceased to be a member of the original family and become an adopted person,

(d)   the child's age, sex, background and any of the child's characteristics which the court or agency considers relevant,

(e)   any harm which the child has suffered or is at risk of suffering, and

(f)   the relationship which the child has with relatives, and with any other person in relation to whom the court or agency considers the question to be relevant, including—

(i)   the value to the child of any such relationship continuing,

(ii)   the ability and willingness of any of the child's relatives, or of any such person, to provide the child with a secure environment in which the child can develop, and otherwise to meet the child's needs,

(iii)   the wishes and feelings of any of the child's relatives, or of any such person, about the child.

(5)   The court or adoption agency must always consider the whole range of powers available to them in the child's case (whether under this Act or the Children Act 1989) and, if it exercises any power, must only exercise the most appropriate one; and the court must not make any order under this Act unless it considers that making the order would be better for the child than not doing so.

(6)   In this section—

. . . references to making an order include dispensing with parental consent.

## 11.3   FREEING FOR ADOPTION

## ADOPTION ACT 1976

### 18.   Freeing child for adoption

(1)   Where, on an application by an adoption agency, an authorised court is satisfied in the case of each parent or guardian of the child that—

(a)   he freely, and with full understanding of what is involved, agrees generally and unconditionally to the making of an adoption order, or

(b)   his agreement to the making of an adoption order should be dispensed with on a ground specified in section 16(2),

the court shall make an order declaring the child free for adoption.

### Re A (A Minor) (Adoption: Contact Order)
### [1993] 2 FLR 645
### Court of Appeal

BUTLER-SLOSS LJ: . . . The effect of an order freeing a child for adoption is to extinguish parental responsibility of those previously endowed with it and thus to bring to an end the relationship between the child and his natural family (see

Adoption Act 1976, s. 12(3)). The child is in a sort of adoptive limbo and parental responsibility is assumed by the adoption agency. . . . The parents become former parents, ss. 18(5), 19 and have no right to make an application under s. 8 of the Children Act 1989. . . .

*Note*

A freeing order cannot be made unless each parent or guardian has consented to the adoption or their consent has been dispensed with (s. 18(2)). Before making the freeing order the court must be satisfied that each parent or guardian has been given an opportunity to make a declaration stating that he or she no longer wishes to be involved in the adoption (s. 18(6)), and must ensure that a father without parental responsibility is not applying for a s. 4 parental responsibility order or a residence order under the CA 1989 (s. 18(7)). A person who wishes to resume parental responsibility may apply for revocation of a freeing order at least 12 months after it has been made if an adoption order has not been made or the child is not living with the prospective adopter (s. 20).

Due to general dissatisfaction with the freeing procedure, the Government proposes to revoke the power to make freeing orders and to introduce new provisions for the placement of children for adoption.

## Department of Health and Welsh Office, *Review of Adoption Law*, Report to Ministers of an Interdepartmental Working Group, 1992

. . .

14.3   At present, it is possible for an agency to seek the court's judgment on the matter of parental agreement at an earlier date by applying for a freeing order before or at about the same time as the child is placed with prospective adopters. A freeing order transfers the parents' parental responsibility to the adoption agency, pending the making of an adoption order. This procedure was originally designed to enable parents to make an irrevocable decision to give up their child at an early stage in the adoption process. In practice, its more common use has been by care authorities seeking to have the question of parental agreement resolved before — or in the early stages of — an adoption placement, so that the parents cannot contest the later adoption application. But freeing is not mandatory, and some agencies place children who are in care with prospective adopters despite parental opposition and without applying for a freeing order, perhaps in part because the court is felt to be more likely to dispense with parental agreement after the child has lived with the prospective adopters for a time.

14.4   Freeing for adoption has attracted much criticism, mainly on account of the delays which are usually involved. We consider that the difficulties associated with freeing are not just procedural ones. Other problems include:

(a)   the court is expected to resolve the question of parental agreement without looking at a particular placement (or proposed placement): there is a danger that courts may contrast the readily apparent shortcomings in the care offered or likely to be offered in future by a child's parents with the care likely to be offered by hypothetically perfect adoptive parents;

(b)   where an order is made prior to the identification of prospective adoptive parents, there is a danger that the child may be left without a family: although the court is not allowed to dispense with parental agreement unless the child is already placed for adoption or the court is satisfied that it is likely that the child will be placed, this is no guarantee that a freed child will be found a suitable adoptive family, and in uncontested cases an order can be made regardless of the likelihood of placing the child;

(c)   a child may also be left without a family if the placement breaks down before an adoption order is made;

(d)   although the agency may apply for a freeing order where the question of parental agreement ought to be resolved prior to placement, there is no requirement for the agency to do so, nor any guarantee that the hearing will take place before the placement has been made.

14.5   Freeing for adoption has been perceived to have some advantages. One reason why some agencies still find it helpful is that the application is by the agency, not the prospective adopters: this is felt to reduce the conflict between the birth family and adoptive family and lessen the risk that the child will later regard his adoptive parents as having 'taken him away' from the birth family. However, the distancing of the prospective adopters from the freeing process may not always work to the advantage of the child: it may in fact be that their closer involvement in the process at the stage when parental agreement is examined would encourage the different parties to discuss matters such as contact and share information about the child's background. . . .

## Department of Health and Welsh Office, *Adoption — A Service for Children*, 1996

. . .

*Placement of children for adoption*
4.2   It was clear from the earlier consultation exercises on the adoption law review that practitioners felt strongly that the provisions in the 1976 Act for freeing children for adoption have not worked well for a number of reasons. (Those reasons are set out fully in the consultation paper 'Placement for Adoption' issued in April 1994).
4.3   Consequently, the power to make freeing orders is to be revoked and new provisions are introduced for placement of children for adoption. The new procedures provide that an adoption agency may only place a child for adoption with the consent of the parent or guardian or under a placement order.

*Placement with parental consent*
4.4   Provisions continue to allow the placement of children for adoption with the consent of the parent or guardian. There are two forms of parental consent to a placement: consent to the child being placed with named prospective adopters, or general consent to the child being placed with any prospective adopters who may be chosen by the adoption agency. It is expected that most parents or guardians will give general consent.
4.5   Parental consent to a child being placed for adoption is not synonymous with their giving consent to an adoption order; these are two distinct stages, each requiring a separate consent to be given. However, consent to the making of a future adoption order can be given at the same time as consent to the child's placement or subsequently before the application to adopt is made. Consent of the mother to adoption may not be given until the child is at least six weeks old.

4.6   It is considered that before giving parental consent to placement or to the making of a future adoption order a parent or guardian should be counselled. It is also considered that the form of the agreement should be prescribed and should be witnessed. In our view the best person to combine these roles would be a reporting officer selected by the adoption agency from the panel of guardians ad litem and reporting officers, although at the moment such persons can only be appointed in specified proceedings by the court. Views on this and other alternatives would be particularly welcome.

4.7   A parent or guardian does not lose parental responsibility for the child until an adoption order is made, although the exercise of that responsibility is to be limited. Where a parent or guardian consents to placement, he will be required at the same time to agree to parental responsibility being given to prospective adopters while the child is placed with them (and in any other case to the adoption agency). The prospective adopters will exercise parental responsibility subject to certain restraints.

*Placement orders*

4.8   Arrangements for placing a child for adoption introduce a new provision — placement orders. Where the parent or guardian does not consent to the placement for adoption and the adoption agency has considered all available options and is satisfied that adoption is in the child's best interests, the matter is to be put to the court at an early stage to enable the court to make realistic decisions about the child's future. The purpose of a placement order is to enable the court to be involved at an early stage in those cases where the agency considers that adoption is in the child's best interests but the parent or guardian is not prepared to give his consent to placement and while other available options for the child's future can also be considered.

4.9   A placement order authorises the adoption agency to place the child for adoption with suitable prospective adopters. An order will not restrict a placement to named prospective adopters even where they are known to the agency; this is to avoid the agency having to go back to court for a new placement order in the event of the first placement breaking down.

4.10   Once a placement order has been made, parental responsibility is given while the child is placed with prospective adopters, to them. Regulations will provide for the names of the prospective adopters to be notified to the court by the adoption agency. Where the child is removed from that placement and subsequently placed with another set of adopters, the court is to be notified of the change. Parental responsibility reverts to the agency when the child is removed and in due course is given to new prospective adopters.

*Placement of children under a care order*

4.11   A placement order will be required for a child who is the subject of a care order; once the placement order is made it is to have the effect of suspending the care order for the duration of the placement order. Where a local authority applies to the court for a care order most courts already require them to provide a care plan for the child. Where the recommendation in the care plan is that the child should be adopted, the authority must also apply for a placement order at the same time as they apply for a care order. (The authority may only make such a recommendation if it is satisfied that adoption is in the child's best interests; the matter must have been put before the agency's adoption panel). Should the placement order be revoked, the care order will automatically revive. This means that where placement for adoption turns out not to be the best solution there is no obstacle to revoking the placement order because the child will remain protected.

4.12   Where the care plan did not originally contain a recommendation that the child be placed for adoption but is revised at a later stage to make such a recommendation, an application for a placement order must be made at this stage. This will usually be heard by the same court which made the care order.

*Placement generally*

4.13   Once a child is placed with prospective adopters whether with the parent's consent or under a placement order, he ceases to be a 'looked after' child under the Children Act. Where the local authority may place a child for adoption, the authority may provide accommodation for him at any time when he is not so placed and during that period he will be a 'looked after' child under that Act.

*Removal provisions*

4.14   Where placement is by consent, the parent may withdraw that consent and require the return of the child (subject to set procedures) at any time up to the time when an application to adopt is made. After that, leave of the court is required. Where a child is placed under a placement order, the parent will not be able to have the child back unless the placement order is revoked. An application to revoke the order by the parent may only be made where the child is not placed with prospective adopters, at least a year has elapsed since the order was made and the court gives leave, being satisfied that there has been a change in circumstances.

*Note*

See clauses 19–39, Draft Adoption Bill 1996, for the proposed new placement procedures and removal provisions.

*Further reading*

Lowe, N., 'Freeing for Adoption — the Experience of the 1980s' [1990] JSWL 220.

## 11.4   CONSENT TO ADOPTION

An adoption order or a freeing order cannot be made unless each parent and guardian agrees to the adoption, although agreement can be dispensed with on one or more of the grounds laid down in s. 16 of the 1976 Act.

### 11.4.1   Grounds for dispensing with consent

### ADOPTION ACT 1976

**16.   Parental agreement**

   (1)   An adoption order shall not be made unless—
      (a)   the child is free for adoption by virtue of an order made—
         (i)   in England and Wales, under section 18;
         . . . or
      (b)   in the case of each parent or guardian of the child the court is satisfied that—
         (i)   he freely, and with full understanding of what is involved, agrees unconditionally to the making of an adoption order (whether or not he knows the identity of the applicants), or
         (ii)   his agreement to the making of the adoption order should be dispensed with on a ground specified in subsection (2).

(2)   The grounds mentioned in subsection (1)(b)(ii) are that the parent or guardian—

  (a)   cannot be found or is incapable of giving agreement;
  (b)   is withholding his agreement unreasonably;
  (c)   has persistently failed without reasonable cause to discharge his parental responsibility for the child;
  (d)   has abandoned or neglected the child;
  (e)   has persistently ill-treated the child;
  (f)   has seriously ill-treated the child (subject to subsection (5)).

(3)   Subsection (1) does not apply in any case where the child is not a United Kingdom national and the application for the adoption order is for a Convention adoption order.

(4)   Agreement is ineffective for the purposes of subsection (1)(b)(i) if given by the mother less than six weeks after the child's birth.

(5)   Subsection (2)(f) does not apply unless (because of the ill-treatment or for other reasons) the rehabilitation of the child within the household of the parent or guardian is unlikely.

### 11.4.2   Withholding agreement unreasonably

Most of the case law on dispensing with agreement is concerned with s. 16(2)(b) of the 1976 Act, i.e. 'is withholding his agreement unreasonably'. The following case (a pre-Adoption Act 1976 case) is the leading authority on the test of reasonableness.

### *In Re W (An Infant)*
[1971] AC 682
House of Lords

*Facts*: W was placed with prospective adopters within a few days of his birth. His mother (unmarried with two other children and living on social security) signed a consent form, but later withdrew her consent. The county court judge dispensed with the mother's agreement on the ground that she was unreasonably withholding her consent to the adoption, and made the adoption order. The Court of Appeal allowed the mother's appeal on the ground that the judge had applied the wrong test of reasonableness. The prospective adopters appealed.

*Held*: allowing the appeal, restoring the order made at first instance and laying down the correct test for reasonableness, that the county court judge had not erred in law.

LORD HAILSHAM: . . . To my mind, this is yet another attempt to improve on the language of the Act of Parliament. Section 5(1)(b) [see now AA 1976, s. 16(2)(b)] lays down a test of reasonableness. It does not lay down a test of culpability or of callous or self-indulgent indifference or of failure or probable failure of parental duty. As the last words in subsection (2) make quite clear, the tests in section 5(1)(b) are quite independent of the test in section 5(2), on which counsel had to some extent plainly modelled his submission. It is not for the courts to embellish, alter, subtract from or add to words which, for once at least, Parliament has employed without any ambiguity at all. I must add that, if the test had involved me in a criticism of the respondent involving culpability or callous or self-indulgent indifference, I might well have come to the same conclusion on the facts as did Sachs and Cross LJJ. But since the test imposed upon me by the statute is reasonableness and not culpability I have come to the opposite conclusion.

The question then remains as to how to apply the correct test. The test is whether at the time of the hearing the consent is being withheld unreasonably. As Lord Denning MR said in *In re L (An Infant)* [[1962] 1 WLR 886]:

> In considering the matter I quite agree that: (1) the question whether she is unreasonably withholding her consent is to be judged at the date of the hearing; and (2) the welfare of the child is not the sole consideration; and (3) the one question is whether she is unreasonably withholding her consent. But I must say that in considering whether she is reasonable or unreasonable we must take into account the welfare of the child. A reasonable mother surely gives great weight to what is better for the child. Her anguish of mind is quite understandable; but still it may be unreasonable for her to withhold consent. We must look and see whether it is reasonable or unreasonable according to what a reasonable woman in her place would do in all the circumstances of the case.

. . .

From this it is clear that the test is reasonableness and not anything else. It is not culpability. It is not indifference. It is not failure to discharge parental duties. It is reasonableness, and reasonableness in the context of the totality of the circumstances. But, although welfare per se is not the test, the fact that a reasonable parent does pay regard to the welfare of his child must enter into the question of reasonableness as a relevant factor. It is relevant in all cases if and to the extent that a reasonable parent would take it into account. It is decisive in those cases where a reasonable parent must so regard it. . . .

I do not understand *In re K (A Infant)* [1953] 1 QB 117 as deciding anything different from what I have said. I specifically endorse the often quoted passage from Jenkins LJ in which he said, at pp. 129–130:

> Prima facie it would seem to me eminently reasonable for any parent to withhold his or her consent to an order (for adoption) 'thus completely and irrevocably destroying the parental relationship. One can imagine cases short of such misconduct or dereliction of duty as is mentioned in section 3(1)(a)' (i.e., of the Adoption Act 1950) in which a parent's withholding of consent to an adoption might properly be held to be unreasonable, but such cases must, in our view, be exceptional.

Exceptional, yes. But the test is still reasonableness, or its opposite, and reasonableness, or its opposite, must be judged, as Russell LJ observed in the instant case [1970] 2 QB 589, 598, and as both counsel agreed, by an objective (as distinct from a subjective) test. Indeed, I cannot myself readily visualise circumstances in which the words 'reason,' 'reasonable' or 'unreasonable' can be applied otherwise than objectively. And, be it observed, 'reasonableness,' or 'unreasonableness,' where either word is employed in English law, is normally a question of fact and degree and not a question of law so long as there is evidence to support the finding of the court. It seems to me that the passage in Jenkins LJ's judgment in *In re K (An Infant)* [1953] 1 QB 117 immediately following that which I have quoted above is too often forgotten and deserves to be better remembered. He said, at p. 130:

> It is unnecessary, undesirable and indeed impracticable to attempt a definition covering all possible cases of that kind. Each case must depend on its own facts and circumstances.

In my opinion, besides culpability unreasonableness can include anything which can objectively be adjudged to be unreasonable. It is not confined to culpability or callous indifference. It can include, where carried to excess, sentimentality, romanticism, bigotry, wild prejudice, caprice, fatuousness or excessive lack of common sense.

This means that, in an adoption case, a county court judge applying the test of reasonableness must be entitled to come to his own conclusions, on the totality of the facts, and a revising court should only dispute his decision where it feels reasonably confident that he has erred in law or acted without adequate evidence or where it feels that his judgment of the witnesses and their demeanour has played so little part in his reasoning that the revising court is in a position as good as that of the trial judge to form an opinion. In my view, by imposing the necessity for a clear prognosis of lasting damage to the child Russell LJ [1970] 2 QB 589, 598, was falling into the same error as the other lords justices in applying to the Act a criterion of construction different from that which the language of the Act in fact prescribes.

I only feel it necessary to add on this part of the case that I entirely agree with Russell LJ when he said, in effect [1970] 2 QB 589, 598, 599, that it does not follow from the fact that the test is reasonableness that any court is entitled simply to substitute its own view for that of the parent. In my opinion, it should be extremely careful to guard against this error. Two reasonable parents can perfectly reasonably come to opposite conclusions on the same set of facts without forfeiting their title to be regarded as reasonable. The question in any given case is whether a parental veto comes within the band of possible reasonable decisions and not whether it is right or mistaken. Not every reasonable exercise of judgment is right, and not every mistaken exercise of judgment is unreasonable. There is a band of decisions within which no court should seek to replace the individual's judgment with his own. . . .

LORD MACDERMOTT: . . . These provisions, by their very nature, show that Parliament cannot have contemplated that the process of adoption would be such as to allow the relationship of parent and child — the blood tie — to be sundered lightly and without good reason. One may therefore assume that it would be contrary to the intention of the statute if a finding of unreasonableness were to be reached on some trivial issue or on grounds which were not clearly established and of substance. Where the natural strength and inherent virtues of the parental bond continue to exist, they must be anxiously regarded in weighing the circumstances relevant to the question of unreasonableness. They are too important and the consequences of adoption too final to let it be otherwise. But, that said, it is also to be noted that these factors are not always present or present to the same extent, and, further, that they will often be best assessed without too much emphasis being placed on purely emotive considerations. It is to be remembered that the statutory process of adoption in English law is aimed at meeting a social need which involves children as well as parents, and that it starts, in the ordinary course, not with the child being taken from his parents because some authority thinks that he would be better off if they were changed but because he has been offered for adoption by his parents (or one of them) or by some person or body acting on their behalf. This is not to say that consent once given may not be retracted, for the legislature has otherwise ordained, but it does, I think, add to the difficulty of reading the word 'unreasonably' in a special sense which includes some degree of blameworthiness. The statutory process does not seem to have a place for such a special meaning or to offer any reason for putting the adopter at the end of the proceedings (including the necessary period of custody) in a position in which, if he is to succeed, he must undertake the additional onus of proving the parent in some way culpable as well as being just unreasonable. And, lastly, the word 'unreasonably' in section 5(1)(b) must, in my view, be read as indicating an objective test, if only to provide a relatively stable criterion for the exercise of the dispensing power. But, if culpability or blameworthiness is to be an added factor, the objectivity of the test will diminish, if it does not disappear, and the yardstick will, in effect, vary from case to case.

My Lords, for these reasons my tentative views based on the Statute itself may be thus summarised:—(1) In section 5(1)(b) the word 'unreasonably' is to be construed according to its natural significance and not as importing words of guilt or misconduct such as 'culpable,' 'blameworthy' or 'a self-indulgent indifference.' (2) So construed, the test for deciding whether consent has been withheld unreasonably is to ask what a reasonable parent, placed in the position of the parent in question, would do. (3) The test is objective. (4) In general, the provisions of the Act require that a finding of unreasonableness should be based on grounds which are well established and of substance. (5) In particular, where the test of unreasonableness falls to be applied in relation to the welfare of the child, the degree of unreasonableness to be proved must be marked in the sense that the parent whose consent is withheld has ignored or disregarded some appreciable ill or risk likely to be avoided or some substantial benefit likely to accrue if the child is adopted.

. . .

*Note*

Lord Hailsham's *dicta* in *Re W* have been referred to in numerous cases; see, e.g., *Re C (A Minor) (Adoption: Parental Agreement: Contact)* [1993] 2 FLR 260; and *Re E (Adoption: Freeing Order)* [1995] 1 FLR 382, CA. See also *Re D (An Infant) (Adoption: Parent's Consent)* [1977] AC 602, 1 All ER 145, where the House of Lords held that the refusal of the father (a practising homosexual) to agree to adoption should be dispensed with on the ground that it was not reasonable.

### 11.4.3 Reform of the grounds for dispensing with agreement

**Department of Health and Welsh Office, *Review of Adoption Law*, Report to Ministers of an Interdepartmental Working Group, 1992**

*Parental agreement*

12.1   We are concerned that at present insufficient weight is given to a parent's lack of agreement. Where it is decided that adoption is in a child's interests, there is in practice very little room left for the court to give any weight to parental views. This cannot be regarded as satisfactory in relation to an order which irrevocably terminates a parent's legal relationship with his or her child.

12.2   The lack of consideration generally given to the importance of parental agreement is sometimes attributable in part to the late stage in the process at which the court is asked to resolve the question of parental agreement. This has frequently been the case where a child is in care and the local authority has decided that there is no prospect of rehabilitating the child with his or her birth parents and has placed the child for adoption. If the local authority applies for a freeing order prior to placement, the question of parental agreement is resolved before the placement begins. But it is also open to the local authority to place the child for adoption without having the court address the question of parental agreement until the adoption application is heard several months later. Even if the parents have had some contact with the child during the placement (which is perhaps more likely to be the case following implementation of the Children Act 1989), the strength of the relationship between the child and prospective adopters at the time of the hearing may present the court with what it regards as a fait accompli. The parent's right to argue, say, that the court should grant a residence order, or that further work should be undertaken to enable the child to return home or to be cared for by relatives, has effectively been overridden by the passage of time. We propose in chapter 14 that where parental agreement is withheld or is likely to be withheld, a placement should not be allowed to proceed until the court has decided whether or not to dispense with parental agreement.

12.3    However, it is still likely to be the case that some parents who decide to give a child up for adoption change their minds before an order is made and want the child back to bring up themselves. Where a child has been separated from the birth mother and has become attached to prospective adoptive parents over a number of months, the mother's chances of securing her child's return are slight. Even where a mother has established that she wants to care for a child, is fit to be a parent and can support the child, the courts are generally unlikely to consider that she is reasonable in contesting the adoption. The welfare of the child has become the paramount consideration.

12.4    Much of the difficulty surrounding this part of the law is associated with the ground used most often for dispensing with parental agreement — that the parent is withholding his agreement unreasonably. The court may dispense with parental agreement if it considers that a hypothetical reasonable parent would agree to the adoption. But it has not been clear how much weight a hypothetical reasonable parent would be expected to place upon the welfare of the child, particularly in the situations described above where a significant relationship has developed between the child and prospective adoptive parents. Even where (in freeing applications) the child has not yet been placed with prospective adoptive parents, there has been a tendency to decide that adoption is in a child's best interests and for this reason alone to dispense with parental agreement on the grounds that it is being unreasonably withheld. This has meant that the test has given paramount weight to the child's welfare, which we consider unsatisfactory when dealing with parental wishes and feelings in relation to so important a step as adoption. It is also unsatisfactory that the parent whose agreement is dispensed with on these grounds thereby acquires what may be perceived as the stigma of being an unreasonable parent.

12.5    Most of the other grounds for dispensing with agreement, although seldom used, are unsatisfactory in that they relate exclusively to shortcomings in parental care rather than to the needs of the child. Where there are faults or shortcomings in parental care, this should not imply that adoption is ipso facto a suitable option for a child. Nor in cases where it is decided that adoption is in a child's best interests should this imply that the parents are necessarily at fault. For instance, a mother whose eldest child has been in care for some years may have other children whom she has shown herself capable of looking after: although the child in care is not at risk of significant harm if he returns home, he may no longer consider himself part of that family and may want to make a fresh start with adoptive parents. Responses to the review largely favoured the removal of fault-based grounds for dispensing with agreement.

12.6    We therefore propose that, of the existing grounds in section 16(2) of the 1976 Act, only (a) ('the parent cannot be found or is incapable of giving agreement') should be retained. The remaining grounds should be replaced by a single test which should apply in all situations where a parent who is capable of giving agreement can be found and is withholding agreement. This test should:

(a)    address the question of the advantages of becoming part of a new family and having a new legal status (rather than the question of where the child should reside);

(b)  focus on the needs of the child rather than any parental shortcomings;

(c)  require the court to be satisfied that adoption is significantly better than other available options and that parental wishes should therefore be overridden.

It might be expressed in terms of the court being satisfied that the advantages to a child of becoming part of a new family and having a new legal status are so significantly greater than the advantages to the child of any alternative option as to justify overriding the wishes of a parent or guardian. The court should consider not just whether the child should go to live with, or continue to live with, the prospective adoptive parents but whether it is in the child's interests to sever his links with the birth family and become part of a new family. This should of course be considered carefully in any proposed adoption, but it is especially important where a child or a parent does not agree to adoption.

12.7  We recommend that the only other ground for dispensing with agreement should be that a parent who agreed to the adoption when a placement order was made has withdrawn that agreement; and that the court considers that there have not been any significant changes since then such as would justify a different outcome.

12.8  It should be absolutely clear that in deciding whether or not to dispense with parental agreement the court should *not* give paramount consideration to the welfare of the child, except in the circumstances described in paragraph 12.7. Where adoption would only be marginally better than another option, the court should allow the fact that a parent does not agree to adoption to tip the balance in favour of the other option.

The Draft Adoption Bill sets out new conditions for dispensing with the consent of a parent or guardian.

## DRAFT ADOPTION BILL 1996

**46.  Parental etc. consent**

(1)  Any consent given by the mother to the making of an adoption order is ineffective if it is given less than six weeks after the child's birth.

(2)  The court cannot dispense with the consent of any parent or guardian of a child to the making of a placement order or adoption order in respect of that child unless—

(a)  the parent or guardian cannot be found or is incapable of giving consent, or

(b)  the court is satisfied that the welfare of the child requires the consent to be dispensed with.

. . .

*Question*

Is the test for dispensing with consent now too child-centred?

### 11.4.4  The child's consent

Under the Adoption Act 1976, the child's consent to adoption is not required; but the Draft Adoption Bill changes this and provides that the child must in certain circumstances give consent.

## DRAFT ADOPTION BILL 1996

**41.  Conditions for making adoption orders**

. . .

(7)  An adoption order may not be made in relation to a person who has attained the age of twelve years unless the court is satisfied that that person—

(a)  freely, and with full understanding of what is involved, consents unconditionally to the making of the order, or

(b)  is incapable of giving such consent.

## Department of Health and Welsh Office, *Review of Adoption Law,* Report to Ministers of an Interdepartmental Working Group, 1992

. . . We do not consider that the need for the child's agreement should in any way
detract from the importance of parental agreement. Adoption has immense implications not just for the child, but for the parents who lose their parental relationship as
a result of the order. Nor would we wish to create the impression that the necessity
for the child's agreement placed responsibility for the decision exclusively upon the
child. Where the agreement of the child is required, it should not override the need
to have parental agreement, nor should it constitute a ground for dispensing with
parental agreement. . . .

## 11.5   OPENNESS IN ADOPTION

As part of a trend towards greater openness in adoption, children have
sometimes been permitted to remain in contact with their natural parents and
their birth family pending and/or after adoption. Furthermore, adult children
may attempt to contact their lost natural parents by consulting their birth
records or the Adoption Contact Register kept by the Registrar General (see
ss. 51 and 51A of the Adoption Act 1976).

## Jolly, Simon, and Sandland, R., 'Political Correctness and the Adoption White Paper'
### [1994] Fam Law 30

. . . From the passage of the first Adoption Act in 1926 the law has been premised on
the 'closed' model of adoption. This holds that the function of adoption is the discreet
reallocation of the unwanted babies of single women to 'respectable' homes. Success
is measured by the invisibility of the 'transplant' of the child. However, over the last
25 years the demography of adoption has changed radically. The easier availability of
contraception and abortion, and the lessening stigma surrounding single parenthood
has led to the much reduced use of adoption for babies, while local authorities have
increasingly used adoption to find homes for older children who would otherwise
have lived out their childhood in residential care. In addition, the adoption of younger
children from outside the UK has increased while the number available for adoption
within the UK has fallen. . . .

## Department of Health and Welsh Office, *Review of Adoption Law,* Report to Ministers of an Interdepartmental Working Group, 1992

. . .

4.1  Adoption has traditionally been a somewhat closed and secretive process in
which many children have been shielded from knowledge about, and contact with,
their birth families. In practice, for many years now, there has been increasing

recognition that a child's knowledge of his or her background is crucial to the formation of positive self-identity, and that adoptive families should be encouraged to be open about the child's adoptive status and the special nature of the adoptive relationship. There has also been a move towards enabling some children to retain contact with their birth families: this may take the form of, say, the exchange of cards on the child's birthday or occasional meetings between the child and former grandparents or siblings.

4.2   Openness can take many different forms, the range and type of which are indicated in the paragraphs below. The extent to which a particular form of openness is likely to be appropriate will vary greatly according to the needs of the child and the circumstances surrounding the adoption. It will very often be a matter for the discretion of the agency or the court to decide exactly what the best approach is likely to be. However, we are concerned that the present law to some extent assumes a closed model of adoption where this is not always the case, nor always appropriate. This is particularly so in the case of access to agency and court records. We have therefore suggested in the context of recommendations concerning the duties and powers of adoption agencies and courts . . . various legislative measures designed to promote and facilitate particular forms of openness.

*Pre-adoption openness*

4.3   The main forms which pre-adoption openness is likely to take are:

(a)   consultation with the child, the parents, any other person with parental responsibility, the child's relatives, and any other relevant person (e.g. a former foster carer) to give them the opportunity to discuss the adoption plan and any possible alternatives to it;

(b)   inviting birth parents and relatives to make known their views about the sort of adoptive family which they would like the child to have;

(c)   encouraging birth parents to share information about their family history and background with the adoptive family and to put onto record the reasons for the adoption, together perhaps with gifts or mementoes for the child;

(d)   possibly arranging for birth parents and prospective adoptive parents to meet each other.

4.4   These types of openness are likely to have many advantages for the child:

(a)   discussion about the child's future may enable more suitable arrangements to be made for the child's care;

(b)   if the child is adopted, the birth family's involvement in the selection of adoptive parents, particularly with regard to race, culture, religion and language, may help to provide greater continuity in the child's upbringing;

(c)   the child is less likely to feel a sense of rejection or desertion by birth parents and family if he or she knows that they contributed in some way to the adoption plan and the choice of adopters, and if he or she has access to information prepared by the parents at the time of the adoption;

(d)   contact between the birth family and adoptive family at this stage may facilitate subsequent exchanges of information (and, where appropriate, other forms of contact).

4.5   Efforts to consult parents and relatives and to involve them in discussion and counselling may help to ease the pain which they may feel in connection with the adoption of a child. Parents may find it easier to come to terms with the sense of loss if they are able to put down in writing the reasons for the adoption and offer mementoes or gifts.

4.6    Adoptive parents may have the opportunity to gain more detailed information about the child's background (e.g. medical history, family details, photographs) which may enable them to parent the child with a fuller understanding of his or her needs.

*Openness in the court process*
4.7    We are concerned that the legal process of adoption often involves unnecessary secretiveness. Court Rules are extremely restrictive as regards disclosure of court records and reports to parties. We discuss below the need to encourage greater disclosure, except where there are compelling reasons to the contrary. There may sometimes be a need to protect the identity of some parties, for instance prospective adoptive parents or birth parents, and it should remain open to the court to make the necessary arrangements to secure anonymity, where appropriate. Anonymity should not be regarded as being necessarily prejudicial to subsequent openness of other kinds. Adoptive parents, for instance, may subsequently choose to pass on news of the child's development to the birth family (via an agency) without fear of undue interference in their parenting of the child if they know that their identity has been kept confidential.

*Exchange of information*
4.8    We understand that many adopted people, regardless of the age at which they are adopted or how happy they have been with their adoptive family, will retain an interest in their background and original family and in the reasons for their adoption. Information about the child's medical history and any relevant information about the birth family's medical history is also highly important. All reasonable efforts should be made at the time of the adoption to record information, to pass it on to adoptive parents and to encourage them to make it available to the child when he or she is of an age to understand it. After an adoption order has been made, arrangements may be made (usually with the assistance of the placing agency) for the adoptive family to keep the birth family informed of the child's development.

*Telling*
4.9    It is essential that adoptive parents tell their children that they are adopted, explain to them what this means, and offer them some information about their background. Adoption agencies generally prepare prospective adoptive parents for these important tasks. It is hoped that it would now be extremely rare for an adopted child to grow up without knowing of his or her adoptive status. We consider that the legislative framework should nonetheless emphasise the importance of telling an adopted child about his or her adoption and background and therefore suggest below duties which agencies and local authorities should have to promote this form of openness.

*Access to identifying information*
4.10    Many adult adopted people experience a need to discover more about their origins, or to try to contact members of their birth family. Many birth relatives, particularly birth mothers, feel a need to find out what has happened to an adopted child, and to see whether the adult adopted person would like to take steps towards re-establishing contact at some level. This is an area of particular sensitivity, which is closely linked to the question of individuals' rights of access to records which contain identifying information about adopted children or former parents or relatives. We discuss below what rights adult adopted people and their birth families should have in this respect, and the services which should be offered to them.

. . .

*Re T (Adoption: Contact)*
[1995] 2 FLR 251
Court of Appeal

*Facts*: The child, who was in care, was placed by the local authority with the prospective adopters. The child's mother consented to the adoption, but wished to remain in contact with the child. The local authority and the guardian *ad litem* supported contact, but were opposed to a contact order being written into the adoption order and were opposed to any s. 8 order being made under the CA 1989. The adopters informally agreed that the mother should see the child two or three times a year. The judge attached to the adoption order an order that there should be contact not less than once a year, because the parties could not agree on the amount of contact and it saved an application having to be made by the mother under s. 10 of the CA 1989 for leave to apply for a contact order once the child was adopted. The adopters appealed against the need for a contact order.
*Held*: allowing the appeal and setting aside the contact order, that the mother's remedy lay in an application under s. 10 of the CA 1989 for leave to apply for a contact order after adoption.

BUTLER-SLOSS LJ: . . . [Counsel for the adopters] has reminded us of various decisions, prior to the Children Act, where both this court and, in particular, the House of Lords have indicated the importance of not interfering with the rights of the adopters, not placing constraints upon the adopters, not fettering them in the difficult task they have in integrating a child into their family. Indeed, Kerr LJ said in *Re M (A Minor) (Adoption Order: Access)* [1986] 1 FLR 51 at p. 60:

> . . . it is only in unusual and perhaps exceptional circumstances that an order combining adoption with access has been made. Indeed, it may well be that such a combined order has never been made unless the position was that both the natural parent and the adopters were agreed, both on the adoption and on the inclusion of an order for access.

There have indeed been cases where such orders have been made at the request of all those concerned with the adoption.
Oliver LJ said in *Re V (A Minor) (Adoption: Consent)* [1987] Fam 57, sub nom *Re V (A Minor) (Adoption: Dispensing with Agreement)* [1987] 2 FLR 89 at p. 107, talking about the conditions of access, which in those days was the only way one could get such an order prior to the Children Act:

> To put it another way, any such condition, if it is not to be repugnant to the notion of adoption, must recognise that, in the ultimate analysis, the question of access or no access is for the adopters to decide in exercise of their parental rights.

Indeed Lord Ackner said in *Re C (A Minor) (Adoption Order: Conditions)* [1989] AC 1, [1988] 2 FLR 159, p. 168A:

> No doubt the court will not, except in the most exceptional case, impose terms or conditions as to access to members of the child's natural family to which the adopting parents do not agree. To do so would be to create a potentially frictional situation which would be hardly likely to safeguard or promote the welfare of the child.

In this case the only argument, really, that remains is whether the once a year, which was agreed to by the adopters and was found to be the right amount of contact by the judge, should be imposed upon these adopters, or whether it should be left to their good sense so that they could be trusted to do what they believe to be in the best interest of their daughter.

[Counsel] for the mother, has one point which he has put to us very effectively, that the mother has consented to adoption, but that her consent to adoption, although it was unconditional, none the less recognised that she would expect to see the child at least once a year, and had hoped to see the child rather more, and that such consent was in the context of this continuing contact in an open adoption. What the judge was doing by making an order was to give her some degree of security. [Counsel for the adopters] says, it seems to me with great force, that that sort of security called for by the mother is inconsistent with the unconditional element of the agreement that she gave under the Adoption Act 1976 and conflicts with the principle that consent to adoption must be, and is certainly seen, in the way in which the mother put her case, to be unconditional. One cannot but recognise, however, that the mother in this case, having consented to her daughter going to be part of a family whom she admires and respects, none the less wishes to have some degree of certainty that she will continue to be in touch with her daughter.

It seems to me that that degree of security that she seeks has to be found in the trust that she must have in these adopters. That is a trust which is undoubtedly held by the local authority and the guardian *ad litem*, because those experts in this field all believe that at this stage of this child's life it is right for her sake that she should continue to see her mother once a year. They have chosen this family on the basis that they also would recognise it was in the interests of this child that she should continue, certainly for the time being, to see her natural mother. These adopters themselves accept that this is right. This is all in the interests of the child, and, of course, an order under s. 8 for contact is made with the welfare of the child of the primary consideration. Nobody is suggesting that if this order is not made then the welfare of this child would not continue to be the primary consideration of these adopters in relation to her continuing contact with her natural mother.

In this particular case, if for some reason the adopters decide that the child should not see her natural mother, that is a flexibility which was implicit in the recommendations of the social workers and the guardian ad litem that there should be no order. As I understand it, for the foreseeable future it is said that there will be contact, but the adopters wish to be in control, responding, as they intend to do, to what the child says, what the child wants, and perhaps, much more importantly what the child needs, in their careful parental estimation.

If there is an order and in due course it looks as though the child does not want to see her mother, or there may be reasons why the child ought not to see her mother, there being a chequered history that the mother has, on the basis of the judge's order it will be the adopters who will have to go back to court and ask for the order to be varied, suspended or for there to be no future contact. That would seem to me to impose upon a family who have chosen to take on the responsibility of this child, with all the burdens as well as all the pleasures that that imposes, an additional burden which is unjust to this adoptive family. I do not see why they should have to go to court.

If they do stop the contact for any reason in the future, it would be reasonable, it would seem to me, that they would give a clear indication to the natural mother as to why they do not think there should be contact either short-term or long-term. They should give their reasons clearly so the mother can study them. If they do not do that, or if the reasons turn out to be inadequate or wrong or unjust, the mother has the right to go to the court and ask for leave to claim the contact that she has had in the past.

She does have a remedy. Judge Heald thought that that need for leave to apply, and all sorts of problems like that, would be met by a s. 8 order. It seems to me that the requirement of leave is a valuable protection, both for the adopters and for the child, and it is one that is very properly in place for that protection in the case of a former parent. If the adopters act unreasonably and that becomes clear to the court, then no doubt the mother would get an order which is appropriate for the time at which this matter comes before the court, bearing in mind the age of the child. Perhaps one matter that I should refer to is in *Re C (A Minor) (Adopted Child: Contact)* [1993] Fam 210, [1993] 2 FLR 431, a decision of Thorpe J, which was a very different case from this, where a mother who had not seen a child for a considerable number of years was applying for contact. Thorpe J proposed a procedure which would, first, require the case to be transferred to the Family Division of the High Court and to involve the Official Solicitor at the leave stage, together with the local authority, before the adopters were troubled with such an application.

That, of course, was a case very different from the present. If the mother does apply for leave her application for leave would be likely to go to the district judge of the local registry and would be considered by the district judge for directions. It may be that in a case such as this, depending entirely on what the facts are at this time, the district judge might think that the procedure provided by Thorpe J in *Re C (A Minor) (Adopted Child: Contact)* (above) was not necessarily appropriate to this case. It would be entirely, of course, within the discretion of the district judge as to how he dealt with it, but he might not feel bound to follow the general propositions put forward by Thorpe J in a rather different type of case.

But in my judgment the prevalence and finality of adoption and the importance of letting the new family find its own feet ought not to be threatened in any way by an order in this case. It is not necessary to make an order, so the quite simple short point is, 'Why make an order where there is no good reason to make it? Unless it is better to make it, you should not make it'. But there are actual reasons not to make the order in my judgment, because it is for the benefit of the child that the adoptive parents should have the feeling that they are not under constraint in doing what they have already said they would do and everybody trusts them to do, but secondly, that if the circumstances change, they should have the flexibility to change with the circumstances and not to be tied to an order.

It is perhaps of some significance that the combined experience of [both counsel] in the Family Division, and I must say my own experience has not thrown up any case where there has been an order imposed upon adopters with which they had not been in agreement — in this particular case the contents of the order were agreed, but the order was not — and I would hesitate to make an order imposing upon adopters that which they are prepared to do in any event, in particular since up to now we do not know of any case where adopters have been ordered to do what they have not wished to do by way of an order. Consequently, for all those reasons, it seems to me that, unusual though it is, his Honour Judge Heald is wrong in this matter and that we should allow the appeal. I would set aside the order for contact and not make any order in its place.

*Note*

See also *Re T (Minors) (Adopted Children: Contact)* [1995] 2 FLR 792, CA, *Re A (A Minor) (Adoption: Contact Order)* [1993] 2 FLR 645, CA; and *Re C (A Minor) (Adoption: Parental Agreement: Contact)* [1993] 2 FLR 260, CA.

### Richards, Margaret, '"It Feels Like Someone Keeps Moving the Goalposts" — Regulating Post-adoption Contact', *Re T (Adopted Children: Contact)*
### [1996] 8 CFLQ 175

. . . A recent study by the Social Services Inspectorate (SSI) of post-adoption contact in the North of England [*Moving Goalposts*, 1995] provides hard evidence of the extent to which openness in its most immediate form has become integral to adoption practice. In approximately 70 per cent of the adoptions arranged by the 37 social services departments and 14 voluntary adoption agencies surveyed in 1994, either direct or indirect contact was maintained between the children adopted and their birth relatives after the order was made. As the study points out, 'The concept of closing a case when the adoption order is granted is becoming less and less appropriate', and the resource implications for agencies in terms of providing post-adoption support for adoptive families and birth parents are now considerable.

It is probably fair to say that for many practitioners — social workers and lawyers — 'openness' is still seen as a gloss on adoption practice rather than as the norm revealed by the above study. There is still, for example, a perception that it is difficult or impossible to recruit prospective adopters who are genuinely prepared to promote contact. The White Paper on adoption nevertheless states, 'the Government intends to ensure that the courts and adoption agencies will assess the most suitable arrangements for contact between the birth family and the child after adoption'.

This is not the place for a critique of the evolution and rationale of the philosophy of openness in adoption, but it is worth noting the extent to which the higher courts have come to endorse it. In Re E *(A Minor) (Care Order)* [[1994] 1 FLR 146] the Court of Appeal overturned a local authority's appication to terminate contact between two young children and their birth parents in order to move towards a closed adoption. Although the local authority argued strongly that contact was of little benefit to the children and that there was no real likelihood of identifying prospective adopters who would countenance continuing contact, the court preferred fairly equivocal medical evidence of the likely benefits of face-to-face contact or at least of its neutral effect. Sir Stephen Brown P commented, in particular, 'The emphasis is heavily placed on the presumption of continuing parental contact' [at p. 151].

The potential benefits for a child of such contact were summarised by Simon Brown LJ in *Re E* in the following terms:

> . . . contact may well be of singular importance to the long-term welfare of the child: first, in giving the child the security of knowing that his parents love him and are interested in his welfare; secondly, by avoiding any damaging sense of loss to the child in seeing himself abandoned by his parents; thirdly, by enabling the child to commit himself to the substitute family with the seat of approval of the natural parents; and fourthly, by giving the child the necessary sense of family and personal identity [at pp. 154 and 155].

There can be no doubt that the Children Act 1989 has largely shaped the current perspective. The presumption of contact created by section 34 means that the court may require a local authority to justify an adoption plan which excludes it. However, recent case-law has begun to raise awkward questions about the assumptions which may now underpin post-adoption contact and about the extent to which the courts are prepared to regulate such arrangements for the sake of the benefits quoted above.
. . .

[After discussing the two *Re T* cases, see above, the author continues . . .]

The two decisions illustrate very well the complexity of adoption practice and what may be perceived as irreconcilable differences of principle. For many practitioners contact is inevitably regarded as a means of facilitating adoptions; not the *quid pro quo* exactly, but a way of enabling birth parents to accept what would otherwise be unacceptable in order to achieve the best possible outcome for the child. Since, however, the law does not allow parental agreement to adoption to be subject to a condition that contact subsequently be allowed, the giving of consent must be an act of faith, and if subsequently that is seen to be betrayed by the adopters, conflict shifts further down the line, to the detriment of, if not outright risk to, the child.

The SSI study demonstrates that adoption agencies are beginning to use written contact agreements and recommends that they should become standard practice in order to avoid confusion, clarify expectations and remove conflict. It is acknowledged that there will be a growing need in future to review and sometimes to re-negotiate agreements already in place. Legal advisers to adoption agencies have difficulty, however, in advising their clients as to the enforceability of such agreements.

*Re T* apart, current judicial opinion leans against enforcement, but that is likely to be a most unsatisfactory position from the point of view of an agency which, after adoption, has no legal status of its own with which to press for contact arrangements to be observed or re-negotiated. Such tension between law and practice is unacceptable in the long term, and it will be interesting to see whether *Re T* sparks off further litigation.

*In whose interests?*

The benefits to the child which contact arrangements imply have already been described. It is also clear, however, that contact arrangements may, in practice, be used as a means of redressing the balance of influence which may otherwise be tilted heavily against birth parents throughout the adoption process. The SSI study identified several cases where the inspectors questioned whose needs primarily the contact arrangement was meeting. Sometimes, for example, information was being provided by the adoptive family to birth relatives, but with no information being reciprocated. In other situations adoption workers referred to 'horse trading', which went on in the pre-order phase, and in which birth parents' representatives saw contact as a bargaining tool. The study points out [at para. 4.10] that:

> Post-adoption contact is not just about meeting the needs of the child. Agencies were regularly faced with the difficult task of balancing the respective needs of the child, the adopters and the birth relatives and in many instances this balance had been achieved to the satisfaction of all parties. Adopters often displayed a remarkable understanding of, and a commitment to meeting, the needs of birth relatives and there was a recognition that contact could help to ease the sense of loss experienced by some birth parents. However, there were other situations where the amount of contact expected by birth relatives was seen as excessive by the adoptive family. This could and indeed did cause stress within the adoptive family and sometimes between the adoptive family and the agency.

This emphasis on the 'adoption triangle' rather than the paramount interests of the child requires adjustment from those more familiar with the philosophy of the Children Act 1989. The child's interests do not alone determine outcomes in adoption. The adopters in learning how to parent someone else's child may need some respite from the pressures imposed by the demands of birth relatives, who themselves must sometimes be prevented from acting out their own sense of loss through the contact arrangements. The Court of Appeal in *Re T* was prepared to adjust the balance of interests in a different way from previously, and it is helpful to have some support for the enforceability of contact agreements. Nevertheless, there are dangers in using contact as a weapon in negotiations with birth relatives or in assuming that indirect contact in particular is to be implied for the sake of others, whether or not it is of benefit to the child. Adoption itself necessitates the legal and emotional separation of children from their birth parents, and unless this is acknowledged and internalised, contact may be harmful to all involved.

*Notes*
1.   Contact may be maintained by attaching an Adoption Act 1976, s. 12(6) condition in an adoption order (not a freeing order), but only in exceptional circumstances (see *Re C (A Minor) (Adoption Order: Conditions)* [1989] AC 1, HL). In *Re S (A Minor) (Blood Transfusion: Adoption Order Conditions)* [1994] 2 FLR 416, CA, it was held inappropriate in the circumstances to attach a condition about blood transfusions to an adoption order, where the adopters were Jehovah's Witnesses. Clause 40 of the Draft Adoption Bill removes the court's power to impose terms and conditions on adoption orders, as '[i]t is unrealistic to make an adoption order conditional upon the fulfilment of certain conditions' (*Review of Adoption Law*, para. 5.8).
2.   Adoption proceedings are 'family proceedings' (see Chapter 7), so that the judge in adoption proceedings has jurisdiction to make a contact order or any other CA 1989, s. 8 order; but as any s. 8 order is terminated by a freeing or adoption order, the court cannot make a contact order in freeing proceedings which is binding on the prospective adopters at the point of adoption (*Re H (A Minor) (Freeing Order)* [1993] 2 FLR 325, CA). After adoption, however, a birth parent or any interested person may apply under s. 10 of the CA 1989 for leave to apply for a s. 8 contact order, although it is difficult to obtain leave (*Re C (A Minor) (Adopted Child: Contact)* [1993] 2 FLR 431, FD).
3.   A local authority may apply for contact to be refused or terminated under s. 34 of the CA 1989 (see Chapter 10), so that an adoption may proceed smoothly.

*Further reading*
Kidd, P., and Storey, P., 'Adoption, Freeing and Contact' [1996] Fam Law 225.
Mullender, A. (ed.), *Open Adoption — the Philosophy and the Practice*, London: British Agencies for Adoption and Fostering, 1991, BAAF Practice Series 19.
Ryburn, M., 'Welfare and Justice in Post-Adoption Contact' [1997] Fam Law 28.
Van Bueren, G., 'Children's Access to Adoption Records — State Discretion or an Enforceable International Right' (1995) 58 MLR 37.

## 11.6   WHO MAY APPLY TO ADOPT?

### 11.6.1   Single persons and married couples

Only single persons and married couples may apply to adopt a child (Adoption Act 1976, s. 14). An applicant must be aged at least 21, except in the case of a step-parent adoption, when the natural parent, not the step-parent, need be only 18 (s. 14(1B)). There is no upper age limit, but some adoption agencies discourage adoptions by those aged over 40.

### 11.6.2   Cohabiting couples

A cohabiting couple cannot apply to adopt a child. The only option available is for one of them to apply to adopt the child and for one or both of them to apply for a s. 8 residence order under the CA 1989, the effect of which will be to give them parental responsibility for the duration of the residence order (see *Re AB (Adoption: Joint Residence)* [1996] 1 FLR 27, FD, where Cazalet J granted an adoption order in respect of one of the cohabitants, and joint residence orders in respect of them both).

## Department of Health and Welsh Office, *Review of Adoption Law*, Report to Ministers of an Interdepartmental Working Group, 1992

*Marital status*

. . .

26.10   In practice, some agencies assess and prepare unmarried couples together, although only one partner may apply for the order and become the child's legal parent. It has been asked whether an unmarried couple should be allowed to adopt jointly. Family structures are changing and more children are born to parents who are not married but are living in stable unions. Under section 4 of the Children Act 1989, an unmarried father may acquire the same parental status as one who is married. On the other hand, unmarried parents do not have the same legal obligations to one another as a married couple have. Should the relationship break down, the caring parent may therefore be less financially secure than if they were married. Furthermore, one of the special features of adoption is that it transfers a child from one family to another and gives the child a legal relationship with all members of the new family, including grandparents, aunts and uncles. However great the commitment of unmarried adoptive parents to a child might be, it is open to question how far their wider families would be willing to accept that child as part of their family.

26.11   It is also important to bear in mind Article 6(1) of the European Adoption Convention which prohibits adoption by unmarried couples. Although some unmarried couples might be suitable adoptive parents for a child, we feel that the security and stability which adopted children need are still more likely to be provided by parents who have made a publicly recognised commitment to their relationship and who have legal responsibilities towards each other. Taking into account also the United Kingdom's international obligations, we consider that it would not be appropriate to allow two unmarried people to adopt jointly.

26.12   The fact that two people are married to each other is not of course in itself a sufficient guide to the likely stability of their relationship. Agencies generally expect applicants to have been married for at least three years, although some are prepared to take into account periods of co-habitation preceding marriage, where there is evidence of it available. We consider that agencies should have flexibility to operate their own criteria in forming views on the likely stability of a marriage, and that this should be the subject of guidance.

26.13   We do not propose any changes to the law relating to single applicants, including lesbians and gay men. There are examples of extremely successful adoptions, particularly of older children and children with disabilities, by single adopters. Some children are only able to settle in single-parent households, as a result of experiences in their early lives.

26.14    Some agencies may place a child with a single applicant who is living with a partner. As a matter of practice, to safeguard the child, they also assess the suitability of the partner. We have suggested above that an unmarried couple should not be allowed to adopt jointly, i.e. that it should not be possible for them to have the same legal relationship towards a child which they would have if they were a married couple adopting together. We do not feel that this is necessarily incompatible with allowing a single person who has a partner to adopt. We recommend that, where assessing a single applicant, agencies should have a duty to assess any other person who is likely to act in a parental capacity towards the adopted child. . . .

*Note and questions*
There is nothing in the Draft Adoption Bill 1996 to allow couples other than spouses to make joint applications for adoption (see clause 43); but the Bill improves the matter slightly, in that a residence order may be made to last until the child reaches majority instead of age 16 as at present. Is there any real objection to a cohabiting couple applying for adoption? What about adoptions by transsexuals, homosexuals and other partnerships?

## 11.6.3    Eligibility and suitability of adopters

**Department of Health and Welsh Office, *Review of Adoption Law*, Report to Ministers of an Interdepartmental Working Group, 1992**

. . .
26.1    Adoption must serve a wide range of children with a wide range of different experiences, circumstances and needs, including children of different racial and cultural backgrounds, different religions, different ages, children with very special needs and children who need to be placed with siblings. Research studies confirm that successful adopters may be equally various. If legislation were to be too prescriptive about the characteristics of those who could be accepted as adopters, the discretion of agencies and courts might be fettered to the extent that some children could not be found families at all. Similarly, to deprive agencies of opportunities to exercise flexibility within reasonable limits could deprive children of the advantages which should flow from the proper exercise on their behalf of sound professional judgements.

26.2    The only limits in present legislation concern the domicile, minimum age and marital status of adopters. We do not propose that there should be any additional statutory criteria.

26.3    The suitability of a person who is eligible by law to adopt a child should be judged primarily according to the needs of a particular child rather than by reference to a notional concept of what makes a good adoptive parent. However, some adoption agencies may apply guidelines to help assess the suitability of people who would like to adopt. Agencies are sometimes criticised by would-be adopters who perceive a lack of consistency between the criteria applied by different agencies. The body of professional experience and practice which constrain and influence decisions are nowhere enshrined in either legislation or guidance where they may be studied and understood by would-be adopters. We consider that it would be helpful for guidance, issued by the Health Departments, to clarify the sort of criteria which agencies may be expected to apply and which would-be adopters can therefore expect to be taken into account. And agencies should be expected to provide would-be adopters with written information explaining the criteria which they apply.

26.4   We recommend that agencies should not be allowed to operate absolute rules governing people's eligibility for consideration as adopters. In other words, a person who meets the statutory criteria for an adoptive parent should not automatically be excluded from consideration on account, say, of his or her age. An agency may, however, decide that, having regard to the needs of the children for whom adoptive families are required and to agency guidelines on suitability, it would not be appropriate to accept that person for consideration.

. . .

*Lower age limits*

26.6   The only age limits prescribed for the adopters in current legislation are that they must be at least 21, or 18 in the case of a parent who is adopting his or her own child jointly with a step-parent. The new type of adoption order for step-parents suggested in paragraph 19.3 would preclude the need for parents to adopt their own child. A single minimum age only would therefore be required, and we recommend that this remain at 21.

*Upper age limits*

26.7   Agencies may not impose strict age limits on adopters, as there is no provision for this in legislation, but they do operate their own age guidelines in relation to people who want to adopt healthy infants. These vary from the early to late thirties, and few agencies will accept applicants over 40 for consideration as adopters for healthy infants. The guidelines reflect the view that it is better for very young children to be placed with adopters who are not older by too wide a margin than most couples starting a family. . . .

*Note and questions*

In *R* v *Secretary of State for Health, ex parte Luff* [1992] 1 FLR 59, QBD, a couple challeged the refusal to allow them to adopt the child because of their age, but they failed. Is it satisfactory that couples in their 40s who would make perfectly good parents are usually refused the opportunity to adopt a child? Is transracial adoption desirable (see *Re JK (Adoption: Transracial Placement)* [1991] 2 FLR 340)?

*Further reading*

Sandlands, R., 'Adoption, Law and Homosexuality' [1993] JSWFL 321.

## 11.7   NON-AGENCY APPLICATIONS

### 11.7.1   Adoption by step-parents

A step-parent may wish to apply for an adoption order in order to create a legal relationship with the step-child. While this may seem to be an advantage for the step-parent, it may sever the legal links between the child and the other side of his or her birth family, which may be detrimental to the child's best interests.

## Department of Health and Welsh Office, *Review of Adoption Law*, Report to Ministers of an Interdepartmental Working Group, 1992

. . .

### 19 Adoption by step-parents

19.1 Where a marriage or relationship breaks down (or a parent dies) and the parent who continues to care for the child subsequently (re-)marries, the parent and step-parent may decide to apply for an adoption order. The step-parent is likely to be effectively sharing responsibility for the care of the child, and the family may wish to seek some legal recognition of the relationship which he or she has with the child. Some applications appear to be based also on a wish for the child to be known by the step-father's surname.

19.2 Adoption by a step-parent and parent severs the legal links between a child and the other side of his or her birth family. There may be circumstances in which this is appropriate, for instance where the other parent has never acted in a parental capacity and the child has never really known any member of that side of the birth family. But where the child has some relationship with the parent, or with his or her relatives, it is unlikely to be in the child's interests for their legal relationship to be extinguished. A parent may agree to adoption simply because he has no interest in the child, or even where he has such an interest and is keen to retain it but wishes to end the payment of maintenance. Where the other parent has died or is no longer in the picture, the possible benefits to the child of retaining a legal relationship with grandparents or other relatives may be overlooked. Of course, the adoption order need not mean severance of practical links. But where the prime motivation behind an adoption application is the wish to cement the family unit and put away the past, this may be confusing and lead to identity problems for the child, especially if (as is statistically not unlikely) the new marriage breaks down. It is also possible that the step-parent's family has little or no involvement or interest in the adopted child, so that the child loses one family without really gaining another. As divorce has become more common, it is less necessary for families to pursue step-parent adoption in order to avoid embarrassment and difficult explanations. We do not consider it appropriate to prevent step-parent adoptions; but there may be ways in which the law can help to discourage inappropriate applications. . . .

The *Review* (para. 19.14) recommended a new type of adoption order for step-parents and that there should be provision for a step-parent adoption order to be undone where the marriage ends in divorce or death and the child is aged under 18. It also recommended (para. 19.8) that step-parents should be able to aquire parental responsibility by agreement. However, the Draft Adoption Bill 1996 does not go so far. Clause 85 inserts the following new subs. (1A) into s. 4 of the CA 1989 and clause 86 inserts a new subs. (5) into s. 12, which may be useful for step-parents instead of applying for an adoption order.

### Children Act 1989, ss. 4(1A) and 12(5) (as inserted by the draft Adoption Bill 1996 clauses 85 and 86)

4.—(1A) Where a child's parent ('parent A') who has parental responsibility for the child is married to a person who is not the child's parent ('the step-parent')—

(a)   parent A, or if the other parent of the child also has parental responsibility for the child, both parents may by agreement with the step-parent provide for the step-parent to have parental responsibility for the child; or

(b)   the court may, on the application of the step-parent, order that the step-parent shall have parental responsibility for the child.

**12.**—(5)   The power of a court to make a residence order in favour of any person includes, where—

(a)   that person would have parental responsibility for the child in question as a result of subsection (2), and

(b)   every other person who has parental responsibility for the child consents, power to direct that the order shall continue in force until the child reaches the age of eighteen (unless the order is brought to an end earlier); and any power to vary a residence order is exercisable accordingly.

*Note*

For a discussion of adoptions by relatives, see the *Review* (1992), paras 20.1–20.5 and for adoption by carers, see the *Review* (1992), paras 21.1–21.3.

*Questions*

Is step-parent adoption really necessary? Is there a danger of too many people having parental responsibility, which may make it impossible for unanimous decisions to be made about the child?

## 11.8   INTERCOUNTRY ADOPTION

**Department of Health and Welsh Office,** *Review of Adoption Law,* **Report to Ministers of an Interdepartmental Working Group, 1992**

46.1   Intercountry adoption has been known since the post-war years, initially as a humanitarian movement in response to the needs of children displaced and suffering through war. More recently, intercountry adoption has tended to develop as a service for childless couples. The growing scale of intercountry adoption and concerns about the welfare of children involved have in recent years prompted many countries — both those from which children are adopted by foreign adopters ('sending countries') and those which receive children from overseas for adoption ('receiving countries') — to consider the need for more effective regulation.

46.2   Intercountry adoption may provide the only opportunity for some children, who have no family and are living in circumstances of deprivation and poverty, of a family life. It is understandable that some people, particularly those who are unable to have children, wish to combine the needs of such children with their own desire for a family. Research suggests that the majority of intercountry adoptions are successful in terms of the adopted person's development and the 'satisfaction' of the adoptive parents and their children.

46.3   However, concerns have arisen about a number of aspects of intercountry adoptions. These have focused around the fact that many intercountry adoptions are arranged without the professional supervision, support and safeguards which are required by the domestic adoption laws of most receiving countries. At its worst, unregulated activity may give rise to corruption, abuse and child-stealing and trafficking. Even where corruption is not involved, there is concern that insufficient attention may be paid to the needs of the child, particularly in terms of the possible risks associated with transracial and transcultural adoption and the importance of information about the child's background.

## Department of Health, *Interdepartmental Review of Adoption Law*, Discussion Paper No. 4, *Intercountry Adoption*, 1992

. . . [I]ntercountry adoption has been known since post-war years, when it was originally seen as a humanitarian response to the needs of young orphaned victims of war. In the last decade or so, however, the emphasis has shifted and it has tended to develop as a service for providing children for childless couples, particularly as the numbers of babies available for adoption in England and Wales has decreased.

Between 1980 and 1989, 170,000 to 180,000 children were involved in intercountry adoptions. 90 per cent came from Korea, India, Colombia, Brazil, Sri Lanka, Chile, the Philippines, Guatemala, Peru and El Salvador (in that order). 85 per cent of those children went to the USA, France, Sweden, the Netherlands, Italy and Switzerland (in that order). During 1990–91 many Romanian orphans were taken from Romania and adopted by people in other countries, and it was that event which highlighted the need for international safeguards to protect children.

A Special Commission, with representatives from more than 50 countries, was set up by the Hague Conference on Private International Law in 1990 in order to develop an International Convention on Intercountry Adoption. The aims of the Commission were first to develop international safeguards to ensure intercountry adoptions only take place where they are in the best interest of the child, and secondly to establish a system of co-operation among Contracting States to ensure that such safeguards are respected. . . .

## The Hague Convention on Protection of Children and Co-operation in Respect of Intercountry Adoption 1993

The States signatory to the present Convention,

*Recognizing* that the child, for the full and harmonious development of his or her personality, should grow up in a family environment, in an atmosphere of happiness, love and understanding,

*Recalling* that each State should take, as a matter of priority, appropriate measures to enable the child to remain in the care of his or her family of origin,

*Recognizing* that intercountry adoption may offer the advantage of a permanent family to a child for whom a suitable family cannot be found in his or her State of origin,

*Convinced* of the necessity to take measures to ensure that intercountry adoptions are made in the best interests of the child and with respect for his or her fundamental rights, and to prevent the abduction, the sale of, or traffic in children,

*Desiring* to establish common provisions to this effect, taking into account the principles set forth in international instruments, in particular the United Nations Convention on the Rights of the Child, of 20 November 1989. . . .

Have agreed upon the following provisions--

**Article 1**
The objects of the present Convention are-

(a) to establish safeguards to ensure that intercountry adoptions take place in the best interests of the child and with respect for his or her fundamental rights as recognized in international law;

(b) to establish a system of co-operation amongst Contracting States to ensure that those safeguards are respected and thereby prevent the abduction, the sale of, or traffic in children;

(c) to secure the recognition in Contracting States of adoptions made in accordance with the Convention.

*Notes*

1. The Convention (arts 6 to 17) provides for the creation of a network of Central Authorities in each Contracting State whose function will be to work together to promote the objects of the Convention and make arrangements for intercountry adoptions.

2. The Convention will be brought into effect in the UK by regulations made under clause 88 of the Draft Adoption Bill, 1996, if enacted, and the text of the Convention will be set out (so far as material) in sch. 2 of the proposed new Adoption Act.

*Further reading*

The following discussion papers were published as part of the 1989 Government Interdepartmental Review of Adoption Law: *The Nature and Effect of Adoption* (1990); *Agreement and Freeing* (1991); *The Adoption Process* (1991); and *Intercountry Adoption* (1992). The following background papers accompanied the discussion documents: *International Perspectives* (1990); *Review of Research Relating to Adoption* (1990); and *Intercountry Adoption* (1992).

Tizard, B., 'Recent Developments in Adoption: Social Work Policy and Research Outcomes' (1994) 4 JCL 50.

# 12 INTERNATIONAL CHILD ABDUCTION

## 12.1 INTRODUCTION

Child abduction is a distressing consequence of family breakdown. It is also a widespread problem due not only to world-wide increases in family breakdown, but also to the growth in international marriages and the greater and easier movement of persons. Two international Conventions exist to combat international child abduction: the Hague Convention on the Civil Aspects of International Child Abduction 1980 (the 'Hague Convention') and the European Convention on Recognition and Enforcement of Decisions Concerning Custody of Children 1980 ('the European Convention'). The UK is party to both Conventions which are effective in the UK by virtue of the Child Abduction Act 1985, the schedules to which contain the texts of the Conventions. Although the Conventions have improved the chances of abducted children being returned to the country from which they have been abducted, many countries are not party to any Convention; and even those who are may sometimes fail to respect the aims of the Conventions.

### Re L (Minors) (Wardship: Jurisdiction)
[1974] 1 WLR 250
Court of Appeal

BUCKLEY LJ: . . . To take a child from his native land, to remove him to another country where, maybe, his native tongue is not spoken, to divorce him from the social customs and contacts to which he has been accustomed, to interrupt his education in his native land and subject him to a foreign system of education, are all acts (offered here as examples and of course not as a complete catalogue of possible relevant factors) which are likely to be psychologically disturbing to the child, particularly at a time when his family life is also disrupted. If such a case is promptly brought to the

attention of a court in this country, the judge may feel that it is in the best interests of the infant that these disturbing factors should be eliminated from his life as speedily as possible. A full investigation of the merits of the case in an English court may be incompatible with achieving this. The judge may well be persuaded that it would be better for the child that those merits should be investigated in a court in his native country than that he should spend in this country the period which must necessarily elapse before all the evidence can be assembled for adjudication here. Anyone who has had experience of the exercise of this delicate jurisdiction knows what complications can result from a child developing roots in new soil, and what conflicts this can occasion in the child's own life. Such roots can grow rapidly. An order that the child should be returned forthwith to the country from which he has been removed in the expectation that any dispute about his custody will be satisfactorily resolved in the courts of that country may well be regarded as being in the best interests of the child.
. . .

*Note*
*Re L* was a kidnapping case, but Buckley LJ's *dicta* have been cited and approved of as being relevant to applications under the Hague and European Conventions.

## UNITED NATIONS CONVENTION ON THE RIGHTS OF THE CHILD 1989

**Article 11**
1. States Parties shall take measures to combat the illicit transfer and non-return of children abroad.
2. To this end, States Parties shall promote the conclusion of bilateral or multilateral agreements or accession to existing agreements.

**Article 35**
States Parties shall take all appropriate national, bilateral and multilateral measures to prevent the abduction of, the sale of or traffic in children for any purpose or in any form.

## 12.2   THE CRIMINAL OFFENCE OF CHILD ABDUCTION

## CHILD ABDUCTION ACT 1984

**1.   Offence of abduction of child by parent, etc.**
   (1)   Subject to sections (5) and (8) below, a person connected with a child under the age of sixteen commits an offence if he takes or sends the child out of the United Kingdom without the appropriate consent.
   (2)   A person is connected with a child for the purposes of this section if—
      (a)   he is a parent of the child; or
      (b)   in the case of a child whose parents were not married to each other at the time of his birth, there are reasonable grounds for believing that he is the father of the child; or
      (c)   he is a guardian of the child; or
      (d)   he is a person in whose favour a residence order is in force with respect to the child; or

(e)   he has custody of the child.

(3)   In this section 'the appropriate consent', in relation to a child, means—

(a)   the consent of each of the following—

(i)   the child's mother;

(ii)   the child's father, if he has parental responsibility for him;

(iii)   any guardian of the child;

(iv)   any person in whose favour a residence order is in force with respect to the child;

(v)   any person who has custody of the child; or

(b)   the leave of the court granted under or by virtue of any provision of Part II of the Children Act 1989; or

(c)   if any person has custody of the child, the leave of the court which awarded custody to him.

(4)   A person does not commit an offence under this section by taking or sending a child out of the United Kingdom without obtaining the appropriate consent if—

(a)   he is a person in whose favour there is a residence order in force with respect to the child; and

(b)   he takes or sends him out of the United Kingdom for a period of less than one month.

(4A)   Subsection (4) above does not apply if the person taking or sending the child out of the United Kingdom does so in breach of an order under Part II of the Children Act 1989.

. . .

*Notes*

*1.*   It is a defence if the person removing the child:

(a)   believed that the other person consented to the removal or would have consented had he or she been aware of all the circumstances; or

(b)   has been unable to communicate with the other person despite taking reasonable steps to do so; or

(c)   the other person has unreasonably refused consent (s. 1(5)).

Defence (c) does not apply if the person who refused consent has a residence order in his or her favour, or the person taking or sending the child out of the UK has done so in breach of a court order (s. 1(5A)). Section 2 makes it an offence for 'other persons' to abduct a child.

*2.*   As child abduction is a criminal offence, it is possible to ask the police to institute an 'All Ports Alert'.

*3.*   In order to avoid committing the offence of child abduction, a parent or other person who wishes to take a child out of the UK must first obtain the consent of the other parent and/or certain other persons, except where that other parent and/or person has a residence order in his or her favour in respect of the child and wishes to take the child out of the UK for less than one month (CA 1989, s. 13). If consent is not forthcoming, then the court's consent must be obtained (see CA 1989, s. 13). When deciding whether to grant consent, the court applies the principles laid down by the Court of Appeal in *Poel* v *Poel* [1970] 1 WLR 1469, i.e. the welfare of the child is the first and paramount consideration, but that leave should not be refused unless the interests of the child and those of the custodial parent are clearly shown to be incompatible. These principles still apply today despite the implementation of the 1989 Act (see *M v A (Wardship: Removal from Jurisdiction)* [1993] 2 FLR 715, FD, *MH v GP (Child: Emigration)* [1995] 2 FLR 106, FD and *H v H (Residence Order: Leave to Remove From Jurisdiction) (Note)* [1995] 1 FLR 529, CA).

## 12.3 THE HAGUE CONVENTION ON THE CIVIL ASPECTS OF INTERNATIONAL CHILD ABDUCTION 1980

The Hague Convention on the Civil Aspects of International Child Abduction 1980 was implemented into English and Scots law by Part I of the Child Abduction and Custody Act 1985 (see sch. 1 for the text of the Convention). For a list of Contracting States, see 12.6 below. The Convention establishes a network of central authorities which 'must co-operate with each other and promote co-operation amongst the competent authorities in their respective States to secure the prompt return of children and to achieve the other objects of this Convention' (art. 7). The Lord Chancellor's Department is the Central Authority in England and Wales, but its functions are performed by the Official Solicitor.

### 12.3.1   The aims, purpose and scope of the Convention

### THE HAGUE CONVENTION ON THE CIVIL ASPECTS OF INTERNATIONAL CHILD ABDUCTION 1980

**The Preamble**
The States signatory to the present Convention,

*Firmly* convinced that the interests of children are of paramount importance in matters relating to their custody,

*Desiring* to protect children internationally from the harmful effects of their wrongful removal or retention and to establish procedures to ensure their prompt return to the State of their habitual residence as well as to secure protection for rights of access,

*Have resolved* to conclude a Convention to this effect, and have agreed upon the following provisions—

**Article 1**
The objects of the present Convention are—

(a)   to secure the prompt return of children wrongfully removed to or retained in any Contracting State; and

(b)   to ensure that rights of custody and of access under the law of one Contracting State are effectively respected in the other Contracting States.

**Article 2**
Contracting States shall take all appropriate measures to secure within their territories the implementation of the objects of the Convention. For this purpose they shall use the most expeditious procedures available.

**Article 4**
The Convention shall apply to any child who was habitually resident in a Contracting State immediately before any breach of custody or access rights. The Convention shall cease to apply when the child attains the age of sixteen years.

## Re M (A Minor) (Child Abduction)
### [1994] 1 FLR 390
### Court of Appeal

BUTLER-SLOSS LJ: . . . The Hague Convention provides a summary procedure for the expeditious return to the country of habitual residence of children who are wrongfully removed to or retained in another Contracting State in order that the courts of the country of habitual residence should should determine their future. . . . The interests of the child in each individual case are not paramount since it is presumed under the Convention that the welfare of children who have been abducted is best met by return to their habitual residence. . . . Provision is made by Article 13 for limited consideration of the welfare of the child. . . .

## B v B (Abduction)
### [1993] 1 FLR 238
### Court of Appeal

SIR STEPHEN BROWN P: . . . [I]t is important when considering applications under the Hague Convention that it should be borne in mind that these are matters which affect the comity of nations. It is a Convention on the civil aspects of *international* child abduction. Its purpose, as the preamble and art. 1 indicate, is to deal summarily with the mischief of taking children from the appropriate jurisdiction in a manner which is considered to be unlawful . . .

## Re E (A Minor) (Abduction)
### [1989] 1 FLR 135
### Court of Appeal

BALCOMBE LJ: . . . [T]he whole purpose of this Convention is . . . to ensure that parties do not gain adventitious advantage by either removing a child wrongfully from the country of its usual residence, or having taken the child, with the agreement of any other party who has custodial rights, to another jurisdiction, then wrongfully to retain that child. . . .

### 12.3.2 What is 'habitual residence' for the purposes of the Convention?

Habitual residence is the connecting factor used in the Convention to determine whether the child comes within the scope of the Convention (see art. 4 at 12.3.1) and whether there has been wrongful removal or retention under art. 3(a) (see 12.3.3). The following case is the leading case on habitual residence.

## In Re J (A Minor) (Abduction: Custody Rights)
### [1990] 2 AC 562
### House of Lords

*Facts*: The parents were UK emigrants to Western Australia where they met and lived together as cohabitants. Their child was born in 1987. When their relationship broke down, the father was told by his solicitor that the mother had sole custody and guardianship of their child, but that he could apply for a custody order. The father indicated an intention to apply but did not do so. Later the mother took the child to England with the settled intention of making a long-term home there for herself and the child. Four days later the father was granted custody by the Australian court and the judge also made a declaration that the child's removal from Australia had been wrongful. The father applied under the Hague Convention for the return of his child. The High Court in England dismissed the father's application, holding that there was no wrongful removal or retention. The Court of Appeal dismissed the father's appeal. He appealed to the House of Lords.

*Held*: dismissing the appeal, that there was no wrongful removal or wrongful retention for the purposes of the Hague Convention, as the mother's removal of the child had caused him no longer to be habitually resident in Western Australia.

LORD BRANDON: My Lords, this appeal concerns the interpretation and application to somewhat special facts of the Convention on the Civil Aspects of International Child Abduction signed at The Hague on 25 October 1980 ('the Convention'). Both Australia and the United Kingdom are parties to the Convention, which was given, with immaterial exceptions, the force of law in the United Kingdom by the Child Abduction and Custody Act 1985.

[After citing the facts his Lordship continued: . . .]

The father's case is that the mother's removal of J from Australia to England, or alternatively her retention of J in England after such removal, was wrongful within the meaning of article 3 of the Convention. The mother's case is that neither her removal of J to England, nor her subsequent retention of him there, was wrongful in that sense.

I consider first the question whether the removal of J from Australia to England by the mother was wrongful within the meaning of article 3 of the Convention. Having regard to the terms of article 3 the removal could only be wrongful if it was in breach of rights of custody attributed to, i.e. possessed by, the father at the time when it took place. It seems to me, however, that since section 35 of the Family Law Act 1975–1979, as amended of Western Australia gave the mother alone the custody and guardianship of J, and no order of a court to the contrary had been obtained by the father before the removal took place, the father had no custody rights relating to J of which the removal of J by the mother could be a breach. It is no doubt true that, while the mother and father were living together with J in their jointly owned home in Western Australia, the de facto custody of J was exercised by them jointly. So far as legal rights of custody are concerned, however, these belonged to the mother alone, and included in those rights was the right to decide where J should reside. It follows, in my opinion, that the removal of J by the mother was not wrongful within the meaning of article 3 of the Convention. I recognise that Anderson J thought fit to make a declaration that J had been wrongfully removed from Australia. I pay to his decision the respect which comity requires, but the courts of the United Kingdom are not bound by it and for the reasons which I have given I do not consider that it was rightly made.

I consider secondly the question whether the retention of J in England by the mother following his removal was wrongful within the meaning of article 3 of the

Convention. Having regard to the terms of article 3 such retention could only be wrongful if, immediately before it took place, it was in breach of rights of custody possessed by the father. In order to decide that question it is necessary to take account of the sequence in time of the relevant events. The first relevant event was the retention of J by the mother after his arrival in England. That began on 22 March 1990 and continued thereafter. The second relevant event was the order of Anderson J giving to the father for the first time guardianship and custody of J. That order was made on 12 April 1990, three weeks after the mother's retention of J began. There may be some doubt whether Anderson J had jurisdiction to make such an order but I shall assume for present purposes that he had. The result was that it was not until 12 April 1990, or such later date as that on which the order was made known to the mother, that her retention of J in England first became in breach of the rights of custody newly conferred on the father by Anderson J. The question then arises whether immediately before that breach occurred, J was habitually resident in Western Australia within the meaning of article 3 of the Convention.

It is not in dispute that, immediately before his removal, J was habitually resident in Western Australia. It was argued for the father that J remained habitually resident in Western Australia despite his removal to and retention in England by the mother with the settled intention that he should reside there with her on a long-term basis. It was argued for the mother that, once she reached England with J on 22 March 1990 and retained him there with the settled intention to which I have just referred, J ceased to be habitually resident in Western Australia and in particular ceased to be so resident well before the date of the order of Anderson J.

In considering this issue it seems to me to be helpful to deal first with a number of preliminary points. The first point is that the expression 'habitually resident,' as used in article 3 of the Conventiont is nowhere defined. It follows, I think, that the expression is not to be treated as a term of art with some special meaning, but is rather to be understood according to the ordinary and natural meaning of the two words which it contains. The second point is that the question whether a person is or is not habitually resident in a specified country is a question of fact to be decided by reference to all the circumstances of any particular case. The third point is that there is a significant difference between a person ceasing to be habitually resident in country A, and his subsequently becoming habitually resident in country B. A person may cease to be habitually resident in country A in a single day if he or she leaves it with a settled intention not to return to it but to take up long-term residence in country B instead. Such a person cannot, however, become habitually resident in country B in a single day. An appreciable period of time and a settled intention will be necessary to enable him or her to become so. During that appreciable period of time the person will have ceased to be habitually resident in country A but not yet have become habitually resident in country B. The fourth point is that, where a child of J's age is in the sole lawful custody of the mother, his situation with regard to habitual residence will necessarily be the same as hers.

In the light of these points the question which has to be posed and answered is not whether, immediately before the continued retention of J became a breach of the father's rights of custody under the order of Anderson J, J had become habitually resident in England. It is rather whether immediately before that time J had already ceased to be habitually resident in Western Australia. To that second question it seems to me that, on the special facts of this particular case, only an affirmative answer can sensibly be given. The mother had left Western Australia with a settled intention that neither she nor J should continue to be habitually resident there. It follows that immediately before 22 March 1990, when the retention of J in England by the mother began, both she and J had ceased to be habitually resident in Western Australia. A fortiori they had ceased to be habitually resident there by 12 April 1990, the date of the order of Anderson J. The consequence is that the continued retention of J in England by the mother was never at any time a wrongful retention within the meaning of article 3 of the Convention.

On the basis that neither the removal of J on the one hand, nor his retention on the other, was wrongful within the meaning of article 3 of the Convention the father's case cannot succeed. It follows that I agree with the decisions of both the courts below and would dismiss the appeal.

*Notes*

1.   Habitual residence has come to be the preferred connecting factor in other family matters, both in international conventions (see, e.g., the Draft Convention on the Protection of Minors at 10.10) and in domestic legislation (see, e.g., s. 44(1), Child Support Act 1991). Lord Brandon's *dicta* on habitual residence are therefore commonly referred to in other contexts.

2.   For a case illustrating the problems of establishing the habitual residence of children, see *Re A (Abduction: Habitual Residence)* [1996] 1 FLR 1, FD).

### 12.3.3   Wrongful removal or retention

## THE HAGUE CONVENTION ON THE CIVIL ASPECTS OF INTERNATIONAL CHILD ABDUCTION 1980

**Article 3**
The removal or the retention of a child is considered to be wrongful where—
      (a)   it is in breach of rights of custody attributed to a person, an institution or any other body, either jointly or alone, under the law of the State in which the child was habitually resident immediately before the removal or retention; and
      (b)   at the time of removal or retention those rights were actually exercised, either jointly or alone, or would have been so exercised but for the removal or retention.
The rights of custody mentioned in sub-paragraph (a) above may arise in particular by operation of law or by reason of a judicial or administrative decision, or by reason of an agreement having legal effect under the law of that State.

**Article 5**
For the purposes of this Convention—
      (a)   'rights of custody' shall include rights relating to the care of the person of the child and, in particular, the right to determine the child's place of residence;
      . . .

### *Re B (A Minor) (Abduction)*
### [1994] 2 FLR 249
### Court of Appeal

WAITE LJ: . . . The purposes of the Hague Convention were, in part at least, humanitarian. The objective is to spare children already suffering the effects of breakdown in their parents' relationship the further disruption which is suffered when they are taken arbitrarily by one parent from their settled environment and moved to another country for the sake of finding there a supposedly more sympathetic forum or a more congenial base. The expression 'rights of custody' when used in the Convention therefore needs to be construed in the sense that will best accord with that objective. In most cases, that will involve giving the term the widest sense possible.

There is no difficulty about giving a broad connotation to the word 'custody'. . . .

*Notes*

1.   'Rights of custody' for the purposes of art. 3 may include *de facto* (i.e. factual) rights of custody, not just legal rights of custody, for in *Re B* the Court of Appeal by a majority distinguished *Re J (A Minor) (Abduction: Custody Rights)* (see 12.3.2) and held that an unmarried father with no legal rights of custody under Australian law had *de facto* rights of custody because he had cared for the child. Peter Gibson LJ, however, dissented, holding that the father had no rights of custody in the Convention sense at the time of the child's removal so that there was no wrongful removal. Neither was there wrongful retention. His Lordship held that the case was indistinguishable from *Re J*.

2.   Where a child is a ward of court, the child's removal may be wrongful as it is a breach of the High Court's 'right of custody' (*Re J (A Minor) (Abduction)* [1992] 1 FLR 276, FD).

*Questions*

1   Could 'rights of custody' be extended to a child-minder, or a foster-parent or any other person caring for a child?

2.   Was *Re J (A Minor) (Abduction: Custody Rights)*, at 12.3.2, correctly decided?

### 12.3.4   Return of children

## THE HAGUE CONVENTION ON THE CIVIL ASPECTS OF INTERNATIONAL CHILD ABDUCTION 1980

**Article 10**

The Central Authority of the State where the child is shall take or cause to be taken all appropriate measures in order to obtain the voluntary return of the child.

**Article 11**

The judicial or administrative authorities of Contracting States shall act expeditiously in proceedings for the return of children.

. . .

**Article 12**

Where a child has been wrongfully removed or retained in terms of Article 3 and, at the date of the commencement of the proceedings before the judicial or administrative authority of the Contracting State where the child is, a period of less than one year has elapsed from the date of the wrongful removal or retention, the authority concerned shall order the return of the child forthwith.

The judicial or administrative authority, even where the proceedings have been commenced after the expiration of the period of one year referred to in the preceding paragraph, shall also order the return of the child, unless it is demonstrated that the child is now settled in its new environment. . . .

### 12.3.5  'Defences' under the Convention

## THE HAGUE CONVENTION ON THE CIVIL ASPECTS
## OF INTERNATIONAL CHILD ABDUCTION 1980

**Article 13**

Notwithstanding the provisions of [Article 12], the judicial or administrative authority of the requested State is not bound to order the return of the child if the person, institution or other body which opposes its return establishes that—

(a)  the person, institution or other body having the care of the person of the child was not actually exercising the custody rights at the time of removal or retention, or had consented to or subsequently acquiesced in the removal or retention; or

(b)  there is a grave risk that his or her return would expose the child to physical or psychological harm or otherwise place the child in an intolerable situation.

The judicial or administrative authority may also refuse to order the return of the child if it finds that the child objects to being returned and has attained an age and degree of maturity at which it is appropriate to take account of its views.

In considering the circumstances referred to in this Article, the judicial and administrative authorities shall take into account the information relating to the social background of the child provided by the Central Authority or other competent authority of the child's habitual residence.

### 12.3.5.1 Acquiescence

### *In Re A (Minors) (Abduction: Custody Rights)*
[1992] Fam 106
Court of Appeal

*Facts*: After divorce, the mother (unbeknown to the father) removed their two sons aged 7 and 5 from Australia to England. Shortly afterwards the father wrote to her expressing his sorrow at what she had done and explaining that although she had acted illegally, he loved the boys too much to fight for their return. His letter said: 'I think you know what you have done is illegal, but I am not going to fight it. I am going to sacrifice myself rather than them.' On the same day, however, he began proceedings under the Hague Convention. It was conceded before the judge in the High Court in England that the removal had been wrongful under art. 3, but the wife argued that the father had acquiesced in the children's removal under art. 13(a) and that there was a grave risk that the children's return would place them in an intolerable situation under art. 13(b). The judge found that the father had not acquiesced and there was no grave risk, and ordered the children's return forthwith under art. 12. The mother appealed.

*Held*: allowing the appeal (Balcombe LJ dissenting), that the father had acquiesced in the children's removal.

LORD DONALDSON MR: I have had the advantage of reading the judgment of Balcombe LJ and agree with it in all respects save one. This is whether on the facts of this case the father, being one of the persons 'having the care of the person of the child . . . subsequently acquiesced in the removal . . .' within the meaning of the Convention. I have no doubt that he did.

Let me say at once that I unreservedly accept the vital importance of protecting children from the harmful effects of their being wrongfully removed from their country of habitual residence, usually clandestinely and often in circumstances calculated to cause them harm. This is the mischief which the Act and the Convention, which is scheduled to the Act, set out to address. They do so by providing for *automatic* return in accordance with article 12 if the issue arises within 12 months of the wrongful removal or retention and, also later, in that case subject to it not having been demonstrated that the child is by then settled in its new environment.

All this demonstrates the agreed international response to a wrongful removal. The child must go back and the status quo ante be restored without further ado. That said, the Convention does itself enter a caveat which is contained in article 13. Before I consider whether it applies in this case, it is I think important to emphasise what is the consequence if it does apply. It is *not* that the court will refuse to order the return of the child to its country or jurisdiction of habitual residence. It is *not* that the court will assume a wardship or similar jurisdiction over the child and consider what order should be made as if the child had never been wrongfully removed or retained. The consequence is only that the court is no longer *bound* to order the return of the child, but has a judicial discretion whether or not to do so, that discretion being exercised in the context of the approach of the Convention.

In the comparatively rare case in which such a judicial discretion falls to be exercised, there will be two distinct and wholly different issues confronting the court. (1) In all the circumstances is it more appropriate that a court of the country to which the child has been wrongfully removed or in which it is being wrongfully retained (country B) should reach decisions and make orders with a view to its welfare or is it more appropriate that this should be done by a court of the country from which it was removed or to which its return has been wrongfully prevented (country A)? (2) If, but only if, the answer to the first question is that the court of country B is the more appropriate court, should that court give any consideration whatsoever to what further orders should be made other than for the immediate return of the child to country A and for ensuring its welfare pending the resumption or assumption of jurisdiction by the courts of that country?

In considering the first issue, the court of country B should approach the matter by giving the fullest force to the policy which clearly underlies the Convention and the Act, namely that wrongful removal or retention shall not confer any benefit or advantage on the person (usually a parent) who has committed the wrongful act. It is only if the interests of the child render it appropriate that the courts of country B rather than country A shall determine its future that there can be any exception to an order for its return. This is something quite different from a consideration of whether the best interests of the child will be served by its living in country B rather than country A. That is not the issue unless paragraph (b) of article 13 applies. The issue is whether decisions in the best interests of the child shall be taken by one court rather than another. If, as usually should be the case, the courts of country B decide to return the child to the jurisdiction of the courts of country A, the latter courts will be in no way inhibited from giving permission for the child to return to country B or indeed becoming settled there and so subject to the jurisdiction of the courts of that country. But that will be a matter for the courts of country A.

I now turn to the point upon which I disagree with Balcombe LJ The issue is whether the father 'consented to or acquiesced in' the wrongful removal of the children. Each case must be considered on its own special facts and the facts of this case are certainly unusual.

In context the difference between 'consent' and 'acquiescence' is simply one of timing. Consent, if it occurs, precedes the wrongful taking or retention. Acquiescence, if it occurs, follows it. In each case it may be expressed or it may be inferred from conduct, including inaction, in circumstances in which different conduct is to be expected if there were no consent or, as the case may be, acquiescence. Any consent or acquiescence must, of course, be real. Thus a person cannot acquiesce in a wrongful act if he does not know of the act or does not know that it is wrongful. It is only in this context and in the context of a case in which it is said that the consent or acquiescence is to be inferred from conduct which is not to be expected in the absence of such consent or acquiescence, that the knowledge of the allegedly consenting or acquiescing party is relevant and, to use the words of Thorpe J, 'the whole conduct and reaction of the husband must be investigated in the round.' Such considerations do not arise in this case because the father's letter of 23 September 1991 is incapable of any construction other than a clearly expressed acquiescence and, unlike *In re A (Minors: Abduction)* [1991] 2 FLR 241, was so construed and believed by the mother. In agreement with Thorpe J, I consider it clear that this was not affected by anything said in the telephone conversation of 24 September 1991. The father cannot be heard to say that he had an intention not to acquiesce which he kept secret from the mother, any more than in other circumstances it would be open to the mother to say, and perhaps to prove, that the father had at one time had an intention to acquiesce which was kept secret from her. On the evidence I think that we are bound to hold that the father acquiesced by writing the letter of 23 September 1991.

The question has been raised of whether an acquiescence can be withdrawn. I think that it cannot, in the sense that once there is acquiescence the condition set out in article 13 is satisfied. On the other hand an apparent acquiescence followed immediately by a withdrawal may lead the court to question whether the apparent acquiescence was real or whether it was the product of emotional turmoil which could not reasonably be interpreted as real acquiescence. That apart, the only relevance of the time which elapses between acquiescence and a purported withdrawal of the acquiescence is in the context of the exercise of a discretion whether to return the child to the jurisdiction of the courts of country A in order to enable those courts to make decisions as to its future. In this case this period lasted from 27 September until 6 December 1991 when the proceedings were served upon the mother.

I would set aside the order of Thorpe J and remit the case to the High Court for a consideration, under the discretion which arises under article 13 of the Convention, of whether the children should or should not be returned to the jurisdiction of the Australian courts. It is only if he decides not to do so, that he will be called upon to consider how to exercise a wardship jurisdiction.

**STUART-SMITH LJ:** Under the provisions of article 12 of the Hague Convention on the Civil Aspects of International Child Abduction, which has force of law in the United Kingdom by virtue of section 1(2) of the Child Abduction and Custody Act 1985, where a child has been wrongfully removed or retained the court of the state to which it has been removed must order its return, if the application is made within a year of the removal or retention. Article 13 provides two exceptions to this rule which, if satisfied, afford a discretion to the court to consider whether or not the child shall be returned. The first exception, so far as it relates to this case is where the father 'had consented to or subsequently acquiesced in the removal or retention.' The reference to consent appears to mean consent prior to the removal or retention and is not relevant here. The question is whether he subsequently acquiesced. Acquiescence means acceptance and it may be either active or passive.

If it is active it may be signified by express words of consent or by conduct which is inconsistent with an intention of the party to insist on his rights and consistent only with an acceptance of the status quo. If it is passive it will result from silence and inactivity in circumstances in which the aggrieved party may reasonably be expected to act. It will depend on the circumstances in each case how long a period will elapse before the court will infer from such inactivity whether the aggrieved party had accepted or acquiesced in the removal or retention.

A party cannot be said to acquiesce unless he is aware, at least in general terms, of his rights against the other parent. It is not necessary that he should know the full or precise nature of his legal rights under the Convention: but he must be aware that the other parent's act in removing or retaining the child is unlawful. And if he is aware of the factual situation giving rise to those rights, the court will no doubt readily infer that he was aware of his legal rights, either if he could reasonably be expected to have known of them or taken steps to obtain legal advice.

If the acceptance is active it must be in clear and unequivocal words or conduct and the other party must believe that there has been an acceptance. This distinguishes this case from *In re A (Minors: Abduction)* [1991] 2 FLR 241 where the husband's language and behaviour was ambivalent and the wife did not believe that the father was agreeing to what she had done. . . .

BALCOMBE LJ (dissenting): . . . The principal issue in this appeal is whether the father, by his letter of 23 September 1991 or otherwise, acquiesced in the mother's removal of the children within the meaning of article 13(a) of the Convention on the Civil Aspects of International Child Abduction. . . .

[After citing the Preamble and arts 1, 3, 12 and 13 of the Convention, his Lordship continued: . . .]

It will be seen that the scheme of the Convention is that, where a child has been wrongfully removed or retained under article 3, then, where the proceedings to recover the child are commenced within a period of less than one year from the date of the wrongful removal or retention, the court of the country to which the child has been taken is under an obligation — there is no discretion — to order the immediate return of the child. However, if consent to — which in the context must mean prior consent — or subsequent acquiescence in the removal or retention of the child by the other parent is established, then, as it was put in argument, the door is unlocked and the court is not then bound to order the return of the child but has a discretion whether or not to do so. The scheme of the Convention is thus clearly that in normal circumstances it is considered to be in the best interests of children generally that they should be promptly returned to the country whence they have been wrongfully removed, and that it is only in exceptional cases that the court should have a discretion to refuse to order an immediate return. It is in that context that I turn to consider the meaning of 'acquiesced' in article 13(a).

The relevant meaning of 'acquiesce' in the *Oxford English Dictionary*, 2nd ed. (1989) is 'To agree tacitly to, concur in; to accept (the conclusions or arrangements of others).' The corresponding meaning of 'acquiescence' is 'Silent or passive assent to, or compliance with, proposals or measures.' Since French and English are both official languages of the Convention, we were referred also to the French version of article 13(a) where the relevant words are: 'Ou avait consenti ou a acquiescé postérieurement' and to a French dictionary definition of 'acquiescer' where the relevant meaning is: 'B. Dans un cont. de nature jur. Donner une adhésion tacite ou expresse à un acte.' We were also referred to a judgment of Deane J in the High Court of Australia in *Orr v Ford* (1989) 167 CLR 316, where, at pp. 337–338, he gave a comprehensive dissertation on the various meanings which 'acquiescence' can have at common law. Since we are here concerned with the meaning of 'acquiesced' in an international convention to which many countries, not only those with a common law background, have adhered, it cannot be right to attempt to construe 'acquiesced' by reference only to its possible meaning at common law or equity. Nevertheless Deane J's first definition, at p. 337, appears to me to have general force:

> Strictly used, acquiescence indicates the contemporaneous and informed ('knowing') acceptance or standing by which is treated by equity as 'assent' (i.e. consent) to what would otherwise be an infringement of rights.

It was common ground before us that acquiescence can be inferred from inactivity and silence on the part of the parent from whose custody, joint or single, the child has been wrongfully removed. In such a case it is in my judgment inevitable that the court would have to look at all the circumstances of the case, and in particular the reasons for the inactivity on the part of the wronged parent and the length of the period over which the inactivity persisted, in order to decide whether it was legitimate to infer acquiescence on his or her part.

However, where as here, it is said that the father's acquiescence was expressed to the mother by the letter of 23 September 1991, it is argued that this was a once for all event and it is impermissible to consider subsequent events, or what was in the mind of the father at the time that he wrote the letter or thereafter. Indeed the argument goes so far as to say that, if the mother had received a letter by the following post making it clear that the father had retracted what he said in his letter of 23 September, and was going to use every legitimate step open to him to have the children returned to Australia, nevertheless he had 'acquiesced' in their wrongful removal, and that the door had been unlocked, so as to give the court discretion whether or not to order the return of the children.

In my judgment this is to give 'acquiesced' far too technical a meaning for the context in which it is used. As I have already said, the main object of the Hague Convention is to require the immediate and automatic return to the state of their habitual residence of children who have been wrongfully removed. To this there are a limited number of exceptions, but it is apparent that the purpose of the exceptions is to preclude the automatic return of the children to the country whence they were removed, only if it can be shown or inferred that this could result in unnecessary harm or distress to the children. In other words, it is to the interests of the children that the exceptions are directed, not (except in so far as these directly affect the interests of the children) the interests of the parents or either of them. In my judgment this requires the court to look at all the circumstances which may be relevant and not, as is here submitted, to the terms of a single letter.

Added force is given to this view by the English and French dictionary definitions of 'acquiesce' which I have quoted above. 'Accept' and 'adhesion' to my mind connote a state of affairs which persists over a period. 'Acquiesce' is not, in my judgment, apt to refer to a single expression of agreement taken in isolation from all surrounding circumstances.

. . .

For these reasons I would uphold the decision of Thorpe J and dismiss this appeal. However, as the other two members of the court take a different view, the appeal will be allowed and the case remitted to the High Court for the exercise of the discretion under article 13(a). It is highly desirable that this should be done without delay. If the boys are to go back to Australia, then the sooner the better.

. . .

*Notes and question*
Wall J in *Re K (Abduction: Child's Objections)* [1995] 1 FLR 977 at p. 985, described Stuart-Smith LJ's judgment, *supra*, as the '*locus classicus*' for the

definition of 'acquiescence'. Whose judgment do you prefer in *In Re A (Minors) (Abduction: Custody Rights)* above?

### Re S (Minors) (Abduction: Acquiescence)
### [1994] 1 FLR 819
### Court of Appeal

*Facts*: The parents were British-born immigrants to Australia. Following the breakdown of their marriage, the mother removed their three children, aged 9, 8 and 4, to England wrongfully under art. 3 of the Hague Convention. Eight months later the father applied for a summary return order under art. 12. The mother resisted the order under art. 13(a) on the ground that the father by delaying in bringing proceedings had acquiesced in the children's removal. The judge held that the father had not acquiesced as he had received wrong legal advice, and accordingly held that he had no jurisdiction to refuse a return order. The mother appealed, contending that the judge had used the wrong test of acquiescence.

*Held*: dismissing her appeal, that the judge had applied the right test of acquiescence and there was no reason to interfere with his decision.

WAITE LJ: . . . Acquiescence is primarily to be established by inference drawn from an objective survey of the acts and omissions of the aggrieved parent. This does not mean, however, that any element of subjective analysis is wholly excluded. It is permissible, for example, to inquire into the state of the aggrieved parent's knowledge of his or her rights under the Convention; and the undisputed requirement that the issue must be considered 'in all the circumstances' necessarily means that there will be occasions when the court will need to examine private motives and other influences affecting the aggrieved parent which are relevant to the issue of acquiescence but are known to the aggrieved parent alone. Care must be taken by the court, however, not to give undue emphasis to these subjective elements: they remain an inherently less reliable guide than inferences drawn from overt acts and omissions viewed through the eyes of an outside observer. Provided that such care is taken, it remains within the province of the judges to examine the subjective forces at work on the mind of the aggrieved parent and give them such weight as the judge considers necessary in reaching the overall conclusion in the totality of the circumstances that is required of the court in answering the central question: has the aggrieved parent conducted himself in a way that is inconsistent with his later seeking a summary return?
. . .

HOFFMANN LJ: . . . The term 'acquiescence' is used in different languages in an international convention. It cannot be construed according to any technical doctrines of English law. The general idea is easy enough to follow. It reflects a very general principle of fairness which must exist in every system of law; that a party should not be allowed to 'blow hot and cold' or in Scottish terminology, 'approbate and reprobate'. But the cases show that this deceptively simple concept may not be all that easy to apply in practice.

In my judgment the reason for the difficulty is that 'acquiescence' in the Convention was not intended to mean something capable of being defined by a single set of necessary and sufficient conditions which must be present in every case. Common sense suggests that acquiescence may take different forms and that something which forms an essential part of acquiescence in one form may not be necessary for acquiescence in another form. In my view the word denotes a cluster of related concepts rather than a single one.

. . . As Butler-Sloss LJ put it in *Re AZ (A Minor) (Abduction: Acquiescence)* [1993] 1 FLR 682 at p. 687:

> Acquiescence has to be conduct inconsistent with the summary return of the child to the place of habitual residence. It does not have to be a long-term acceptance of the existing state of affairs.

. . .

As I have already indicated, I reject the submission that acquiescence is a single concept. I accept that the labels 'active' and 'passive' may one day have to be reconsidered in a case in which, in the light of something which has gone before, an omission is on the facts a plain and unequivocal choice not to pursue the Convention remedy. It may also be that some future case will show that two categories are not sufficient. But for the purposes of the present case they serve well enough.

I think that where the conduct relied upon is inactivity, it would be unjust not to take into account the reasons, whether they were known to the other party or not. Suppose, for example, that shortly after the abduction the applicant suffers an incapacitating illness of which the abductor knows nothing. I do not accept that his resulting inaction could fairly be described as acquiescence. Equally, I do not think that a party can be said to have acquiesced by doing nothing if he reasonably thought, on the basis of the advice he had been given, that there was in practice nothing which he could do. I do not think that this amounts, as [counsel] contended that the judge had done, to examining whether the applicant had subjectively acquiesced. If a person knowing all the objective facts and looking at the matter in the round would infer from the applicant's inactivity that he had acquiesced, it does not matter that he had actually intended all the time to pursue the summary remedy. But the advice which the applicant received and his knowledge of his rights are objective facts and I think that the judge was entitled to take them into account. It follows that he did not misdirect himself and his conclusion that there was no acquiescence cannot in my judgment be disturbed.

I therefore agree that the appeal should be dismissed.

NEILL LJ: . . . From the wording of Art 13 and from the authorities to which Waite LJ has referred it is plain:

(1)   that as the words 'subsequently acquiesced in' appear in an international convention one cannot have regard to any technical rules of English domestic law or to any special meanings which may be given to 'acquiescence' when, for example, principles of equity are applied in English courts;

(2)   that it is legitimate to have regard to other official languages of the Convention, if to do so is of assistance;

(3)   that as the words 'subsequently acquiesced in' follow the words 'consented to' acquiescence includes, though it is not limited to, consent given after the time of removal or retention. As Lord Donaldson MR put the matter in *Re A (Minors) (Abduction: Custody Rights)* [1992] Fam 106 at p. 123C, sub nom *Re A (Minors) (Abduction: Acquiescence)* [1992] 2 FLR 14 at p. 29E: 'Consent, if it occurs, precedes the wrongful taking or retention. Acquiescence, if it occurs, follows it . . .';

(4)   that it is for the party opposing the child's return to establish that the other party had consented to or subsequently acquiesced in the removal or retention.

It follows therefore that though in other contexts the word 'acquiescence' may suggest approval which is silent or tacit rather than expressed, in the Convention the phrase 'acquiesced in' includes both conduct which involves the taking of active steps as well as conduct which amounts to complete inactivity. The conduct to be examined may cover a wide spectrum. Accordingly, provided the terms 'active acquiescence' and 'passive acquiescence' are not allowed to become rigid categories or substituted for the general term 'acquiesced' in the Convention I see no objection to their use. Indeed they are of value as demonstrating that acquiescence may take a number of different forms.

Where the parent opposing the return raises the issue of consent or acquiescence the court will scrutinise the conduct of the applicant to see whether that conduct is consistent with the claim for a summary order. The court will look at all the circumstances.

. . .

The conduct of the applicant must be looked at objectively. However, with one exception to which I shall come later, the court should admit evidence to explain conduct which otherwise might indicate acquiescence. Thus, for example, a long period of silence or a failure to reply to a communication from the other parent where an answer would be expected may be capable of explanation. The applicant might have been ill or in some other way disabled from taking any action.

It was strongly argued on behalf of the mother that it was necessary to look at the conduct of the applicant parent through the eyes of someone in the position of the other parent. As I understand the Convention, however, the court is primarily concerned, not with the question of the other parent's perception of the applicant's conduct, but with the question whether the applicant acquiesced in fact. It is to be remembered that the jurisdiction of the requested State is based on the premise that the original removal or retention of the child was wrongful. The proof of consent or acquiescence does not extinguish the jurisdiction to order the return of the child; it merely debars the applicant from obtaining a summary order under Art. 12 as of right. It follows therefore that the court should make its own assessment of the applicant's conduct, and the impact of that conduct on the wrongdoer is of relevance only to the extent that the wrongdoer cannot establish that the applicant acquiesced if he or she did not believe that the applicant had done so: see *Re A and Another (Minors: Abduction)* [1991] 2 FLR 241 at p. 249 *per* Fox LJ: *Re A (Minors) (Abduction: Custody Rights)* [1992] Fam 106 at p. 120B, sub nom *Re A (Minors) (Abduction: Acquiescence)* [1992] 2 FLR 14 at p. 26D *per* Stuart-Smith LJ.

It is also clear, however, that where the applicant has made some unambiguous communication to the other parent which, looked at objectively, constitutes acquiescence in the removal or retention the applicant is not allowed to withdraw that communication or to rely on some unexpressed reservation. Thus in *Re A (Minors) (Abduction: Custody Rights)* the majority of the Court of Appeal held that once there is acquiescence then, in the words of Lord Donaldson at p. 123G, 'the condition set out in Art. 13 is satisfied'. But the reason why the applicant is not entitled to withdraw or add some explanation is because, looked at objectively, the communication is unequivocal and is sufficient and conclusive evidence of acquiescence.

I turn to the facts of the present case. I am satisfied that looking at the judgment of Singer J as a whole he applied the right test to the facts before him. I can see no sufficient reason to interfere with his decision. Accordingly I too would dismiss the appeal.

## Re AZ (A Minor) (Abduction: Acquiescence)
[1993] 1 FLR 682
Court of Appeal

SIR DONALD NICHOLLS V-C: . . . I add only a brief comment on the concept of acquiescence in the removal or retention of a child. The context is an exception to the general Convention rule of summary and speedy return of a child who has been wrongfully removed to or retained in another contracting State. If the person who had care of the child consented to the removal or retention he cannot afterwards, when he changes his mind, seek an order for the summary return of the child pursuant to the Convention. Likewise if he acquiesces. It seems to me that the underlying objectives of the Convention require courts to be slow to infer acquiescence from conduct which is consistent with the parent whose child has been wrongly removed or retained perforce accepting, as a temporary emergency expedient only, a situation forced on him and which in practical terms he is unable to change at once. The Convention is concerned with children taken from one country to another. The Convention has to be interpreted and applied having regard to the way responsible parents can be expected to behave. A parent whose child is wrongly removed to, or retained in, another country is not to be taken as having lost the benefits the Convention confers by reason of him accepting that the child should stay where he or she is for a matter of days or a week or two. That is one edge of the spectrum.

At the other edge of the spectrum the parent may, again through force of his circumstances, accept that the child should stay where he or she is for an indefinite period, likely to be many months or longer. There is here a question of degree. In answering that question the court will look at all the circumstances and consider whether the parent has conducted himself in a way that would be inconsistent with him later seeking a summary order for the child's return. That is the concept underlying consent and acquiescence in Art. 13. That is the touchstone to be applied.

I am not able to accept that, in applying this test, there cannot be acquiescence unless the parent knew, at least in general terms, of his rights under the Convention. Whether he knew or not is one of the circumstances to be taken into account. The weight or importance to be attached to that circumstance will depend on all the other circumstances of the particular case.

. . .

*Notes*

1.   If the court is satisfied that there is acquiescence, it must then exercise its discretion to decide whether to return the child, taking into account the child's welfare and all the circumstances of the case (see *Re A (Minors) (Abduction: Acquiescence) (No. 2)* [1993] 1 All ER 272, CA).

2.   For other cases on acquiescences, see, e.g., *Re R (Child Abduction)* [1995] 1 FLR 725, CA; *W v W (Child Abduction: Acquiescence)* [1993] 2 FLR, FD; and *Re R (Child Abduction: Acquiescence)* [1995] 1 FLR 716, CA.

### 12.3.5.2   Grave risk of physical or psychological harm etc.

The burden of establishing a defence under art. 13(b), as under art. 13(a), is a heavy one for a parent to discharge. A high degree of intolerability must be established in order to bring into operation art. 13(b) (see Balcombe LJ in *Re A (Minors) (Abduction: Acquiescence)* [1993] Fam 106, [1992] 2 FLR 14, CA, and Sir Stephen Brown P in *B v B (Abduction)* [1993] 1 FLR 238, CA).

## Re C (A Minor) (Abduction)
[1989] 1 FLR 403
Court of Appeal

*Facts*: The child, aged 4, was taken from Australia to England by the mother despite a consent order having been made on marriage breakdown that neither parent would remove the child from Australia without the consent of the other. The father brought proceedings in the English High Court under the Hague Convention for the child's return. The mother argued that there was no wrongful retention or removal; but even if there were, there was a grave risk that the child's return would expose him to psychological harm under art. 13(b). She argued that as she would not accompany the child back to Australia, she would herself be creating the risk of harm under art. 13. The judge dismissed the application. The father appealed.

*Held*: allowing the appeal and ordering the child's return, that there was wrongful removal but art. 13 did not apply as, if the mother's argument were to succeed, it would defeat the purpose of the Convention and be contrary to international relations.

BUTLER-SLOSS LJ: . . . The grave risk of harm arises not from the return of the child, but the refusal of the mother to accompany him. The Convention does not require the court in this country to consider the welfare of the child as paramount, but only to be satisfied as to the grave risk of harm. I am not satisfied that the child would be placed in an intolerable situation if the mother refused to go back. In weighing up the various factors I must place in the balance and as of the greatest importance the effect of the court refusing the application under the Convention because of the refusal of the mother to return for her own reasons, not for the sake of the child. Is a parent to create the psychological situation and then rely on it? If the grave risk of psychological harm to a child is to be inflicted by the conduct of the parent who abducted him, then it would be relied upon by every mother of a young child who removed him out of the jurisdiction and refused to return. It would drive a coach and four through the Convention, at least in respect of applications relating to young children. I, for my part, cannot believe that this is in the interests of international relations. Nor should the mother, by her own actions, succeed in preventing the return of a child who should be living in his own country and deny him contact with his other parent. . . .

LORD DONALDSON MR: . . . We have also had to consider art. 13, with its reference to 'psychological harm'. I would only add that in a situation in which it is necessary to consider operating the machinery of the Convention, some psychological harm to the child is inherent, whether the child is or is not returned. This is, I think, recognized by the words 'or otherwise place the child in an intolerable situation' which cast considerable light on the severe degree of psychological harm which the Convention has in mind. It will be the concern of the court of the State to which the child is to be returned to minimize or eliminate this harm and, in the absence of compelling evidence to the contrary or evidence that it is beyond the powers of those courts in the circumstances of the case, the courts of this country should assume that this will be done. Save in an exceptional case, our concern, i.e. the concern of these courts, should be limited to giving the child the maximum possible protection until the courts of the other country, Australia in this case, can resume their normal role in relation to the child.

. . .

*Note*

A grave risk that return would expose the child to physical or psychological harm was established in *Re F (Child Abduction: Risk if Returned)* [1995] 2 FLR 31, CA. See also *B v B (Abduction)* [1993] 1 FLR 238, CA; *Re L (Child Abduction) (Psychological Harm)* [1993] 2 FLR 401, FD; *Re G (Abduction: Psychological Harm)* [1995] 1 FLR 64, FD; *N v N (Abduction: Article 13 Defence)* [1995] 1 FLR 107, FD and *Re M (A Minor) (Child Abduction)* [1994] 1 FLR 390, CA, disapproving *B v K (Child Abduction)*, [1992] 2 FCR 606, [1993] Fam Law 17.

### 12.3.5.3 Child objects to being returned

The court may refuse to order the child's return if he or she objects to being returned and has attained an age and degree of maturity at which it is appropriate to take account of the child's views (art. 13(b)).

### *In Re S (A Minor) (Abduction: Custody Rights)*
#### [1993] Fam 242
#### Court of Appeal

*Facts*: On her parents' divorce the child, a girl aged 10 with a severe stammer and associated behavioural problems, was taken from France to England by her English mother who alleged that she feared violence from the father. She later added the additional reason of the child's speech problem. In England the child's stammer and behaviour problems disappeared. The father applied under the Hague Convention for the child's return. The mother accepted that she had removed the child wrongfully, but argued under art. 13 that (i) there was a grave risk that the child's return would expose her to physical or psychological harm, and (ii) the child objected to being returned and had reached the age and degree of maturity at which it was appropriate to take account of her views. The judge refused to make the order sought on the basis of ground (ii). The father appealed.

*Held*: dismissing the father's appeal and refusing the application for return, that the child had attained an age and degree of maturity at which it was appropriate to take account of her views. There was no ground for interfering with the trial judge's finding that there were exceptional circumstances which warranted a refusal to return the child to France.

BALCOMBE LJ: [After citing art. 13, Balcombe LJ continued: . . . ]

*The construction of article 13*

It will be seen that the part of article 13 which relates to the child's objections to being returned is completely separate from paragraph (b), and we can see no reason to interpret this part of the article, as we were invited to do by [counsel], as importing a requirement to establish a grave risk that the return of the child would expose her to psychological harm, or otherwise place her in an intolerable situation. Further, there is no warrant for importing such a gloss on the words of article 13, as did Bracewell J in *In re R (A Minor: Abduction)* [1992] 1 FLR 105, 107–108:

> The wording of the article is so phrased that I am satisfied that before the court can consider exercising discretion, there must be more than a mere preference expressed by the child. The word 'objects' imports a strength of feeling which goes far beyond the usual ascertainment of the wishes of the child in a custody dispute.

Unfortunately Bracewell J was not referred to the earlier decision of Sir Stephen Brown P in *In re M (Minors)* (unreported), 25 July 1990, in which he rightly considered this part of article 13 by reference to its literal words and without giving them any such additional gloss, as did Bracewell J in *In re R*.

As was also made clear by Sir Stephen Brown P in *In re M*, the return to which the child objects is that which would otherwise be ordered under article 12, viz., an immediate return to the country from which it was wrongfully removed, so that the courts of that country may resolve the merits of any dispute as to where and with whom it should live see, in particular, article 19. There is nothing in the provisions of article 13 to make it appropriate to consider whether the child objects to returning in any circumstances. Thus, to take the circumstances of the present case, it may be that S would not object to returning to France for staying access with her father if it were established that her home and schooling are in England, but that would not be the return which would be ordered under article 12.

*The establishment of the facts necessary to 'open the door' under article 13*

The questions whether: (i) a child objects to being returned; and (ii) has attained an age and degree of maturity at which it is appropriate to take account of its views, are questions of fact which are peculiarly within the province of the trial judge. [Counsel] submitted that the child's views should not be sought either by the court welfare officer or the judge, until the evidence of the parents has been completed. We know of no justification for this submission. She also asked us to lay down guidelines for the procedure to be adopted in ascertaining the child's views and degree of maturity. We do not think it is desirable that we should do so. These cases under the Hague Convention come before the very experienced judges of the Family Division, and they can be relied on, in those cases where it may be necessary to ascertain these facts, to devise an appropriate procedure, always bearing in mind that the Hague Convention is primarily designed to secure a speedy return of the child to the country from which it has been abducted.

It will usually be necessary for the judge to find out why the child objects to being returned. If the only reason is because it wants to remain with the abducting parent, who is also asserting that he or she is unwilling to return, then this will be a highly relevant factor when the judge comes to consider the exercise of discretion.

Article 13 does not seek to lay down any age below which a child is to be considered as not having attained sufficient maturity for its views to be taken into account. Nor should we. In this connection it is material to note that article 12 of the United Nations Convention on the Rights of the Child 1989 (Treaty Series No. 44 of 1992 (Cm. 1976)), which has been ratified by both France and the United Kingdom and had come into force in both countries before Ewbank J's judgement, provides:

> 1. States parties shall assure to the child who is capable of forming his or her own views the right to express those views freely in all matters affecting the child, the

views of the child being given due weight in accordance with the age and maturity of the child. 2. For this purpose, the child shall in particular be provided the opportunity to be heard in any judicial and adminstrative proceedings affecting the child, either directly, or through a representative or an appropriate body, in a manner consistent with the procedural rules of national law.

In our judgment, no criticism can be made of the decision by Ewbank J to ascertain S's views, nor of the procedure which he adopted for that purpose. There was evidence which entitled him to find that S objected to being returned to France and that she had attained an age and degree of maturity at which it was appropriate to take account of her views. Those are findings with which this court should not interfere.

*The exercise of the discretion under article 13*

The scheme of the Hague Convention is that in normal circumstances it is considered to be in the best interests of children generally that they should be promptly returned to the country whence they have been wrongfully removed, and that it is only in exceptional cases that the court should have a discretion to refuse to order an immediate return. That discretion must be exercised in the context of the approach of the Hague Convention: see *In re A (Minors) (Abduction: Custody Rights)* [1992] Fam. 106, 122E *per* Lord Donaldson of Lymington MR.

Thus, if the court should come to the conclusion that the child's views have been influenced by some other person, for example the abducting parent, or that the objection to return is because of a wish to remain with the abducting parent, then it is probable that little or no weight will be given to those views. Any other approach would be to drive a coach and horses through the primary scheme of the Hague Convention. Thus in *Layfield* v *Layfield* (unreported), 6 December 1991, in the Family Court of Australia, Bell J ordered an 11-year-old girl to be returned to the United Kingdom because he found that, although she was of an age and degree of maturity for her wishes to be taken into account, he believed that those wishes were not to remain in Australia per se, but to remain with her mother who had wrongfully removed the girl from the United Kingdom to Australia. On the other hand, where the court finds that the child or children have valid reasons for their objections to being returned, then it may refuse to order the return.

Thus in *In re M (Minors)*, 25 July 1990, the court refused to order the return of three children aged 11, 9 and 8 to America. In the course of his judgment Sir Stephen Brown P said:

I am, however, concerned for the children. I find that they do object to being returned and that each of them has attained an age and a degree of maturity at which it is appropriate to take account of their views. I feel that I must take account of their views. Their views are not however determinative of the position and I have to consider how far they should affect me. I feel that I should give effect to their objection in this case in the light of the fact that they give valid reasons, in my judgment, for objecting to going back to America into the care of their father, because of his former conduct. I consider that he has materially admitted this. I do not therefore propose to order their return. That is the sole extent of the order that I make. I do not determine custody rights or access rights or any other rights as between the parties. But in the light of the children's objections to being returned, I decline to order their return under the terms of the Hague Convention and the provisions of the Child Abduction and Custody Act 1985.

A similar result was reached in *Wilson* v *Challis* (unreported), 19 March 1992, where Judge Foran, sitting in the Ontario Court (Provincial Division) (East Region) and following the decision in *In re M,* refused to order the return of an 11-year-old boy to his father in England for what appeared to be good and valid reasons.

In the present case S objected strongly to being returned to France. Her reasons had substance and were not merely a desire to remain in England with her mother. This court cannot interfere with the judge's exercise of his discretion unless he took into account some irrelevant factor, left out of account some relevant factor or was plainly wrong: see *G* v *G (Minors: Custody Appeal)* [1985] 1 WLR 647. It could not seriously be suggested that Ewbank J took into account any irrelevant factor. . . . In these circumstances we are quite unable to say that his decision not to return S to France, even having regard to the father's undertakings, was plainly wrong.

Nothing which we have said in this judgment should detract from the view, which has frequently been expressed and which we repeat, that it is only in exceptional cases under the Hague Convention that the court should refuse to order the immediate return of a child who has been wrongfully removed. This is an exceptional case and accordingly we dismiss this appeal.

Similar observations are found in the judgment of Waite J, as he then was, in *P* v *P (Minors) (Child Abduction)* [1992] 1 FLR 155, at p. 161:

. . . The whole jurisdiction under the Convention is, by its nature and purpose, peremptory. Its underlying assumption is that the courts of all its signatory countries are equally capable of ensuring a fair hearing to the parties, and a skilled and humane evaluation of the issues of child welfare involved. Its underlying purpose is to ensure stability for children, by putting a brisk end to the efforts of parents to have their children's future decided where they want and when they want, by removing them from their country of residence to another jurisdiction chosen arbitrarily by the absconding parent.

It would be contrary to that underlying assumption and purpose to give the Convention an interpretation which allowed the absconding parent to insist, as of right, that the Convention's mandatory procedures for a child's return should be suspended while detailed investigation was made into the child's views, the terms and circumstances in which, and the persons to whom, they had been expressed, and — perhaps in borderline cases — the medical and psychological factors involved in gauging the child's degrees of maturity. Of course, there may be instances in which precisely such an investigation will be found necessary, but I suspect they will be rare. When they do arise, it will be because the judge, exercising his discretion in exceptional circumstances, thinks that such an investigation is necessary, and not because one or other parent has exercised any supposed right to insist upon it. . . .

*Notes*

1. See also *Re M (A Minor) (Child Abduction)* [1994] 1 FLR 390, CA, where Butler-Sloss LJ stressed that the court must be 'vigilant to ascertain and assess the reasons for the child not wishing to return to the parent living in the State of habitual residence'. In *Re K (Abduction: Child's Objections)* [1995] 1 FLR 977, FD, the children were ordered to be returned to the USA, despite one of them, a girl aged 7, being terrified of returning.

Waite J stated that he considered a child aged 7 as being on the borderline for the purposes of refusing return because of the child's wishes, but nevertheless invited the duty court welfare officer to report on her.

2.   In *Re M (A Minor) (Abduction: Child's Objections)* [1994] 2 FLR 126, the Court of Appeal held *obiter* that a child may be made a party to a Convention application in an exceptional case (*Re M* was such a case as the dispute was between the mother and child, not the mother and father).

3.   As Hague Convention proceedings are summary and speed is of the essence, the court will usually refuse to hear oral evidence in respect of a child's wishes (see *Re K (Abduction: Child's Objections)* [1995] 1 FLR 977, FD).

4.   It is quite common for the court to accept undertakings from one or both parents (e.g., to return the children, to provide accommodation, travel costs and maintenance), but undertakings 'must not be used by parties to try to clog or fetter, or, in particular, to delay the enforcement of a paramount decision to return the child' (Butler-Sloss LJ in *Re M (Abduction: Undertakings)* [1995] 1 FLR 1021, CA).

### 12.3.6   Rights of access

Access rights may be secured under art. 21 of the Hague Convention, but art. 21 confers no jurisdiction on the court to determine access matters or to recognise or enforce foreign access orders. It merely provides for executive cooperation in the enforcement of such recognition as national law allows, e.g., by the Lord Chancellor's Department making arrangements for finding a solicitor, applying for legal aid and instituting proceedings in the High Court under s. 8 of the CA 1989 (*In Re G (A Minor) (Enforcement of Access Abroad)* [1993] 2 WLR 824, CA, and *Practice Note* [1992] 1 WLR 586).

### Anton, A., 'The Hague Convention on International Child Abduction'
(1981) 30 ICLQ 554–55

. . . The Convention contains no mandatory provisions for the support of access rights comparable with those of its provisions which protect breaches of rights of custody. . . . It was felt not only that mandatory rules in the fluid field of access rights would be difficult to devise but, perhaps more importantly, that the effective exercise of access rights depends in the long run more upon the goodwill, or at least the restraint, of the parties than upon the existence of formal rules. Article 21, therefore, establishes open-textured rules for assisting parties to secure the effective exercise of access rights by seeking the intervention of central authorities. . . .

*Note*

Anton was the Chairman of the Conference which drafted the Hague Convention.

## 12.4   THE EUROPEAN CONVENTION ON RECOGNITION AND ENFORCEMENT OF DECISIONS CONCERNING CUSTODY OF CHILDREN 1989

The European Convention on Recognition and Enforcement of Decisions Concerning Custody of Children 1989 ('the European Convention') is a Council of Europe Convention, which was implemented into UK law by Part II of the Child Abduction and Custody Act 1985 (see sch. 2 to the Act for the text of the Convention). For Contracting States, see 12.6 below.

### *Re A (Foreign Access Order: Enforcement)*
[1996] 1 FLR 561
Court of Appeal

WAITE LJ: . . . Although the Hague Convention and the European Convention are different treaties to which effect is given by different parts of the Child Abduction and Custody Act 1985, the underlying policy is the same. It is to settle the lives of children. The Hague Convention seeks to do that by avoiding the disruption suffered when a child is abducted from the jurisdiction of habitual residence. The European Convention seeks to spare children the unsettling effect of a potential conflict of orders for custody or contact in different jurisdictions.

Although both Conventions contain provision for ascertaining the views of children old enough to make a judgment of their own, neither Convention makes such views conclusive, and the terms of both are sufficiently stringent to make it plain that the signatory States did not intend that the underlying policy of the Convention should be eroded by a proliferation of supposedly hard cases.

Just as the Hague Convention makes mandatory the return of a wrongfully abducted child in all circumstances save those for which exceptional provision is made in Art. 13, so the European Convention, by s. 15 of the Act and Art. 7, makes mandatory the recognition and enforcement in England of foreign custody and contact orders in all circumstances, save those for which exceptional provision is made in Art. 10.

. . .

*Note*

In *Re A (Foreign Access Order: Enforcement)*, the Court of Appeal, allowing the appeal, made an order giving recognition to a French access order and making it enforceable in England, and held that the case did not come within the exception provided by art. 10 and that the radical change made to the French order by giving the father staying access in England amounted to a review as to the substance of the foreign decision, which was specifically prohibited by art. 9(3).

## THE EUROPEAN CONVENTION ON RECOGNITION AND ENFORCEMENT OF DECISIONS CONCERNING CUSTODY OF CHILDREN 1989

**Article 1**
For the purposes of this Convention:
. . .

(c) 'decision relating to custody' means a decision of an authority in so far as it relates to the care of the person of the child, including the right to decide on the place of his residence, or to the right of access to him;

(d) 'improper removal' means the removal of a child across an international frontier in breach of a decision relating to his custody which has been given in a Contracting State and which is enforceable in such a State; 'improper removal' also includes:

(i) the failure to return a child across an international frontier at the end of a period of the exercise of the right of access to this child or at the end of any other temporary stay in a territory other than that where the custody is exercised;

(ii) a removal which is subsequently declared unlawful within the meaning of Article 12.

## Article 7
A decision relating to custody given in a Contracting State shall be recognised and, where it is enforceable in the State of origin, made enforceable in every other Contracting State.

## Article 9
(1) . . . recognition and enforcement may be refused only if:

(a) in the case of a decision given in the absence of the defendant or his legal representative, the defendant was not duly served with the document which instituted the proceedings or an equivalent document in sufficient time to enable him to arrange his defence; but such a failure to effect service cannot constitute a ground for refusing recognition or enforcement where service was not effected because the defendant had concealed his whereabouts from the person who instituted the proceedings in the State of origin;

(b) in the case of a decision given in the absence of the defendant or his legal representative, the competence of the authority giving the decision was not founded:

(i) on the habitual residence of the defendant; or

(ii) on the last common habitual residence of the child's parents, at least one parent being still habitually resident there; or

(iii) on the habitual residence of the child;

(c) the decision is incompatible with a decision relating to custody which became enforceable in the State addressed before the removal of the child, unless the child has had his habitual residence in the territory of the requesting State for one year before his removal.

. . .

(3) In no circumstances may the foreign decision be reviewed as to its substance.

## Article 10
(1) . . . recognition and enforcement may also be refused . . . on any of the following grounds:

(a) if it is found that the effects of the decision are manifestly incompatible with the fundamental principles of the law relating to the family and children in the State addressed;

(b) if it is found that by reason of a change in the circumstances including the passage of time but not including a mere change in the residence of the child after an improper removal, the effects of the original decision are manifestly no longer in accordance with the welfare of the child;

(c) if at the time when the proceedings were instituted in the State of origin:

(i) the child was a national of the State addressed or was habitually resident there and no such connection existed with the State of origin;

(ii)   the child was a national both of the State of origin and of the State addressed and was habitually resident in the State addressed;

(d)   if the decision is incompatible with a decision given in the State addressed or enforceable in that State after being given in a third State, pursuant to proceedings begun before the submission of the request for recognition or enforcement, and if the refusal is in accordance with the welfare of the child.

**Article 12**
Where, at the time of the removal of a child across an international frontier, there is no enforceable decision given in a Contracting State relating to his custody, the provisions of this Convention shall apply to any subsequent decision, relating to the custody of that child and declaring the removal to be unlawful, given in a Contracting State at the request of any interested person.

**Article 15**
(1)   Before reaching a decision under paragraph (1)(b) of Article 10, the authority concerned in the State addressed:

(a)   shall ascertain the child's views unless this is impracticable having regard in particular to his age and understanding; and

(b)   may request that any appropriate enquiries be carried out.

. . .

*Notes*
1.   A person wishing to have a custody decision recognised or enforced in another Contracting State may apply to the central authority in any Contracting State (art. 4) (in England, the Lord Chancellor's Department), which must take appropriate steps without delay, *inter alia*, to institute proceedings to discover the child's whereabouts, to secure the recognition or enforcement of the decision, to secure delivery of the child to the applicant where enforcement is granted, and to inform the requesting authority of the measures taken and their results (art. 5).
2.   Decisions on access, and custody decisions dealing with access, must also be recognised and enforced subject to the same conditions which apply to custody decisions, but the competent authority of the State addressed may fix the conditions for the implementation and exercise of the right of access taking into account, in particular, undertakings given by the parties on this matter (art. 11). Where there is no decision as to access or where recognition or enforcement of a custody decision has been refused, the central authority of the State addressed may apply to its competent authorities for a decision on the right of access if the person claiming a right of access so requests (art. 11(3)).
3.   For examples of applications under the European Convention, see *Re L (Child Abduction: European Convention)* [1992] 2 FLR 178, FD; *Re K (A Minor) (Abduction)* [1990] 1 FLR 387, FD; *Re F (A Minor) (Custody: Foreign Order)* [1989] 1 FLR 335, FD; and *Re G (A Minor) (Child Abduction: Enforcement)* [1990] 2 FLR 325, FD.

## 12.5   NON-CONVENTION CASES

Where children from non-Convention countries are brought into England and Wales, applications for their return are decided by the High Court in wardship (see Chapter 7).

## Re F (A Minor) (Abduction: Custody Rights)
[1991] Fam 25
Court of Appeal

*Facts*: Under Israeli law both parents were joint guardians and had joint custody of the child, including a right to determine the child's place of residence. When their marriage broke down, the father took their second child from Israel to England without the mother's knowledge and in breach of her right of custody. The Israeli court granted the mother custody, care and control and ordered the child's immediate return to his mother. The father was granted interim custody, care and control of the child by an English county court judge, who concluded that the child had not been removed in breach of a prior court order and that the child should not be returned to Israel on the facts of the case. The judge also ordered that the mother be restrained from moving the child from the jurisdiction. The mother appealed.

*Held*: allowing the appeal and ordering the child's immediate return, that although Israel was not a party to the Hague Convention, the general principles of that Convention applied to the extent that in normal circumstances it was in an abducted child's best interests that he should be returned to his country of habitual residence so that custody matters could be decided there. On the facts the child's removal had been in breach of a right of custody and there were no contra-indications such as those contained in art. 13 of the Hague Convention requiring the retention of jurisdiction, and no risk of persecution or discrimination or any evidence that the Israeli courts would adopt an approach to the child's future which differed from that of the English court.

LORD DONALDSON MR: This is an international child abduction case. It is not, however, one to which the Child Abduction and Custody Act 1985 applies because Israel has not yet been named in an Order in Council made under section 2, and may indeed not be party to the Hague Convention on the Civil Aspects of International Child Abduction 1980 to which that Act gives effect. Nevertheless, like all international child abduction cases, it is in a special category.

. . .

If this had been a Convention case, there would have been no argument. The father's action in bringing B to England was a 'wrongful removal' within the meaning of the Convention, having been undertaken in breach of the mother's rights of custody under the law of B's habitual place of residence immediately before the removal. There are no contra-indications, such as those contemplated by article 13. But this is not a Convention case and the question inevitably arises of the extent to which Convention principles are applicable.

I agree with Balcombe LJ's view expressed in *G v G* (unreported) 26 May 1989; Court of Appeal (Civil Division) Transcript No. 527 of 1989, that, in enacting the Act of 1985, Parliament was not departing from the fundamental principle that the welfare of the child is paramount. Rather it was giving effect to a belief

that in normal circumstances it is in the interests of children that parents or others should not abduct them from one jurisdiction to another, but that any decision relating to the custody of children is best decided in the jurisdiction in which they have hitherto normally been resident.

This decision was not drawn to the judge's attention, although she was referred to two earlier cases, *In re H (Infants)* [1966] 1 WLR 381 and *In re G (A Minor) (Wardship: Jurisdiction)* [1984] FLR 268, in which children were ordered to be returned. She distinguished those cases upon the grounds that in each case there had been orders by foreign courts relating to the children prior to their removal and that in *In re G* the family had no fixed ties with England, although the mother was of English nationality. In the instant case, by contrast, she held that the father had important ties with England and that not all B's ties were with Israel.

For my part, I consider that the existence of prior orders by a foreign court is of little, if any, significance so long as the removal was in breach of rights of custody. The existence of a prior order would do no more than affirm and reinforce those rights. So far as ties with England are concerned, this is one of the matters which falls to be considered by the court charged with resolving the dispute between parents. It does not point to the English courts as the court appropriate for that purpose.

Similarly, I reject the judge's reliance upon her view of B's future. As she put it, 'this is not a case where his future is inevitably tied up with Israel. It might be so, but that is not an inevitable certainty.' That is something which has to be taken into account by the appropriate court, be it English or Israeli, but does not point to one rather than the other.

Finally, the judge expressed doubts as to the extent to which the father is free to return to Israel without adverse consequences as a result of his abduction of B. If, for example, he were imprisoned, this would deprive B of his father's care and attention for a period. Quite apart from the fact that this involves the father being allowed to rely upon his own wrong, it ignores the fact that, so long as B remains in England, he is cut off from his mother and elder brother. In fact, the criminal charges were instituted in Israel by the mother when she discovered that B had been abducted, and we are told that she does not intend to press those charges. Of course, it will be for the Israeli authorities to decide what difference that makes.

There is no evidence that the Israeli courts would adopt an approach to the problem of B's future which differs significantly from that of the English courts. It is not a case in which B or his father are escaping any form of persecution or ethnic, sex or other discrimination. In a word, there is nothing to take it out of the normal rule that abducted children should be returned to their country of habitual residence.

The welfare of the child is indeed the paramount consideration, but it has to be considered in two different contexts. The first is the context of which court shall decide what the child's best interests require. The second context, which only arises if it has first been decided that the welfare of the child requires that the English rather than a foreign court shall decide what are the requirements of the child, is what orders as to custody, care and control and so on should be made.

In my judgment, the judge mixed the two questions. Thus, in her judgment, having distinguished *In re G* [1984] FLR 268 on the basis that the parents were of different nationalities but the mother, though English, had no fixed ties with Britain, she continued:

> In this case the applicant clearly has important ties with this country notwithstanding his conversion and acceptance of dual nationality. It could not be said that on common sense all B's ties are with Israel. As regards the future and B, this is not a case where his future is inevitably tied up with Israel. It might be so but that is not an inevitable certainty.

In other words, she was saying that, if one possible outcome of any proceedings, whether in Israel or England, would be that B might remain in England, the English courts should retain jurisdiction.

This is an error in principle. Possible outcomes have no bearing on which court should decide. Which court should decide depends, as I have said, on whether the other court will apply principles which are acceptable to the English courts as being appropriate, subject always to any contra-indication such as those mentioned in article 13 of the Convention, or a risk of persecution or discrimination, but prima facie the court to decide is that of the state where the child was habitually resident immediately before its removal.

I would allow the appeal accordingly and order the immediate return of B to Israel.

*Note*
Israel is now a party to the Hague Convention.

### Re M (Abduction: Non-Convention Country)
### [1995] 1 FLR 89
### Court of Appeal

*Facts*: The two children, aged 4 and 2, were born in Italy of an English mother and an Italian father. On marriage breakdown, the mother, having been advised by her Italian lawyer that she stood little chance of obtaining custody in Italy, brought the children to England and sought a residence order from the English court. The father obtained an interim order in Italy that they live with him, but custody was vested in the Italian local authority. The father applied for and was granted a peremptory return order by Wilson J in the High Court after a short adjournment to sort out practical arrangements which Wilson J was concerned about, and after the father had given undertakings. The mother appealed, introducing fresh evidence to show that the arrangements made in Italy regarding the matters which had concerned Wilson J were inadequate.

*Held*: dismissing the appeal, that the principles which applied in Hague Convention cases were also *prima facie* to be applied in non-Convention cases. There was sufficient material before Wilson J for him to be satisfied that a return order would be in the best interests of the girls and his decision was vindicated by the new evidence.

WAITE LJ: . . . The principles upon which the courts act in non-Convention cases are now well settled. They can, I think, be summarised in this way. First, the underlying assumptions which the court applies prima facie to every case are those which underlie the Hague Convention itself, namely that the best interests of children are normally best secured by having their future determined in the jurisdiction of their habitual residence and sparing them the distress and disruption which they are liable to suffer if one parent abducts them from the home jurisdiction in order to secure a tactical, or a supposed juridical, advantage in a competing jurisdiction: see *Re S (Minors) (Abduction)* [1993] 1 FCR 789 and *D v D (Child Abduction: Non-Convention Country)* [1994] 1 FLR 137.

Secondly, in acting by analogy with the Convention the court takes account of those matters which it would be relevant to consider under Art. 13.

Thirdly, it is of the essence of the jurisdiction to grant a peremptory return order that the judge should act urgently. That means that the court has no time to go into matters of detail. The case has to be viewed from the perspective of a quick appraisal of its essential features. Any risk of injustice suffered by the abducting parent as a result of limiting the scale of the survey in the interests of speed is minimised by the adoption in the Court of Appeal of a policy which, while discouraging appeals that attempt to reargue the merits, allows some relaxation of the rule in *Ladd* v *Marshall* 1954] 1 WLR 1489. That relaxation is applied to the extent necessary to enable this court to determine whether there are any matters not dealt with at first instance which might have materially affected the judge's decision, had he been aware of them.

Fourthly, in this area — as in many others — the principle of comity applies. It is assumed, particularly in the case of States which are fellow members of the European Union, that such facilities as rights of representation, means of collecting information through independent sources and welfare reports, and opportunities of giving evidence and of interrogating the other side, all of which are necessary to place the court in a position to determine the best interests of the child concerned, will be secured as well within one State's jurisdiction as within another.

Against that background of principle I now turn to the facts of this case. . . .

Wilson J was right, in my judgment, to refuse an adjournment for further investigation. [Counsel for the mother] criticised him for having put what might be called the 'spirit of the Convention considerations' ahead of his duty to give paramount considerations to the girls' welfare. To put it in that way shows, with respect, a confusion of the issue. The paramountcy of the welfare of the child in these cases arises at every stage from the first preliminary to the last adjudication. The fact that there is jurisdiction to grant a peremptory return order in child abduction cases where the Convention does not apply, is itself based upon nothing else but an appreciation of the general demands of the best interests of all children. It assumes that in the absence of special circumstances, it will best serve the immediate welfare of the abducted child to have its long-term interests judged in the land from which it was abducted. When that principle is taken with the general principle of comity which applies between civilised countries, and especially between partners in the European Union, an element of trust is bound to become involved. Judges in one country are entitled, and bound, to assume that the courts and welfare services of the other country will all take the same serious view of a failure to honour undertakings given to a court (of any jurisdiction), failure to maintain financially, failure to afford contact, and so on. It is to be assumed that the courts in every country will not hesitate to intervene to enforce whatever orders, or to direct whatever inquiries, are called for in the children's best interests. In that process every judge is bound to take into full and careful account what his or her colleague has already ordered in antecedent proceedings in another jurisdiction.

The judge was, therefore, right to act as he did. He had enough material before him to be satisfied that a return order would accord with the best interests of the girls. His decision has been, if anything, vindicated, and has certainly not at all been put in doubt, by the new evidence. I would dismiss the appeal.

*Note*
Italy is now a party to the Hague and European Conventions.

## Beevers, Kisch, 'Child Abduction — Welfare or Comity?'
[1996] Fam Law 365

The case of *Re M (Abduction: Peremptory Return Order)* [1996] 1 FLR 478 brings into question, once again, the exact principles upon which non-Convention child abduc-

tion cases should be decided. The purpose of this article is to suggest that it is time the Court of Appeal stopped developing this area of law by analogy with the Hague Convention on the Civil Aspects of International Child Abduction, and reasserted the paramountcy of the welfare principle as latterly laid down by the Children Act 1989.
. . .

Integral to the principles underlying the Hague Convention is the acceptance of comity between the nations of the Hague Conference. This acceptance is based on the understanding that most of the member States of the Hague Conference (and all of the contracting States to this Hague Convention) base their decisions on the upbringing of children on the 'best interests' of the individual child principle. This is underlined in the preamble to the Convention itself:

> The States signatory to the present Convention, . . . Firmly convinced that the interests of children are of paramount importance in matters relating to their custody . . .

This is not true of many countries in the world. Alternative principles include a presumption or, indeed, an irrefutable right that the parent of one sex or other will have custody of any children; or that custody is decided on grounds of social 'fitness' or 'unfitness' of one of the parents regardless of their parenting ability (see Dyer 'Report on International Child Abduction' in Hague Conference on Private International Law, *Actes et Documents de la Quatorzième Session, Tome III, Child Abduction*, 1982, at p. 22). For example, under Islamic law the custody of a 10-year-old boy would most certainly be given to the father. International comity is not, and never has been, the principle of law upon which to decide to return a child to the jurisdiction of his habitual residence. The principle underlying the peremptory return order is a forerunner of the underlying principle of the Hague Convention outlined above, in that it is normally in the best interests of the child for the courts of habitual residence to decide on the future of that child. The welfare of children should not be subjected to considerations of international comity; quite the reverse, international comity must give way where the welfare of the child so requires.

To return to the facts of *Re M (Abduction: Peremptory Return Order)*, from the small amount of information given in the report it would seem that the decision to return the two children to the United Arab Emirates could easily be reconciled with the welfare principle. The children had been born and brought up in Dubai in a family environment which also contained members of their mother's family. There was no evidence to suggest that the children would suffer in any way by returning to the jurisdiction of the country of their habitual residence. Whatever the decision, however, the legal principle upon which it must be made is the welfare principle, and not considerations of international comity.

*Notes*
1. In *Re M (Abduction: Peremptory Return Order)* [1996] 1 FLR 478, CA, in which two brothers aged 2 and 10 were ordered to be returned to Dubai so that the issues could be dealt with there, Waite LJ said that underlying the whole purpose of the peremptory return order is 'a principle of international comity under which judges in England will assume that facilities for a fair hearing will be provided in the court of the other jurisdiction' and that very exceptional circumstances would be needed to depart from that general principle.

*2.* In *Re P (A Minor)(Abduction)* (1996) *The Times*, 19 July (abduction from Bombay to England by mother), the Court of Appeal, allowing the mother's appeal, held that where a child was abducted to England from a non-Convention country, the English court, in considering whether or not the child should be ordered to be returned to the country where she habitually resided, should give paramount consideration to the overall welfare of the child. Ward LJ held that the judge had wrongly considered himself bound to apply the spirit of the Convention in a non-Convention case, and concluded, applying by analogy art. 13, that he should order the child's return unless the mother established to a high decree of satisfaction that the child would thereby be exposed to a grave risk of physical or psychological harm. The authorities stated that in a non-Convention case the welfare of the child was the only consideration that governed the courts. To elevate art. 13 into some test was to fly in the face of those authorities. See also *D* v *D (Child Abduction: Non-Convention Country)* [1994] 1 FLR 137, CA (child's return to Crete refused as the mother was pregnant and not prepared to return), and *S* v *S (Child Abduction: Non-Convention Country)* [1994] 2 FLR 681, FD.

*3.*   Where a child is taken from England and Wales to Scotland or Northern Ireland, an English court order (e.g., a CA 1989, s. 8 order) can be enforced and recognised in those countries (see FLA 1986, ss. 1 and 25–29).

*4.*   Where a child has been abducted into England and Wales, the English courts have jurisdiction to make s. 8 orders under the CA 1989 if the child is: habitually resident in England and Wales; or present in England and Wales and is not habitually resident in any part of the United Kingdom (FLA 1986, s. 2(2) and 3). The High Court has jurisdiction under its inherent jurisdiction and its wardship jurisdiction to make orders if the child is habitually resident in England and Wales, or present here and not habitually resident elsewhere in the UK or certain dependent territories, or present here and the court considers the immediate exercise of its powers necessary for the child's protection (FLA 1986, s. 2(3), read with s. 1(1)(d) and s. 3(1)); see *Re A (Wardship: Jurisdiction)* [1995] 1 FLR 767, FD).

*Question*
How paramount is the welfare of the child in non-Convention cases?

## 12.6   CONTRACTING STATES TO THE HAGUE AND
## EUROPEAN CONVENTIONS

| *State* | *Convention* |
|---|---|
| Argentina | Hague |
| Australia | Hague |
| Austria | Hague and European |
| Bahamas | Hague |
| Belgium | European |
| Belize | Hague |
| Bosnia and Herzegovina | Hague |
| Burkina Faso | Hague |
| Canada (most states) | Hague |
| Chile | Hague |
| Columbia | Hague |
| Croatia | Hague |
| Cyprus (Southern) | Hague and European |
| Denmark | Hague and European |
| Ecuador | Hague |
| Finland | Hague and European |
| France | Hague and European |
| Germany | Hague and European |
| Greece | Hague and European |
| Honduras | Hague |
| Hungary | Hague |
| Iceland | European |
| Israel | Hague |
| Italy | Hague and European |
| Luxembourg | Hague and European |
| Macedonia | Hague |
| Mauritius | Hague |
| Mexico | Hague |
| Monaco | Hague |
| Netherlands | Hague and European |
| New Zealand | Hague |
| Norway | Hague and European |
| Panama | Hague |
| Poland | Hague and European |
| Portugal | Hague and European |
| Republic of Ireland | Hague and European |
| Romania | Hague |
| Slovenia | Hague |
| Spain | Hague and European |
| St Kitts and Nevis | Hague |
| Sweden | Hague and European |
| Switzerland | Hague and European |

| *State* | *Convention* |
|---|---|
| United Kingdom | Hague and European |
| United States of America | Hague |
| Yugoslavia | Hague |
| Venezuela | Hague |
| Zimbabwe | Hague |

*Further reading*

Bruch, C., 'Child Abduction and the English Courts', in Bainham, A., Pearl, D., and Pickford, R. (eds), *Frontiers of Family Law*, 2nd edn, Chichester: John Wiley, 1995.

Bruch, C., 'The Central Authority Role and the Hague Child Abduction Convention: A Friend in Deed' (1994) 28 Fam LQ 35.

Hamilton, C., and Standley, K. (eds), *Family Law in Europe*, London: Butterworths, 1995.

McClean, D., and Beevers, K., 'International Child Abduction — Back to Common Law Principles' [1995] 7 CFLQ 128.

Standley, K., 'International Child Abduction: the Hague and European Conventions' [1991] 3 JCL 137.

Stone, P., 'The Habitual Residence of a Child' [1992] 4 JCL 170.

Mears, M., 'Removal of Children from the Jurisdiction' [1989] Fam Law 322.

# INDEX